AF882598

Getting to Brexit

Legal Aspects of the Process of the UK's Withdrawal from the EU

Jennifer A. Hillman and Gary Horlick,
Editors

Getting to Brexit

Legal Aspects of the Process of the UK's Withdrawal from the EU

Jennifer A. Hillman and Gary Horlick,

Editors

Published by the Institute of International Economic Law
Georgetown Law
Washington, DC

The Institute of International Economic Law

The Institute of International Economic Law (IIEL) is the focal point for the study of international economic law at Georgetown University and one of the leading centers for international economic law and policy in the world. Founded in 1999 by the late University Professor John H. Jackson, the IIEL's objective is to facilitate thoughtful and scholarly research and teaching, convene stakeholder meetings and conferences bringing together public and private sector leaders, and offer Executive Education on a broad range of subjects that concern the law of international economic activity. Originally focused on trade, the Institute's portfolio has grown to include leading capabilities and international renown in a range of areas including investment and arbitration, financial regulation, tax, business and monetary law. The Institute actively approaches these fields as interrelated and at times overlapping policy spheres that impact how law is devised, practiced and enforced.

IIEL hosts fora for policy debate and research with a wide range of international organizations, firms, NGOs and government agencies, and welcomes new partnerships. The Institute also contributes to the analysis of today's most pressing global economic law and policy issues, via its Issue Brief Series, among other mechanisms.

Institute of International Economic Law
Georgetown Law
600 New Jersey Avenue, NW
Washington, DC 20001
lawiiel@georgetown.edu
http://iielaw.org

Copyright © 2018 Institute of International Economic Law
All rights reserved
Printed in the United States of America

Names: I. Hillman, Jennifer A., Editor
II. Horlick, Gary, Editor
Title: Getting to Brexit: Legal Aspects of the Process of the UK's Withdrawal from the EU
Subjects: Law -- European Union, international trade, World Trade Organization, commercial policy
ISBN-13:978-0692167014 (Institute of International Economic Law)
ISBN-10:0692167013

Table of Contents

Preface

In the fall of 2016, less than eight weeks after the unexpected results of the June 23, 2016 British referendum in favor of leaving the European Union (EU), my colleague and long-time Georgetown Law adjunct professor Gary Horlick and I launched the first law course of which we are aware focused solely on the depth and breadth of legal issues that arise and will need to be addressed in the course of the United Kingdom (UK)'s journey to remove itself from the treaties and institutions that make up the EU. We understood then (and believe that the events of the last year have only underscored) that Brexit has the potential to be one of the most significant international economic law events of our lifetimes.

That first 2016 seminar focused on the EU law applicable to a wide-range of issues, how that particular law was transposed into the UK—whether through the enactment of free-standing UK law or through direct effect, and what, if any, of the EU law would remain as binding law in a post-Brexit UK. The course further examined what the UK can or should do to fill any holes created in their legal framework as a result of Brexit and what new or different obligations might be placed on the EU or its institutions in a post-Brexit world. All of the work was done at a time when many questioned whether the UK would go through with its withdrawal intentions and invoke Article 50 of the Treaty on the European Union. One result was a book, *Legal Aspects of Brexit*, published in early 2017 containing edited versions of the student papers with an introductory note outlining the state of Brexit events at that time.

Fast forward to the spring of 2018 and a second seminar at Georgetown Law on Brexit—this time taught with the certain knowledge that the Article 50 withdrawal provision had indeed been invoked on March 28, 2017, thereby starting the two-year withdrawal clock ticking. The focus of the seminar therefore shifted to how exactly the withdrawal process would work and to a more specific and detailed analysis of the two major legal texts affecting Brexit: 1) the European Commission's Draft Agreement on the Withdrawal, and 2) the UK's European Union (Withdrawal) Bill, formerly described as the "Great Repeal Bill." The first text (Draft Withdrawal Agreement) was released in its color-coded format on March 19, 2018, outlining agreements in principle (text in green or yellow) or proposals by the European Commission (text in white) on the key withdrawal issues of citizens' rights, financial contributions by the UK to the EU, the Irish border, and the establishment of a transition period between Brexit day, March 29, 2019, through December 31, 2020, during which EU law will continue to apply in and to the UK. The second text, the UK's repeal bill, which received Royal Assent on June 26, 2018, gives legal effect to the UK's decision to leave the bloc by repealing the 1972 legislation that took the UK into the EU (known then as the European Communities) and "grandfathers" European rules and regulations into the British statute books.

As such, the focus of the chapters of this book are on the interpretation and implication of those two legal texts—what exactly does the Draft Withdrawal Agreement and the UK's repeal bill mean for the future relationship between the UK, the EU and the rest of the world across a range of trade and economic issues? What are the key sticking points in reaching a final withdrawal agreement? What is the timing and process for implementing such a final deal? What law and policy issues remain under debate in the UK under its repeal bill? What is likely to happen during the 21-month transition period? Each of the following chapters reflects the work done by the Georgetown Law students in our seminar to answer these questions and more. They are broadly grouped into those papers addressing issues that fall to the UK to address in the immediate future as part of its repeal process, those addressing implications of the Draft Withdrawal Agreement, and those which must be addressed in any understandings on the future relationship between the UK, the EU and the rest of the world.

Our path to making this course a reality was substantially aided by the enthusiasm and tireless work of our research assistant, Aditi Rao, who immediately set to work tracking down sources and materials, keeping us and our students updated on all major events in the Brexit firmament. Ms. Rao crafted the introduction to this book. She also continued to add materials to our initial collection, ultimately organizing them into a roadmap to guide anyone interested in examining any Brexit issue to the most relevant sources of information on each particular topic. That roadmap is available on the website of Georgetown Law's Institute of International Economic Law (www.iiel.org).

Jennifer Hillman and Gary Horlick
Washington, DC
August 2018

Acknowledgments

The authors gratefully acknowledge the contributions and support from our smart and diligent research assistant, Aditi Rao, without whom this book and its roadmap to the many sources of information about Brexit would not have been possible; our guest lecturers, Hannah Young and Emma Coppack, of the UK Department of Exiting the EU (DExEU) who shared significant insights on both the procedural and substantive dilemmas facing the UK as it seeks to simultaneously craft both a withdrawal package and agreements for future relationships; Damien Levie, the Head of the Trade and Agriculture Section of the European Union delegation to the United States, who outlined the variety of agreements that could be fashioned under EU law and procedures to respond to both the UK's formal invocation of Article 50 and EU member state concerns over preserving the integrity of the Union; Timothy Wedding, one of the lead negotiators from the Office of the United States Trade Representative (USTR), who explained the hopes and immediate requirements for the US in forming a new relationship with the UK and in working to maintain US rights with the soon-to-be EU-27; Lee Godown, Vice-President of General Motors Corporation, who described how a large multinational business adapts to and prepares for an eventual Brexit; and John Cooke, Chairman, Liberalization of Trade in Services Committee, TheCityUK, who greatly aided our understanding of Brexit's implications for the financial services industry and for those reliant on the right to "passport" their services from the UK to continental Europe; to Professor Christopher Brummer and Christine Washington at the Georgetown Law Center's Institute of International Economic Law (IIEL) for their enthusiastic support for this project; to Betsy Kuhn and Alina Schmidt for their tireless work in proofreading and formatting this book; to Ines Hilde for her creativity in designing the cover; and last, but certainly not least, to those students brave enough to take this class, who enlivened the debate and taught us much about the tremendous complexities of Brexit and the transition process: Eike Bleckwenn, Joshua Blume, Aure Demoulin-Bouchier, Saray Leon, Tendai Mukau, Shengxiang Ni, Joshua Newton, Cameron Peek, Worthington Phillips, Philipp Ruppert, Alexandra Stanley, Catherine Tassin de Montaigu, Amelia Theisen, Caitlin Thomas, Kanzanira Thorington, Jacob Travers, Yasutaka Tsuji, Ariane Yvon, and Minxi Wang.

Jennifer A. Hillman
Gary Horlick

INTRODUCTION

ADITI RAO AND JENNIFER HILLMAN

On 29 March 2017, by way of a letter from UK Prime Minister Theresa May to European Council President Donald Tusk, the UK officially notified the EU of its intent to withdraw under Article 50 of the Treaty of the European Union ["TEU"].[1] This letter formally triggered the process that has come to be known as 'Brexit,' following the unexpected result of the British Referendum of June 2016, in which 52 percent of those voting had cast ballots in favor of leaving the EU. The road to this official notification and the road since has been a tortuous one, with numerous twists and turns along the way. Beginning with the complexity surrounding the scope of Article 50 and its implications for the UK's parliamentary system to the contentious border issue between Ireland and Northern Ireland, Brexit has launched a series of novel legal questions. Picking up from *Legal Aspects of Brexit*,[2] which discussed Brexit in its early phases, this book seeks to examine how some of those legal issues have evolved, how others have emerged, and where Brexit's road may be headed.

I. ARTICLE 50 OF THE TFEU

At the very outset, Article 50 of the TFEU, the provision which establishes the right and process of exit from the EU, has proven to be legally challenging. In fact, the some of the drafters of Article 50 say they never envisioned that this provision would be used[3] and perhaps, as a result, the precise scope of Article 50 and its implications for the UK's parliamentary system have raised many legal questions.

These issues came to the fore in 2016, when two UK citizens challenged Prime Minister Theresa May's contention that the Crown, acting through the executive in the form of the Secretary of State for Exiting the EU, could use its prerogative powers to invoke Article 50 and thereby convey the UK's intention to withdraw from the EU. The claimants argued that Article 50 could only be triggered by Parliament, an assertion that was upheld in the UK's High Court as well as in the

---

[1] HM Government, "Prime Minister's Letter to Donald Tusk triggering Article 50," 29 March 2017.

[2] *Legal Aspects of Brexit*, Jennifer Hillman and Gary Horlick (eds.), IIEL (2017).

[3] See Christopher Hooton & Jon Stone, "Brexit: Article 50 Was Never Actually Meant to be Used, Says Its Author" *Independent* (July 26, 2016).

nation's highest court, the UK Supreme Court.[4] The court reasoned that since legislation had been enacted by both Houses of Parliament for the UK to join the then European Communities (precursor to the EU) and to establish the process for EU law to become domestic law in the UK, that EU law could not be displaced or repealed solely through the exercise of the Crown's prerogative power—effectively stating that if it took an Act of Parliament to enter the EU, it also takes an Act of Parliament to exit.[5]

Further, the Supreme Court decision resulted in two important conclusions: first, it accepted the uncontested proposition that Article 50 is irrevocable, such that once it is invoked, the request to start the withdrawal process cannot be taken back and; second, that the invocation of Article 50 cannot be made conditional, so the ultimate withdrawal from the EU does not depend on a subsequent approval by the UK Parliament of the terms of the withdrawal agreement worked out between the UK and the EU.[6]

Following the Supreme Court decision, legislation was introduced into both the House of Commons, the UK's lower house of Parliament, as well as the House of Lords, the Parliament's upper chamber, which prompted contentious debates between the two. The May government sought and the House of Commons passed a "clean" bill that simply authorized the withdrawal, while the House of Lords amended the legislation to include a guarantee of the rights of EU citizens in the UK to remain after Brexit, but the Lords finally backed down and the bill authorizing the invocation of Article 50 (without any provisions on citizens' rights) received Parliamentary approval on March 14, 2017.[7]

II. LEGISLATION EMERGING FROM THE UK-EU NEGOTIATIONS

While much of both the substance and the process of Brexit remains murky, it has become clear that Brexit will involve three elements that will be completed largely in sequential order: (1) a Withdrawal Agreement to establish key elements of the "divorce," including citizens' rights, financial contributions by the UK to the EU, and the Irish border; (2) a transition deal to cover the relationship between the UK and the EU

---

[4] R (on the application of Miller and another) (Respondents) v Secretary of State for Exiting the European Union (Appellant), Hilary Term, 2017, UKSC 5 On appeals from: 2016, EWHC 2768 (Admin) and 2016, NIQB 85.

[5] Id.

[6] Id.

[7] The 134-word bill ("the Prime Minister may notify, under Article 50(2), the United Kingdom's intention to withdraw from the EU") received Royal Assent on March 16, 2017, European Union (Notification of Withdrawal) Act 2017.

immediately after the withdrawal; and (3) a framework for a future relationship which will outline the final terms of post-transition EU-UK relations. The first two will likely be done in a single formal document (the Withdrawal Agreement) and the third will most likely not be completed by the March 29, 2019 deadline ("Brexit Day") and will therefore have to take the form of a political declaration for now, with the details to be worked out during the transition period. It is expected that those details will include a further transition period well beyond December 2020 for the implementation of whatever trade, economic and security cooperation arrangements are agreed under such a framework.

The first two of these steps has thus far resulted in two landmark pieces of legislation—the Draft Withdrawal Agreement[8], as proposed by the European Union and released on March 19, 2018 and the UK's "Great Repeal Bill," now known as the European Union (Withdrawal) Act, which was passed by the UK Parliament and received Royal Assent on June 26, 2018.[9]

A. WITHDRAWAL AGREEMENT

Article 50 specifies that the EU "shall negotiate and conclude an agreement with [the withdrawing] State, setting out the arrangements for its withdrawal . . ."[10] It goes on to note that such an agreement "shall be concluded on behalf of the [EU] by the Council, acting by a qualified majority, after obtaining consent of the European Parliament."[11]

As such, the Draft Withdrawal Agreement requires approval of the European Parliament (by simple majority) and approval of the Council by qualified majority vote (20 of the 27 Member States representing at least 65 percent of their combined population), along with approval in the UK under UK law. Given the time that it will take to obtain these approvals, it is likely that the final text of the Draft Withdrawal Agreement will need to be completely agreed upon before the end of 2018 in order to allow time for the approval processes to be completed by March 29, 2019 ("Brexit Day") when the agreement needs to take

---

[8] EU Commission, Draft Agreement on the withdrawal of the United Kingdom of Great Britain and Northern Ireland from the European Union and the European Atomic Energy Community TF50 (2018) 35, 19 March 2018. ("Draft Withdrawal Agreement").

[9] European Union (Withdrawal) Act of 2018, c. 16. ("EU Withdrawal Act") Two additional pieces of Brexit-related legislation are also pending in the UK: 1) the Taxation (Cross-Border Trade) Bill, which deals with import and export tariffs, and 2) the Trade Bill, which provides the authority to make changes necessary to rollover existing trade agreements.

[10] Article 50(2) TEU.

[11] Article 50(2) TEU.

effect. At 11 p.m. (UK time) on Brexit Day, the UK will cease to be an EU Member State. It will then be a third country for the purpose of the EU Treaties and EU law. Failure to obtain this approval (and a comparable approvable on the UK side) would mean that there would be no withdrawal agreement and the UK would abruptly leave the EU on March 29, 2019 under the terms of Article 50(3)—"the [EU] treaties shall cease to apply."[12]

The Draft Withdrawal Agreement was published by the European Commission on February 28, 2018 but later released in a color-coded version setting forth agreements in principle (text in green if agreed to or yellow if agreed in principle) or European Commission proposals not yet agreed to (text in white) on the key withdrawal issues of citizens' rights, financial contributions by the UK to the EU, the Irish border, and the establishment of a transition period between Brexit Day through December 31, 2020. Although the UK officially departs the EU on March 29, 2019, the Withdrawal Agreement is meant to provide a structured and graduated process, which in some sense lessens the blow of Brexit, allows for various parties to prepare for a new paradigm, and buys additional time for negotiations regarding a future relationship agreement.

The Draft Withdrawal Agreement contains six Parts and has two protocols attached. It addresses a range of issues, and per a joint statement published on June 19, 2018, the parties are in agreement regarding a majority of the provisions.[13] Broadly, the parties agree that during the transition period, the UK will not be a member of the EU but will participate in all of the common commercial policies including maintaining the same external tariffs and the UK will continue to pay into the EU's budget. The UK shall in effect remain an EU Member state for EU and UK law purposes for the entirety of the transition period and all EU law shall continue to apply to the UK. Notably, certain key issues have been agreed upon—free movement of persons is recognized, so EU citizens shall continue to enter the UK during the transition period, and CJEU decisions shall remain applicable on all matters until December 31, 2020.[14]

From the outset, a major area of concern has been what to do with the soon-to-be-required border between Northern Ireland (UK and not-

---

[12] Article 50(3) TEU.

[13] See EU Commission, Joint Statement from the negotiators of the European Union and the United Kingdom Government on progress of negotiations under Article 50 TEU on the United Kingdom's orderly withdrawal from the European Union, TF50 (2018) 52, 19 June 2018.

[14] See Articles 2, 8-18, 82 of Draft Withdrawal Agreement

EU post Brexit) and Ireland (member of the EU). Both sides would prefer that the border be minimally intrusive, not inflame past disputes, and support the free flow of goods and services, while respecting the integrity of the European Union. A traditional border with customs and immigration checks would not meet those goals while the absence of any clear border controls would likely not protect the integrity of the EU or be consistent with EU law. The original text of the Draft Withdrawal Agreement suggested a backstop arrangement—that Northern Ireland (but not the rest of the UK) would remain aligned with the EU's customs union and single market in the absence of any other agreement during the transition period. This solution appears to mitigate—at least for the moment—any trade issues that would arise from the absence of a border between Northern Ireland and Ireland. It is unlikely, if UK's past public assertions are anything to go by, that it will agree to this proposal, given that it could result in Northern Ireland being more closely aligned with Ireland than it is with the rest of Britain—a proposition that is largely untenable to certain members of Prime Minister May's ruling coalition. The UK has put forward a variety of alternatives, but they have been met with considerable skepticism both within the UK and by the EU in terms of their workability at both a practical and a political level. However, in the absence of any other agreement, it appears that the default will be the EU's solution.

Beyond the Irish border, one of the agreed-upon (green text) set of provisions in the Draft Withdrawal Agreement are those spelling out a transition period following the date of the UK's exit through December 31, 2020.[15] If it is agreed and formally adopted, the provisions dealing with the transition period will govern the UK's relationship with the EU from the date of entry into force of the Withdrawal Agreement (March 30, 2019) until December 31, 2020.[16] Most importantly, the provisions provide that during the transition period, EU law (subject to certain carve outs) shall continue to apply to the UK and shall create rights and obligations for the UK and all UK residents, companies and other entities as if the UK was still a member of the EU.[17] Moreover, the Draft

[15] Articles 121 – 126, Draft Withdrawal Agreement

[16] Like the rest of the provisions, those governing the transition period can only take effect if the Draft Agreement is formally adopted following the required approval processes.

[17] Article 122, Draft Withdrawal Agreement ("Unless otherwise provided in this Agreement, Union law shall be applicable to and in the United Kingdom during the transition period.") The carve outs are largely those related to European Parliament related election and citizen initiative rights (Article 11(4) TEU, Articles 20(2)(b), 22 and 24 of TFEU) and to those EU initiatives that the UK opted not to join (Euro zone –

Withdrawal Agreement defines EU "law" very broadly, including within its scope the treaties that establish the EU (TEU, TFEU and Euroatom); all of the protocols set forth pursuant to those treaties; the Charter of Fundamental Rights; the general principles of EU law; all international agreements the EU has entered into; and the acts adopted by the bodies, offices or agencies of the EU. As a result of the transition provisions contained in the Draft Withdrawal Agreement, this broad swath of EU law will continue to have direct effect in the UK, and the principle of supremacy will apply, even though the UK will not be a member of the EU during the transition period.[18] The provisions also state that any references to Member States in EU law, including EU law as implemented by Member States, is to be understood as including the UK during the transition period.[19]

As such, the transition provisions resolve a number of contentious issues, at least during the 21-month transition period, including the following:[20]

1. *Free Movement of Persons* – The UK had originally sought a limitation to rights for EU nationals to bring family members into the UK during the transition period and for oversight by the Court of Justice of the European Union (CJEU) over such free movement to end on Brexit Day. The transition provisions call for no exceptions to the free movement of persons and no limitations on the jurisdiction of the CJEU.[21] As such, the UK will continue to permit the entry of EU citizens and their families throughout the transition period.
2. *UK Negotiation of Its Own International Agreements* – Among the sequencing difficulties facing the UK has been that so long as it is a member of the EU and its customs union, only the European Commission can negotiate trade agreements and all tariffs must be established on a customs-union wide basis, leaving the UK unable to fulfill one of the many promises of Brexit—the ability to negotiate

Protocol No. 15, Schengen visa system – Protocol No. 19 and freedom, security, and justice cooperation – Protocol no. 21).

[18] Article 122(3) of the Draft Withdrawal Agreement provides that EU law "shall produce in respect of and in the United Kingdom the same legal effects as it produces" within the EU and its Members States.

[19] Article 122(6), Draft Withdrawal Agreement.

[20] A number of additional transition issues are discussed in the chapters in this book, including fisheries (Chapter 10), border arrangements(Chapter 11), free movement of persons (Chapter 12), trade remedies policy (Chapter 13), and implications for national security (Chapter 14).

[21] Article 126, Draft Withdrawal Agreement. "During the transition period . . . the Court of Justice of the European Union shall have jurisdiction as provided for in the Treaties."

its own free-trade agreements with other countries.[22] The transition provisions give the UK the ability to negotiate, sign and ratify (but not to bring in to force) agreements during the 21-month transition period.[23]

3. *Jurisdiction of the CJEU* – Among the other drivers of Brexit was the UK's desire to get out from under the jurisdiction of the CJEU.[24] However, the transitional provisions provide for CJEU jurisdiction on all matters during the transition period.[25]

4. *UK Participation in EU Decision Making* – Brexit and a transition period always raised concerns in the UK that it would be subject to EU law (and required to continue to pay into the EU budget) but would have no say in the decisions made by the EU. As a result, the UK long sought consultation rights within various EU institutions and agencies and decision-making powers where such decisions would result in the effective operation of EU law in the UK during the transition period. The EU, for its part, largely viewed the March 29, 2019 Brexit Day as the date on which the UK ceases to be a Member State and therefore ceases to have participation rights in the EU decision making process. The transition provisions strike a compromise, allowing the UK to be consulted on EU legislative proposals during the transition and for UK representatives to attend meetings of the EU bodies, agencies or institutions if participation by non-EU Member States is permitted by the agreements applicable to those institutions, but without voting rights.[26] In recognition of the difficulty of binding the UK to decisions it did not make, the transition provisions also permit the UK to opt out of EU decisions on foreign policy if "for vital and stated reasons of national policy."[27]

Another sticking point that the Draft Withdrawal Agreement does not address is the possibility of an extension of the transition period. That is, what happens if the UK is unprepared to 'actually' exit on

---

[22] Quotes on desire for FTA with US and others; shape our own economic future.

[23] Article 124(4), Draft Withdrawal Agreement. ". . . during the transition period, the United Kingdom may negotiate, sign, and ratify international agreements entered into in its own capacity in the areas of exclusive competence of the Union, provided those agreement do not enter into force or apply during the transition period, unless so authorized by the Union."

[24] Boris Johnson, UK Foreign Secretary, "We can't remain subject to the European Court of Justice and that's part of taking back control of our laws." BBC Radio, February 27, 2018.

[25] Article 122(3), Draft Withdrawal Agreement.

[26] Articles 123 and 124(2)(b), Draft Withdrawal Agreement.

[27] Article 124(6), Draft Withdrawal Agreement.

December 31, 2020? What will the status quo be if a future trading arrangement is not agreed upon by that date? Particularly given the legal issues and technical delays that have surrounded Brexit, the absence of any provision either extending the transition period or stipulating the applicable rules and procedures in the event of a cliff edge seems particularly concerning. The EU insisted on December 31, 2020 as the end-date because it coincides with the completion of its current seven-year budget cycle. Already, politicians on both sides of the Channel are suggesting that an extension may be needed, although moving the transition into the next EU budget period raises significant financial questions.[28] Clearly, if both sides agree to extend the transition period *before* the Draft Withdrawal Agreement has been formally agreed to, such changes are entirely permissible and within the control of the UK and EU negotiators. If, however, the change is sought after the Withdrawal Agreement has been formally approved, extension is much less certain, particularly if such an extension agreement is considered a "mixed-competence" agreement requiring approval of all of the EU Member states in addition to the Council.

A final Withdrawal Agreement should be completed in October or November of 2018, which should give enough time for ratification by the European Parliament, the European Council acting by qualified majority (20 of the other 27 Member States). For the Agreement to come into effect in the UK, the UK Parliament will need to enact primary legislation to implement the Agreement. The government has proposed bringing forward its draft Withdrawal Agreement and Implementation Bill (the WAI Bill), which will need to be passed before exit day on 29 March 2019, so that the transition comes into effect the moment the UK leaves the EU.

B. THE UK'S EUROPEAN UNION (WITHDRAWAL) ACT 2018

As of 26 June 2018, the second major piece of Brexit legislation, the EU (Withdrawal) Act[29] ["the Act"] (formerly referred to as the [Great] Repeal Bill), has been passed as law in the UK. The primary purpose of

---

[28] *Tories Divided Over Extension to Brexit Transition Period,* Daily Mail (July 1, 2018), http://www.dailymail.co.uk/wires/pa/article-5905935/Tories-divided-extension-Brexit-transition-period.html, "UK Business Secretary Greg Clark "refuses to rule out" extension of Brexit transition period"; Joe Watts, *Brexit: Brussels set to push for six-month extension to UK's transition period out of EU,* Independent (May 12, 2018), https://www.independent.co.uk/news/uk/politics/transition-period-brexit-eu-theresa-may-a8347731.html, "The EU is to push for an optional six-month extension to the Brexit transition period to be built in to the UK's withdrawal agreement."

[29] See *supra* note 9, EU Withdrawal Act

the Act is to repeal the 1972 European Communities Act[30], the legislation that gave direct force to EU Treaties, regulations and decisions in the UK. This ends the impact of EU law within the UK. The Act also retains about 12,000 pieces of existing EU regulations by transferring them to the UK statute books but offers Parliament the power to amend such laws as it deems appropriate in the context of Brexit. Additionally, the Act legislates on a variety of other issues: it officially sets exit day for 11 p.m. (UK time) on March 29, 2019; mandates Parliamentary approval of the outcome of the Draft Withdrawal Agreement currently being negotiated between the UK and the EU; considers how coordination is to operate between the devolved administrations in Scotland, Wales and Northern Ireland in the context of new legislation; and provides that the judgements of the European Court of Justice that were made prior to Brexit Day will continue to be binding in domestic law insofar as it relates to any retained EU law.[31]

The lead-up to the passing of the Act was fraught with ping pong contests between the House of Commons and the House of Lords, the latter having proposed a variety of amendments to the legislation. Two notable amendments that have carried forward into the Act, albeit with significant changes, relate to what is known as 'the meaningful vote' and the Northern Ireland border issue. At the core of the 'meaningful vote' issue is the discord between the House of Lords and May's government over the role of Parliament in the event of a no-deal Brexit—a situation where the government does not reach a deal with the EU, or in a situation where MPs reject the deal that government does eventually broker. The House of Lords sought to push for the ability of MPs to 'approve' or exercise discretion on the government's decision in the event of a no-deal Brexit, which May's government was ultimately successful in rejecting. Although the Act currently reads as a win for May's government, it comes with a few concessions. Section 13(1) of the Act now provides that the Withdrawal Agreement can only be ratified subject to stipulated conditions, namely approval by Parliament and enactment of an act which permits the implementation of the Withdrawal Agreement. Although the Act mandates parliamentary involvement, approval, and control, it also ultimately leaves the power to specify the terms of the Withdrawal Agreement and a future trading arrangement with the EU in the hands of the government, thus finding a compromise on the issue of a 'meaningful vote.'

---

[30] European Communities Act of 1972.

[31] See Articles 1-3, 7, 10, 13, 19, EU Withdrawal Act.

As far as the Northern Ireland border issue is concerned, the Act states that the UK government must not do anything which is incompatible with the Northern Ireland Act 1998, and therefore, may not build any physical infrastructure or checks and controls between Northern Ireland and the Republic of Ireland.[32] In the absence of any physical border though, it would seemingly be hard for the UK to enforce its own trade regulations, and the only feasible result would be retaining the customs arrangement with the EU. However, the provision of the Act is subject to an agreement between the UK and the EU, so it remains to be seen how the UK-EU negotiations are likely to adhere to the provisions of the Act.

C. FUTURE UK-EU TRADE RELATIONSHIP

The 21-month period stipulated in the Draft Withdrawal Agreement is meant to offer enough time to negotiate a future trading relationship between the EU and the UK. However, it is currently unclear what the nature of this relationship will be. A few different models have been considered including: (a) the Norway model, under which the UK would retain access to the EU's single market (goods, services, capital and people) upon joining the European Economic Area Agreement (EEA) and working out an agreement that would include continued payments into the EU budget and continued jurisdiction of the CJEU; (b) the FTA model, based on the example of the Canadian-EU Trade Agreement (CETA); and (c) the Turkey model, based on the EU's customs union with Turkey. However, in May's Mansion House speech of March 2, 2018, all such models were rejected in a push for a 'customs partnership,' a novel trading arrangement that would extend beyond the scope of a regular free trade agreement while rejecting some of the elements of the Norway model.[33] Key elements of this unique approach include reciprocal binding commitments, an open border with Ireland, full recognition of standards thereby facilitating customs procedures, and the ability to negotiate independent trade policies with non-EU countries post-Brexit.

The EU, on the other hand, has a different vision in mind. In an assertive response to May's proposal, the EU noted that an exit from the EU would necessarily lead to 'frictions in trade' and that the negative economic consequences were inevitable results of the UK's vote.[34] Further, 'A non-member of the Union, that does not live up to the same

[32] Article 10(2)(b), EU Withdrawal Act.

[33] "Our Future Economic Partnership with the European Union: PM Speech," Prime Minister's Office, March 2, 2018.

[34] European Council, Article 50 Guidelines, Brussels, March 23, 2018, para. 4.

obligations as a member, cannot have the same rights and enjoy the same benefits as a member.'[35] Therefore, the only possible outcome of negotiations that the EU deems available would be an FTA and not an arrangement as broad or as deep as May's proposal. The EU appears to envision an FTA that would address trade in goods, with an attempt to maintain zero tariffs and no quantitative restrictions with appropriate accompanying rules of origin, customs cooperation, preserving the regulatory and jurisdictional autonomy of the parties and integrity of the EU Customs Union, disciplines on TBT and SPS measures, a framework for voluntary regulatory cooperation, and trade in services, with the aim of allowing market access to provide services under host state rules.[36]

In July 2018, and perhaps in response to the red lines set by the EU, the May government published a new proposal, its White Paper on the future relationship between the United Kingdom and the European Union following a weekend retreat at Chequers to hash out the proposal among her cabinet.[37] Although May's Cabinet signed on to the Chequers proposal, which calls for a UK-EU FTA under a 'common rulebook,' the proposal met with alarm and disdain from many others, including some in May's Cabinet and a number of her own MPs. May's Foreign Secretary Boris Johnson and her Secretary of State for Exiting the EU, David Davis, both resigned in protest over what they saw as too soft a Brexit enshrined in the Chequers proposal and the accompanying White Paper.

The White Paper sets forth three pillars for future cooperation between the UK and the EU: (1) an economic partnership; (2) a security partnership; and (3) a cross-cutting cooperation arrangement, all overseen by a joint governance structure modelled on CETA and other trade agreements. The economic partnership calls for tariff-free trade in goods with a "common rulebook" for regulatory standards for such goods, a "new customs arrangement" that treats the UK and the EU as one customs union, a new mobility framework for the movement of people, a new arrangement to facilitate services and digital trade and a new regulatory arrangement for financial services. As such, the plan is likely to harmonize standards while phasing out customs checks and controls between the UK and EU.[38] The proposal seems to advocate for no changes in the trade relationship for goods, but separate and new arrangements for services, including financial services. The notion of

[35] Id.
[36] Id.
[37] HM Government, "The future relationship between the United Kingdom and the European Union," July 12, 2018.
[38] Id.

maintaining adherence to EU regulatory standards and customs-union-esque provisions is a prospect that is not sitting well with hardline Brexit supporters and those that preferred May's initial stance set forth in her September 22, 2017 Florence speech outlining a plan for a "new era of cooperation and partnership between the UK and the EU."[39]

It remains to be seen, given the differing visions of a future agreement both between the UK and the EU and within the UK itself, how the lines will finally be drawn and what compromises will be made. No matter whether the final agreement is a soft Brexit or a hard one, the impact of a new paradigm on the private sector is likely to be significant and exacerbated by the existence of major supply chains for many producers spanning both the UK and other EU countries. Take the supply chain of BMW, an automobile company, as an example. Production of BMW cars requires a number of components to cross the English Channel as many as four times before a vehicle is fully built. In the wake of Brexit, it is likely that such back and forth across the Channel will be met with additional duties and/or customs regulations, which is likely to create bottlenecks at the border. Even in a zero-tariff regime, potential bottlenecks caused by additional processing or regulatory procedures are like to cause significant manufacturing delays.[40] Such hindrances to the private sector are likely to complicate life for the vast majority of both UK and EU businesses. While the transition period could serve as a potential preparation period for these companies, it is essential for a future trading arrangement to account for such regulatory challenges.

III. UK RELATIONS WITH NON-EU COUNTRIES

The aftermath of Brexit is likely also to have severe impacts on non-EU countries. This is particularly the case for countries with which the EU already has FTAs. For starters, agreements with non-EU countries will no longer apply to the UK once it leaves the EU. The Draft Withdrawal Agreement addresses this issue and mandates the UK to retain its obligations in EU treaties with non-EU countries through the transition period.[41]

---

[39] "A new era of cooperation and partnership between the UK and the EU: PM speech," Prime Minister's Office, September 22, 2017.

[40] Burkhard Riering. "BMW task force prepares for worst-case Brexit." Automotive News Europe. 16 June 2018.

[41] Article 124(1), Draft Withdrawal Agreement."1. Without prejudice to Article 122(2), during the transition period, the United Kingdom shall be bound by the obligations stemming from the international agreements concluded by the Union, or by Member

The general premise is the UK is to be treated (at least by the EU) as though it remains a member of the EU through the end of the transition period. However, many of the EU's international agreements are with non-EU states, raising the clear question of the degree to which such third parties must or will agree to also treat the UK as if it were still a member of the EU through December 31, 2020. In a footnote to Article 124(1) of the Draft Withdrawal Agreement, it is agreed that "the Union will notify the other parties to these agreements that during the transition period the UK is to be treated as a Member State for the purpose of these agreements."[42] However, such a notification will not in itself create an obligation for third countries to continue to treat the UK as though it remained a member state of the EU. The clear hope by the UK and the EU is that since third countries have an interest in preserving stability in commercial relations, they will also continue to treat the UK as if it were a member of the EU, as least for purposes of any FTAs between the EU and a third country. But what happens if they don't? Many will have to consider their internal legal processes and may not have an automatic way to quickly change the parties to its agreements to include the UK once it is no longer a formal member of the EU.

No requirement to recognize the UK as party during the transition period

Most of the agreements at issue clearly provide that the parties to the agreement are the EU and its Member States, on the one hand, and the third-party country on the other. And the UK will cease to be a party to such agreements once it is no longer a member of the EU, which will be on March 29, 2019.[43] Whether the various third-party countries will agree

---

States acting on its behalf, or by the Union and its Member States acting jointly as referred to in Article 2(a)(iv)."

[42] Article 124(1) (footnote), Draft Withdrawal Agreement. The EU currently has 36 international trade (including a Free Trade Agreement with South Korea) or economic partnership agreements in place, 46 agreements partly in place (including Free Trade Agreements with Canada, Colombia, Ecuador and Peru), eight agreements pending (including Free Trade Agreements with Japan, Singapore and Vietnam), five agreements being updated and 21 agreements being negotiated. http://ec.europa.eu/trade/policy/countries-and-regions/negotiations-and-agreements/#_in-place.

[43] Scholars looking at the text and the territorial scope of the EU's FTAs and similar agreements agree that the UK ceases to be a party to the FTA from the date when it ceases to be a formal member of the EU, which is March 29, 2019. See, for example, Kim, Jay, "Is the United Kingdom Still a Party to the EU-Korea FTA After Brexit," *Legal Aspects of Brexit,* Hillman, Jennifer and Gary Horlick (eds), IIEL (2017), pp. 61-87; Ana Poienaru, Stefanija Savic, and Morgan McCabe, Trade Lab, "Brexit and the EU -Canada Comprehensive Economic and Trade Agreement: Implications for the European Union, the United Kingdom and Canada," https://www.tradelab.org/single-post/2018/03/02/

to effectively deem the UK to still be a member of the EU may vary depending on whether their internal legal procedures permit them to do so and on the products traded between the UK and the third party.

One of the significant issues for the UK will be that many of its products are produced with numerous components or services from other EU member states. So long as the UK is "deemed" to be a member of the EU, its goods would likely continue to satisfy the rules of origin contained in the various trade agreements that spell out what portion of the work, or value-added or components must come cumulatively from the EU member states in order for the good to be considered "Made in the EU" for purposes of receiving duty free treatment under the FTA. Similarly, if the EU is exporting goods containing a substantial amount of input materials or value from the UK, its goods may no longer meet the FTA rule-of-origin thresholds.[44] If the third-party to an FTA perceives that it has been or will soon be flooded with duty-free imports as a result of the FTA, that third party might decide not to deem the UK to be a member of the EU after March 29, 2019. If so, those goods that no longer meet the rule of origin requirements would be subject to the normal Most Favored Nation (MFN) tariffs that were applicable before the FTA was put in place.

Issues Where Third Parties May Not Wish to Treat UK as an EU Member

Other third-parties may also have reasons not to treat the UK as a member of the EU beyond March 29, 2019. For example, those countries facing anti-dumping or countervailing duties on their exports as a result of a finding by the European Commission that their exports were dumped or subsidized and were causing material injury to the domestic producers in the EU may object to the continuation of such duties, particularly those applied by the UK. Given that the anti-dumping and countervailing duty rules at the World Trade Organization (WTO) require that each country imposing such duties must first conduct its own investigation of allegedly dumped or subsidized imports, if the UK wishes to maintain any such duties after March 29, 2019, it must conduct its own investigations. Similarly, the EU may have to re-do its trade remedy determinations if its injury determinations included data from

Brexit-and-the-EU---Canada-Comprehensive-Economic-and-Trade-Agreement-Implications-for-the-European-Union-the-United-Kingdom-and-Canada.

[44] The issue of rules of origin is explored in Chapter 16, Jacob Travers, "The Impact of Rules of Origin on the UK's Post-Brexit Trade Relationships."

UK companies or its export price calculations included sales made in the UK.[45]

Another example may be sanitary or phytosanitary (SPS) measures put in place to protect EU farmers and food producers from diseases that could affect their plants or animals. WTO rules permit such restrictions if they are based on a scientific assessment by the EU that certain imports pose a threat to EU plants, animals or food safety. However, those EU-wide risk assessments may not necessarily support the continuation of import restrictions by the UK. For example, the EU often restricts the import of oranges from countries such as South Africa and the United States based on a concern over the importation of oranges with the fungal infection Citrus Black Spot, since the disease might be spread to Spain's orange groves. But given the climate in the UK, it does not have commercial orange groves that could be affected by Citrus Black Spot and therefore no basis to maintain the EU's restrictions. As such, South Africa or the United States or other citrus producing countries may have an incentive not to deem the UK a member of the EU after March 29, 2019.[46]

Although the footnote to Article 124(1) reflects the EU's attempts to ensure continuity of UK's status as an EU Member insofar as it applies to treaties with non-EU countries, such efforts may not be enough – both for legal reasons and for the economic and trade issues noted above. One option is for the UK to seek to replicate all of the affected treaties. However, this is both a time-intensive and arduous process. As an alternative, the UK has proposed using the interpretive tool codified in Article 31 of the Vienna Convention on the Law of Treaties (VCLT) to urge non-EU countries to regard the UK as an EU Member State. Article 31 provides that a treaty is to be interpreted in its context, which can include a subsequent agreement between the parties regarding its interpretation or application. The UK proposes applying this provision to interpret the terms 'European Union' or 'EU Member State' to include the UK.[47] It is uncertain whether non-EU countries can or will observe this process.

---

[45] The issue of the potential carryover of anti-dumping measures is explored in depth in Chapter 13, Shengxiang Ni, "EU Trade Remedy Policy in the Wake of Brexit – A Case Study of the Steel Industry."

[46] The of SPS measures in a post-Brexit world is explored in depth in Chapter 6, Alexander Stanley, "Brexit and SPS Measures: Implications for the UK."

[47] HM Government, Technical Note: International Agreements During the Implementation Period. 8 February 2018.

UK Trade Agreements with Third Countries

The UK repeatedly cited its freedom to negotiate bilateral arrangements with non-EU countries as a key outcome of Brexit. Such 'taking back' of power is codified in Article 124(4) of the Draft Withdrawal Agreement.[48] However, in practice, it is unclear whether the provision will necessarily allow the UK to exert such power. Given the significance of UK-EU relations to global business and trade, it is unlikely that non-EU countries will sign binding agreements with the UK if they are uncertain of the future relations between the UK and the EU. Much of the investment in the UK is dependent on ready access to both UK and EU markets. The absence of certainty of such unfettered access for goods and services "Made in the UK" to the EU market may limit the real negotiating power that the UK will be able to wield during the transition period. Further, it could extend the timeline for bilateral trading agreements beyond the transition period, which could have severe impacts on the UK's economy.

IV. INTRA-UK DYNAMICS

Debates over how to do Brexit have also resulted in a range of intra-UK skirmishes. May's government has been subject to pressures from a range of sources. From the very beginning, the Supreme Court's Article 50 decision and the delays in the House of Parliament have posed stumbling blocks to the government's authority to take Brexit-related decisions. In addition, backlash from the House of Lords at various instances has been challenging. While the Lords have more or less ultimately backed down in their stance towards May's government, the pushback has multiple ramifications on intra-UK dynamics, delays the Brexit process, and potentially affects the UK's bargaining power in negotiations with the EU.

Further, from a political perspective, the Northern Ireland issue runs deep. As a result of a loss of seats during a snap election in 2018, May's government was forced to enter into an agreement with Northern Ireland's Democratic Unionist Party (DUP) in order to retain its political position. Such a coalition potentially increases the political pressure on May's government to resolve Irish border issues in a manner that would be suitable to pro-Brexit DUP's concerns, which means ensuring that the alignment on standards and regulatory issues is stronger between

---

[48] Article 124(4), Draft Withdrawal Agreement. "Notwithstanding paragraph 3, during the transition period, the United Kingdom may negotiate, sign and ratify international agreements entered into its own capacity in the areas of exclusive competence of the Union provided those agreements do not enter into force or apply during the transition period, unless so authorized by the Union."

Northern Ireland and Britain than it is between Northern Ireland and Ireland. The current if-all-else-fails backstop in the Draft Withdrawal Agreement does just the opposite, effectively creating a border in the Irish Sea.

Finally, and more recently, May's government has been subject to blow-ups from within. The sudden resignations of David Davis and Boris Johnson have forced some government reshuffling at a critical time when greater progress to resolve both outstanding disagreements over the Draft Withdrawal Agreement and the crafting of a framework for the future relationship between the UK and the EU is desperately needed. It remains to be seen how this intra-UK upheaval is likely to affect negotiations with the EU, but these developments also raise questions regarding governance of the UK once—and, as it increasingly appears, if—Brexit does indeed happen.

V. CONCLUSION

With the two-year time clock for Brexit ticking away, questions and concerns over where Brexit is headed become more urgent. The recent developments in the UK raise the specter of an inability to garner enough votes in the Parliament for any particular approach, leaving the UK (and everyone else) in the worst of all worlds—a hard exit. If the Parliament cannot agree on some form of a withdrawal package, then the automaticity of Article 50—"the Treaties shall cease to apply"—will kick in on March 29, 2019, with no transition period and no backstops in place to bridge the many legal gaps that will be created. As such, planning for the transition—whether under the terms of the Draft Withdrawal Agreement with its 21-month transition period or not—becomes essential. From the resolution of the Irish border, to the implications for data flows, regulatory measures, professional qualifications for workers, financial services trade and future relationships between the UK, the EU and the rest of the world, the slate of issues that must be discussed, debated and resolved remains large. The chapters that follow are designed to do just that—to spell out transition issues that must be considered and addressed if the chaos that could otherwise result is to be avoided.

PART I:

UK's Post-Brexit "To Do" List

CHAPTER 2: THE UK'S AGRICULTURAL DOMESTIC SUPPORT COMMITMENT AT THE WTO AFTER BREXIT

ARIANE YVON

INTRODUCTION

All commitments of the United Kingdom ("UK) at the World Trade Organization ("WTO"), are currently contained in the WTO schedule of the European Union ("EU"). At the end of the Brexit transition period in December 2020, the EU's WTO schedule will no longer be applicable to the UK.[1] The EU's existing quantitative commitments will therefore have to be split up between the EU and the UK before that date, with the approval of all WTO Members. One of these commitments covers the subsidization of the agricultural sector. Under the WTO Agreement on Agriculture ("AoA"),[2] the maximum levels of the most trade-distorting kind of domestic support[3] (called the Amber box support or Aggregate Measurement of Support) that WTO Members can provide to their farmers in any year are bound by a scheduled overall "aggregate" cap referred to as Bound Total Aggregate Measurement of Support ("BTAMS").

The UK and the EU announced that the BTAMS of the EU28 ("EU28 BTAMS") would be apportioned between them.[4] If all WTO Members agree to such apportionment, the question remains how the UK and the EU will proceed to split up the EU BTAMS.

The first part of this chapter provides a background on the issue, including an explanation on the AoA discipline on domestic support. The second part analyses the stakes underlying the apportionment of the

---

[1] *Recommendation for a Council authorizing the opening of negotiations with a view to apportioning the Union's WTO concessions on Tariff Rate Quotas annexed to the General Agreement on Tariffs and Trade 1994 in view of the withdrawal of the United Kingdom from the Union*, May 22, 2018, European Commission, at 1, https://eur-lex.europa.eu/resource.html?uri=cellar:-86068319-5dd9-11e8-ab9c 01aa75ed71a1.0021.02/DOC_1&format=PDF.

[2] Agreement on Agriculture, April 15, 1994, Marrakesh Agreement Establishing the World Trade Organization, Annex 1A, 1867 U.N.T.S. 410. [Not reproduced in I.L.M.].

[3] Under the AoA domestic support refers to agricultural subsidies other than export subsidies.

[4] *Joint letter from the EU and the UK Permanent Representatives to the WTO*, October 11, 2017, https://ec.europa.eu/commission/sites/beta-political/files/letter_from_eu_and_uk_-permanent_representatives.pdf.

EU BTAMS between the EU and the UK. Finally, the last part details potential ways to proceed.

I. BACKGROUND

A. *UK'S AGRICULTURAL POLICY (OR POLICIES) POST-BREXIT*

On average, 50 to 80% of a British farmer's income comes in the form of agricultural subsidies.[5] These subsidies are currently provided in the UK through an EU legislative framework, the Common Agricultural Policy ("CAP"). The CAP is a system of subsidies and support programs for agriculture which combines direct payments to farmers together with market supports. The UK will continue to apply the rules of the CAP during the transition period until December 2020 but will be operating outside of the CAP under any scenario after that.[6]

While the UK will be free to design its own agricultural policy after the transition period, the UK government has already guaranteed that farming subsidies will be protected at the current EU level until 2022 (end of the current Parliament) in each part of the UK.[7] After that however, direct payments will be phased out in England and replaced by a new "environmental land management system" based on the idea of paying farmers "public money for public goods."[8]

Whether there will be only one post-Brexit UK agricultural policy or several agricultural policies remains uncertain. Agricultural policy in the UK is currently subject to EU policy making and devolved to Scotland, Wales and Northern Ireland, meaning that the money received from the EU is administered by national governments.[9] What will happen to the agricultural competency after Brexit is currently a debated question. The EU Withdrawal Bill, currently before Parliament, proposes that devolved agricultural competency returns to Westminster, allowing some of them

---

[5] *Brexit: Future UK agriculture policy*, House of Common Library Briefing Paper by Emma Downing, Sarah Coe, January 31, 2018, at 3, https://www.parliament.uk/documents/-commons-library/Brexit-UK-agriculture-policy-CBP-8218.pdf.

[6] *Id.*

[7] *Farming for the next generation*, Speech of Secretary of State Michael Gove at the Oxford Farming Conference on January 4, 2018, https://www.gov.uk/government/speeches/-farming-for-the-next-generation.

[8] *Health and Harmony: the future for food, farming and the environment in a Green Brexit*, Department for Environment, Food and Rural Affairs, February 27, 2018, at 7, https://assets.publishing.service.gov.uk/government/uploads/system/uploads/attachment_data/file/684003/future-farming-environment-consult-document.pdf.

[9] *Id.* at 59.

to be "released".[10] The Scottish and Welsh Governments, however, have opposed this on constitutional and practical grounds.[11]

B. AOA'S DOMESTIC SUPPORT DISCIPLINE

Shaping the new post-Brexit agricultural support policy (or policies) will require the UK to go through a process of negotiation at the WTO. As discussed in the introduction, the subsidization of the agricultural sector is disciplined at the international level by the AoA, one of the many agreements negotiated during the Uruguay Round which took effect on 1st January 1995. The Agreement is made up of three 'pillars': market access,[12] export competition,[13] and domestic support. All WTO Members, except least developed countries (LDCs), were required to make commitments in all these areas in order to liberalize agricultural trade.

AoA's discipline on domestic support starts from the fact that different types of subsides are presumed to afford different degrees of protection.[14] AoA classifies domestic support measure based on their presumed trade distorting nature into three boxes: Green box, Blue box and Amber box.[15]

---

[10] *See EU Withdrawal Bill: Clause 11 and the devolution deadlock*, Institute for Government, March 20, 2018, https://www.instituteforgovernment.org.uk/explainers/eu-withdrawal-bill-clause-11-devolution.

[11] *Id.*

[12] Regarding market access the most difficult negotiations, not discussed in this chapter, are related to the apportionment of the EU's tariff rate quotas (TRQs). The task of extracting the UK's TRQs from the EU's is already contentious. On October 11, 2017, the EU and the UK informed WTO Members that they agreed to apportion TRQs on the basis of historical trade flows. The plan has been rejected by various WTO Members. On May 22, 2018, the European Commission released a draft to be approved by EU Member States that would allow the Commission (and also the UK) to start talks with other Members of the WTO on separating TRQs between EU and the UK.

[13] The third pillar, "export competition" includes export subsidies and three areas of policy that may contain hidden subsidies: government involvement in export credit and insurance, food aid, and state trading exporting enterprises. Under the 2015 Nairobi Ministerial Decision on Export Competition, WTO Members, including the EU, have agreed to eliminate their scheduled export subsidies and to discipline the three other components. Export Competition Ministerial Decision of 19 December 2015, Ministerial Conference Tenth Session Nairobi, WT/MIN(15)/45 WT/L/980. On October 17, 2017, the EU submitted a revised goods schedule to the WTO for certification (document G/MA/TAR/RS/506) confirming the elimination of export subsidies. Unless the UK oppose the Nairobi Decision, this should be implemented without any problem.

[14] *See Domestic support in agriculture: the boxes,* WTO website, https://www.wto.org/english/tratop_e/agric_e/agboxes_e.htm.

[15] *Id.*

Green box and Blue box supports are excluded from all WTO discipline, meaning that WTO Members are free to provide Green box and Blue box subsidies without any limitation. Green box support is presumed to have "no, or at most minimal, trade distorting effects"[16] while Blue box support is presumed to have trade distorting effect but less than Amber box support.[17] Green box support includes decoupled payments, defined as direct payments to farmers based on production in a historic and fixed reference period and not linked to current production or price.[18] Decoupled payments are classified as Green box support because they do not influence production decisions of farmers receiving payments. Green box support also includes disaster relief, domestic food aid and environmental programs.[19]

All other agricultural support is classified as Amber box support, presumed to be production and trade distorting.[20] Amber box support is also referred to as Aggregate Measurement of Support. In any year, the Current Total AMS ("CTAMS") calculated for each country[21] must not exceed its scheduled BTAMS.[22] Amber box support includes coupled payments, which unlike decoupled payments, are based on current production or price and may affect the decision making process of farmers.[23] Amber box support also includes price support regimes, which are government assistance in maintaining the levels of market prices regardless of supply or demand.

The EU28 BTAMS is equal to the BTAMS of the EU12 ("EU12 BTAMS)[24] plus the BTAMS of every EU Member having joined the EU after the Uruguay Round.[25] The EU28 BTAMS, notified to the Committee on Agriculture in November 2015 after Croatia joined the

---

16 AoA Annex 2.

17 Details are set out in Paragraph 5 of AoA Article 6.

18 *Domestic support in agriculture: the boxes, supra* note 14.

19 *Domestic support in agriculture: The boxes,* WTO website, https://www.wto.org/english/tratop_e/agric_e/agboxes_e.htm.

20 *See* AoA Article 6.

21 CTAMS covers all Amber box support provided, irrespective of whether such support is only granted for a subset of agricultural commodities or whether it was available to all agricultural production. The *de minimis* exemption excludes from the CTAMS calculation support that across all the relevant support programs amounts for less than 5% of the total value of the production of a specific commodity (product-specific support), or 5% of the value of total production (non-product specific support). *See* AoA, Article 4.

22 *See* AoA Article 6.1 and 6.3.

23 *Domestic support in agriculture: the boxes, supra* note 14.

24 The BTAMS of each WTO Member (including the EU12 and the new EU Member States) is based on the amount of support it provided during a base period (1986-88) plus a reduction commitment of 20% for developed countries and 13% for developing countries.

25 *See* for a detailed explanation: Lars Brink, *UK Brexit and WTO farm support limits,* July 13, 2016, http://capreform.eu/uk-brexit-and-wto-farm-support-limits.

EU, amounts to 72,378 billion euros.[26] The UK and the EU informed that they agreed to apportion between them the EU28 BTAMS on the basis of an objective methodology.[27] The methodology chosen is likely to be influenced by the stakes of the negotiation.

II. THE STAKES OF THE NEGOTIATION

The stakes of the negotiation between the EU and the UK for the apportionment of the EU BTAMS can be discerned from (A) the current use by the EU and the UK of Amber box support and (B) post-Brexit UK's interests in BTAMS.

A. THE EU AND UK' CURRENT USE OF AMBER BOX SUPPORT

As discussed above, the domestic support commitments taken by WTO Members during the Uruguay Round do not cover all kind of subsidies, but rather limit only the most trade distorting kind: Amber box support.

1. The EU's use of Amber box support

Domestic support data provided to the WTO reveals that the EU makes very small use of Amber box support. In its last notification to the Committee on Agriculture for the marketing year 2014-2015 dated March 5, 2018, the EU declared a cumulated amount of Green and Blue box subsidies of 68,135.6 billion euros for an amount of Amber box support of only 6,642.3 billion euros.[28] Exempted Green box and Blue box support therefore represent 91% of the total domestic support provided in the EU while non-exempted Amber box support represents only 9%. Such disproportion mostly results from the 2003 CAP reform and subsequent sectorial reforms, which decoupled most of the existing direct aid, moving most of the Amber and Blue box support to the Green box.[29] As a result, the EU does not make full use of its BTAMS, with a large gap between its CTAMS (6,642.3 billion euros) and its BTAMS (72,378 billion euros).[30]

---

26 Committee on Agriculture, *Notification of European Union for the marketing year 2012/2013 of domestic support*, November 2, 2015, GG/AG/N/26. On October 17, 2017, the EU submitted for certification a revised draft schedule for EU28 (document G/MA/TAR/RS/506).

27 *Joint letter from the EU and the UK Permanent Representatives to the WTO*, *supra* note 4.

28 Committee on Agriculture, *Notification of European Union for the marketing year 2014/2015 of domestic support,* March 5, 2018, G/AG/N/EU/43.

29 *WTO Agreement on Agriculture,* Fact Sheet on the European Union, European Parliament, January 1, 2018, http://www.europarl.europa.eu/atyourservice/en/-displayFtu.html?ftuId=FTU_3.2.7.html.

30 *See* Committee on Agriculture, *Notification of European Union for the marketing year 2014/2015 of domestic, supra* note 28.

2. The UK's use of Amber box support

The distribution of the UK's domestic support between AoA boxes is not provided in the EU notifications to the Committee on Agriculture, which do not indicate the repartition between boxes for each EU Member State. However, data published by the EU Commission and the UK government provides a general idea of the structure of the UK's domestic support.[31] The UK's agricultural expenditure is currently divided into three main categories.

The first and most important one, accounting for 79% of the UK's total agricultural expenditure in 2017, is direct payments.[32] Direct payments are provided under Pillar 1 of the CAP, known in England as the Basic Payment Scheme. In 2017, 97% of these direct payments were provided in the form of decoupled payments, classified under the AoA as Green box support, while only 1.7% were provided under the form of coupled payments, likely to be classified as Amber box support.[33]

The second biggest part of the UK's agricultural expenditure, accounting for 19% of the UK's total agricultural expenditure in 2017, is rural development. Rural development is provided under Pillar II of the CAP and aims at promoting economic, environmental and social development.[34] Pillar II support is notified by the EU at the WTO as Green box support.[35]

Finally, the third category of the UK's agricultural expenditure, accounting for only 2% of it in 2017, is market measures.[36] Market measures, usually provided under the form of prices support, fall within the Amber box.

While the classification between AoA boxes at the WTO is the result of more complex and precise calculations, the above numbers provide a rough approximation of the UK's Amber box support, which would have been only 4% of the UK's total agricultural expenditure in 2017.

The small use of Amber box support by both the EU and the UK suggests that the apportionment of BTAMS may not be the most

---

[31] *See* The UK Statistical Factsheet, European Commission, May 2018, at 4, https://ec.europa.eu/agriculture/sites/agriculture/files/statistics/factsheets/pdf/uk_en.pdf; Agriculture in the United Kingdom 2017, National Statistics, Department for Environment, Food and Rural Affairs, May 31, 2018, at 79, https://assets.publishing.service.gov.uk/government/uploads/system/uploads/attachment_data/file/712317/AUK-2017-31may18.pdf.

[32] *Id.*

[33] *Id.*

[34] *Second pillar of the CAP: rural development policy,* Fact Sheet on the European Union, European Parliament, April 2018, http://www.europarl.europa.eu/atyourservice/en/-displayFtu.html?ftuId=FTU_3.2.6.html.

[35] *See* Committee on Agriculture, *Notification of European Union for the marketing year 2014/2015 of domestic, supra* note 28.

[36] The UK Statistical Factsheet, *supra* note 31.

contentious part of the renegotiation of the UK's commitments at the WTO. However, the UK's interests in this negotiation cannot be reduced to its current use of Amber box support considering that the UK will have to shape a completely new agricultural subsidies policy outside of the CAP after Brexit, and that the negotiation of BTAMS must be thought of in a wider context of trade-offs in the UK's negotiations with the EU as well as with other WTO Members.

B. *POST-BREXIT UK'S INTERESTS IN BTAMS*

1. Reasons for the UK not to want to negotiate a large share of the EU BTAMS

a. The need to prioritize claims in the context of negotiations with the EU

The negotiation of the UK BTAMS will necessarily play a role in the trade-offs game with the EU. While at first glance the EU has little interest in high BTAMS as its CTAMS represents only 9% of its BTAMS, the EU will not offer the UK a large BTAMS without any concession in return. In this context, the UK may have to set up priorities in the renegotiation of its commitments under the AoA. The UK may decide to abandon its claim on BTAMS to gain leverage in the negotiation of the apportionment of EU's tariffs rate quotas (TRQs) on agricultural products.[37]

b. The necessity of a cautious stance regarding WTO Members

Since the EU BTAMS is a WTO commitment, WTO Members will have to agree to the fact that the UK and the EU can apportion between them the EU BTAMS as well as on the methodology used. If splitting up the EU BTAMS between the EU and the UK may reduce the EU's ceiling, WTO Members have little reason to contest at first glance. However, some Members may see the renegotiation of the UK's domestic support commitment as an opportunity to revive their complaints about the inequality underlying the inherent domestic support WTO framework. There are two main points of contention at the WTO concerning the AoA's discipline on domestic support. Firstly, Members that provided large amount of domestic support prior to the completion of the Uruguay Round have retained very high AMS caps, especially the EU.[38] Secondly the exclusion of Blue box subsidies from

[37] *See supra* note 12 for a short explanation on the negotiation between the EU and the UK on TRQs.

[38] Christian Lau and Colette Van der Ven, *The WTO Agreement on Agriculture*, Chapter 7 in Business Guide to Trade and Investment, Volume 1 International Trade, International Chamber of Commerce, 2017, at 192.

the calculation of CTAMS undermined the effectiveness of the AoA's subsidy reduction obligations by excluding precisely the type of domestic support most utilized by developed countries including the EU: compensation payments.[39] In such a contentious context, some WTO Members may decide to contest the mere fact that the UK is entitled to any BTAMS or could oppose the methodology proposed by the EU and the UK to split up the EU BTAMS, in the same way they recently pushed back on EU/UK plan to split up TRQs.[40]

In such a context, the UK may prefer not to enter in any sharp debate at the WTO regarding BTAMS, unless absolutely necessary for its future domestic policy. And apparently, this does not seem to be the case.

c. The absence of need of a large BTAMS

If the UK is likely to put its negotiation priorities on areas other than its BTAMS, it is because the UK apparently does not need a large BTAMS.

Firstly, at that point of the Brexit process, the UK does not send signals of an increase of its Amber box support. In its consultation paper on post-Brexit farming policy, the UK government set out its ambitions for what it deems a "Green Brexit", with a phasing out of direct payments and the implementation of a new "environmental land management system" in England, based on the idea of paying farmers for their work to enhance the environment and invest in sustainable food production.[41] Any agricultural support provided under a scheme that pays farmers for delivering environmentally beneficial outcomes would likely qualify as Green box support. As a result, if such policy path is followed, the UK would not need a large BTAMS to implement its domestic support policy.

In addition, the *de minimis* exemption rule under the AoA provides the UK with some policy space to offer Amber box support to its farmers without any limiting constraint.[42] A study conducted by Professor Alan Matthews[43] shows that, as a result of the *de minimis*

---

[39] *Id.* at 191.

[40] *See supra* note 12 for a short explanation on the negotiation between the EU and the UK on TRQs. *See e.g., Resistance to joint proposal to WTO leaves UK and EU divided*, The Guardian, April 25, 2018, https://www.theguardian.com/politics/2018/apr/25/-resistance-to-joint-proposal-to-wto-leaves-uk-and-eu-divided-us-australi-reject-brexit-trade-plans.

[41] *Health and Harmony: the future for food, farming and the environment in a Green Brexit, supra* note 8, at 7.

[42] The *de minimis* exemption rule is explained in note 16.

[43] Alan Matthews is professor Emeritus of European Agricultural Policy in the Department of Economics at Trinity College, Dublin, Ireland.

exemption, the UK could provide up to £2,310 million in domestic support to its farmers that would not be counted in the UK BTAMS.[44]

Considering that the UK may not need a large BTAMS to implement its proposed domestic support policy, the UK may decide to put its negotiation priorities with the EU and with WTO Members on other areas. Some other factors however predict that the UK may not want to accept a too constraining domestic support commitment at the WTO.

2. Reasons for the UK to want a large share of the EU BTAMS

a. An agricultural sector unable to survive without domestic support

The UK may not want to tie its hands at the WTO considering the fact that it may have to rely on farm subsidies to maintain its agricultural sector in the coming years.

While the pro-Brexit campaign heavily relied on the post-Brexit UK's freedom from participating to the EU budget, it remains that a big part of the money sent to Brussels currently comes back to the UK in the form of multi-million pounds of agriculture subsidies. While Brexit will free the UK from paying money to the EU budget, it will not free the UK from the necessity to pay money to its farmers. In fact, the UK will probably have to provide more domestic support than it did while in the EU if it wants its agricultural sector to stay sustainable. As discussed above, on average, 50 to 80% of a British farmer's income comes in the form of agricultural subsidies.[45] And despite this high level of subsidization of the UK farmers under the CAP, 26% of British farms failed to break even in 2016.[46] Such a critical situation occurs despite the fact that British farmers are currently protected from low-priced imports by the EU's Common External Tariff. After Brexit, the UK's import tariffs subject to Free Trade Agreements ("FTAs") negotiations are likely to drop. In such a context, it is hard to conceive how the UK's farms, already struggling to prosper, may survive in a context of fiercer competition without at least an equivalent level of support from the UK government.

And if the UK decides to increase its level of farm subsidies, there is no guarantee that it would do so using only Green or Blue box subsidies.

---

[44] Alan Matthews, *Establishing the UK's non-exempt limit on agricultural support after Brexit*, January 29, 2017, http://capreform.eu/establishing-the-uks-non-exempt-limit-on-agricultural-support-after-brexit/.

[45] *Brexit: Future UK agriculture policy*, House of Common Library Briefing Paper, *supra* note 5.

[46] Allan Beattie, *Brexit and agriculture: British farmers to plough new course*, The Financial Times, January 14, 2018, https://www.ft.com/content/e33d5f12-f462-11e7-8715-e94187b3017e.

Some policy instruments classified as Amber Box support may be really useful in the context of a fierce international competition, especially coupled payments, administered support prices and deficiency payments.[47] By negotiating a large amount of BTAMS, the UK would ensure itself sufficient domestic policy space to use these tools if needed.

b. Potential internal tensions

In addition, the UK may not want to add constraining international commitments to potential internal tensions. As discussed above, there are already some tensions on the exercise of the agricultural competency between Westminster and the devolved administrations in Scotland, Wales and Northern Ireland, with the Scottish and Welsh Governments refusing to recommend legislative consent for the EU Withdrawal Bill.[48] Such tensions on the exercise of the agricultural policy power predict strong disagreements on the substance of the agricultural policies chosen. If Westminster takes back legislative power concerning agricultural policy, there is no guarantee that the proposed policy would be supported by the three devolved administrations. In fact, disagreements are likely to arise from the important differences in needs between the agriculture in England and those in the devolved territories.[49] As the UK BTAMS will be binding for England, Scotland, Wales and Northern Ireland, the UK may want it to be large enough to give the government sufficient policy space to settle internal tensions.

c. The instability of the agricultural market

The agricultural commodities market, sometimes affected by pests and the vagaries of weather, is characterized by large price swings. Due to this instability, governments are sometimes forced to intervene, and having a less constraining commitment at the WTO would allow the UK to react to such unexpected circumstances.

d. BTAMS as a leverage in FTA negotiations

The UK Government has proposed to negotiate a series of FTAs with non-EU countries. Having a large BTAMS and a large amount of subsidies at the time of these negotiations could provide the UK with bargaining power, allowing it to offer the reduction of its domestic support in exchange for instance of large TRQs or small external tariffs.

---

[47] *See* Matthews, *supra* note 44.

[48] *Health and Harmony: the future for food, farming and the environment in a Green Brexit*, *supra* note 8.

[49] *See* Michael Keating, *the Repatriation of Competences in Agriculture after Brexit, Study: Uncertain Post-Brexit Future for Farmers in Scotland, Wales and Northern Ireland*, Centre on Constitutional Change, January 2018. In this research study, Michael Keating shows that the variation in need is in part due to the fact that respectively, 85, 81 and 70% of farmland in Scotland, Wales and Northern Ireland are in 'areas of natural constraint' such as hill farms, compared with only 17% of farmland in England.

III. THE POSSIBLE OUTCOMES OF THE NEGOTIATION

The UK and the EU have two principal options for apportioning the EU BTAMS, which would have to be approved at the WTO: (A) reconstructing what the UK BTAMS would have been during the Uruguay Round and deducting this amount from the EU28 BTAMS, (B) finding an allocation key to split up the amount of either the EU12 BTAMS or the EU28 BTAMS.[50]

Whichever option is chosen, the EU and the UK will also have to agree (and negotiate WTO approval) on the euros/pounds sterling rate, assuming that the UK BTAMS will be expressed in pounds sterling. The UK and the EU may agree on an exchange rate specifically for the purpose of splitting up the EU BTAMS (*e.g*, the average exchange rate between ECU and pound in 1986-1988) or they could agree on an exchange rate for the renegotiation of all the UK's WTO commitments (*e.g*, the exchange rate at the moment of withdrawal from the EU).

A. OPTION 1: RECONSTRUCTING WHAT THE UK BTAMS WOULD HAVE BEEN DURING THE URUGUAY ROUND

The key objective of the negotiation at the Uruguay Round has been to discipline and reduce domestic support while at the same time leaving great scope for governments to design domestic agricultural policies. In order to establish a basis for reductions, WTO Members set out the support they had provided to agriculture during the base period of 1986 to 1988 (referred to as Base Total AMS). Developed-country Members then committed to reduce their Base Total AMS by 20% over the six-year implementation period (1995-2000) to obtain their Bound Total AMS (BTAMS).

One way to determine the UK BTAMS after Brexit could be to take the amount of domestic support provided in favor of agricultural producers in the UK during the average 1986-88 base period, and reduce it by 20%. This amount could then be deducted from the EU28 BTAMS. Such methodology would have the clear advantage of providing an amount for the UK BTAMS which would not to be the result of a bilateral bargain between the EU and the UK but that would rather exactly reflect what the UK would have been entitled to as an individual country during the Uruguay Round.

This option, that requires to determine the UK contribution to the EU12 BTAMS, has major drawbacks regarding its feasibility, underlined

---

[50] This chapter elaborates on propositions from Dr. Lars Brink and Prof. Alan Matthews. *See* Brink *supra* note 25 and Matthews *supra* note 44.

and partially resolved by Dr. Lars Brink.[51] He explains that the EU's 1986-88 support was not in the form of easily traceable budgetary payments, but rather in the form of price gaps, which were then multiplied by the EU total production to get the market price support component of the product's AMS. If the EU and the UK have the data to reconstruct the level of support provided specifically by the UK during the base period 1986-88, this could be a first option for them to apportion the EU28 BTAMS.

B. OPTION 2: SPLITTING UP THE EU BTAMS USING AN ALLOCATION KEY

The UK and the EU could also (1) agree on an objective allocation key and (2) apply it to split up the amount of the EU BTAMS, which could be either the amount of the EU12 BTAMS or the amount of the EU28 BTAMS. This chapter provides (3) the potential UK BTAMS as a result of the various possible combinations (allocation key/amount divided).

1. The possible allocation keys

This chapter analyses four potential objective keys of allocation: (a) the UK's share of EU agricultural output (b) the UK's share of EU agricultural expenditures (c) the UK's share of EU CTAMS (d) the UK's share of EU holdings.

a. The UK's share of EU agricultural output

One possible way to split up the EU BTAMS, proposed by some scholars,[52] would be to do so in proportion of the UK's share of EU total agricultural output. If such an allocation key is chosen by the EU and the UK, it would likely be contested at the WTO.

WTO Members' BTAMS have been determined on the basis of their level of domestic support on a base period (1986-88). Using the UK's share of EU agricultural output to determine the UK BTAMS would amount to using a complete different basis for the UK than for the other WTO Members.

In addition, linking a country's agricultural output to its domestic support commitment could be criticized as such. WTO Members' efforts to reduce trade-distorting subsidies consist in large part in disconnecting domestic support from production. As such, establishing a clear link between agricultural output and domestic support could be contested at the WTO.

---

[51] Dr. Lars Brink is an affiliated with the Global Issues Initiative at Virginia Tech University and a leading expert on domestic support issues in the WTO Agreement on Agriculture. *See* Brink, *supra* note 25.

[52] *See* Alan Matthews, *WTO dimensions of a UK 'Brexit' and agricultural trade*, January 5, 2016, http://capreform.eu/wto-dimensions-of-a-uk-brexit-and-agricultural-trade/.

b. The UK's share of EU agricultural expenditures

Another key that could be used to split up the EU BTAMS between the EU and the UK is the UK's share of EU agricultural expenditures. Unlike the prior option, using the UK's share of EU agricultural expenditures would have the advantage of using for determining the UK BTAMS a basis similar than the one used to determine other WTO Members' BTAMS, namely the level of domestic support at a given time. Some WTO Members could criticize this choice, noting that the UK's agricultural expenditure is an artificial number amounting to its receipt of CAP payments. And the EU Member States' receipts of CAP payments are not the result of any specific formula but rather the result of non-transparent negotiations in the context of agreeing to the overall ceilings for the EU budget.

If the rationale of the first allocation key (*i.e.* the UK's share of EU agricultural output) and the rationale of the second one (*i.e.* the UK's share of EU agricultural expenditures) seem to differ, the stakes of the choice between the two are not high. The amount of the UK's agricultural expenditure is almost equal to the amount of the UK's receipt of CAP payments, and the latter (despite not being the result of any defined formula) is partially based on historic trends of agricultural output. As a result, the UK's share of EU agricultural expenditure is quite close to the UK's share of EU agricultural output (*see* table below on p15).

c. The UK's share of EU CTAMS

Another way to split up the EU BTAMS between the EU and the UK would be to do so accordingly to the UK's share of EU CTAMS. The EU and the UK could indeed decide to determine how much the UK contributes to the total EU use of Amber box support and to apply this percentage to divide the EU BTAMS.

This option is the one that is the most likely to be accepted by other WTO Members. In addition of using for determining the UK BTAMS a basis similar than the one used to determine other WTO Members' BTAMS, such method would reflect the UK's use of Amber Box support rather than the UK's use of domestic support regardless of the AoA boxes.

d. The UK's share of EU holdings

Finally, one last key that could be used to apportion the EU BTAMS is the UK's share of EU holdings. This could be an objective way to allocate EU BTAMS based on the EU and the UK's needs without linking domestic support to production. However as for the UK's share of EU agricultural output, WTO Members could oppose that option, denouncing the fact that the UK BTAMS would be set on a basis that was not the one used for determining other WTO Members' BTAMS, namely a level of domestic support at a given period.

Once the allocation key is chosen, it would be applied either to the amount of the EU28 BTAMS or to the amount of the EU12 BTAMS.

2. The amount to which the allocation key should be applied: EU12 BTAMS or EU28 BTAMS?

The EU and the UK already expressed their will to apportion the amount of the EU28 BTAMS.[53] As discussed above, the EU28 BTAMS is equal to the EU12 BTAMS plus the BTAMS of every EU Members States having joined the EU after the Uruguay Round, which amounts to 72,378 billion euros. Splitting up this amount seems to be the simplest option. It would avoid any question regarding the application of the chosen allocation key (*see* paragraph below). However, this option is likely to be contested at the WTO on the ground that such a number, notified to the Committee on Agriculture in 2015,[54] has never been officially accepted by WTO Members so far. The EU has however submitted for certification a revised draft schedule for the EU28 on October 17, 2017 (document G/MA/TAR/RS/506). Some WTO Members could also claim that splitting up the EU28 BTAMS would provide the UK with a portion of BTAMS that it is not entitled to receive. The EU28 BTAMS is indeed constituted in part of the BTAMS of the EU Members States that have joined the EU after the Uruguay Round. As under the AoA every WTO Member has been only entitled to a BTAMS equal to its domestic support during the base period 1986-1988 reduced by 20% and not anything more, some WTO Members could claim that the UK is only entitled to a portion of the EU12 BTAMS (calculated based on the EU12 domestic support) and not to a portion of the EU28 BTAMS. If the apportionment of the EU28 BTAMS is contested at the WTO, the UK and the EU may have to split up the amount of the EU12 BTAMS.

The EU12 BTAMS amounts to 61,204 billion ECU. If the decision is made to apportion the amount of the EU12 BTAMS, the EU and the UK would then have to decide how to apply the allocation key to this amount. More precisely, they would have to decide whether the UK's share of any allocation key should be the UK's share of EU12 (*e.g.*, the UK's share of EU12 agricultural output) or the UK's share of EU28 (*e.g.*, the UK's share of EU28 agricultural output). If the amount serving as a

---

[53] *See Joint letter from the EU and the UK Permanent Representatives to the WTO*, *supra* note 4. "Similarly, we intend that the EU's *current* annual and final bound commitment level specified for domestic agricultural support be apportioned between the future EU and the UK on the basis of an objective methodology." (emphasis added).

[54] Committee on Agriculture, *Notification of European Union for the marketing year 2012/2013 of domestic support*, *supra* note 26.

basis for the apportionment is the EU12 BTAMS rather than the EU28 BTAMS, it could seem logical to determine the UK's share of EU12 of any allocation key rather than the UK's share of EU28 of any allocation key. If the option of using the UK's share of EU12 of any allocation key to split up the EU12 BTAMS is chosen, a sub-question raises: should the UK's share of EU12 used be the UK's share of EU12 today (the UK's share of EU12's agricultural output in 2018) or the UK's share of EU12 during 1986-88 base period (the UK's share of EU12's agricultural output in 1986-88)? In the table provided below (*see* p15), the UK's share of EU12 of any allocation key is based on the most recent data, assuming that if data from 1986-88 were collected and analysed for the purpose of the BTAMS negotiation, the UK and EU would choose to reconstruct what the UK BTAMS would have been during the Uruguay Round (*see* above Option 1).

3. Potential results

The table below provides the amounts of potential UK BTAMS depending of the different combinations of allocation key and amount apportioned.

UK's potential BTAMS (in billions EUR)[55]

Allocation key / Amount apportioned		UK's share of EU CTAMS*	UK's share of EU agricultural output (9,1% of EU12 and 7.2% of EU28 in 2017)	UK's share of EU28 agricultural expenditures (9.5% of EU12 and 6.7% of EU28 in 2017)	UK's share of EU holdings (4.3% of EU121.7% of EU28 in 2013)
Splitting up the EU12 BTAMS (61,204)	By using UK's share of EU12	X	5,569.6	5,814.4	2,680.7
	By using UK's share of EU28	X	4,406.7	4,100.7	1,040.5
Splitting up the EU28 BTAMS by using UK's share of EU28 (72,378)		X	5,221.2	4,849.3	1,230.4

[55] Numbers provided are calculated from data provided by the EU Commission in the section "Agriculture in the European Union and the Member States - Statistical factsheets", available at https://ec.europa.eu/agriculture/statistics/factsheets_en.

* As mentioned above, the EU notifications to the WTO Committee on Agriculture do not provide the contribution by Members states to the EU CTAMS. The UK's share of AMS mainly corresponds to amount of the UK's share of EU's direct payments falling under AMS and the UK's share of EU's production of products subject to administered prices.

IV. CONCLUSION

At the end of the transition period, the UK will leave the CAP and will be free to set its own agricultural policy. This freedom will be limited by the AoA, which imposes a maximum level of trade distorting domestic support for each country, referred to as its BTAMS. The international constraints that the UK will face in setting its new domestic support regime will depend on the outcome of its negotiation with the EU and other WTO Members regarding the apportionment of the EU28 BTAMS. Despite the fact that the EU does not make full use of its BTAMS, the EU is unlikely to provide a large BTAMS to the UK upon its request without any trade-offs. Whether the UK will and should give up any claim on BTAMS to gain bargaining power on other areas of negotiations is not straightforward. While the UK does not seem to need a large BTAMS considering its current use of Amber box support, the uncertainty surrounding Brexit effects on the UK's international trade in food and the UK's need to have as much leverage as possible to negotiate its future trade deals may incentivize the UK not to abandon its "right" to have a large BTAMS too easily.

Whatever it will be, the UK's position on domestic support during the coming trade negotiations will send a clear message on the UK's ambitions for its agricultural sector post-Brexit. The UK lost self-sufficiency in food long ago and has a current important trade deficit in food and drinks.[56] Its agricultural sector accounts today for less than 1% of the UK's total output and is apparently unable to survive without state intervention. In such a context, the UK government's proposal to reduce direct payments to farmers could be read as implicitly announcing that the UK government is ready to sacrifice its agricultural sector on the altar of a liberalized economy, promoting non-farming rural activity based on tourism and industry which creates jobs without needing continuous subsidies.

[56] The UK has a trade deficit in food and drinks of £23 billion pa – of which £18 billion with the EU27. *Brexit: Future UK agriculture policy*, House of Common Library Briefing Paper, *supra* note 5 at 5.

Chapter 3: Safeguarding the United Kingdom's Financial Services Sector in Preparation for Brexit

Caitlin Thomas

I. Introduction

Nearly two years post-referendum, over a year since Article 50 was triggered, and less than a year out from the prospects of Brexit Day One, the picture remains far from clear as to just what March 29, 2019 holds for the UK. The information that *is* available is vague, often conflicting, and liberally mixed with political grandstanding. For those interested in researching the topic, this might be mildly frustrating. But for those whose businesses are at stake, the looming deadline may be cause for outright alarm. And when the economic output of those businesses accounts for over a tenth of the economy, it makes sense for others to join in that alarm.

To get a sense of the current state of confusion, one needs only read the headlines. Articles entitled "Brexit details taking too long to agree, warns City chief"[1] and "Philip Hammond says transition deal has ended fears of Brexit-inspired banker exodus,"[2] appear just days apart. Seeing "UK fund houses record big drop in investment professional hires" alongside "London Remains Graduates' Choice for Financial Services Careers,"[3] leaves one wondering just what those graduates will do once they arrive. Finally, there are still those calling for a second referendum

---

[1] Oliver Ralph and Caroline Binham, *Brexit details taking too long to agree, warns City chief*, THE FINANCIAL TIMES (Apr. 19, 2018) https://www.ft.com/content/ff640da6-43e2-11e8-803a-295c97e6fd0b.

[2] Alexandra Rogers, *Philip Hammond says transition deal has ended fears of Brexit-inspired banker exodus*, CITY A.M. (Apr.21, 2018) http://www.cityam.com/284434/philip-hammond-says-transition-deal-has-ended-fears-brexit.

[3] *London Remains Graduates' Choice for Financial Services Careers*, ONREC (Apr. 13, 2018) http://www.onrec.com/news/news-archive/london-remains-graduates-choice-for-financial-services-careers.

that would reverse the "leave" decision,[4] as well as the possibility that a new government will head those calls.[5]

The situation becomes even more complex and grave when business constraints are added into the mix. There is little room for spontaneity in business planning and decisions often must be made months if not years in advance. The result is that the UK and its financial services sector need a plan, and fast. While it is the UK government that is best placed to secure a long-term softening of Brexit's effects, it is the industry itself which will likely have to take up the mantle of protecting the sector's viability in the short-run. This chapter will examine the current state of affairs under EU membership, the implications of a 'hard Brexit,' possible post-Brexit scenarios, and the preparations to be made by market participants and negotiators alike.

II. THE CURRENT SYSTEM

The EU's Single Market for services is founded upon two core principles provided for in the Treaty on the Functioning of the European Union (TFEU).[6] Article 56 of the TFEU provides for the freedom to furnish services across borders by prohibiting restrictions where there is establishment in a member state.[7] Article 56 also allows for the extension of this freedom to nationals of third countries who are established within the EU,[8] a concession soon to be highly important to the UK. Article 49 of the TFEU provides for the freedom of establishment, on which the provision of cross-border services is predicated.[9] For the purposes of this chapter, the freedom for businesses to establish "branches or subsidiaries" is most relevant.[10]

---

[4] Donald McRae, *Brexit makes no sense and Britain should vote again, says Jürgen Klopp*, THE GUARDIAN (Apr. 23, 2018) https://www.theguardian.com/football/2018/apr-/23/brexit-makes-no-sense-and-britain-should-vote-again-says-jurgen-klopp.

[5] Robert Hutton and Thomas Penny, *Labout Not Ruling Out Second Brexit Referendum, McDonnell Says*, BLOOMBERG (Apr. 20, 2018) https://www.bloomberg.com/news/-articles/2018-04-20/mcdonnell-says-labour-not-ruling-out-second-brexit-referendum.

[6] *Single Market for Services*, EUROPEAN COMMISSION (last updated Apr. 25, 2018) https://ec.europa.eu/growth/single-market/services_en.

[7] Consolidated Version of the Treaty on the Functioning of the European Union art. 56, May 9, 2008, 2008 O.J. (C 115) 70 [hereinafter TFEU].

[8] *Id.*

[9] TFEU art. 49.

[10] *Id.*

Starting with the First Banking Directive of 1977,[11] a variety of EU directives and regulations have built upon the two freedoms to give rise to the Single Market in services we see today. The current framework additionally includes numerous technical standards and a role for European Supervisory Authorities (ESAs), who ensure harmonization across the domestic supervisory authorities applying those technical standards.[12] While there is certainly an abundance of EU legislation in the area, it is important to remember that "[t]he current EU regulatory framework of financial services is largely based on global standards."[13] Such standards may place an upward limit on just how much regulatory divergence will be possible between the EU and a post-Brexit UK. This reality may be beneficial to negotiators navigating the uncertainties of defining the future relationship between the EU and UK.

The main event when it comes to the Single Market for services is "passporting." A "passport":

> is attached to the license to operate as a financial institution granted by the home regulator. On the basis of their authorisation in the Member State of establishment ('home state'), financial institutions are allowed to operate in all other Member States. The 'host' Member State may thus not impose any additional requirements, although in certain instances additional conduct-of-business rules may apply. In order for a financial institution to operate in another Member State on the basis of the European passport, it needs to conclude a 'notification procedure': it has to notify the competent authority in its home Member State of its intention to operate in another Member State and the competent authority will consequently notify the competent authority in the host Member State.[14]

---

[11] Council Directive 77/780, 1977 O.J. (L 322) (ECC).

[12] *European Supervisory Framework*, EUROPEAN SECURITIES AND MARKETS AUTHORITY (last visited Apr. 29, 2018) https://www.esma.europa.eu/about-esma/governance/european-supervisory-framework; The Commission drafts the technical standards in consultation with the relevant ESAs, including "the European Banking Authority (EBA) where it concerns banks, the European Securities and Markets Authority (ESMA) where it concerns markets and securities, and the European Insurance and Occupational Pensions Authority (EIOPA) where it concerns insurers and pension funds."; *Implications of Brexit on EU Financial Services*, at 22, European Parliament, Directorate-General for Internal Policies, Policy Department A: Economic and Scientific Policy (Study, Jun. 2017).

[13] *Implications*, *supra* note 12, at 22.

[14] *Id.*

The acceptance of "home state" authorization by the "host state" (facilitated by a harmonization of rules), is a type of mutual recognition and underpins the entire Single Market for services system.[15] A single firm may have several passports depending on the services it provides and the number of member states in which it provides those services.[16] More than 5,400 UK firms and more than 8,000 EU firms currently use financial services passports, with UK firms holding a total of 336,421 passports.[17]

In contrast to member state businesses, third-country businesses are required to make one of two difficult and expensive choices. They must either establish a subsidiary (a legally separate entity) in a member state and then make use of passporting, or else obtain the individual authorization of each member state in which they intend to provide services.[18] Currently "no country outside the EU enjoys full passporting rights into the EU"[19] and so the need for UK firms to establish subsidiaries and obtain EU authorizations is increasingly likely, as is an increase in the cost of financial services.

III. THE STAKES

When it comes down to it, "no deal" will be a very *big* deal for the financial services sector and, consequently, the UK. Having just discussed the importance of passporting to the industry, it should be known that Prime Minister May has ruled out the possibility of

---

15 MARCIN SZCZEPANSKI, EUROPEAN PARLIAMENTARY RESEARCH SERVICE, UNDERSTANDING EQUIVALENCE AND THE SINGLE PASSPORT IN FINANCIAL SERVICES: THIRD-COUNTRY ACCESS TO THE SINGLE MARKET 3 (Briefing Feb. 2017) http://www.europarl.europa.eu/RegData/-etudes/BRIE/2017/599267/EPRS_BRI(2017)599267_EN.pdf.

16 KAREL LANNOO, CENTRE FOR EUROPEAN POLICY STUDIES, EU FINANCIAL MARKET ACCESS AFTER BREXIT 5 (Policy Brief, Sept. 2016), https://www.ceps.eu/system/files/Brexit%20and%20the%20financial%20sector_0.pdf.

17 Damian Fantato, *May rules out passporting for financial services post Brexit*, THE FINANCIAL TIMES ADVISER (Mar. 5, 2018) https://www.ftadviser.com/regulation-/2018/03/05/may-rules-out-passporting-for-financial-services-after-brexit/

18 SZCZEPANSKI, *supra* note 15, at 4.

19 THECITYUK, A PRACTITIONER'S GUIDE TO BREXIT: EXPLORING ITS CONSEQUENCES AND ALTERNATIVES TO EU MEMBERSHIP 7 (Sept. 9, 2016) https://www.thecityuk.com/assets/2016/Reports-PDF/A-practitioners-guide-to-Brexit.pdf.

continuing the practice post-Brexit.[20] In a recent report by Oliver Wyman and Clifford Chance, it was predicted that the financial services sector of the UK would take "by far the biggest hit" and "incur about a third of the extra 'red tape' costs" of Brexit.[21] This is not entirely surprising given just how integral the industry is to the UK economy. Financial services account for nearly 12% of the UK's GDP, the jobs of almost 2.2 million people across the country, and the largest source of tax revenue by sector.[22] Although loss estimates have recently been revised downward, the UK stands to lose between 5,000 and 10,000 banking and insurance jobs[23] and as many as 20,000 jobs in financial services overall.[24] Finally, and to further illustrate the magnitude of the UK's exposure to finance-related Brexit upheaval, 96 trillion pounds worth of derivatives will be at risk if contracts cannot be serviced on Day One.[25]

It is worth noting that the painful effects of Brexit will not be cabined to just one side of the Channel. "London has developed over the last quarter century as the wholesale financial centre for the EU"[26] and the "EU relies on the UK for three-quarters of its hedging activities, three-quarters of its foreign exchange, half its lending and half its

---

[20] "She said: 'We are not looking for passporting because we understand this is intrinsic to the single market of which we would no longer be a member. It would also require us to be subject to a single rule book, over which we would have no say.'" Damian Fantato, *May rules out passporting for financial services post* Brexit, THE FINANCIAL TIMES ADVISER (Mar. 5, 2018) https://www.ftadviser.com/regulation/2018/03/05/may-rules-out-passporting-for-financial-services-after-brexit/.

[21] Hannah Smith, *Financial services to be worst hit by Brexit*, THE FINANCIAL TIMES ADVÍSER (Mar. 12, 2018) https://www.ftadviser.com/investments/2018/03/12/uk-financial-services-tops-five-sectors-to-be-hit-hardest-by-brexit/.

[22] THECITYUK, *supra* note 19, at 4.

[23] Catherine Lafferty, *Fewer finance jobs to go with Brexit, UK bank chief says*, FUNDS EUROPE (Apr. 20, 2018) http://www.funds-europe.com/news/fewer-finance-jobs-to-go-with-brexit-uk-bank-chief-says.

[24] Marrianne Curphey, *Brexit: what lies ahead for the UK's financial services?*, RELOCATE MAGAZINE (Apr. 11, 2018) https://www.relocatemagazine.com/articles/brexit-what-lies-ahead-for-the-uks-financial-services-mcurphey-spr18.

[25] Silla Brush, *Banks Told by EU to Fix Their $134 Trillion Brexit Headache*, BLOOMBERG (Apr. 24, 2018) https://www.bloomberg.com/news/articles/2018-04-24/banks-told-by-eu-to-solve-their-134-trillion-brexit-headache.

[26] LANNOO, *supra* note 16, at 2.; "A wholesale financial centre provides for the refinancing of local financial centres, of which there are many in Europe, and financial services for corporations, governments and institutional investors."

securities transactions."[27] According to the Global Financial Centres Index 21, London is the top ranked global financial center, with the next EU city not coming in until the twelfth position.[28] Furthermore, alterations to the current industry structure may well complicate and ultimately undermine regulatory coherence.[29] The consequence of such complications is the creation of systemic risk, which will not be purely European, but rather global in scope.[30]

Even if a "hard Brexit" is averted, a deal reached too late could mean that firms have already made unnecessarily extreme changes because they had to deal with the practical realities of business.[31] It can take over 18 months to set up a bank subsidiary and as many as 6 to 12 months to obtain a banking license from the selected member state's regulator and the European Central Bank (ECB).[32] Even expanding pre-existing subsidiaries is likely to require regulatory approval,[33] in addition to a huge influx of capital.[34] So what has been the response of the UK-located financial firms? Large players like Barclays,[35] Goldman Sachs,[36] JP

---

27 Patrick Jenkins, *How the City finally raised its voice over Brexit*, THE FINANCIAL TIMES (Oct. 2, 2017), https://www.ft.com/content/69764310-971f-11e7-8c5c-c8d8fa6961bb?utm_source=facebook.

28 *Implications*, *supra* note 12, at 44.

29 Mark Taylor, *'Equivalency' Regime Will Not Ease Brexit Fears, City Warns*, LAW 360 (Nov. 9, 2017), https://www.law360.com/articles/983648/-equivalency-regime-will-not-ease-brexit-fears-city-warns.

30 *Id.*; *see also* Jenkins, *supra* note 27.

31 Jenkins, *supra* note 27.

32 Francesco Canepa, *Fewer than 10 UK-based banks have asked for EU license as Brexit looms: sources*, REUTERS (Sept. 6, 2017) https://www.reuters.com/article/us-britain-eu-banks-ecb/fewer-than-10-uk-based-banks-have-asked-for-eu-license-as-brexit-looms-sources-idUSKCN1BH143.

33 *Id.*

34 Jenkins, *supra* note 27.

35 Martin Arnold and Dan McCrum, "Barclays plans to split euro trading hub over Brexit, Shift highlights level of uncertainty in London's position as dominant centre," THE FINANCIAL TIMES (Apr. 8, 2018) https://www.ft.com/content/07e374c4-3b00-11e8-b7e0-52972418fec4 ("The British bank is planning to make Dublin its main EU hub outside London, adding 150 to 200 more staff in a new office building in the Irish capital. It is also beefing up its legal status to become a standalone subsidiary with its own capital and regulatory oversight.").

36 "US firm Raymond James 'discussed shifting London brokerage to Frankfurt,' The wealth manager and investment banking firm opened its office in the German city last summer," BT (Apr. 10, 2018) http://home.bt.com/news/uk-news/us-firm-raymond-james-discussed-shifting-london-brokerage-to-frankfurt-11364263553096 ("... employs

Morgan,[37] Morgan Stanley,[38] and even law firms,[39] have already begun to put Brexit plans into action. Several EU cities have been the beneficiaries of these moves, with Frankfurt, Berlin, Dublin,[40] and Paris[41] featuring prominently. That said, as recently as April 12th, "[l]eading bankers" admonished that "Britain [has] yet to feel the real impact of Brexit which will undermine its status as a global finance center as companies prepare to shift jobs out of London to preserve access to Europe's single market,"[42] indicating that the worst may be yet to come.

IV. THE DRAFT WITHDRAWAL AGREEMENT AND FUTURE RELATIONSHIP

Part Four of the draft withdrawal agreement first published in February of this year, provides for a transition period to begin when the agreement enters into force and end on December 31, 2020.[43] This termination date was sooner than the UK had hoped, a pill not made easier to swallow by the fact that the agreement provided for no mechanism to extend the transition period.[44] EU law will continue to

---

6,500 UK staff – is set to at least double its Frankfurt workforce to 400 through a mixture of relocations and local recruitment ….").

[37] *Id.* ("… has 16,000 staff in the UK, will ramp up operations at a number of its EU sites with plans to move up to 1,000 London front and back office roles across its offices.").

[38] *Id.* ("… is understood to have plans to relocate 200 of its 6,000 UK staff to Frankfurt, while Citigroup notified its bankers that it may need to create 150 roles at its Frankfurt offices as well as those in Amsterdam, Dublin, Luxembourg, Madrid and Paris.").

[39] Rose Walker, *Hogan Lovells Launches London Trade Practice Ahead of Brexit*, LAW.COM (Apr. 16, 2018) https://www.law.com/international/2018/04/16/hogan-lovells-launches-london-trade-practice-ahead-of-brexit/?slreturn=20180322104341.

[40] Jenkins, *supra* note 27.

[41] *Fintech firms must cash in on Frankfurt opportunities*, INDEPENDENT.IE (Apr. 15, 2018) https://www.independent.ie/business/irish/fintech-firms-must-cash-in-on-frankfurt-opportunities-36807388.html.

[42] Andrew MacAskill and Lawrence White, *Top bankers warn London's status as a global finance center at risk from Brexit*, REUTERS (Apr. 12, 2018) https://www.reuters.com/article/us-britain-eu-banks/top-bankers-warn-londons-status-as-a-global-finance-center-at-risk-from-brexit-idUSKBN1HJ2FA.

[43] *Draft Agreement on the withdrawal of the United Kingdom of Great Britain and Northern Ireland from the European Union and the European Atomic Energy Community*, at 74, COM (Mar. 19, 2018).

[44] Alex Barker and Mehreen Khan, *UK and EU agree 'decisive step' with 21-month Brexit transition: Northern Irish single market backstop 'will apply unless another solution is found'*, THE FINANCIAL TIMES (Mar. 19, 2018) https://www.ft.com/content/493af6d6-2b53-11e8-9b4b-bc4b9f08f381.

apply during this time, preserving the status quo, but losing the UK its voice in any decision-making processes.[45]

While the final agreement is expected in October 2018,[46] it still faces several hurdles. The agreement must be passed as a bill in the UK and approved by the EU, which will require approval by the European Parliament and passage by the European Council, before it may take effect.[47] The October date poses two significant problems: 1) businesses will not know that the transition period is binding until that time and 2) should the agreement fail, only five months will then remain until the March 29, 2019 deadline. On the first point, the Bank of England (BoE) and the Financial Conduct Authority (FCA) have said that EU firms providing services in the UK could rely on the transition period, even if it failed to become legally binding.[48] Unfortunately, EU regulators have failed to make reciprocal assurances to UK firms providing services within the EU.[49] While Chancellor Phillip Hammond believes the current commitment to a transition period is enough to keep jobs in the UK,[50] others remain skeptical due to the lack of legal certainty.[51] As for the second problem, some have said that a "year is the bare minimum" needed for businesses to effect their hard Brexit contingency plans.[52] If

---

[45] *Id.*

[46] *EU, UK Negotiators Begin Prep for Next Chapter in Brexit Talks*, INT'L CENTRE FOR TRADE AND SUSTAINABLE DEVELOPMENT, 22 BRIDGES 12 (Apr. 12, 2018) https://www.ictsd.org/bridges-news/bridges/news/eu-uk-negotiators-begin-prep-for-next-chapter-in-brexit-talks.

[47] *Brexit: the draft withdrawal agreement*, UK PARLIAMENT, COMMONS LIBRARY BRIEFING (Mar. 26, 2018) https://researchbriefings.parliament.uk/ResearchBriefing-/Summary/CBP-8269#fullreport.

[48] Caroline Binham, *Bank of England more optimistic on risk of City exodus post Brexit*, THE FINANCIAL TIMES (Apr. 19, 2018) https://www.ft.com/content/83dcaffe-43c8-11e8-803a-295c97e6fd0b.

[49] *Id.*

[50] Larry Elliott, *Hammond: Brexit transition deal has averted City job losses, Chancellor gives upbeat assessment of state of UK economy at IMF meeting*, THE GUARDIAN (Apr. 20, 2018) https://www.theguardian.com/politics/2018/apr/20/hammond-brexit-transition-deal-city-job-losses-uk-economy-imf.

[51] *Reaction to the Brexit transition deal between UK and EU*, REUTERS (Mar. 19, 2018) https://www.reuters.com/article/us-britain-eu-deal-instant-view/reaction-to-the-brexit-transition-deal-between-uk-and-eu-idUSKBN1GV1KC.

[52] Mark Taylor, *'Equivalency' Regime Will Not Ease Brexit Fears, City Warns*, LAW 360 (Nov. 9, 2017), https://www.law360.com/articles/983648/-equivalency-regime-will-not-ease-brexit-fears-city-warns.

that is the case, five months will be far from adequate and Brexit may prove far more painful than necessary.

With respect to any future relationship agreement, the EU's draft negotiating guidelines are telling. While there is promising language on creating a "balanced, ambitious and wide-ranging free trade agreement,"[53] this positive start quickly devolves into the warning that "[s]uch an agreement cannot however offer the same benefits as Membership and cannot amount to participation in the Single Market or parts thereof."[54] Then the guidelines address trade in services specifically, stating that it should be approached

> with the aim of allowing market access to provide services under host state rules, including as regards right of establishment for providers, to an extent consistent with the fact that the UK will become a third country and the Union and the UK will no longer share a common regulatory, supervisory, enforcement and judiciary framework."[55]

This language sounds no better than the treatment currently offered by the EU to third-countries, none of which are starting from the point of regulatory alignment enjoyed by the UK. The uncertainty surrounding the withdrawal and future relationship agreements should be kept in mind when considering the potential Brexit solutions that follow.

V. THE OPTIONS

This section will discuss four (of the many) possible post-Brexit scenarios for the UK: a "hard Brexit" (no deal), the equivalence regime, membership in the European Economic Area (EEA), and a free trade or other bespoke agreement.

A. NO DEAL

Much has been said about the difficulty of quantifying just how painful a hard Brexit would be.[56] This is largely due to the fact that it remains unclear just how much business currently taking place in the UK will be replicated within the EU, by UK firms or otherwise.[57] Although few firms have made such moves thus far, the incidence of relocation is

---

[53] *European Council (Art. 50) (23 March 2018) – Guidelines*, EUROPEAN COUNCIL 3 (Mar. 7, 2018).

[54] *Id.*

[55] *Id.* at 4.

[56] *See Implications*, *supra* note 12, at 50.

[57] *Id.*

expected to rise as March 2019 nears.[58] There is, however, an argument, the so called "ecosystem" argument, that the City of London is unique in such a way that its role is not capable of complete replication within the EU.[59] This ecosystem is composed of London's language, legal system, highly-skilled work force, ancillary services, and even culture, all of which are said to make economies of scale uniquely possible within the City.[60] To the degree to which this hypothesis holds true, we might expect to see diminished flows of business to the EU or perhaps workarounds that allow continued access to the London ecosystem.

What *is* known is that a great deal of EU legislation currently applicable to financial services activities will no longer be applicable on Day One should the UK exit without a deal. Such changes will roughly include the:

- European Market Infrastructure Regulation (EMIR), Markets in Financial Instruments Regulation (MiFIR), Securities Financing Transactions Regulation (SFTR), and Settlement Finality Directive (SFD) within post-trade financial services (including derivatives, central counterparties, and trading repositories);[61]
- Capital Requirements Directive (CRD IV), Capital Requirements Regulation (CRR), and directive on payment services within the field of banking and payment systems;[62]
- Markets in Financial Instruments Directive (MiFID) rules on investment services and activities in the field of markets in financial instruments;[63]

---

[58] JOINT COMMITTEE REPORT ON RISKS AND VULNERABILITIES IN THE EU FINANCIAL SYSTEM, JOINT COMMITTEE OF THE EUROPEAN SUPERVISORY AUTHORITIES 10 (Apr. 2018) https://esas-joint-committee.europa.eu/Publications/Reports/Joint%20Committee%20Risk%20Report.pdf.

[59] *Implications*, *supra* note 12, at 50.

[60] *Id.*

[61] *Notice to Stakeholders: Withdrawal of the United Kingdom and EU Rules in the Field of Post-Trade Financial Services*, EUROPEAN COMMISSION, DIRECTORATE-GENERAL FOR FINANCIAL STABILITY, FINANCIAL SERVICES AND CAPITAL MARKETS UNION 1 (Feb. 8, 2018).

[62] *Notice to Stakeholders: Withdrawal of the United Kingdom and EU Rules in the Field of Banking and Payment Systems,* EUROPEAN COMMISSION, DIRECTORATE-GENERAL FOR FINANCIAL STABILITY, FINANCIAL SERVICES AND CAPITAL MARKETS UNION 1 (Feb. 8, 2018).

[63] *Notice to Stakeholders: Withdrawal of the United Kingdom and EU Rules in the Field of Markets in Financial Instruments*, EUROPEAN COMMISSION, DIRECTORATE-GENERAL

- Solvency II Directive and Insurance Distribution Directive in the fields of insurances and reinsurance;[64]
- Undertakings for Collective Investment in Transferable Securities (UCITS) and Alternative Investment Fund Managers (AIFM) Directives in the field of asset management;[65]
- Statutory Audit Directive in the field of statutory audit;[66]and
- Credit Rating Agencies (CRA) Regulation in the field of credit rating agencies.[67]

Although certain pieces of financial regulation may allow for delegation back to UK offices of particular operational functions, [68] financial services arrangements seen today will be largely altered as the UK takes on third-country status with respect to the pieces of legislation listed above.

The other unhappy reality of a no-deal scenario will likely be trade in financial services on the General Agreement on Trade in Services (GATS) terms,[69] though again it is unclear exactly what this might mean. The GATS commitments are a positive list that can be changed unilaterally, take no direct effect in domestic legislation, and are subject to the time-consuming Dispute Settlement Understanding.[70] While the

---

FOR FINANCIAL STABILITY, FINANCIAL SERVICES AND CAPITAL MARKETS UNION 1 (Feb. 8, 2018) [hereinafter *Field of Markets in Financial Instruments*].

[64] *Notice to Stakeholders: Withdrawal of the United Kingdom and EU Rules in the Field of Insurance/REinsurance*, EUROPEAN COMMISSION, DIRECTORATE-GENERAL FOR FINANCIAL STABILITY, FINANCIAL SERVICES AND CAPITAL MARKETS UNION 1 (Feb. 8, 2018).

[65] *Notice to Stakeholders: Withdrawal of the United Kingdom and EU Rules in the Field of Asset Management*, EUROPEAN COMMISSION, DIRECTORATE-GENERAL FOR FINANCIAL STABILITY, FINANCIAL SERVICES AND CAPITAL MARKETS UNION 1 (Feb. 8, 2018) [hereinafter *Field of Asset Management*].

[66] *Notice to Stakeholders: Withdrawal of the United Kingdom and EU Rules in the Field of Statutory Audit*, EUROPEAN COMMISSION, DIRECTORATE-GENERAL FOR FINANCIAL STABILITY, FINANCIAL SERVICES AND CAPITAL MARKETS UNION 1 (Feb. 8, 2018).

[67] *Notice to Stakeholders: Withdrawal of the United Kingdom and EU Rules in the Field of Credit Rating Agencies*, EUROPEAN COMMISSION, DIRECTORATE-GENERAL FOR FINANCIAL STABILITY, FINANCIAL SERVICES AND CAPITAL MARKETS UNION 1 (Feb. 8, 2018).

[68] *Field of Markets in Financial Instruments*, at 4; *Field of Asset Management*, at 4.

[69] *The future UK-EU relationship*, House of Commons, Exiting the European Union Committee 46 (Fourth Report of Session 2017-19, Apr. 4, 2018) https://publications.parliament.uk/pa/cm201719/cmselect/cmexeu/935/935.pdf.

[70] *The Consequences of Brexit on Services and Establishment: Different Scenarios for Exit and Future Cooperation*, European Parliament, DIRECTORATE-GENERAL FOR INTERNAL

UK has retained its WTO membership, it is uncertain whether the UK will need to submit new commitments or whether EU commitments will be attributed to the UK following its departure from the Union.[71] Furthermore, the GATS Annex on Financial Services allows for the restriction of "cross-border financial services on the basis of prudential controls,"[72] leaving UK financial services firms open to further potential discrimination. Unsurprisingly, trade on GATS terms is seen as one of the worst possibilities of a hard Brexit.[73] However, what is more likely than a future relationship marked solely by trading on GATS terms, is trade in financial services under the equivalence regime.

B. EQUIVALENCE

The equivalence regime is the name given to the "piecemeal access to the single market"[74] afforded by "[s]ome 15 acts [which] contain 'third-country provisions' that empower the Commission … to decide on the equivalence of foreign rules and supervision for EU regulatory purposes."[75] The goals of the regime are to balance a liberalizing of financial markets around converging international standards while maintaining financial stability and consumer protections.[76] An equivalence decision, in the "form of an implementing or delegated act,"[77] is reached by the Commission (often in consultation with ESAs) which takes a risk-based approach to assessing the supervisory and regulatory framework of a third country.[78] Equivalence decisions are "tailored to the needs of each specific act,"[79] are discretionary on the part

---

POLICIES, POLICY DEPARTMENT A: ECONOMIC AND SCIENTIFIC POLICY 14 (Study, Jun. 2017) http://www.europarl.europa.eu/RegData/etudes/IDAN/2017-/602035/IPOL_IDA(2017)602035_EN.pdf.

71 *Id.*

72 *Implications*, *supra* note 12, at 15.

73 *The Consequences*, *supra* note 70, at 14.

74 SZCZEPANSKI, *supra* note 15, at 1.

75 *EU equivalence decisions in financial services policy: an assessment*, EUROPEAN COMMISSION 4 (Commission Staff Working Document, Feb. 27, 2017) https://ec.europa.eu/info/sites/info/files/eu-equivalence-decisions-assessment-27022017_en.pdf.

76 *Id.* at 5.

77 *Recognition of non-EU financial frameworks (equivalence decisions)*, EUROPEAN COMMISSION (accessed Apr. 25, 2018) https://ec.europa.eu/info/business-economy-euro/banking-and-finance/international-relations/recognition-non-eu-financial-frameworks-equivalence-decisions_en.

78 *EU equivalence decisions in financial services policy*, *supra* note 75, at 8.

79 *Id.* at 7.

of the EU (as they may be altered or withdrawn at any time), and may be either full or partial, indefinite or time limited, and applicable to an entire regulatory framework or solely specified entities, products, etc.[80]

Equivalence is less than ideal because not all financial services-related EU acts contain equivalence provisions[81] and even those that do, do not necessarily provide for market access. The result is that equivalence is incapable of replicating the status quo achieved under passporting. So which financial service activities could benefit from equivalence and which will not? The Directorate-General for Internal Policies' Economic and Scientific Policy Department within the Commission, reached the following conclusions for UK financial services:

- UK financial institutions will be allowed to cater for professional investors throughout the EU only if the European Commission will declare the UK rules and supervision to be equivalent to MiFID II. But Member States will have national discretion to allow UK financial institutions to provide services limited to their territory to EU retail investors (and to EU professional investors in the absence of an equivalence decision);
- UK AIFs will either need an EU AIFM to market their units or shares to professional investors, or they need to be authorised by the national authorities of the Member State, where they want to pursue their activities.[82]

Because an approximation of passporting rights may be attained for certain financial services, it is likely that equivalence will be "less costly than the 'hard Brexit' scenario,"[83] though relocation will still be necessary for a significant number of service providers.[84]

Another substantial drawback to the equivalence route is the time that it would take to effect. Obtaining an equivalence decision has historically taken anywhere from two to four years.[85] This timeline would not necessarily be shortened by current regulatory alignment. While there is a possibility that the process could be expedited (discussed below), this

---

[80] *Id.* at 9.

[81] *Id.* at 8.

[82] *Implications*, *supra* note 12, at 11-12.

[83] *Id.* at 55.

[84] *Id.* at 59 ("This is true in particular for wholesale banking activities (CRD IV) and also for some investment banking activities (MiFiD II) and some asset management activities (AIFMD and UCITS).").

[85] SZCZEPANSKI, *supra* note 15, at

discussion will now turn to an option that offers more immediate certainty to financial services businesses: EEA membership.

C. EEA MEMBERSHIP

The EEA Agreement brings together EU Member States and three EEA European Free Trade Agreement (EFTA) states (Iceland, Lichtenstein, and Norway).[86] Joining the EEA would "theoretically provide[] full access to all areas of the Single Market"[87] and for this reason may be seen as a superior option to equivalence.[88] The UK would first need to join the EFTA and then apply to become a party to the EEA Agreement, approval pending the ratification of all parties under Article 128(2) of the EEA Agreement.[89]

While membership may be the least disruptive and easiest to effect option given that it is available off-the-shelf,[90] there are significant hurdles to joining from the UK perspective. Although the UK would be subject to the EFTA Court rather than the CJEU (an intolerable arrangement from the UK perspective), it would be required to accept all EEA-relevant EU legislation.[91] This would make the UK a rule taker, even though it may retain an opportunity to influence EEA policy.[92] Furthermore, the UK would have to accept the four freedoms, with the freedom of movement of persons constituting a significant point of contention.[93] While Articles 112 and 113 of the agreement have been used by Lichtenstein to restrict rights of residency, the UK's immigration concerns extend beyond residency to include the right to work within the UK.[94] Regardless, it is unlikely the UK could take similar steps given its size.[95] Additionally, the UK would have to make financial

---

[86] *The future UK-EU relationship*, *supra* note 68, at 30.

[87] THECITYUK, *supra* note 19, at 16.

[88] *Implications*, *supra* note 12, at 63.

[89] *Id.* at 16.

[90] *The future UK-EU relationship*, *supra* note 69, at 5.

[91] *Implications*, *supra* note 12, at 62.

[92] *Id.*

[93] *Norwegian lessons for Brexit Britain: Theresa May's government is firmly against the Norway model. Yet it offers many advantages, even for Brexiteers*, THE ECONOMIST (Feb. 22, 2018) https://www.economist.com/news/britain/21737266-theresa-mays-government-firmly-against-norway-model-yet-it-offers-many-advantages-even; Articles 112 and 113 have been used by Lichtenstein to restrict rights of residency, but the UK is unlikely to do likewise given its size. *The future UK-EU relationship*, *supra* note 69, at 38.

[94] *The future UK-EU relationship*, *supra* note 69, at 38.

[95] *Id.*

contributions to the EU, another sticking point that featured prominently in referendum rhetoric.[96] While Norway makes only three-fourths the contribution of the UK on a per capita basis,[97] and Prime Minister May has admitted that payments will be necessary for continued access to certain EU programs,[98] further contributions will be difficult to sell politically. Next, it is worth considering that the UK is starting from a point of regulatory alignment with the EU. Divergence from EU legislation, which to some degree is a substantial likelihood following the UK's exit, could result in the country being "taken to the EFTA Court by the EFTA Surveillance Authority and found to be in breach of the Agreement."[99] Finally, and perhaps most importantly, Prime Minister May has explicitly rejected EEA membership as an option for the post-Brexit UK.[100] While the ready availability of EEA membership is certainly attractive, the rigidity of its requirements makes a bespoke agreement even more attractive.

D. Free Trade or Other Bespoke Agreement

Although the EU negotiating guidelines currently call for an "ambitious and wide-ranging free trade agreement,"[101] the treatment of such a possibility will be relatively brief in this chapter as a free trade agreement, though certainly the long-term goal, cannot respond to the exigencies of the timeline with which the UK financial services sector is currently faced.

The recent Comprehensive Economic and Trade Agreement (CETA) between the EU and Canada has received a great deal of attention as a possible model for the UK-EU future relationship.[102] Hailed as the "EU's most ambitious trade agreement to date,"[103] CETA does contain attractive advancements, including an innovative dispute settlement tribunal and enhanced protection of the right to regulate for

---

96 *Norwegian lessons for Brexit Britain*, *supra* note 93.

97 *Id.*

98 *The future UK-EU relationship*, *supra* note 69, at 32.

99 *Id.* at 35.

100 *Implications*, *supra* note 12, at 12.

101 *European Council (Art. 50) (23 March 2018) – Guidelines*, EUROPEAN COUNCIL 3 (Mar. 7, 2018).

102 *See The Consequences of Brexit on Services and Establishment*, *supra* note 69, at 13; THECITYUK, *supra* note 19, at 18.

103 *The Consequences of Brexit on Services and Establishment*, *supra* note 70, at 13.

party governments.[104] Reality, however, stands in the way of any free trade agreement serving as the savior for the financial services industry. Such an agreement would likely take years to conclude and the fact that "[p]ast EU FTAs and CETAs … have never covered right of establishment, passporting or cross-border services in any sense that would replicate the UK's current degree of full access to the EU Single Market,"[105] means that the Canadian CETA is at best a rough jumping off point for the future relationship structure.

What the UK is really looking for in a bespoke agreement is mutual recognition, which Brexit Secretary David Davis has described as an arrangement where "each side would trust each other's regulations and the institutions that enforce them.'"[106] Collaborating lobby groups and lawyers have floated potential formats for just such a free trade deal for financial services, using "mutual access" as the agreement's foundation.[107] However, existing provisions for mutual recognition between the EU and third countries have fallen far short of replicating the current passporting arrangement.[108] Any such initiative, for its novelty, is therefore all the more politically contentious and open to EU accusations of "cherry picking."

There are several elements that should be included in the free trade or bespoke agreement eventually reached between the UK and EU. First, the agreement should be innovative enough to allow financial firms to continue servicing clients on both side of the Channel in as close an approximation to the pre-Brexit status quo as possible. The aim here should be an understanding that causes the least economic damage within a highly integrated market. Second, and in contrast to the nature of equivalence decisions issued by the Commission, the arrangement must be non-discretionary on the part of the EU. While an equivalence decision has never yet been revoked, the option would leave the UK comparatively powerless and UK firms in a vulnerable position.

---

[104] Roy Millen and Mark Klaver, *Dispute Resolution under CETA: A New Investment Court for Canada and Europe*, LEXOLOGY (Dec. 15, 2016) https://www.lexology.com/library/-detail.aspx?g=e46e5848-0761-468e-ac02-64d7a03c4edd.

[105] THECITYUK, *supra* note 19, at 18.

[106] John Glover, *U.K.'s New Brexit Gotta-Have is 'Mutual Recognition'*, BLOOMBERG (Feb. 23, 2018) https://www.bloomberg.com/news/articles/2018-02-23/u-k-s-new-brexit-gotta-have-is-mutual-recognition-quicktak.

[107] Jenkins, *supra* note 27 ("The plan, devised in collaboration with the City of London Corporation, lobby group TheCityUK and lawyers at Hogan Lovells, has been cautiously welcomed by some EU 27….").

[108] *Id.*

Furthermore, the mutual recognition provided for in the free trade agreement should be predicated on an equivalence of outcome rather than rule homogeneity. The latter arrangement would require the UK to be a rule taker and would be at odds with the referendum result's goals. Next, the agreement must provide for a dispute settlement mechanism for *material* divergences in regulation. The materiality requirement is key as the two parties begin from a point of regulatory alignment and a little divergence will be an inescapable reality moving forward. Finally, as evidenced by EU and EEA membership requirements, an arrangement including market access will also likely involve some financial contribution on the part of the UK, but this should not be allowed to stand in the way of a mutually advantageous agreement that protects the viability of such a critical sector.

VI. RECOMMENDATIONS

UK negotiators aiming to bolster confidence within the UK financial services sector have several top priorities before them. As an initial matter, negotiators should proceed with an eye to obtaining (1) a reciprocal pledge from the EU to that made by the BoE and FCA for respecting the transition period, whether or not it becomes legally binding, and (2) the inclusion of an automatic transition period extension provision within the withdrawal agreement. Both of these steps would allow businesses to calmly prepare for the future while the UK and EU carve out their future relationship.

It would appear that the continued prevalence of hard Brexit fears is increasingly present in negotiators' minds as the BoE and ECB have recently announced a joint working group that would "focus on the potential disruption to the financial services industry when Britain ceases to be an EU member…."[109] While "Brussels officials emphasised that the move was … not a signal that risks of a breakdown in talks were actually increasing,"[110] it is impossible to ignore the fact that tough issues like the Irish border remain and could derail an orderly withdrawal.[111]

---

[109] Phillip Inman, *Bank of England and ECB set up group to address Brexit fears*, THE GUARDIAN (Apr. 27, 2018) https://www.theguardian.com/business/-2018/apr/27/bank-of-england-and-ecb-set-up-group-to-address-brexit-fears.

[110] Jim Brunsden, *UK and EU financial regulators to examine hard Brexit impact*, THE FINANCIAL TIMES (Apr. 27, 2018) https://www.ft.com/content/710143f6-4a1f-11e8-8ee8-cae73aab7ccb.

[111] Huw Jones, *UK, EU banking regulators team up in case of cliff-edge Brexit*, REUTERS (Apr. 27, 2018) https://uk.reuters.com/article/uk-britain-eu-banks/uk-eu-banking-regulators-team-up-in-case-of-cliff-edge-brexit-idUKKBN1HY1VI.

Furthermore, EU rhetoric on a deal specifically aimed at financial services is rapidly deteriorating. The EU's Chief Negotiator, Michel Barnier, has recently downplayed the distress that the EU would feel in a world without full market access for the UK and "made clear that the EU would never accept … May's plan for a special access regime based around a broad commitment to adopt financial rules that have the same effect as those in the EU."[112] The chances for a future relationship based upon mutual recognition are thus looking increasingly doubtful.

Additionally, European Commission Vice President Valdis Dombrovskis has continued to promote the equivalence route.[113] Dombrovskis has clarified that the "improved equivalence" mentioned in a set of draft guidelines for EU negotiators actually means "adapting equivalence when applied to a country that is systemic for the EU."[114] The equivalence regime is certainly in need of improvement, though Dombrovskis' prescription is hardly imaginative enough. Instead the UK should be pushing for what has been called "preemptive equivalence."[115] Preemptive equivalence would mean that, on Day One, equivalence decisions are in place that allow the covered financial services to conduct their business as per the decisions.[116] While this would provide access short of that currently enjoyed by UK financial services firms, preemptive equivalence would provide for a state of affairs vastly superior to that which would be seen under a no-deal scenario.

A. PREEMPTIVE EQUIVALENCE

There is some precedent for the preemptive equivalence approach. For example, the Commission granted equivalence decisions on

---

[112] Mehreen Khan and Jim Brunsden, *Michel Barnier quashes UK hopes of special access to EU markets*, THE FINANCIAL TIMES (Apr. 26, 2018) https://www.ft.com/-content/ad96d948-4975-11e8-8ee8-cae73aab7ccb.

[113] Huw Jones and Marc Jones, *EU downplays prospect of bespoke Brexit trade deal for banks* , REUTERS (Apr. 24, 2018) https://uk.reuters.com/article/uk-britain-markets-dombrovskis/eu-downplays-prospect-of-bespoke-brexit-trade-deal-for-banks-idUKKBN1HV0TH.

[114] *Id.*

[115] *Implications, supra* note 12, at 55.

[116] Stephen Booth and Vincenzo Scarpetta, *How the UK's financial services sector can continue thriving after Brexit*, OPEN EUROPE (Oct. 17, 2016) https://openeurope.org.uk/-intelligence/britain-and-the-eu/how-the-uks-financial-services-sector-can-continue-thriving-after-brexit/.

Solvency II prior to the directive coming into effect.[117] Switzerland obtained an equivalence decision under Solvency II on June 5, 2015, nearly half a year before the directive took effect.[118] The second of the enumerated points in the Switzerland decision reads, "[e]ven though the Solvency II Directive will be fully applied from 1 January 2016, the Commission may already adopt the present Delegated Decision as indicated under Article 311 of the Solvency II Directive."[119] Article 311 in turn provides that the "Commission may adopt delegated acts and regulatory and implementing technical standards prior to the date referred to in the third paragraph,"[120] which again names the January 1st application date. Following the Switzerland decision, Japan, Australia, Bermuda, Brazil, Canada, Mexico, and the United States were also able to secure equivalence decisions prior to the Directive's effective date.[121] Given the starting point of regulatory alignment that exists between the EU and UK, granting preemptive equivalence need not take nearly as long as past decisions by the Commission. Therefore, if the Commission began assessing UK regulatory structures now, there is potential for preemptive equivalence decisions to be in place prior to the UK's ultimate departure from the EU.

Dombrovskis' point, however, should not be entirely disregarded. If the current level of integration between the UK and EU were to continue following Brexit, as would be ideal from a financial services perspective, that would necessarily mean increased vulnerability for the EU as the UK would suddenly be outside of its legislative power. This concern might be addressed in a number of ways. For instance, the Commission could include a provision making the equivalence decisions it issues for the UK time limited rather than indefinite. This would allow the several years

---

117 Vincenzo Scarpetta, *Understanding regulatory equivalence – an effective fall-back option for UK financial services after Brexit?*, OPEN EUROPE (Oct. 19, 2016) https://openeurope.org.uk/today/blog/understanding-regulatory-equivalence-an-effective-fall-back-option-for-uk-financial-services-after-brexit/.

118 *Commission Delegated Decision (EU) 2015/1602 of 5 June 2015 on the equivalence of the solvency and prudential regime for insurance and reinsurance undertakings in force in Switzerland based on Articles 172(2), 227(4) and 260(3) of Directive 2009/138/EC of the European Parliament and of the Council*, Sept. 29, 2015 O.J. (L 248).

119 *Id.*

120 Council Directive 2009/138, 2009 O.J. (L 335) 1 (EC).

121 *Implementing and delegated acts on Directive 2009/138/EC of the European Parliament and of the Council of 25 November 2009 on the taking-up and pursuit of the business of Insurance and Reinsurance (Solvency II) (Text with EEA relevance) - Equivalence Decisions*, EUROPEAN COMMISSION (last visited May 18, 2018).

undoubtedly required for a more robust trade agreement to be concluded between the UK and EU. Alternatively, or perhaps additionally, the decisions could provide for regular reassessment of the continued equivalence of UK measures over the coming years. This would allow for the EU to mitigate the risk that the UK will be tempted to de-regulate in order to attract business once it has exited the EU and moved beyond its legislative control. Such negotiations would clearly be an area ripe for creativity and as an equivalence regime would necessarily entail some continued form of EU discretion, the Commission is free to be as flexible as it likes and as the situation may require. As was outlined above, creativity and compromise are in the interests of both parties given the economic significance of the financial services sector and the level of market integration between the EU and UK.

It is true that pursuing preemptive equivalence might be a risky approach. Preemptive equivalence may have the potential to detract from or even halt free trade agreement negotiations as it provides a more immediate and, admittedly, EU-friendly solution. However, it is also possible that a preemptive equivalence agreement could instead serve as a backstop while future relationship negotiations continue. For instance, draft withdrawal agreement language on Northern Ireland "will apply unless, or until, another solution is found."[122] There is no reason that preemptive equivalence decisions might not be given similar treatment in the hopes that a more far reaching free trade agreement would be adopted before the equivalence decisions became necessary. Constructing those decisions would undeniably be much more time consuming than issuing the language the two parties have come forward with on Northern Ireland, but it can hardly be doubted that the certainty gained would be worth the effort. Again, creativity and flexibility are available within the equivalence regime and will be key to making such a regime work for the two parties.

Unfortunately, it must be admitted that equivalence will not solve all of the financial services sector's problems and that other measures will be needed to dull Brexit's damaging consequences. For example, the passporting system is most critical to wholesale banking ("banking services between merchant banks and other financial institutions"[123]), but CRD IV does not currently provide for equivalence.[124] Additionally,

---

122 Alex Barker and Mehreen Khan, *supra* note 44.

123 *Wholesale Banking*, INVESTOPEDIA, https://www.investopedia.com/-terms/w/wholesalebanking.asp (last visited May 24, 2018).

124 Stephen Booth and Vincenzo Scarpetta, *supra* note 116.

there are certain exceptional cases, like that of Lloyd's of London within the otherwise relatively secure insurance sector.[125] The former problem can be solved by either pushing for the institution of equivalence within CRD IV or a bespoke agreement that secures the "main elements of [the] CRD IV passport."[126] Unique issues similar to that presented in the latter example will be best addressed through the use of bilateral agreements.[127]

VII. CONCLUSION

As this chapter has already cautioned, there are long-term goals to be pursued with respect to a future trading relationship for financial services, and then there are hard constraints, posed by time and business practicalities, that demand a more immediate response than can be provided by a deeply negotiated international agreement. Neither of the two most simple solutions present a realistic option for the UK moving forward. A "no deal" scenario is simply irrational from either the UK or EU perspective as it would entail great financial pain on both sides. EEA membership, on the other hand, has already been dismissed as a political impossibility within the UK, although it is an off-the-shelf solution that could be implemented relatively rapidly.

According to the Commission, "[t]he primary responsibility to prepare for Brexit remains with market participants."[128] As a practical matter, this is likely true and means that businesses, on the individual level, will need to make the tough decisions that best serve their interests. Affected businesses will need to examine their exposures (and, most importantly, their aversion to risk) and act accordingly as the March 2019 deadline approaches. This will likely mean the relocation of certain operations onto the European continent through branching or else the creation of subsidiaries. Both options will require hefty expenditures of time and capital. At the same time, negotiators must continue to work towards a free trade or other bespoke deal. This is essential both because (depending on the creativity of said negotiators) it is the best hope for protecting the viability of the UK financial services sector in the long run, and because doing otherwise would likely rock the industry. Any such shock would lead to a dramatic uptick in relocations, increasing the costs of furnishing financial services and damaging economies and businesses alike.

---

125 *Id.*

126 Vincenzo Scarpetta, *supra* note 117.

127 *Id.*

128 Phillip Inman, *supra* note 109.

Once again, however, more immediate and less aspirational actions are required and, fortunately, within negotiators' power. First, negotiators need to obtain reciprocal political commitments on a transition period, legally binding or otherwise. Next, they must negotiate for automatic extensions to the transition period in the event that no future relationship agreement were reached prior to the period's termination. Automatically extending the transition period will prevent businesses from being confronted with cliff edge scenarios. Finally, negotiators should work to secure preemptive equivalence where such equivalence is available and expand existing financial legislation to include such measures where it is not. The current equivalence regime allows for flexibility in the timing and content of decisions and thus can be used to reach a mutually beneficial arrangement for the two parties as they work toward a long-term solution. These steps will allow businesses to carefully plan rather than make hasty relocation decisions and allow the UK government the breathing room it needs to achieve the quality free trade agreement that is required to secure it the least financially damaging arrangement moving forward.

CHAPTER 4: BREXIT AND MUTUAL RECOGNITION OF PROFESSIONAL QUALIFICATIONS: A STUDY OF EU-27 NURSES IN THE UK

AMELIA THEISEN

I. INTRODUCTION

In the run up to the referendum in which the United Kingdom (UK) voted to leave the European Union (EU), immigration and the National Health System (NHS) were recurring themes.[1] At the intersection of the topics of immigration and the NHS is a unique group of individuals: citizens from the remaining twenty-seven member states of the EU (EU-27) who work as nurses in the UK. Although this group may seem small (approximately 21,000[2]), they play a vital role in the UK health system. These workers currently reap the benefits of EU integration. Because of the EU's free movement of people,[3] they can move to and work in the UK without a visa. Because of EU law,[4] they qualify as nurses in the UK without any re-training and with minimal processes for recognition. Given these two separate but interconnected benefits, the future of EU-27 nurses in the UK will depend on two separate but interconnected inquiries: how they can immigrate to the UK and how can they qualify as nurses. This chapter focuses on qualifications, but examines immigration controls in relation to the efficacy of qualification recognition.

The UK and the EU-27 are currently negotiating Britain's exit (Brexit) from the EU. This withdrawal agreement, discussed below, will govern the relationship between the UK and the EU-27 during a

---

[1] *See* BRIEFING ROOM, http://www.voteleavetakecontrol.org/briefing.html (last visited Apr. 8, 2018); Lord Ashcroft, *How the United Kingdom voted on Thursday...and why*, LORD ASHCROFT POLLS (June 24, 2016), http://lordashcroftpolls.com/2016/06/how-the-united-kingdom-voted-and-why/.

[2] Carl Baker, *NHS staff from overseas: statistics*, HOUSE OF COMMONS LIBRARY (Feb. 7, 2018), https://researchbriefings.parliament.uk/ResearchBriefing/Summary/CBP-7783#fullreport.

[3] Consolidated Version of the Treaty on the Functioning of the European Union art. 21, Mar. 30, 2010, 2010 O.J. (C 83/57).

[4] Directive 2005/36/EC of the European Parliament and of the Council of Sept. 7, 2005 on the recognition of professional qualifications, 2005 O.J. (L 255/23). *See also* Directive 2013/55/EU of the European Parliament and of the Council of Nov. 2013 amending Directive 2005/36/EC on the recognition of professional qualification and Regulation (EU) No 1024/2012 on administrative cooperation through the Internal Market Information System ('the IMI regulation'), 2013 O.J. (L 354/132).

transition period leading up to the actual withdrawal. Such a transition period is important because of the complex nature of the relationship and the strict timeline envisioned by Article 50 of the Lisbon Treaty, which provides for the exit of an EU member state. The current draft of the withdrawal agreement includes protections for the recognition of EU-27 nurses, among other professionals, during a transition period.

The future of EU-27 nurses' in the UK will likely consist of two groups: those who arrive before and during the transition period, and those who wish to migrate after. The withdrawal negotiations protect the future livelihood of EU-27 nurses currently in the UK and those who enter during the transition period. However, the ability of EU-27 nurses to live and work in the UK after the transition period will be shaped by the future relationship of the EU and the UK, as well as the future immigration policy of the UK. Although the recognition of professional qualifications may be achieved through any variation of future relationship, the efficacy of this recognition will depend on an immigration system that fosters the ability of nurses to enter. The ultimate inclusion of a system to continue recognizing nursing qualifications after the transition will depend on the political and economic interests of the UK and the EU.

This chapter analyzes a specific subset of workers who benefit from mutual recognition of professional qualifications: nurses. The EU qualifications recognition framework is more expansive than nurses, and it covers a variety of other professions, including doctors and veterinarians. This case study is unique given the political and economic factors surrounding the employment and migration of EU-27 nurses. Though unique, the analysis may be shifted and adapted to incorporate or focus on other professions.

II. BEFORE BREXIT: FOUNDATION FOR MUTUAL RECOGNITION

The EU is a single market, which guarantees, among other things, free movement of people. According to EU treaty law, citizens of one EU member state can freely move to and work in another EU member state, for the most part, without visa restrictions.[5] As a result of the free movement of people, EU-27 nurses are exempt from the UK's tiered, points-based immigration system. Citizens of the European Economic Area (EEA) are also exempt from the UK's system.[6] Three countries are members of the EEA, but not members of the EU: Iceland,

---

[5] Consolidated Version of the Treaty on the Functioning of the European Union art. 45, Mar. 30, 2010, 2010 O.J. (C 83/65-66).

[6] Agreement on the European Economic Area art. 28, 1994 O.J. (L 1) 12.

Liechtenstein, and Norway.[7] Swiss nationals are also exempt from the UK immigration system because Switzerland is part of the single market.[8]

While EU members have ceded some state sovereignty regarding their immigration system because of the incorporation of free movement of people, each EU member state, including the UK, maintains its own immigration policy for non-EU/EEA migrants. The UK has a tiered, points-based immigration system. The tiers represent different types of immigration (business people, inventors, and those with exceptional skill; skilled migrants; students; and temporary workers).[9] Each tier consists of different opportunities to allocate points to an applicant based on certain characteristics. In each tier, an applicant must obtain a requisite amount of points in order to be eligible for a visa.

Nurses migrating to the UK from non-EU/EEA countries currently fall within Tier 2 of the UK's immigration system: skilled migrants. To be eligible under Tier 2, an applicant must have an offer of employment, typically with a salary of at least £30,000 or the government's "appropriate rate" (whichever is higher).[10] There are some exceptions to those salary requirements, principally for "new entrants."[11] There is also an exception for nurses making at least £20,800.[12] These exceptions are vital because the current standard salary range for an NHS nurse is between £22,128 and £28,746, well under the standard £30,000 requirement.[13] NHS recently announced a pay increase, but the exact details are unclear.[14]

---

[7] *See generally*, *Countries in the EU and EEA*, GOV.UK, https://www.gov.uk/eu-eea (last visited June 7, 2018).

[8] *Id.*

[9] *See generally*, *Visas and Immigration*, GOV.UK, https://www.gov.uk/browse/visas-immigration (last visited June 7, 2018).

[10] *Tier 2 (General) visa - Eligibility*, GOV.UK, https://www.gov.uk/tier-2-general/eligibility (last visited Apr. 30, 2018).

[11] *See New Tier 2 Salary Requirements*, SMITH STONE WALTERS, (Dec. 8, 2016) https://smithstonewalters.com/2016/12/08/higher-tier-2-salary-requirements/ ("New Entrants are defined as new applicants to the Tier 2 (General) visa category who are either under 26 years of age, are switching from Tier 4 visa, or have been hired through a milkround recruitment process").

[12] *Tier 2 of the Points Based System—Policy Guide*, UK VISAS & IMMIGRATION, (Jan. 11, 2018), https://assets.publishing.service.gov.uk/government/uploads/system/uploads/attachment_data/file/673762/Tier_2_Policy_Guidance_01_2018__2_.pdf.

[13] *Agenda for Change*, HEALTH CAREERS, (last visited Apr. 18, 2018), https://www.healthcareers.nhs.uk/working-health/working-nhs/nhs-pay-and-benefits/agenda-change-pay-rates. There are opportunities for increased pay for chief nurses and other roles.

[14] *NHS Pay Increase Good but Doesn't Go Far Enough*, THE RECRUITER, (Mar. 22, 2018), http://www.recruiter.co.uk/news/2018/03/nhs-pay-increase-good-doesn't-go-far-enough-say-recruiters.

In addition to the eligibility requirements, applicants from non-EU/EEA countries face high fees to apply for a Tier 2 visa. The exact cost depends on the applicant's nationality (citizens from Turkey and Macedonia, two countries applying for EU membership, often have reduced fees), the applicant's whereabouts (whether s/he is already in the UK), the type of work (shortage occupation), and the duration of the stay. One of the lowest-cost application fees is £409 and it is a reduced fee for citizens of Turkey or Macedonia for up to three years in a shortage occupation.[15] Generally, a non-EU/EEA immigrant will spend closer to £1000 for a Tier 2 visa.[16] Moreover, an applicant must also have £945 in a bank account for ninety days before even applying, or a sponsor's confirmation of financial support.[17] None of these requirements apply for EU/EEA applicants.

Although the single market guarantees the ability to move and work, the single market alone is not sufficient to allow any EU citizen to work *any* job in another member state. Certain jobs have qualifications, such as nursing; these jobs require licenses, certifications, or some similar recognition of competency. The EU adopted a directive on the recognition of professional qualifications in 2005 (Qualifications Directive),[18] which covered nurses among other professions.[19] The Qualifications Directive was the result of years of increasing attempts to create a mutual recognition system throughout the EU. Through this directive, an EU member state recognizes the qualifications of nurses trained in another EU member state. The Qualifications Directive has EEA relevance, thus applying to the EEA member countries as well. The Qualifications Directive is also the foundational law introducing what is now known as the European Professional Card, an electronic procedure coordinated through the EU's Internal Market Information System that allows regulatory authorities to cooperate and communicate about

---

[15] *Tier 2 (General) visa – Overview*, GOV.UK, https://www.gov.uk/tier-2-general (last visited Apr. 30, 2018).

[16] *Id.*

[17] *Tier 2 (General) visa - Eligibility*, GOV.UK, https://www.gov.uk/tier-2-general/eligibility (last visited Apr. 30, 2018).

[18] Directive 2005/36/EC of the European Parliament and of the Council of Sept. 7, 2005 on the recognition of professional qualifications, 2005 O.J. (L 255/23); *see also* Directive 2013/55/EU of the European Parliament and of the Council of Nov. 2013 amending Directive 2005/36/EC on the recognition of professional qualification and Regulation (EU) No 1024/2012 on administrative cooperation through the Internal Market Information System ('the IMI regulation'), 2013 O.J. (L 354/132).

[19] The Qualifications Directive covers a number of other professionals as well. The analysis set forth in this paper may be useful foundation for an analysis of another profession. Nurses are uniquely interesting because of the context of NHS as a factor in Brexit and the current staffing concerns that the NHS faces.

mutual recognition.[20] The European Professional Card is one method of recognition, but applicants can have their qualifications recognized without it as well.

The Nursing and Midwifery Council (NMC) is the regulatory body within the UK that oversees the recognition of nursing qualifications. NMC has a streamlined process for nurses covered by the Qualifications Directive to join the registry. The current difference for EU/EEA-qualified nurse applicants and non-EU/EEA-qualified nurse applicants is stark, in terms of both procedural and financial burdens. For EU/EEA nurses, the application fee is £110 and a registration fee of £120 (if the application is recognized), while the total cost for non-EU/EEA applicants is currently £1415.[21] While EU/EEA applicants are still required to demonstrate knowledge of English, they are exempt from both the test of competence and the objective structured clinical evaluation, both of which non-EU/EEA applicants must complete. Those evaluations contribute to a substantial portion of the overall cost for non-EU/EEA applicants. NMC requires registered nurses to revalidate their registration every three years in a fairly straightforward and cost-free process.[22]

III. TRANSITION PERIOD: PROTECTION FOR CURRENT EU-27 NURSES IN THE UK

On February 28, 2018, the European Commission published the "Draft Agreement on the withdrawal of the United Kingdom of Great Britain and Northern Ireland from the European Union and the European Atomic Energy Community" (Draft Withdrawal Agreement).[23] Part Two of the Draft Withdrawal Agreement focuses on

---

[20] Directive 2005/36/EC of the European Parliament and of the Council of Sept. 7, 2005 on the recognition of professional qualifications, 2005 O.J. (L 255/26) at Preamble (32); *see also* Directive 2013/55/EU of the European Parliament and of the Council of Nov. 2013 amending Directive 2005/36/EC on the recognition of professional qualification and Regulation (EU) No 1024/2012 on administrative cooperation through the Internal Market Information System ('the IMI regulation'), 2013 O.J. (L 354/132); *European Professional Card*, EUROPEAN COMMISSION (Apr. 2, 2018), http://ec.europa.eu/growth/-single-market/services/free-movement-professionals/european-professional-card_en.

[21] *Trained outside the EU/EEA*, NURSING & MIDWIFERY COUNCIL (Nov. 21, 2017), https://www.nmc.org.uk/registration/joining-the-register/trained-outside-the-eueea/.

[22] *Registering as a nurse or midwife in the UK: Information for applicant trained in the European Union or the European Economic Area*, NURSING & MIDWIFERY COUNCIL, 6, https://www.nmc.org.uk/globalassets/sitedocuments/registration/registering-nurse-or-midwife-inside-eu2.pdf.

[23] *European Commission Draft Agreement on the withdrawal of the United Kingdom of Great Britain and Northern Ireland from the European Union and European Atomic Energy Community*, (Feb. 28, 2018), https://ec.europa.eu/commission/sites/beta-political/files/draft_-withdrawal_agreement.pdf.

citizens' rights, with Articles 25 through 27 particularly about professional qualifications. On March 19, 2018, the UK released its own draft withdrawal agreement of the same name.[24] Although the UK voiced concerns about other facets of the Draft Withdrawal Agreement, it agreed to the section covering professional qualifications.

The three articles represent three distinct but connected areas of agreement. Article 25 provides for the recognition of professional qualifications, before the end of the transition period, that are governed by the Qualifications Directive (including nurses).[25] The transition period is currently planned to last until December 31, 2020.[26] It covers both EU-27 citizens working in the UK and UK citizens working in EU-27 member states. Article 26 provides that a competent authority shall examine any application for recognition introduced *before* the end of the transition period.[27] Finally, Article 27 sets forth an agreement for administrative cooperation between the UK and EU member states in order to facilitate mutual recognition of those applications submitted before the end of the transition period.[28] This cooperation includes access by the UK to the Internal Market Information System, which is particularly useful in recognizing professional qualifications of European Professional Cardholders. In sum, the Draft Withdrawal Agreement's provisions will protect those who are already in the UK or arrive and submit their qualifications before the transition period ends. The Draft Withdrawal Agreement also contains provisions guaranteeing the right of residency for EU-27 citizens residing in the UK through the transition period.[29]

Reaching consensus on withdrawal is no small feat. The two parties are clearly focused on protecting the rights of their citizens. This apparent consensus belies some continued disagreement between the EU and the UK regarding dispute resolution. The parties agree to a specialized committee on citizens' rights that will oversee the regulatory process.[30] Despite a general agreement on the protection of EU citizens in the UK and UK citizens in the EU, the jurisdiction of the Court of Justice for the European Union (CJEU) remains a contentious issue. However, this issue is likely of minimal consequence in the realm of

---

[24] *Draft Agreement on the withdrawal of the United Kingdom of Great Britain and Northern Ireland from the European Union and European Atomic Energy Community*, (Mar. 19, 2018), https://www.gov.uk/government/uploads/system/uploads/attachment_data/file/691366/20180319_DRAFT_WITHDRAWAL_AGREEMENT.pdf.

[25] *Id.* at art. 25.

[26] *Id.* at art. 121.

[27] *Id.* at art. 26.

[28] *Id.* at art. 27.

[29] *Id.* at arts. 8-21.

[30] *Id.* at art. 157.

nursing qualifications. Although the CJEU has heard many cases on the Qualifications Directive, they are not particularly pertinent to nursing qualifications.[31]

The general consensus should offer some relief to the 21,000 EU-27 nurses currently working and living in the UK, and any EU-27 nurses who arrive during the transition period. However, the agreement does not create, or even indicate, a framework for future EU-27 nurses wishing to work in the UK after the UK leaves the EU.

IV. COMPETING CONCERNS: UK INTERESTS AND EU INTERESTS

EU-27 nationals currently account for roughly seven percent of NHS nurses—approximately 21,000 nurses.[32] One third of EU-27 national nurses work in London.[33] EU-27 nurses are admittedly a small group living and working in the UK. However, they are an essential component to the NHS, which is facing serious staffing concerns.[34] The Royal College of Nursing has extolled the benefits and contributions of EU-27 nurses, and has voiced concern for their future post-Brexit.[35] Unison, the public service union, has voiced similar concerns.[36] Against the backdrop of the economic demand for EU-27 nurses is the political reality of Brexit. The referendum focused on taking back control. In particular, those who voted to leave the EU wanted to regain control over immigration and borders.[37] Prime Minister May has confirmed this attitude by announcing, "free movement of people will come to an end and [the UK] will control the number of people who come to live [there]."[38] Without free movement of people, the efficacy of any mutual

---

[31] InfoCuria – Case-law of the Court of Justice, CURIA, https://curia.europa.-eu/jcms/jcms/j_6/en/ (search terms "nurse" and "2005/36).

[32] Carl Baker, *NHS staff from overseas: statistics*, HOUSE OF COMMONS LIBRARY, Feb. 7, 2018, https://researchbriefings.parliament.uk/ResearchBriefing/Summary/CBP-7783#fullreport.

[33] *Id.*

[34] Laura Donnelly, *Number of EU nurses registering to work in Britain falls by 90 per cent*, THE TELEGRAPH, (Nov. 2, 2017), https://www.telegraph.co.uk/news/2017/11/02/number-eu-nurses-registering-work-britain-falls-90-per-cent/.

[35] *Nursing staff from the European Union*, ROYAL COLLEGE OF NURSING, https://www.rcn.org.uk/employment-and-pay/nursing-staff-from-the-european-union (last visited Apr. 30, 2018).

[36] *Nurse and midwife numbers dragged down by Brexit effect*, UNISON, (Apr. 25, 2018), https://www.unison.org.uk/news/2018/04/nurse-midwife-numbers-dragged-brexit-effect/.

[37] Lord Ashcroft, *How the United Kingdom voted on Thursday…and why*, LORD ASHCROFT POLLS (June 24, 2016), http://lordashcroftpolls.com/2016/06/how-the-united-kingdom-voted-and-why/.

[38] *PM speech on our future economic partnership with the European Union*, GOV.UK, (Mar. 2, 2018), https://www.gov.uk/government/speeches/pm-speech-on-our-future-economic-partnership-with-the-european-union.

recognition of nursing qualifications will be shaped by the immigration controls. Mutual recognition can certainly exist without free movement (discussed below), but whether it would be sufficient to address the UK's economic needs is questionable.

Moreover, it is not only the UK's political and economic interests at play. The foundation of the mutual recognition of professional qualifications is reciprocity. The UK has a clear economic incentive to recognize EU nursing qualifications: the regulatory requirements are already aligned, and the UK is facing a staffing problem. However, the EU does not necessarily face the same sort of incentives. It is difficult to quantify how a lack of UK nurses in the EU-27 would impact that economy. Between 1997 and 2016, the European Regulated Professionals Database (a system that records EU nationals seeking recognition of qualifications to practice in other EU member states) recorded 35,800 submissions from applicants with UK qualifications and 29,149 approvals.[39] The third largest number of applicants during that span (1997-2016) came from UK-trained nurses (3,270).[40] Although this number is small, UK professionals generally are among the most mobile nationalities in the EU.[41] Those UK nurses presently working in the EU-27 will maintain their qualification under the Draft Withdrawal Agreement. However, after the transition, EU law will no longer recognize immigrating UK nurses' qualifications absent an agreement. While the EU may lose potential migration from UK nurses, the difference may be made up by other EU-27 nurses who will no longer be able to migrate to the UK through free movement of people.

Economic considerations do not exist in a vacuum; there are also political considerations. The EU is able to connect the countries of Europe only as long as it maintains its members. The EU works because of its members; the members share the benefits, but also the burdens of the union. In order to achieve harmonization across the diverse countries, certain compromises must be made. For many countries, free movement of people is a compromise. Immigration is generally considered a pillar of state sovereignty and EU member states have ceded this sovereignty—in part—by acquiescing to free movement of people. Although it comes at a cost of state sovereignty, free movement of people has economic benefits because migrants, particularly in the services sector, can facilitate trade and investment, and thus serves an

---

[39] Meghan Benton, Safe or Sorry? Prospects for Britons in the European Union after Brexit, Migration Policy Institute, Nov. 2017, 14.

[40] *Id.*

[41] *Id.*

important role in the functioning of the Single Market.[42] If the UK can gain the benefits of harmonization, such as mutual recognition of certain professional qualifications, without the cost of free movement of people, it could set a difficult precedent for the EU. Recently, there has been concern that other countries may also seek an exit, though none has actively pursued that option as of yet.[43] Although the EU may lose some potential UK nurses, the EU may also not want to incentivize further exits from the union by giving the UK a better deal outside of the union than it had within the union—which would be mutual recognition of qualifications without the free movement of people.

On the other hand, the EU may also favor a mutual recognition agreement (MRA) with the UK, even without free movement of people because MRAs foster international trade, particularly in services. The EU generally favors MRAs, both within the union and with third countries. Within the EU, the member states have strengthened their own framework in recent years to better serve their citizens.[44] As discussed in more detail below, the EU has focused on incorporating MRAs in their latest trade agreements, with various degrees of success.[45] MRAs within bilateral trade agreements do not typically accompany free movement of people.

V. THE ROAD AHEAD: HOW MUTUAL RECOGNITION CAN FIT IN A NEW RELATIONSHIP

The Draft Withdrawal Agreement sets out a framework for protecting the professional qualifications of EU-27 citizens in the UK throughout the transition period. However, the withdrawal is merely the first stage of the UK's separation from the EU. The next step will be for the UK and the EU to broker some form of agreement regarding their future relationship. The future relationship is an open question with a number of possibilities available. Any possible agreement can potentially

---

[42] Camino Mortera-Martinze and Christian Odendahl, What free movement means to Europe and why it matters for Britain, Centre for European Reform, Jan. 2017, 2.

[43] Sam Meredith, "Nexit, Frexit or Grexit? The countries that could follow Britain out of the EU," CNBC, https://www.cnbc.com/2017/02/13/nexit-frexit-or-grexit-the-countries-that-could-follow-britain-out-of-the-eu.html (Feb. 13, 2017).

[44] Directive 2013/55/EU of the European Parliament and of the Council of Nov. 2013 amending Directive 2005/36/EC on the recognition of professional qualification and Regulation (EU) No 1024/2012 on administrative cooperation through the Internal Market Information System ('the IMI regulation'), 2013 O.J. (L 354/132).

[45] Howard Davies, *EUA Special Update on EU Trade Agreements and on the Recognition of Professional Qualifications*, EUROPEAN UNIVERSITY ASSOCIATION, (June 2016), http://www.eua.be/Libraries/publications-homepage-list/eua-special-update-on-eu-trade-agreements-and-on-the-recognition-of-professional-qualifications.pdf?sfvrsn=4.

include an MRA on professional qualifications, but the incorporation of such agreement will depend on the political will of both parties.

First, the UK and the EU might not reach an agreement about their relationship before the transition period ends. In the event of a "no deal" situation, the two parties will revert back to World Trade Organization (WTO) standards. The WTO is an intergovernmental organization for regulating international trade; it is a forum for trade negotiations. The General Agreement on Trade in Services (GATS) expanded this trading system to include the service sector. Specifically, the UK can continue to pursue MRAs under GATS Article VII.[46] Under GATS Article VII, subject to nondiscrimination,

> a Member state may recognize the education or experience obtained, requirements met, or licenses or certifications granted in a particular country. Such recognition, which may be achieved through harmonization or otherwise, may be based upon an agreement or arrangement with the country concerned or may be accorded autonomously.[47]

This provision of GATS would leave the UK open to negotiating for professional recognition with the EU or with other countries. Such agreements may be unilateral or multilateral. Based on the NMC guidelines, the UK currently does not have specialized recognition systems for nursing qualifications with countries other than EU members, EEA members, and Switzerland. So although the UK can pursue other MRAs under GATS Article VII, it has not done so for nurses.

The EU's system for mutual recognition is especially progressive, but MRAs are not particularly uncommon. MRAs have expanded since GATS; they may stand alone, even as a bilateral agreement concerning a single profession, or they may be part of a more expansive free trade agreement (FTA) or a regional trade agreement.[48] Another progressive example of an MRA system, similar to the EU, is the Trans-Tasman Mutual Recognition Arrangement between Australia and New Zealand, two countries that certainly have a unique relationship.[49] Other attempts

---

46 GATS: General Agreement on Trade in Services, Apr. 15, 1994, Marrakesh Agreement Establishing the World Trade Organization, Art. VII, 1869 U.N.T.S. 183 (1994).

47 *Id.* at art. VII(1).

48 *See* Trade Committee, Service Providers on the Move: Mutual Recognition Agreements, ORGANIZATION FOR ECONOMIC COOPERATION AND DEVELOPMENT, TD/TC/WP(2002)48/FINAL (Feb. 6, 2003).

49 *Recognition of qualifications*, NEW ZEALAND FOREIGN AFFAIRS AND TRADE, https://www.mfat.govt.nz/en/countries-and-regions/australia/new-zealand-high-

have been more tentative. The North American Free Trade Agreement (NAFTA), for example, includes an annex encouraging, but not requiring, mutual recognition.[50]

GATS plays other roles in determining the ability of nurses to work in foreign countries, besides allowing for MRAs. In particular, each WTO member creates a GATS schedule of its commitments in various service sectors (nurses actually fall within the "Business Services" sector). Mode 4 of the GATS schedules covers the presence of natural persons, such as nurses. Currently, the EU's GATS schedule covering nurses in Mode 4 is complex and includes certain restrictions for some member states and not for others.[51] Importantly, these restrictions do not apply to nurses from other member states—only for nurses from countries outside of the EU. The details of the UK and the EU GATS schedules and the future status of them are beyond the scope of this chapter, but the schedules will be an additional consideration in the ability of EU-27 nurses to work in the UK.

In a "no deal" scenario, the UK would need to negotiate with the EU in order to have UK nursing qualifications recognized within the EU-27. However, the UK has transposed the Qualifications Directive into its own domestic law.[52] The EU has both primary and secondary legislation.[53] Primary legislation includes treaty law, which provides for the foundation of free movement. Secondary legislation includes regulations, directives, and decisions, which stem from the principles of the treaties. Regulations are binding and become immediately enforceable, without the member states transposing them into domestic law. On the other hand, directives, like the Qualifications Directive, set out a goal for member states, but it is up to each member state to achieve those goals, typically by implementing domestic legislation. Because the Qualifications Directive has been transposed into domestic law, the UK

---

commission/living-in-australia/recognition-of-qualifications/ (last visited Apr. 30, 2018).

[50] North American Free Trade Agreement, Annex 1210.5, Dec. 17, 1992.

[51] Council for Trade in Services, *Communication from the European Communities and its Member States – Certification – Draft consolidated GATS Schedule*, S/C/W/273* (Oct. 9, 2006), *available at* http://trade.ec.europa.eu/doclib/docs/2012/november/tradoc_150087.pdf

[52] For the seventy-nine measure through which the UK has transposed the Qualifications Directive, *see* National transposition measures communicated by the Member States concerning: Directive 2005/36/EC of the European Parliament and of the Council of 7 September 2005 on the recognition of professional qualifications (Text with EEA relevance), EUR-LEX: ACCESS TO EUROPEAN UNION LAW, http://eur-lex.europa.eu/legal-content/EN/NIM/?uri=CELEX:32005L0036&qid=1523897464697 (select United Kingdom) (last visited Apr. 30, 2018).

[53] *See generally*, *EU Law*, EUROPEAN UNION, https://europa.eu/european-union/law_en (last visited June 7, 2018).

will likely continue to recognize EU/EEA qualifications unless and until Parliament changes its law. But the recognition will not be reciprocated because the remaining EU member states will only recognize other EU member states—not third countries, which the UK will be post-Brexit.

Alternatively, the UK may pursue a relationship with the EU that is similar to Norway or Switzerland. Norway is a member of the EEA and its citizens thus benefit from free movement of people[54] and mutual recognition of qualifications.[55] Switzerland maintains its unique relationship with the EU through a series of bilateral agreements, including an Agreement on the Free Movement of People.[56] The Qualifications Directive currently applies to Switzerland based on Annex III of the Agreement on the Free Movement of People.[57] Although the Norway model and the Switzerland model are both possibilities, they are unlikely choices for the UK to pursue. Both options will put the UK in the position of a rule-taker. The UK will be subject to the EU directive, but not in a position to change it. Because of the administrative cost of the professional qualifications recognition system (particularly the European Professional Card and the accompanying database), the UK may even be required to continue contributing to the EU budget, a politically difficult concession to make. Prime Minister May has specifically noted that a Norway model will not work due to the continuation of the free movement of people,[58] which would also rule out a Switzerland model.

Prime Minister May has also expressed doubt regarding an FTA because it could mean a reduction in market access.[59] Despite her reservation, an FTA could be a strong option for the UK in order to

---

[54] Agreement on the European Economic Area art. 28, 1994 O.J. (L 1) 12.

[55] Agreement on the European Economic Area art. 30, 1994 O.J. (L 1) 12; *see also* Agreement on the European Economic Area – Annex VII Recognition of Professional Qualifications, http://www.efta.int/media/documents/legal-texts/eea/the-eea-agreement/Annexes%20to%20the%20Agreement/annex7.pdf.

[56] *Agreement on the Free Movement of Persons*, STATE SECRETARIAT FOR EDUCATION, RESEARCH AND INNOVATION, https://www.sbfi.admin.ch/sbfi/en/home/bildung-/recognition-of-foreign-qualifications/legal-basis-for-the-recognition-of-foreign-qualifications/swiss-eu-bilateral-agreement-on-the-free-movement-of-persons.html (last visited Apr. 30, 2018).

[57] *Agreement on the Free Movement of Persons*, STATE SECRETARIAT FOR EDUCATION, RESEARCH AND INNOVATION, https://www.sbfi.admin.ch/sbfi/en/home/bildung/-recognition-of-foreign-qualifications/legal-basis-for-the-recognition-of-foreign-qualifications/swiss-eu-bilateral-agreement-on-the-free-movement-of-persons.html (last visited Apr. 30, 2018).

[58] *PM speech on our future economic partnership with the European Union*, GOV.UK, (Mar. 2, 2018), https://www.gov.uk/government/speeches/pm-speech-on-our-future-economic-partnership-with-the-european-union.

[59] *Id.*

maintain continued mutual recognition of nursing qualifications. The EU-Canada Comprehensive Economic and Trade Agreement (CETA) contains a mutual recognition provision covering certain professions and a provision for a Joint Committee on Cooperation for the Recognition of Qualifications.[60] It is unclear how exactly CETA's MRA will progress given the novelty of the trade agreement. In the negotiation of an FTA between the UK and the EU, the parties will need to push for a MRA and ensure that nurses are covered as regulated professions. Unlike the Norway and Switzerland examples, CETA does not include an agreement on free movement of persons. It is a unique example of mutual recognition of professional qualifications within an FTA. MRAs are not present in the EU's previous FTAs, but the EU is focused on incorporating such agreements into future trade deals, both bilateral and multilateral.[61] For example, the creation of a framework for mutual recognition of professional qualifications is a stated goal of the EU in its negotiations on the Transatlantic Trade and Investment Partnership,[62] if the agreement ever moves forward.

Yet another option for the future EU-UK relationship is a customs union. Much to the chagrin of Prime Minister May's cabinet, the House of Lords voted for an amendment to the European Union Withdrawal Bill requiring that the government provide "a statement about the steps it had taken on a customs union."[63] Notably, this amendment has only passed the House of Lords and does not actually require a customs union, but rather an explanation for the lack of a customs union. To this point, the EU has three customs unions (with Turkey, Andorra, and Monaco), none of which includes mutual recognition of professional qualifications and also none of which includes the free movement of people.[64] A customs union does not solve the UK's potential concerns

---

[60] Comprehensive Economic and Trade Agreement between Canada, of the one part, and the European Union and its Member States, Can.-EU, Oct. 30, 2016.

[61] Howard Davies, *EUA Special Update on EU Trade Agreements and on the Recognition of Professional Qualifications*, EUROPEAN UNIVERSITY ASSOCIATION, (June 2016), http://www.eua.be/Libraries/publications-homepage-list/eua-special-update-on-eu-trade-agreements-and-on-the-recognition-of-professional-qualifications.pdf?sfvrsn=4.

[62] Directives for the Negotiation on the Transatlantic Trade and Investment Partnership between the European Union and the United States of America, Council Doc. 11103/13 of 17 June 2013, para. 17, http://data.consilium.europa.eu/doc/document/ST-11103-2013-DCL-1/en/pdf.

[63] *Ministers braced for new vote on customs union after Lords defeat*, THE GUARDIAN, (Apr. 19, 2018), https://www.theguardian.com/politics/2018/apr/19/ministers-braced-for-new-vote-on-customs-union-after-lords-defeat.

[64] *See Customs unions*, EUROPEAN COMMISSION, https://ec.europa.eu/-taxation_customs/business/calculation-customs-duties/rules-origin/customs-unions_en (last visited Apr. 30, 2018).

about mutual recognition, but it also would not impede the UK from seeking a separate MRA under GATS Article VII.

Finally, Prime Minister May has expressed her desire for a unique relationship between the UK and the EU, unlike that between other countries.[65] In a bespoke deal, the mutual recognition of professional qualifications will simply be one of countless topics that will need to be negotiated. The UK should, however, ensure that mutual recognition is incorporated into the deal. The UK would benefit economically from the mutual recognition of professional qualifications, particularly of nurses. Because such a deal will be unique, it is difficult to predict the exact contours; however, a provision on mutual recognition may be incorporated into such agreement, just as it has been incorporated into FTAs, such as CETA.

The key issue facing the UK will be the tension between recognizing nursing qualifications and withholding free movement of people. Whatever mutual recognition the UK and the EU do or do not reach, recognition of qualifications is only one part of the equation. If the UK wishes to continue attracting nurses, the UK must create an immigration system that adequately facilitates the migration of nurses. The current system for non-EU nurses hoping to migrate to the UK is expensive (high fees) and onerous (many steps including a job offer). Typically immigration is considered a pillar of sovereignty that exists outside international agreements like FTAs and customs unions. Thus it would presumably be for the UK to decide its own immigration policy, which is unlikely to include free movement of people, but could contain special categories or point allocations for EU-27 citizens.

The UK may also decide that it is simply not politically wise (or feasible) to continue mutual recognition. With the staffing shortages, this decision could have negative consequences for the NHS. The UK could explore options of mutual recognition arrangements with other third countries. However, the UK and the EU currently have regulatory equivalence—unlike the UK and other third countries. This current equivalency makes the EU an ideal partner in an MRA, more so than other potential third countries.

VI. CONCLUSIONS

Nurses are but one of many professions regulated by the Qualifications Directive and other EU directives. They represent a small case study of the effects of Brexit and the challenges in reconciling the many goals of the UK in its future relationship with the EU. Brexit is a

---

[65] *PM speech on our future economic partnership with the European Union*, GOV.UK, (Mar. 2, 2018), https://www.gov.uk/government/speeches/pm-speech-on-our-future-economic-partnership-with-the-european-union.

battle being fought on multiple fronts: politically, economically, and legally. The issue of professional qualifications will be a battle between what is economically ideal and what is politically feasible. Economically, EU-27 nurses, as well as EU-27 doctors and staff, play an important role within the NHS.[66] Politically, the results of the referendum indicate reluctance on the part of the UK to pursue any professional qualifications recognition system that requires free movement of people. Although mutual recognition of nursing qualifications can fit into any of the various options for the future EU-UK relationship, the efficacy of a mutual recognition system is inherently tied to the free movement of people. The EU has shown a willingness to pursue MRAs without free movement of people; however, the EU's previous negotiations have had limited success so far and have not been clouded by the politics of Brexit.

Besides the legal logistics of allowing EU-27 nurses to work in the UK, there is another question: will they even want to work there? According to an analysis of the NMC registrar, in the first year after the Brexit vote, the number of EU-27 nurses who came to the UK to work dropped from 10,000 to 1,000.[67] According to the European Regulated Professions Database, the number of decisions on nurses' applications in 2014-2015 and 2015-2016 were over 15,000 and over 18,000 respectively; the number in 2016-2017 was less than 10,000.[68] Even if the UK and the EU agree to mutual recognition of nursing qualifications and the UK creates a visa system that will meaningfully allow EU-27 nurses to immigrate, EU-27 nurses simply may not come to work in the UK. The current downturn in applications may reflect the current level of uncertainty. But it may also reflect a growing feeling of disconnect between EU-27 citizens and their soon-to-be former member state, the UK. A battle for continued recognition of nursing qualifications may not be worth the challenge of negotiation if EU-27 citizens no longer want to live and work in the UK.

---

[66] *See Brexit and the NHS*, THE UK IN A CHANGING EUROPE, (Mar. 14, 2018), http://ukandeu.ac.uk/research-papers/brexit-and-the-nhs/.

[67] Laura Donnelly, *Number of EU nurses registering to work in Britain falls by 90 per cent*, THE TELEGRAPH, (Nov. 2, 2017), https://www.telegraph.co.uk/news/2017/11/02/number-eu-nurses-registering-work-britain-falls-90-per-cent/.

[68]Statistics – Professionals Moving Abroad (Establishment), EUROPEAN COMMISSION, http://ec.europa.eu/growth/tools-databases/regprof/index.cfm?action=stat_overall&b_services=false (last visited May 4, 2018) (search based on "general care nurse" recognition regime).

CHAPTER 5: THE UK DUAL-USE EXPORT CONTROL REGIME POST-BREXIT

CAMERON PEEK

The current European Union (EU) and United Kingdom (UK) regimes for controlling exports of dual-use[1] goods present a balance of two critical policy goals typical of all export control regimes. One goal is the maximization of economic welfare by promoting international competitiveness; both the EU and UK want to encourage their producers to stay competitive in the international arena by allowing them to export their goods as much as possible.[2] The other goal is maintaining national security; the EU wants to protect the security interests of all its Member States, and similarly the UK wants to protect its own security interests, by preventing their respective producers from either intentionally or unwittingly equipping actors who seek to harm international peace and security with the tools to do so.[3] Where private sector producers deal in dual-use goods, the EU, UK, and other EU Member States use export controls to require that their producers apply for and receive a license before engaging in export activity, thereby helping ensure that these goods do not fall into the wrong hands.

The UK's decision to leave the EU presents two types of challenges to both the EU and the UK's ability to meet these policy goals. The first set of challenges relates to potential legal gaps or confusion regarding legal liability when exporting dual-use goods post-Brexit. The second set relates to issues inherent to the divergence of the two regimes. This paper aims to present and analyze these challenges and make recommendations for how the UK might best respond to them. Part I will present a brief background on export controls and their importance in the EU and the UK. Part II will identify and explain the relevant provisions under EU and UK law which comprise the current export control regime. Part III

---

[1] "Dual-use" goods are goods which have both civilian and military applications. While the EU also employs controls on other types of goods (for example, military-goods or non-hazardous waste), this paper will focus only upon Brexit's effects on the EU and UK's respective dual-use export control regimes. *See generally* EUROPEAN COMMISSION – POLICIES, INFORMATION AND SERVICES, http://ec.europa.eu/trade/import-and-export-rules/export-from-eu/dual-use-controls (last visited May 11, 2018).

[2] *Cf. European Parliament Directorate-General for External Policies: Workshop on Dual Use Export Controls*, at 48 (Oct. 2015), http://www.europarl.europa.eu/RegData/etudes-/STUD/2015/535000/EXPO_STU(2015)535000_EN.pdf.

[3] *Cf. id.*

will describe the two sets of previously mentioned challenges in detail, including potential recommendations for how these challenges may be mitigated. Finally, Part IV will summarize the most appropriate recommendations from Part III to recommend an overall course of action the UK should take in relation to effectuating its export control regime post-Brexit.

I. BACKGROUND ON THE IMPORTANCE OF EXPORT CONTROLS IN THE EU AND THE UK

It is important that the EU and the UK continue to maintain effective export control laws to balance economic growth with national security interests for three reasons. 1) Dual-use goods are an important part of the EU and UK economies, 2) The EU and the UK have hard law obligations to implement effective export controls, and 3) The EU and the UK have soft law obligations to implement effective export controls necessary to support their international efficacy.

A. DUAL-USE GOODS ARE AN IMPORTANT PART OF THE EU AND UK ECONOMIES.

Although dual-use goods are not typically documented by EU customs officials as an industry unto themselves, EU customs data suggest that trade in dual-use goods comprises a significant portion of total EU exports. According to a 2015 report commissioned by the European Commission, in 2014 total trade in dual-use related exports from the EU could be estimated at approximately €1.1 trillion (approximately 7% of total EU GDP), €623 billion of this being intra-EU trade, and €476 billion being extra-EU trade.[4] This comprised approximately 24% of the value of total extra-EU exports for 2014.[5]

This data was produced by algorithmically assigning tariff codes to related export control categories.[6] However, in reality, tariff codes do not directly correspond to regulated dual-use goods.[7] Thus, these figures significantly overestimate the actual value of EU dual-use goods exports, and more realistically represent the upper bound of the possible value of the EU dual-use industry.[8] When readjusting the estimation to account

---

[4] *See Final Report: Data and Information Collection for EU Dual-Use Export Control Policy Review*, at 48 (Nov. 6, 2015), http://trade.ec.europa.eu/doclib/docs/2016/september/-tradoc_154962.PDF [hereinafter *EU Dual-Use Data*]; *See also European Union Data*, THE WORLD BANK, https://data.worldbank.org/region/european-union (last visited May 11, 2018) (estimating 2014 EU GDP at 18.6 trillion USD, or 15.6 trillion EUR).

[5] *See EU Dual-Use Data*, *supra* note 4.

[6] *See id.*

[7] *Id.*

[8] *Id.* at 13.

for tariff code inconsistencies, and after excluding exports to countries which do not require license applications due to the existence of general authorizations, the realistic value of extra-EU dual-use trade was estimated at €180 billion, or 3.9% of total EU exports.[9]

Unfortunately, the 2015 report did not disaggregate data by Member State, and neither the UK Department for the Economy nor the Department for International Trade keep statistics allowing for easy extrapolation of the value of the UK dual-use industry. However, if taking 3.9% as an average value of dual-use exports for all EU Member States, it seems likely that the UK, a considerably developed and complex economy, and the second largest economy in the EU, would fall somewhere above this 3.9% average.[10] This seems even more likely when considering that the UK is the world's second largest exporter of defense and security goods, which might be thought of as a proxy indicator for industries dealing in dual-use goods.[11]

B. THE EU AND THE UK HAVE HARD LAW OBLIGATIONS TO IMPLEMENT EFFECTIVE EXPORT CONTROLS.

Export controls are a recognized obligation under international law. U.N. Security Council Resolution 1540, the Chemical Weapons Convention and the Biological Weapons Convention require effective controls be implemented to deter proliferation of nuclear, biological and chemical weapons.[12] The UK is a member of the U.N. and a signatory to both conventions. Similarly, any obligations the EU possesses under these sources of international law are unrelated to the UK's status as an EU member. Thus, neither the EU nor the UK's obligations under international law to maintain effective export controls will change due to Brexit.

---

[9] *See id.*

[10] *See Share of Member States in EU GDP*, EUROPEAN COMMISSION: EUROSTAT (Oct. 4, 2017), http://ec.europa.eu/eurostat/web/products-eurostat-news/-/DDN-20170410-1.

[11] *See UK Defence and Security Export Statistics for 2016*, UK DEP'T FOR INT'L TRADE (OCT. 24, 2017), https://www.gov.uk/government/publications/uk-defence-and-security-export-figures-2016/uk-defence-and-security-export-statistics-for-2016#summary (last visited May 11, 2018).

[12] *See* S.C. Res. 1540, ¶ 3 (Apr. 28, 2004); *See also* Convention on the Prohibition of the Development, Production, Stockpiling and Use of Chemical Weapons and on Their Destruction, Jan. 13, 1993, 1974 U.N.T.S. 45; Convention on the Prohibition of the Development, Production and Stockpiling of Bacteriological (Biological) and Toxin Weapons and on their Destruction, Apr. 10, 1972, 1015 U.N.T.S. 163.

C. THE EU AND THE UK HAVE SOFT LAW OBLIGATIONS TO IMPLEMENT EFFECTIVE EXPORT CONTROLS NECESSARY TO SUPPORT THEIR INTERNATIONAL EFFICACY.

Implementing dual-use export controls poses an especially difficult policy challenge because collective international action is needed for controls to be effective. Where one country prohibits exports of a certain good and another does not, the first country fails to achieve either of the previously mentioned policy goals—economic welfare is harmed because exports are prohibited and bad actors can procure prohibited goods all the same. For controls to be effective, all countries which can produce goods of concern must employ similarly effective controls to assuage fears that foreign producers will undercut domestic regimes.[13] To this end, the nations concerned about the proliferation of weapons of mass destruction participate in multilateral coordinative bodies, creating soft law obligations to adhere to and promote inter-compatibility of their respective export control regimes. Most noteworthy are the Wassenaar Arrangement, the Australia Group, the Nuclear Suppliers Group, and the Missile Technology Control Regime.[14]

Notably, only countries are members of these coordinative bodies; the UK is a member of them all, and the EU of none.[15] Thus, Brexit will not have any effect upon either the UK or the EU's international obligations under any of these coordinative bodies.[16]

---

[13] *See* Quentin Michel & Ian Stewart, *Brexit and Strategic Trade Controls: Key Implications*, KING'S C. LONDON CTR. FOR SCI. AND SECURITY STUDIES: PROJECT ALPHA (May 3, 2017), https://projectalpha.eu/brexit-and-strategic-trade-controls-key-implications (noting that the possibility of divergence of the EU and UK export control regimes presents a risk of unhealthy competition and a "race to the bottom.").

[14] *See generally* THE WASSENAAR ARRANGEMENT, https://www.wassenaar.org (last visited May 11, 2018); NUCLEAR SUPPLIERS GROUP, http://www.nuclearsuppliersgroup.org/en/ (last visited May 11, 2018); THE AUSTRALIA GROUP, http://www.australiagroup.net/en/ (last visited May 11, 2018); *The Missile Technology Control Regime at a Glance*, ARMS CONTROL ASSOCIATION, https://www.armscontrol.org/factsheets/mtcr (last visited May 11, 2018).

[15] This is not to say these bodies are entirely unrelated to the EU export control regime. Conversely, because most EU member states are members of all four organizations, the EU's implementation of its export control laws is heavily influenced by the outcomes agreed upon in these organizations. *See* Council Regulation 428/2009, Annex I, 2009 O.J. (L 134) ("[Annex I] implements internationally agreed dual-use controls including the Wassenaar Arrangement, the Missile Technology Control Regime (MTCR), the Nuclear Suppliers' Group (NSG), the Australia Group and the Chemical Weapons Convention (CWC)").

[16] *See* Clif Burns, *A Brief Brexplanation of Brexit and Brexport*, EXPORTLAWBLOG (June 24, 2016), https://www.exportlawblog.com/archives/7887 (last visited May 11, 2018).

II. THE CURRENT EU DUAL-USE EXPORT CONTROL REGIME

The primary legal basis for control of exports of dual-use goods in the EU emanates from Council Regulation 428/2009 ("EC 428/2009").[17] This regulation defines the broad parameters under which each Member State must implement their export control regimes. However, it leaves the actual implementation of export control enforcement to Member States, and allows Member States to modify the obligations imposed by the regulation within certain parameters.[18] Thus, it is easiest to understand the current interaction between the EU and UK regimes by first looking at what the EU regime requires, and then looking at how the UK regime implements these requirements, as well as its own.

A. THE EU REGIME: COUNCIL REGULATION 428/2009

As previously noted, EC 428/2009 provides the substantive legal basis for EU export controls. It has been periodically amended to update its coverage of goods, but substantively it has not changed since it was originally implemented.[19]

At the broadest level, EC 428/2009 requires authorization be granted before any EU exporter export any items listed in Annex I (appended to EC 428/2009).[20] Here, EC 428/2009 defines an "export" as items which leave the customs territory of the EU.[21] Thus, it does not apply to intra-EU transfers of dual-use goods. Annex I lists goods to be controlled according to ten separate categories, such as Nuclear Materials, Facilities and Equipment (Category 0) or Aerospace and Propulsion (Category 9).[22] Annex I is periodically updated to reflect changes in sensitivity of dual-use goods.[23]

Beyond this broad requirement, EC 428/2009 also requires authorization for export of items which do not fall under Annex I under several specific scenarios, such as, but not limited to, when the destination is subject to an embargo or economic sanctions, or when the

---

[17] Council Regulation 428/2009, 2009 O.J. (L 134) [hereinafter *EC 428/2009*].

[18] *See European Parliament Directorate-General for External Policies: Workshop on Dual Use Export Controls*, at 12 (Oct. 2015), http://www.europarl.europa.eu/RegData/etudes/-STUD/2015/535000/EXPO_STU(2015)535000_EN.pdf.

[19] For the most notable amendments to EC 428/2009, see Council Regulation No 1232/2011, 2011 O.J. (L 326) (primarily expanding EU General Export Authorisations and updating language for clarity); Council Regulation No 388/2012, 2012 O.J. (129) (primarily updating Annex I).

[20] *EC 429/2009* Art. 3.

[21] *Id.* Art. 2(2).

[22] *Id.* Annex I.

[23] *See* Council Regulation No 388/2012, 2012 O.J. (L 129) (replacing Annex I with an updated version).

exporter knows the non-controlled items will be used for a military purpose.[24]

EC 428/2009 allows for two categories of General Export Authorisations (GEAs)—carve-out categories which remove the need to apply for authorization—in order to ease regulatory burdens.[25] The first category are EU GEAs issued by the European Commission which can be used by any EU producer.[26] There are currently six types of EU GEA: 1) exports to Australia, Canada, Japan, New Zealand, Norway, Switzerland and the United States, 2) certain dual-use items to certain destinations, 3) exports of goods for repairs/replacements, 4) temporary exports for exhibitions or fairs, 5) telecommunications, and 6) chemicals.[27] The second category, National GEAs, are issued by national authorities, but can still be claimed by any EU producer, so long as the terms of the National GEA comport with EC 428/2009.[28] Where an exporter intends to export dual-use goods which fall under either of these GEAs, the exporter simply notes this on their exporting paperwork and notifies the appropriate national authorities.

In addition to GEAs, EC 428/2009 allows for two other types of authorization: Global Export Authorisation and Individual Export Authorisation.[29] Both authorizations are issued by national authorities to individual exporters on a case-by-case basis. The difference between the two is that global authorizations are granted to one exporter to allow them to export an entire category of dual-use goods to multiple foreign users, and individual authorizations are granted to one exporter to export one type of dual-use good to one foreign user.[30] Individual authorizations are the most common type of authorization, accounting for over 75% of total authorizations.[31]

Some goods are of such a sensitive nature that allowing national governments to implement general authorizations would present a security risk. Such goods are listed in Annex IV, essentially establishing an exception to the GEA exceptions.[32] For items under this list, export

---

24 *See id.* Art. 4.

25 *Id.* Art. 9.

26 *See id.* Annex II, *amended by* Council Regulation No 1232/2011, 2011 O.J. (L 326) (adding type 2 through 6).

27 *Id.*

28 *See id.* Art. 9.

29 *Id.*

30 *See Briefing: Implementation Appraisal of Control of Trade in Dual-Use Items* at 3, EUROPEAN PARLIAMENTARY RESEARCH SERVICE (Sept. 2016), http://www.europarl.europa.eu/-RegData/etudes/BRIE/2016/587340/EPRS_BRI%282016%29587340_EN.pdf.

31 *See id.* at 5.

32 *See EC 428/2009* Art. 22; *EC 428/2009* Annex IV.

authorization is required even when transferring the items to other EU member states (a rare restriction on one of the EU's core freedoms, the free movement of goods).[33]

Finally, perhaps the most important aspect to maintaining intra-EU effectiveness of nationally implemented export controls, EC 428/2009 also requires Member States and exporters keep detailed records of export activity and establish mechanisms by which Member States directly cooperate and share information with other Member States relating to the enforcement of export controls.[34] These information sharing systems are put in place "to eliminate the risk that possible disparities in the application of export controls to dual-use items may lead to a deflection of trade," addressing the collective action problem by assuaging concerns that certain Member States may unfairly choose not to enforce controls in order to gain a competitive advantage.[35] Furthermore, this record keeping and information sharing contributes to what are known colloquially as "catch-all controls"—EU-wide databases which aim to help EU Member States compile information to collectively identify end-users who cannot be trusted to receive future exports or re-exports of dual-use goods.[36]

B. THE UK REGIME: THE EXPORT CONTROL ACT OF 2002 AND EXPORT CONTROL ORDER OF 2008

As a Regulation issued by the European Commission, EC 428/2009 represents binding law applicable to all EU Member States.[37] It is itself a sufficient form of legal authority for the UK to implement its entire export control regime. However, beyond EC 428/2009, the UK has two additional independent bases of legal authority to regulate exports from its borders: The Export Control Act of 2002 ("the Export Control Act") and the Export Control Order of 2008 ("the Export Control Order").[38]

While the language of Export Control Act and Export Control Order may differ from EC 428/2009, they provide substantially the same legal authority to EC 428/2009 as previously described, such that the

---

[33] *EC 428/2009* Art. 22.

[34] *EC 428/2009* Art. 19; *EC 428/2009* Art. 20.

[35] *EC 428/2009* Art. 19.

[36] *See* Steve Osborne, *Brexit and Export Controls: Challenges Facing the UK and the EU in Controls and Enforcement, and the Implications for Proliferation and National Security*, KING'S C. LONDON CTR. FOR SCI. AND SECURITY STUDIES: PROJECT ALPHA (Jan. 31, 2018), https://projectalpha.eu/brexit-and-export-controls-challenges-facing-the-uk-and-the-eu-in-controls-and-enforcement-and-the-implications-for-proliferation-and-national-security/#_ftnref2 [hereinafter *Brexit and Export Controls: Challenges Facing the UK*].

[37] *European Union Regulations*, EUR-LEX, https://eur-lex.europa.eu/legal-content/EN/TXT/?uri=LEGISSUM%3Al14522 (last visited May 11, 2018).

[38] *See* Export Control Act 2002, c. 28 (UK); Export Contr. Order of 2008 No. 3231 (UK).

removal of EC 428/2009 should not inhibit the UK's legal authority to regulate exports.[39] The only significant difference is that the Export Control Order goes beyond what is regulated under Annex I of EC 428/2009, and implements its own additional schedule of dual-use controls, listed in Schedule 3.[40]

However, an important consequence of the fact that the Act, the Order and EC 428/2009 are different legal authorities is that certain UK regulations implemented by the UK Secretary of State derive their power from these authorities on separate bases.[41] Where the UK Secretary of State has implemented regulations pursuant to the authority of EC 428/2009, this could lead to confusion post-Brexit regarding what regulations still apply, and what regulations must be re-implemented pursuant to valid authority in either the Act or the Order.

C. EU/UK EXPORT CONTROLS UNDER THE WITHDRAWAL AGREEMENT

Ancillary to the question of "what will happen to export controls after Brexit" (discussed below in Part III) is "when will these changes occur?" Under the Withdrawal Agreement proposed on March 19, 2018, all changes to export control laws expected to occur and outlined in Part III will occur, on March 29, 2019, Brexit day.[42] At that point, unless otherwise implemented into UK law, EC 428/2009 will become ineffective in the UK, with one exception.

After the withdrawal and during the entire transition period, the UK will be required to continue to adhere to EC 428/2009 Article 19, regarding administrative cooperation and exchange of information concerning export controls.[43] This obligation will extend beyond the transition period under two types of circumstances. First, the UK and all Member States will be required to complete all administrative cooperation procedures between the UK and the Member state launched before, but extending beyond, the end of the transition period.[44] Second,

---

[39] *See Brexit and Export Controls: Challenges Facing the UK, supra* note 36.

[40] *See* Export Control Order of 2008, No. 3231, sch. 3 (UK).

[41] For discussion of the implications of UK regulations deriving power from separate authorities, see *infra* Part III.

[42] *See Draft Agreement on the withdrawal of the United Kingdom of Great Britain and Northern Ireland from the European Union and the European Atomic Energy Community*, EUROPEAN COMMISSION: TASK FORCE FOR THE PREPARATION AND CONDUCT OF THE NEGOTIATIONS WITH THE UNITED KINGDOM UNDER ARTICLE 50 TEU (Mar. 19, 2018), https://ec.europa.eu/commission/sites/beta-political/files/draft_agreement_coloured.pdf [hereinafter *Withdrawal Agreement*].

[43] *See Withdrawal Agreement*, *supra* note 41, Art. 93; *Withdrawal Agreement*, *supra* note 41, Annex y+2 ¶ 4.

[44] *See Withdrawal Agreement*, *supra* note 41, Art. 93(1).

for three years following the transition period, where administrative cooperative procedures are initiated between the UK and an EU Member state after the transition period has ended, but concern facts that occurred during the transition period, the UK will still need to comply with its obligations under EC 428/2009 Article 19.[45]

III. THE CHALLENGES PRESENTED BY BREXIT AND RECOMMENDATIONS FOR UK/EU ACTION

Brexit will present both large and small challenges to the continued effectiveness and enforcement of UK/EU export control laws. Generally, these challenges can be separated into two categories: (1) those emanating from legal gaps and confusion, and (2) those emanating from divergence of the EU and UK regimes.

A. CHALLENGES EMANATING FROM LEGAL GAPS AND CONFUSION

1. Northern Ireland remaining in the EU customs union will render EU and UK export controls ineffective as applied against each other.

The issue of what is to become of Northern Ireland is one of the most pervasive challenges related to Brexit. Here, it will complicate the implementation of export control laws as well. Under the draft Withdrawal Agreement, Northern Ireland is to continue to remain a part of the EU customs union.[46] However, because the EU's customs regulations and EC 428/2009 define "exports" as items which leave the customs territory of the EU, on the day after Brexit all transfers of goods between the UK and EU will become "exports," fully subject to all export licensing requirements.[47] Thus, Northern Ireland remaining both a part of the territory of the UK as well as part of the EU customs union is fundamentally incompatible with the UK and the EU's respective abilities to maintain consistent control of dual-use goods as applied to each other. So long as Northern Ireland stays a part of the EU customs union, dual-use controlled goods can flow freely from any part of the UK into Northern Ireland (export control laws do not apply to movement of goods within the same country), and then to any other part of the EU (as permitted by EC 428/2009 and in keeping with the fundamental freedom of movement of goods). The opposite (goods flowing from the EU into the UK via Northern Ireland) will be true as well.

---

[45] *See id.* Art. 93(2).

[46] *See id.* Art. 4.

[47] *See* Council Regulation No 2913/92, 1992 O.J. (L 302) Art. 161; *EC 428/2009* Art. 2(2).

Recommendation: the problem presented by only Northern Ireland remaining in the EU customs union is not unique to export controls—it pervades practically all Brexit trade issues. Here, it is likely a solution can be reached in which the EU and the UK negotiate a system of mutual recognition of each other's regimes during the process of negotiating how to solve larger trade issues (such as the assessment of tariffs between the EU and the UK for goods passing through Northern Ireland). This system would likely require the EU and the UK apply heightened scrutiny to all dual-use goods entering/exiting the UK and the EU from Northern Ireland. The EU could do this by adding a section to Annex IV relating to Northern Ireland, and the UK could pass similarly strict authorization requirements specific to Northern Ireland. Unfortunately, this solution would add regulatory burdens where none previously existed. Where these burdens lead to the treatment of Northern Ireland as distinct from the UK, such a solution is unlikely to be warmly accepted.

Absent some kind of agreement, the only other feasible way to solve this issue is for the UK to adopt some kind of "Norway Model" agreement with respect to its export control regime. This would require the UK maintain total regulatory alignment with the EU export control regime, such that, effectively, the UK would still be subject to all EU export control regulation decisions.[48] An outright adoption of the Norway Model seems unlikely, given that May has outright discounted it on numerous occasions, stating that it "impose[s] unsustainable constraints on [the UK's] democracy."[49] Still, unlikely though it may be, a "Norway-plus" or "Norway-minus" arrangement specific to regulation of export controls could potentially provide a way forward.

2. EU GEAs will become ineffective in the UK, and UK National GEAs will also become ineffective.

The general authorizations to export goods under all six EU GEAs derive their authority from EC 428/2009. Thus, on Brexit day, when EC 428/2009 becomes ineffective, all UK dual-use goods previously exported under this type of authorization will face the added burden of requiring an export license.

Additionally, the UK currently recognizes fifteen National GEAs, referred to under UK law as "Open General Export Licenses" (OGELs).[50] OGELs are enacted by the UK Secretary of State to carve

---

[48] *See Brexit and Export Controls: Challenges Facing the UK*, *supra* note 36.

[49] *See In full: Theresa May's speech on future UK-EU relations*, BBC.COM (Mar. 2, 2018), https://www.bbc.com/news/uk-politics-43256183.

[50] *See* Information on measures adopted by Member States in Conformity with Articles 5, 6, 7, 9, 10, 17 and 22 of Council Regulation (EC) No 428/2009, 2016 O.J. (C 304) ¶

out categories of exports, and certain destinations for which export licenses are not required (even though the goods involved technically fall under the purview of EC 428/2009).[51] However, fourteen of the current UK OGELs derive their legal efficacy from EC 428/2009. For example, the OGEL for Chemicals states,

> This is a general export authorisation under the terms of Article 9(2) of Council Regulation (EC) No. 428/2009. This authorisation, in accordance with Article 9(2) of that Regulation, is valid in all Member States of the European Community and is a Community Licence for the purposes of the [Export Control Order 2008].[52]

Only one OGEL derives its legal authority from the Export Control Order 2008—the OGEL for shipment of military and dual-use goods to UK forces deployed in non-embargoed destinations. This OGEL states simply, "The Secretary of State, in exercise of powers conferred by article 26 of the Export Control Order 2008 (the Order), hereby grants the following Open General Export Licence."[53] As the fourteen other OGELs were all enacted pursuant to solely EC 428/2009, these OGELs will technically become ineffective on Brexit day, exposing any UK exporters who currently export under such OGEL authorization to legal uncertainty.

Recommendation: The first problem (EU GEAs losing efficacy in the UK) can be solved through appropriate legislation. This may not be as simple as copy-pasting EC 428/2009 into UK law under the Repeal Bill—at the very least, terminology referring to the EU would need to be changed to avoid confusion.[54] Alternatively, the same effect could be

---

6.9 (Aug. 20, 2016) http://trade.ec.europa.eu/doclib/docs/2016/-august/tradoc_154880.pdf. For details of these 15 orders, see also Open General Export Licenses (OGELs), UK Gov't (Jul. 28, 2017) https://www.gov.uk/-government/collections/open-general-export-licences-ogels#dual-use-open-general-export-licences (last visited May 11, 2018). For a description of EC 428/2009's authorization for EU Member States to enact National GEAs, see *supra* Part II (1).

51 *See* Open General Export Licenses, UK Gov't (Jul. 28, 2017) https://www.gov.uk/government/collections/open-general-export-licences-ogels#dual-use-open-general-export-licences (last visited May 11, 2018).

52 Open General Export Licence (Chemicals), Dep't for Int'l Trade, UK, ¶ 1, Aug. 27, 2009 (*last updated* Apr. 6, 2018).

53 Open General Export License (Military and Dual Use Goods: UK Forces deployed in non-embargoed destinations), Dep't for Int'l Trade, UK, p. 1, Apr. 11, 2018.

54 *See Legislating for the United Kingdom's Withdrawal from the European Union* at 13, DEP'T FOR EXITING THE EUROPEAN UNION (Mar. 2017), https://assets.publishing.service.gov.uk/government/uploads/system/uploads/attachment_data/file/604516/-Great_repeal_bill_white_paper_accessible.pdf [hereinafter *Legislating UK Withdraw from*

achieved by having the UK Secretary of State issue new OGELs to cover those types of transactions previously covered by EU GEAs.

The second problem (UK OGELs becoming ineffective) can be solved in the same manner. As the Export Control Act and Export Control Order provide the UK with sufficient legal authority to authorize OGELs, this issue can be fixed by the UK Secretary of State simply reissuing the fourteen OGELs to make clear that they are supported by effective legal authority.

3. **UK export controls based on the EU Dual-Use List will become ineffective.**

As previously described, the UK publishes its own dual-use list (Export Control Order Schedule 3), going beyond what is required by the EU dual-use list (Annex I of EC 428/2009). However, Schedule 3 is not duplicative of Annex I; it provides further regulation of additional goods.[55] Thus, the UK currently derives its legal authority to regulate all Annex I goods solely from EC 428/2009. On Brexit day, if UK authorities take no action, technically all Annex I goods would no longer require authorization, leaving a massive gap in export control regulations.

Recommendation: The UK Parliament could include Annex I and appropriate provisions from EC 428/2009 in the Repeal Bill planned to be passed as a result of Brexit.[56] However, in doing so, the UK should keep in mind that all its current materials published to guide its exporters in complying with UK export controls should be similarly updated. For example, the UK Strategic Export Control Lists (published as guidance to exporters looking to export dual-use goods), currently distinguishes between the UK Dual-Use List and the EU Dual-Use List.[57] Unless all these forms of guidance are similarly consolidated to reflect the efficacy of UK law regarding both lists by Brexit day, exporters (especially new exporters) will likely become confused about how to properly comply with UK export control laws.

4. **The Export Control Act and Export Control Order reference the EC 428/2009, which will create confusion for UK exporters.**

The Export Control Act and Export Control Order make numerous references to EC 428/2009, the EU, and the European Communities, which may create confusion about the efficacy of the Act and Order

---

the EU] (planning for the conversion of EU law into UK law to avoid large holes in the UK statute book).

[55] *See* Export Control Order of 2008, No. 3231, sch. 3 (UK).

[56] *See Legislating UK Withdraw from the EU, supra* note 54.

[57] *See UK Strategic Export Control Lists* at 1, Dep't for Int'l Trade, UK (Mar. 5, 2018), https://assets.publishing.service.gov.uk/government/uploads/system/uploads/attachment_data/file/685044/controllist20180305.pdf.

post-Brexit. One example, Section 5(2) of the Export Control Act will become particularly incoherent because of Brexit. This section currently states that "[export] controls of any kind may be imposed for the purpose of giving effect to any EU provision or other international obligation of the United Kingdom."[58] Here, "international obligations," is defined as including "an obligation relating to a joint action or common position adopted, or a decision taken, by the Council under Title V of the Treaty on European Union."[59]

These types of discrepancies are not crisis-level issues, as even without correcting them the Export Control Act will continue to provide the UK with legal authority to effect controls on dual-use exports.[60] However, unless amended, post-Brexit this provision would seem to suggest that the UK could impose export controls solely pursuant to EU provisions or international obligations undertaken by the EU, a clearly absurd result which may confuse new exporters.

Recommendation: This issue can be fixed by legislation amending the original bills. However, as the Export Control Act and Export Control Order are UK statutes, they do not come under the scope of the Repeal Bill as it is currently conceived.[61] The work of amending these statutes, and similar UK statutes which refers to EU law, will present another burden to the already resource-strapped UK Parliament.

B. CHALLENGES EMANATING FROM DIVERGENCE OF THE TWO REGIMES

1. UK producers will require export licenses when exporting dual-use goods to the EU, and vice versa.

As previously mentioned in Part III (1)(i), on Brexit day all transactions of dual-use goods between the UK and EU will become subject to the requirements of both EU and UK export control laws.[62] This will impose a significant burden on both EU and UK producers of dual-use goods, especially where such producers were not even considered exporters before Brexit because their transactions pre-Brexit were solely limited to transfers between the UK and other EU Member States. As such transactions will become subject to increased legal liability and transaction costs, a certain amount of trade will be deterred or diverted elsewhere as a result.

---

[58] Export Control Act 2002, c. 28 § 5(2) (UK).
[59] *Id.* § 5(3).
[60] *Id.* § 5(4)-(7).
[61] *See Legislating UK Withdraw from the EU*, *supra* note 54 (the Repeal Bill aims to convert EU law into UK law, not amend UK law).
[62] *See* Council Regulation No 2913/92, 1992 O.J. (L 302) Art. 161; *EC 428/2009* Art. 2(2).

Recommendation: If the UK were to adopt the Norway Model of regulatory adherence, there may be room to solve this problem through EU-UK mutual recognition of each other's regimes. Absent such unlikely agreement, the EU and the UK could mitigate a degree of this increased regulatory burden by expanding current GEAs. The EU could add the UK to GEA No EU001 (the EU GEA for trusted allies).[63] Similarly, the UK Secretary of State could issue a broad OGEL for exports to the EU. This is not ideal, as even GEAs do not apply to some categories of goods which currently enjoy free movement within the EU.[64] However, mutually adding each other to each other's respective general authorizations would be the minimum the UK and the EU could do to keep from imposing unnecessary burdens on their own dual-use exporters.

2. **Divergent regimes will detract from the efficacy of each regime, and the termination of cooperative information between the EU and UK will detract from the efficacy of catch-all controls.**

Brexit will introduce uncertainty into the general international regime for dual-use export control due to the inevitability that over time the UK and EU schemes will diverge.[65] The tendency towards divergence over time could drive temptations for both the EU and the UK to weaken its controls on certain goods to gain a competitive edge, thereby detracting from the overall efficacy of the efforts of all nations to control exports of dual-use goods.[66]

Similarly, with the exclusion of the UK from the EU regime, the UK will be prevented from contributing to or benefiting from the EU's collaborative and information sharing processes which promote the efficacy of catch-all controls.[67] Such processes are only as effective as the information contained within them; thus, the removal of the UK from the system will necessarily detract from the overall benefit each EU Member States currently derives from it.

Recommendation: The only way to avoid these negative effects is to establish some method of cooperative interaction which would continue to deter both the EU and the UK from engaging in a "race to the bottom," and promote information sharing and cooperation between the UK and EU Member States as it does currently. A mutual recognition

---

63 *See* EC 428/2009 Annex II Part 3.

64 For a list of goods which require a license regardless of GEA EU001 status, see EC 428/2009 Annex II Part 2.

65 *See Brexit and Export Controls: Challenges Facing the UK*, *supra* note 36.

66 *See id.*

67 *See EC 428/2009* Art. 19; *EC 428/2009* Art. 20.

of regimes is one option to achieve this goal, the UK adopting the Norway model of regulatory adherence is another. Additionally, the UK and the EU may decide to establish a separate agreement whereby the UK participates in the EU regime with respect to information sharing only. If the UK intends to maintain regulatory sovereignty, this agreement would likely be the most practical option.

IV. SUMMARY OF RECOMMENDATIONS FOR UK ACTION TO MITIGATE BREXIT CHALLENGES

As soon as possible, the UK should confirm with the EU the status of their post-Brexit export control regimes as they are affected by Northern Ireland remaining in the EU customs union. Ideally, the UK and the EU can agree on a system of mutual recognition of the efficacy of each other's regimes such that transfers of dual-use goods between the UK and the EU can continue unimpeded, as though they were still intra-EU transfers. If no agreement is reached, the UK could consider adopting the Norway Model of complete regulatory compliance with the EU's export control regime in order to deal with the problem presented by Northern Ireland and avoid placing increased regulatory burdens on UK exporters of dual-use goods to the EU. Should this prove politically impossible, the EU and the UK should make all efforts possible to reduce the imposition of new regulatory burdens, including updating their respective General Export Authorisations, for the benefit of both their producers.

As Brexit approaches, the UK Parliament should prepare legislation to update the Export Control Act and Export Control Order to mitigate any confusion regarding the post-Brexit legal environment. Similarly, the Repeal Bill should incorporate Annex I and relevant portions of EC 428/2009 to avoid any regulatory gaps. At the same time, the UK Department for International Trade should survey and update its materials providing guidance on export control compliance to reflect expected changes in the law to reduce confusion amongst exporters going forward.

Finally, the UK and the EU should negotiate to agree on a system which would allow the UK to continue to cooperate and engage in information sharing with EU Member States to maintain the current strength of catch-all controls.

CHAPTER 6: BREXIT AND SPS MEASURES: IMPLICATIONS FOR THE UNITED KINGDOM

ALEXANDRA STANLEY

In 2000, mad cow disease sparked panic across Europe.[1] Mad cow disease has no cure, and leads to a brain disorder that causes blindness, a loss of physical coordination and speaking abilities, and severe memory loss, resulting in death about two years after contracting the disease.[2] After the spread of the disease through France, Germany, and Spain, beef sales dropped fifty percent.[3] Public concern about the outbreak was so severe that a safety hotline in Germany was created specifically to address calls about the disease.[4] At one point, the hotline collapsed due to the volume of callers.[5] Public health concerns regarding chlorine-washed chicken, hormones in beef, and genetically modified crops have also arisen in the EU.[6]

In 2010, citrus black spot (CBS) was found in North America for the first time.[7] CBS does not cause any health problems, but creates black spots on the rinds of citrus fruit so that they cannot be sold in major markets and can only be sold at a deeply discounted price in a less

[1] Daley, Suzanne. "Mad Cow Disease Panicking Europe as Incidents Rise." *The New York Times*, 1 Dec. 2000, www.nytimes.com/2000/12/01/world/mad-cow-disease-panicking-europe-as-incidents-rise.html.

[2] "Creutzfeldt-Jakob disease: symptoms." NHS Choices. July 21, 2015. https://www.nhs.uk/conditions/creutzfeldt-jakob-disease-cjd/symptoms/.

[3] *Id.*

[4] Daley, *supra note 1*.

[5] *Id.*

[6] *See* Capeluoto, Susanna. "European Activists Say They Don't Want any U.S. 'Chlorine Chicken.'" NPR. Sept. 30, 2014. https://www.npr.org/sections/thesalt/2014/09/30/351774240/european-activists-say-they-dont-want-any-u-s-chlorine-chicken; Emmott, Robin. "Europe's Fear of GM Food and Meat from Cattle Raised with Growth Hormones Sows Divide." Scientific American. https://www.scientificamerican.com/article/europes-fear-of-gm-food-and-meat-from-cattle-raised-with-growth-hormones-sows-divide/; Chow, Lorraine. "16 European Nations Vote Against GMO Crops." EcoWatch. Mar. 27, 2017. https://www.ecowatch.com/eu-nations-vote-against-gmo-crops-2332080511.html.

[7] Dewdney, et. al. "Citrus Black Spot in Florida." Citrus Industry. July 2010. http://www.crec.ifas.ufl.edu/extension/trade_journals/2010/2010%20July%20citrus%20black%20spot.pdf.

sensitive market.[8] It also results in up to a fifty percent reduction in yield.[9] The decline in fruit prices followed by destruction of fruit-bearing trees causes catastrophic losses for citrus growers and countries like South Africa where citrus exports make up a significant portion of their economy. For example, in 2014 when South Africa faced a total ban of its citrus fruits in the EU, it lost an estimated 323 million USD in exports.[10] While CBS doesn't result in the death of humans, it can destroy citrus farmer's livelihoods and even entire sectors of national economies. Diseases with similar impacts include medfly, wheat and barley blight, and citrus canker. With the shipment of products around the world, diseases like mad cow and CBS can spread from one country to dozens of others in a matter of days. They can destroy human, plant, and animal health, as well as the livelihoods of farmers and of economic sectors. Although these diseases have vastly different effects, all of them are regulated by sanitary and phytosanitary (SPS) measures.

While these diseases remain sources of public concern, the UK government has ignored the implications of Brexit on SPS measures that would enable it to combat such issues. Currently, the EU implements SPS measures rather than individual member states. Unless the UK considers what must be done to implement SPS measures into its national framework, the UK will be left with no SPS measures on exit day. A complete lack of SPS measures would leave the UK vulnerable to diseases like mad cow and CBS, and potentially harmful foods like genetically modified crops and beef with growth hormones. To avoid a public health crisis, the UK should consider how to implement SPS measures at a national level. This chapter will examine whether it is possible to implement the EU's SPS measures in the UK and what is needed to successfully do so. In part 1, this chapter provides a brief introduction to SPS measures. Part 2 considers what agencies and capacities the UK must have in order to implement the EU's SPS measures into its national law consistent with the World Trade

---

[8] Halueendo, K.L.M.E. "Impact Assessment of Citrus Black Spot, Guignardia Citricarpa Kiely, in Southern Africa and an Alternative Approach in Management Strategies." University of Pretoria. Pg. 3. July 2008. https://repository.up.ac.za/bitstream/handle/2263/29581/dissertation.pdf?sequence=1.

[9] Graham, Jim. "Citrus Black Spot: lessons from Brazil." Citrus Industry. Pg. 1. Nov. 2010. http://www.crec.ifas.ufl.edu/extension/trade_journals/2010/2010_Nov_blackspot_brazil.pdf.

[10] Potelwa, Xolisiwe Yolanda. "Socio-economic implication of Citrus Black Spot on South African citrus exports to the European Union Market." University of Pretoria. July 2017. Pg. 49. https://repository.up.ac.za/bitstream/handle/2263/63281/Potelwa_Economic_2017.pdf?sequence=1.

Organization's Agreement on Sanitary and Phytosanitary Measures. Part 3 examines the political and economic considerations the UK should take into account when determining whether to keep or discard an SPS measure. Part 4 examines whether WTO rules allow the post-Brexit UK to keep the EU's SPS measures and remain in compliance with international law. Due to the large numbers of SPS measures that must each be analyzed by the UK, this chapter does not seek to make any wholesale predictions regarding the UK's future SPS scheme, nor does it address potential questions regarding the EU's ability to retain its SPS measures post-Brexit.[11] Instead, it lays out the challenges the UK will face when incorporating SPS measures into its national system.

I. WHAT ARE SPS MEASURES?

SPS measures are any measure applied to protect animal and human health from food risks and diseases, to protect animals and plants from pests and diseases, and to prevent or limit territorial damage from pests.[12] They must be based on science, and based on international standards or risk assessments.[13] Measures may take a variety of forms, from "laws, decrees regulations, requirements and procedures" to "packaging and labeling requirements."[14] These measures vary greatly in geographic specificity, from bans on poultry from Okanogan County farms North of US 97, WA 20, and S,[15] to bans on sheep and goat meat from any European Union member state.[16] They also vary in their restrictiveness, ranging from total bans of a product to production process or labeling requirements. Any good not meeting a country's SPS requirements can be turned away at the border.

---

[11] If any of the EU's risk assessments were based solely on risks to pests or diseases likely to take hold in the UK, the SPS measure arising from that risk assessment presumably must be rescinded upon Brexit. The potential for questions to be raised by WTO members about EU SPS measures is one the EU should prepare for.

[12] United Nations. "The WTO Agreement on the Application of Sanitary and Phytosanitary Measures." *United Nations Treaty Collection*. New York: United Nations, 1994. Annex A. 6 May 2018. Web.

[13] *Id.*

[14] *Id.*

[15] United States Department of Agriculture Food Safety and Inspection Service. "HPAI Banned Areas." https://www.fsis.usda.gov/wps/wcm/connect/b5c86033-ba6a-40f8-8fe3-f6d25eecdcd4/Okangoan_County_01292015.pdf?MOD=AJPERES.

[16] European Commission Market Access Database. "SPS: Sanitary and Phytosanitary Issues: Sheep and goat meat market access to USA." 12 Feb., 2018. http://madb.europa.eu/madb/sps_barriers_details.htm?isSps=true&barrier_id=13623.

II. SPS MEASURES IN THE EU AND UK

A. CURRENT EU FRAMEWORK FOR SPS MEASURES

The European Commission is the executive arm of the EU responsible for overseeing the enforcement of international treaties, including the World Trade Organization's SPS Agreement, which lays out the requirements for SPS measures.[17] Within the Commission, there are policy departments known as Directorates-General.[18] The Directorate General for Health and Food Safety (SANTE) is responsible for developing and implementing the Commission's policies on SPS measures.[19] There are three expert groups in SANTE that are each responsible for different aspects of SPS measures: an advisory group that consults with stakeholders about proposed measures, scientific committees that help to create the measure, and a health policy forum that consults with public health stakeholders like NGOs and international organizations about proposed measures.[20] These groups act in concert to create SPS measures, which SANTE then sends notification of to the World Trade Organization (WTO).

SPS measures take the form of EU regulations.[21] Regulations and regulatory agency decisions at the EU level take direct effect within member states without requiring any national legislation, as opposed to directives, which must be implemented into national law in order to take effect.[22] Therefore, there is little domestic law regarding SPS measures in the UK. The UK's Repeal Bill will cut off EU law in the UK on exit day, March 29, 2019.[23] As such, in the absence of grandfathering or transitions, almost no SPS measures will exist in the UK after Brexit. This legal vacuum could have severe consequences unless the UK quickly imposes specific SPS measures. Pests and plants banned by the EU would be allowed in, spreading diseases and overtaking native plants. Animals and animal products with different diseases, and foods

---

[17] "European Commission: Overview." European Union. *European Commission.* europa.eu/european-union/about-eu/institutions-bodies/european-commission_en.

[18] *Id.*

[19] "Health and Food Safety: Responsibilities." Directorate-General SANTE. *European Commission.* https://ec.europa.eu/info/departments/health-and-food-safety_en# responsibilities.

[20] "Food: Expert Groups." European Union. *European Commission.* https://ec.europa.eu/food/expert-groups_en.

[21] *See, e.g.,* Regulation No. 853/2004 of the European Parliament and of the Council. L 139/55. April 29, 2004.

[22] "Regulations, Directives and other acts." European Union. https://europa.eu/european-union/eu-law/legal-acts_en.

[23] European Union (Withdrawal) Bill. HL Bill 79.

containing banned substances would be able to enter the UK, spreading illness to both animals and humans. In short, without SPS measures, the UK would be completely vulnerable to the pests and diseases that SPS measures have prevented from entering the UK for over twenty years.

B. THE REPEAL BILL

Fortunately, the Repeal Bill prevents this from happening. The Repeal Bill repeals the 1972 European Communities Act, ends the power of the European Court of Justice in the UK, and incorporates direct EU legislation into national law.[24] It has already passed the House of Commons and is currently in the House of Lords.[25] Once both Houses agree upon a final version of the Bill, it will receive Royal Assent and become an Act of Parliament.[26] Article 3 of the Bill incorporates direct EU legislation, including regulations, into the UK's domestic law after Brexit.[27] As a result of Article 3, all SPS measures will be incorporated into the UK's domestic law automatically on exit day, March 29, 2019.[28] While there is no exact count, there are approximately 12,000 EU regulations in force (including amending, delegated, and implementing regulations), which will enter into UK domestic law.[29] As Prime Minister May has said, "all EU laws will transfer into British law . . . and then we can unpick them one by one as we please."[30] However, this "unpicking" cannot occur until after the transition period.

C. THE TRANSITION PERIOD

The draft Withdrawal Agreement between the UK and the EU lays out the terms of the "divorce" and provides for a 21-month transition period after the UK's exit from the EU, beginning on March 29, 2019 and ending on December 31, 2020.[31] During this period EU law remains

---

24 *Id.*

25 "European Union (Withdrawal) Bill 2017-19." https://services.parliament.uk/bills/2017-19/europeanunionwithdrawal.html.

26 "Consideration of Amendments." UK Parliament. www.parliament.uk/about/how/laws/passage-bill/commons/coms-consideration-of-amendments/.

27 Withdrawal Bill, *supra note 23*, at art. 3.

28 *Id.*

29 HM Government, "Legislating for the United Kingdom's withdrawal from the European Union", (White Paper) Cm 9446, March 2017.

30 Wooding, David. "We'll Rule Britannia: Theresa May plans to scrap EU laws as she unveils new Great Repeal Bill to claw back power from the European courts." The Sun. Oct. 1, 2016. https://www.thesun.co.uk/news/politics/1893464/theresa-may-plans-to-scrap-eu-laws-as-she-unveils-new-great-repeal-bill/.

31 "European Commission Draft Withdrawal Agreement on the withdrawal of the United Kingdom of Great Britain and Northern Ireland from the European Union and the

the default law for the UK unless otherwise specified, and the UK remains bound to the international agreements concluded by the EU.[32] Any new EU laws referencing member states will also apply to the UK until December 31, 2020.[33] This means that the UK will remain bound by the EU's current SPS measures and any SPS measures it implements until the end of the transition period.

While the withdrawal agreement essentially deems the UK a member of the EU during this two-year period, only the UK and EU have agreed to this arrangement. What remains to be seen is whether other countries will agree to honor this arrangement and recognize the UK as a member of the EU until December 31, 2020. In regard to SPS measures, some countries may not want to honor the transition period. For example, the US may not want to consider the UK part of the EU after exit day on March 29, 2019, because it would like to be able to send beef with growth hormones to the UK, which is currently banned by an EU SPS measure. South Africa may not want to consider the UK part of the EU either because they would like to ship citrus with CBS to the UK, which is currently prohibited by an EU SPS measure.

In addition to potential disagreements from countries about the transition period, keeping all SPS measures for an additional two years will anger some UK citizens while reassuring others. Complaints of the EU's overregulation sparked calls for Brexit. For instance, the UK Independence party called EU measures, "a regulatory straightjacket in virtually every aspect of the rural economy, from controls on pesticides and food labeling, to veterinary and animal transportation" costing an estimated "billions of pounds per annum."[34] *The Daily Telegraph* called deregulation "a key advantage of Brexit" that "can be used to boost internal trade and lower costs."[35] Keeping SPS measures during the transition period may be especially egregious to some, because it will force the UK to keep SPS measures to protect countries in a customs union it is no longer part of. For example, the EU's citrus black spot measure allowing only citrus from CBS free areas and production sites where no CBS infected fruit was found by inspectors forces consumers

---

European Atomic Energy Community. European Commission. TF50 (2018) 33. Feb. 28, 2018. Art.121.

[32] *Id.* arts. 122.1, 124.1.

[33] *Id.* art. 122.6

[34] Clarke, Philip, Cooper, Olivia. "UK Farms would Prosper Outside EU, UKIP Claims." *Farmers Weekly*, vol. 151, no. 19, 2009, pp. 16. *ProQuest*, https://0-.search.proquest.com.gull.georgetown.edu/docview/224690912?accountid=36339.

[35] Bourne, Ryan. "We can End the Era of Stifling Regulations." *The Daily Telegraph*, Jan 27, 2017, pp. 16. *ProQuest*, https://0-search.proquest.com.gull.georgetown.edu/docview/1862017108?accountid=36339.

to pay for more expensive citrus.[36] Yet the citrus measure was implemented to protect citrus in Spain, Greece, and other citrus producing EU countries, so during the transition period UK consumers will be paying to protect an industry that lies outside of their borders.

For UK citizens who wanted to exit the EU because of concerns about overregulation, keeping all EU regulations during the transition period negates the purpose of Brexit. Yet the same farmers angered by certain EU SPS measures may be relieved to hear that EU SPS measures aimed at preventing the entry of mad cow disease and hoof and mouth will remain in place during that time. Because overregulation was an important part of why the UK voted to leave the EU, after the transition period the UK will have to repeal some SPS measures to make good on its Brexit campaign promises of deregulation. But what agency in the UK will determine this, and how?

D. NEW FRAMEWORK FOR SPS MEASURES

The Parliament has the power to repeal regulations converted by the Repeal Bill after they become domestic law.[37] Since there are approximately 12,000 technical measures regulating specific products, the legislature will likely designate an agency to determine which measures should be kept and which discarded. It will also likely need an agency similar to SANTE and its Committees that can create, implement, and monitor the UK's own SPS measures.[38] It is unlikely that any agency in the UK currently has the capacity to replace SANTE. The UK may have to create such an agency, and then recruit, hire, and train people to staff it, conduct risk assessments, and construct appropriate measures. It will take time and money to create both the institutional and human capacity to create a fully functioning SPS regime. Alternately, the UK could decide to create a small agency to implement SPS measures largely on the basis of international standards or on the basis of other country's risk assessments. This would require less money and fewer staff, and may be a better short-term option while the UK is dealing with all of the other implications of Brexit.

---

[36] Fisher, Martyn. "RSA citrus industry suspends EU exports." *Fresh Produce Journal.* Sept. 9, 2014. http://www.fruitnet.com/fpj/article/162629/rsa-citrus-industry-suspends-exports-to-eu

[37] Repeal Bill White Paper, *supra note 29*, pg. 10.

[38] See, for example, "A Brexit Act in 19 ¾ Pages," for a list of main EU agencies and bodies that the UK would cease to be a member of or eligible for benefits from. Allen & Overy, LLP. Aug. 30, 2016. http://www.allenovery.com/Brexit-Law/Documents/Macro/AO_GLIU_-_A_Brexit_Act_Aug_2016.pdf.

1. Legal Implementation

As it stands now, if the Repeal Bill becomes law all EU SPS measures will be grandfathered into UK domestic law immediately after exit day. However, in order to function within the UK's domestic legal framework, the text of SPS measures adopted from the EU may have to be amended. To this end, the Repeal Bill creates the power to make secondary legislation that allows a Minister of the Crown to "prevent, remedy or mitigate" by regulation "any failure of retained EU law to operate effectively, or any other deficiency in retained EU law."[39] These ministers will be given the power to amend legislation that won't function properly if incorporated wholesale into the UK's national law.[40] Any changes will be approved by Parliament through either the negative or affirmative procedure.[41] The negative procedure doesn't require debate, while the affirmative procedure requires debate and approval by both Houses.[42] The more often that Parliament uses the affirmative procedure, the slower the process of amending regulations. The government currently estimates that necessary corrections will require 800 to 1,000 statutory instruments.[43] This means that ministers will be making up to 1,000 statutory corrections, each of which Parliament will then have to pass, making secondary legislation a potentially time intensive process. According to the UK, all secondary legislation amending EU laws so that they function in the UK will be finished before exit day.[44] This will likely require considerable time and a large workforce to accomplish, as there are 12,000 SPS measures to sort through in less than one year.

There are a number of changes that secondary legislation may need to address. First, SPS measures usually cross-reference other EU laws, so the UK will have to find a corresponding UK law to replace it with. Many of the measures reference Commission Directives, which the UK already had to implement in its national laws and should therefore be simple to cross-reference. But cross-referencing other legislation that took direct effect in the UK will be more difficult as such measures will not have prior domestic legal counterparts. The measure will only recently have been converted into UK law as a result of the Repeal Bill and will have to be found in its new converted form in UK law before being applied to the measure at hand. Second, a lot of text may need to be taken out

---

[39] European Union (Withdrawal) Bill. HL Bill 79. Art. 7.1.

[40] Repeal Bill White Paper, *supra note 29*, pg. 24.

[41] *Id.*

[42] *Id.*

[43] *Id.*

[44] Repeal Bill White Paper, *supra note 29*, pg. 21.

completely as it references EU processes that will no longer apply to the UK. For example, the UK will no longer need to inform the European Commission when it comes into compliance with a directive regarding a SPS measure. The UK will not have to await further Council decisions regarding SPS measures, nor will they have to ensure that their domestic laws for third country imports are not more favorable than those for intra-community imports.[45]

III. DETERMINING WHICH SPS MEASURES TO KEEP

As all of the EU's SPS measures will be implemented into the UK's domestic law if the Repeal Bill goes into force, the UK will have to determine which measures it wants to keep. The UK should devote considerable time to this determination for political and economic reasons, and analyze each SPS measure separately to determine which measures to keep.

Politically, concerns about expensive overregulation by the EU were a major part of the "leave" platform.[46] The Conservative party may be heavily criticized if it chooses to keep most SPS measures in place. Alternately, many SPS measures are done for legitimate health reasons, and some people may fear a public health crisis if the government repeals certain SPS measures about food safety. This analysis will also likely be heavily impacted by whether the border between Ireland will be hard or soft. If the latter, uniformity in SPS measures between the EU and UK may be necessary. Ireland aside, the UK also wants to maintain a close relationship with the EU and be its "strongest friend and partner,"[47] yet any differentiation in SPS measures between the UK and EU will slow down trade across the UK-EU27 border as UK products or onward shipped goods will have to be inspected for compliance with the EU's SPS measures and vice versa. This will also be an important consideration to take into account. In the international sphere, it would be wise for the UK to maintain certain SPS measures, like those regarding chlorinated chicken and beef hormones, which can serve as bargaining chips in future trade negotiations with countries like the US.

Economically, SPS measures are barriers to trade that slow national economic growth, yet sometimes they are worth the economic impact

---

[45] Council Directive 81/602/EEC, of July 31 1981, No. L 222/32.

[46] Boris Johnson's Speech on the EU Referendum. May 9, 2016. http://www.conservativehome.com/parliament/2016/05/boris-johnsons-speech-on-the-eu-referendum-full-text.html.

[47] Theresa May's Florence Speech. Sept. 22, 2017. https://www.gov.uk/government/speeches/pms-florence-speech-a-new-era-of-cooperation-and-partnership-between-the-uk-and-the-eu.

because they protect consumers. The effects EU's SPS measures have on US exports to the EU are a telling example of how SPS measures increase the cost of trade. One researcher estimated that reducing non-tariff measures like Technical Barriers to Trade (TBT) and SPS measures would account for as much as 80% of the economic gains of an EU and US trade agreement.[48] In 2015, the EU's SPS measures for beef exports had estimated effects of approximately 497 million USD in forgone trade.[49] For pork, the forgone trade was 1.829 billion, for poultry it was 145 million, corn 612 million, vegetables 479 million, and fruits 467 million.[50] While these estimates don't reflect the predicated gains from removing these barriers because of certain secondary effects like supply constraints, these numbers still show astounding potential growth for the UK if it were to get rid of most SPS measures.[51] It is important that the UK take these economic considerations into account when determining which measures to keep, especially because of fears that Brexit will create an economic depression in the UK.

In addition to creating trade barriers between countries, SPS measures increase costs for consumers. SPS measures increase compliance, inspection, and operational costs for importers, which in turn are shifted to consumers by increasing the price of the product affected by the measure. For example, poultry from the US costs approximately 20% less than European poultry yet is currently banned by the EU's SPS measures so that consumers are forced to pay the more expensive price for European chicken.[52] Sometimes consumers are willing to shoulder the expense resulting from SPS measures they feel protect their health. For instance, studies show that EU consumers are concerned about hormones in food production and are willing to pay premiums for hormone-free beef.[53] Yet other times, consumers feel that

---

[48] Centre for Economic Policy Research (CEPR). 2013. "Reducing Trans-Atlantic Barriers to Trade and Investment." Pg. vii. http://trade.ec.europa.eu/doclib/docs/2013/march/tradoc_150737.pdf.

[49] Shawn Arita, Lorraine Mitchell, and Jayson Beckman. "Estimating the Effects of Selected Sanitary and Phytosanitary Measures and Technical Barriers to Trade on U.S.-EU Agricultural Trade." USDA. Nov. 2015. Pg. 30.

[50] *Id.*

[51] *Id.* pg. 31.

[52] Clark, Ross. "Ignore the scare stories from Remainers over chlorinated chicken." The Spectator. July 24, 2017. https://blogs.spectator.co.uk/2017/07/ignore-the-scare-stories-from-remainers-over-chlorinated-chicken/.

[53] Lusk, J., M. Jamal, L. Kurlander, M. Roucan, and L. Taulman. 2005. "A Meta-Analysis of Genetically Modified Food Valuation Studies." *Journal of Agricultural and Resource Economics* 30(1): 28-44; Tonsor, G.T., T.C. Schroeder, J.A. Fox, and A. Biere. 2005. "European Preferences for Beef Steak Attributes." *Journal of Agricultural and Resource Economics*, 367-380.

such measures are unnecessary and would rather have access to cheaper products. The UK should look carefully at consumer beliefs in regard to different SPS measures and determine whether most consumers think that the protection an SPS measure grants is important enough to pay a premium for. The UK will also have to determine the main concerns of farmers and fishers in regard to what plants diseases, pests, and invasive species could harm their industry if allowed in. The removal of certain SPS measures will decrease the cost of imports for consumers, a politically savvy move that will also fulfill promises made during the leave campaign. Yet removing certain SPS measures could spark outcry by impacted industries that enjoy the protection of the SPS measure or consumers concerned about health safety. Determining which measures to keep and discard will be a careful balancing act.

The first measures that the UK should repeal are those relating to pest and plant diseases that cannot survive in the UK's climate or hurt any plants in the UK. One such example is the citrus black spot (CBS) SPS measure. CBS only occurs in subtropical regions that receive rain in the summer.[54] The UK does not export any citrus on a commercial scale, and is the 6th largest importer of citrus in the world. Because it doesn't grow citrus and is not a subtropical climate, the UK has no risk of getting CBS and has no reason to keep the measure. Ending the EU's ban on fruits with CBS will considerably decrease the citrus prices for consumers in the UK.[55] Without costly CBS control measures diverting about 11% of value for citrus going to the UK, South African citrus will likely come into the UK at a significantly lower price, fulfilling a promise of Brexit.[56]

Unlike the CBS measures, the UK may want to keep the EU's SPS measures on mad cow disease. As there is still no cure for mad cow disease and it has not been completely eradicated worldwide, SPS measures banning beef from countries where mad cow disease is found remain important. As shown by history, consumers would rather go without beef than eat beef that may be infected. Therefore, the UK should and likely will keep the EU's mad cow disease SPS measures. The final issue is whether the UK may keep such measures and remain in

---

[54] "Citrus Black Spot." USDA. https://www.aphis.usda.gov/aphis/ourfocus/planthealth/plant-pest-and-disease-programs/pests-and-diseases/citrus-health-response-program/CT_Black_spot

[55] One study shows that prices of citrus from South Africa have been 20% higher from 2012-2015 than they were from 2007-2011 to help "defray the costs of additional CBS controls measures" that cost approximately 11% of the value of exports to the EU to implement. "CBS controls remain threat to South Africa citrus to EU despite recent expansion." EPA Monitoring. Aug. 28, 2017. http://epamonitoring.net/cbs-controls-remain-threat-to-south-africa-citrus-exports-to-eu-despite-recent-expansion/.

[56] *Id.*

compliance with the World Trade Organization's Agreement on Sanitary and Phytosanitary Measures.

IV. SPS MEASURES AND THE WTO

The World Trade Organization (WTO) is an organization run by its member governments to facilitate international trade.[57] There are currently 164 members, including the UK and the EU.[58] The EU has been a WTO member since January 1, 1995, and the UK has also been a member in its own right since 1947, as one of the original members of GATT.[59] As such, the UK will remain part of the WTO even after its withdrawal from the EU. The obligations of member states are laid out in approximately thirty agreements on everything from trade in goods and services, to dispute settlement, to the environment and health.[60] One such agreement is the Agreement on Sanitary and Phytosanitary (SPS) Measures. The SPS Agreement gives every country the right to decide how much risk they want to take on, including zero risk, which would result in a full ban.[61] However, the measure must be geared to achieving the country's desired level of risk, not more.[62] So while countries have the right to ban something, their measure must meet the standards discussed in the risk assessment section. As such, it is unclear whether the UK's adoption of the EU's SPS measures will comply with the requirements of the SPS Agreement.

A. NOTIFICATION REQUIREMENT OF THE SPS AGREEMENT

The SPS Agreement requires members to notify the WTO of any new SPS measures under consideration and publish all measures already in force.[63] All measures must be based upon a risk assessment unless the measure conforms to an international standard created by the Codex Alimentarius, the World Organization for Animal Health, and the FAO's Secretariat of the International Plant Protection Convention.[64] The European Commission currently fulfills these requirements by notifying

---

57 "What is the WTO?" World Trade Organization. https://www.wto.org/english/thewto_e/whatis_e/whatis_e.htm.
58 *Id.*
59 "Members and Observers." World Trade Organization. https://www.wto.org/english/thewto_e/whatis_e/tif_e/org6_e.htm.
60 "Understanding the WTO." World Trade Organization. https://www.wto.org/english/thewto_e/whatis_e/inbrief_e/inbr03_e.htm
61 *See* "Agreement on the Application of Sanitary and Phytosanitary Measures."
62 *Id.*
63 *Id.*, Annex B.
64 "EC Measures Concerning Meat and Meat Products (Hormones). Report of the Appellate Body. AB-1997-4. Pg. 71.

the WTO of all SPS measures within the EU and conducting risk assessments.[65] Now that the UK will no longer be part of the EU, it may have to send out new notifications of SPS measures that it intends to keep and conduct its own risk assessments.

1. Sending Notifications

Article 7 of the SPS Agreement requires members to notify and provide information on SPS measures in accordance with Annex B. Notifications are required for all measures, with exceptions for measures that are "substantially the same" as an international standard, guideline, or recommendation, and don't have a "significant effect" on the other Members' trade.[66] There is no definition as to what constitutes a "significant effect," but the Transparency Provision Handbook suggests notifying measures where the effect of a proposed measure is uncertain, "for the sake of increased transparency."[67]

All members must have a single central government authority responsible for such notifications, designated as the "notification authority." In most circumstances, the notification authority must submit a notification for a new measure or the change of an existing measure to the WTO Secretariat.[68] It must then give countries a reasonable time to make comments in writing, discuss country comments upon request, and take comments and discussions into account when deciding whether to adopt or amend a measure.[69] The notification authority must also provide additional relevant information on the measure when requested.[70] In sum, notification authorities act as liaisons between the country implementing a measure and the county concerned by the measure.

SANTE currently notifies all SPS measures to the WTO on behalf of EU member states.[71] The UK has no country-specific notification authority and will have to create one in order to comply with its notification requirement. The UK will have to identify a "central government authority" to serve as the notification authority.[72] The notification authority need not have experts on its staff but should have

---

65 https://www.wto.org/english/thewto_e/countries_e/european_communities_e.htm

66 "How to apply the transparency provisions of the SPS Agreement." (Handbook.) World Trade Organization. Sept. 2002. ¶ 32.

67 *Id.* ¶ 41.

68 *Id.* ¶¶ 42-45.

69 *Id.*

70 *Id.* footnote ¶26.

71 Enquiry Points/Notification Authorities. World Trade Organization. http://spsims.wto.org/en/EnquiryPointsNotificationAuthorities/Search?countryCode=U918&filter=.

72 Handbook, *supra note 67*, ¶ 1.

relationships with the experts who will be writing SPS measures.[73] Establishment of a notification authority should be simple because the authority serves a secretarial role that does not require any technical expertise.

The real difficulty of the notification requirement lies in determining whether the UK has any entitlement to the EU's notifications. Can the UK tell the WTO that all of the EU's notifications still apply to the UK? The UK could argue that the EU's applications continue to apply to the UK because the UK was a member of the EU when it sent the notification, so it was as if the UK sent the notifications to the WTO itself. The UK could also argue that it does not have to submit new notifications because the regulations will not have any effect on trade. The world has been subject to all EU SPS measures already, and up until March 29, 2019, the world will continue to have to follow EU SPS measures when shipping to the UK.[74] Any EU measures that the UK chooses to adopt will not have a "significant effect" on other Member's trade because it will just be maintaining the status quo. This argument will likely only work if the UK does not add any new SPS measure or increase the protection level of certain SPS measures. Conversely, opponents will say that these measures came into the UK through direct effect, so the UK's national system had nothing to do with it. Since the EU notified these measures without any input from the UK, the UK should not be able to adopt the EU's notifications as their own. Ultimately this will probably be sorted out through negotiation at an SPS Committee meeting.

If the UK chooses to keep some measures and discard others, some kind of notification will probably be necessary so that countries know which measures the UK is keeping. Perhaps these notifications could be less formal than the standard notification, listing the current EU measures that the UK will keep without allowing for public comment on them. While this would be easiest for the UK, other member governments to the WTO may not find this acceptable. They may want to challenge some of the EU's existing measures that act as barriers to trade and convince the UK either not to adopt those measures or to adopt less stringent measures. Because member governments run the WTO, they may require the UK to issue standard notifications for all SPS measures it rolls over from the EU. Director General Azevedo has

---

[73] *Id.* ¶ 11.

[74] Depending upon whether third countries honor the transition agreement struck between the UK and the EU, this date would be 21 months later, on December 31, 2020.

already noted that the UK will have to renegotiate and re-file its tariff and GATS schedules, so it may also have to re-file its SPS notifications.[75]

Notifications are supposed to be made "when a draft with the complete text of a proposed regulation is available" with enough time for comments from other members to be taken into account and amendments made to the text.[76] The Transparency Provision Handbook recommends at least 60 days between notification of a measure and its entry into force.[77] Therefore, the UK should put out all notifications at least 60 days before the transition period ends and its measures come into force. Since it may have to send new notifications for every EU measure that it keeps, the next issue is whether it may use the EU's notification as its own.

2. Text of the Notification

While the notification authority sends notifications to the WTO, someone with knowledge of the measure should write the notifications.[78] This will likely create a competency issue for the UK. SANTE, which currently formulates measures and writes and sends notifications, is an EU institution located in Luxembourg.[79] The UK has no experience with formulating measures or writing notifications. Since it hasn't formulated SPS measures itself, it may be difficult to find someone within the UK who knows enough about the measures to write an accurate notification. The UK could copy and paste the explications from EU's notifications, but many of the EU's SPS measures have been changed by subsequent addenda and revisions, so simply copying prior notifications would result in inaccurate descriptions. Whoever in the UK is placed in charge of creating notifications will therefore need some knowledge of the specifics and scientific underpinnings of each SPS measure in order to adequately characterize them in light of all the changes they may have gone through over the years.

The best team for this is likely the UK's current enquiry point, the International Team for Better Regulation at the EU International located at the Department for Environment Food and Rural Affairs (DEFRA).[80]

---

[75] "Azevedo addresses World Trade Symposium in London on the state of global trade." World Trade Organization News. (Dec. 22, 2016). https://www.wto.org/english/news_e/spra_e/spra126_e.htm.

[76] Handbook, *supra note 67*, ¶ 42.

[77] *Id.* ¶ 42.

[78] *Id.* ¶ 48.

[79] "Directorate-General SANTE." European Commission. https://ec.europa.eu/info/departments/health-and-food-safety_en.

[80] "Enquiry Points/Notification Authorities." SPS Information Management System. http://spsims.wto.org/en/EnquiryPointsNotificationAuthorities/Search?countryCode=C826&filter=.

Enquiry points are responsible for replying to country inquiries by getting answers from relevant bodies.[81] In the absence of any other body concerned with SPS measures in the UK, presumably the international team at DEFRA knows more about SPS regulations than any other agency. While this makes sense, enquiry points serve a mostly secretarial role, and without DEFRA being able to contact the EU committees that created SPS measures they may not know enough to write the notifications. With this shortcoming in mind, DEFRA should begin to work with the EU to prepare their notifications and continue to do so during the transition period while they are still bound by the EU's current SPS measures and therefore have access to SANTE.[82]

In addition to changing the description of notifications, this team may also have to change the legal document attached to the notification. The UK will have to attach a regulation to its notification, and it may not be entitled to attach a regulation published by the Official Journal of the European Union. It may instead have to transpose all EU SPS measures into its own UK Journal and format before notification. This will likely need to be done during the transition process, as the Repeal Bill recognizes that measures coming into the UK may need to be changed in order to operate effectively.

In order to operate effectively within the UK, the regulations will need to be re-numbered so that they conform to the UK's legislative system, including cross-references to other regulations in any regulatory text. This will become complicated because the UK will be simultaneously notifying member states about regulations cross-referencing other regulations that are also going through the notification process. By maintaining the cross-references in the document attached to the notification, which it must do for the regulation to make sense, the UK will have to assume that the measures will go through without amendment, even though one of the reasons for the notification process is to consider amendments suggested by other countries. Assuming that all measures will go through without changes thus negates one of the purposes of the notification process.

The success of the UK in this area will depend on the WTO member states' willingness to indulge the UK's legal fiction. If the WTO decides to hold the UK strictly to the purpose of the notification process, it could require the UK to notify in waves. The first wave would be foundational SPS measures that don't reference other measures and upon which many other measures are based. Each successive wave would build upon the

---

[81] Handbook, *supra note 67*, ¶15.

[82] Draft Withdrawal Agreement, *supra note 31*, art. 122.6.

other so that measures being notified would only include references to already implemented regulations that have gone through the notification process. This would be time-consuming and would require intricate analysis of each measure and its relationship with all other measures. If WTO members are lenient, they may allow all measures to be notified at the same time, creating the appearance of compliance with the notification requirement, but failing to fulfill a purpose of the notification requirement. While this depends on the political situation at the WTO, the UK must fulfill other legal requirements of the SPS Agreement that are not capable of being solved through politics.

B. RISK ASSESSMENT REQUIREMENT OF THE SPS AGREEMENT

In addition to notification of potential SPS measures, the SPS Agreement also requires SPS measures to be based on a risk assessment and be done to protect plant, animal, or human health in the territory of the member.[83] If a WTO panel or the Appellate Body finds that a measure does not meet these two requirements, the measure must be gotten rid of, or amended by conducting a new risk assessment tailored to the UK. The WTO will not examine the appropriateness of an SPS measure unless a member state challenges it using the dispute settlement mechanism. Knowing this, the UK can hedge its bets and roll over uncontroversial and small SPS measures without conducting any analysis as to its continued relevancy on the assumption that the measure will not be challenged.

Many measures will likely have to be discarded or changed, because what might have been a good policy for a customs union that allowed the free movement of goods will likely be unnecessarily restrictive for a country separated from the rest of the world by water. Overall, measures related to human and animal health will be easier to keep because they are less dependent on geography. UK citizens will want the same health protections they had in the EU regardless of whether they are considered part of the EU or not.

Determining whether a measure meets the requirements of the SPS Agreement will require an in-depth measure-by-measure analysis. Countries can only apply SPS measures to protect their own country, so the UK will have to discard any measure that seeks to protect plants or animals not found within the UK's borders.[84] While this takes some measures off the board, the vast majority of measures must go through further analysis to determine whether they may be kept.

---

[83] *See* Beef-Hormones, *supra note 65*, ¶ 71; SPS Agreement, *supra note 62*, art. 2.3.
[84] *Id.* art. 2.3.

To conduct this analysis, the UK must first determine whether it will have to redo all risk assessments done by the EU. There is one situation in which a risk assessment is not required. If a measure "conforms to" international standards, a rebuttable presumption is created that this measure is necessary to protect public health and consistent with the requirements of the SPS Agreement.[85] Acceptable international standard-setting organizations are the World Organization for Animal Health, the Codex Alimentarius, and the Food and Agriculture Organization of the United Nation's Secretariat of the International Plant Protection Convention.[86] "Conformed to" means "full compliance," "adoption" or "incorporation" and is therefore a high standard requiring that a measure "embody the international standard completely" and "convert[] it" into a domestic measure.[87] If a member meets this high standard, the burden of proof shifts to the complainant to show that the measure is inappropriate.[88] It is unlikely that a challenge based on a conforming measure would be successful because international standards usually reflect scientific consensus unless such measure is not related to any product found within the UK.[89] Therefore, if any EU measures "conform to" international standards, the UK will likely be able to keep these so long as they apply to plant animal or human health in its territory. For measures not conforming to an international standard a risk assessment is required.[90]

1. "An Assessment"

Article 5.1 specifies that SPS measures must be based on "an assessment." "An" is an indefinite article that "refer[s] to something not

---

[85] *Id.* arts. 5.1, 5.2, 2.2. "India- Measures Concerning the Importation of Certain Agricultural Products." WT/DS430/AB/R. June 4, 2015. ¶ 5.6.

[86] "Sanitary and Phytosanitary Measures." World Trade Organization. https://www.wto.org/english/tratop_e/sps_e/sps_e.htm.

[87] Beef-Hormones, *supra note 65*, pg. 170; *WTO Technical Barriers and SPS Measures*. Rudiger Wolfrum, Peter-Tobias Stoll, Anja Seibert-Fohr. Max Planck Commentaries on World Trade Law. 2007. pg. 422.

[88] *Id.*

[89] *Id.*

[90] Article 3.3 is in the disjunctive, requiring a risk assessment for a member's determination of an appropriate level of protection but not if the member provides a scientific justification. However, the Appellate Body in EC-Hormones (¶ 175) found this interpretation to be incorrect, because the final sentence requires that both scientific justification and member determination be consistent with the other provisions of the SPS Agreement, and the footnote defining scientific justification includes a risk assessment. Article 5 requires a risk assessment, so a risk assessment must be conducted for all SPS measures, regardless of whether they are originally based on science or member preference.

specifically identified . . . but treated as one of a class."[91] Because assessment is modified by "an," the Member imposing a measure need not conduct its own risk assessment but can apply a risk assessment conducted by another country. The Appellate Body in Beef Hormones reinforced this interpretation, saying that a "SPS measure might well find its objective justification in a risk assessment carried out by another Member, or an international organization."[92] However, the risk assessment must also be "appropriate to the circumstances," so the member doesn't have unfettered discretion in which risk assessment to adopt.[93]

2. "Based on"

Article 5 requires members to "ensure that their sanitary or phytosanitary measures are based on an assessment." The Appellate Body in Hormones noted that the term "based on" could encompass a variety of meanings.[94] However, it struck down the Panel's interpretation, which read "based on" to mean "conform to."[95] The Appellate Body found that the ordinary meaning of "based on" means "stands" "founded," "built upon" or "supported by" another thing.[96] A measure must therefore be "founded" upon a risk assessment, but need not "conform" to that risk assessment. Since this is a less rigorous standard than conformity, an SPS measure may be "based on" a risk assessment where "only some, not all, of the elements of the standard are incorporated into the measure."[97] The measure may also deviate from the risk assessment to a certain extent by taking into account non-scientific factors like economics, politics, and public preference.[98] Therefore "based on" requires only an "objective situation that persists and is observable between an SPS measure and a risk assessment."[99] In other words, there must be a "rational relationship" between the measure and the risk assessment.[100]

Since SPS measures do not need to "conform" to the risk assessment, the UK should be able to carry over the EU's SPS measures even if certain parts of the risk assessment are no longer applicable to

---

91 "An." Oxford English Dictionary. http://www.oed.com.proxygt-law.wrlc.org/view/Entry/4?rskey=m2RjIg&result=2&isAdvanced=false.
92 Beef-Hormones, *supra note 65*, ¶ 190.
93 SPS Agreement, *supra note 62*, art. 5.2.
94 Beef-Hormones, *supra note 65*, ¶ 163.
95 *Id.*
96 *Id.*; India-poultry, *supra note 86*, ¶ 5.77.
97 Beef-Hormones, *supra note 65*, ¶ 163.
98 *Id.*
99 *Id.* ¶ 189
100 *Id.* ¶ 193.

the UK, as only some of the elements need to be incorporated into the measure. This is especially so considering that the UK may take into account non-scientific factors like economics, and it has a strong interest in maintaining the EU's SPS measures in order to lower trade barriers. Therefore, even though certain parts of the EU's risk assessment will not be applicable to the UK, the UK has considerable leeway to argue that its SPS measures have a rational relationship and are "based on" the EU's risk assessment.

3. "Appropriate to the Circumstances"

Article 5.1 requires that the risk assessment be "appropriate to the circumstances," which gives countries some flexibility in the way they carry out risk assessments.[101] This phrase "confers a right and obligation on WTO Members to assess the risk, on a case by case basis, in terms of product, origin and destination, including, in particular, country specific situations."[102] It also includes a temporal element, as a change in circumstances at a later date could mean the risk assessment is no longer appropriate to the circumstances.[103]

The UK is most likely to be challenged on this requirement. In regard to the temporal element, the EU's risk assessment is likely no longer appropriate because the UK's circumstances have changed dramatically. Instead of being part of a regional group encompassing a number of different climates and geographies, the UK is no longer part of a customs union and has only one climate and geography. Furthermore, the origin and destination considerations of the risk assessment have also changed, as the UK will likely no longer be part of the single market. Before Brexit, the EU's broader risk assessment was appropriate to the UK because of the single market. Even when the UK wasn't susceptible to certain risks because once inside the UK, products would be shipped from the UK to other countries throughout the EU that were susceptible to the risk without being stopped. As the UK will likely no longer be part of the single market, this risk assessment may not be appropriate to the circumstances because products will be subject to reexamination upon entry into the EU.[104] Overall, determining whether

---

101 *Id.* ¶ 129; "Australia- Measures Affecting Importation of Salmon" WT/DS18/R ¶ 8.57; Gruszczynski, Lukasz. *Regulating Health and Environmental Risks under WTO Law.* Oxford University Press. 2010.

102 *Id.* ¶ 8.71

103 Scott, Joanne. *The WTO Agreement on Sanitary and Phytosanitary Measures.* Oxford University Press. 2007.

104 This depends on whether there will be a hard border in Ireland. If there is a hard border, then this remains true. If there is a soft border, as seems desired by both sides, there will be a similar situation to the open market in terms of danger of the spread of diseases to products. Once a product crosses from the UK to Ireland, then it could

a measure complies with the requirements of the WTO is a time-intensive process that will require intricate analysis.

V. CONCLUSION

Despite their importance to health and safety, SPS measures have, so far, gone unaddressed in Brexit negotiations. Instead, they remain like Gordian knots waiting to be unraveled. With no clear positions articulated by either the UK or the EU on this issue, this chapter presents the considerations the UK will face in developing its SPS regime. SPS measures involve three main considerations: what agencies and capacities the UK must have to implement such measures, the political and economic issues the UK should take into account when determining which measures to keep, and whether the WTO will allow the UK to keep the EU's SPS measures. As this chapter has shown, within these categories lie many complex, fact-intensive questions that will have to be considered individually for each of the hundreds of SPS measures. In short, the UK should begin considering what its own SPS regime will look like as soon as possible in order to be prepared for the end of the transition period on December 31, 2020.

potentially cross to the EU without further checks, potentially making the EU's risk assessments appropriate to the UK's circumstances.

CHAPTER 7: BESPOKE AGREEMENT TO SAVE BESPOKE FASHION

CATHERINE TASSIN DE MONTAIGU

I. INTRODUCTION

London Fashion Week—a perfect illustration of the four freedoms embodied in four days of catwalks flooded by couture-clad models draped in Italian fabric, sewn by Spanish seamstresses, paid for with capital from France, all under a British house name that is likely predominately staffed by European Union [EU] citizens.[1] Although the UK fashion sector has steadily grown into one of the most valuable industries on the island, bringing in more than fifteen times the fishing industry,[2] Brexit will ultimately wreak havoc on the creative industry in a multitude of ways. The UK's eventual exclusion from the free movement of students and tuition subsidization under the EU's Erasmus scheme will severely drain the pool of talent available to fashion schools and designers that rely on eager students willingness to work for experience.[3] Beyond blocking the pipeline for future talent, businesses urge both parties to come to an agreement on maintaining the free movement of people—arguing that forcing the Scandinavian designer based in London to pick "home" or their professional future must be avoided at all costs.[4] Further, leaders in the FashTech industry—the businesses exploring the intersection of fashion, technology, and ecommerce—warn that companies headquartered in London such as ASOS, Farfetch, Matches, and Net-A-Porter that experience any design-to-consumer shipping delays may lead to relocation within the EU.[5] While this chapter will primarily focus on intellectual property [IP] rights and the effect a lapse

---

[1] Ben Chapman, *London Fashion Week highlights the industry's Brexit problem*, INDEPENDENT (February 17, 2017), http://www.independent.co.uk/news/business/news/london-fashion-week-brexit-immigration-controls-clothing-industry-a7586511.html.

[2] Olivia Pinnock, *British Fashion Industry Voices Brexit Concerns in White Paper*, FORBES, (May 3, 2018), https://www.forbes.com/sites/oliviapinnock/2018/05/03/british-fashion-industry-voices-brexit-concerns-in-white-paper/#32e01dae803d.

[3] Brexit and the Impact on the Fashion Industry, FASHION ROUNDTABLE, March 29, 2018, at 6, phttps://www.fashionroundtable.co.uk/news/2018/4/1/fashion-roundtable-brexit-and-the-impact-on-the-fashion-industry-paper.

[4] *Id.* at 6.

[5] *Id.* at 5.

would have on the spring 2019 London Fashion Week—as a £28bn[6] per year industry that employs roughly 1 million people—any changes to the status quo will have major implications on the industry on both sides of the pond.

Part II will summarize the current landscape of fashion in the United Kingdom, its' relationship to the European continent, the effects Brexit has had on the industry to date, and expose the slew of issues that are sure to reveal themselves as the transition period comes to an end. Part III will uncover the current protection offered under EU law. Part IV will first outline the IP rights available under UK law during the transition period, then the rights available under international law, and lastly will offer some insight into what kind of bespoke agreement the two parties should agree to and will suggest various points of leverage that can yield an ideal arrangement. Although UK fashion houses stand to lose a lot should a beneficial deal not come to fruition, the EU undoubtedly has more fashion companies that stand to suffer should the Crown fail to input reciprocal protection after Brexit.

II. THE EFFECTS OF BREXIT ON UK FASHION

While cost of a jumper purchased in a "High Street" shop may vary widely compared to an illustrious couture wedding gown designed by Londoner Jenny Packham, the value of the fashion industry to the Crown is clear. The United Kingdom's fashion industry contributes around £28 billion per year, provides around 880,000 jobs, and had a 4.7% gross value added [GVA] contribution—per calculations conducted in 2015 in the "Value of Fashion" study produced by Oxford Economics.[7] Growth for the industry prior to the referendum—in June 2016—was at 6% annually and predicted to surpass £32 billion by 2020.[8] However, numbers are now reflecting a mere 1.2% growth in the wake of glacial negotiation and lack of predictability.[9]

---

[6] Charlie Porter, *After Brexit, which way for fashion?*, FINANCIAL TIMES (June 30, 2016), https://www.ft.com/content/8f288762-3316-11e6-bda0-04585c31b153.

[7] Response to Industrial Strategy Green Paper, BRITISH FASHION COUNCIL, April 17, 2017, http://www.britishfashioncouncil.com/uploads/files/1/British%20Fashion%20Council%20Response%20Industrial%20Strategy%20Green%20Paper.pdf.

[8] Your UK, FASHION ROUNDTABLE, https://www.fashionroundtable.co.uk/political-intelligence/, *see also* Lowdown on Fashion Industry in all 650 Constituencies in the UK, FASHION ROUNDTABLE, https://static1.squarespace.com/static/5a1431a1e5dd5b754be2e0e9/t/5a1d70838165f542d60ac2ad/1511878792447/Comp+%28fixed+numbers%29+4.pdf.

[9] Your UK, FASHION ROUNDTABLE, https://www.fashionroundtable.co.uk/political-intelligence/.

With as little as 33.3 kilometers between England and France, it is no surprise that the current EU share of exports in the fashion industry is at a staggering 60%.[10] Exports of clothing to the EU was at 4.762 billion, while exports to non-EU was 1.470 billion in 2016.[11] However, imports of clothing from the EU was at a whopping 5.395 billion dollars in 2016.[12] Should the parties fail to negotiate a "free trade" deal, the UK businesses will be subjected to the EU's current tariff bindings which vary, but reach as much as 17% in duties for "Footwear, Gaitors & the like" to 5.3% in duties for "Wool…and woven fabric"—a predominate product of the Scottish industry.[13] Although, in the absence of an agreement, the UK's average tariff is set to jump to 12% for most types of fashion-related products destined for the EU market.[14]

London Fashion Week is one of the four premier trade shows that showcases unique local and foreign designers' latest collection. The event is held twice a year: once in February debuting fall and winter designs and another in September unveiling the latest in spring and summer trends. Viewed as equal to its' counterparts in New York, Paris, and Milan—the event boasts a media value of about £600m for the February 2017 LFW, including pre-and-post coverage.[15] Outside of the tourism driven to the city by the two events, 4 out of 5 visitors cite the reason they choose to travel to London is due to fashion—as a part of the cultural and creative industries.[16] Although the cumulative effects of Brexit are yet to be seen, Business of Fashion reports that the British Fashion Council, among others, argues "that losing EU protections against intellectual property could significantly impact the fashion industry […] 'effectively closing down London Fashion Week as a platform to promote British businesses' if designers or companies had to register and show their designs in the EU first to benefit from its intellectual property protections."[17] London Fashion Week may not be a competitive or advisable option anymore for UK brands and the

---

10 *Id.*

11 Apparel market United Kingdom (UK) - Statistics & Facts, STATISTA, https://www.statista.com/topics/3348/apparel-market-in-the-uk/.

12 *Id.*

13 World Trade Organization, EU Tariff Binding Schedule, https://www.wto.org/english/tratop_e/tariffs_e/tariff_data_e.htm

14 *Id.*

15 Response Industrial Strategy Green Paper, BRITISH FASHION COUNCIL, April 17, 2017, citing data collected by Precise Media Monitoring.

16 *Id.* citing GLA economics.

17 Limei Hoang, *Triggering Article 50: What Brexit Means for Fashion*, BUSINESS OF FASHION (March 29, 2017), https://www.businessoffashion.com/articles/intelligence/triggering-article-50-what-does-brexit-mean-for-fashion.

international designers that would forgo IP protection in the EU-27 simply because they identify with the unique style of the event.[18]

Beyond the clear implications that potential trade barriers will have, Brexit may affect EU citizens' access and funding to the top design schools in the region thereby limiting the talent available to elite fashion houses such as Burberry or Alexander McQueen. Subjecting these businesses to anything from changes to rules of origin, the use of geographic indicators, varying textile import and export quotas or tariffs, requiring visa sponsorships, changing the level of IP protection, or something else will have a wide range of effects on the industry's bottom line.

III. IP PROTECTION UNDER EU LAW

"Fashion" and all it includes can take a multitude of forms, from a 3-dimentional shoe or a 2-dementional form such as a unique pattern. While protection for trademarks, copyrighted work, and patents are fairly traditional, the European Union has developed a unique scheme—the Registered and Unregistered Design Protection—to guard products that may not fall into any of those categories. Due to the temporary nature of fashion and the unique publicity provided during fashion week, the free unregistered design right has become the premier mechanism for guarding designers' work.

The scheme, found in Regulation (EC) No 6/2002, protects "designs", "products", and "complex products" for a maximum period of three years starting from the date on which the design is first made available to the public in any of the EU countries.[19] Whether a design has been "made public" would be fairly easily accomplished in these circumstances as it only requires publishing, exhibition, or having been used in trade.[20] A design includes "the appearance of the whole or a part of a product resulting from the features of, in particular, the lines, contours, colours, shape, texture and/or materials of the product itself and/or its ornamentation."[21] A product is "any industrial or handcraft item, including *inter alia* parts intended to be assembled into a complex product, packaging, get-up, graphic symbols and typo- graphic typefaces...."[22] A complex product is defined as a "'complex product' means a product which is composed of multiple components which can be replaced permitting disassembly and re-assembly of the product."[23] In

---

18 *Id.*
19 Council Regulation 6/2002, art. 11(a), (EC).
20 *Id.* art. 11(b).
21 *Id.* art. 3(a).
22 *Id.* art. 3(b).
23 *Id.* art. 3(c).

order to be protected, the design must be both novel[24] and possess an individual character.[25]

As a regulation, the rights set forth are directly applicable—without need for domestic governmental implementation—in all of the EU member states and can be enforced in all countries as well. The regulation is particularly useful because all of which is featured during London Fashion Week would likely fall within the three categories. The ability to avoid the expensive time-consuming registration process is ideal considering the feasibility of doing so during the six months between shows and that each design may not merit the financial commitment attached to the prolonged procedure. However, should a piece prove to be particularly popular for a prolonged period of time, then brands can register their design and will be protected for up to 25-years.[26]

Although the designs themselves are artistically valuable and certainly need protection, most pieces sold to the general public are more affordable derivatives of the styles showcased during fashion week but simply affixed with the brand's name or logo. As one can imagine, trademark protection is particularly important to combat the manufacture and sale of counterfeit goods. Under EU law, "any signs, in particular words, including personal names, or designs, letters, numerals, colours, the shape of goods or of the packaging of goods, or sound"[27] that is distinguishing one producer's good from another will be registerable.[28] The registered trademark will prohibit the sale of a product under the same name or through the use of your unique logo within the EU.[29] Although established companies will likely not have any lapse in coverage, trademark protection for newly established brands or designers in the UK will likely be forced to simultaneously double-register. Under article 10(4) of Regulation (EU) 2017/1001, a UK trademark holder would only be able to prevent the sale of counterfeited items produced by EU citizens or third parties exporting into the EU from if registered under this scheme.[30] Further, if another person or company is using a similar mark within the EU that a UK holder created earlier—the UK holder would have to file a "seniority" application, thereby imposing a secondary procedure on an already burdened party.[31]

[24] *Id.* art. 5.
[25] *Id.* art. 6.
[26] *Id.* art. 12.
[27] Parliament and Council Regulation 2017/1001, art. 4 (EU).
[28] *Id.* art. 6.
[29] *Id.* art. 9(3).
[30] *Id.* art. 10(4).
[31] *Id.* art. 39.

Due to the large number of world-renowned fashion houses being located within the EU, it is not surprising that the block has a robust anti-counterfeit scheme that allows the customs administration to detain goods suspected of infringing on IP rights.[32] The accusing party need only submit an application for action with the competent national customs authorities and they will either detain, donate, or destroy the goods depending on the outcome of the infringement case.

A niche segment of fashion has seen surges in growth due to the ever-changing habits and needs of consumers: smart fabrics. A company may invest in research and development which yields the invention of textiles that contain materials or are constructed to retain or expend heat, that do not wrinkle, are particularly breathable, or even change composition when exposed to different elements. In the case of e-textiles, embedded electronics sustained by batteries can modify the color using cognitive technology, including the ability to "communicate, transform, conduct energy and even grow."[33] For a beautiful example, see Zac Posen's Cinderella-esque ball gown made with a custom fiber optic woven organza worn by the luminous Claire Danes at the 2016 Met Gala.[34]

An EU patent would prevent third parties from making, using, or selling an invention for a given period depending on the type of invention.[35] Hopeful patent holders have three options: apply for a national patent in each EU country, apply for a unitary patent through the European Patent Office (EPO), or apply for protection under the Patent Cooperation Treaty enforced by the World Intellectual Property Organization.[36] Identical to most patent protection schemes, the item must be novel, have an inventive step or be non-obvious, and be capable of an industrial application.[37] Although the unitary patent "has

---

[32] Defend your rights, THE EUROPEAN COMMISSION, https://ec.europa.eu/taxation_customs/business/customs-controls/counterfeit-piracy-other-ipr-violations/defend-your-rights_en.

[33] Rebecca Gaddis, *What Is The Future Of Fabric? These Smart Textiles Will Blow Your Mind*, FORBES (May 7, 2014), https://www.forbes.com/forbes/welcome/?toURL=https://www.forbes.com/sites/forbesstylefile/2014/05/07/what-is-the-future-of-fabric-these-smart-textiles-will-blow-your-mind/&refURL=https://www.google.com/&referrer=https://www.google.com/, *see also* Victoria McClellan, *Cognitive Marchesa dress lights up the night*, IBM (October 27, 2016), https://www.ibm.com/blogs/internet-of-things/cognitive-marchesa-dress/

[34] Cara Kelly, *Marchesa, Zac Posen and Claire Danes light up the Met Gala red carpet*, USA TODAY (May 2, 2016), https://www.usatoday.com/story/life/entertainthis/2016/05/02/claire-danes-wore-light-up-cinderella-dress-met-gala/83858594/.

[35] Your Guide to IP in Europe, EUROPEAN IPR HELPDESK, https://www.iprhelpdesk.eu/sites/default/files/.../EU-IPR-Guide-IP-in-Europe.pdf

[36] *Id.* at 57

[37] *Id.*

international character…national laws govern the registration in each territory. A granted European patent is then a 'bundle of national patents that must be validated at the national IP offices of the countries selected by the applicant for it to be effective.'"[38] Albeit somewhat duplicitous, the benefit lies in the cost-saving fee scheme where an applicant need only file one registration under a single fee payment system to benefit from the 20-year protection.[39] Although patents for smart fabrics are less likely to be held by traditional designers, failure to provide a transparent and easily-navigable patent system would certainly harm the burgeoning field within the UK.

Fashion—an unlikely beneficiary of intellectual property rights—stands to lose a great deal should no deal yield a lapse in protection and no mutual recognition.

IV. IP PROTECTION POST BREXIT

A. IP PROTECTION DURING THE TRANSITION PERIOD

Like many other industries housed in the UK and the EU, predictability is the commodity no one possesses. Further, business is no longer segmented into pre-and-post Brexit but now includes the dreaded "transition period." The transition period is the time in which UK law will be comprised of EU law that has been implemented through the legislative process since the UK's accession to the EU that is not terminated in the Repeal Bill but may be maintained in the Withdrawal Bill.

The most valuable IP protection—the unregistered community design—as a regulation would in theory go unscathed by Brexit upon the mass EU-to-UK law conversion provided for in article 2 of the Repeal Bill.[40] However, the nature of the right requires EU recognition. Simply providing the right to UK citizens or perhaps even to the EU citizens in the UK, would only provide half of the puzzle. Although there is a UK Unregistered Design right, it falls short of the EU equivalent and only applies to 3D shapes and configuration.[41] In attempting to minimize transaction costs and lack of coverage, the goal must be to include patterns and also cover the appearance of the "whole or part of a design

---

[38] *Id.* at 19.

[39] *Id.*

[40] European Union (Withdrawal) Bill, https://publications.parliament.uk/pa/bills/-cbill/2017-2019/0005/18005.pdf.

[41] Copyright, Designs and Patents Act 1988, Part III, Chapter 1, Article 213(3), www.legislation.gov.uk/ukpga/1988/48/pdfs/ukpga_19880048_en.pdf.

including lines, contours, colors, shape, texture, materials, features of ornamentation" as provided for in the EU Unregistered Design Regulation.

While implementing a new UK unregistered design protection scheme that mimics more closely the EU system would close that gap, a more important development for the industry would be to maintain the status quo and fashion a reciprocity scheme as between the two countries. Without a such an agreement, there may be a chilling effect on the UK industry and trade shows like London Fashion week. The short-term protection, because it does not require registration, would require a party seeking protection to feature their garment or accessory first in the most valuable jurisdiction—the EU—thereby risking lapse in protection in the UK due to priority EU disclosure. As a point of leverage, there are more EU fashion companies selling to UK citizens and its tourists than there are UK companies selling in the EU. One can imagine that telling Chanel that the designs they featured in Paris fashion week will go unprotected in the UK would not go over well.

Trademarks are protected within the UK under the Trademarks Act of 1994. However, under this scheme, trademark protection would be limited to the borders under the control of the Crown.[42] As a piece of legislation implementing an EU directive, it thankfully offers the same level of protection as its counterpart: the EU Trademark under the European Union Intellectual Property Office.[43] Again, in order to avoid the hassle of double-registry, an immediate reciprocal recognition with shared access to the each other's' database would be advisable. However, as most trademarks are made public upon approval, access to the databases may not be necessary.[44]

Patents will be protected under the Patent Act of 1977 and the amendments provided under the Patents Act of 2004. Similar to the Trademark Act, the legislation emulates the EU counterpart and maintains the domestic registration and enforcement mechanisms. Although solutions to any potential gaps in coverage as between UK and EU legislation are presently unclear, the UK government has agreed to accede to the Unitary Patent and Unified Patent Court treaties.[45] Although viewed as perhaps a step back into the arms of the EU, UK businesses will benefit from protecting their "invention in up to

---

[42] Trademarks Act 1994, https://www.legislation.gov.uk/ukpga/1994/26/pdfs/ukpga_19940026_en.pdf.

[43] *Id.*

[44] *See* Search for a trademark, UK GOVERNMENT, https://www.gov.uk/search-for-trademark.

[45] The Unitary Patent and Unified Patent Court, UK GOVERNMENT, https://www.gov.uk/guidance/the-unitary-patent-and-unified-patent-court

25 EU countries with a single unitary patent."[46] This new system is poised to reduce on transaction costs such as translation and allow a party to "challenge and defend unitary patents in a single court action through the Unified Patent Court."[47]

Under the Draft Withdrawal Agreement, intellectual property rights are covered in Articles 50 through 57. Article 50 specifically deals with the unregistered community design right which effectively delays the inevitable cliff-edge.[48] As imagined, most rights are only discussed within the scope of the transition period and for those provisions in green—only remain in effect if they are established prior to the end of the transition period. The articles highlighted in green, have been "agreed at negotiators' level and will only be subject to technical legal revisions."[49] Not surprisingly, the agreement fails to address how any rights will be retained afterwards. As such, current international treaties may be the only mechanism by which UK companies can maintain protection moving forward.

B. IP PROTECTION UNDER INTERNATIONAL LAW

The EU and the UK are both parties to the World Intellectual Property Organization (WIPO), the WTO Agreement on Trade-Related Aspects of Intellectual Property Rights (TRIPS), and recently the Unitary Patent and Unified Patent Court.

WIPO is a specialized agency under the United Nations.[50] With 191 members, it is one of the most expansive mechanisms for protecting intellectual property.[51] Trademarks are covered under the Madrid System, which allows a party presently in a member state's territory or citizen of a member state to file one application and pay one set of fees to benefit from the protection in over 100 countries.[52] Although it minimizes costs related to the application, it does allow parties to avoid the "validation" process that each trademark must undergo in order to be effective.[53] Industrial designs are covered under the Hague System, which allows a single application and fee system but only provides

---

[46] *Id.*

[47] *Id.*

[48] Article 50 Draft Withdrawal, February 28, 2018, https://ec.europa.eu/-commission/sites/beta-political/.../draft_withdrawal_agreement.pdf.

[49] *Id.*

[50] WORLD INTELLECTUAL PROPERTY ORGANIZATION, http://www.wipo.int/about-wipo/en/.

[51] *Id.*

[52] Your Guide to IP in Europe, at 7.

[53] *Id.* at 7.

coverage in 65 territories.[54] Similarly, this system is subject to national authentication.[55] Lastly, Patents are covered under the Patent Cooperation Treaty which allows the singular application and fee system in order to gain coverage in the 152 contracting parties.[56]

The Agreement on Trade-Related Aspects of Intellectual Property Rights, recently amended on January 23 of this year, is an agreement under the purview of the World Trade Organization.[57] Part 2 covers, among other things, copyrights,[58] trademarks,[59] geographical indications,[60] industrial designs,[61] and patents.[62] Part 3 outlines the enforcement mechanism, part 4 sets out the transferability of rights, and part 5 empowers the WTO to resolve disputes under the Dispute Settlement Understanding. While the WTO has proven to be a valuable mechanism to combating barriers to international trade, as a state-only system, private parties would be forced to notify their government and hope it would subsume their claim. This type of litigation is impractical for the fashion industry given the short-term applicability or need and the transaction costs associated with filling the gap in understanding the system as a whole.

The benefit of a reciprocal trade deal is undoubtedly revealed in providing businesses with the predictability that the industry is desperately lacking. The Fashion Round Table asserts that "in the fashion industry, for every £1 the government invests in trade show support, almost £70 comes back to the UK in export revenue."[63] Reciprocity in all aspects of intellectual property is key and failure to conclude a deal is not a viable option for any creative industry within the United Kingdom.

---

54 *Id.* at 15.

55 *Id.*

56 PCT—The International Patent System, WORLD INTELLECTUAL PROPERTY ORGANIZATION http://www.wipo.int/pct/en/.

57 THE WORLD TRADE ORGANIZATION, https://www.wto.org/english-/tratop_e/trips_e/trips_e.htm.

58 The Trade-Related Aspects of Intellectual Property Rights, April 15, 1994, Annex 1C of the Marrakesh Agreement Establishing the World Trade Organization, art. 9-14.

59 *Id.* art. 15-21

60 *Id.* art. 22-24

61 *Id.* art. 25-26

62 *Id.* art. 27-34

63 Political Intelligence, FASHION ROUNDTABLE, https://www.fashionroundtable.co.uk-/political-intelligence/

V. CONCLUSION

Come late February 2019 when the designers, models, and eager attendees flood the city of London the last thing on their minds should be Brexit. Lapse in coverage of these artist's intellectual property will not only harm the industry as a whole but the Crown's economy as well. Baroness Goudie boldly stated on March 15th of this year, "My Lords… Organisations such as fashion week will disappear from London. The amount of GDP that fashion week brings to this country is enormous…Will the Government assure those industries that they are welcome here, and do so quite quickly, otherwise they will look to go to Paris and Milan, because they are asking and baiting them to come?"[64]

Although no industry has gone unscathed by the separation, a potential positive effect of this uncertainty is the expansion of London fashion week to London fashion week festival—shifting the focus from exclusively on designers to attendees.[65] The festival will not only showcase the various designs but also have catwalks dedicated to "trends," provide luxe on-site shopping, and give attendees access to the bright minds of the industry through their wide array of panels.[66] This move appears to be evidence of their strategy to keep their competitive edge, grow its market value, and promote confidence during this turbulent time.

Industry leaders have consistently put fashion at the forefront of the government's agenda. The British Fashion Council, the Creative Industries Council, the Anti-Counterfeiting Group, and the UK's Department for Digital, Culture, Media & Sport all must work together to ensure the vulnerable industry's intellectual property is protected, the fight against counterfeit products does not go unattended, and London Fashion Week maintains its stature as one of the premier fashion displays of the world. Reciprocity must be a key ingredient in the bespoke agreement to save bespoke fashion.

---

64 789 Parl Deb HL (March 15, 2018) col. 1768-70 (UK), available at https://hansard.parliament.uk/Lords/2018-03-15/debates/1F6F792A-11C5-4463-B154-B00476E4D322/BrexitFashionIndustry.

65 LONDON FASHION WEEK FESTIVAL, http://londonfashionweekfestival.com-/about/overview/.

66 *Id.*

CHAPTER 8: THE RIPTIDE GROWS STRONGER: EFFECTS OF THE CJEU'S RULING IN *ACHMEA* ON BREXIT

JOSHUA BLUME

I. INTRODUCTION

Many of the individual member states within the EU have a long and storied history with bilateral investment treaties (BITs).[1] That history now includes more than one hundred individual operative BITs.[2] Strangely, that tide has quickly begun to push the other way, as several decisions by the Court of Justice of the European Union (CJEU) have changed the ability of individual countries to enforce individual BITs, especially between themselves and other EU member states.[3] Perhaps the most monumental of these cases is the recent decision in *Achmea BV v. Slovak Republic*.[4] While monumental for the EU as a whole, the decision will have a powerful impact on the UK as it continues with the Brexit process.

At first blush, Brexit might seem as though it could provide the UK a timely opportunity to enhance its global position as the seat of arbitral proceedings and enforcement. This is because the UK currently has 13 BITs in force with fellow EU member states.[5] That means of the remaining 27 Member States, nearly half of them will have a BIT with the UK after Brexit. The problem is, however, that the European Commission (EC) has strong feelings about intra-EU BITs and is actively campaigning to invalidate them. Depending on how the British government is able to negotiate the exit of the UK from the EU, those 13 BITs could be rendered meaningless. That could happen as part of the negotiations themselves or because the EU takes action to invalidate intra-EU BITs completely before the UK is able to finalize its withdrawal process and break free of EU rulings and regulations. What might have been a purely academic discussion on the issue became much more

[1] *See, e.g.*, Gesetz zu dem Vertag vom 25. November 1959 zwischen der Bundesrepublik Deutschland und Pakistan [Germany-Pakistan BIT], BGBL II, 793.

[2] 2013 O.J. C 131, 2-97.

[3] *See, e.g.*, Achmea B.V. v. The Slovak Republic, UNCITRAL, PCA Case No. 2008-13 (formerly Eureko B.V. v. The Slovak Republic).

[4] *Id.*

[5] Poland, Romania, Bulgaria, Czech Republic, Croatia, Hungary, Malta, Cyprus, Lithuania, Slovakia, Slovenia, Estonia, and Latvia.

relevant, however, after the *Achmea* decision was made by the CJEU. As described in this chapter, the *Achmea* decision may well be the brightly burnished tip to the European Commission's (EC) spear—a spear that will almost certainly cut down intra-EU BITs as constituted.

In order to sufficiently analyze this issue, the chapter begins by first analyzing the history of intra-EU BITs, with a specific reference to the UK's intra-EU BITs. Next, the chapter proceeds to analyze the competing goals and powers of the EC and the individual member states with reference to investment law and enforcement. Thirdly, the chapter looks to the governing law within the EU, with respect to investment treaties and negotiations, before *Achmea*. After drawing on this background, the chapter analyzes the antecedent facts in *Achmea*, followed by a legal analysis of the decision, including commentary on how the outcome is likely to affect the UK immediately. Finally, the chapter concludes by looking toward Brexit and comparing and assessing some of the most viable the options available to the UK.

II. BACKGROUND ON INTRA-EU BITS

For years, BITs have been seen as tools for developing countries to attract investment from more developed countries.[6] Furthermore, BITs provide a formal treaty that provides for certain defenses and protections that might otherwise be unenforceable in less developed countries.[7] That is what originally drove Germany to sign the first-ever BIT with Pakistan in 1959.[8] However, 1959 was long before the European Community had grown into the European Union, and long before it became the 27+1 member state institution it is today. After the fall of Soviet Union, many of the Western European states signed investment treaties with former Soviet states and satellites.[9] The initial goal was to encourage economic growth and capitalism in the post-Soviet states, but the treaties remained, even after those countries began to join their western allies in the reformed EU.[10] That is why the majority of the UK's 13 intra-EU BITs are made of up of Eastern European, post-Soviet states.[11] As the EU has

---

[6] *See, e.g.*, Office of the United States Trade Representative, *Bilateral Investment Treaties*, https://ustr.gov/trade-agreements/bilateral-investment-treaties (last visited May 28, 2018) (making this argument, along with several others).

[7] *Id.*

[8] *See generally*, Jeswald W. Salacuse, *BIT by BIT: The Growth of Bilateral Investment Treaties and Their Impact on Foreign Investment in Developing Countries*, 24 INT'L LAW. 655-657.

[9] *Five EU countries asked to terminate intra-EU bilateral investment treaties*, INS. TIMES, June 18, 2015.

[10] *Id.*

[11] For a full list of UK's BITs *see United Kingdom*, INV. POL'Y HUB, http://investmentpolicyhub.unctad.org/IIA/CountryBits/221 (last visited May 28, 2018).

grown, however, so have the opinions of the EC, the EU Commission, the EU Council, and the CJEU. The next section analyzes the growth and genesis of those perspectives.

III. EC'S GOALS COMPETING WITH MEMBER STATES

A natural tension between any supranational body and its members is the division of competencies. Within the EU, there are several issues where the states retain sole competency;[12] Other issues are the sole competency of the EU;[13] and, finally, there are some things where there is shared competency. During the negotiations on the Singapore free trade agreement (Singapore-FTA) the CJEU was forced to make just those types of determinations.[14]

A. ISSUES OF BITS WITHIN THE EU

According to the European Commission, Singapore is the EU's 17th largest trading partner—just in terms of goods—and the value of trade in services has been accelerating rapidly over the past decade.[15]As such, the EU had been keen to negotiate a free trade agreement (FTA) with Singapore. Due to member state concerns with the "new generation" FTA, the European Commission submitted a request to the CJEU for "an opinion to determine whether the EU has exclusive competence enabling it to sign and conclude" an FTA with Singapore.[16] The main holding of the CJEU was that "as it stands," free trade agreements can "only be concluded by the EU and the Member States jointly."[17] There were only two issues, however, that the CJEU found were not the exclusive competence of the EU; those issues were "non-direct foreign investment" and the "regime governing dispute settlement between investors and States."[18] This decision became monumental with regard to the EU-Canada Comprehensive Economic and Trade Agreement (CETA), which failed to receive the necessary votes from the state of Wallonia within Belgium for this exact reason.[19] In fact, the negotiations remained stalled for months, and while there has since been an official

---

[12] National security is one example of this.

[13] Negotiating external trade agreements is an example of this.

[14] European Commission, *Countries and Regions: Singapore*, http://ec.europa.eu/trade/-policy/countries-and-regions/countries/singapore/ (last visited May 28, 2018).

[15] *Id.*

[16] CJEU, 2017, Opinion 2/15, 1.

[17] *Id.* at 2.

[18] *Id.*

[19] Maia de la Baume, *Walloon Parliament rejects CETA deal*, POLITICO, Oct. 14, 2016.

signature of the agreement, the applicable pieces of the investment chapter still remain in contention and may be removed by the CJEU.[20]

Beyond future negotiations, however, the Singapore-FTA decision also underscored the exclusive competence of member states to facilitate ongoing investor state dispute settlement (ISDS) and to maintain their intra-EU agreements.[21] This is contrasted with the EU's total competence to negotiate actual ISDS provisions in future trade agreements, as well as the exclusive competence of the EU to negotiate BITs with third-countries.[22] Therefore, on a moving-forward basis, no EU country has the competence to negotiate BITs with other countries. Instead, the member states simply retain authority to oversee ISDS proceedings in their own state.[23]

1. The EC's Dream Lives On

Recent events have surprisingly shown that just because the apex court has made a determination on these issues does not mean that the EC is willing to accept the status quo.[24] In fact, the EC has played off the *Singapore-FTA* decision as yielding a type of smaller authority to the states—and when read between the lines, this is not just smaller; it is interpreted and explained as a sort of melting iceberg, with slowly diminishing authority.[25] One paper, though written a few years before the decision, explains much of what the EC has intended to do if granted the opportunity: eliminate intra-EU BITs and unify the EU with respect to the Washington, New York, and other ISDS conventions.[26] Certainly, the EC's actions have shown dedication to completing at least the first part of that prognostication.

Another author argued, in 2015, that the EU would being to push for an overhaul of the BIT language it used in international agreements, a push that would set the EC's objectives at odds with at least some

---

[20] Erin Brown, *CETA is in effect (mostly): what you need to know*, NORTON ROSE FULBRIGHT, Sept. 2017.

[21] *See generally*, European Commission, *Factsheet: The Opinion of the European Court of Justice on the EU-Singapore Trade Agreement and the Division of Competences in Trade Policy*, Sept. 2017, http://trade.ec.europa.eu/doclib/docs/2017/september/tradoc_156035.pdf.

[22] *Id.*

[23] European Commission, *Investment*, http://ec.europa.eu/trade/policy/accessing-markets/investment/ (last visited May 28, 2018).

[24] For background, *see* James Killick et al., *EU Court confirms EU competence on wide range of trade areas in onion on EU-Singapore FTA*, WHITE & CASE: May 17, 2017, https://www.whitecase.com/publications/alert/eu-court-confirms-eu-competence-wide-range-trade-areas-opinion-eu-singapore-fta.

[25] *See generally, e.g.*, European Commission, *Factsheet: The Opinion of the European Court of Justice on the EU-Singapore Trade Agreement and the Division of Competences in Trade Policy*, Sept. 2017, http://trade.ec.europa.eu/doclib/docs/2017/september/tradoc_156035.pdf.

[26] 2010 COM 343, 10, *Communication from the Commission to the Council, the European Parliament, the European Economic and Social Committee and the Committee of the Regions.*

individual member states.[27] In fact, in the wakes of the *Micula* decision, the EC specifically requested that states terminate all intra-EU BITS.[28] This change in posture by the EC has become problematic for many states and could also cause a stalemate between Poland and the rest of the Union due to Poland's refusal to join ICSID by signing the Washington Convention.[29] Instead, the EC would merely achieve the death of ISDS protections within the EU in the short term—a point argued by Wolfgang Alschner in a 2014 paper focused on consolidation versus contradiction.[30] However, since Alschner argued that point, ISDS has become increasingly politically toxic within the EU. Now any future ISDS provisions or agreements will require the recalcitrant Wallonia region, to give assent before entry into force. Indeed, the path forward on positive ISDS protections seems littered with political mines and virtually impossible to pass.[31]

2. September 2016 – the Gloves Come Off

In September 2016, the EC opted for a much more forward approach than a slow death when it notified Austria, Netherlands, Romania, Slovkia, and Sweden that their intra-EU BITs were "likely to create scenarios of illegal state aid under EU law."[32] The EC argued this was because the "special bilateral protections enjoyed by the citizens and companies of the signatory states" violated the TFEU.[33] Some, including the Centre for Economic Performance at LSE have argued this is a prominent issue for Brexit, as "it is likely that Brexit will have a negative impact on the UK's FDI" to the tune of reduced FDI inflows to the UK by "around 22" percent.[34] Indeed, while some authors are more sanguine about the future of third-country BITs after Brexit, the general trend leading up to *Achmea* does not provide a comforting picture for the UK's

---

[27] Catharine Titi, *International Investment Law and the European Union: Towards a New Generation of International Investment Agreements*, 26 EUR. J. INT'L. L. 639.

[28] European Commission, *Press Release: Commission asks Member States to terminate their intra-EU bilateral investment treaties*, June 18, 2015, available at http://europa.eu/rapid/press-release_IP-15-5198_en.htm.

[29] *List of Member States – ICSID/3*, WORLD BANK, https://icsid.worldbank.org-/en/Pages/icsiddocs/List-of-Member-States.aspx (last visited May 28, 2018).

[30] *See generally*, Wolfgang Alschner, *Regionalism and Overlap in Investment Treaty Law: Towards Consolidation or Contradiction?*, 17 J. INT'L. ECON. L. (2014) 271 (stating explicitly that "the EU seeks to avoid overlap altogether and instead starts EU investment relations with third countries on a clean slate by replacing existing BITs").

[31] *See, e.g.*, *Wallonia is adamantly blocking the EU's trade deal with Canada*, ECONOMIST, Oct. 22, 2016 (describing the protests in Wallonia).

[32] Adrian Jones et al., *Legal Considerations for the UKs Investment and Trade Treaties After Brexit*, CROWELL & MORING, May 20, 2017.

[33] *Id.*

[34] Dechert LLP, *Why Brexit is Not Bad News for UK Based Litigation*, DECHERT, December 2016.

post-Brexit position.[35] Thus, while many might have imagined that Brexit would provide the UK with a comparative advantage on investment and enforcement issues, timing will be everything as the EU continues to bring blow-dryers to an already melting ice sculpture.

IV. GOVERNING LAW BEFORE *ACHMEA*

While the *Singapore-FTA* decision did provide an instructive groundwork for both the EC as well as member states, one should keep in mind that the EC has been moving toward an increasingly integrated single market for years now.[36] Unified investment provisions and agreements would be a big step in that direction. That said, the EC will likely continue to prioritize invalidating all awards from a losing state to a winning investor within the EU. The *Micula* decision provided just that opportunity for the EC to step in, so they did.

A. MICULA *STATE AID DECISION*

For years, ICSID has been considered one of the most potent and durable investment tribunals, in great part because it provides enforceable and mutually cognizable awards.[37] It is just this type of "recognition and enforcement" that makes the organization such an attractive venue for investors hoping to recoup lost profits and investments.[38] The EC looked at this structure and certainly began to strategize how to take out this foundational pillar.[39] The issue presented itself in *Micula & Ors v. Romania & Anor* in January 2017.[40] The Miculas were Swedish investors who had made significant investments in

---

[35] *See, e.g.*, Jose-Ignacio Saldana, *A Snapshot of the Status of the UK's Bilateral Investment Treaties and the Related International Arbitration After Brexit*, 39 MICH. J. INT'L L., http://www.mjilonline.org/a-snapshot-of-the-status-of-the-uks-bilateral-investment-treaties-and-related-international-arbitration-after-brexit/#_ftn9.

[36] *See*, European Commission, *Internal Market, Industry, Entrepreneurship and SMEs: The Europena Single Market*, https://ec.europa.eu/growth/single-market_en (last visited May 28, 2018).

[37] World Bank, *Recognition and Enforcement – ICSID Convention Arbitration*, ICSID, https://icsid.worldbank.org/en/Pages/process/Recognition-and-Enforcement-Convention-Arbitration.aspx (last visited May 28, 2018).

[38] *Id. See also generally*, Katharina Diel-Gligor, *The Enforcement of ICSID Awards: Revolutionary or Ineffective?*, 15 AM. REV. INT'L ARB. 439 (2011) (discussing strengths and weaknesses of ICSID award enforcement).

[39] As one author has written, this also came at a time when the EC was ramping up efforts to take down investment arbitration through amicus curiae generally, but Micula provided an especial opportunity. *See generally*, Fernando Dias Simoes, *A Guardian and a Friend? The European Commission's Participation in Investment Arbitration*, 25 MICH. ST. INT'L L. REV. 233 (2017).

[40] In re Arbitration Act of 1966 [2017] EWHC 31 (Comm), [2017] Bus LR 1147, [2017] WLR(D) 35.

Romania.[41] The arbitral body found in favor of the Miculas and awarded approximately $116 million (USD)[42] to the investors for a violation of fair and equitable treatment and a failure to render a minimum standard of treatment—including denial of justice.[43] Annulment proceedings were filed, and on February 26, 2016, the ICSID annulment panel upheld the award.[44] Everything appeared to be going according to plan for the Miculas.

All of that was until the EC decided to get involved. As two authors have noted, the EC saw in Micula a particularly good opportunity to target ISDS between two EU member states.[45] On March 30, 2015, the EC issued a Final Decision[46] barring payment of the award because it would constitute State aid within the definition provided by Article 107(1) of the Treaty on the Functioning of the European Union (TFEU).[47] The Miculas appealed the decision in the UK and argued for *res judicata*—requesting that the terms of the 1966 Act be enforced to require Romania to pay out the remainder of the reward.[48] The UK court found difficulty applying any such decision without review by the CJEU; therefore, the court ultimately stayed the award and submitted the case to the CJEU.[49]

While the *Micula* case remains pending before the CJEU, the Miculas have failed to recoup on their multi-million dollar investment from nearly a decade ago in a former soviet state. The case has become a touchstone for the ISDS enforcement turmoil within the EU.[50] *Micula* has also sent shockwaves throughout the investor communities, with one author noting that "the application of the ICSID Convention within the EU [has become] seriously endangered by the EC."[51] Other authors have

---

[41] *See generally*, *Id.*

[42] Note, after awards of legal and panel fees, the total award is around $250 million USD. *See* Alejandro I. Garcia & Herbert Smith Freehills, *Breach of Fair and Equitable Treatment Standard (ICSID)*, THOMPSON REUTERS (Jan. 15, 2014).

[43] *Investment Dispute Settlement: Micula v. Romania*, INVESTMENT POLICY HUB, http://investmentpolicyhub.unctad.org/ISDS/Details/180 (last visited May 28, 2018)

[44] *Id.*

[45] *See* Daniele Gallo & Fernanda Nicola, *The External Dimensions of EU Investment Law: Jurisdictional Clashes and Transformative Adjudication*, 39 FORDHAM INT'L L.J. 1081, 1108-10 (2016)

[46] 2015 O.J. (L. 1470) 43.

[47] 2012 O.J. (L. 326) 47.

[48] *See* In re Arbitration Act of 1966 [2017] EWHC 31 (Comm), [2017] Bus LR 1147, [2017] WLR(D) 35.

[49] *Id.* While this is a complex and important decision, this chapter does not give it any more treatment due to a limitation on space.

[50] *See generally*, Monique Govens, *The Micula Case: When ISDS Messes with EU Law*, BEUC, Oct. 27, 2014 (presenting an informative narrative on this perspective).

[51] Nikos Lavranos, *A new Micula-type case on the horizon?*, ISDS PLATFORM, Jan. 25, 2018, https://isds.bilaterals.org/?a-new-micula-type-case-on-the.

even opined about the dangers the *Micula* decision creates within U.S. courts.[52]

B. THE UK'S THREE CASES UNDER THE UK-CZECH REPUBLIC BIT

All of this might seem academic at this point, especially since the CJEU has yet to rule on the *Micula* case, but the fact that things are so much in motion should matter that much more to the UK as they continue to negotiate their exit and continued relationship with the EU. The UK needs to ensure that it has clarity on the future of intra-EU, as well as external, third-country BITs.

There is another, more immediate reason for the UK to be concerned with the growing riptide against ISDS: there are three pending cases under the UK-Czech Republic BIT.[53] Those three cases were all objected to by the Czech Republic for purposes of jurisdiction.[54] In each of the three cases, the Czech Republic argued that the BIT was illegal because it conflicted with EU law.[55] The arbitral tribunals in each of the cases disagreed with this argument and found that the BIT and the EU treaties "did not cover the same subject matter."[56] This was important because under Article 59 of the Vienna Convention on the Law of Treaties (VCLT) it meant that the more recently agreed upon treaty (the EU treaty) could not overrule the older treaty (UK-Czech BIT).[57] But as the *Micula* decision shows, the findings by the arbitral panel may be irrelevant now, as many investors may find it impossible to recover their losses.

In fact, in the *WNC Factoring* case, the tribunal noted just this, "concluding their analysis on the EU law argument by recognizing that EU law may shift" as the EC and the CJEU continue to rule on these issues.[58] In short, tribunals within the EU are faced with the daunting issue of no longer holding gravity, sway, or retaining finality in their decisions. Additionally, the interoperability of awards among ICSID

---

52 *See generally, e.g.*, Abby Cohen Smutny et al., *Enforcement of ICSID Convention Arbitral Awards in U.S. Courts*, 43 PEPP. L. REV. 649, 659-665; *see also*, James Berger & Charlene Sun, *Rift Among US Courts In Enforcing Int'l Arbitration Awards*, Law360 Aug. 20, 2015.

53 WNC Factoring Ltd v. The Czech Republic (PCA Case No. 2014-34); I.P. Busta & J.P. Busta v. The Czech Republic (SCC V 2015/014); and Anglia Auto Accessories Limited v. The Czech Republic (SCC V 2014/181).

54 *Id.*

55 Angeline Welsh, *Grappling with Jurisdictional Issues under the UK-Czech Republic BIT*, LEXIS PSL ARB., May 8, 2017.

56 *Id.*

57 *Id.*

58 *Id.*

signatories may also be a in jeopardy as other states begin to either look on with concern or interest.[59]

V. VIEWS ON HOW THE CJEU'S DECISIONS MIGHT AFFECT BREXIT NEGOTIATIONS

Micula has since become a turning point, according to many authors, for the EU.[60] Furthermore, the time between the *Micula* and *Achmea* decisions has been transformative and is very important to understand before analyzing *Achmea*. Because *Achmea* was so recently decided, it is also critical to analyze what many scholars and practitioners had written on the subject of intra-EU BITS, especially with regard to Brexit. This body of literature, though still limited, provides important insight into how earth-shattering the *Achmea* decision truly is.

A. *INITIAL CONCERNS AND LOOKING FORWARD, BEYOND THE EU*

From the moment the UK referendum on Brexit was passed, academics and legal practitioners have been contemplating and opining on the meaning of Brexit for the UK and the EU's BITs going forward.[61] Much of the initial concern has been with regard to the EU's ongoing treaties with Brazil, Russia, India, China, South Africa, Singapore, Malaysia, Indonesia, and Mexico.[62] All of these FTAs, with the notable exception of Singapore (see above) were concluded prior to the entry into force of the Lisbon Treaty in 2009.[63] Thus, both the longevity of the ISDS provision of those treaties within the EU as well as the transferability to the UK after Brexit are deeply concerning to many.[64] This is important for the UK to consider, because if it wishes to make a new trade agreement with the EU, it will need to think seriously about the durability of any ISDS provisions—and that is still assuming the UK can get EU-wide agreement on the position despite intractable voters in Wallonia.

---

[59] *See* James Berger & Charlene Sun, *Rift Among US Courts In Enforcing Int'l Arbitration Awards*, Law360 Aug. 20, 2015 (noting the interest of some U.S. Court in applying these same rules).

[60] *See generally, e.g.*, Dominik Moskvan, The Clas of Intra-EU Bilateral Investment Treaties with EU Law: A Bitter Pill to Swallow, 22 COLUM. J. EUR. L. 101.

[61] See, e.g., James Rogers, Simon Goodall & Cara Dowling, *Brexit and investor-state dispute settlement*, NORTON ROSE FULBRIGHT, June 2017.

[62] Aidan O'Neill, *Brexit, Bits, and Enforcement*, MATRIX CHAMBERS 2.

[63] *Id.*

[64] *See, e.g.*, *Id.*

B. *THE UK'S INTENTIONS POST-BREXIT*

While the stated intention of the UK government is to keep many of the rules and regulations—and even political opinions—of the EU, several authors have noted the UK's intent to retain ISDS.[65] These thoughts and opinions are critical because the draft withdrawal bill[66] fails to treat BITs going forward, and the Title III on dispute settlement provides no language on investment disputes.[67] Not everyone in the UK is happy about this perspective, and some have voiced their concerns loudly because the UK will be forced to renegotiate many of the trade deals it had while in the EU.[68] That said, much of this analysis—from both sides—assumes that the UK is able to make this determination on its own before an intra-EU BIT wipeout. That is why, as some have argued, the UK should continue to seriously entertain the option of an expedited exit.[69] While considered a poor option for many other issues, it may be legitimate here given the EC's push to invalidate the UK's intra-EU BITs specifically.[70]

C. *THE RAIN CLOUD, FOLLOWING LIKE A SHADOW*

Any desire to leave expeditiously to protect current intra-EU BITs post-Brexit should be met with the harsh awakening to the current authority the EU retains over the UK. The depth and breadth of long-standing agreement regarding the importance of investor protections has not meant much to the EC or the CJEU; in fact, neither has written much about the estimated 190 intra-EU BITs other than to argue for their demise.[71] One author, Dr. Lavranos, the Secretary General of the European Federation for Investment Law and Arbitration, has stated this worry specifically.[72] He posits that the UK post-Brexit cannot simply

---

[65] *See, e.g.*, Phillip Inman, *Voting for Brexit Hasn't Saved Us From Secretive Trade Deals*, OBSERVER (Feb. 4, 2017).

[66] *See generally*, TF50 (2018) 33 – Commission to EU 27, Draft Withdrawal Agreement, 28 Feb. 2018.

[67] However, it should be noted that Title III Article 14 technically addresses financial investments, but the current language really only addresses fraud. *Id.*

[68] Swati Dhingra and Thomas Sampson, *Life After BREXIT: What are the UK's options outside the European Union*, CTR. ECON. PERFORMANCE, 10, Feb. 2016.

[69] Sophie Nappert & Nikos Lavranos, *BREXIT: Implications for the EU Reform of ISDS*, PRACTICAL L., 2, Oct. 15, 2016.

[70] *Brexit Bonanza, Lawyers encouraging corporations to sue UK & EU member states*, CORPORATE EUROPE OBSERVATORY, Sept. 25, 2017, https://corporateeurope.org/international-trade/2017/09/brexit-bonanza-lawyers-encouraging-corporations-sue-uk-eu-member-states (due to the potential "bonanza" of claims facilitated through the UK after Brexit).

[71] Cecilia Olivet, Intra-EU Bilateral Investment Treaties, TRANSLAT'L INST., Feb. 1, 2013.

[72] Nikos Lavranos, *UK Post-Brexit Cannot Escape the Impact of EU Law and of the Court of Justice of the EU*, EFILA BLOG, https://efilablog.org/2017/09/26/uk-post-brexit-

ignore the impact of EU law as well as the continued pressure from the CJEU.[73] Dr. Lavranos also specifically notes that the impact of both the *Achmea* and *Micula* decisions—both still pending when he wrote his paper—would likely be significant.[74]

Another issue he highlights is the pending Wallonia questions submitted to the CJEU on the Investment Court System (ICS) and its compatibility with EU law under CETA.[75] That system is a fundamental piece of CETA and could put other trade agreements in jeopardy—such as the EU's FTA with Vietnam.[76] It also would rob the most likely avenue for a continued investment protection regime in a future trade agreement with the UK post-Brexit, and, potentially even worse, the decision could invalidate the ICS after the UK has already left the EU, causing even more disillusionment and uproar with the investment system in the EU.[77] Dr. Lavranos concludes by stating that the UK needs "a reality check" as it continues with the Brexit negotiations—a check that will require great attention to both the trend and positions of the CJEU and EC.[78]

VI. FACTUAL BACKGROUND ON THE *ACHMEA* CASE

As with any investment tribunal case, the background is key in understanding both the panel and the final rulings. Furthermore, it is important to understand the various options that were available to the CJEU, the positions of the parties, and the suggested legal analysis provided by the Advocate General.

A. *BACKGROUND*

Dutch insurer Eureko (later renamed Achmea) brought proceedings against Slovakia in 2008 on the basis that Slovakia had violated the substantive treaty standards under the Netherlands-Slovakia BIT.[79] The complaint arose when Slovakia renationalized their health system, which Eureko claimed caused an indirect expropriation of Eureko's Slovak insurance business.[80] The arbitral panel agreed with Eureko and required

cannot-escape-the-impact-of-eu-law-and-of-the-court-of-justice-of-the-eu/(Sept. 26, 2017).

[73] *Id.*

[74] *Id.*

[75] *Id.*

[76] *Id.*

[77] *Id.*

[78] *Id.*

[79] Global Investment Protection, *Intra-EU BITs Before the Court of Justice of the EU*, http://www.globalinvestmentprotection.com/2016/05/24/intra-eu-bits-before-the-court-of-justice-of-the-eu/ (last visited May 29, 2018).

[80] *Id.*

Slovakia to pay damages.[81] A final award of €22.1 million was rendered by the ad-hoc arbitral tribunal constituted under the UNCITRAL rules in Frankfurt, Germany.[82]

B. SET-ASIDE PROCEEDINGS IN GERMANY

As with any arbitral decision under the UNCITRAL rules, Slovakia was able to assert its rights to set-aside the award.[83] In those proceedings before the German lower court, Slovakia claimed that its accession to the EU in 2004 superseded the commitments it had made in the Netherlands-Slovakia BIT.[84] It referenced three different provisions within the TFEU—Articles 344, 267, and 18—as grounds for the illegality of the BIT. Because these claims are addressed at length below, it suffices to say that the Frankfurt Regional Court rejected the annulment claim by Slovakia.[85] Slovakia then appealed the decision to the Bundesgerichtshof—Federal Supreme Court (BGH) in Karlsruhe—which stayed the proceedings and submitted three preliminary questions to the CJEU on the basis of Articles 344, 267, and 18 of the TFEU.[86]

C. TFEU PROVISIONS IN CONTENTION:

Because the premise of Slovakia's position rested on the interpretation of the TFEU, the BGH was legally barred from interpreting the TFEU. As such, the BGH referred the three main questions on interpretation of Articles 344, 267, and 18 to the CJEU.

1. Article 344

As interpreted by the BGH, the premise of Article 344 of the TFEU is to mandate that all disputes between Member States be referred directly and exclusively to the CJEU.[87] The language of the provision specifies that the "interpretation or application of the Treaties to any method of settlement" outside of the settlement methods provided

---

[81] *Achmea B.V. v. The Slovak Republic* ICSID Case No. 2008-13 (2012).

[82] Clement Fouchard & Marc Krestin, *The Judgement of the CJEU in Slovak Republic v. Achmea – A Loud Clap of Thunder on the Intra-EU BIT Sky!*, KLUWER ARB. BLOG, Mar. 7, 2018.

[83] Oberlandsgericht [OLG] Dec. 18, 2014, BGH – AZ | ZB 2/15 (Ger.) available at https://www.italaw.com/sites/default/files/case-documents/italaw7079.pdf.

[84] Global Investment Protection, *Intra-EU BITs Before the Court of Justice of the EU*, http://www.globalinvestmentprotection.com/2016/05/24/intra-eu-bits-before-the-court-of-justice-of-the-eu/ (last visited May 29, 2018).

[85] *Id.*

[86] Bundesgerichtshof [BGH] [Federal Court of Justice] Mar. 3, 2016, (Ger.) available at http://juris.bundesgerichtshof.de/cgi-bin/rechtsprechung/document.py?Gericht=bgh&Art=en&client=12&nr=74612&pos=0&anz=1&Blank=1.pdf.

[87] TFEU Article 344 (2012 O.J. (L. 326) 194).

under the TFEU.[88] Slovakia and the EC had been pushing the envelope on this language, arguing that while the language only specifies the member states, it should also apply to disputes between an investor of one state with another member state.[89] The BGH reasoned with the lower court and believed the award should be enforced; however, the BGH felt it necessary to seek confirmation from the CJEU.[90]

2. Article 267

Article 267 requires that national courts refer questions on the EU governing treaties and application of law to the CJEU.[91] It provides, in part, that the CJEU "shall have jurisdiction to give preliminary rulings" regarding the "interpretation of the Treaties."[92] The BGH referred this question to the CJEU to help ensure uniformity where there are difficult questions, such as the interpretation of Article 344 to ISDS as there was here.[93] This would really only come into play, the BGH argued, if the CJEU answered their first question on Article 344 in the negative.[94] The reason for this is because the CJEU has typically not viewed arbitral panels as courts under the definition of the TFEU; therefore, in order to ensure that Article 267 is interpreted by tribunals on a going-forward-basis correctly, the BGH asked this question.[95] Because the BGH agreed with the lower court and did not see Article 344 as an impediment, nor did it view Article 267 as a roadblock for tribunals, it saw no ongoing concern for tribunals to render ISDS judgements but felt it was important for the CJEU to clarify the law in this area.[96]

3. Article 18

Finally, the BGH asked the CJEU to answer a question with regard to Article 18, but only if the first two questions on 344 and 267 were

---

88 *Id.*

89 Global Investment Protection, *Intra-EU BITs Before the Court of Justice of the EU*, http://www.globalinvestmentprotection.com/2016/05/24/intra-eu-bits-before-the-court-of-justice-of-the-eu/ (last visited May 29, 2018).

90 *Id.*

91 TFEU Article 344.

92 *Id.*

93 Global Investment Protection, *Intra-EU BITs Before the Court of Justice of the EU*, http://www.globalinvestmentprotection.com/2016/05/24/intra-eu-bits-before-the-court-of-justice-of-the-eu/ (last visited May 29, 2018).

94 Bundesgerichtshof [BGH] [Federal Court of Justice] Mar. 3, 2016, (Ger.) available at http://juris.bundesgerichtshof.de/cgi-bin/rechtsprechung/document.py?Gericht=bgh&Art=en&client=12&nr=74612&pos=0&anz=1&Blank=1.pdf.

95 Global Investment Protection, *Intra-EU BITs Before the Court of Justice of the EU*, http://www.globalinvestmentprotection.com/2016/05/24/intra-eu-bits-before-the-court-of-justice-of-the-eu/ (last visited May 29, 2018).

96 *Id.*

returned negatively.[97] Article 18 explicitly prohibits discrimination based on nationality.[98] Because Slovakia and the EC had argued that a BIT grants the "right to use investment arbitration only to the nationals of the states," it provided a privileged, discriminatory benefit to the citizens of only specific nationalities.[99] This was the one area the BGH ceded some ground on but argued that while it may be discrimination, that could easily be prevented so long as the nationality provisions within the BITs were interpreted to apply to EU citizens generally and not nationals of a specifically related member state.[100]

D. THE ADVOCATE GENERAL'S OPINION

When a case is referred to the CJEU, an Advocate General is assigned to the case to render a legal opinion that will aid the court's decision.[101] In this case, a former judge on the CJEU, Advocate General (AG) Wathelet was appointed.[102] In his analysis, AG Wathelet reasoned that the ISDS "mechanisms in bilateral investment agreement between EU Member States… are compatible with the EU legal system."[103] AG Wathelet arrived at this conclusion by working backward, starting with Article 18, which he argued applied to intra-EU BITs with language like the Netherlands-Slovakia BIT (Art. 8) much like bilateral double taxation treaties, and are therefore compatible with EU law.[104] He then proceeded to explain that Article 267 is not violated because the tribunals can be considered courts of the member states.[105] Finally, AG Wathelet argued

---

[97] *Id.*
[98] TFEU Article 18 (2012 O.J. (L. 326) 56).
[99] Global Investment Protection, *Intra-EU BITs Before the Court of Justice of the EU*, http://www.globalinvestmentprotection.com/2016/05/24/intra-eu-bits-before-the-court-of-justice-of-the-eu/ (last visited May 29, 2018).
[100] Bundesgerichtshof [BGH] [Federal Court of Justice] Mar. 3, 2016, (Ger.) available at http://juris.bundesgerichtshof.de/cgi-bin/rechtsprechung/document.py?Gericht=bgh&Art=en&client=12&nr=74612&pos=0&anz=1&Blank=1.pdf.
[101] Opinion of Advocate General, Case C-284/16, Sept. 19, 2017.
[102] TFEU Article 18 (2012 O.J. (L. 326) 56).
[103] Advocate General of the European Court of Justice issues opinion on compatibility of intra-EU investor-State dispute resolution with EU law, FIETTA LLP, http://www.fiettalaw.com/pil_news/advocate-general-of-the-european-court-of-justice-issues-opinion-on-compatibility-of-intra-eu-investor-state-dispute-resolution-with-eu-law/ (last visited May 29, 2018) citing TFEU Article 18 (2012 O.J. (L. 326) 56).
[104] Ivaylo Dimitrov, Digesting the AG Wathelet Opinion in Case C-284/16 Slowakische Republik v. Achmea BV Is it a Trap?, KLUWER ARB. BLOG, Oct. 7, 2017, http://arbitrationblog.kluwerarbitration.com/2017/10/07/digesting-ag-wathelet-opinion-case-c-28416-slowakische-republik-v-achmea-bv-trap/.
[105] *Id.*

that Article 344 was not violated because ISDS disputes "do not concern the interpretation or application of the EU treaties."[106]

VII. THE CJEU'S DECISION IN *ACHMEA*

Before even getting to the questions of the BGH, the CJEU sent a signal flare up that would highlight the general trend readily apparent in the rest of the case: EU law is characterized by the fact that it comes from the governing treaties, and those treaties always supersede the national laws and treaties of the individual member states.[107] The rest of the opinion is rather brief and to the point, and the EU wastes no time essentially adjoining itself to the opinions of Slovakia and the EC.[108] The CJEU did this by grouping the questions under Articles 267 and 344 together, first noting that no arbitral tribunal can ever be considered or classified as a court of a member state within the meaning of Article 267.[109] The court then went on to explain that while future rulings, such as set-aside proceedings or enforcements of awards, could be considered under the jurisdiction of EU courts vis-à-vis Articles 344 and 267, the operative part of the tribunal, which often must look to EU law and regulation, fails to meet the necessary requirements.[110] Therefore, any ISDS tribunal established pursuant to the Netherlands-Slovakia BIT cannot accurately opine as to EU law.[111] This statement has been considered by many to be the true "thunderclap" of the decision.[112]

VIII. IMPLICATIONS FOR THE UK

While volumes could be written on the implications of *Achmea* within the EU, the focus of this chapter is on how this decision will affect the UK before, during, and after Brexit. Because the UK has 13 intra-EU BITs, there is a significant risk that many of those same ISDS provisions might be tossed into the furnace with the Netherlands-Slovakia BIT, and while the *Micula* decision might at least explain to investors what they can expect down the line, *Achmea* may cause immediate distortions for the UK. Those distortions are likely bound to grow, however, as the UK is currently on track to continue applying the EU's rules—notably new

---

106 *Id.*

107 Case C-284/16, Slovak Republic v. Achmea BV, 2018 E.C.L.I. 158.

108 *See* Szilárd Gáspár Szilágyi, The CJEU Strikes Again in Achmea. Is This the End of Investor-State Arbitration under Intra-EU BITs?, IELP Blog, Mar. 7, 2018, https://isds.bilaterals.org/?the-cjeu-strikes-again-in-achmea.

109 Case C-284/16, Slovak Republic v. Achmea BV, 2018 E.C.L.I. 158.

110 *Id.*

111 *Id.*

112 Clement Fouchard & Marc Krestin, *The Judgement of the CJEU in Slovak Republic v. Achmea – A Loud Clap of Thunder on the Intra-EU BIT Sky!*, KLUWER ARB. BLOG, Mar. 7, 2018.

CJEU rulings—while negotiating a going-forward agreement after withdrawal.

A. *THE PROBLEM OF TRANSITION FOR THE UK*

The problem for the UK is that it will be in a "transition period" of at least two years,[113] and because the EU is likely to be reluctant to allow the UK continued access to the EU market without compliance to CJEU decisions, the UK is attached directly to the *Achmea* decision and will be forced to comply with the now-looming *Micula* decision. Depending on what happens during that period of time, it is also likely to taint the negotiations for the UK-EU "bespoke" agreement.[114] Additionally, the UK must remember that it has long been a staunch advocate for free trade within the EU; thus, when the UK finally retreats into its transition period, it will likely no longer have a voice in the EU decision-making process. Yet, the UK will still be forced to apply the decisions and rulings until a going-forward agreement is reached.[115] In fact, some have argued this would be a perfect opportunity for the EU to "punish" the UK either in regulation or through reduced market access in order to discourage other member states from exiting the union.[116]

B. *PUNISHMENT AND THE CHANCES OF KILLING THE UK'S INTRA-EU BITS FOREVER*

Perhaps the biggest worry for the UK should be that as part of this "punishment," the EC may be able to convince other member states to wholly invalidate all intra-EU BITs. After all, several other states, especially former Soviet-states like Slovakia, have a vested interest in this area, as do others like Spain—who has recently seen a swath of ISDS tribunal requests.[117] In the end, if those political forces are able to rally a sufficient number of other member states to their cause, the group could invalidate all of the UK's intra-EU BITs before they are able to escape the EC and CJEU's authority, and if the UK is forced to cancel its intra-EU BITs during this period of time, it will be virtually impossible to resurrect them due to all of the problems outlined above.

---

113 *See generally*, Aidan O'Neill, *Brexit, Bits, and Enforcement*, MATRIX CHAMBERS 2.

114 Svenja O'Donnell, *May Insists on 'Bespoke' Trade Deal in Face of EU's Rebuttal*, BLOOMBERG, Dec. 19, 2017.

115 *Id.*

116 Silva Amaro, *Many in Europe Wish to Punish the UK for Leaving the EU, Says Luxembourg Finance Minister*, CNBC, Jan. 24, 2018.

117 Anne-Karin Grill & Sebastian Lukic, *Towards a Post-Arbitration Age: The European Commission's Fast-Track Reform of Investment Dispute Settlement*, KLUWER ARB. BLOG, Dec. 11, 2017, http://arbitrationblog.kluwerarbitration.com/2017/12/11/towards-post-arbitration-age-european-commissions-fast-track-reform-investment-dispute-settlement./

IX. CONCLUSION: THE UK'S MOST PALATABLE OPTIONS

While the period of transition will certainly be fraught with concerns, issues, and worries for the UK, the Brexiteers should be thinking and strategizing on their various paths forward. While a "hard" versus "soft" Brexit will certainly implicate ISDS options afterward, this important sector of investment may be a large enough issue for the UK to strategize around, instead of adding it in at the end.[118] And no matter how "flimsy" the CJEU's decision may be legally, the UK should consistently keep in mind the power the court has to drive policy.[119]

A. KEEPING THE CURRENT ROAD

Regardless of how the transition period looks—and inferring that the BITs themselves stay at least formally intact—the UK will need to start thinking about how they are going to negotiate with the EU on a look-forward basis. Because the member states do not have competence to negotiate trade agreements, the UK will be forced to continue with its current trade agreements.

B. TAKING THE HIGH ROAD

In the event that the UK is forced to invalidate its BITs, or, on the other hand, should they feel so inclined as to negotiate with the EU, there is one major benefit they could receive. Namely, the UK would be able to have a BIT with other western European countries, such as Spain. The terms would likely be less favorable than their current BITs; however, such an agreement would be far more inclusive, and it would make the EU happy—at least for now. Therefore, this could be seen as a major piece of leverage the UK has over the EU in its Brexit negotiations.

C. FINAL NOTE: LOOMING DANGER

Even if the UK makes it through the transition period with its Intra-EU BITs still alive, future arbitral decisions could just as easily be invalidated by the CJEU. Given the Court's willingness to invalidate the tribunal's findings in *Achmea*, the UK should anticipate that any future case before the CJEU could easily invalidate all BITs with the UK. This essentially means that the UK must think strategically, as it can use its decades of experience within the EU to structure and facilitate a durable

---

[118] *Brexit: What Are the Options?*, BBC, last updated Jun. 12, 2017, http://www.-bbc.com/news/uk-politics-37507129.

[119] Philippe Pinsolle & Isabelle Michou, *Arbitration: The Achmea v. Sloviakia Judgement of the CJEU, is it really the end of the Intra-EU Investment Treaties?*, DALLOZ-ACTUALITE, Mar. 7, 2018, English available at https://www.quinnemanuel.com/media/1418711/the-achmea-judgement-ending-intra-eu-investment-treaties.pdf.

and reliable investment review and enforcement body. Because of this specific complexity, the UK has a significant amount of leverage and knowledge it can use to springboard investment from the rest of the world into the EU, especially into the former Soviet states. As such, at least in this one respect, Brexit may still provide a hopeful opportunity to the UK that no other country would have a comparable opportunity to enjoy.

CHAPTER 9: BREXIT AND THE EU-US BEEF HORMONES DISPUTE: HOW THE UK CAN MAINTAIN THE IMPORT BAN ON HORMONE-TREATED BEEF FROM THE US

YASUTAKA TSUJI

I. INTRODUCTION

The European Union (EU) and the United States (US) have engaged in a long-standing dispute over the EU's decision to ban hormone-treated meat. A series of dispute settlement proceedings and decisions in the World Trade Organization (WTO) is still ongoing. Currently, the parties are implementing the "Memorandum of Understanding" (MOU), which tries to resolve the dispute in phases. This chapter explores the impact of Brexit on the dispute, including the timing of the imposition of the EU import ban on the United Kingdom (UK), whether the UK will maintain the import ban, and whether the MOU still applies to the UK after the Brexit. Then this chapter discusses how the UK can roll over the MOU with the US, what the procedural and substantive risks are for the UK in the new MOU negotiation, and what the UK should do to avoid the risk. This chapter also focuses on the UK's status during the transition period regarding the implementation of the import ban, application of the MOU, and the UK's ability to negotiate with the US, based on the current draft of the Withdrawal Agreement between the UK and the EU.

This section provides a brief overview of the Beef Hormones dispute, focusing on the UK's position within the dispute and what the EU and the US have agreed to in the MOU. Then the section reviews the current status of the Brexit negotiation between the UK and the EU.

II. BEEF HORMONE DISPUTES IN THE WTO

Since the EU imposed an import ban on hormone-treated beef in 1980's, the US has repeatedly imposed retaliatory tariffs on EU products. The EU import ban and the US retaliation was disputed in the WTO twice, but the parties failed to settle the dispute. The UK has taken part in the EU import ban, but the UK has uniquely been an opponent of the ban within the EU. The timeline below provides a brief overview of the history of the dispute. This timeline helps readers who are not familiar with the issue understand the history and current status of the issue.[1]

Timeline of the EU-US Beef Hormones Dispute

A. *USE OF GROWTH HORMONE IN MEAT PRODUCTION*

Growth-promoting hormones are used widely in beef production in the US and in other meat-exporting countries because they allow animals to grow larger and more quickly on less feed and fewer other inputs, thus reducing production costs, but also because they produce a leaner carcass

[1] Source of the timeline: Renée Johnson, Cong. Research Serv., R40449, The US.-EU Beef Hormone Dispute, (Jan. 14, 2015).

more in line with consumer preferences for diets with reduced fat and cholesterol.[2] Growth-promoting hormones include compounds that either naturally occur in an animal's body or mimic naturally occurring compounds. Estradiol, progesterone, and testosterone (three natural hormones), and zeranol and trenbolone acetate (two synthetic hormones), are absorbed through an implant on the animal's ear.[3]

B. EU IMPORT BAN ON HORMONE-TREATED BEEF

The European Commission (EC) enacted its ban on both the production and importation of meat derived from animals treated with growth-promoting hormones in the early 1980s.[4] This ban restricts the use of natural hormones to therapeutic purposes, bans the use of synthetic hormones, and prohibits imports of animals and meat from animals that have been administered the hormones.[5] The commission has justified its ban as necessary to protect consumer health and safety.[6] This position initially evolved, in part, as a reaction to reports in the 1970s over the illegal use of dethylstilboestrol in veal production in France, and consumer concerns that this was linked to reports of hormonal irregularities in Italian adolescents.[7] These events contributed to a general climate in Europe that was suspicious of the use of hormones in livestock production.[8]

C. EC-HORMONES CASE (WTO DS 26)

In response to the EU's initial ban on hormone-treated meat in the 1980s, the US first invoked the General Agreement on Tariffs and Trade (GATT) dispute settlement process in 1986-1987 under the Tokyo Round's Technical Barriers to Trade Agreement, and also threatened to implement retaliatory tariffs on selected EU imports.[9] This action delayed full implementation of the EU ban until January 1, 1989. Once the ban was implemented, the US instituted retaliatory tariffs (100% ad

---

[2] Johnson, at page 1, citing National Cattlemen's Beef Association (NCBA), "Fact Sheet: Growth Promotant Use in Cattle Production."

[3] Johnson, at page 1, citing USDA, Food Safety and Inspection Service, "Beef ... from Farm to Table." The implanted hormone is time-released and is effective for 90 to 120 days.

[4] Johnson, at page 2, citing Council Directives 81/602 (July 1981), 88/146 (7 March 1988), 88/299 (17 May 1988).

[5] *Id.*

[6] Johnson, at page 2.

[7] *Id.*

[8] *Id.* at page 3.

[9] *Id.* at page 5.

valorem) on EU imports valued at $93 million, which stayed in effect until May 1996.[10] Earlier in 1996, both the US and the EU had separately requested WTO consultations in an attempt to resolve the dispute.[11]

In August 1997, the WTO dispute settlement panel released its report agreeing with the US that the ban violated several provisions of the WTO Sanitary and Phytosanitary (SPS) Agreement.[12] Specifically, the EU ban was found to violate SPS requirements that such measures:

- be based on international standards, guidelines or recommendations (Article 3.1);
- be based on a risk assessment and take into account risk assessment techniques developed by the relevant international organizations (Article 5.1); and
- avoid arbitrary or unjustifiable distinctions that result in discrimination or a disguised restriction on international trade (Article 5.5).[13]

The EU appealed the ruling, and in February 1998, the WTO Appellate Body found that the EU ban did contravene the EU's obligations under the SPS Agreement, but left open the option for the EU to conduct a risk assessment of hormone-treated meat.[14] A WTO arbitration panel ruled subsequently that 15 months from the date of the decision (i.e., May 13, 1999) would be a reasonable period of time for the EU to conduct its assessment.[15] However, the EU did not complete its scientific review by the May 1999 deadline. Nevertheless, the EU decided not to consider removing the ban before conducting the additional review. This led the way for the US to retaliate by imposing its current trade sanctions against US imports of EU products starting in July 1999, with its retaliatory tariffs (100% ad valorem) on EU imports valued at about $116.8 million per year as authorized by the WTO arbitrators.[16]

---

10 *Id.*

11 *Id.*

12 *Id.*

13 *Id.*, citing Panel Report, *EC Measures Concerning Meat and Meat Products (EC-Hormones)*, WTO Doc. WT/DS26/R/USA (adopted Aug. 18, 1997) at paras. 8.74-81, 8.162, 8.248.

14 Appellate Body Report, *EC-Hormones*, WTO Doc. WT/DS26/AB/R ; WT/DS48/AB/R (adopted Jan. 16, 1998) at paras. 2.245-246.

15 Johnson, at page 5.

16 Johnson, at pages 5, 11.

D. UK OBJECTION TO THE IMPORT BAN

The UK has opposed the EU import ban since 1996.[17] In 1999, the commission voted unanimously to continue its ban, with only the Agriculture Minister of the UK voting to end the ban.[18] The UK's position is based on 1999 and 2006 Veterinary Products Committee reports produced by UK's independent experts committee. The UK committee concluded that the scientific evidence in the European scientific committee on veterinary measures relating to public health (SCVPH) report did not support the EU's ban on the use of hormonal growth promoters.[19] To present, the Agriculture Minister of the UK repeatedly announced the UK's objection to the import ban and communicated the UK's support to US position against the import ban.[20] As a result, the UK has been exempt from the retaliatory tariff by the US, both in the initial retaliatory tariff imposed in 1999 and the increased retaliatory tariff proposed in 2009.[21]

E. US-CONTINUED SUSPENSION CASE (WTO DS 320)

In 2003, the EU announced that its scientific review had concluded that estradiol-17β was carcinogenic and that the current state of knowledge did not make it possible for the five other hormones to provide a quantitative assessment of their risks to consumers.[22] Accordingly, in 2003, the EU issued a new directive and revised its ban to permanently ban estradiol-17β and provisionally ban the five other hormones.[23] The EU claims the decision to provisionally ban the five other hormones is necessary while the European Commission seeks more complete scientific information.[24] The EU claims that its actions replacing its original ban with a provisional ban comply with its WTO obligations under Article 5.7 of the SPS Agreement.[25] US trade and veterinary officials have repeatedly rejected the EU studies, claiming that

---

17 The Guardian, *UK resists ban on beef hormones* (Mar. 16, 1996), The Guardian, *Britain overruled as EU tightens hormone-beef ban* (May. 19, 1996).

18 Johnson, at page 4.

19 UK's Veterinary Products Committee, *VPC Report - Risk Associated with the Use of Hormonal Substances in Food Producing Animals*, July 2006, and *Sub Group on Hormonal Growth Promoters*, October 1999.

20 Joe Watson, *UK says hormone-treated beef is safe to eat, but it remains banned* (Jul. 6, 2006), The Guardian, *Policy and Politics: Brown backs US on hormone beef* (Jun. 12, 2000), The Guardian, *UK escapes beef retaliation* (Jul. 20, 1999).

21 64 Fed. Reg. 40,638 (Jul. 27, 1999), 74 Fed. Reg. 4,265 (Jan. 23, 2009).

22 Johnson, at page 5.

23 *Id.* at page 6.

24 *Id.*

25 *Id.*

the scientific evidence is not new information nor does it establish a risk to consumers from eating hormone-treated meat.[26]

Claiming that its ban is justified and in compliance with its WTO obligations, the EU has continued to initiate counteractions against the US (and Canada), stating that there is no longer a legal basis for the US to impose trade sanctions against the European Union.[27] In 2005, the EU initiated new WTO dispute settlement proceedings against the US and Canada.[28] The March 2008 Panel report cited fault with all three parties (EU, US, and Canada) on various substantive and procedural aspects of the dispute.[29] The Panel found that the EU had not presented sufficient scientific evidence to justify the import ban, including the EU's 2003 risk assessment report.[30] The Panel faulted the US and Canada for maintaining their imposed trade sanctions.[31] The Panel found that both parties had made procedural violations under the WTO Dispute Settlement Understanding (DSU) because of unilateral actions they had taken.[32] Both parties filed appeals citing procedural errors and disagreements with the panel findings.

In October 2008, the WTO Appellate Body issued a mixed ruling that allows for the continued imposition of trade sanctions on the EU by the US and Canada, but also allows the EU to continue its ban on imports of hormone-treated beef.[33] The Appellate Body report reversed the Panel decision that the EU import ban is incompatible with the WTO law.[34] However, the Appellate Body refrained from analyzing the compatibility of EU's 2003 directives with the rulings of *EC – Hormones* in light of the numerous flaws in the Panel's analysis and the highly contested nature of the facts.[35] The WTO Appellate Body recommended that the parties initiate a compliance panel proceeding under Article 21.5 of the DSU to determine whether the EU is in compliance with its WTO obligations in the underlying beef hormones dispute.[36]

---

[26] *Id.*
[27] *Id.*
[28] *Id.*
[29] Panel Report, *United States - Continued Suspension of Obligations in the EC - Hormones Dispute (US-Continued Suspension)*, WTO Doc. WT/DS320/R (adopted Mar. 31, 2008).
[30] *Id.* at paras. 7.573-579.
[31] *Id.* at paras. 7.250,251.
[32] *Id.* at paras. 7.245,847-851.
[33] Appellate Body Report, *US-Continued Suspension*, WTO Doc. WT/DS320/AB/R (adopted Oct. 16, 2008).
[34] *Id.* at para. 616.
[35] *Id.* at paras. 620, 735.
[36] *Id.* at para. 737.

III. THE 2009 MEMORANDUM OF UNDERSTANDING REGARDING THE IMPORTATION OF HORMONE-TREATED BEEF AND INCREASED DUTIES APPLIED BY THE US

In late December 2008, the EU requested consultations under Article 21.5. The negotiation between the EU and the US faced difficulties as the United States Trade Representatives (USTR) announced changes to the list of EU products subject to increased tariffs under the dispute, adding countries and raising the tariff on select products in January 2009. [37] The EU responded by preparing to challenge the US in the WTO.[38] On May 13, 2009, following a series of negotiations, the EU and the US signed the MOU.[39]

A. *WHAT THE PARTIES AGREED IN THE MOU*

The MOU tries to resolve the dispute in three phases. During the implementation of the MOU, parties will not request the establishment of a WTO panel under DSU 21.5 for noncompliance with the rulings of *EC-Hormones*.[40]

In Phase 1, the EU will provide tariff rate quota (TRQ) of 20,000 MT at zero duty for beef produced without growth-promoting hormones ("High-Quality Beef" or HQB).[41] A tariff rate quota allows enhanced access to a market for a limited quantity of goods by virtue of a low in-quota tariff.[42] Once this quota is filled, subsequent imports are still permitted, but must apply the full tariff.[43] For HQB, the in-quota tariff is zero whereas the full quota is the sum of ad valorem duty of 12.80% and specific duty of 176.80 euros per 100 kg.[44] This full quota amounts to 2,700 to 4,700 euros per ton.[45] In return for the TRQ, the US will delay implementation of the increased retaliatory duties for

---

37 73 Fed. Reg. 66,066 (Nov. 6, 2008), 74 Fed. Reg. 4,264 (Jan. 23, 2009).

38 European Commission, *WTO Dispute Settlement: EU Prepares WTO Action over Trade Sanction Law*, Trade Issues (Jan. 15, 2009).

39 EC-Hormones, Joint Communication from the European Communities and the United States (MOU), WTO Doc. WT/DS26/28 (Sep. 30, 2009).

40 Art.7.1 of the MOU.

41 Art.2.1,2 of the MOU.

42 Chris Downes, *The Post-Brexit Management of EU Agricultural Tariff Rate Quotas*, https://ssrn.com/abstract=2874371 (Nov. 21, 2016) at page 742.

43 *Id.*

44 European Commission Directorate-General for Trade, EU Tariffs, http://madb.europa.eu/madb/euTariffs.htm

45 Peter Ungphakorn, *The Hilton beef quota: a taste of what post-Brexit UK faces in the WTO*, https://tradebetablog.wordpress.com/2016/08/10/hilton-beef-quota/ (Posted Aug. 10, 2017, Updated Nov. 25, 2016).

certain EU imports decided on in January 2009.[46] In Phase 2, the EU will expand the TRQ to 45,000 MT and the US will suspend all retaliatory duties imposed in connection with WTO dispute settlement proceedings in *EC-Hormones*.[47] In Phase 3, the EU will maintain the same level of TRQ as in Phase 2 and the US will cease all of the retaliatory duties, leading to the possible longer-term resolution of the dispute.[48]

As part of Phase 1, the EU opened the TRQ for 20,000 MT imports of HQB in August 2009[49] and the US officially terminated its plan to increase retaliatory duties in September 2009.[50] The parties transitioned to Phase 2 when the US terminated the retaliatory tariffs under the *EC-Hormones* dispute in May 2011[51] and the EU increased the HQB quota to 48,200 MT in June 2012.[52] In October 2013, the parties agreed on the revised MOU which extends Phase 2 instead of proceeding to Phase 3.[53] The EU-US Beef Hormones dispute has been raised as an issue as part of the Transatlantic Trade and Investment Partnership (TTIP) negotiations between the US and the EU, which started in 2013 but has been stalled since 2016.[54]

B. EU IMPORT OF HIGH-QUALITY BEEF UNDER THE TRQ

Administration of the duty-free TRQ on HQB has been the main issue in the implementation of the MOU. First of all, it should be noted that the amount of the TRQ is very small compared with US exports and US, EU and UK domestic production. The initial TRQ of 20,000MT only amounts to 2.3% of total US exports and 0.2% of total US domestic production of beef in 2009. Even after the TRQ is increased to 48,200 MT, it only amounts to 3.7% of total US export and 0.4% of total US production in 2017.

---

46 Art.2.3 of the MOU.

47 Art.2.4 of the MOU.

48 Art.2.5 of the MOU.

49 Council Regulations No 617/2009 of 13 July 2009 opening an autonomous tariff quota for imports of high-quality beef.

50 74 Fed. Reg. 48,808 (Sep. 24, 2009).

51 76 Fed. Reg. 30,987 (May 27, 2011).

52 EU Regulation (EU) No. 464/2012. Canada and the EU signed a similar MOU in connection with the WTO dispute '*European Communities-Measures Concerning Meat and Meat Products (Hormones)*' (DS 48) on March 17, 2011, adding 3,200 MT to the 45,000 MT from the US-EU agreement in two steps.

53 EC-Hormones, Joint Communication from the European Union and the United States, WT/DS26/29 (Apr. 17, 2014).

54 United States Trade Representatives, *Transatlantic Trade and Investment Partnership (T-TIP)*, https://ustr.gov/ttip (last visited on Apr. 13, 2018).

Beef Export and Production (MT)[55]

	HQB TRQ	US Export	US Production	EU Production	UK Production
2009	20,000	877,592	11,885,209	7,765,580(p)	849,860
2010	20,000	1,043,084	12,034,305	7,968,370(c)	924,470
2011	20,000	1,263,282	11,977,832	7,896,220(c)	935,520
2012	48,200	1,112,435	11,845,020	7,579,010	882,560
2013	48,200	1,174,069	11,751,490	7,271,380	847,660
2014	48,200	1,167,435	11,074,821	7,317,680(c)	877,580
2015	48,200	1,028,395	10,817,362	7,582,590	883,210
2016	48,200	1,159,245	11,507,185	7,798,270(p)	911,660(p)
2017	48,200	1,297,980	11,938,098	7,795,730(p)	899,220

Another key aspect of the duty-free TRQ under the MOU is that it is not US specific. Rather it is *erga omnes* quota, which means it is open to all countries. Neither party explains why it is *erga omnes*. In addition, the consultation process under the WTO DSU is confidential.[56] Nevertheless, it can be stipulated that the parties had to abide by WTO principles and not to prejudice the rights of other trading partners in order to avoid challenges to the WTO consistency of the TRQ.[57] Article 3 of the MOU provides that the European Commission implements and administers TRQ in accordance with Article 13 of the GATT.[58] This means that the TRQ on HQB has to be designed in a

55 US statistics – Source: USDA, World Agricultural Outlook Board, "World Agricultural Supply and Demand Estimates" and supporting materials. For the production data, data for Beef and Veal are combined.

EU statistics – Source: Eurostat. (p): provisional. (c): confidential - some member states' data were confidential, so the sum excludes those countries' data. In 2011 and 2012, Bulgaria's productions were unavailable. In 2014, Estonia's production was unavailable.

56 Understanding on Rules and Procedures Governing the Settlement of Disputes (DSU), Marrakesh Agreement Establishing the World Trade Organization, Annex 2, 1869 U.N.T.S. 401, 33 I.L.M. 1226 (Apr. 15, 1994) Art. 4.6.

57 Australia and New Zealand participated in the consultation as third country. They might have pressured EU and US to open the duty-free TRQ to other countries.

58 Art. 3 of the MOU.

non-discriminatory fashion, and in principle, be open to the benefit of all supplying countries.[59] If the quota is to be allocated, the EC must either reach an agreement with all supplying countries or allocate shares among them on the basis of past performance.[60]

Although the TRQ was open to all supplying countries, it was designed to favor the US and Canada. The definition of "High-Quality Beef" that is eligible for the TRQ is beef that has been produced and marketed according to specific procedures which are practiced by US and Canadian producers.[61] For example, the TRQ requires beef to be grain-fed, but most producers in the Southern hemisphere were producing grass-fed beef at the time the TRQ was created.[62]

As a result, the US was the principal supplier in the first three quota years.[63] However, the Southern Hemisphere suppliers managed to re-tool their industries to produce the HQB in several years. Imports from Australia and Uruguay increased rapidly while imports from the United States declined.[64] With total imports under the quota capped at 45,000 MT, growth in the shares of any of the supplying countries comes at the expense of the other suppliers. Imports from Australia, Uruguay, and Argentina have grown consistently since 2012, and although imports from Australia are slowing down, they will be more than offset by continued growth from Uruguay and Argentina.[65] Thus, the US share declined from 98.8% (2009) to 32.6% (2016).[66] According to the US beef industry, under the TRQ, the EU imports 18,000 metric tons from the US, and the UK imports about 1,500 metric tons in 2016.[67]

---

[59] General Agreement on Tariffs and Trade 1994 (GATT 1994), Marrakesh Agreement Establishing the World Trade Organization, Annex 1A, 1867 U.N.T.S. 187, 33 I.L.M. 1153 (Apr. 15, 1994). Art. XIII.

[60] *Id.*

[61] FrantiniVergano, *Trade Prospectives*, Issue No. 9 of 4 (May 2012), Art.4 of the MOU.

[62] Vergano.

[63] National Cattlemen's Beef Association, *Request to Reinstate Action Taken in Connection with European Union Measures Concerning Meat and Meat Products*, Section 301 Committee Rebuttal Comments, Fed. Docket No. USTR-2016-0025 (Mar. 8, 2017).

[64] *Id.*

[65] *Id.*

[66] United States Trade Representatives, *Section 301 Hearing Regarding Request To Reinstate Action Taken in Connection with the European Union's Measures Concerning Meat and Meat Products*, Fed. Docket No. USTR-2016-0025 (Feb. 15, 2017, statement by Thad Lively, Senior Vice President, US. Meat Export Federation) at page 31.

[67] *Id.* No data found regarding other exporting countries.

In response to the declining US export under the TRQ, in December 2016, the USTR launched a process to reinstate the retaliatory tariff against the EU.[68] After the Section 301 Committee hearings were held in February 2017, however, no further development has been made under the Trump Administration. Still, such US actions indicate that the US has a strong interest in the TRQ despite its small amount.

IV. BREXIT

Article 50 of the Treaty on European Union (TEU) provides that "[a]ny Member State may decide to withdraw from the Union in accordance with its own constitutional requirements."[69] On June 23, 2016, the British referendum turned out in favor of leaving the EU.[70] Following the referendum, on March 29, 2017, the UK triggered Article 50 of the TEU by notifying the EU its intent to withdraw, and thus officially kicked off the process for the UK to formally exit the EU.[71] Since Article 50.3 of the TEU provides that the EU Treaties would cease to apply to the withdrawing State from the date of entry into force of the withdrawal agreement or two years after the notification of the intent to withdraw, the UK will leave the EU by March 29, 2019.

The Brexit negotiation between the UK and the EU started on June 19, 2017.[72] The negotiations were split into two broad "phases."[73] Phase 1 focused on withdrawal issues, including citizens' rights, the financial settlement, and the impact of Brexit on the island of Ireland. The two sides agreed that only once "sufficient progress" had been reached on Phase 1, would negotiations move on to Phase 2, focusing initially on transition, and then on the framework for future relations between the UK and the EU.[74]

---

68 81 Fed. Reg. 95,724 (Dec. 28, 2016).

69 European Union, *Consolidated version of the Treaty on European Union* (TEU), 2008/C 115/01 (Dec. 13, 2007) Art. 50.

70 Alex Hunt & Brian Wheeler, *Brexit: All you need to know about the UK leaving the EU*, BBC NEWS, Apr. 25, 2017, http://www.bbc.com/news/uk-politics-32810887.

71 *Id.*

72 UK Department for Exiting the European Union, *Negotiations start today to form a new partnership with the EU*, https://www.gov.uk/government/news/david-davis-opening-remarks-at-the-start-of-eu-exit-negotiations-in-brussels (Jun. 19, 2017).

73 UK Parliament, *Brexit negotiations*, https://www.parliament.uk/business/committees/committees-a-z/lords-select/eu-select-committee-/inquiries/parliament-2017/scrutiny-of-brexit-negotiations/brexit-negotiations/ (last visited on Apr. 1, 2018), European Council, European Council (Art. 50) guidelines for Brexit negotiations, http://www.consilium.europa.eu/en/press/press-releases/2017/04/29/euco-brexit-guidelines/ (Apr. 29, 2017) at para. 4.

74 *Id.*

On December 8, 2017, both parties jointly announced that they had reached an agreement in principle on Phase 1 of the negotiations and moved on to the next phase of negotiations.[75] On March 19, 2018, the UK and the EU agreed on the terms of the transition period.[76] The draft Withdrawal Agreement states that the transition period will last from Brexit day on March 29, 2019, to December 31, 2020.[77]

The discussions in this chapter are based on the draft Withdrawal Agreement, which was published on March 19, 2018.[78] However, it should be noted that "[n]egotiations under Article 50 TEU will be conducted in transparency and as a single package. In accordance with the principle that nothing is agreed until everything is agreed, individual items cannot be settled separately."[79] Therefore, agreements in principle negotiated so far will not be finalized until the Brexit negotiations as a whole are concluded.

A. WILL THE UK MAINTAIN THE IMPORT BAN AFTER BREXIT?

In exploring the post-Brexit development of the Beef Hormones dispute, the first key question is whether the UK will maintain the import ban on hormone-treated beef after Brexit by enacting its own legislation. Currently, the import ban is implemented by the EU Council Directive 96/22/EC.[80] EU Directives are binding as to the result to be achieved upon each Member State to which it is addressed, but leave to the national authorities the choice of form and methods.[81] Thus, directives are not directly applicable and need to be incorporated or implemented through national legislation. In the UK, the import ban is implemented by the statutory instruments called the Animals and Animal Products (Examination for Residues and Maximum Residue Limits) Regulations.[82]

---

[75] Joint report on progress during phase 1 of negotiations under Article 50 TEU on the UK's orderly withdrawal from the EU (Dec. 8, 2018).

[76] BBC News, *The UK and EU agree terms for Brexit transition period*, http://www.bbc.com/news/uk-politics-43456502 (Mar. 19, 2018).

[77] Art.121 of the draft Withdrawal Agreement.

[78] BBC News, *The UK and EU agree terms for Brexit transition period*, http://www.bbc.com/news/uk-politics-43456502 (Mar. 19, 2018).

[79] European Council, *European Council (Art. 50) guidelines for Brexit negotiations*, http://www.consilium.europa.eu/en/press/press-releases/2017/04/29/euco-brexit-guidelines/ (Apr. 29, 2017) at para. 2.

[80] EU Council Directive 96/22/EC.

[81] European Union, *Consolidated version of the Treaty on the Functioning of the European Union* (TFEU), 2008/C 115/01 (Dec. 13, 2007) Art. 288.

[82] The Animals and Animal Products (Examination for Residues and Maximum Residue Limits) (England and Scotland) Regulations 2015, the Animals and Animal Products (Examination for Residues and Maximum Residue Limits) Regulations (Northern Ireland) 2016.

In this section, I would analyze the legal effect of Brexit on the EU Directive and the UK statutory instrument.

1. The UK Will Maintain the Import Restriction During the Transition Period

According to the latest draft of the Withdrawal Agreement, the EU law will remain applicable to the UK during the transition period including the EU directives.[83] Therefore, the UK has to maintain the import restriction on hormone-treated beef as required by the EU Council Directive 96/22/EC until the end of 2020.

2. The UK Plans to Grandfather the EU Import Ban

After the Transition period, the EU law will cease to apply to the UK, including EU directives. Therefore, the UK will have a choice whether to maintain the import ban on the hormone-treated beef. I argue that the UK is likely to maintain the import ban after Brexit because it provides more legal stability, and policy and economic concerns favor the import ban.

B. LEGAL STABILITY CONCERN FAVORS THE STATUS QUO

The function of current UK law will be determined by the Withdrawal Bill that will ensure that the UK statute book is able to function after the Brexit.[84] According to the factsheets on the Withdrawal Bill published by the UK Department for Exiting the European Union, the Bill will preserve the laws that were made in the UK to implement the EU obligations, such as the laws which implement EU directives.[85] The EU directives themselves will not be preserved because they do not form part of the UK domestic law and have already been implemented in domestic law where required.[86] As of April 2018, the UK legislation that implements the import ban on hormone-treated beef is not exempted from this grandfather policy.[87] In addition,

---

[83] Art.122 of the draft Withdrawal Agreement.

[84] Department for Exiting the European Union, *The Withdrawal Bill Factsheet 1: General*, https://www.gov.uk/government/uploads/system/uploads/attachment_data/file/678328/Factsheet_1-_General.pdf (Published on Jul. 13, 2017 and last updated on Mar. 15, 2018).

[85] Department for Exiting the European Union, *The Withdrawal Bill Factsheet 2: Converting and preserving law*, https://www.gov.uk/government/uploads/system/uploads/attachment_data/file/678329/Factsheet_2_-_Converting_and_Preserving_law.pdf (Published on Jul. 13, 2017 and last updated on Mar. 15, 2018).

[86] *Id.*

[87] Department for Exiting the European Union, *Information about the Withdrawal Bill*, https://www.gov.uk/government/publications/information-about-the-withdrawal-bill (Published on Jul. 13, 2017 and last updated on Mar. 15, 2018).

exempting the EU import ban from grandfathering will be contrary to the purpose of preserving and converting the EU law, which is to prevent significant gaps in the UK law before and after Brexit and to maximize certainty and stability.[88]

C. Policy Considerations Also Favor the Import Ban

In addition to the legal stability concern, the UK House of Lords' report summarizes the UK's policy considerations. The UK Minister of State for Agriculture and Food recognizes a mixed UK consumer reaction toward maintaining the import ban. While many consumers favor rigorous food safety controls, price greatly affects consumer behavior as US beef is much cheaper than UK beef.[89] The UK Chief Veterinary Officer (CVO) points out that even if the UK were not bound by the EU law and policy after Brexit, there is a possibility of US retaliation if the UK maintains the import ban.[90] But the CVO also raises a concern that admitting hormone-treated beef into UK market may pose a challenge to trade between the UK and the EU.[91] In addition to these considerations raised by the report, UK beef producers will strongly support the import ban. As the statistics below indicate, the UK production price of beef is higher than the US, Australia, and Uruguay, the countries which currently utilize the most of the TRQ on HQB. In addition, the UK is a net importer of beef. Most of the imports are from other EU members, mainly Ireland. The production prices of Australia and Uruguay are even cheaper than Ireland. Therefore, if the UK lifts the import ban, the UK would experience a surge in imports which may put the domestic producers in jeopardy.

---

[88] Department for Exiting the European Union, *The Withdrawal Bill Factsheet 1: General*, https://www.gov.uk/government/uploads/system/uploads/attachment_data/file/678328/Factsheet_1-_General.pdf (Published on Jul. 13, 2017 and last updated on Mar. 15, 2018).

[89] House of Lords European Union Committee, *Brexit: agriculture*, 20th Report of Session2016-17 (May 3, 2017) at paras. 135-137.

[90] *Id.* at para. 138.

[91] *Id.* at paras. 139.

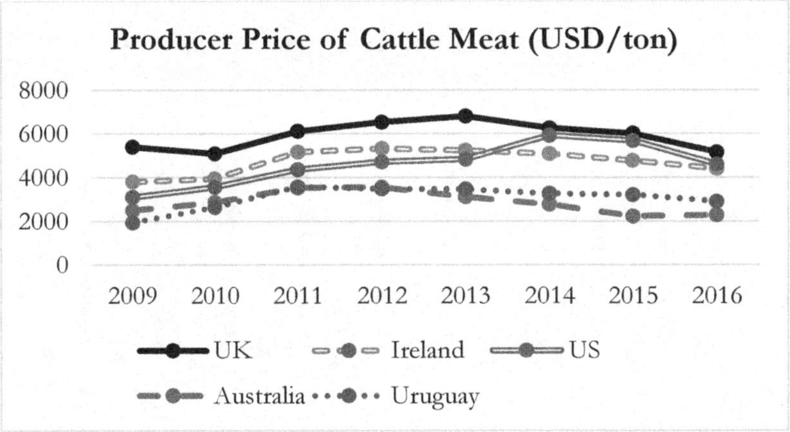

[92]

	UK	Ireland	US	Australia	Uruguay
2009	5397.4	3804.3	3105.3	2500.4	1942.1
2010	5094.2	3950.6	3566.7	2870.2	2648.7
2011	6114.4	5163.8	4370.2	3537.0	3581.3
2012	6532.1	5325	4719.3	3561.8	3487.8
2013	6797.7	5228.2	4835.1	3122.1	3468.0
2014	6256.4	5076	5917.5	2772.8	3268.1
2015	6012.7	4767.3	5686.0	2235.0	3214.0
2016	5155.6	4400.8	4603.5	2285.8	2910.7

[92] FAO STAT.

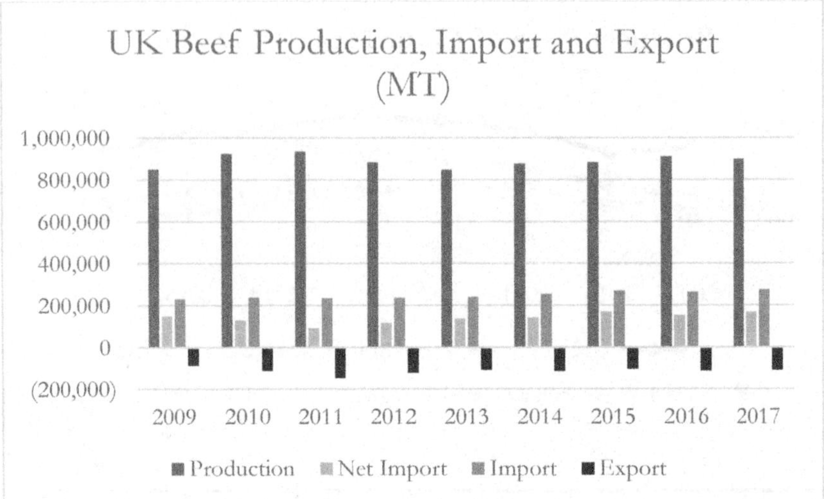

	UK Production	UK Net Import	UK Import			UK Export
				EU	Non-EU	
2009	849,860	147,419	230,832	188,286	42,545	83,412
2010	924,470	127,905	238,026	204,995	33,031	110,120
2011	935,520	91,711	235,358	210,007	25,351	143,647
2012	882,560	116,497	236,267	213,377	22,891	119,770
2013	847,660	135,978	241,289	209,758	31,531	105,311
2014	877,580	142,570	254,830	227,306	27,524	112,260
2015	883,210	169,165	269,656	244,715	24,941	100,491
2016	911,660(p)	153,150	263,578	242,680	20,898	110,428
2017	899,220	168,607	275,258	259,460	15,797	106,651

[93]

In sum, considering these factors, the UK is likely to maintain the import ban after Brexit because it provides more legal stability, and policy and economic concerns favor the import ban. On the other hand, it should be noted that maintaining the import ban after Brexit will be contrary to the past UK position against the import ban on hormone-treated beef, which led the US to exclude the UK from the retaliatory

[93] Production data – Source: Eurostat. (p): provisional.
Import and export data – Source: UK Agriculture & Horticulture Development Board, *UK Statistics*.

tariffs. The UK should expect strong US opposition against retaining the import ban.

V. AFTER BREXIT, THE UK COULD NOT BE A PARTY TO THE MOU

The next question is whether the UK remains a party to the MOU after Brexit. If the UK maintains the import ban, then the UK would want to maintain its membership in the MOU, which enables the UK to succeed in the efforts between the EU and the US to resolve the dispute.

A. THE LEGAL CHARACTERISTICS OF THE MOU: DOES IT CREATE BINDING OBLIGATIONS?

In order to answer the question regarding the impact of Brexit on the MOU, the legal characteristics of the MOU need to be analyzed first. Specifically, the issue is whether the MOU falls within the definition of "treaty" under the Vienna Convention of the Law of Treaties 1969 (VCLT)[94] and thus creates obligations that would be binding under international law. Such question arises because a memorandum of understanding is often used to avoid legally binding obligations under international law, but sometimes a treaty is named a memorandum of understanding.

The Oxford Guide to Treaties provides a framework to distinguish a memorandum of understanding from a treaty.[95] In addition to formality requirements under the VCLT, the guide suggests there must be evidence of an intention to conclude a treaty. According to the ILC Commentary[96] on its draft which became the VCLT, in the definition of "treaty," the phrase "governed by international law" embraces the element of an intention to create obligations under international law.[97] In order to determine whether parties have such intention, the ICJ in the Aegean Sea Continental Shelf case held that the intention must be

---

[94] United Nations, *Vienna Convention on the Law of Treaties*, United Nations, Treaty Series, vol. 1155 (May 23, 1969), at page 331. Under Art. 2.1. (a) of the VCLT, "Treaty" means an international agreement concluded between States in written form and governed by international law, whether embodied in a single instrument or in two or more related instruments and whatever its particular designation.

[95] Anthony Aust, *Alternatives to Treaty-Making: MOUs as Political Commitments*, in THE OXFORD GUIDE TO TREATIES 46 (Duncan B. Hollis ed., 2012).

[96] *Id.* See also A Watts, *The International Law Commission 1949–1998* (OUP, Oxford 004) vol II, 621–4.

[97] Aust, at page 48, Art. 2(1)A of VCLT.

gathered from the terms of the instrument itself and the circumstances of its conclusion.[98]

1. Terminology and form of the text

Although the law of treaties does not require a treaty to be in any particular form or to use special wording,[99] most countries now follow a practice of manifesting their intention to conclude a treaty by consciously employing a fairly standard form and mandatory terminology such as "shall," "agree," "undertake," "rights," "obligations," and "enter into force." In contrast, when they do not intend to conclude a treaty, but rather a memorandum of understanding, instead of "shall" they use a less mandatory term, such as "will"; such terms as "agree" or "undertake" are avoided; the instrument is expressed to "come into operation" or "come into effect"; and most of the final clauses usually found in treaties are omitted or simplified.[100] The US Department of State's Guidance on Non-Binding Documents similarly instructs US negotiators to distinguish uses of terms between treaties and memorandum of understandings.[101] Here, the use of terms in the EU-US MOU is somewhat mixed. Although the forehead of the MOU avoids the term "agreement," its texts use "will" instead of "shall." The MOU lacks entry into force provisions. The MOU uses the term "obligation" and "parties." Finally, its texts are organized in a treaty-like manner using the term "article."

2. Express provisions as to non-legally binding status

In many cases, negotiating States will clearly evince an intention to conclude an MOU instead of a treaty through language in the text itself.[102] The US Department of State's guidance suggests that "it may be useful for a non-binding document to include a disclaimer in the text of the document expressly providing that it is not legally binding under international law."[103] Here, however, the EU-US MOU does not contain such a disclaimer.

3. Circumstances in which the instrument was concluded

If the form, terminology, or express terms of the instrument do not contain enough evidence of the intention of the authors as to its status, it is necessary to consider any evidence of the practice of the States, the

---

98 Aust, at page 48, citing *Aegean Sea Continental Shelf Case (Greece v Turkey)* [1978] ICJ Rep 40, 39–44; H Thirlway, 'The Law and Procedure of the International Court of Justice 1960–1989' (1991) 62 BYBIL 13–15 (interpreting the intention of the parties in the Brussels Communiqué of 31 May 1975).

99 Aust, at page 48.

100 *Id.*

101 US. Department of State, *Guidance on Non-Binding Documents*, https://www.state.gov/s/l/treaty/guidance/ (last visited on Apr. 14, 2018).

102 Aust, at page 50.

103 US. Department of State, *Guidance on Non-Binding Documents.*

circumstances in which the instrument was drawn up, and the subsequent acts of the States, such as registration or non-registration.[104] Here, the MOU was negotiated as a consultation under Article 4 of the WTO DSU to resolve the dispute, and the MOU was notified to the WTO, while it was not registered with the United Nations as a treaty. The parties implemented respective obligations after the conclusion of the MOU. Thus, although the EU and the US did not follow the typical procedure to enter into a treaty, they acted in a treaty-like manner under the MOU. International tribunals may find the parties' intentions to enter into treaties from the parties' such behavior.

In sum, the analysis of these factors does not provide a clear answer as to whether the EU-US MOU is a treaty. Although the parties use the term "obligation" and the text is organized in a treaty-like manner, the MOU lacks some typical formalities of treaties such as entry into force provisions and the term "agreement" in the forehead. Neither party explains its intent as to the nature of the MOU. It is unclear whether international tribunals would find the MOU is a treaty.

However, even if tribunals find that the EU-US MOU is not a treaty, the MOU still creates a legally binding obligation under the fundamental international law principle of good faith. Under the principle, where a clear statement or representation is made by State A to State B, which then in good faith State B relies upon it to its detriment, State A is estopped from going back on its statement or representation.[105] Similarly, if two states choose to record the settlement of a dispute between them in a memorandum of understanding rather than in a treaty, each is clearly estopped from denying that the terms of the settlement are binding.[106] Here, the EU provided the TRQ on HQB and the US ceased the retaliatory tariffs as part of the settlement after the WTO rulings. Such mutual reliance between the parties and parties' intentions to settle the dispute create legally binding obligations on both sides. In conclusion, the MOU creates legally binding obligations on the EU and the US even if it is not a treaty.

B. THE UK WILL HAVE TO IMPLEMENT ITS OBLIGATIONS UNDER THE MOU DURING THE TRANSITION PERIOD

Now I turn to the question as to how obligations created by the MOU bind the UK during the implementation of Brexit and after Brexit.

---

104 Aust, at page 51.

105 Aust, at page 69.

106 *Id.*

Regarding the transition period, Article 124.1 of the draft Withdrawal Agreement states that the UK "shall be bound by the obligations stemming from the international agreements concluded by the Union,"[107] and "[t]he Union will notify the other parties to these agreements that during the transition period, the United Kingdom is to be treated as a Member State for the purpose of these agreements."[108] Therefore, the UK will be obligated to provide the TRQ on HQB as an obligation under the MOU during the transition period, i.e. until the end of 2020. On the other hand, the US will only be notified of such arrangement and will not be obligated to regard the UK as a party to the MOU. Thus, the US will not be obligated to suspend the retaliatory tariffs against the UK (although the UK is already exempt) and refrain from requesting the establishment of a WTO panel under DSU 21.5 for noncompliance with the rulings of *EC-Hormone*. This is a risk for the UK because the US can file a new WTO claim even during the transition period if the US expects the UK would maintain the import ban after Brexit.

C. THE UK WILL NO LONGER BE A PARTY TO THE MOU AFTER BREXIT

After the transition period ends, the legal consequences of Brexit on the UK as a party to the MOU should be determined by referring to the text of the MOU itself. According to Article 31 of the VCLT, a "treaty shall be interpreted in good faith in accordance with the ordinary meaning to be given to the terms of the treaty in their context and in light of its object and purpose."[109] Even if the MOU is not regarded as a treaty, it should be reasonable to apply by analogy the rules for the interpretation of treaties in so far as they are not at variance with the non-legally binding nature of a memorandum of understandings.[110] The forehead of the MOU states that the United States and the European Commission have reached an understanding as documented in the Memorandum of Understanding.[111] In provisions of the MOU, the US and the EU are referred to as the "Parties."[112] Thus, after the UK loses membership to the EC, a plain reading of the text of the MOU does not support the UK's membership to the MOU. Therefore, the UK will no longer be a party to the MOU after the transition period ends in 2020.

---

107 Art.124.1. of the draft Withdrawal Agreement.

108 Note to Art.124.1. of the draft Withdrawal Agreement.

109 Art. 32 of the VCLT.

110 Aust, at page 62.

111 Forehead of the MOU.

112 Art. 1 of the MOU.

D. CONSEQUENCE: ANOTHER US CLAIM IN THE WTO AGAINST THE UK

Loss of membership to the MOU has several consequences for the UK, as it will no longer be bound by the obligation to the US and vice versa. First, the UK will no longer be required to take part in the EU TRQ on HQB. Second, the US will not be obligated to suspend the retaliatory duties imposed in connection with *EC–Hormones*, although the UK is already exempt. Third, both the UK and the US will no longer be obligated to refrain from requesting the establishment of a WTO panel for noncompliance with the rulings of *EC-Hormones* against each other.

Due to these consequences, what actions the parties may take depends on whether the UK maintains the import ban on hormone-treated beef. If the UK abandons the import ban, the US will not need to take any actions against the UK. However, as discussed in section 3.2., the UK plans to grandfather EU law, likely including the import ban on hormone-treated beef. Then the US will have two strategies. First, the US may claim that the UK is bound by the WTO rulings in *EC–Hormones* and *US–Continued Suspension*, according to the principle of succession under the Vienna Convention on Succession of States in respect of Treaties.[113] Under Article 34 of the Convention, in the case where a part or some parts of the territory of a State is separated in order to form one or more States, whether the predecessor State continues to exist, any treaty in force at the time of the succession of the State on the entire territory of the predecessor State shall remain in force on each successor State so formed.[114] Since obligations to implement the WTO DSB rulings stem from the DSU of the WTO Agreements,[115] the US may claim the principle of succession obligates the UK to implement the rulings in *EC–Hormones* and *US–Continued Suspension.* In addition, the MOU which obligated the US to refrain from requesting the establishment of a WTO panel for noncompliance with the rulings of *EC-Hormones* no longer applies against the UK. The second strategy for the US is to initiate a separate case against the UK. In either of the two scenarios, the UK will be in a tough position to establish that the current import ban under the EU's 2003 directive is consistent with the rulings in *EC–Hormones*, which WTO Appellate Body did not decide in the *US–*

---

[113] UN General Assembly, *Vienna Convention on Succession of States in respect of Treaties* (Nov. 6, 1996).

[114] Art. 34 of the Vienna Convention on Succession of States in respect of Treaties.

[115] Art. 21 of the DSU.

Continued Suspension. In addition, the US would attack the UK politically, as the UK has repeatedly objected to the EU import ban based on reports produced by the UK's independent experts committee.[116]

VI. How the UK and the US Can Roll Over the MOU

In order to maintain the import ban on hormone-treated beef and avoid US claim in the WTO after Brexit, the UK would need to roll over the MOU with the US and maintain the status quo. But rolling over the MOU cannot be done by simply copying and pasting. The question is how the UK would take the TRQ obligation.

A. What Will the Future UK-EU Trade Relationship Look Like?

Regarding whether the UK and the US would roll over the MOU, the first question is what the future UK-EU trade relationship will look like. If the UK remains in the EU single market with respect to the trade in beef, then the MOU needs to be amended to include the UK as a party because the MOU would need to address how the TRQ on HQB would be administered when imported HQBs would freely move between the UK and the EU. On the other hand, if the UK exits the EU single market, then the UK needs to consider rolling over the MOU into its own agreement with the US. On this point, in March 2018, the UK Prime Minister May stated that the UK is leaving the EU single market.[117] Therefore, the UK would need to negotiate its own agreement with the US.

B. When Can the UK and the US Start the Negotiation?

If the UK seeks to roll over the MOU with the US, when can the UK start the negotiation with the US? Since the EU has exclusive competence over customs union and common commercial policy,[118] only the EU has the power to negotiate and enter into trade agreements

---

[116] In *EC-Hormones*, the Appellate Body addressed the question of whether a Member should carry out its own risk assessment for a SPS measure:

"Article 5.1 does not insist that a Member that adopts a sanitary measure shall have carried out its own risk assessment … The SPS measure might well find its objective justification in a risk assessment carried out by another Member, or an international organization."

Appellate Body Report, *EC-Hormones*, para. 190. Therefore, it is legally possible for the UK to rely on the EU scientific reports instead of its own and maintain the import ban, but the UK should expect political backlash from the US.

[117] GOV.UK, *PM speech on our future economic partnership with the European Union* (Mar. 2, 2018).

[118] Art.3.1 of TFEU.

with non-EU countries.[119] Therefore, the UK is prohibited from entering into trade negotiation as long as the UK is bound by EU law. But the UK Withdrawal Agreement is likely to allow the UK to start trade negotiations as early as the transition period, although the UK will be bound by EU law during that period. Under Article 124.4 of the draft Withdrawal Agreement, the UK "may negotiate, sign and ratify international agreements entered into in its own capacity in the areas of exclusive competence of the Union, provided these agreements do not enter into force or apply during the transition period, unless so authorized by the Union."[120] Thus, the UK can start the negotiation with the US once the transition period begins on March 29, 2019, provided that the UK and the EU reach final agreement on the Withdrawal Agreement.

C. HOW WILL THE UK TAKE THE TRQ OBLIGATIONS?

When the UK and the US start the negotiation, they will focus on how the UK will take the TRQ obligations under the new MOU. There are procedural and substantive issues. The procedural issue is whether WTO law for modification of the tariff schedule applies. Currently, the TRQ on HQB is provided by the EU autonomously under Article 2 of the MOU and the amount of the TRQ is stated solely in the MOU. The TRQ is not incorporated in the EU's tariff schedule certified by the WTO, since the EU's tariff schedule was last certified in December 2016, reflecting its 2004 expansion from 15 to 25 members,[121] while the TRQ on HQB was created in 2009. On October 17, 2017, the EU circulated revised goods "schedules" for all its 28 members. If no WTO member objects, these could be certified in three months. The documents using the code number G/MA/TAR/RS/506 are visibly listed on the WTO website but remain unavailable to the public until they are certified.[122] If the TRQ on HQB is incorporated into the EU's WTO schedule, the TRQ needs to be modified in accordance with Article 28 of the GATT. Under Article 28 of the GATT, a country can modify concessions in negotiation with other relevant trading partners with the aim to "maintain the general level of reciprocal mutually advantageous concessions, not less favourable to trade than...prior to such

---

119 Art.3.2 of TFEU.

120 Art.124.4 of the draft Withdrawal Agreement.

121 Peter Ungphakorn, *12 years on, EU's certified WTO goods commitments now up to date to 2004*, https://tradebetablog.wordpress.com/2017/02/04/after-12-years-eu-25-goods-commitments/#eu25 (Posted Feb. 4, 2017, Updated Oct. 22, 2017).

122 *Id.*

negotiation."[123] Thus, if the UK has to go through the Article 28 process, the UK has to negotiate not only with the US but also with other exporters such as Australia, Uruguay, Argentina, and New Zealand. The Article 28 process will put the UK in a danger of protracted negotiations with multiple opponents and in a danger of rapid retaliation by the opponents under Article 28.3 of the GATT.[124]

The substantive issue is how to determine the amount of the new TRQ amount. The UK would argue to set the amount smaller than the current TRQ in order to protect domestic beef producers by minimizing the increase of beef imports. For example, the UK would propose to separate the UK's share from the current EU TRQ. On the other hand, the US, and other beef exporters—if they join the negotiation—would insist on setting the TRQ at the same or at a greater amount than the current EU-US MOU. Especially when the UK has to go through the GATT Article 28 process, the modification of the concession cannot be less favourable to trade than prior to such negotiation.[125] The exporter countries would argue that the value of the EU's commitment lies not only in the quantity, but in its geographical reach and flexibility in terms of accessing different country markets, including the UK.[126] Therefore, the countries would insist on simply splitting the current EU TRQ because it would diminish the level of concession and violate Article 28 of the GATT. The UK should expect highly political negotiations to reach an agreement on the amount of the TRQ.

D. CAN THE EU REQUEST THE US RENEGOTIATION OF THE MOU TO REDUCE THE TRQ OBLIGATION?

The last question regarding the future implementation of the MOU is whether the EU can request that the US renegotiate the MOU in order to reduce the TRQ obligation after Brexit. In response to its shrink of its beef market, the EU may request the US to rebalance the concession. Although the EU is legally allowed to request renegotiation, it would face a difficult negotiation.

Again, the first issue is whether WTO law for modification of tariff schedule applies. If the TRQ on HQB is incorporated into the EU's WTO schedule, the EU has to negotiate not only with the US but also with other exporters under Article 28 of the GATT. The EU would face protracted negotiations with a danger of retaliations.[127] If the TRQ on

123 Art.28 of the GATT 1994, Downes, at page 748.

124 Downes, at pages 754, 755.

125 Art.28 of the GATT 1994.

126 Downes, at page 747.

127 In fact, a US-led group of countries has rejected a plan agreed by the UK and the EU to split their WTO quotas after Brexit. On September 26, 2017, the US, Argentina,

HQB is not incorporated into EU's WTO schedule, the amendment of the total amount of the TRQ will be governed solely by the MOU. The amendment provision of the MOU says only "by mutual agreement in writing" and there are no other requirements.[128] The EU would request the US to modify the TRQ based on this provision.

Similar to the UK-US negotiation, the EU will face a tough negotiation with the US on the EU's new TRQ obligation. The US would not agree to decrease the amount of the TRQ arguing that: 1) the EU should not request the adjustment of the TRQ amount upon a change in EU membership because the EU did not increase the TRQ on HQB when the EU expanded in 2013; 2) the amount of the TRQ is already too small considering the size of the EU beef market and US beef exports to the world, and 3) the US share within the TRQ is declining and the US is not receiving enough of the benefit it bargained for. For these reasons, contrary to the EU's purpose for the renegotiation, renegotiating the MOU may lead to an increase in the TRQ amount. Given the fact that the current TRQ amount is very small compared to the EU beef market, the EU is unlikely to request the US to renegotiate the MOU.

VII. CONCLUSION

Although the UK will not be obliged to take part in the EU import ban after Brexit is implemented, the UK is likely to maintain the import ban because of legal stability and policy and economic concerns. If it does so, the UK would face very difficult negotiations with the US to roll over the EU-US MOU, especially in negotiations for the UK's new TRQ obligation. The likelihood of a more complicated negotiation process should be expected. If the latest EU tariff schedule submitted to the WTO, which is currently undergoing a certification process, incorporates the TRQ on HQB, the negotiation will be even more complicated as the exporting countries other than the US would join the negotiation. If the UK fails to roll over the MOU, the UK would face a danger of new WTO claims challenging the UK import ban and a danger of retaliation. Both scenarios would cause harm to the UK economy.

Brazil, Canada, New Zealand, Thailand, and Uruguay submitted a jointly signed letter to the UK and the EU, addressing their objection. IEG Policy, *US leads growing opposition to EU-UK WTO tariff rate quota plan*, https://iegpolicy.agribusinessintelligence.informa.com/PL051037/US-leads-growing-opposition-to-EUUK-WTO-tariff-rate-quota-plan (Oct. 5, 2017).

[128] Art.5.5 of the MOU.

A possible strategy for the UK is to negotiate the TRQ under the proposed UK-US Free Trade Agreement (UK-US FTA) negotiations. Under the FTA, the UK can provide the US a country-specific TRQ instead of *erga omnes* TRQ. This may expedite the process with the US, which is the largest actor in the dispute. In fact, the past two rounds of the UK-US dialogue for post-Brexit trade relationships have raised the issue of SPS and agricultural trade.[129] Even in the UK-US FTA negotiations, the UK should expect strong US opposition to the import ban on hormone-treated beef and strong US demand for increased market access, given the long history of the dispute and the US's interest in it.

---

[129] International Centre for Trade and Sustainable Development, *Preparations for Post-Brexit Trade Deals Continue with US, Australia*, Bridges, Volume 22 - Number 11, https://www.ictsd.org/bridges-news/bridges/news/preparations-for-post-brexit-trade-deals-continue-with-us-australia (Mar. 29, 2018).

PART II:

Implications of the Draft Withdrawal Agreement

CHAPTER 10: BREXIT AND THE FUTURE OF EUROPEAN FISHERIES

AURE RENZA DEMOULIN-BOUCHIER

INTRODUCTION

"We want our waters back."—Nigel Farage[1]

Fishermen have long had an outsized voice in politics. British fishermen are no exception. In June 2016, as part of the "Leave" (the EU) campaign, Nigel Farage, then leader of the Independence Party, led a flotilla of fishermen up the Thames to protest European fishing quotas.[2] Although the UK fishing industry only employs an estimated grand total of 11,000 people, fishermen were some of the most outspoken proponents of Brexit.[3] One survey conducted before the referendum thus found that over 90 percent of fishermen wanted to leave the Union.[4]

That is because under the Common Fisheries Policy (CFP)—the fishing policy of the European Union—EU countries' fishing fleets can fish anywhere in European waters, including in UK waters, so long as they respect CFP fishing quotas.[5] The policy imposes quotas on all EU fishermen (including Brits until the end of the transition period), and grants access to the 200-mile exclusive economic zone around the UK

---

[1] Nigel Farage was the leader of the UK Independence Party (UKIP) from 2006 to 2009 and again from 2010 to 2016. He reportedly said: "We want our waters back!" when, in June 2016, he joined fishermen to sail up the Thames to Westminster with a flotilla of fishing vessels as part of the Fishing for Leave campaign. *See e.g.* Adam Withnall, *Nigel Farage and Sir Bob Geldof Clash over Brexit Flotilla in 'Battle for the Thames,'* INDEPENDENT, June 15, 2016, *available at: https://www.independent.co.uk/news/uk/politics/nigel-farage-and-sir-bob-geldof-clash-over-brexit-flotilla-in-battle-for-the-thames-a7083106.html.*

[2] Adam Withnall, *Nigel Farage and Sir Bob Geldof Clash over Brexit Flotilla in 'Battle for the Thames,'* INDEPENDENT, June 15, 2016, *available at: https://www.independent.co.uk/news/uk/politics/nigel-farage-and-sir-bob-geldof-clash-over-brexit-flotilla-in-battle-for-the-thames-a7083106.html.*

[3] *E.g.*, House of Commons Library, Briefing Paper, UK Sea Fisheries Statistics, Elise Uberoi, Dec. 5, 2017, at 7, [hereinafter UK Sea Fisheries Statistics], accessible at: file:///Users/auredemoulin/Desktop/SN02788.pdf.

[4] Michael Acton, *Britain Seeks to Take Back Control in Brexit Fisheries Fight*, THE FINANCIAL TIMES, Nov. 28, 2017, accessible at: https://www.ft.com/content/4f21072a-c87f-11e7-ab18-7a9fb7d6163e.

[5] "The Common Fisheries Policy (CFP)," European Commission, 29 May 2015.

coastline to all EU fishing vessels.[6] Only a 12-mile zone is preserved for the exclusive use of UK boats.[7] When campaigning for "Leave," British fishermen thus hoped that a Brexit would force foreign ships out of UK waters.[8]

Unfortunately, EU fishermen are campaigning for the exact opposite. Michel Barnier, the EU's chief negotiator for Brexit talks, is himself acutely aware of the weight that EU fishermen could carry in politics: in 2009, as France's Agriculture and Fisheries Minister, he was forced to offer French fishermen a four million Euros subsidy package to stop the blockage of French ports in a dispute over fishing quotas.[9] Fishermen's interests are thus also on the Union's radar, and the overall balance of interests leaves EU officials dubious that the UK will insist on major fishing quota changes when push comes to shove.[10] In that respect, London's concession in a March 2018 Draft Agreement that British fishermen would not be granted a larger share of British fish during the post-Brexit transition period has already begun to prove the EU right.[11]

This chapter examines the potential fates of EU and British fisheries after Brexit, with a particular focus on future fishing rights. Indeed, the UK's withdrawal from the European Union will impact access to fishing grounds in UK and EU waters, current fishing agreements with third party-countries, and fishing quotas. Trade in fisheries products and fishermen's rights will also very much be affected: these complex issues are somewhat out of the scope of such a short analysis, but this chapter will address them briefly to give the reader an overview of the complex, multifaceted, and interconnected nature of the issues facing the fishing industry after Brexit. This chapter also makes note of the future for trade in fish products and fishermen's rights, which will be addressed in the

---

[6] *Id.*

[7] Peter Foster, *What would Brexit Mean for British Sovereignty?*, DAILY TELEGRAPH, June 8, 2016 available at: http://www.celebratethought.com/wp-content/uploads/2016/07/Daily-Telegraph-on-soveriegnty-and-EU-8-June-2016.pdf.

[8] Nigel Hunt, *UK Fisherman Expect a Post-Brexit Bonanza - But There's a Catch*, INDEPENDENT, Sep. 19, 2017, accessible at: https://www.independent.co.uk/news/business/news/uk-fishing-industry-brexit-eu-subsidies-fishermen-european-union-market-a7954641.html.

[9] J.B., *Les Pêcheurs du Nord Lèvent le Blocage de tous les Ports*, LE PARISIEN, Le Figaro, Apr. 16, 2009, accessible at: http://www.lefigaro.fr/actualite-france/2009/04/16/01016-20090416ARTFIG00302-pecheurs-une-aide-de-4-millions-pas-plus-de-quotas-.php.

[10] Michael Acton, *Britain Seeks to Take Back Control in Brexit Fisheries Fight*, THE FINANCIAL TIMES, Nov. 28, 2017, accessible at: https://www.ft.com/content/4f21072a-c87f-11e7-ab18-7a9fb7d6163e.

[11] *UK Set to Back Down Over Fishing Quotas During Brexit Transition*, accessible at: https://www.ft.com/content/89ef8760-2931-11e8-b27e-cc62a39d57a0.

general withdrawal agreement, in order to encourage Brexit negotiators to think of these rights in conjunction with fishing access rights, which will most likely be addressed in a separate agreement and are, therefore, too often thought of in isolation.

The chapter first gives some background on UK and EU fishing and on the applicable law (I). The chapter then briefly discusses the impact that Brexit negotiations on primary issues, such as commerce, free enterprise, individual freedoms, and conflict resolution will have on trade in fishing products and fishermen's rights (II). Finally, this chapter focuses on the core fishery issue of regulation of access to UK and EU waters for fishing purposes: in particular, this chapter reviews the Draft Withdrawal Agreement proposed by the EU in March 2018, discusses the main conflicting interests that will weigh on the negotiations, and makes recommendations as to what an ad hoc fisheries agreement between the EU and the UK should look like (III).

I. EU AND UK FISHING: BACKGROUND INFORMATION

This section is meant to give the reader context for the ongoing Brexit negotiations over fisheries. It starts with some of the relevant data regarding the British fishing industry and foreign fishing in UK waters (A). The section will then explore the law applicable to European fisheries, including the Union's Common Fisheries Policy (B) and the international framework, especially the UN Convention on the Law of the Sea (C). Finally, the section will explore whether the Court of Justice of the EU, which currently has jurisdiction over fisheries-related disputes, will continue to play a role in the resolution of such conflicts (D).

A. EU AND UK FISHING IN NUMBERS

"We are sitting in the middle of some of the best fishing grounds in the world."
—Bertie Armstrong[12]

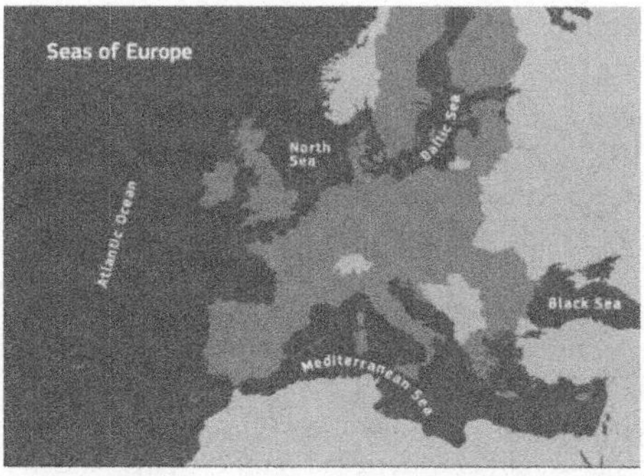

Figure 1: The Seas of Europe. Source: https://ec.europa.eu/fisheries/sites/fisheries/files/docs/body/pcp_en.pdf

[12] Bertie Armstrong is the CEO of the Scottish Fishermen's Federation.

Before diving into the core issues that Brexit will generate for fishermen, let us set the stage for the negotiation. Four major players dominate the EU fishing industry and will have the most at stake: Spain, which produced 1.2 million tons of fish in 2015, the UK and Denmark, with 0.9 million tons each, and France with 0.7 million tons.[13] These four countries accounted for half of the total EU production in 2015.[14]

These numbers are significant because the fishing fleets of the UK, Denmark, and France are all most active in the same sector, the North East Atlantic, and made up 47.7 percent of EU catches in the region in 2015.[15] Spain, which is very active in most sectors, also fishes in the North East Atlantic. In fact, in 2016, 74.3 percent of EU-28 catches were taken from the region.[16]

This is what bothers UK fishermen: the majority of fish and shellfish in UK waters seems to be caught by EU boats.[17] A study by the NAFC Marine Centre at the University of the Highlands and Islands thus estimates that between 2012 and 2014 about 58 percent of fish caught in UK waters was landed by boats from other EU countries.[18] This is said to represent about 650,000 tons worth over 400 million pounds per year. In the same period, UK fishing boats only landed an estimated average of 90,000 tons per year in other EU Member States' waters.[19]

British waters are so popular because they currently are home to many popular species of fish, including 88 percent of the adult population of the North Sea herring, Europe's most popular fish by

---

13 EUROSTAT, FISHERY STATISTICS, http://ec.europa.eu/eurostat/statistics-explained/index.php/Fishery_statistics [hereinafter FISHERY STATISTICS]

14 Damian Carrington, *Hard Brexit would mean more and cheaper British fish - but there's a catch*, Apr. 24, 2018, https://www.theguardian.com/environment/2018/apr/24/hard-brexit-would-mean-more-and-cheaper-british-fish-but-theres-a-catch. Other EU nations may actually have even more at stake: fleets from Ireland, Belgium, and the Netherlands catch 35-35% of their fish in UK waters. Ireland also imports a lot of fish from the UK, which could drive prices up to 9%.

15 FISHERY STATISTICS, *supra* note 13.

16 *Id.*

17 Ian Napier, Fish Landings from the United Kingdom's Exclusive Economic Zone, and UK Landings from the European Union's EEZ, University of the Highlands and Islands, October 2016, https://www.nafc.uhi.ac.uk/t4-media/one-web/nafc/research/document/eez-reports/report-uk-eez-2016-10-11-final.pdf.

18 *Id.*

19 UK Sea Fisheries Statistics, *supra* note 3. Similarly, the Marine Management Organisation estimates that in 2015, UK fishing boats landed between 94,000 and 149,000 tons from the Exclusive Economic Zones of other EU Member States, worth £90 -169 million. This suggests that about 16% of all fish and shellfish landed by UK vessels into the UK and abroad that year was caught in other EU Member States' waters. *See* Marine Management Organisation, Provisional statistics – UK fleet landings from other EU Member States' water: 2015.

weight. And yet, British fishermen have to contend with Danish and Dutch boats holding the largest quota shares for North Sea herring.[20]

Figure 2: North Sea Herring Stock

As detailed further in this chapter, the region is partially managed by the EU, since the EU has control over its territorial waters (see Figure 3). However, the region is also managed—in cooperation with the EU—

by a regional organization, the North East Atlantic Fisheries Commission (or NEAFC), which is mostly comprised of non-EU Member States, and which maintains control over fishing opportunities in the area (see Figure 4). Contracting Parties to the NEAFC include Denmark (in respect of the Faroe Islands and Greenland), the European Union, Iceland, Norway, and Russia.[21] The organization establishes binding management measures and an enforcement scheme aimed at preserving marine resources in its area of authority.

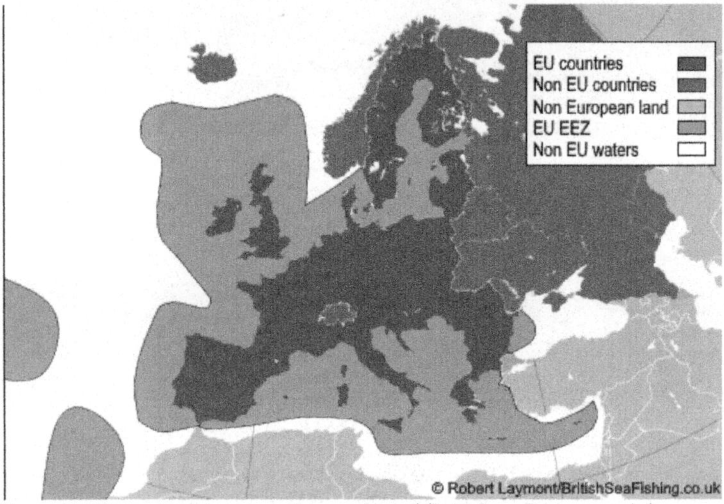

Figure 3: EU territorial waters. Source: http://britishseafishing.co.uk/common-fisheries-policy-cfp/

As such, non-EU countries will also impact the balance of interests in Brexit negotiations. For instance, Norway, with a hefty fish production of 3.5 million tons, and Iceland, with 1.3 million tons, both produce more than any State in the Union.[22] The two countries' total added production volume was equivalent to three quarters of the total EU-28 production, and because their fishing grounds overlap with the EU's, they will definitely be voices to contend with.[23]

---

[20] At approximately 17 percent and 17.5 percent, respectively.

[21] NORTH-EAST ATLANTIC FISHERIES COMMISSION, https://www.neafc.org/ (last visited June 8, 2008).

[22] FISHERY STATISTICS, *supra* note 13.

[23] *Id.*

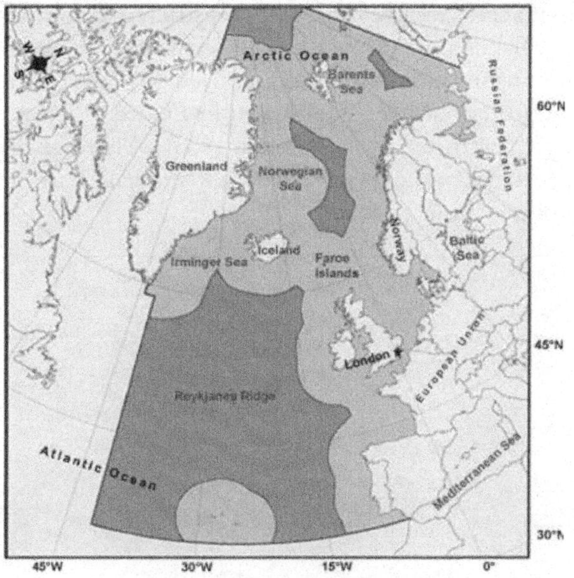

Figure 4: Zone Managed by NEAFC

These non-EU countries' voices especially matter because most species caught in the North East Atlantic are highly migratory and are therefore "shared stocks"—stocks that migrate through different countries' territorial waters and are therefore shared amongst these countries' fishermen. Herring is by far the most caught species in the area, representing almost 23 percent of total EU catches in 2016, followed by mackerel at 12.3 percent, sprat at 11.9 percent, blue whiting, and cod.[24] These five species make up over 55 percent of EU catches in the North East Atlantic and most of them are highly migratory. As explained below in this chapter, the exploitation of shared stocks requires a fair amount of international cooperation. Indeed, coordinating fishing opportunities to prevent over-fishing, especially in spawning grounds, is key to preserving sustainable fishing opportunities. In 2012, a "mackerel war" already broke out between the UK, Faroe Islands, and Iceland, which led to overfishing.[25] The herring, for example, nurses in Dutch and Danish waters before migrating to British waters.[26] The Danish have

---

[24] *Id.*

[25] Joshua Chaffin, *The Brexit catch for North Sea cod,* The Financial Times, May 11 2017, https://www.ft.com/content/404cc4a8-3402-11e7-bce4-9023f8c0fd2e.

[26] Michael Acton, *Britain Seeks to Take Back Control in Brexit Fisheries Fight*, THE FINANCIAL TIMES, Nov. 28, 2017, accessible at: https://www.ft.com/content/4f21072a-c87f-11e7-ab18-7a9fb7d6163e.

stated that if access to UK waters were restricted, fishermen would target the younger fish in unrestricted areas.[27] Smaller fish could not be destined to human consumption, but could be used for different purposes, such as manufacturing fish oil.[28] As shown in Figure 5 below, many species are already over-fished, a situation that EU Member States and non-Member States from the North Atlantic Region alike are trying to remedy through conservation efforts.

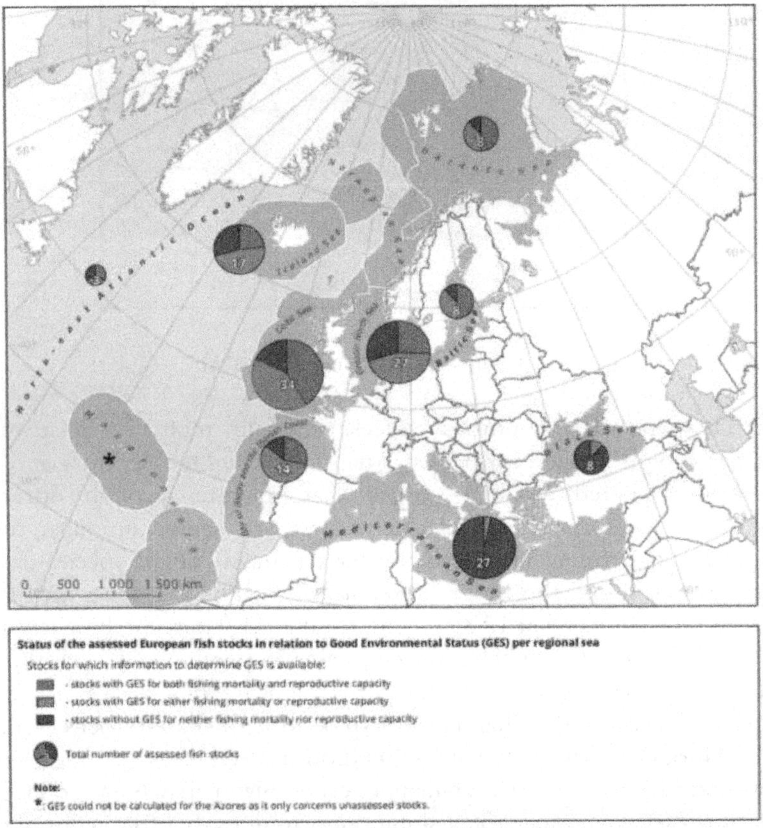

Figure 5: Status of the assessed European fish stocks in relation to Good Environmental States (GES) per regional sea. Source::https://www.eea.europa.eu/data-and-maps/figures/total-catch-in-ices-and-gfcm-fishing-regions-of-europe-in-3

[27] *Id.*
[28] *Id.*

Highly migratory stocks further require cooperation because they not only migrate across borders throughout their life cycle, their migration pattern can also change over the years. Returning to the example of the very popular North Sea herring illustrates that point. Today the herring reaches adulthood in British waters. However, in the 1980s and 1990s, the majority of adult North Sea herring lived in Norwegian waters. Their migration pattern could move back.[29] With global warming impacting water temperatures, other fish like cod have already migrated north.[30]

Future trade opportunities and tariffs will also influence negotiations over rights to access fishing grounds: UK fishermen would have no interest in obtaining increased fishing opportunities in British waters if they were unable to sell the resulting surplus. Unfortunately for UK fishermen, due to differing consumption preferences between European states when it comes to fish, the UK, which has been a net importer of fish since 1984, imports most of the fish that Brits consume from the EU, while exporting most of the UK's production to EU Member States.[31] For instance, in 2016, UK imports were highest for tuna,[32] cod,[33] and shrimps and prawns,[34] species that are fished by French and Spanish boats, but not by UK vessels (see Figure 6). Tariffs the UK imposes on fish when it exits the EU will thus mostly negatively impact the price of fish sold in the UK. This issue would be compounded by the fact that in a hard Brexit scenario, increases in catches would be for species such as blue whiting, herring, and sand eels, which are of very little interest to UK consumers.[35]

---

29 *Id.*

30 Nigel Hunt and Sybille de La Hamaide, *UK fishermen see Brexit bonanza, but there's a catch*, Reuters, Sept. 19, 2017, https://www.reuters.com/article/us-britain-eu-fishing-insight/uk-fishermen-see-brexit-bonanza-but-theres-a-catch-idUSKCN1BU0IQ.

31 UK Sea Fisheries Statistics, *supra* note 3 at 9.

32 The UK imported more than 120,000 tons of tuna in 2016. UUK Sea Fisheries Statistics, *supra* note 3 at 9.

33 The UK imported 120,000 tons of cod in 2016. UK Sea Fisheries Statistics, *supra* note 3 at 9.

34 The UK imported more than 80,000 tons of prawns in 2016. UK Sea Fisheries Statistics, *supra* note 3 at 9.

35 Damian Carrington, *Hard Brexit would mean more and cheaper British fish - but there's a catch*, Apr. 24, 2018, https://www.theguardian.com/environment/2018/apr/24/hard-brexit-would-mean-more-and-cheaper-british-fish-but-theres-a-catch.

FR		
Yellowfin tuna	41 809	7.9%
Hake	32 348	6.1%
Scallop	30 977	5.9%
Herring	30 142	5.7%
Skipjack tuna	29 432	5.6%
Sardine	27 519	5.2%

T which reaches adulthood in British waters nowadays

ES		
Skipjack tuna	128 027	14.2%
Sharks	92 452	10.2%
Hake	88 801	9.8%
Yellowfin tuna	85 794	9.5%
Sardine	49 024	5.4%
Mackerel	47 010	5.2%

UK		
Mackerel	163 801	26.5%
Herring	93 569	15.2%
Scallop	45 038	7.3%
Haddock	39 742	6.4%
Crab	30 936	5.0%

Figure 6: Main Species Caught by Member States (2013).
Source: https://ec.europa.eu/fisheries/sites/fisheries/files/docs/body/pcp_en.pdf

Similarly, most UK exports go to the EU and will now have to contend with increased competition from non-EU countries exporting the same species. For example, UK Salmon, the UK's main export,[36] will now have to contend with Norwegian competition, which, until now, had to build EU tariffs into its prices, something UK fisheries have not had to do for decades.[37]

[36] The UK exported more than 100,000 tons of salmon in 2016, closely followed by mackerel (more than 80,000 tons) and herring (40,000 tons). UK Sea Fisheries Statistics, *supra* note 3 at 9.

[37] KLUGE, *8 things you should know about Brexit and Norwegian fisheries*, Jul. 29, 2017 https://www.kluge.no/en/recent/news/2017/brexit-and-norwegian-fisheries/.

B. *INCEPTION OF THE COMMON FISHERIES POLICY AND OF THE QUOTA SYSTEM*

"*We get a very unfair share of quota allocations.*" —George Eustice[38]

The idea of a Common Fisheries Policy dates back to the inception of the European Economic Community, the EU's predecessor. The community had already gained competences over fisheries policy pursuant to Article 38 of the 1957 Treaty of Rome, which stated that "the operation and development of the common market for agricultural products, [which include products of fisheries,][39] must be accompanied by the establishment of a common ... policy among the Member States."[40] The more formal Common Fisheries Policy (CFP) thereafter came into force in 1983.[41]

The Common Fisheries Policy gave exclusive competence to the Community to manage conservation responsibilities within all Member States' combined Exclusive Economic Zones (EEZ).[42] Thus, the policy aims, among other similar goals, to achieve long-term maximum sustainable yield of EU fishing stocks, and in order to do so, manages

---

38 George Eustice is a pro-Brexit British Conservative Party politician. He was first elected at the 2010 general election as the MP for Camborne and Redruth, and was reelected in 2015. He was the 2013 Parliamentary Under Secretary of State for Farming, Food and the Marine Environment, and the 2015 Minister of State for Agriculture, Fisheries and Food. The Guardian reported that he stated: "In the Channel, North Sea and far south-western waters we get a very unfair share of quota allocations . . . In the Celtic Sea, France gets nearly three times our allocation of dover sole, roughly four times more cod and five times more haddock." Arthur Neslen, *Leaving EU could end 'unfair' French fishing quotas, says minister*, THE GUARDIAN, Jun. 1, 2016, https://www.theguardian.com/environment/2016/jun/01/leaving-eu-could-end-unfair-french-fishing-quotas-says-minister.

39 Treaty of Rome, art. 38 §1, Mar. 25, 1957.

40 *Id.* art. 38 §4. The Treaty of Lisbon enshrined fisheries conservation policy as one of the of the EU's exclusive competences, though the General Fisheries Policy remains a shared competence. *See* Consolidated Treaty on the Functioning of the European Union, arts. 3(d), 4(d).

41 Griffin Carpenter and Richard Kleinjans, New Economics Foundation, Who Gets to Fish?, The Allocation of Fishing Opportunities in EU Member States, 17, accessible at: http://neweconomics.org/wp-content/uploads/2017/03/Carpenter-Kleinjans-Who-gets-to-fish-16.03.pdf [hereinafter Who Gets to Fish?].

42 *Id.*

fishing opportunities, landing obligations,[43] and fleets. The policy also encourages the industry through various market interventions.[44]

Most relevant to this chapter, the policy sets quotas of each species of fish that can be caught within a given area of EU waters.[45] First, the Council of Ministers relies on scientific advice[46] to set the Total Allowable Catch (or TAC) on a yearly basis, or two-yearly basis for deep-sea stocks.[47] These quotas are then apportioned between Member States based on each country's traditional share.[48] For each stock, a different allocation percentage per EU countries is applied: it is known as the "relative stability key."[49]

The quota each Member State receives is based largely on catch records in those areas between 1973 and 1978, before the Common Fisheries Policy came into effect.[50] As this chapter later discusses, the UK is especially critical of this particular system because until 1976,[51] UK fleets fished in the waters around Iceland, which is not an EU member. UK fishermen thus argue that they were not awarded a large enough

---

[43] Landing obligations attempt to curtail discarding. Discarding is the practice of returning unwanted catches to the sea—either dead or alive—because they are undersized, because the fisherman has no quota, or because there is no demand for the species caught. The 2013 CFP reform aims at eliminating this practice through the introduction of the landing obligation, whereby all catches of regulated commercial species on-board must be landed and counted against quota. *See* European Commission, Discarding and the Landing Obligation, accessible at: https://ec.europa.eu/fisheries/cfp/fishing_rules/discards_en.

[44] Who Gets to Fish?, *supra* note 41, at 17.

[45] *See* European Commission, The Common Fisheries Policy (CFP), available at: https://ec.europa.eu/fisheries/cfp_en.

[46] TACs are set through a multi-stage process involving several institutions. Every year, Member States submit data on fish stocks. The International Council for the Exploration of the Seas (ICES), an intergovernmental scientific body, subsequently carries out annual stock assessments, which it formulates into scientific advice on recommended levels of fishing to achieve the CFP's objectives. An advisory committee reviews the scientific advice issued, before passing it on to the Commission. The Scientific Technical Economic Committee (STECF) also makes recommendations to the Commission. The Commission then formulates proposals on TAC levels. Finally, the European Council of Ministers, which has full legal discretion, establishes a regulation that sets fishing opportunities for the following year. *See* Who Gets to Fish?, *Supra* note 41, at 17.

[47] *See* Who Gets to Fish?, *supra* note 41, at 17.

[48] European Commission, Fishing Quotas, accessible at: https://ec.europa.eu/fisheries/cfp/fishing_rules/tacs_en.

[49] "Fishing opportunities allocated to Member States shall ensure relative stability of fishing activities of each Member State for each fish stock or fishery. The interests of each Member State shall be taken into account when new fishing opportunities are allocated." Regulation (EU) No 1380/2013, art. 16(1).

[50] Who Gets to Fish?, *supra* note 41, at 18.

[51] At the time, fishing limits around Iceland did not yet extend to 200 miles.

portion of EU quotas. After TACs have been set, it is up to Member States to decide how to distribute their allocations to their fishermen.[52] Although it may seem far-fetched, the relative stability key method is designed to keep the levels of fishing per area relatively stable.

Ironically, the UK's departure from the EU could lead to the dissolution of the relative stability system that UK fishermen have so hated. Indeed, if the UK does decide to close off access to its waters to other EU Member States, the EU will do the same, and fishing quotas currently attributed to the UK within the EU (about 30 percent of fishing opportunities in the EU) will have to be redistributed among other remaining Member States.[53] Some Member States might refuse to re-apportion these fishing opportunities by using the relative stability key because the system was adopted in a specific historical context in which the UK's presence in the Union was a determinant factor.[54] They might argue that the system should be reviewed since the circumstances that justified it have dramatically changed.[55]

Finally, it is worth noting that the CFP's formula is not the only determinant for fishing opportunities allocated to UK fishermen. Some stocks are also shared, agreed upon, and jointly managed with non-EU countries, thus allowing for more efficiency and a more sustainable management of highly migratory stocks.[56] Agreements made by the EU with non-EU countries are thus also responsible for the presence of foreign fishermen, for instance Norwegian fishermen, in UK waters.

---

[52] Who Gets to Fish?, *supra* note 41, at 18.

[53] European Parliament, Directorate-General for Internal Policies, Research for PECH Committee - Common Fisheries Policy and Brexit, 15, 2017, accessible at: http://www.europarl.europa.eu/RegData/etudes/STUD/2017/601981/IPOL_STU(2017)601981_EN.pdf, [hereinafter Common Fisheries Policy and Brexit].

[54] *Id.*

[55] *Id.*

[56] *Id.*

C. *THE INTERNATIONAL FRAMEWORK*

"We will be an independent coastal state."—Theresa May[57]

Upon withdrawing from the EU, the UK will automatically become an independent coastal state bound by international obligations.[58] The most comprehensive law for international fishing is the United Nations Convention on the Law of the Sea (UNCLOS), which the UK is a party to.[59] UNCLOS includes provisions for the establishment of sovereignty of coastal states over territorial waters, rules of free passage, measures on the conservation of biological resources, and the provision of an international dispute settlement mechanism.[60]

Most importantly to UK fishermen, UNCLOS allows nations to establish an Exclusive Economic Zone (EEZ) of up to 200 nautical miles from their coast—or, when other sovereigns exist within a 200-mile radius,[61] up to the median line between the two coasts.[62] Countries have sovereignty over their EEZ to exploit its living and non-living resources. Therefore, now that the UK is leaving the EU, it will exit the EU's EEZ and theoretically can have control of all fish within its own EEZ as well as over who harvests it.[63] These provisions and the ability to control which fleets enter UK waters are what the British fishing industry is most excited about when it comes to Brexit.

However, membership in UNCLOS also comes with a number of international obligations, which are not far removed from objectives the CFP was aiming to respect.[64] First, the UK will be required to enact

[57] Theresa May currently serves as Prime Minister of the UK and has been Leader of the Conservative Party since 2016. During an appearance before the Commons Liaison Committee in March 2018, she stated: "We must get ourselves into an independent coastal state and be ready to run our own fish. . . . We will be an independent coastal state." *E.g.*, Mark Chandler, *Theresa May insists Britain WILL take back control of fishing after Brexit*, EXPRESS, Mar. 27, 2018, https://www.express.co.uk/news/politics/937885/brexit-news-fishing-theresa-may-Liaison-Committee-transition.

[58] *E.g.*, Common Fisheries Policy and Brexit, *supra* note 53.

[59] The UK is party to the Convention on its own, as well as through the European Union's membership. *See* Chronological lists of ratifications of, accessions and successions to the Convention and the related Agreements, UNITED NATIONS, OCEANS & LAW OF THE SEA, last updated: 03 April 2018, accessible at: http://www.un.org/depts/los/reference_files/chronological_lists_of_ratifications.htm

[60] Who Gets to Fish?, *supra* note 41 at 16.

[61] The UK will have to limit its EEZ to the median line between Britain and France, and Britain and Ireland, for example.

[62] *E.g.*, Who Gets to Fish?, *supra* note 41 at 16.

[63] United Nations Convention on the Law of the Sea, art. 62(4), 10 December 1982.

[64] *See* Common Fisheries Policy and Brexit, *supra* note 53 at 15.

measures designed to maintain or restore stocks to levels that can produce the maximum sustainable yield.[65] The country will thus need to determine the total allowable catch, which should reflect the best scientific advice available of living resources within its EEZ.[66] Consequently it will be for the UK Government to develop and implement a domestic fisheries policy after withdrawal from the EU.

Moreover, UNCLOS Article 63(1) imposes an obligation on states in whose waters the same stock occurs (shared stock), to co-operate in the management of these stocks.[67] Although there are no precise guidelines as to how this needs to be done, the obligation nonetheless exists.[68] This obligation is echoed in the Fish Stocks Agreement of 1995. These agreements thus impose an obligation to co-operate with respect to the management of species that are highly migratory or straddle the EEZ of coastal states and the adjacent high seas (straddling stocks), such as mackerel.[69] The cooperation can be done through sub-regional fisheries management organization, or directly through bilateral negotiations, and must rely on scientific data to preserve the sustainability of stocks.[70] Unfortunately for British seafarers, most of the fish found in UK waters are shared with the UK, Norway, and/or the Faroe Islands.[71] The UK will thus also need to engage in bilateral and multilateral negotiations with its neighbors after Brexit.

Furthermore, Article 62(3) of UNCLOS requires that if a coastal state is not capable of harvesting the entire allowable catch, it must allow access to states whose nationals have habitually fished in a given EEZ where a surplus exists.[72] EU Member States could rely on this article to claim a right to continued access to the UK EEZ if the UK were to close off access entirely.[73] Michael Gove has already announced that British fishermen would not be able to land all of the fish in British territorial

---

[65] *Id.*, art. 61(2).

[66] United Nations Convention on the Law of the Sea, art. 61(1), 10 December 1982. *See* Who Gets to Fish?, *supra* note 41.

[67] United Nations Convention on the Law of the Sea, art. 63, 10 December 1982; Agreement for the implementation of the provisions of the United Nations convention on the law of the sea, art. 8, 10 December 1982.

[68] *See* Common Fisheries Policy and Brexit, *supra* note 53 at 17.

[69] Agreement for the implementation of the provisions of the United Nations convention on the law of the sea, art. 5, 10 December 1982.

[70] Brexit: Fisheries, Chapter 3: A new legal baseline, Parliament.uk, 2016, https://publications.parliament.uk/pa/ld201617/ldselect/ldeucom/78/7806.htm.

[71] *Id.*

[72] United Nations Convention on the Law of the Sea, art. 62(3), 10 December 1982.

[73] *Id.*

waters, and that some form of access would thus have to be granted to vessels from other countries.[74]

Finally, some European nations may also make a claim to historic access rights to fishing in UK waters.[75] Before EU law came into effect, the 1964 London Fisheries Convention gave rights to vessels that had fished these waters between 1953 and 1963 to fish in the 6 to 12 nautical mile limit.[76] Most scholars are skeptical that this Convention would be resurrected, since EU law superseded it.[77] Even if it were, the UK would be able to withdraw. However, the withdrawal would take two years, which could have diplomatic consequences for Brexit negotiations.[78]

The UK may, however, be advantaged by some of its international obligations. The UK may, for example, be able to gain a seat at the Atlantic Fisheries Commission, which sets quotas for the North Sea fish, and where the EU only has one representative, despite speaking for 28 nations.

D. THE CJEU AND ITS POTENTIAL ROLE IN FUTURE DISPUTES

"We want to take back control of our laws."—Theresa May[79]

The Court of Justice of the European Union (or CJEU) is the Union's judicial authority. Save for a few exceptions, the scope of its competence does not usually include the settlement of disputes involving third countries.[80] Moreover, the UK has been adamant that it would no longer accept CJEU jurisdiction, especially when it comes to fishery

---

[74] *Brexit: Gove confirms foreign access to UK fishing grounds*, BBC, Aug. 3, 2017, http://www.bbc.com/news/uk-scotland-scotland-politics-40814377.

[75] Valentin Schatz, *Brexit and fisheries access - Some reflections on the UK's denunciation of the 1964 London Fisheries Convention*, EJIL, Jul. 18, 2017, https://www.ejiltalk.org/brexit-and-fisheries-access-some-reflections-on-the-uks-denunciation-of-the-1964-london-fisheries-convention/; Brexit: Fisheries, Chapter 3: A new legal baseline, Parliament.uk, 2016, https://publications.parliament.uk/pa/ld201617/ldselect/ldeucom/78/7806.htm.

[76] *Id.*

[77] *Id.*

[78] *Id.*

[79] In her March 2018 Mansion House speech, which set out her vision for the UK's relationship with the EU after Brexit, Theresa May said: "We want the freedom to negotiate trade agreements with other countries around the world. We want to take back control of our laws. We also want as frictionless a border as possible between us and the EU . . ." *In full: Theresa May's speech on future UK-EU relations*, BBC NEWS, Mar. 2, 2018, https://www.bbc.com/news/uk-politics-43256183.

[80] *See* Common Fisheries Policy and Brexit, *supra* note 53 at 28.

disputes between British and EU citizens, companies, or authorities.[81] The CJEU will retain jurisdiction over disputes involving UK interests until the country agrees to a withdrawal agreement, but it will be necessary to devise dispute settlement procedures for after the UK's withdrawal.[82] The EU and the UK should also formulate a system to give effect to any pending CJEU cases at the time of withdrawal.

Looking at other agreements concluded by the EU with third countries may help in imagining what the future UK-EU relationship might look like. For internal market questions (free movement of fishermen and of products), current practice suggests the dispute could be submitted to the CJEU by mutual agreement or could be solved through consultation, mediation, or arbitration as dictated by a new potential UK-EU agreement on dispute settlement.[83] By way of example, the EU Turkey Agreement allows for CJEU jurisdiction when unanimously agreed by the EU-Turkey Association Council.[84] However, that is unlikely considering the UK has expressed its strong desire to remove itself from the jurisdiction of the CJEU in the future, and its recognition that future relations will require some dispute settlement mechanism.[85]

In the case of disputes related to fisheries activities (discards, fishing opportunities, quotas, etc.), the CJEU would once again be unlikely to settle disputes, (a UK-EU agreement providing for such a measure would be a novelty).[86] Other options include means of dispute settlement provided in Part XV of UNCLOS, which would be used exceptionally as they are intended for states and international organizations, rather than for individuals, the International Tribunal for the Law of the Sea (ITLOS), which is open to individuals, or through friendly settlement.[87] This last option is what current EU fisheries agreements provide for.

---

[81] Elizabeth Piper, *Britain outlines plans to break free of European Court after Brexit*, REUTERS, Aug. 22, 2017, https://www.reuters.com/article/us-britain-eu-court-idUSKCN1B22GU.

[82] *See* Common Fisheries Policy and Brexit, *supra* note 53 at 28.

[83] *Id.* at 29.

[84] *Id.* at 29, *citing* V. SKOURIS, "The Role of the Court of Justice of the European Union in the Development of the EEA Single Market," in EFTA Court (ed.), *The EEA and the EFTA Court,* Hart Publishing, 2014, pp. 3-12; D. SARMIENTO, "Prejudiciales especiales. Auge y fenomenologia de los regimenes atipicos de la cuestion prejudicial europea", in R. Alonso Garcia and J.I Ugartenmendia Eceizabarrena (eds.), *La cuestion prejudicial,* European Inklings, No. 4, 2014, pp. 111-112.

[85] *See* Common Fisheries Policy and Brexit, *supra* note 53 at 29, *citing* White Paper, February 2017: Ending jurisdiction of EU Court in UK and recognition that future relationship agreement will need dispute resolution mechanisms.

[86] *See* Common Fisheries Policy and Brexit, *supra* note 53 at 30.

[87] *Id.*

Unfortunately, these mechanisms only provide for the suspension of the agreement if the dispute cannot be resolved.[88]

II. IMPACT OF THE WITHDRAWAL AGREEMENT ON FISHERIES

"If they get free access to the European market, we should also have free access to fish in the British fishing zone."—Niels Wichmann[89]

Although fisheries are a somewhat over-politicized issue compared to their low economic weight, they will not be a central issue in Brexit negotiations. However, fisheries will still be strongly conditioned by the terms of any withdrawal agreement on other core issues, such as the internal market or fundamental freedoms. Indeed, the fate of the internal market will determine that of British fishery products' access to the EU market and vice versa (A). Likewise, negotiations will impact the freedom to set up fishery businesses in the UK (B) and the free movement of fishermen (C).

These core issues will be negotiated separately from any specific agreement regarding access rights to fishing grounds and apportionment of fishing quotas. They are complex and multifaceted, and as such, their deep analysis is outside the scope of this chapter. This being said, this chapter still briefly addresses them to give the reader an overview of the context in which future ad hoc agreements about fishing grounds will be negotiated. Negotiators will need to consider the way these issues are resolved in order to form a consistent framework, which ensures, for example, that the freedom of movement of fishery products is linked to free access to waters and resources, and vice versa.

A. RIGHT TO TRADE IN FISH PRODUCTS

Trade in fish products between the EU and the UK after Brexit will be foremost affected by the imposition of new tariffs, where the UK currently trades with the EU tariff-free. Moreover, where, until now, the UK benefited from tariffs negotiated by the EU with third-parties, London will now have to negotiate its own tariffs. Although the ability to freely negotiate tariffs was one of the main reasons why so many Brits supported Brexit, analysts tend to agree that the odds are not in the UK's

---

[88] *See Id.*, EU-Morocco fisheries agreement, arts. 7-15, 2006; EU-Senegal fisheries agreement, arts 7-13.

[89] Nigel Hunt and Sybille de La Hamaide, *UK fishermen see Brexit bonanza, but there's a catch*, Reuters, Sept. 19, 2017, https://www.reuters.com/article/us-britain-eu-fishing-insight/uk-fishermen-see-brexit-bonanza-but-theres-a-catch-idUSKCN1BU0IQ. Niels Wichmann is the Head of the Danish Fishermen's Association.

favor. In any case, the UK is likely to start paying tariffs on many of its fisheries' products or to face a very long and difficult negotiation: By waz of example, Norway still pays tariffs on its exports of many processed fish, such as salmon, to the EU, and the EU's deal with Canada took 7 years to negotiate.[90] Time spent negotiating will be costly since WTO tariffs on fish and shellfish exports before a deal is hashed out could cost the UK's fishing industry up to 100 million pounds a year.[91] These new tariffs will be problematic for Brits who consume fish products, and most of all, they will be problematic for UK fishermen.

They will be problematic for British consumers because, as aforementioned, two-thirds of the fish consumed in the UK is imported. A large portion of the British consumption of fish is actually imported from the European Union.[92] Trade barriers resulting from a hard Brexit—that is, the type of Brexit that fishermen are asking for—would impose a higher price on most fish products offered to UK consumers.[93]

Moreover, a hard Brexit, which would keep foreign fishermen out of UK waters, would not only lead to British vessels landing more fish, it would also lead to a corresponding drop in UK-caught fish prices.[94] That drop in price would actually lead to a drop in UK fishermen's earnings. Indeed, research conducted at Wageningen University & Research (WUR) in the Netherlands found that if a hard Brexit came to pass, UK vessels could land up to 15 percent more fish, worth 250 million pounds, in the five years following the transition period. However, according to the researchers these additional landings would not be sufficient to compensate for the increased supply driving prices down.[95]

---

[90] *See E.g.*, Common Fisheries Policy and Brexit, *supra* note 53 at 36; KLUGE, *8 things you should know about Brexit and Norwegian fisheries*, Jul. 29, 2017 https://www.kluge.no/en/recent/news/2017/brexit-and-norwegian-fisheries/.

[91] Elizabeth Truss, *We must not lose our voice in EU fishing policy*, THE NATIONAL FEDERATION OF FISHERMEN'S ORGANISATION, May 13, 2016, http://nffo.org.uk/eu-referendum/2016/05/13/we-must-not-lose-our-voice-in-eu-fishing-policy.

[92] *E.g.*, Damian Carrington, *Hard Brexit would mean more and cheaper British fish - but there's a catch*, Apr. 24, 2018, https://www.theguardian.com/environment/2018/apr/24/hard-brexit-would-mean-more-and-cheaper-british-fish-but-theres-a-catch.

[93] Wageningen University & Research, Impact of hard Brexit on European fisheries, April 2018, https://www.wur.nl/upload_mm/6/3/7/f745b912-2409-4184-ac19-dbd71d019edd_Brexit%20MAGNET.pdf.

[94] Damian Carrington, *Hard Brexit would mean more and cheaper British fish - but there's a catch*, Apr. 24, 2018, https://www.theguardian.com/environment/2018/apr/24/hard-brexit-would-mean-more-and-cheaper-british-fish-but-theres-a-catch.

[95] It is also worth noting that by exiting the European Union, UK fishermen will lose EU subsidies. Subsidies to the fishing sector are equivalent to 50 percent of the value of the total fish catch by the EU in the same year. Spain, France, Denmark, the UK, and Italy

Of course, British fish farms, which also export most of their products, and the fish processing industry, which relies on imports, would also be affected.[96] The fish processing industry would also be hit by Norwegian fish companies, which currently process a lot of their fish in the UK in order to avoid EU tariffs on processed fish products, leaving the UK once the country no longer has tariff-free access to the European market.[97]

More bad news for British fisheries, the UK's withdrawal from the Union may also level out the playing field when it comes to fish exports towards the EU, and lead to more intense competition between Nordic countries and the UK as the UK loses preferential access to the common market.[98]

Proponents of the hard Brexit in the fishing industry, however, continue to believe that the scenario would be a better deal for the UK. They posit that although prices may drop, they would eventually recover, as the UK's processing industry also rebuilds.[99]

Whether or not they are right may ultimately not matter. Indeed, tariffs will not apply only to fish. With fishing trade representing only 0.4% of the UK's GDP, British negotiators are more worried about trade tariffs being applied to other major sectors. The imposition of new tariffs could thus push the UK to use access to British waters as a bargaining chip for lower trade tariffs in other areas. The March 2018 Draft Agreement is only one element confirming this scenario.

B. EU INVESTMENTS IN FISHERIES IN THE UK

Many EU companies made investments in UK fisheries based on the expectation that the UK would remain within the European Union.[100] This scenario is now being shaken up. The UK's withdrawal from the EU could lead UK-registered EU ships to lose their British flag, that is

---

receive the most fishing subsidies. *See* Oceana, The European Union and Fishing Subsidies,
http://oceana.org/sites/default/files/reports/EU_Subsidies_Report_Fact_Sheet_FINAL.pdf.

[96] Damian Carrington, *Hard Brexit would mean more and cheaper British fish - but there's a catch*, Apr. 24, 2018, https://www.theguardian.com/environment/2018/apr/24/hard-brexit-would-mean-more-and-cheaper-british-fish-but-theres-a-catch.

[97] KLUGE, *8 things you should know about Brexit and Norwegian fisheries*, Jul. 29, 2017 https://www.kluge.no/en/recent/news/2017/brexit-and-norwegian-fisheries/.

[98] *Id.*

[99] Damian Carrington, *Hard Brexit would mean more and cheaper British fish - but there's a catch*, Apr. 24, 2018, https://www.theguardian.com/environment/2018/apr/24/hard-brexit-would-mean-more-and-cheaper-british-fish-but-theres-a-catch.

[100] Common Fisheries Policy and Brexit, *supra* note 53, at 19.

to say, the registration of their ship in the UK.[101] As such, ships that were previously able to share in UK quotas in the past may not be able to do so anymore. Brexit will also engender greater complexity and higher costs for EU fishermen involved in activities in UK waters due to differences between UK and EU regulations, and will likely generate difficulties for EU companies in cooperating, investing, or merging with British fishing companies.[102]

Today, a large number of vessels with capital from EU Member States now operate under the British flag. This practice is the result of the former British policy requiring only that a vessel be owned by a subject or by a company incorporated and headquartered in the UK for it to be registered in a British register.[103] Due to quota hopping —the practice of registering a EU ship in the UK in order to receive a share of UK quotas—British authorities tightened the conditions for granting British registration to fishing boats in a 1988 Act of Parliament.[104] This decision led to a legal battle that reached the CJEU, which declared the British Act to be in contravention with EU law.[105] EU ships continued to register in the UK en masse thereafter.

However, freed from the constraints of European law, the rule of the internal market, and CJEU case law, British authorities will have the freedom they need to incorporate restrictive measures aimed at limiting the registration of vessels in their Register.[106] Therefore, the UK's withdrawal could dramatically change the circumstances under which registrations are taking place. Vessels could have to recover their flag of origin, consequently losing their investments. On the other hand, the British Government may also decide to preserve freedom of establishment at least in some sectors, and perhaps in the fishing industry. As a less stringent measure, the Government could seek to ensure that domestic quotas deliver benefits to the UK by strengthening the "economic link," which is a set of conditions vessels using UK quotas must comply with to demonstrate that the quotas benefit UK communities.[107]

Because of business owners' expectations associated with investments in British ships when the UK was a Member State, it is

---

101 *Id.*

102 *Id.*

103 *Id.*

104 Requiring 75% of the capital and 75% of the crew to be British or a Member State national, excluding the nationals of certain Member States subject to a transitional period (Merchant Shipping Act, 1988).

105 *Factortame* line of cases, 1991.

106 Common Fisheries Policy and Brexit, *supra* note 53, at 19.

107 *Id.*

argued that investors should be protected from the negative impacts of Brexit. While the EU will likely fight for the protection of its citizen's "acquired rights," it is still unclear what the UK will acquiesce to in the final withdrawal agreement.[108] However, denying these protections could give rise to numerous legal claims in which investors sue for jurisdictional protection of their "substantive legitimate expectation."[109]

C. FREEDOM OF MOVEMENT OF FISHERMEN

The right to free movement of persons will be one of the first and most important issues in the EU-UK negotiations. As the UK regains its competence in matters of immigration with regard to EU Member State nationals, it could decide to put an end to the free movement of persons. Some EU seafarers, either self-employed or employed in UK-based fishing companies live and work in the UK. They will most likely be adversely affected by any withdrawal agreement. The UK could decide to make immigration procedures burdensome for EU fishermen if its end goal is to nationalize British fisheries' activity. Indeed, in addition to potentially needing a passport, visa, or work and residence permit to travel between their country of origin and their place of work, they may face new labor regulations and altered social security systems. Indeed, many acts of labor law harmonization, usually offering stronger protections than the preexisting standards in the country and coordination of social security systems, will cease to apply if they are not replaced by a specific EU-UK agreement.

Fortunately, all is not lost for EU seafarers. First of all, European fishermen will continue to enjoy and acquire rights arising from their European citizenship during the transition period and until an agreement regulating the UK's withdrawal from the EU is entered into. Moreover, if the UK chooses a formula similar to those established with EFTA countries, the current EU regulations on Social Security could be kept in place.[110] Finally, the EU is likely to defend the existence of acquired rights by all workers, including fishermen, who rooted their lives in the UK.[111]

---

108 *Id.*

109 Violation of substantive legitimate expectation is a recognized cause of action in the UK.

110 Common Fisheries Policy and Brexit, *supra* note 53, at 22.

111 However, the right for seafarers to remain and work in the country under the same conditions they currently enjoy will most likely not be considered an acquired right that could be invoked before the British courts. Indeed, although Art. 70 of the Vienna Convention ensures respect for rights acquired whilst a treaty is in force and following its termination, most authors hold that this guarantee is limited to states (the parties to treaties) and does not affect individuals. This interpretation is based on the International Law Commission's own commentary to this provision, as well as the evolution of

Whatever the outcome, negotiations should be swift in order to eliminate uncertainty and to encourage reciprocity in the legal treatment of Member State nationals in the UK, and British nationals in the EU.

III. RIGHT TO FISH: AGREEMENTS ON ACCESS TO FISHING GROUNDS AND QUOTAS

This section addresses the balance of powers in the negotiation of fishing rights and fishing quotas in the North East Atlantic post-Brexit. A provisional agreement was reached in March 2018, setting the stage until the end of 2020 (A). The way fishing opportunities will be apportioned after 2020 remains to be negotiated. This section will thus examine some of the most prominent actors that will likely weigh in on these negotiations (B) before making a set of recommendations (C).

A. THE MARCH 2018 PROVISIONAL AGREEMENT

"At least through the implementation period nothing will change."
—Iain Duncan Smith[112]

The threat of an unfavorable deal when it comes to fisheries materialized with the publication on February 28, 2018 of a provisional agreement on the terms of a 21-month period ending on December 31, 2020. The agreement will likely be signed in 2019. An updated color-coded version of the Draft Withdrawal Agreement was published on March 19th, indicating which articles are provisionally agreed, subject to re-drafting, or not agreed.[113]

---

international case law. See note 19. Other interpretations, taking into account the now changed historical context during which the International Law Commission wrote its commentary argue that individuals could have acquried these rights. In any case, the freedom of movement for persons will not be negotiated in bilateral negotiations with different Member States, as that would be contrary to the principle of sincere cooperation (Art 4(3) TEU).

[112] Iain Duncan Smith is a former Tory leader. He was Secretary of State for Work and Pensions from 2010 to 2016. He told the BBC: "There does seem to be a real concern . . . It appears that at least through the implementation period nothing will change and I think that will be a concern and the government clearly has to deal with that because a lot of MPs are very uneasy about that right now." Daniel Boffey, Anushka Asthana and Lisa O'Carroll, *Theresa May under fire over Brexit transition deal*, THE GUARDIAN, Mar. 19, 2018, https://www.theguardian.com/politics/2018/mar/19/uk-and-eu-agree-terms-for-brexit-transition-deal.

[113] Draft Agreement on the withdrawal of the United Kingdom of Great Britain and Northern Ireland from the European Union and the European Atomic Energy Community, accessible at: https://ec.europa.eu/commission/sites/beta-political/files/draft_agreement_coloured.pdf [hereinafter Withdrawal Agreement].

The UK started out with an ambitious negotiation agenda. With regards to fisheries, the country wanted to be able to control fishing in UK waters during the transition period. EU negotiators described this demand as "wild," and as "one of the most ambitious requests relating to the transition period."[114] They flatly rejected it. Instead, Brussels offered to consult UK authorities and to give them the opportunity to provide comments when the EU will set the TACs in British waters.[115] London begrudgingly accepted. The article is currently color-coded as provisionally agreed.

Theresa May expectedly faced protest and disapproval over what was perceived to be a concession on a high-profile Brexit demand. Tories in Scotland and Scottish fishermen especially expressed their disappointment with this outcome. Nigel Farage even called for the Prime Minister's removal from office.[116] The agreement is open for re-negotiation for 2021 on. The sections below detail the interests of some of the main players in the negotiations going forward.

---

114 THE FINANCIAL TIMES, https://www.ft.com/content/89ef8760-2931-11e8-b27e-cc62a39d57a0.

115 Withdrawal Agreement, *supra* note 113 at art. 125. The EU also proposed, though that portion is still subject to negotiations, that the provisions of Union law on the production and marketing of agricultural and fisheries products shall apply to the UK in respect to Northern Ireland. Withdrawal Agreement, *supra* note 113 at art. 5.

116 Daniel Boffey, *Theresa May under fire over Brexit transition*, THE GUARDIAN, Mar. 19, 2018, https://www.theguardian.com/politics/2018/mar/19/uk-and-eu-agree-terms-for-brexit-transition-deal

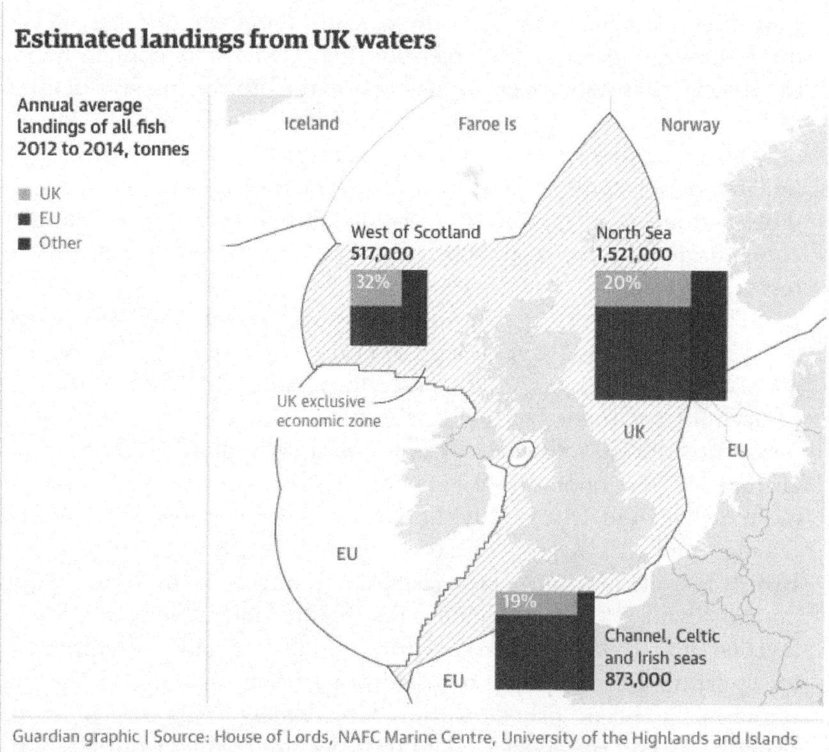

Figure 7: Estimated Landing from UK Waters

B. Primary Interests Weighing in on Negotiations Going Forward

1. UK

"We need to be a fully independent coast state looking after and taking advantage of our most excellent natural resources in our waters"—Bertie Armstrong[117]

The UK's sensitivity when it comes to fisheries-related issues derives at least in part from what may, at first sight, seem like an imbalance in benefits derived from the CFP between the EU and the UK. Indeed, EU fleets have been taking an average of 760,000 tons of fish from UK

---

[117] Darren Hunt, *If Brexit 'falls off a cliff' EU won't get a 'FIN OF FISH' blasts leading UK fishermen*, EXPRESS, Apr. 13, 2018, https://www.express.co.uk/news/uk/945133/Brexit-news-UK-EU-fishing-Theresa-May-European-Union-fisheries-CFP. Bertie Armstrong is the CEO of the Scottish Fishermen's Federation.

waters a year, while the UK only catches about 90,000 tons.[118] From these numbers breeds the perception that UK waters contain most of the resources and that reciprocal access is thus to the massive detriment of UK fishermen.[119] This is why Fishing for Leave demands that access only be negotiated "when absolutely necessary."[120] The group hopes that new restrictions will allow British trawlermen to catch more than three times as much fish as they are currently able to, which, they argue, will compensate for the comparatively small losses caused by the EU restricting access to its EEZ.[121]

Though it is correct that non-British EU vessels land more catches in UK waters than UK vessels do in non-UK EU waters, the fishermen are not necessarily right. As discussed throughout this chapter, they need to account for other factors. For instance, the UK only possesses 13 percent of the EU's total sea area, but is already allocated 30 percent of current EU fish quotas.[122] What's more, Britain currently exports most of its fish to the EU, and if the UK unilaterally extends its exclusive fishing waters, EU Member States could retaliate by putting up tariffs on British fish. This is what 60 coastal communities from 9 EU Member States (Spain, France, Belgium, the Netherlands, Germany, Poland, Sweden, and Ireland) are asking for.[123] Finally, rising sea temperatures are spurring the northward migration of stocks, such as cod, that have traditionally been fished within UK waters.[124] Some of British fishermen's favorite species could thus become extinct from UK waters in coming years, and the UK would lose out much from a non-reciprocal deal. These are the numbers that EU negotiators have in mind when discussing the future of fisheries with the UK.

---

[118] Verity Ryan, *Britain can have its 'fish cake' and eat it, says Government minister on fishing after Brexit*, THE TELEGRAPH, Feb. 27, 2018, https://www.telegraph.co.uk/politics/2018/02/27/britain-can-have-fish-cake-eat-says-government-minister-fishing/.

[119] *E.g.*, *Id.*

[120] Njodr AB, *Fishing for Leave House of Lords Submission Summary*, FISHING FOR LEAVE, Oct. 12, 2016, http://ffl.org.uk/fishing-for-leave-house-of-lords-submission-summary/.

[121] *Id.*

[122] Arthur Neslen, *Leaving EU could end 'unfair' French fishing quotas, says minister*, THE GUARDIAN, Jun. 1, 2016, https://www.theguardian.com/environment/2016/jun/01/leaving-eu-could-end-unfair-french-fishing-quotas-says-minister.

[123] Paola Tamma, *EU fishermen weigh in on Brexit tug-of-war*, EURACTIV, Oct. 25, 2017, https://www.euractiv.com/section/uk-europe/news/eu-fishermen-weigh-in-on-brexit-tug-of-war/.

[124] Peter Hetherington, *Net loss: Why Brexit could spell disaster for fishing*, THE NEW EUROPEAN, Feb. 20, 2018, http://www.theneweuropean.co.uk/top-stories/peter-hetherington-on-brexit-s-impact-on-british-fishing-industry-1-5396375.

Moreover, the fishing industry contributes less than 0.5 percent to the UK's total GDP.[125] Fishing communities are, of course, visible: In two of the EU's largest fishing ports, Fraserburgh, a 13,000 people town in Scotland, and Peterhead, a town of 19,000 souls, 40 percent of employment derives from the fishing industry. However, this visibility and hyper-mediatization is unlikely to outweigh British negotiator's need for an issue to trade for concessions in more economically significant areas in the end.

2. EU Bloc: Focus on Denmark and France

"We have to defend access to waters for artisanal and coastal fishing."
—Stephane Travert[126]

The EU holds some powerful cards in Brexit negotiations regarding fisheries. Perhaps most importantly, British companies currently export, mostly to EU states, 75 percent of the catches they land in UK waters.[127] This figure has made EU negotiators skeptical that the UK would seek to change much the current balance between quotas and market access. However, because the UK imports most of the fish for its own consumption from Europe, the EU also stands to lose from a poor deal.

Two EU countries stand to lose a lot from a poor deal and will weigh heavily on Brussels' position when it comes to fisheries: Denmark and France. Indeed, in 2015, Denmark made up a 14.1 percent share, and France a 10.3 percent share of the total EU fish production.[128] The Danish Prime Minister has expressed Danish interests in retaining access to the North Sea after the UK exits the Union, and has vowed to make access rights for fisheries a top priority in the Brexit negotiations.[129]

---

125 *Will Britain's fishermen be better off after Brexit?*, FINANCIAL TIMES, Jul. 3, 2017, https://www.ft.com/content84f51c84-5fe2-11e7-91a7-502f7ee26895.

126 *France eyes post-Brexit deal to keep fishing in UK waters*, THE LOCAL, Jul. 18, 2017, https://www.thelocal.fr/20170718/france-eyes-post-brexit-deal-to-keep-fishing-in-uk-waters.

Stephane Travert has been France's Minister of Agriculture since June 2017.

127 Camilla Canocchi, *EU trade is 'key' to success of UK fish industry as 75% of home-caught fish is exported - and majority of fish eaten by Britons is imported*, THIS IS MONEY, Dec. 17, 2016, http://www.thisismoney.co.uk/money/news/article-4043758/EU-trade-key-success-UK-fish-industry-75-home-caught-fish-exported-majority-fish-eaten-Britons-imported.html.

128 FISHERY STATISTICS, *supra* note 13.

129 Chloe Kerr, *Denmark PM DEMANDS access to UK waters after Brexit and vows to make fishing TOP PRIORITY*, EXPRESS, Mar. 23, 2018, https://www.express.co.uk/news/world/935762/brexit-news-fishing-north-sea-scotland-denmark-rasmussen-comments.

Indeed, Danish fishermen rely heavily on catches off the coast of Scotland, and Danish authorities have complained that the UK was making a balanced deal difficult to develop because of the multiple red lines it is drawing with regards to fishing rights and other high stakes issues.[130] In preparation for the worst, the country has reportedly built a case against the UK based on historic fishing rights dating back to the 1400s, should the UK close off its waters to Danish fleets.[131]

French authorities have also expressed their hopes for a balanced deal that would preserve French fishermen's rights to fish in UK waters and would allow for both sides to thrive. Unfortunately, among British seafarers' many complaints concerned the "disproportionately large" share of total fish catches allocated to France.[132] Some of the numbers are striking and arouse public opinion: An extreme example is that of Eastern Channel cod, of which the UK was allocated 9 percent, while France received an 84 percent share.[133] Thus, French fishermen are worried, and probably rightfully so. In some French towns, up to 80 percent of the fish, especially sole, cod, and turbot comes from the British side, about a two-hour boat ride away.[134] In light of EU seafood producers' tight connections with the UK, Travert, the French Minister for fisheries, has taken a less aggressive stance than Danish officials and advocated for finding a way to give Britain access to the single market, hoping that this might result in increased access rights to UK fishing grounds.[135] It is reasonable to posit that the EU would position itself at a midway point between these two stances, attempting to reach a

---

130 *Id.*

131 Valentin Schatz, *Brexit and fisheries access - Some reflections on the UK's denunciation of the 1964 London Fisheries Convention*, EJIL, Jul. 18, 2017, https://www.ejiltalk.org/brexit-and-fisheries-access-some-reflections-on-the-uks-denunciation-of-the-1964-london-fisheries-convention/; Daniel Boffey, *Denmark to contest UK efforts to 'take back control' of fisheries*, THE GUARDIAN, Apr. 18, 2017, https://www.theguardian.com/politics/2017/apr/18/denmark-to-contest-uk-efforts-to-take-back-control-of-fisheries.

132 Arthur Neslen, *Leaving EU could end 'unfair' French fishing quotas, says minister*, THE GUARDIAN, Jun. 1, 2016, https://www.theguardian.com/environment/2016/jun/01/leaving-eu-could-end-unfair-french-fishing-quotas-says-minister.

133 Abigail Morris, *'Life will be HARD!' French fisherman in PIECES as Britain to FINALLY get its water back*, EXPRESS, Jan. 18, 2018, https://www.express.co.uk/news/uk/906529/Brexit-news-latest-fishing-policy-UK-EU-European-Union-French-fisherman.

134 Joanna Kakissis, *Brexit Leaves French Fishermen on the Hook*, NPR, Sep. 11, 2017, https://www.npr.org/sections/thesalt/2017/09/11/548963126/brexit-leaves-french-fishermen-on-the-hook.

135 *France eyes post-Brexit deal to keep fishing in UK waters*, THE LOCAL, Jul. 18, 2017, https://www.thelocal.fr/20170718/france-eyes-post-brexit-deal-to-keep-fishing-in-uk-waters.

mutually beneficial agreement through talks, while maintaining a firm attitude.

3. Scotland

"The EU's stance is arrogant, absurd and nonsensical"—Simon Collins[136]

Scottish fishermen, fishing associations, and politicians alike have all been staunch proponents of the UK regaining full control of its territorial waters through Brexit.[137] They reacted violently to the EU's Draft Withdrawal Agreement, which calls for the UK to remain within the CFP until 2020. After Michael Gove confirmed that some foreign trawlers would still have access to UK waters after Brexit, Scottish Environment Secretary Fergus Ewing urged UK ministers to refrain from trading access to Scotland's water post-Brexit for other concessions from the EU. This position may not be the wisest. Many foreign boats in Scottish waters are actually exploiting deep-water fish stocks, such as grenadier, that British populations do not consume. Hence, fishing towns, such as Lochinver, the second largest fishing port in Scotland, have become dependent on large Spanish and French vessels, which exploit the differing fish preferences in the EU, and fish there for their own domestic markets. Without these foreign ships, employment opportunities would plummet, and the port might die.[138]

A further thorny issue for Scotland is that of competence over fishery policy once the UK leaves the EU bloc. In a speech in 2017, Theresa May explained she expected a rebalancing of powers across the UK after Brexit. In a policy paper dated December 2016 on Scotland's Place in Europe, her Government had proposed to repatriate power over fishery-related issues to the Scottish Parliament.[139] However, the Cabinet Office withdrew this promise when it published a list of 24 areas,

---

[136] Michael Settle, *Scottish fishermen reject Brussels' "arrogant and absurd" plan to maintain current access to UK waters post Brexit*, THE HERALD, Mar. 7, 2018Simon Collins is a member of the Shetland's Fishermen's Association.

[137] *E.g.*, *EU fishing deal 'far from acceptable' to Scottish industry*, BBC, Mar. 19, 2018, http://www.bbc.com/news/uk-scotland-scotland-politics-43458081.

[138] Peter Hetherington, *Net loss: Why Brexit could spell disaster for fishing*, THE NEW EUROPEAN, Feb. 20, 2018, http://www.theneweuropean.co.uk/top-stories/peter-hetherington-on-brexit-s-impact-on-british-fishing-industry-1-5396375.

[139] Imrie, Brexit, powers and the Scottish Parliament: The case of agriculture and fisheries, University of Strathclyde Glasgow, available at: https://strathprints.strath.ac.uk/60231/; https://www.telegraph.co.uk/politics/2018/03/07/scottish-fishermen-react-fury-eu-demand-unchanged-access-uk/.

including fisheries and quotas, which would be subject to centralized UK-wide common agreements for consistency.[140]

Scotland is thus pushing May to adopt a stronger stance towards fisheries. Whether or not the weight of that voice is sufficient to influence her, it at least `makes clear that there will be political repercussions if she does not listen.

4. Norway

"Our largest trading partner for white fish is the UK."—Per Sandberg[141]

Contrary to the UK, where fisheries have only marginal economic significance, fisheries are one of the most important economic sectors in Norway.[142] At the moment, cooperation between Norway and the EU is based on a bilateral framework agreement from 1981, which provides for mutual access, quota arrangements—especially on North Sea stocks—and joint fisheries-management measures.[143] Norway uses its access to the EU's EEZ especially to fish in UK waters. Brexit thus has Norway concerned with access to the British market and to fishing opportunities in UK waters.

The Norwegian government has backed the EU's insistence—now reflected in the Draft Withdrawal Agreement—that quotas for UK waters remain in force during the transition period in order to avoid any legal vacuum. Indeed, the talks between the UK, EU, and Norway over fishing rights, especially in the North Sea, are likely to be complex and

---

[140] Simon Johnson, *Scottish fishermen react with fury to EU demand for unchanged access to UK waters*, THE TELEGRAPH, Mar. 7, 2018, https://www.theguardian.com/politics/2018/mar/09/brexit-scotland-and-wales-face-battle-for-fish-and-farm-policy.

[141] Ariane Sohrabi-Shiraz, *Give us ACCESS! Norway fears losing BILLIONS without UK waters as cost of Brexit hits home*, EXPRESS, Nov. 7, 2017, https://www.express.co.uk/news/world/876535/Brexit-news-latest-Norway-fish-exports-UK-North-Sea-Per-Sandberg; Daniel Boffey, *Norway backs EU fishing policies remaining during Brexit transition*, THE GUARDIAN, Jan. 12, 2018, https://www.theguardian.com/environment/2018/jan/12/norway-backs-eu-fishing-policies-remaining-brexit-transition. Per Sandberg is a Norwegian Politician and has served as the Minister of Fisheries since December 2015.

[142] Ariane Sohrabi-Shiraz, *Give us ACCESS! Norway fears losing BILLIONS without UK waters as cost of Brexit hits home*, EXPRESS, Nov. 7, 2017, https://www.express.co.uk/news/world/876535/Brexit-news-latest-Norway-fish-exports-UK-North-Sea-Per-Sandberg; Daniel Boffey, *Norway backs EU fishing policies remaining during Brexit transition*, THE GUARDIAN, Jan. 12, 2018, https://www.theguardian.com/environment/2018/jan/12/norway-backs-eu-fishing-policies-remaining-brexit-transition.

[143] *Id.*

would be difficult to conclude before the end of the transition period.[144] New legal and institutional frameworks for managing joint fish stocks in the North Sea will need to be reached, and issues will include how to organize access to fish in each other's waters, cooperation on surveillance and control, and maybe the inception of a system to exchange fishing opportunities.

The UK will finally have the opportunity to negotiate its own fisheries agreement directly with Norway, which many British seafarers are actually excited for. Unfortunately, the outcome of a poor deal, or no deal at all between the UK and Norway could mean much more than reduced fishing opportunities for both British and Norwegian fishermen. Indeed, if a sustainable way to manage stocks is not agreed upon, stocks may be depleted within a few years as countries overfish on spawning grounds within their EEZ. Finally, as much as the UK will gain from Norwegian fishermen not entering UK waters anymore, British fishermen will lose their own access to Norwegian waters. Although some expect the UK will attempt to trade access to its market for access to Norwegian waters, Mr. Sandberg, minister of fisheries in Norway, has said that Norway "never negotiate[s] quotas in exchange for market access."[145] Luckily, Norway will have incentives to discuss with the UK: the UK, with its important consumption of white fish, is the biggest market for fish and seafood from Norway (taking 50-55 percent of total export volumes).

5. Fish Conservation Activists

"Brexit must not mean lower protection for marine life" — Catherine Weller[146]

Finally, as aforementioned, reopening negotiations on quotas could have dangerous implications for only recently achieved sustainable fishing. Michael Gove has claimed that the UK's exit from the CFP would allow the UK to manage its waters more sustainably.[147] Theresa May echoed this sentiment, stating that despite the UK's withdrawal from the CFP, governments should continue to collaborate over the

---

144 *Id.*

145 Ariane Sohrabi-Shiraz, *Give us ACCESS! Norway fears losing BILLIONS without UK waters as cost of Brexit hits home*, EXPRESS, Nov. 7, 2017.

146 *Fisheries laws must continue to tackle overfishing after Brexit,* CLIENTEARTH, Mar. 15, 2017, https://www.clientearth.org/fisheries-laws-must-continue-tackle-overfishing-brexit/. Catherine Weller is the Head of Biodiversity Programme at ClientEarth.

147 Paola Tamma, *EU fishermen weigh in on Brexit tug-of-war*, EURACTIV, Oct. 25, 2017, https://www.euractiv.com/section/uk-europe/news/eu-fishermen-weigh-in-on-brexit-tug-of-war/.

management of shared stocks with a view to achieve sustainability while granting a fairer allocation of fishing opportunities for the UK fishing industry.[148]

However, Ocean conservation activists explained that it took years to get a commitment from EU Member States to reduce catches to their maximum sustainable yield. They believe, probably rightfully so, that no individual country would have taken this decision unilaterally. Although the countries have been able to negotiate for sustainable fishing practices across state lines, doing so within the EU with the help of EU institutions has allowed for much more effective coordination, and more sweeping measures. To reward these efforts, statistics have shown that stocks of overfished species were building back up.

Unfortunately, taking a short-term political vision instead of a long-term sustainable approach may lead to poor fishing opportunities for every party concerned.[149] If the UK closes off its waters, non-UK fleets that currently fish highly migratory and shared stocks in UK waters because that is where fish reach their optimal size, may decide to fish in waters where the same species are present at a suboptimal level of development. For example, Danish waters are a breeding ground for herrings, which then migrate to UK waters when they have reached their adult size. If this scenario came to pass, the herring population could be severely depleted in just a few years.

C. RECOMMENDATIONS

Unfortunately, withdrawal from the EU will not eliminate the UK's need and obligation to negotiate fishing quotas or possible transfers or exchanges thereof, but rather will increase it. The UK will not only need to renegotiate with the EU while upholding its international obligations, it will also cease to be a party to fisheries agreements signed by the EU on behalf of the Member States, and will need to renegotiate these agreements again, where it deems appropriate. The facts and balance of interests highlighted in this chapter tend to point to necessary action and reasonable negotiating positions the UK is likely to eventually accept.

First and foremost, the UK will need to enter into an ad-hoc fisheries agreement with the EU bloc. Indeed, the EU is likely to link market access to the right to fish in the UK's EEZ, since in the past, the bloc

---

148 *Scots fishermen slam EU call for access to UK waters*, BBC, Mar. 7, 2018, http://www.bbc.com/news/uk-scotland-scotland-politics-43319132.

149 Arthur Neslen, *Leaving EU could end 'unfair' French fishing quotas, says minister*, THE GUARDIAN, Jun. 1, 2016, https://www.theguardian.com/environment/2016/jun/01/leaving-eu-could-end-unfair-french-fishing-quotas-says-minister.

has used market access as a means to negotiate for fishing interests.[150] This is an opportunity the UK may not want to pass up considering it runs a net trade surplus with the EU in fish products. In any case, the UK is likely to start paying tariffs on many of its fisheries' products considering that even Norway still pays tariffs on many fish products it exports to the EU.

Secondly, the UK will need to enter in bilateral negotiations for fisheries agreements with relevant countries,[151] whom the EU already had agreements with. For instance, the UK fishes beyond the UK coastal zone in Norwegian and Faroes waters pursuant to an EU-negotiated agreement worth 23 billion pounds to the UK. Some commentators believe the UK will have difficulty striking deals that are as favorable as what it currently has through the EU once it loses the bloc's collective bargaining power. Nevertheless, the UK will have to try.

Thirdly, the UK will need to develop its own fishing regulations to maintain stocks, reach sustainability, and remain in compliance with international law obligations. Regulators will have their work cut out since so many of the stocks present in UK waters are highly migratory and shared with other nations. This work will prove that much harder politically considering that fishermen were hoping to leave behind the EU's stringent regulations.

Fourthly, most commentators seem to agree that whatever agreement is reached between the UK and the EU, it should include clauses establishing transitional periods in order to enable a progressive and gradual transition from a regime of equal access to a preferential regime based on historical rights and reciprocity. Many countries are likely to exert pressure over UK authorities to see such a transition period enacted, and have already partially succeeded in that endeavor, as exemplified in the Draft Withdrawal Agreement.

Finally, it is of paramount importance that the UK recognize the need to include provisions for reciprocal access in both a EU deal, and in any deal struck with non-EU countries. Reciprocal access will not only be expected because of the precedent set by other non-EU coastal states in the region, it will also allow to maximize efficiency for specialized

---

150 For example when it banned Faeroese herring from the internal market in order to convince the Faroe Islands to reduce its herring quota. KLUGE, *8 things you should know about Brexit and Norwegian fisheries*, Jul. 29, 2017 https://www.kluge.no/en/recent/news/2017/brexit-and-norwegian-fisheries/; Elizabeth Truss, *We must not lose our voice in EU fishing policy*, THE NATIONAL FEDERATION OF FISHERMEN'S ORGANISATION, May 13, 2016, http://nffo.org.uk/eu-referendum/2016/05/13/we-must-not-lose-our-voice-in-eu-fishing-policy.

151 Probably Norway, Iceland, Russia, The Faroe Islands, and Greenland.

fleets, and will largely contribute to sustaining highly migratory stocks.[152] It will also credit the UK with some diplomatic and political capital with the EU and with other nations it negotiates with, something the country will be in dire need of to negotiate other big ticket items.

Unfortunately, if this is the course the UK ultimately chooses, political repercussions for the Government who accepts such a deal may be somewhat crippling.

[152] If the UK chose not to cooperate with neighboring coastal states and closed its waters to foreign vessels, shared fish stocks, which represent most commercial species around the coast of Britain, would become overfished. The move would thus not only be damaging to diplomatic relations, but also to the fishing industry because it would jeopardize stock preservation. Reciprocity would also favor efficiency as it would enable vessels that are specialized in fishing for certain stocks or in certain waters to maximize their fishing patterns.

CHAPTER 11: AVOIDING A BORDER ON THE ISLAND OF IRELAND AFTER BREXIT

WORTHINGTON PHILLIPS

SUMMARY OF THE ISSUE AND PROPOSED SOLUTION

This chapter offers a solution of how to avoid a hard border on the island of Ireland when the UK exits the EU. Specifically, this chapter is concerned with the movement of goods, rather than people, over that border.[1] The first part of this analysis begins with clearly defining the problem. This chapter stipulates the crux of the border issue is one commonly seen in multiparty negotiations. In other words, the problem here is that there are four parties with different underlying interests. The challenge is to find a solution that harmonizes those underlying interests.[2] The underlying interests of the four relevant parties; the UK, the EU, Northern Ireland (NI), and Irish Republic (RoI); can be teased out from the official statements they have released, and an understanding of their context. They are as follows:

United Kingdom Interests

(i) Belfast agreement must be adhered to; (ii) Northern Ireland must remain part of the UK; (iii) reject free movement of people; (iv) build infrastructure to check rules of origin (ROO); (v) seeking mutual recognition with the EU.

European Union Interests

(i) Belfast agreement must be adhered to; (ii) RoI must remain part of the EU; (iii) prohibit the UK from cherry-picking freedoms; (iv) build infrastructure to check ROO; (v) allow Northern Ireland into the EU single market.

---

[1] The movement of people has been taken addressed by the Common Travel Agreement (CTA) since 1922, and all parties have confirmed the agreement will remain in place after the UK exits the EU. Joint report from the negotiators of the European Union and the United Kingdom Government on progress during phase 1 of negotiations under Article 50 TEU on the United Kingdom's orderly withdrawal from the European Union. (EC) 8 Dec. 2017, 9. https://ec.europa.eu/commission/publications/draft-withdrawal-agreement-withdrawal-united-kingdom-great-britain-and-northern-ireland-european-union-and-european-atomic-energy-community_en.

[2] Roger Fisher, William Ury, Bruce Patton, *Getting To YES: Negotiating Agreement without Giving In*, 11 (3rd ed. 2011) (articulating one of the principles to successful negotiations is to find the underlying interests of relevant parties, and build a solution around those interests.).

Northern Ireland (and DUP) Interests

(i) Belfast agreement must be adhered to; (ii) frictionless access to the UK market; (iii) refuses to be *more* aligned with the RoI/EU than with the UK.

Irish Republic Interests

(i) Belfast agreement must be adhered to; (ii) frictionless access to the EU market; (iii) ship goods to the EU via land route in the UK; (iv) seek more Island unification.

These interests do not have to result in a zero-sum game. However, harmonizing these interests does require creativity. This chapter proposes the following solution:

(i) Northern Ireland and the Irish Republic form a single market economy in which the UK and the EU give mutual recognition to each other's regulations regarding the import of goods into the Island.

(ii) Imports to the Island comply entirely with either the UK or the EU regulations, and will receive access to the Island and the respective market of the regime complied with.

(iii) the EU and the UK edit the tariffs based on rules of origin and:

(a) allow free movement of goods originating on the Island into their respective market

(b) apply appropriate tariffs to the rest of the world

(iv) the EU and the UK utilize 21st century technology for screening goods before they enter their respective markets

I. WHY THERE CAN NOT BE A PHYSICAL BORDER BETWEEN NORTHERN IRELAND AND THE IRISH REPUBLIC

The peace agreement signed in 1998 between Northern Ireland and The Irish Republic called for no border.[3] If a hard border returns, the 'troubles' may also return.[4] Both the EU and the UK have explicitly stated that abiding by the Belfast Agreement is paramount.[5] The question is how to abide by the Belfast Agreement when the UK exits the EU.

---

[3] Northern Ireland Office, The Belfast Agreement, (Apr. 10, 1998) https://www.gov.uk/government/publications/the-belfast-agreement.

[4] *E.g.*, Reuters Staff, *Northern Ireland police demand extra resources for post-Brexit*, Reuters (May 31, 2018) https://www.reuters.com/article/us-britain-eu-nireland/northern-ireland-police-demand-extra-resources-for-post-brexit-idUSKCN1IW2U7?il=0 ("Authorities on both sides of the now-open frontier fear a return to a hard border, complete with customs and other checks, could be a target for militant groups behind the violence that afflicted Northern Ireland until a peace deal in the late 1990s.").

[5] Joint report from the negotiators of the European Union and the United Kingdom Government on progress during phase 1 of negotiations under Article 50 TEU on the United Kingdom's orderly withdrawal from the European Union. (EC) 8 Dec. 2017, 7. https://ec.europa.eu/commission/publications/draft-withdrawal-agreement-withdrawal-united-kingdom-great-britain-and-northern-ireland-european-union-and-european-atomic-energy-community_en.

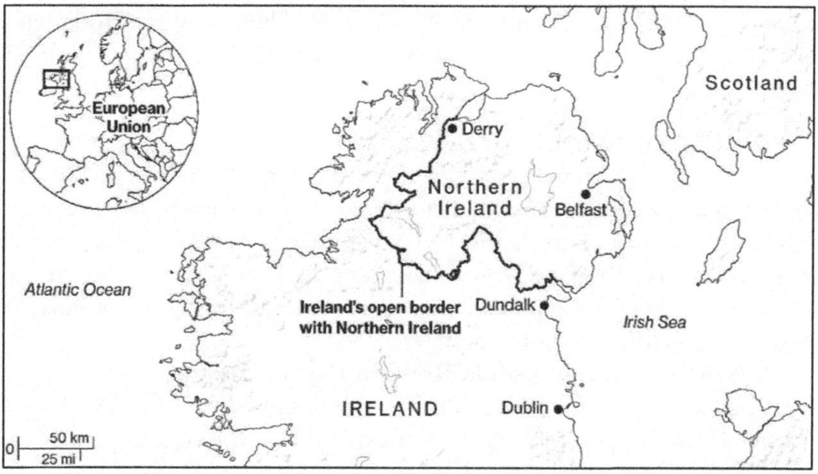

II. WHAT IS THE PURPOSE OF CUSTOMS?

A proposal suggesting a mutual recognition scheme necessitates a discussion on what the purpose of customs is. This will help define what features need to be mutually recognized between the EU and the UK in regards to the import of goods into the Island. Customs is needed to (i) define a goods classification and origin status for tax and regulations; (ii) determine if the good satisfies a health and safety regulation; (iii) collect a tariff duty and VAT.[6] This proposal suggests that goods imported into the Island of Ireland can satisfy all elements of either the UK or the EU regulations. In other words, the proposal is not suggesting that goods can satisfy the health and safety standards of the EU while paying the tariff duty of the UK. An import to the Island must either comply with the full set of UK regulations or the full set of EU regulations. This element must be agreed to in order to ensure there is no border on the Island.

III. IDENTIFYING UNDERLYING INTERESTS OF THE PARTIES INVOLVED

As stated earlier, the crux of solving the border issue is understanding and harmonizing the underlying interests of the different parties involved. Those interests are most accurately identified through

---

[6] *E.g.*, *Customs basics: why does Customs exist?*, (May 12, 2018 4:13 PM) https://www.macocustoms.com/nl/node/852; *What are Rules of Origin*, World Customs Organization, (May 12, 2018 4:15 PM), http://www.wcoomd.org/en/topics/-origin/instrument-and-tools/comparative-study-on-preferential-rules-of-origin/specific-topics/general-topics/roo-agr-atiga.aspx

official government statements. An understanding of these underlying interests will equip us with forming a proper solution acceptable to all parties.[7]

A. *UNITED KINGDOM INTERESTS*

While the UK has a few red lines, it would be wise for the UK government to compromise and seek creative solutions to minimize the degree of separation from the EU where it can. This not only makes economic sense, but political sense as well. It makes political sense, because the leave vote won by a narrow majority, showing the populace's unwillingness to see a hard Brexit.[8]

1. Northern Ireland must Remain Part of the UK

The hard stance by Prime Minister Theresa May and the DUP, who she needs the support of,[9] have been explicit that the sovereignty of the

---

[7] All parties demand that the Belfast Agreement is adhered to. Rather than articulating that in the body of text for each party, here are relevant sources: Joint report from the negotiators of the European Union and the United Kingdom Government on progress during phase 1 of negotiations under Article 50 TEU on the United Kingdom's orderly withdrawal from the European Union. (EC) 8 Dec. 2017, 7. https://ec.europa.eu/-commission/publications/draft-withdrawal-agreement-withdrawal-united-kingdom-great-britain-and-northern-ireland-european-union-and-european-atomic-energy-community_en (articulating that EU and UK agree the Belfast Agreement must be adhered to); *e.g.*, Connal Parr & Edward Burke, *Brexit: What are the issues surrounding Northern Ireland's border and could it scupper UK's EU withdrawal?*, Independent, (Dec. 5, 2017) https://www.independent.co.uk/news/uk/politics/brexit-latest-northern-ireland-border-republic-dup-arlene-foster-theresa-may-david-davis-eu-a8093171.html (reporting that while the DUP wants to avoid a hard border, the party has also stated it wants to leave the customs union along with the rest of the UK. Also reporting that Irish Foreign Minister Simon Coveney said: "We have always been clear that our preference is to avoid a hard border through a wider future relationship agreement between the EU and the U.K., a view we share with the British government.); *see also* HM Government, Additional Data Paper: Northern Ireland Trade Data and Statistics, Aug. 2017, 1, 8, https://www.timloughton.com/sites/www.timloughton.com/files/2017-09/Additional_Data_Paper_-_Northern_Ireland_Trade_Data_and_Statistics__2_.pdf (which provides the following economic statistics: value of goods sold by businesses in NI to RoI was £2.7 billion in 2015; total value of goods imported from Ireland was £1.8 in same time period; Irish Revenue commissioners estimate that 177,000 heavy goods vehicles and 208,000 light vans cross the border between NI and RoI each month; the Dept. of Transportation estimates that in 2015, there were 6.4 million tonnes of freight carried by Northern Ireland HGVs (heavy goods vehicles) between Northern Ireland and Ireland. All these stats are to indicate the economic interconnectedness of NI and RoI.).

[8] Donald McRae, *Brexit makes no sense and Britain should vote again, says Jürgen Klopp*, The Guardian (Apr. 23, 2018), https://www.theguardian.com/football/2018/apr/23/brexit-makes-no-sense-and-britain-should-vote-again-says-jurgen-klopp (stating the ratio of leave to remain votes to be 51.9% to 48.1%.).

[9] Alex Hunt, *Theresa May and the DUP deal: What you need to know*, BBC, (June 26, 2017) http://www.bbc.com/news/election-2017-40245514; see also, MPs, Lords & offices, Current State of the Parties, https://www.parliament.uk/mps-lords-and-offices/mps/current-state-of-the-parties/ (stating that the DUP holds ten seats, and that

United Kingdom must not be interfered. This is the primary reason why the backstop option of putting the border on the Irish Sea proposed in the EU Draft Withdrawal Agreement has received so much backlash from the UK government.[10]

2. Reject Free Movement of People

It was commonly reported that significant portions of the Brexit campaign focused on fears and anxiety over immigrants into the UK.[11] Additionally, in her speech to the Conservative Party Conference in October 2016, the Prime Minister set out several 'red lines' for the Government's approach to the negotiations, which included ending the 'freedom of movement for EU citizens into the UK.'[12]

3. Retain Ability to Check Goods for ROO

Even if the UK and the EU reach a grand FTA that allows for tariff-free trade in goods, there will still be need for infrastructure to check for ROO. Without such infrastructure, there will be nothing to prevent a third country from using the EU as a backdoor into the UK avoiding the UK regulatory regime, and vice versa. For this reason, maintaining the status quo with no border between these two sovereigns is not a realistic option. Note that this interest is equally shared by the EU.[13]

4. Seeking Mutual Recognition with the EU

A full mutual recognition regime would be desirable by the UK. Theresa May has stated "we must ensure that, as now, products only need to undergo one series of approvals, in one country, to show that

---

May's Conservative party holds 316. In order to have half of the 650 votes in Parliament the two parties have formed a 'confidence and supply' agreement, in which the DUP will support the Conservatives.).

[10] Prime Minister's Office, PM speech on our future economic partnership with the European Union, Mar. 2, 2018, https://www.gov.uk/government/speeches/pm-speech-on-our-future-economic-partnership-with-the-european-union (May stating that "I want to make one final point. Just as it would be unacceptable to go back to a hard border between Northern Ireland and Ireland, it would also be unacceptable to break up the United Kingdom's own common market by creating a customs and regulatory border down the Irish Sea.").

[11] Richard Hall, *How the Brexit campaign used refugees to scare voters*, PRI (June 24, 2016), https://www.pri.org/stories/2016-06-24/how-brexit-campaign-used-refugees-scare-voters; Nicholas Watt, *EU referendum: Vote Leave focuses on immigration*, BBC (May 25, 2016), http://www.bbc.com/news/uk-politics-eu-referendum-36375492.

[12] Mar. 29, Parl Deb HC (2018) col. 10, https://publications.parliament.uk-/pa/cm201719/cmselect/cmexeu/935/935.pdf

[13] Guidelines (EC) EUCO XT 20001/18 of 23 Mar. 2018, art. 50, 2018 (BXT 25) 2, http://data.consilium.europa.eu/doc/document/XT-20001-2018-INIT/en/pdf (stating that "divergence in external tariffs and internal rules as well as absence of common institutions and a shared legal system, necessitates checks and controls to uphold the integrity of the EU Single Market as well as of the UK market.").

they meet the required regulatory standards. To achieve this we will need a comprehensive system of mutual recognition."[14] However, the EU may be unwilling to provide full mutual recognition, because it may incentive leave votes in other member states. As such, a more subtle recognition regime is preferable, which this proposal offers.

B. EUROPEAN UNION INTERESTS

There is good reason to think the EU is the most important party in the negotiations, because it holds the most amount of leverage.[15]

1. Irish Republic Must Remain in the EU

Although most would assume this interest is self-evident and not worth mentioning, it should be noted that the UK's interest in maintaining sovereignty over Northern Ireland was equally self-evident, but ignored.[16] Furthermore, this interest is important to point out as it is directly related to the solution proposed by this chapter.

2. Prohibit the UK from Cherry-Picking Freedoms

If the EU gives the UK too good a deal, there will be added incentive for Frexit, Nexit, etc.[17] If the UK gets too good a deal, there will also be criticism from third party nations already trading with the EU.[18] As such,

---

[14] Prime Minister's Office, PM speech on our future economic partnership with the European Union, Mar. 2, 2018, https://www.gov.uk/government/speeches/pm-speech-on-our-future-economic-partnership-with-the-european-union.

[15] Deepak Malhotra, *A Definitive Guide to the Brexit Negotiations*, Harvard Business Review, (Aug. 5, 2016) https://hbr.org/2016/08/a-definitive-guide-to-the-brexit-negotiations (reasoning that "a 'no deal' (or a deal that hurts trade, to be more precise) is much worse for the UK than it is for the EU." because 44% of UK trade goes to the EU, while 10% of EU trade goes to the UK.).

[16] European Commission Draft Withdrawal Agreement on the withdrawal of the United Kingdom of Great Britain and Northern Ireland from the European Union and the European Atomic Energy Community (EC) 28 Feb. 2018, 98-99, https://ec.europa.eu/commission/publications/draft-withdrawal-agreement-withdrawal-united-kingdom-great-britain-and-northern-ireland-european-union-and-european-atomic-energy-community_en (stating that the EU recognizes the "rights and obligations of Ireland under the rules of the Union's internal market and customs union must be fully respected' and the EU is 'desiring to create a common regulatory area on the island of Ireland.").

[17] Dominic Evans & Marton Dunai, *Nexit, Frexit or Italeave? British vote fires up EU's 'Outers'*, Reuters (June 24, 2016), https://www.reuters.com/article/us-britain-eu-outers-all-idUSKCN0ZA2LP (articulating that the Brexit vote has resulted in louder calls for referendums in other EU countries.).

[18] Mar. 29, Parl Deb HC (2018) col. 7, https://publications.parliament.uk/pa/-cm201719/cmselect/cmexeu/935/935.pdf (in which the UK house of commons recognizes "in respect of both trade and non-trade agreements, other countries will take a close interest in the mix of rights and obligations that constitute any future relationship with the UK and may see any special deals for the UK as a precedent. Countries such as Switzerland and Norway will examine closely any agreement between the UK and the EU to see if it contains better terms than their current arrangements. This, in itself, may limit the EU's room for manoeuvre in terms of what it is prepared to offer the UK.").

the EU cannot allow the UK to cherry-pick freedoms of the single market, and importantly cannot allow the UK to have free movement of goods without free movement of people.[19]

3. Keeping Northern Ireland in the EU single market

The EU's proposal for the border issue is curious. It allows both (a) Northern Ireland to remain in the European Union Customs Union (EUCU) and (b) tariff-free, unlimited movement of goods between the UK and Northern Ireland if those goods (c) comply with EU regulations.[20] For now, we will simply take note of this, and address the possibility of it being realized in the following section.

C. NORTHERN IRELAND INTERESTS[21]

1. Frictionless Access to the UK Market

Like the UK's red line on keeping Northern Ireland within its sovereignty, this Northern Ireland demand is another reason why the current backstop option proposed by the EU is unattainable.[22]

---

[19] Guidelines (EC) EUCO XT 20001/18 of 23 Mar. 2018, art. 50, 2018 (BXT 25) 7, http://data.consilium.europa.eu/doc/document/XT-20001-2018-INIT/en/pdf (in which the EC states "any agreement with the UK will have to be based on a balance of rights and obligations, and ensure a level playing field. A non-member of the Union, that does not live up to the same obligations as a member, cannot have the same rights and enjoy the same benefits as a member. The EC recalls that the four freedoms are indivisible and that there can be no "cherry picking" through participation in the Single Market based on a sector-by-sector approach, which would undermine the integrity and proper functioning of the Single Market.").

[20] European Commission Draft Withdrawal Agreement on the withdrawal of the United Kingdom of Great Britain and Northern Ireland from the European Union and the European Atomic Energy Community (EC) 28 Feb. 2018, 99-100, https://ec.europa.eu/commission/publications/draft-withdrawal-agreement-withdrawal-united-kingdom-great-britain-and-northern-ireland-european-union-and-european-atomic-energy-community_en (in which the EU proposes that there will be no customs duties (Chapter III, Art. 4, Paragraph 3), quantitative restrictions (Chapter III, Art. 4, Paragraph 4), or taxes (Chapter III, Art. 4, Paragraph 5) on goods between the UK and the EU in regards to NI, as long as those goods comply with the provisions of EU law on goods (Chapter III, Art. 4, Paragraph 1) and EU customs legislation (Chapter III, Art. 4, Paragraph 2)).

[21] Note that at the time of this writing there was no single party or coalition in power in Stormont, the Northern Irish legislature. Still, the DUP's views are the most important of the two parties who historically share power in Stormont, as Sinn Féin abstains from taking their seats in Westminster. *See* Ben Kelly, *Northern Ireland Latest: How did power-sharing at Stormont collapse and what happens if talks break down?*, Independent, (Feb. 14, 2018) https://www.independent.co.uk/news/uk/politics/northern-ireland-talks-latest-updates-stormont-power-sharing-deal-what-deal-look-sinn-fein-dup-deal-a8207916.html.

[22] William Booth, *Northern Ireland has become an unexpected hurdle for Brexit*, The Washington Post, (Feb. 28, 2018) https://www.washingtonpost.com/world/northern-ireland-has-

2. Refuses to be *More* Aligned with the ROI/EU than with the UK

This chapter stipulates that it is uncertain how uncompromising the DUP is in regards to fully leaving the EUCU. On the one hand, it's often reported that the DUP wants to leave the customs union along with the rest of the UK, despite the majority of people in Northern Ireland voting to remain in the EUCU.[23] On the other hand, the DUP's official texts state it wants a comprehensive free trade and customs agreement with the EU, and a frictionless border with the Irish Republic.[24] This official text of the party currently keeping Prime Minister May in power indicates that achieving the solution proposed here may not have to wait until the next election in Northern Ireland.

Although achieving both goals (leaving the EUCU and having a comprehensive customs agreement with the EU) is unattainable, it is possible to achieve the goals set forth in the official texts: a frictionless border with RoI, and a comprehensive free trade and customs agreement with the EU. Achieving these goals will require the DUP compromising on their status of Northern Ireland in the EUCU. This chapter is offering a reasonable solution for Northern Ireland in this regard by allowing both the UK and EU customs regulatory regime to be established on the whole Island, which allows Northern Ireland to be aligned to the EU no more than it is aligned to the UK.

---

become-an-unexpected-hurdle-for-brexit/2018/02/28/7efd54e4-1c94-11e8-98f5-ceecfa8741b6_story.html?utm_term=.979049d89a45 ("The DUP leader in Parliament, Nigel Dodds, on Wednesday described the latest E.U. proposals as 'ludicrous' and said that if enacted, the treaty would be 'catastrophic' for Northern Ireland. We did not leave the EU to oversee the breakup of the UK.").

[23] Connal Parr & Edward Burke, *Brexit: What are the issues surrounding Northern Ireland's border and could it scupper UK's EU withdrawal?*, Independent, (Dec. 5, 2017) https://www.independent.co.uk/news/uk/politics/brexit-latest-northern-ireland-border-republic-dup-arlene-foster-theresa-may-david-davis-eu-a8093171.html (reporting that while the DUP wants to avoid a hard border, the party has also stated it wants to leave the customs union along with the rest of the UK.); Aisling Moloney, *How did Northern Ireland vote on Brexit?*, Metro (Dec. 6, 2017) https://metro.co.uk/2017/-12/06/northern-ireland-vote-brexit-7136444/ (reporting that 55.8% of voters in Northern Ireland opted to remain in the EU during the Brexit vote.).

[24] The DUP Manifesto for the 2017 Westminster Election, *Standing Strong for Northern Ireland*, 2017, 6 http://www.mydup.com/publications/view/2017-westminster-manifesto (stating that among the DUP aims is a "frictionless border with the Irish Republic' and a 'comprehensive free trade and customs agreement with the EU.").

D. Irish Republic Interests

1. Frictionless Access to the EU Market

RoI naturally demands that at the end of Brexit, it retains full access to the EU market.[25]

2. Ship Goods to the EU via a Land Route in the UK

A clear majority of goods sold from RoI to the EU market use a land route over the UK, and as such the Irish government would greatly appreciate a proposal that would allow their businesses to continue using that route.[26] The proposal laid out here would allow goods made in RoI to have frictionless access to the UK, and subsequently to the EU market.

3. Seeking More Island Unification

It's been openly admitted by the Irish government and Irish people for there to be a united Island.[27] It seems that this desire will materialize at some point. The only option currently on table is the EU Draft Withdrawal agreement, in which the border is put in the Irish Sea. That proposal will likely result in Island unification as the people become more accustomed to no checks between Northern Ireland and the Irish Republic and increased checks between Northern Ireland and the UK. Admittedly, the proposal here will also likely result in Island unification in the future for the same reasons. However, with this proposal that reality will be realized in a more subtle and gradual way, because the UK will have influence over the Island as well.

IV. Highlight Solutions Commonly Proposed, and Why They Will Not Work

The UK's relationship with the EU will be unique, and as such no current model of a relationship between the EU and a third party will

---

[25] Foilseachán Rialtas na hÉireann, Ireland and the negotiations on the UK's withdrawal from the European Union, The Government's Approach (May 2017) 4, https://merrionstreet.ie/en/EU-UK/Key_Irish_Documents/Government_Approach-_to_Brexit_Negotiations.pdf (stating that Ireland's "priorities are clear...securing Ireland's future in a strong European Union.").

[26] Joshua Posaner & Emmet Livingstone, *Brexit burns Ireland's British bridge to EU markets*, Politico (Aug. 17, 2017), https://www.politico.eu/article/cargo-food-production-producers-brexit-burns-irelands-british-bridge-to-eu-markets/ ("It is impossible to overstate the importance of the British transit route: Some 80 percent of the Irish road freight that reaches mainland Europe passes through the U.K.").

[27] Judith Vonberg, *Irish Prime Minister says he aspires to a 'united Ireland'*, CNN (Jan. 2, 2018), https://www.cnn.com/2018/01/02/europe/varadkar-united-ireland-intl/index.html (reporting that the Irish Prime Minister, Leo Varadkar, stated "Our constitution aspires to there being a united Ireland. I share that aspiration.").

work. However, all of the models provide useful lessons as to what may or may not work for the border issue specifically, and the trading relationship more generally.

A. EU DRAFT WITHDRAWAL AGREEMENT

The solution offered by the EU, if no other deal is reached, is to place the border on the Irish Sea, which results in Northern Ireland being considered part of the 'customs territory' of the EU.[28] Conceptually, this is an easy solution, but it poses overly burdensome political, and social problems. Theresa May, and the DUP have stated a border on the Irish Sea is just as unacceptable as a physical border that violates the Belfast agreement.[29] Despite the proposal's unacceptable nature, it highlights the reality that the EU must have influence in Northern Ireland because of two facts: (i) there must not be a border on the Island, and (ii) the Irish Republic will remain part of the EU. These facts are also recognized in the solution proposed here.

B. FREE TRADE AGREEMENT

Even if a grand FTA is reached between the UK and the EU allowing for tariff free movement of goods, as the EU guidelines have suggested is possible,[30] border infrastructure is still necessary.

---

[28] European Commission Draft Withdrawal Agreement on the withdrawal of the United Kingdom of Great Britain and Northern Ireland from the European Union and the European Atomic Energy Community (EC) 28 Feb. 2018, 99-100, https://ec.europa.eu/commission/publications/draft-withdrawal-agreement-withdrawal-united-kingdom-great-britain-and-northern-ireland-european-union-and-european-atomic-energy-community_en (in which the EU proposes that there will be no customs duties (Chapter III, Art 4, Paragraph 3), quantitative restrictions (Chapter III, Art. 4, Paragraph 4), or taxes (Chapter III, Art. 4, Paragraph 5) on goods between the UK and the EU in regards to NI, as long as those goods comply with the provisions of EU law on goods (Chapter III, Art. 4, Paragraph 1) and EU customs legislation (Chapter III, Art 4, Paragraph 2).).

[29] Prime Minister's Office, PM speech on our future economic partnership with the European Union, Mar. 2, 2018, https://www.gov.uk/government/speeches/pm-speech-on-our-future-economic-partnership-with-the-european-union, (Theresea may stating "just as it would be unacceptable to go back to a hard border between Northern Ireland and Ireland, it would also be unacceptable to break up the United Kingdom's own common market by creating a customs and regulatory border down the Irish Sea."); Connal Parr & Edward Burke, *Brexit: What are the issues surrounding Northern Ireland's border and could it scupper UK's EU withdrawal?*, Independent, (Dec. 5, 2017) https://www.independent.co.uk/news/uk/politics/brexit-latest-northern-ireland-border-republic-dup-arlene-foster-theresa-may-david-davis-eu-a8093171.html (reporting that while the DUP wants to avoid a hard border, the party has also stated it wants to leave the customs union along with the rest of the UK.).

[30] Guidelines (EC) EUCO XT 20001/18 of 23 Mar. 2018, art. 50, 2018 (BXT 25) 4, http://data.consilium.europa.eu/doc/document/XT-20001-2018-INIT/en/pdf (in which the EC states that they'll be aiming to establish a "balanced, ambitious and wide-ranging FTA…[which includes] trade in goods, with the aim of covering all sectors and

Specifically, border infrastructure will be necessary so the UK and the EU can check goods for rules of origin. If such infrastructure is lacking, it will be too easy for third parties to use the UK as a backdoor into the EU, and vice versa. Thus, a simple FTA will not avoid having an Irish border. However, it is good to note that the EU is willing to accept an FTA, in exchange for a few compromises on part of the UK - especially in terms of fishing rights.[31] This is a relevant point, because it points out that the EU will be accepting of this subtler proposal, in which there is only free trade between Northern Ireland and the EU.

C. NORWAY MODEL

It is often suggested that the UK should look to the Norway model as guidance for its exit.[32] It is agreed that there are a good number of benefits with this option - e.g. would give the UK access to the single market, allow the UK to set their own customs duties with third party nations, and would give the U.K. a chance to influence EU regulations. However, cutting against those benefits is that UK would have to accept free movement of people, pay into the EU budget, and would have no legal recourse if their suggestions in EU regulations are ignored. Although there are reports that the majority of people in the UK would accept free movement of people in return for free trade of goods/services,[33] the fact remains that the UK populace voted to exit the EU, and was heavily influenced by fears of immigration.[34] More

---

seeking to maintain zero tariffs and no quantitative restrictions with appropriate accompanying rules of origin In the overall context of the FTA, existing reciprocal access to fishing waters and resources should be maintained.").

[31] Guidelines (EC) EUCO XT 20001/18 of 23 Mar. 2018, art. 50, 2018 (BXT 25) 4, http://data.consilium.europa.eu/doc/document/XT-20001-2018-INIT/en/pdf (in which the EC states that they'll be aiming to establish a 'balanced, ambitious and wide-ranging FTA…[which includes] trade in goods, with the aim of covering all sectors and seeking to maintain zero tariffs and no quantitative restrictions with appropriate accompanying rules of origin In the overall context of the FTA, existing reciprocal access to fishing waters and resources should be maintained.").

[32] *The right way to do Brexit*, The Economist, (Feb. 22, 2018), https://www.economist.com/news/leaders/21737271-britain-can-take-back-control-europe-without-cutting-all-ties-right-way-do-brexit (an opinion piece stating that it would be wise for the UK to mimic much of the Norway model for the time being, and perhaps alter the arrangement further down the line if the UK finds it unacceptable.).

[33] *The right way to do Brexit*, The Economist, (Feb. 22, 2018), https://www.economist.com/news/leaders/21737271-britain-can-take-back-control-europe-without-cutting-all-ties-right-way-do-brexit ("A majority of all voters, including a third of those who voted to leave, would accept free movement in return for free trade.").

[34] Richard Hall, *How the Brexit campaign used refugees to scare voters*, PRI (June 24, 2016), https://www.pri.org/stories/2016-06-24/how-brexit-campaign-used-refugees-scare-

importantly, the UK government has come out explicitly against adopting the Norway model.[35] Finally, a Norway model, is insufficient to solve the border issue, as there are still checks of goods between Sweden and Norway, which the environment of the Island will not accept.[36] Still if all other solutions, including the one proposed in this chapter, fail, the UK would be able to quickly negotiate into the EEA, as it is an 'off the shelf' model.[37] In short, the UK can do much worse than the Norway model, but there is hope it can do better.

D. CANADA MODEL

Some hold out hope that the UK achieves a model similar to Canada, because Canada has achieved FTAs on some goods, and by some measures it is "the most ambitious trade agreement that the EU has ever concluded."[38] However, that list of goods is limited, and would not come near replicating the breadth of an FTA that the UK is seeking.[39]

---

voters; Nicholas Watt, *EU referendum: Vote Leave focuses on immigration*, BBC (May 25, 2016), http://www.bbc.com/news/uk-politics-eu-referendum-36375492.

[35] Prime Minister's Office, PM speech on our future economic partnership with the European Union, Mar. 2, 2018, https://www.gov.uk/government/speeches/pm-speech-on-our-future-economic-partnership-with-the-european-union (in which May states that "existing models for economic partnership either do not deliver the ambition we need or impose unsustainable constraints on our democracy. For example, the Norway model, where we would stay in the single market, would mean having to implement new EU legislation automatically and in its entirety – would also mean continued free movement.").

[36] Mar. 29, Parl Deb HC (2018) col. 4, https://publications.parliament.uk/pa/-cm201719/cmselect/cmexeu/935/935.pdf (in which the UK House of Commons recognizes "The Norway-Sweden border has been held up as an example of a possible model for the Northern Ireland-Ireland border...The two countries have been cooperating on how to manage the border for several years, but there are still checks and there is physical infrastructure.").

[37] Mar. 29, Parl Deb HC (2018) col. 5, https://publications.parliament.uk/pa/-cm201719/cmselect/cmexeu/935/935.pdf (in which the UK House of Commons recognizes "The Government has rejected applying for EEA Membership because its view is that this entails accepting both free movement and EU law. Should the negotiations on a deep and special partnership not prove successful, EFTA/EEA membership remains an alternative and would have the advantage of continuity of access for UK services. The EEA option is available off-the-shelf and could be negotiated relatively quickly.").

[38] European Commission proposes signature and conclusion of EU-Canada trade deal (July 5, 2016) trade.ec.europa.eu/doclib/press/index.cfm?id=1524 (in which the trade deal is described by the EU Commission.).

[39] Mar. 29, Parl Deb HC (2018) col. 5, https://publications.parliament.uk/pa-/cm201719/cmselect/cmexeu/935/935.pdf (in which the UK House of Commons recognizes "The Comprehensive Economic and Trade Agreement (CETA) between the UK and Canada is an arrangement designed to meet the trading objectives of both Canada and the EU. It does not eliminate all tariffs and provides for market access some way short of Single Market participation. The trading relationship between the UK and the EU is very different and so a "CETA-style" agreement with the UK would need to

Additionally, like an FTA, this agreement fails to give a solution for the border issue. This is to reiterate the point that while a trade agreement on goods will be helpful, it is not sufficient for solving the border issue, because there will remain a need to check for ROO, and that goods fit within the parameters of a regulatory regime.

E. Swiss Model

The UK will not get the same deal that Switzerland has. There are several reasons for concluding this. Firstly, those deals were accomplished over many years, and were done through a great number of bilateral investment treaties. Conversely, the UK has until December 2020 to get a deal together. More importantly, the EU has explicitly stated it cannot allow the UK to get access to the Swiss model.[40] This red line by the EU should not be surprising. If the EU gave the UK too good a deal, there will be added incentive for Frexit, Nexit, Grexit, Italeave, etc.[41] Even if the UK could access such a model, it's unlikely they would take it as Switzerland accepts some free movement of people, and still checks for goods at the border.

F. Turkey Model

The Turkey model provides some useful illustrations of what will and will not work. Turkey has a customs union agreement covering some goods, it is bound by EU's Common External Tariff, but not involved in setting the direction of the EU's Common Commercial Policy. Additionally, Turkey is unable to automatically secure market access via the EU's FTAs, whereas those third countries have automatic access to Turkey's market.[42] A lack of access to help set EU policy, or a lack of

---

reflect markets that are already very much more integrated. A cut and paste of CETA would not be a good deal for the UK or the EU.").

40 Mar. 29, Parl Deb HC (2018) col. 3, https://publications.parliament.uk/pa/-cm201719/cmselect/cmexeu/935/935.pdf (in which the UK House of Commons states "Relates between Switzerland and the EU are governed by a series of bilateral agreements and negotiations towards an institutional framework have been ongoing for a number of years. While we were told the EU would not be willing to replicate such an arrangement for the UK, it is clear that Switzerland has been able to establish its own unique arrangement with the EU.").

41 Dominic Evans & Marton Dunai, *Nexit, Frexit or Italeave? British vote fires up EU's 'Outers'*, Reuters (June 24, 2016), https://www.reuters.com/article/us-britain-eu-outers-all-idUSKCN0ZA2LP (articulating that the Brexit vote has resulted in louder calls for referendums in other EU countries.).

42 Mar. 29, Parl Deb HC (2018) col. 5, https://publications.parliament.uk/-pa/cm201719/cmselect/cmexeu/935/935.pdf (in which the UK house of commons highlights aspects of Turkey's trade relationship with the EU).

market access to EU's FTAs would likely be viewed as unacceptable by the UK.

G. Implementing a Smart Border between Ireland and Northern Ireland

Some have suggested using a smart border between Ireland and Northern Ireland, which uses a de minimis amount of physical infrastructure at the border.[43] While this proposal includes some nuanced approaches, such as doing checkpoints away from the border,[44] it will still result in the need for personnel and some sort of physical infrastructure, which will provide targets to bomb, and not meet the commitment made in the joint agreement from December 2017.[45]

H. The UK Remains in the Customs Union

The idea of the UK remaining in the customs union has been advocated by many, including the UK House of Lords.[46] What this would entail is uncertain. However, like Norway, it would likely entail paying into a budget and accepting movement of people, which the UK will not accept. If the UK could somehow negotiate with the EU to allow the UK into the customs union without free movement of people, it would solve all relevant problems. However, this seems too difficult to achieve, and the proposal here is a subtler way to ensure no border, while also giving the UK the independence it voted for.

I. A Second Referendum

Like the customs union proposal, a second referendum could solve the whole issue if the population voted to remain in the EU. There is a decent argument that the following factors would legitimize a second referendum: (i) small margin voted in favor of Brexit [51.9% - 48.1%]; (ii) those who voted in favor of Brexit may not have understood the

---

[43] *Smart Border 2.0: Avoiding a hard border on the island of Ireland for Customs control and the free movement of persons* (Nov. 2017), http://www.europarl.europa.eu/RegData/etudes/-STUD/2017/596828/IPOL_STU(2017)596828_EN.pdf.

[44] *Smart Border 2.0: Avoiding a hard border on the island of Ireland for Customs control and the free movement of persons*, at 9 (Nov. 2017), http://www.europarl.europa.eu/RegData-/etudes/STUD/2017/596828/IPOL_STU(2017)596828_EN.pdf.

[45] John Campbell, *Ireland sceptical of 'smart border' solution*, BBC (Mar. 10 2018), http://www.bbc.com/news/world-europe-43356568 (explaining that any personnel or physical infrastructure would violate the December agreements); Peter Kellner, *'Technology' cannot make a hard border in Ireland soft*, Independent, (Mar. 6, 2018), https://www.independent.co.uk/voices/irish-hard-border-soft-brexit-technology-theresa-may-a8242461.html (explaining that the soft border technology will still require personnel and some phsyical infrastructure which will be targets for terrorisim).

[46] Heather Stewart, Brexit bill: May under pressure after two big defeats in Lords, The Guardian (Apr. 18), https://www.theguardian.com/politics/2018/apr/18/ministers-to-announce-brexit-climbdown-as-they-face-lords-defeat.

implications, partly because no one thought about them (it's evident no one important seriously thought about the Irish border before the vote), and partly because there were inaccurate statements made to induce people to vote leave.[47] However, May has made it clear that Brexit means Brexit, and there will be no second referendum.[48] Consequently, the best proposals recognize this hard fact, and try to make the best of it.

V. PROPOSED SOLUTION

As stated, the solution proposed here is conceptually easy to grasp. The first step is to realize that there are only three hard red lines that must be respected: (i) there must be no border on the Island; (ii) there must be free trade between Northern Ireland and the UK; (iii) there must be free trade between the EU and the Irish Republic. The solution proposed here meets those goals. To reiterate, the proposal consists of (i) forming a single market on the Island; (ii) The EU and UK give mutual recognition to each other in regards to Northern Ireland and the Irish Republic; (iii) goods originating on the Island (and receiving the appropriate documentation to ensure they did originate there) get access to both the UK and the EU markets; (iv) importers to the Island choose to comply *entirely* with either UK or EU regulations; (v) the EU and the UK use 21st century technology to retain the ability to check goods for ROO to ensure goods from the other's sovereignty are not getting unfettered access into their markets.

This solution, while not proposed anywhere else, is drawing elements from the proposals outlined above.

A. *HOW THIS SOLUTION DRAWS FROM OTHER PROPOSALS*

This solution takes a page from the EU draft withdrawal agreement by recognizing that there must be an Island economy, which has access to the EU. This is because of two red lines: (i) there must be no border, (ii) the Irish Republic is staying in the EU. However, that reality also necessities the UK to have Island access, because Northern Ireland is staying part of the UK. This proposal recognizes that. In other words,

---

[47] Donald McRae, *Brexit makes no sense and Britain should vote again, says Jürgen Klopp*, The Guardian (Apr. 23, 2018), https://www.theguardian.com/football/2018/apr/23/brexit-makes-no-sense-and-britain-should-vote-again-says-jurgen-klopp.

[48] Department for International Trade, UK is open for business like never before: Speech by Secretary of State for International Trade Liam Fox to the Sage conference (July 27, 2016) https://www.gov.uk/government/speeches/uk-is-open-for-business-like-never-before (stating that the Prime Minister has "affirmed that 'Brexit means Brexit'. There will be no backtracking. No second guessing and no second referendum.").

like the Good Friday Agreement, this proposal is one where everyone wins, because no one wins.

While some of the proposals mentioned above are good from a technical standpoint (namely: the UK receiving full mutual recognition; the UK staying in the customs union; the UK having a second referendum; or the UK entering the EEA) there is great political difficulty with all of them. These political challenges come mostly in the form of either: the EU's unwillingness to grant the UK too good a deal, or the inability of the UK government to reach a consensus. This proposal allows a more nuanced and compromising step to solving the trade issue generally and the border issue specifically. For example, this proposal allows the Island to be a testing bed for a full scale mutual recognition system, or customs union, or what the landscape could look like without Brexit. In other words, the rest of the UK will be able to look on Northern Ireland to see what advantages and disadvantages occur in Northern Ireland, and perhaps those observations will influence the rest of the UK to reconsider their position within the EU. Speaking only hypothetically, if the UK leaves the EU, and subsequently observes the benefits Northern Ireland receives by staying part of the UK and the EU, it may influence the UK to ask for acceptance back into the EU. Such a situation would solidify the EU's strength for a long time to come, as all will have noticed that remaining part of the EU greatly outweighs the disadvantages.

Finally, this solution draws from the Norway-Sweden border and other examples regarding the use of 21st century technology to help mitigate the inevitable friction that will be felt as Island businesses export to the UK/EU. The details of this part of the proposal are explained in the following section.

B. 21ST CENTURY TECHNOLOGY AT THE UK AND THE EU BORDERS

Most elements of the proposed solution are immediately understood by those familiar with basic tenets of International Law/Trade. However, the element of using 21st century technology on the UK and the EU border, which is necessary to help mitigate the inevitable increase of friction when trading between the Island and either the EU or the UK, is worthy of a detailed discussion because of its greater unfamiliarity to novices and experts in the field.

Recall that the proposed solution recognizes the need for the UK and the EU to check any goods coming from the Island to ensure they originated on the Island. This clearance procedure will result in increased fiction for businesses trading between the Island and the UK/EU. The use of 21st century technology will allow for Island businesses to get pre-clearance into the UK and the EU markets, which will help decrease the amount of friction those businesses would feel because of the proposed solution. The 21st century technology this proposal recommends comes in three elements: (i) trusted trader program; (ii) pre-clearance; and to a lesser extent (iii) a 'gateway solution'.

There are several reasons why some doubt the validity of using state of the art technology for border control. One reason is that some have not heard of it before, so are naturally suspicious. Others may be wary of its cost. However, the concepts involved in 21st century technology are not novel. The EU has been using a Trusted Traders program for some time. However, this program is underutilized in the UK and Ireland, but well used in Germany, France and Italy.[49] Additionally, the pre-clearance regime is in use on the Norway-Sweden border which requires exporters to give pre-arrival information at least one hour prior to arrival at the border. Reports of goods moving over the Norway-Sweden border state that "most goods traffic travelling across the border are cleared, on average, within 3-9 minutes, with longer waiting times at peak periods."[50]

The following discussion will highlight key aspects of the 21st century technology proposed, and explain why those elements would be helpful in this proposal.

1. Trusted Traders

Trusted Trader programs, also known as Authorised Economic Operator (AEO) programmes, are based upon the World Customs Organizations Framework of Standards to Secure and Facilitate Global Trade (SAFE).[51] This concept is based off a principle that "companies

[49] *Smart Border 2.0: Avoiding a hard border on the island of Ireland for Customs control and the free movement of persons*, at 22 (Nov. 2017), http://www.europarl.europa.eu/RegData/etudes-/STUD/2017/596828/IPOL_STU(2017)596828_EN.pdf ("Both the UK and Ireland have a trusted trader programmes under the umbrella of the EU's Authorised Economic Operator programme, which has its current legal basis in Article 39 of the Union Customs Code (UCC). The EU programme has three sub-classifications: AEO Customs Simplifications; AEO security and safety; and AEO Customs simplifications/Security and safety. The UK and Ireland AEO programmes are currently underutilised. The UK currently has 604 AEO companies (no separate figures for NI) under all three of the EU AEO sub-classifications. Ireland has 139 AEO companies. By comparison, Germany has 6,000 AEOs in all classifications, France 1,453 and Italy 1,238.").

[50] *Smart Border 2.0: Avoiding a hard border on the island of Ireland for Customs control and the free movement of persons*, at 30 (Nov. 2017), http://www.europarl.europa.eu/RegData/etudes-/STUD/2017/596828/IPOL_STU(2017)596828_EN.pdf.

[51] WCO, SAFE: Framework of Standards to Promote and Facilitate Global Trade, June 2015, http://www.wcoomd.org/en/topics/facilitation/instrument-and-tools/tools-/~/media/55F00628A9F94827B58ECA90C0F84F7F.ashx; *see also Smart Border 2.0:*

that are able to meet specific compliance and/or security standards in their day-to-day operations will receive benefits in their trade across borders, both for imports and exports...including expedited clearance, reduced documentary and physical checks, and benefits under Mutual Recognition Agreements (MRA) with other customs jurisdictions."[52]

Island companies could simply as a trusted trader, and with the pre-clearance system described below, get close to frictionless access into the EU and UK markets. These trusted traders may need to be randomly inspected while traveling in the UK or the EU to help ensure compliance and that the UK goods are not being smuggled into the EU and vice versa.

2. Pre-Clearance

A key piece in the proposal offered is to allow the release of goods prior to clearance by customs and other agencies. The idea is that based on pre-arrival information goods can be released and a full declaration made within a defined time period after release.[53] To establish advance clearance, the customs regime of the EU and the UK would require implementing as close to a fully electronic environment as possible, which allows for the electronic submission and receipt of documents and payments.

As companies are transporting their goods to/from the Island, those companies can provide the appropriate customs authorities with the appropriate paperwork to get pre-clearance. Note that this system would be useful not only for trade from the Island, but would be helpful for trade across the globe, which helps to justify the cost of establishing the technology.

3. Gateway Solution

Just as the Irish Republic would benefit from being able to use the UK as a land route to the EU market to decrease transit times, the EU would likely benefit if it had the same ability to use the UK as a land route to the Island. Although this chapter's proposal does not necessitate EU businesses to be able to use the UK as a land route to the Island, there is technology in use that would allow for it. 'The Gateway solution' uses existing infrastructure, like mobile networks, for Customs and Government related information messages to and from businesses

---

Avoiding a hard border on the island of Ireland for Customs control and the free movement of persons, at 22 (Nov. 2017), http://www.europarl.europa.eu/RegData/etudes/STUD/2017-/596828/IPOL_STU(2017)596828_EN.pdf.

[52] *Smart Border 2.0: Avoiding a hard border on the island of Ireland for Customs control and the free movement of persons*, at 22 (Nov. 2017), http://www.europarl.europa.eu/-RegData/etudes/STUD/2017/596828/IPOL_STU(2017)596828_EN.pdf.

[53] *Smart Border 2.0: Avoiding a hard border on the island of Ireland for Customs control and the free movement of persons*, at 24 (Nov. 2017), http://www.europarl.europa.eu/RegData/-etudes/STUD/2017/596828/IPOL_STU(2017)596828_EN.pdf.

involved in import and/or export. It was first tested by Swedish Customs for AEO at the Sweden-Norway border in 2003-2005. It can also be used to follow vehicles in real time through GPS positioning.[54] This technology could be used to monitor when/where shipping containers are opened and ensure that goods from the EU are not being opened on UK territory without authorization. To reiterate - this element is not necessary, but is simply available as an added 'sweetener' to the deal for the EU, who may have businesses that wish to use the UK as a land route to the Island market. Another benefit of utilizing this technology is that it could mitigate the fear that Irish exporters, who use the UK route to the EU, do not have their shipping containers opened and then have UK goods smuggled into that Irish shipping container, to get free access into the EU market.

C. ILLUSTRATIVE HYPOTHETICALS

To assist in understanding the model proposed, the following discussion will go through a few hypotheticals to illustrate how the system would work.

1. Hypothetical A: American business exports to the UK

Here the good would receive appropriate documentation from the UK customs illustrating that it is compliant with UK regulations. (note the documentation can be given in advance, if the border technology discussed above is implemented.) The good has access to the UK market (England, Wales, Scotland), and because it meets UK standards, it has access to the Island economy. However, customs authorities on continental Europe will prohibit the item, unless it complies with EU regulations.

2. Hypothetical B: American business exports to the EU

This is the same situation as Hypothetical A, except that the positions of the UK and the EU are reversed.

3. Hypothetical C: American business exports to the Island

The exporter will choose to comply either with UK or EU regulations in their entirety. If the exporter complies with UK regulations, the good will receive the appropriate documentation indicating it is cleared by UK customs, just as it done now. The good will then get access to the Island and the UK. However, the good will not get automatic access into the EU market. Alternatively, if the exporter decides upon arriving at the Island to comply with EU regulations, it will

---

[54] *Smart Border 2.0: Avoiding a hard border on the island of Ireland for Customs control and the free movement of persons*, at 25 (Nov. 2017), http://www.europarl.europa.eu/RegData/-etudes/STUD/2017/596828/IPOL_STU(2017)596828_EN.pdf.

receive the appropriate documentation and get access to the EU market along with the Island.

4. Hypothetical D: UK business exports to the Island

Here, the good will receive appropriate documentation showing that it originated in the UK just as is done now.[55] The good will receive access to the Island, but will not receive automatic access into the EU market.

5. Hypothetical E: EU business exports to the Island

This is the same situation as Hypothetical D, except that the positions of the UK and the EU are reversed.

6. Hypothetical F: Island business exports to the UK or the EU

The Island business will receive a country of origin document, and receive access to the UK and the EU market.

D. Why the Relevant Parties will Accept this Proposal

While this solution is not perfect, this chapter stipulates it achieves all of the parties' minimum requirements in a deal, and then some. This section will articulate why the four relevant parties will be satisfied with this proposal.

1. United Kingdom

Firstly, the UK is satisfied because it still has unfettered access to the market of Northern Ireland. Its hard line on freedom of people is not impeded. It has the infrastructure ability to ensure it's getting a fair deal with the EU, and not allowing third parties to get a backdoor entrance into the UK via the EU. Lastly, the proposal would provide a testing bed for mutual recognition between the UK and the EU, which this chapter stipulates should be a long term goal of the UK. In fact, Theresa May has said she desires mutual recognition between the UK and the EU.[56]

---

[55] Chamber International, *European Community (EC) Certificate of Origin Completion Guide: Guide to completing European Community Certificates of Origin and other documents*, (May 12, 2018, 12:45 PM), https://www.chamber-international.com/exporting-chamber-international-/documentation-for-export-and-import/certificates-of-origin/certificates-of-origin-european-community/the-certificate-of-origin-completion-guide-european-community/ (advising that when exporters fill out documentation to receive Certificate of Origin 'Box 3' requires the 'Country of Origin' to be listed, and an example reads as follows: "For goods originating in the European Community the designation should read "European Community" followed by the particular member state(s), e.g. "European Community - United Kingdom", and that "area groupings (e.g. EFTA) are not acceptable." This indicates that UK and EU businesses are already required to list their country of origin on goods.).

[56] Prime Minister's Office, PM speech on our future economic partnership with the European Union, Mar. 2, 2018, https://www.gov.uk/government/speeches/pm-speech-on-our-future-economic-partnership-with-the-european-union (May stating that "when it comes to goods, a fundamental principle in our negotiating strategy should be

This solution simply provides a more subtle compromise by giving mutual recognition only on the Island. It should also be noted that a mutual recognition system between the UK and the EU will be easier to establish than most other mutual recognition agreements established. Unlike the majority of the world's mutual recognition systems, the UK and the EU will be diverging in their regulations as opposed to converging. Theoretically, it ought to be easier to maintain similar outcomes in regulations than would otherwise be the case. As promising as it is for these parties to achieve mutual recognition, it must be recognized there are difficulties with it, and this proposal of starting small by implementing a mutual recognition regime on the Island helps to mitigate those difficulties.

2. European Union

Just as the UK maintains unfettered access into Northern Ireland, the EU will maintain unfettered access into the Irish Republic. The EU is not allowing the UK 'to cherry pick freedoms' because the UK is not getting full access to the EU market. Like the UK, the EU can ensure goods comply with the EU regulations before entering continental Europe. The EU retains full market access to Northern Ireland (which would be required with any solution, because there must be no Island border, and the EU cannot lose access to the Irish Republic), but also realizes that this feature requires a compromise - namely giving the UK full access to the Irish Republic. This is surely not the EU's most desired outcome, but it's the logical consequence of its unique geographical and oncoming political relationship with the UK. Refusing to accept this compromise may result in strained tensions, or worse, between either the EU and the UK or between Northern Ireland and the Irish Republic. Accepting this compromise of mutual recognition will result in all parties having mutual respect for each other.

Some may argue that the UK is getting too good a deal out of this proposal. Namely, that the UK is not only leaving the EU as it wanted, but it's taking the Irish Republic with it. This is not accurate. The UK maintains *access* to the Irish Republic, while the EU maintains access to Northern Ireland. This chapter stipulates that both parties can agree that this is a balanced compromise.

3. Northern Ireland

Northern Ireland demands unfettered access to the UK market, while also maintaining a North-South relationship with the Irish

---

that trade at the UK-EU border should be as frictionless as possible...to acheive this we will need a comprehensive system of mutual recognition.").

Republic. There are limited ways these goals can be achieved: (i) Brexit does not happen; (ii) the UK remains in the EUCU; (iii) the UK and the EU establish mutual recognition with each other. Option (i) is immediately discounted. Theresa May has laid a hard line down that 'Brexit means Brexit', and 'there will be no second referendum.'[57] The second option is equally unattainable, because neither the UK nor the EU will accept it. The UK won't accept it, because it would prohibit the UK from being able to set their own trade agreements with third countries. The EU won't accept the UK staying in the customs union if the UK refuses free movement of people. The third option is the most logical solution, and is supported by high ranking officials on the UK side.[58] However, it may be too much for the EU to provide mutual recognition to the entire UK regulatory regime, despite both parties starting off with the same laws in place. The reason for the EU's unwillingness to do this stems from the likelihood that other EU nations will consider exiting if they see the UK with a good deal after Brexit. As a result, this proposal provides a middle ground in which the mutual regulatory regime is confined to the Island, allowing for expansion of it later on if need be.

4. Irish Republic

The Irish Republic retains frictionless access to the EU market. Also, because Irish businesses retain access to the UK market, they get the added benefit of being able to use the UK as a land route when shipping to the EU, which as stated previously is of great value for transportation times.[59] It must be acknowledged that the Irish Republic is arguably losing out because there will undoubtedly be added friction when they ship goods to the EU, because the EU will now need to check goods coming from the Island to ensure they originated on the Island. However, this disadvantage is mitigated in a few ways. Firstly, the use of

---

[57] Department for International Trade, UK is open for business like never before: Speech by Secretary of State for International Trade Liam Fox to the Sage conference (July 27, 2016) https://www.gov.uk/government/speeches/uk-is-open-for-business-like-never-before (stating that the Prime Minister has "affirmed that 'Brexit means Brexit'. There will be no backtracking. No second guessing and no second referendum.").

[58] Prime Minister's Office, PM speech on our future economic partnership with the European Union, Mar. 2, 2018, https://www.gov.uk/government/speeches/pm-speech-on-our-future-economic-partnership-with-the-european-union (May stating that "when it comes to goods, a fundamental principle in our negotiating strategy should be that trade at the UK-EU border should be as frictionless as possible...to acheive this we will need a comprehensive system of mutual recognition.").

[59] Joshua Posaner & Emmet Livingstone, *Brexit burns Ireland's British bridge to EU markets*, Politico (Aug. 17, 2017), https://www.politico.eu/article/cargo-food-production-producers-brexit-burns-irelands-british-bridge-to-eu-markets/ ("It is impossible to overstate the importance of the British transit route: Some 80 percent of the Irish road freight that reaches mainland Europe passes through the U.K.").

21st century technology on the EU continental border will allow Irish businesses to get advance clearance by EU customs. Secondly, the Irish Republic, like Northern Ireland, is maintaining access to a much larger global trading network than would otherwise be possible. This is because they can benefit from trade agreements made by *both* the UK and the EU. These upsides substantially outweigh the added cost of having to endure slightly longer wait times getting into the EU market. Finally, and perhaps most appealing to the Irish Republic, is that this proposal recognizes and builds the foundation for a future unified Island (but not too much Island unification to scare off the DUP and others in Northern Ireland).

VI. CONCLUSION

Brexit presents a web of problems, many of which were not fully contemplated before a narrow majority voted to leave. This is especially true of the Irish border. Although the solution proposed here would change the landscape of Europe, and the UK, so would every other possible solution to the chaos that Brexit brings forth. However, unlike the other proposed solutions, this one incorporates a calculation of every party's interest to find a possible solution. Every party is making sacrifices, and getting something great in return. The UK is sharing limited "sovereignty" in Northern Ireland with the EU, while in return the UK maintains access to the Irish Republic. The EU is likewise sharing some "sovereignty" over the Irish Republic with the UK, while maintaining access to Northern Ireland. Northern Ireland is implicitly becoming more aligned with the Irish Republic than the UK, but at the same time maintains access to both the UK and the EU and any FTAs those sovereign entities form. Also, Northern Ireland maintains frictionless access to its main trading partner, the Irish Republic. The Irish Republic, will see slightly more friction in their trade to the EU, but that is mitigated with 21st century technology, maintaining frictionless access to Northern Ireland, benefiting from trade deals the UK and the EU make, and the Irish Republic is getting closer to realizing some of its deeper goals: Island unification.

Chapter 12: Re-dividing Europe: Key Topics in the Legal and Economic Consequences of Brexit on the Low-Wage Economy of the European Single Market

Tendai Mukau

Introduction

On June 23, 2016, the citizens of the United Kingdom of Great Britain and Northern Ireland voted to undertake a legally unprecedented endeavour -to withdraw from the most complicated and integrated intergovernmental institution in history, the European Union, directly affecting the legal status of at least 2.9 million EU27 citizens and nearly 700,000 UK citizens residing in EU27 Member States.[1] Immigration is the most controversial issue in the Brexit debate – indeed the dispositive reason the UK voted to leave the Union. Accordingly, it appears there is a reasonable chance that prospective EU workers who are not UK citizens will be subject to general UK immigration law when the UK formally leaves the Union. Barring radical alterations to the UK immigration regime, there will be a dramatic effect on certain sectors of the British labour economy, particularly on the lower-skilled and lower-paid industries, notably agriculture and construction. A "Hard" Brexit may also significantly affect the labour economies and welfare regimes of key sending Member States, *i.e.* Central and Eastern European Member States.

Section I of this chapter will begin with an exposition of the scope of Free Movement of People in the European Union. Section II will transition to a discussion of the economic pressures and demographic shifts that occurred in the EU following its post-2004 expansion eastwards when the A8 states joined the EU in 2004.[2] This section will

---

[1] Patricia Mindus, European Citizenship After Brexit (2017) at 31. Furthermore, between May 2004 and 2011, data indicate the overwhelming majority of EU27 migration to the UK consisted of migration from Central and Eastern Europe. 62% of such migrants were from Poland, 11% from Lithuania, and 10% were from Slovakia. They also overwhelmingly skewed young. 43% were under the age of 25, and 81% were under the age of 35. Catherine Barnard, *Enforcement of Employment Rights by Migrant Workers in the UK*, *in* Migrants at Work, Immigration and Vulnerability in Labour Law, 195 (Catheryn Costello & Mark Freedland QC eds. 2014).

[2] Particularly, this applies to the A8 Member States, which all joined the EU in 2004. (The three Baltic States: Estonia, Latvia, and Lithuania, the Visegrád (V4 Group) Member States: Poland, Hungary, Czechia, and Slovakia, and the Yugoslav successor state of

establish the salience of the issue of immigration in the 2016 Brexit referendum and how immigration speaks to a high likelihood of a "Hard Brexit" with respect to immigration. In Section III of this chapter, the discussion will shift to the current legal situation concerning Free Movement of People in the interim period between the triggering of Article 50 of the Treaty on the European Union (hereinafter "TEU") and the date at which the withdrawal of the UK from the EU becomes legally effective. Section III will also discuss the UK immigration system to which EU27[3] citizens would be subject in a Hard Brexit "cliff edge" scenario. Section IV will provide an overview of the labour shortages currently facing the UK and underscore some of the main challenges a Hard Brexit would impose on the British economy. This section also endeavours at observations which may form a basis for legal recommendations with respect to negotiating Brexit and the needs of the UK economy. Section V discusses some of the potential positive and negative economic and political consequences for the sending Member States through the return home of their citizens and their loss of access to low-wage sectors of the UK labour market, with a particular emphasis on remittances. Finally, Section VI will conclude with final observations. This chapter will largely focus on Poland as it is unambiguously the most significant EU27 Member State with respect to Brexit and the low-wage economy in the European Single Market. The reader should bear in mind that, as of publication, Brexit remains a dynamic event, negotiated in real time, and thus the legal situation and figures should always be re-referenced to ensure that they are current.

Slovenia.) A2 Member States (Bulgaria and Romania), accedding in 2007 are also relevant to this discussion.

[3] Unless otherwise specified, reference to the rights of EU27 workers applies to citizens of the European Economic Area states (Iceland, Norway, Lichtenstein) and also Switzerland, (these four together comprising the European Free Trade Area (EFTA)) although for the purpose of low-wage migration to the UK, this distinction is likely of little practical relevance.

I. THE DEVELOPMENT OF THE *ACQUIS COMMUNAUTAIRE* ON FREE MOVEMENT OF PEOPLE & LABOUR

A. *THE RIGHT OF RESIDENCE IN THE EUROPEAN UNION*

EU primary and secondary law[4] elucidate the scope of the rights attendant to the Free Movement of People in the European Union, (and to a large extent the European Economic Area (hereinafter "EEA") and European Free Trade Area (hereinafter "EFTA")), one of the four "Fundamental Freedoms" of the EU, and they apply to the constituent states that form the European Union (hereinafter "Member States").[5] The culmination of the entire body of EU primary and secondary law on any issue creates the *acquis communautaire* on any legal issue of EU law. Perhaps the closest analogue in US jurisprudence to the *acquis communautaire* is the US *corpus juris* -how international law, the US Constitution, federal, state, and local statutes, regulations, and common law all together speak to any legal matter in a particular jurisdiction.

The EU treaties explicitly provide for the free movement of people as among the foundational principles of the EU[6] and key to "European integration."[7] The Lisbon Treaty of 2009, which implemented the Treaty on Functioning of the European Union (hereinafter "TFEU"), explicitly affirms the right of travel and residence of EU citizens within the EU.[8]

---

[4] Primary law consists of the three Treaties of the European Union: the aforementioned TEU, the Treaty on the Functioning of the European Union [hereinafter "TFEU"] and the Charter of Fundamental Rights of the European Union. Secondary Law is the body of decisions handed down by the Court of Justice of the European Union (hereinafter "CJEU,") the supreme judicial organ of the EU, well as the Regulations, Directives, and Opinions of the European Commission interpreting the scope and application of the legal rights and principles of the European Union. Given that the status of law requires the application of both primary and secondary law together, it makes sense to discuss them in concert with each other.

[5] The UK, unlike most EU Member States, is *not* part of the Schengen Zone. This allows the UK to maintain permanent border controls and regulate Third Country migration, and indeed vet all persons, at ports of entry. There has been a widespread and erroneous conception, encouraged by the Leave Campaign, that exiting the EU will allow the UK to start exercising control over Third Country migration. The Schengen Agreement is legally independent from the EU, and the UK has retained the right to regulate the inflow of non-EEA residents in the course of its membership in the EU.

[6] Consolidated Version of the Treaty on the Functioning of the European Union, [hereinafter "TFEU"] Art. 80 at 78, [2012] O.J. C. 326/47; *Id.* Art. 3(2) at 17.

[7] Treaty on the European Union [hereinafter "TEU"], Preamble at 15-16, [2012] O.J. C. 326/13.

[8] TFEU, *supra* note 6, Arts. 20-23 at 56-68. Several specific rights of EU citizens are enumerated in Part II of the TFEU, for example, the right to "protection by the diplomatic or consular authorities of any Member State, on the same conditions as the nationals of that State"); *Id.* Art. 20(c) at 57. It also confers certain political rights. *See Id.* Art. 20(b) (granting "the right to vote and to stand as candidates in elections to the

Article 41(1) thereof affirms that "every citizen of the Union has the right to move and reside freely within the territory of the Member States"[9] and Article 41(2) extends those rights to Third Country nationals *residing legally* in Member States.[10] The right to free movement is also referenced in Charter of Fundamental Rights and Freedoms[11] in its preamble.[12] The "Citizens' Rights Directive," the most important piece of secondary EU law with respect to EU immigration rights, largely defines the scope of free movement rights, which are technically not absolute under EU law. EU citizens and their family members enjoy a right to reside for three months without restriction[13] with right to indefinite if working,[14] studying, training, qualify as certain types of job-seekers, otherwise can financially maintain themselves and are not a "burden" on the resources of the host state.[15] EU citizens also enjoy a right to permanent residence in any Member State after 5 years of residence therein, subject to some

---

European Parliament and in municipal elections in one's Member State of residence, under the same conditions as nationals of that State."); *Id.* Art. 20(d) (granting "the right to petition the European Parliament, to apply to the European Ombudsman, and to address the institutions and advisory bodies of the Union in any of the Treaty languages and to obtain a reply in the same language.").

[9] *Id.* Art. 41(1) at 404.

[10] *Id.* Art. 41(2) at 404.

[11]The rights in the charter are guidance for legislative interpretation and cannot independently be invoked as a basis for a claim to a right in European Union jurisprudence, but the Charter is nonetheless an important symbolic document and instrumental in interpreting EU law from a teleological method of interpretation in view of these espoused rights and principles. Charter on Fundamental Rights of the European Union, Arts. 51-53 at 21, [2000] O.J. C. 364/391.

[12] *Id.* Preamble at 395.

[13] Directive 2004/38/EC Of The European Parliament And Of The Council Of 29 April 2004 On The Right Of Citizens Of The Union And Their Family Members To Move And Reside Freely Within The Territory Of The Member States Amending Regulation (EEC) No 1612/68 And Repealing Directives 64/221/EEC, 68/360/EEC, 72/194/EEC, 73/148/EEC, 75/34/EEC, 75/35/EEC, 90/364/EEC, 90/365/EEC and 93/96/EEC [hereinafter "Citizens' Rights Directive"], Art. 6(1) at 92, [2004] O.J. L. 158/77 (affirming that "Union citizens shall have the right of residence on the territory of another Member State for a period of up to three months without any conditions or any formalities other than the requirement to hold a valid identity card or passport."). There are reservations for health, safety, and public policy considerations. TFEU, Art. 20(d) at 57. *Id.* 45(3) at 66; Citizens' Rights Directive, Recital (22) at 84. The definition of "family member" is a developing area of EU law. *See e.g.* C-673/16, *Coman and Others v. Romania*, ¶ 58(1)-(2), [2018] ECLI:EU:C:2018:385 (interpreting this right to include same-sex spouses in certain situations). This June 2018 CJEU judgment is not yet published in an official EU journal as of writing.

[14] *Id.* Art. 7(1)(a) at 93.

[15] *Id.* Art. (7)(b)-(c) at 93.

conditions.[16]

A series of directives and decisions have further elucidated the scope of the right to free movement,[17] and the Court of Justice of the European Union (hereinafter "CJEU") broadly interprets such rights under the Treaty documents. The oft-cited line in EU jurisprudence associated with this right is written into the CJEU decision of *Grzelczyk v. Centre public d'aide sociale d'Ottignies-Louvain-la-Neuvve*, in which the Court remarked "Union citizenship is destined to be fundamental status of nationals of the Member States."[18] CJEU jurisprudence even extends residence rights to Third Country nationals in some narrowly circumscribed cases, teleologically interpreting TFEU Art. 20 to ensure that EU citizens are able to exercise their residence rights in practice.[19]

The CJEU has encumbered the scope of its subject matter jurisdiction so as to limit the application of EU law to those situations which are "wholly internal" -having no "connecting factors to European Union law"[20] and those in which it is not imperative to allow Third Country nationals to reside within a Member State in order for an EU citizen to exercise his or her right of residence in the EU generally.[21] In light of the *acquis communautaire* on Free Movement, it appears that the stand-alone right of residence of the Third Country nationals is limited to situations in which the refusal of residence and work permits to the Third Country national would constructively force an EU citizen to leave

---

[16] *Id.* Art. 16(1) at 105. There are also restrictions and caveats throughout the Citizens' Rights Directive that may limit an EU citizen's residence rights.

[17] The Treaty of Maastricht, signed in 1993 was the first step in making the EU a political Union rather than simply and economic and customs union PAUL CRAIG & GRÁINNE DE BÚRCA, EU LAW TEXTS CASES, AND MATERIALS, Chapter 23 Citizenship of the European Union, (6th ed. 2015) at 852.

[18] C-184/99, *Rudy Grzelczyk v. Centre public d'aide sociale d'Ottignies-Louvain-la-Neuve*, [2001] E.C.R. I-6229, ¶ 32 at 6242.

[19] The *Zambrano* decision offers a teleological explanation for this interpretation of TFEU Art. 20, explaining that refusal to grant the parents [the presumable guardians] of EU-citizen children or refusing the parents work permits would have the effect of constructively compelling EU citizen dependents on guardians (in the present case, minor children) to leave the Member State, abrogating a child's right to reside in the member State granted by Art. 20. Case C-34/09, *Ruiz Zambrano v. Office National de L'emploi*, [2011] E.C.R. I-1177, ¶ 44 at 1252. Third Country nationals must be granted entrance and ability to obtain work permits in the Member State insofar as it is necessary to allow EU citizens who are dependent minors to exercise their EU rights. *Id.*

[20] *Marat Deceri et al. v. Ministerium für Inneres*, [2011] E.C.R. I-11339, ¶ 39 at 11362.

[21] "Refusal of request of EU citizen wanting to bring non-EU citizen to third member State, does not infringe upon requestor's right of residence because such refusal is not sufficient in itself to support the view that the Union citizen will be forced to leave Union territory if such a right is not granted."C-256/11, *Deceri*, *supra* note 20, ¶ 68 at 11369.

the EU,[22] notwithstanding any separate freestanding grounds under the European Court of Human Rights, which the court in *Deceri v. Ministerium für Inneres* (Austria) left as an open question.[23] There are, however, several limitations to this right in the context of "public policy, public security or public health."[24]

B. RIGHT TO SEEK EMPLOYMENT

Attendant to the right of Free Movement of People is the remarkable right of EU citizens to generally seek employment within any EU Member State, free from discrimination based on national citizenship. While explicitly stated in the TFEU, secondary law has elaborated upon the rights of EU workers[25] within arguably wide scope. In a practical sense, this is the linchpin of Free Movement rights as the ability to freely live in another Member State, for most people, is dependent upon the ability to secure employment.

Article 45 TFEU provides that "(1) Freedom of movement for workers shall be secured within the Union"[26] and "(2) such freedom of movement shall entail the abolition of any direct or indirect

---

[22] *See* CRAIG & DE BÚRCA, at 869 (noting that the case outcomes turned on whether the Third Country was necessary to sustain the EU citizen's existence within the EU).

[23] *See Deceri*, supra note 20, ¶ 69 at 11370, ¶ 72 at 11371.

[24] TFEU, *supra* note 6, Art. 45(3) at 66. In *Gaydarov*, for instance, restricting free movement rights on the basis of a serious crime, such as drugs-trafficking would be a lawful and proportionate invocation of a public policy exception. In this case, the CJEU held: "To invoke public policy the state must justify three conditions: "(i) the personal conduct of that national constitutes a genuine, present and sufficiently serious threat affecting one of the fundamental interests of society, (ii) the restrictive measure envisaged is appropriate to ensure the achievement of the objective it pursues and does not go beyond what is necessary to attain it and (iii) that measure is subject to effective judicial review permitting a determination of its legality as regards matters of fact and law in the light of the requirements of European Union law."). C-430/10, *Gaydarov v. Direktor na Glavna direktsia 'Obranitelna politsia' pri Ministerstvo na vatreshnite raboti*, ECLI:EU:C:2011:749 ¶ 43, [2011] (no page number available). *See also* note 13.

[25] The CJEU has ruled that it shall determine who is a worker to avoid politicization. C-75/63 *Hoekstra v. Bestuur der Befrijfsvereniging voor Detailhandel en Ambachten*, [1964] E.C.R. I-177, 184. Work must be "genuine" and not "on such a small scale as to be regarded as purely marginal and ancillary" which can be justified as a "genuine economic activity." C-53/81, *Levin v. Staatssecretaris van Justitie* [1982] E.C.R. 1035 ¶ 17 at 1050. A worker is an EU worker when receiving private or public support is irrelevant so long as the worker pursues "effective and genuine work." C-139/85 *Kemf v. Staatsecretaris van Justitie* [1986] E.C.R. 1741 ¶ 16 at 1751. For an expanded body of caselaw on the definition of a "worker," *see generally* C-456/02 *Trojani v. CPAS* [2004] E.C.R. I-7573; C-413/01, *Nonni-Orasche v. Bundesminister für Wissenschaft, Verkehr, und Kunst*, [2003] E.C.R. I-13187. There is a respective *acquis communautaire* for job-seekers. *See e.g.* C-292/89, *R. v. Immigration Appeal Tribunal, ex parte Antonissen*, [1991] E.C.R. I-745.

[26] TFEU, *supra* note 6, Art. 45(1) at 65.

discrimination based on nationality between workers of the member States as regards to employment, remuneration and other conditions of work and employment."[27] Additionally, Member States must recognise relevant work experience gained in other Member States[28] and must also mutually recognise skills qualifications.[29] Furthermore, Member States are not permitted discriminate against EU citizens through tax policy[30] or conditions of employment, including "eligibility for employment, remuneration and other conditions of work or dismissal."[31]

As with Free Movement rights, there are limitations to the right to be free from discrimination in employment. Member States can rely on national security as a limitation to the Free Movement of People, as an Article 346 derogation provided in if proportional.[32] For example, in *Schiebel Aircraft GmbH v. Bundesminister für Wirtschaft, Familie und Jugend*, the CJEU determined that, in line with the concept of "shared competence," the courts of a Member State could undertake an analysis of whether a national security derogation provided in TFEU Art. 346(1)(b) could be invoked as necessary to "protect its essential security interests" of the state in a case concerning citizenship requirements for a "managing partner" of a business wishing to conduct a transaction involving the sale of armaments.[33] States are also permitted to discriminate on the basis of nationality in the hiring of public employees.[34]

---

[27] *Id.* Art. 45(2) at 66.

[28] Case C-224/01, *Köbler v. Republik Österreich*, [2003] E.C.R. I-10290, ¶ 74 at 10317, (determining that "absolute refusal to recognise periods served as a university professor in a Member State other than the Republic of Austria impedes freedom of movement for workers established in Austria inasmuch as it is such as to deter the latter from leaving the country to exercise that freedom.)."

[29] Judgement of the Court of 28 June 1977 in Case 11/77 185 C. O.J. 2, 3 (1977) (holding that "[a] national of a new Member State who holds a qualification recognised by the competent authorities of the member State of establishment as equivalent to the qualification issued and required in that State enjoys the right to be admitted . . . under the same conditions . . . without being required to satisfy additional conditions.").

[30] "Free Movement of People: Commission to Tackle Tax Discrimination Against Mobile EU Citizens," EUROPEAN COMMISSION, (Jan. 20, 2014), http://europa.eu/rapid/press-release_IP-14-31_en.htm.

[31] C-34/97, *Commission v. France*, [1998] E.C.R. I-5343, ¶ 4 at 5343.

[32] C-474/12, *Schiebel Aircraft GmbH v. Bundesminister für Wirtschaft, Familie und Jugend.* [2014] E.C.R. 395 O.J. C. 6 ¶ 40, (holding "It is for the national court . . . to verify whether the Member State which, in order to justify that legislation, relies on the derogation allowed under Article 346(1)(b) TFEU is able to show that such derogation is necessary in order to protect its essential security interests.") Similar carveouts exist in other European Free Movement agreements. *See e.g.* AGREEMENT BETWEEN THE EUROPEAN COMMUNITY AND ITS MEMBER STATES, OF THE ONE PART, AND THE SWISS CONFEDERATION, OF THE OTHER, ON THE FREE MOVEMENT OF PERSONS, Art. 5, 2002 O.J. L. 144/6, at 17.

[33] *Id.*

[34] *Id.* 45(4), at 66.

II. BREXIT IS SUBSTANTIALLY LIKELY TO BE HARD WITH RESPECT TO THE FREE MOVEMENT OF PEOPLE

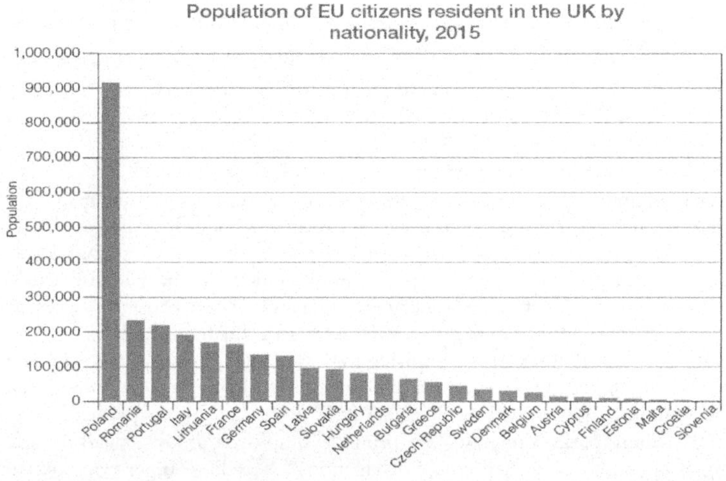

Angst in the UK concerning immigration is clearly connected to the motivation to leave the European Union in dispositive measure. As of 2017, 2.9 million non-UK Europeans reside in the UK, an overwhelming share of whom come from relatively low-wage post-communist Member States, in particular, Lithuania, and Romania, Poland,[35] 16.5% of whom are Polish, a thirteen-fold increase from 2004 and 2017.[36] Although the rate of net *immigration* has fluctuated between the years 1992 and 2017, the values have always been positive, meaning that on balance, the UK has added to its EU resident population every year.[37]

The prevailing reason why immigration has become the most salient political and economic issue in Brexit[38] and among the reasons why a Hard Brexit on immigration will have a significant effect on the UK economy is because employers from various sectors of the UK low-wage

---

35 BBC, *Reality Check: How Many EU Nationals Live in the UK?*, (Jul. 8, 2016), http://www.bbc.com/news/uk-politics-uk-leaves-the-eu-36745584; Migrants in the UK An Overview, (Feb 21, 2017), http://www.migrationobservatory.ox.ac.uk/resources/briefings/migrants-in-the-uk-an-overview/.

36 Katarzyna Dulewicz, *The Leadup to Brexit and the Post-Brexit Employment Law Landscape: The Impact on Multinational Employers Across the Globe*, 27 EMP. & INDUS. REL. L. 34, 36 (2017).

37 *Id.*

38 This general view is shared by numerous scholars. *See e.g.* McIndoe, Pledger, & Wright, *Immigration, in* DOING BUSINESS AFTER BREXIT A PRACTICAL GUIDE TO THE LEGAL CHANGES, (Tse ed. 2017) at 113.

economy[39] demonstrate a strong preference for EU27 workers, particularly those from Poland, due to their perceptions that these migrants are better workers than British workers. Such perceptions are numerous, and include perceptions that Polish workers are more willing to: accept work for which they are overqualified,[40] assume labour-intensive jobs,[41] accept an unpredictable quantity of[42] and more irregular[43] working hours. Employers also perceive those workers as

---

[39] Labour migrants from A8 tend to be heavily represented in manufacturing, construction, agriculture, and hotel/restaurant-related work. Brückner et al., "Labour Mobility Within the EU in The Context of Enlargement and The Functioning of The Transitional Arrangements," Final Report commissioned for the Employment, Social Affairs and Equal Opportunities Directorate General of the European Commission, (2009), at 152, http://doku.iab.de/grauepap/2009/LM_finalreport.pdf.

[40] Data indicate that Polish workers applying for low-skilled jobs tend to be higher-skilled than native UK applicants and were willing to accept a higher mismatch between their own skills and their job. *Id.* at 119. Brückner et al. find that "[t]his is particularly the case in the UK, where NMS-8 migrants are primarily employed in low skilled occupations, working as operatives or in elementary occupations (exceeding 60 per cent compared to only 18 per cent of UK-born workers). At the same time, NMS migrants have higher education levels (two years more) than UK-born workers, suggesting 'that in some senses NMS migrants are 'underemployed' relative to their education' (Upward, 2008)." *Id.* at 153. Additionally, Polish workers applying for low-skilled jobs tend to be better educated than their UK counterparts, willing to accept a higher degree of over-qualification for a position, and are highly regarded as workers. MIGRATION ADVISORY COMMITTEE, "Migrants in Low-Skilled Work the Growth of EU and non-EU Labour in Low-Skilled Jobs and its Impact on the UK," (Jul. 2014), at 118-19.

[41] *See UK Farmers Wonder Who'll Get the Harvest In*, POLITICO, (Aug. 18, 2016), https://www.politico.eu/article/uk-farmers-wonder-wholl-get-the-harvest-in-agriculture-migration-brexit-labour/. One survey indicated that only one out of every 50 applicants at a well-known fast food chain was British. Julia Kollewe, *The British Jobs Brexit Makes it Hard to Fill*, THE GUARDIAN, (Mar. 25, 2017), https://www.theguardian.com/business/2017/mar/25/brexit-eu-nationals-exodus-jobs-recruitment. Chairman of British Summer Fruits, a lobbying agency for the berries industry, remarked that "[t]he £1.2bn industry relies virtually 100% on workers from Europe because British workers 'do not want to get up at 6am and work on their hands and knees all day.'" Lisa O'Carroll, *supra* note 134.

[42] This working agreement often referred to as a "zero hours" contract are largely undesired by native UK workers and present issues for UK nationals who are re-entering the workforce from previously drawing on unemployment benefits. *Jonathan Fortes, Immigration and the UK—EU Relationship, in* THE ECONOMICS OF UK-EU RELATIONS : FROM THE TREATY OF ROME TO THE VOTE FOR BREXIT, at 123-25, (Campos & Frabrizio, eds. 2017); Kimiko De Freytas-Tamura, *Exodus of Foreign Workers Leaves British Employers in the Lurch*, N.Y. TIMES, (Dec. 16, 2017), https://www.nytimes.com/2017/12/16/-world/europe/britain-european-union-farming-immigration-labour-shortage.html.

[43]*See* In addition to a good attitude, honesty and reliability, "work ethic" is often, and especially those in this context, often expressed as a willingness to endure long working hours, work "antisocial" hours, and work extra hours with little to no notice, not belong to a union and generally being flexible and able to meet the employers demands and desires, even with modest compensation. *See generally id.* at 127-135 (noting the job characterizes, such insufficient hours and lack of predictability, poor conditions).

demonstrating a greater degree of flexibility in terms of willingness to relocate within the UK for work, relative to native UK workers, particularly in comparison with low-skilled Britons.[44]

In addition to the competitive traits related to the quality of work prospective workers are willing to take on, UK employers in some industries also perceive some A8 workers as possessing superior "work ethic" traits in the course of work,[45] including better punctuality, politeness, and being better self-starters.[46] Employers sometimes perceive them as more reliable and harder-working than their British counterparts.[47] This also suggests that Central and Eastern workers are more likely also to endure the attendant depravations and hardships associated with a good "work ethic."[48] Employers also regard Central and Eastern European labour migrants as possessing, on balance, better soft skills than UK workers,[49] a skill set which may be emphasised as hiring criteria in certain low-skilled industries more than in high-skilled ones.[50]

What the evidence appears to bear out is that Poles and other

---

[44]*See* Fortes, *supra* note 42 at 186, "Migrants in Low-Skilled Work the Growth of EU and non-EU Labour in Low-Skilled Jobs and its Impact on the UK," supra note 40 at 123-25; Kimiko De Freytas-Tamura, *supra* note 42.

[45]*See* "Migrants in Low-Skilled Work the Growth of EU and non-EU Labour in Low-Skilled Jobs and its Impact on the UK," at 121-22.

[46] *Id.* at 120. One interviewee noted: "Migrants have a very strong attitude towards work. For them it's not all about the money. If I asked them to work extra hours with no notice, they will say yes and do it happily with no complaints. They are very loyal given the chance … Of course, some British can be like this. Take [employee], he's a good example of that same kind of mentality – he's a good person and loyal. But he's an older worker, the younger ones don't seem to be the same." *Id.*

[47], "Migrants in Low-Skilled Work the Growth of EU and non-EU Labour in Low-Skilled Jobs and its Impact on the UK," *supra* note 40 at 118, 121.

[48] *See supra* note 46; *See id* at 168. As a note of editorial clarity, the intent here is not to suggest that a willingness to accept degrading conditions and decreased autonomy, whether by virtue of cultural character or economic necessity means that such traits are objectively virtuous or that workers who exhibit them are inherently superior to workers who are unwilling to exhibit such traits or that society should revere and accept such traits as normal. Rather, this point is only to demonstrate that such traits are more attractive to employers. These traits can be perniciously manipulated when immigrant workers are singled out for negative disparate treatment. *See e.g. id.* at 130 (suggesting that employers or supervisors take advantage of immigrant workers). This perhaps a combination of conventional discrimination and a rational calculation, knowing that they can get away with asking certain immigrants to do more than British workers.

[49] *Id.* at 120; *Id.* at 3 (noting that "[m]igrants," are generally perceived by employers to possess better "soft skills.")

[50] "Migrants in Low-Skilled Work the Growth of EU and non-EU Labour in Low-Skilled Jobs and its Impact on the UK," *supra* note 40 at 120. *See also id* at 110 (noting that "[r]esearch has shown that some care service users actively express a preference for personal qualities over formal qualifications.")

migrants are not simply "taking all the jobs" and there are none left for Britons, but rather that there is a high degree of structural unemployment in the UK labour market which Poles fill, as Polish labour does pose as harsh competition for low-skilled work in the UK.[51] However, it must be noted that there does also appear to be an explicit bias against UK workers in some cases, at least in some sectors.[52] While some of those critical of the current immigration environment in the UK acknowledge that it may indeed be the case that labour migrants fill positions that Britons themselves will not take, there is evidence to suggest that British employers do engage in pernicious practices, some of whom *do* actively discriminate against British workers, knowing that they will be able to profit off of the relatively more complacent foreign workers.[53] In fact, there is now a substantial body of evidence suggesting that UK employers have illicitly taken advantage of some foreign workers in measure so egregious[54] as to conceivably rise to the level of labour trafficking.

A. *WHY DO THEY COME? WAGES AND PURCHASING POWER ARBITRAGE BETWEEN THE UK AND A8 STATES IN THE LATE 2010S*

There are clear and substantial economic reasons why Poles and other similarly-situated labour migrants are willing to endure less certain terms of employment, jobs for which they are overqualified, and lower-quality working conditions discussed above. These reasons centre around the macroeconomic disparities between purchasing power parity and wages which translate into substantially more attractive "real" wages

---

[51], "Migrants in Low-Skilled Work the Growth of EU and non-EU Labour in Low-Skilled Jobs and its Impact on the UK," *supra* note 40 at 118-19, https://assets.publishing.service.gov.uk/government/uploads/system/uploads/attachment_data/file/333083/MAC-Migrants_in_low-skilled_work__Full_report_2014.pdf.

[52] *Id.* at 121. *See also id.* at 132, (noting "[f]or example, in the food industry Scott . . . found a very clear low-wage hiring queue divide between migrants, especially between Central and Eastern European, and UK workers. That study, based on interview and survey evidence, identified a strong preference among labour-intensive horticultural employers for migrants and strong prejudice against UK workers . . ."

[53] "It may be the case, as some have argued, that many young people discount hospitality or care industries as beneath them . . . .yet I have heard horror tales of hotel management deliberately cutting hours of young British workers and adding hours to migrant workers who do not complain about deductions from earnings that almost certainty take people below the minimum wage." *Chris Bryant's Speech on Immigration: Full Text,* NEW STATESMAN, (Aug. 12, 2013), https://www.newstatesman.com/politics/2013/08/chris-bryants-speech-immigration-full-text.

[54] *See* Barnard, *supra* note 1 at 203-206.

in the UK relative to some sending states.[55] A cursory analysis into the disparity between economic environments in relevant sending states and the UK provides insight into the major economic forces driving migration to the UK and the willingness of migrant workers to endure less favourable conditions than their British counterparts. Using data from 2015 as an example, the average wage of EU-A8 migrants was £ 9.33/hr for men and £ 9.13/hr for women.[56] This translates into an average annual rate of 49.36 Polish Złoty (zł)[57]/hour for men and 48.30 zł/hr for women, based on the average annual exchange rate over the course of 2015.[58] While this may be relatively low in a UK context, based on available wage date from 2015, the average hourly wage in Poland was 23.84 zł/hr (or according to the average 2015 exchange rate, equivalent to 4.51 £/hr).[59] This means that, on average, an Polish worker being paid an average A8 migrant salary probably earned about twice what he or she would earn in Poland in real terms, at least within the period of time that this set of data is current. This arbitrage is probably amplified many-fold for A8 labour migrants from outside major cities in relatively poorer

---

[55] *See*, "Migrants in Low-Skilled Work the Growth of EU and non-EU Labour in Low-Skilled Jobs and its Impact on the UK," *supra* note 40 at 126-27. This particularly makes sense in the context of understanding the enormous PPP differential among even the lowest-paid migrant workers in the UK.

[56] The Migration Observatory, "Characteristics and Outcomes of Migrants in the UK Labour Market," (Mar. 23, 2017), http://www.migrationobservatory.ox.ac.uk/resources/briefings/characteristics-and-outcomes-of-migrants-in-the-uk-labour-market/. The British Pound Sterling (GBP) [hereinafter "£" or "British Pound."]

[57] Although Poland is in the EU, it still uses its national currency, the Złoty (zł).

[58] The average exchange rate between the £ and zł was 0.19 £/zł, or conversely, 5.29 zł/£ (averaging the month average exchange rates for 2015). X-RATES, https://www.x-rates.com/average/?from=PLN&to=GBP&amount=1&year=2015. This figure was obtained by averaging the monthly data.

[59] According to the Polish Statistical Office, the average monthly gross wage in 2015 was 3899.78 zł. STAT.GOV.PL, "Average Monthly Gross Wage and Salary in National Economy 1950-2016," (Feb. 9, 2018), https://stat.gov.pl/en/topics/labour-market/working-employed-wages-and-salaries-cost-of-labour/average-monthly-gross-wage-and-salary-in-national-economy-1950-2017,2,1.html. According to the Organisation for Economic Co-operation Development (OECD), the average Polish worker worked 1963 hours/year, yielding an average of 163.58 hours/month. Organization for the Co-operation and Economic Development, "Hours Worked," https://data.oecd.org/emp/hours-worked.htm. The monthly wages were then divided by the 163.58 hr/month. The result of these figures is an average hourly rate of 23.84 zł/hr in 2015. For the conversion of these figures to £ in 2015, *see* note 58. Fortes notes that "[m]igration from some EU countries -e.g. Poland -appears to respond quite quickly and substantially to exchange rate changes, presumably because migrants compare the salaries that they could earn at home to what the can earn here (and, in part, remit back to family)." Fortes, *supra*, note 42 at 19.

regions, where local average wages (and the price of goods and services) may fall far below the national average.

Wages paid in the UK to the Polish worker are also bolstered by the a "currency multiplier effect" created through a particular type of currency arbitrage resulting from a misalignment of Purchasing Power Parities (PPP) between the UK and Poland on one hand and the actual rate of exchange on the other. For example, using data for 2017, the PPP differential between the UK and Poland, meant that each British Pound earned and remitted to Poland can be construed as "overvalued" by 172.6%, or 1.726 times more valuable than the same Pound earned and spent in the UK.[60] Simply put, every British Pound a Polish worker remits home was worth almost twice much[61] as it would be to a UK worker not remitting that money. Put in the most simple terms, a British worker (who would spend her earnings in the relatively "expensive" UK economy, in which goods and services are relatively expensive) may consider minimum, or near minimum, wage earnings a paltry sum. But the same humble earnings (earned in British Pounds) would be quite substantial to a migrant worker who takes these earnings aggregated over the course of months or years, converts them into local currency, and spends them (or sends them to associates to be spent) in the economy of the sending state.[62] Assuming similar PPP disparities exist between the UK and most other sending Member States,[63] low-wage labour will remain attractive to those who either remit earnings to the A8 or intend to save up their earnings and either relocate back home or to another EU27 jurisdiction in which the cost of living is cheaper than that in the

---

[60] According to OECD data Poland's 2017 purchasing power parity index was 1.798, and the UK's was 0.713, using the USD as a reference. Organisation for Economic Co-operation and Development, "Purchasing Power Parities (PPP)," https://data.oecd.org/conversion/purchasing-power-parities-ppp.htm#indicator-chart. Therefore, using the 2017 PPP rates of the UK against Poland, yields an implied exchange rate of 1 £ to 2.52 zł. The actual average 2017 exchange rate was about 1 £ to 4.35 zł. *See* X-RATES, "Monthly Averages Polish Zloty [sic] per 1 British £ Monthly Average,"https://www.xrates.com/average/?from=GBP&to=PLN&amount=1&year=2017. From these figures, one could deduce that every £ earned in the UK market would be worth about 173% (1.73 times) more when that £ is spent back in Poland (after conversion into local currency).

[61] I will refer to this as the "currency multiplier effect." There are many perspectives of analysing economic phenomena. This is simply one perspective, but is by no means an authoritative assessment of purchasing power and relative strength of currency.

[62] This type of currency flow is a known as a remittance.

[63] *See* note 64 for a few examples of calculations of this effect in key sending states.

UK.[64] This is *a fortiori* the case for A8 workers sending money earned as British Pounds to poorer regions of the sending states where the PPP may fall far below the national average.

---

[64] This phenomenon can be observed in other A8 countries which send a significant number of labour migrants to the UK. Barnard, *supra* note 1 at 196. For example, in Lithuania, which uses the Euro, the implied exchange rate based on 2017 PPP data (UK PPP=0.713, Lithuanian PPP =0.461) would be 1 £ to 0.63 € (in the Lithuanian economy), however the 2017 nominal (actual) exchange rate was 1 £ to 0.88 €. STATISTA, "Euro (EUR) to British Pound Sterling (GBP) Average Annual Exchange Rate from 1999 to 2017," https://www.statista.com/statistics/412806/euro-to-gbp-average-annual-exchange-rate/; This would make every £ remitted to and spent in Lithuania "overvalued" by a factor of 1.40, or 140%. For Latvia, the implied exchange rate based on 2017 PPP data (UK PPP=0.713, Latvia PPP =0.501) would be 1 £ to 0.70 €. The actual average exchange rate was 1 £ to 0.88 €. *Id.* Therefore, the every Pound earned would "overvalued" by a factor of 1.26, or 126% (once converted to Euros) in the Latvian economy. The 2017 PPP differential between the UK (PPP=0.713) and Romania (1.696), using the USD as a reference, suggests that the implied exchange rate is 1 £= 2.38 Romanian Leu. OECD, "Purchasing Power Parities Indicator Chart," https://data.oecd.org/conversion/purchasing-power-parities-ppp.htm#indicator-chart. Using data from 2017, the nominal (actual) 2017 average £ to Romanian Leu exchange rate was 1£ to 4.56 Romanian Leu. X-RATES, https://www.x-rates.com/average/?from=EUR&to=RON&amount=1&year=2017. Because the implied exchange rate is 1.92 times higher than the actual exchange rate, this means that for 2017, on average, each Pound earned in the UK was "overvalued" by a factor of 1.92, or 192% when spent in the Romanian economy. *See also* Mereuta, "Mobilising Migrant's Skills and Recourses – The Case of Romania," for "The Economic Impact of Emigration in Latvia and the Other Baltic Countries: Challenges and Policy Implications, for "The Economic Impact of Emigration in Latvia and the Other Baltic Countries: Challenges and Policy Implications, " a collaboration between the OECD and the Ministry of Foreign Affairs of Latvia, (Dec. 17, 2012), *in Coping with Emigration in Baltic and Eastern European Countries*, OECD, (2013) at 48 (noting [m]igrants went not to the closest countries, but to the countries where they could earn the most (*e.g.*, through informal trading or employment) or where study was likely to provide the greatest return . . ."). If Brexit turns out to be hard however, *ceteris paribus*, this "currency multiplier effect" may be diminished. Due to likely decreased trade volumes that the UK's leaving of the customs union and single market will cause as a result of the imposition of tariffs between the UK and the EU, value of the Pound may fall against the Euro and Polish Złoty. Dimitrios Syrrakos, *Economic Impact and Manufacturing*, *in* DOING BUSINESS AFTER BREXIT A PRACTICAL GUIDE TO THE LEGAL CHANGES, *supra* note 38 at 41. By proxy, effects on the Euro will affect the Złoty because the Złoty is hard-pegged to the Euro. *Id.* at 34. This would render money earned in British Pounds less valuable than it would have been had the Pound remained stronger against the Euro and Złoty. However, it seems likely that the PPP disparities are still significant enough, and the UK economy is large and diversified enough that the Pound will remain strong even a fairly substantial decline in trade with the EU keep the PPP labour arbitrage attractive to A8 labourers.

B. *BREXIT ON IMMIGRATION WILL BE HARD: CURRENT STANCE OF THE UK GOVERNMENT, POLITICAL LEADERSHIP, AND POPULATION ON POST-BREXIT IMMIGRATION*

1. The UK Government

While both the EU and UK are eager to continue a relationship with each other, for the foreseeable future, it appears that the relationship is destined for a significantly altered legal regime which will curtail Free Movement of People between the UK and EU27 -in essence, a significantly "hard" Brexit with respect to immigration. The UK population[65] and the two major UK parties, the Conservative "Tory" party (along with their new Democratic Unionist colleagues) as well as the Labour Party, unequivocally support a Brexit which limits immigration. The official Conservative position supports a Brexit which reduces immigration,[66] and the current government, headed by Conservative Theresa May, has made its position on immigration clear in its white paper,[67] promising to "design [the UK] immigration system to ensure that [it is] able to control the numbers of people who come [to the UK] from the EU. In future, therefore, *the Free Movement Directive will no longer apply and the migration of EU nationals will be subject to UK law.*"[68] Prime Minister May has said that Brexit allows the UK to cut immigration[69] to 100,000 persons per year, from the current rate of a net gain of 330,000 (however these numbers include students many of whom eventually leave).[70] Prime Minister May's position is, if anything,

---

[65] Interestingly, during the earlier 1975 referendum on whether the UK should remain in the European Economic Community, voters more concerned about immigration were more likely to vote to remain in the European Economic Community, the previous iteration of the EU. *See* Fortes, *supra* note 42 at 177.

[66] "[W]e continue to believe that no deal is better than a bad deal for the UK. . . .We will control immigration and secure the entitlements of EU nationals in Britain and British nationals in the EU." CONSERVATIVES.COM, "The Conservative and Unionist Party Manifesto 2017," at 36, https://www.conservatives.com/manifesto.

[67] "However, in the last decade or so, we have seen record levels of long-term net migration in the UK, and that sheer volume has given rise to public concern about pressure on public services, like schools and our infrastructure, especially housing, as well as placing downward pressure on wages for people on the lowest incomes. The public must have confidence in our ability to control immigration. It is simply not possible to control immigration overall when there is unlimited Free Movement of People to the UK from the EU." "The United Kingdom's Exit from and New Partnership With the EU," White paper of the Office of the Prime Minister, (Feb. 2017), at 25.

[68] *Id.* at 25. Emphasis added.

[69] Saim Saeed, *Theresa May Pledges to Cut Immigration to "Tens of Thousands,"* POLITICO, (Aug. 17. 2017), https://www.politico.eu/article/theresa-may-pledges-to-cut-immigration-to-tens-of-thousands-uk-election-2017.

[70] Dulewicz, *supra* note 36 at 36.

likely to harden given the coalition her government formed with the nationalist, Eurosceptic, Northern Ireland-based Democratic Unionist Party, which has likewise indicated its desire to "control immigration."[71] Given the current status of negotiations, some lawyers believe that it appears that the EU is not likely to join EEA or EFTA in the foreseeable future,[72] and even it were a likely possibility, it is highly unlikely that EFTA would allow the UK to join *not* accepting Free Movement, and even if it were willing to accept such a deal, EFTA would face enormous pressure from the EU not to accept it. The EU would consider such an agreement, essentially rewarding the UK for leaving the EU on terms unfair to the EU, unacceptable.

2. Public Opinion

The UK government position is unlikely to change due to a popular mandate to reduce immigration. In 2016, immigration was the issue of most concern to Britons.[73] In 2013, 56% wanted immigration reduced "a lot," 77% wanted immigration reduced "a little,"[74] and in 2014, a slight majority were "concerned with EU immigration."[75] Finally, if recent legislation is any indication, Parliament's mood is in lockstep with May's government and public opinion.[76]

3. Support for Brexit from the Political Opposition

Even if somehow Labour gains control of the UK government during the negotiating phase of Brexit, Brexit is unlikely to reverse course with respect to Free Movement as it is not at all a significant leap to

---

[71] The Democratic Unionist Party platform has stated, in its 2017 Manifesto, that "[t]he DUP sees no value in the attempts by some to keep re-running the referendum. Instead, we want to get on with the work to make it a success; to write our own laws; to deliver on the vision of a Global UK with new free trade deals; to control immigration; to deliver policies for farming and fishing shaped to our needs; to lift the burden of unnecessary regulation." *Our Plan for Northern Ireland The DUP Manifesto for the 2017 Northern Ireland Assembly Election*, (Feb. 17, 2017), at 4, http://www.mydup.com/images/-uploads/publications/DUP_Manifesto_2017_v2_SINGLES.pdf.

[72] "Brexit EEA: Q&A," Travers Smith, (Jul. 11, 2017), https://www.traverssmith.com/news-publications/brexit/resources/brexit-eea-q-a/.

[73] The Migration Observatory, "UK Public Opinion Toward Immigration: Overall Attitudes and Level of Concern," (Nov. 28, 2016), at 3, http://www.migrationobservatory.ox.ac.uk/wp-content/uploads/2016/04/Briefing-Public_Opinion_Immigration_Attitudes_Concern.pdf.

[74] *The United Kingdom's Exit from and New Partnership With the EU*, *supra* note 67 at 4.

[75] *Id.* at 6.

[76] "The ratcheting up of criminalization is of great symbolic and practical importance . . . It also reinforces a public discourse of national community that potentially legimates xenophobic agendas. He is rallying call of 'British Jobs for British Workers' provides cover for a range of political programmes, not all of the benign." Alan Bogg, *Brexit, Labour Law and the Twilight of Liberalism*, *in* THE NEW FOUNDATIONS OF LABOUR LAW 49-51, (Ahlberg & Brun eds. 2017).

conclude that Labour does support a Brexit which reduces immigration. Labour leader Jeremy Corbyn has been critical of intra-EU labour migration to the UK[77] and the Labour Party's Manifesto states: "Labour accepts the referendum result and a Labour government will put the national interest first. We will prioritize jobs and living standards, build a close new relationship with the EU . . ."[78] From a trade unionist perspective, the type of work frequently undertaken by agricultural workers, the so-called "zero hours contracts,"[79] is the type of working arrangement which can clearly be seen as a negative by-product of malign labour liberalisation associated with the EU, possibly engendering "Brexiteer" sentiments among economically left-wing detractors of such arrangements. Other figures in Labour, such as former Shadow Immigration Minister, Chris Bryant, have spoken out against the current labour regime in such populist terms.[80] Further considering that Corbyn has recently announced his abandonment of any attempt to remain in the European Single Market,[81] the EU would have little leverage on the UK from the perspective of Labour.

---

[77] LABOR.ORG.UK, "Negotiating Brexit," https://labour.org.uk/manifesto/negotiating-brexit/#second. In a January 2017 interview, Labour Party Leader Jeremy Corbyn told the BBC that he did not consider immigration numbers too high, but claimed that "[t]he right to work here would be something that would have to be negotiated" and the "grotesque exploitation" of workers has had a detrimental effect on wages." He also said: "What we don't want to do is turn Britain into a bargain-basement economy on the shores of Europe where we continuously reduce corporation taxation, encourage a low-wage economy. . . . Instead what we want is a high-value economy with skilled jobs promoting high-quality exports." BBC, *Jeremy Corbyn Outlines Plan to 'Cap' Boardroom Pay*, (Jan. 10, 2017), http://www.bbc.com/news/uk-politics-38568116. Corbyn also stated "what there wouldn't be is the wholesale importation of underpaid workers from central Europe in order to destroy conditions, particularly in the construction industry."
Adam Beckett & Adam Payne *Jeremy Corbyn Does Not 'Believe' In Ending Free Movement After Brexit, Leading Momentum Activist Claims*, (Aug. 11, 2017), BUSINESS INSIDER, http://www.businessinsider.com/jeremy-corbyn-does-not-believe-in-ending-free-movement-after-brexit-leading-momentum-activist-claims-2017-8.

[78] Labour Party Manifesto, *Negotiating Brexit*, (undated) https://labour.org.uk/-manifesto/negotiating-brexit/.

[79] Juliet McMahon, Michelle O'Sullivan, Tom Turner, Lorraine Ryan, Jonathan Lavelle, Caroline Murphy, Mike O'Brien, & Patrick Gunnigle, *Zero Hours Work and the Role of the Law in Ireland, in* THE NEW FOUNDATIONS OF LABOUR LAW, at 147.

[80] "It may be the case, as some have argued, that many young people discount hospitality or care industries as beneath them . . . .yet I have heard horror tales of hotel management deliberately cutting hours of young British workers and adding hours to migrant workers who do not complain about deductions from earnings that almost certainty take people below the minimum wage." *Chris Bryant's Speech on Immigration: Full Text*, NEW STATESMAN, (Aug. 12, 2013), https://www.newstatesman.com/politics/2013/08/chris-bryants-speech-immigration-full-text.

[81] Simon Johnson, *Jeremy Corbyn: UK Must Reject Full EU Single Market Membership*, THE Telegraph, (Mar. 9, 2018), https://www.telegraph.co.uk/news/2018/03/09/jeremy-corbyn-labour-must-reject-full-eu-single-market-membership.

4. EU has Little Leverage to Persuade the UK to Maintain Free Movement of People

The UK government appears to be yielding to domestic pressure not to pursue a customs union,[82] (*ergo* the single market as well).[83] Seeing as it has rejected access to the free movement of goods[84] and to some degree services,[85] European leaders will have dramatically reduced leverage to pressure the UK to maintain Free Movement of People by withholding access to the Single Market in ongoing negotiations towards a final agreement.[86] Even if the UK government were to abandon its mandate to decrease EU27 immigration and join the EEA or EFTA, it would have to adhere to Single Market rules without having a say in the rulemaking process.[87] Lack of representation in the decision-making EU

---

[82] Adam Payne *Theresa May Is Set to Surrender to Cabinet Brexiteers in Customs Union Row*," BUSINESS INSIDER, (May 11, 2018), http://www.businessinsider.com/theresa-may-is-set-to-surrender-to-cabinet-brexiteers-in-customs-union-row-2018-5; Eleanor Garnier, *Brexit: Government Insists UK Will Leave* Customs Union, (Apr. 23, 2018), http://www.bbc.com/news/uk-politics-43860453.

[83] A customs union with harmonised external tariffs is a necessary condition for a single market. Many scholars also believe that a true single market cannot exist without Free Movement of People.

[84] Dulewicz, *supra* note 36 at 35.

[85]"Services are not directly included in a customs union (they are subject to neither tariffs nor customs controls) but have become increasingly embedded in goods production. Therefore, a customs union could indirectly affect trade in services industries, for example, in parallel to exporting cars, an automotive firm might also provide financial services." *Id.* at 47.

[86] The position of EU27 leaders and the EU's position, articulated by Brexit Negotiator, Michel Barnier, is that the UK cannot enjoy the benefits of access to the Single Market, e.g. no tariffs, duties or customs, and reject Free Movement of People for EU citizens into the UK. *See e.g.* Michel Barnier: Speech of Michele Barnier, European Commission Negotiator for Brexit, at Hannover Messe, (Apr. 23, 2018), http://europa.eu/rapid/press-release_SPEECH-18-3511_en.htm. ("[A]ny change from the UK must respect our principles, the principles we have built with the UK over 45 years. In particular, the four freedoms of the Single Market go together. They are all indivisible. You cannot have free movement of services without free movement of goods, and so forth. And you cannot have free movement of goods without free movement of people.."); James Randerson, *EU Won't Break the Single Market for Brexit UK* (Jul. 7, 2018), POLITICO, https://www.politico.eu/article/michel-barnier-brexit-customs-eu-wont-break-the-single-market-for-brexit-uk/; David Connolly, *Merkel: No Single Market Without Free Movement for EU Citizens*, SKY NEWS, (Jan 9, 2017), https://news.sky.com/story/merkel-no-single-market-without-free-movement-for-eu-citizens-10723535; Ian Wishart, *EU Heavyweights Will Block UK Single-Market Bid, Spain* Says, BLOOMBERG, (Jun. 26, 2018), https://www.bloomberg.com/news/articles/2018-06-26/eu-heavyweights-will-block-u-k-single-market-bid-spain-says.

[87] Dulewicz, *supra* at 36. However, if the UK were able to join the EEA or EFTA, it could largely access the Single Market without necessarily having to accept Free Movement of People. Lichtenstein is an EFTA Member and extremely tightly controls immigration. *See* "Ausländer und Passampt," (APA), LANDESVERWALTUNG FÜRSTENTUM LICHTENSTEIN,

institutions would be more pronounced for the UK than the current European Free Trade Association states (Iceland, Norway, Lichtenstein, and Switzerland) due the UK's large population.[88] In sum, given current popular opinion in the UK and the UK government's current negotiating posture, it would appear improbable and politically irrational (at least from the perspective of a UK politician facing re-election) to pursue a deal in which the *acquis communautaire* of Free Movement of People is preserved.

III. LEGAL CONSEQUENCES OF HARD BREXIT

A. *CURRENT LEGAL SITUATION*

In the immediate future, the legal situation has been relatively stabilised. Until the UK formally withdraws from the EU, EU law continues to apply to the UK and the UK remains subject to all the adjudicatory bodies of the EU in the resolution of disputes falling under the ambit of EU law. In its March White Paper, the UK Government declared its intention to transpose the *acquis communautaire* into UK law[89] in the "Repeal Bill," (the legislative bill currently working its way through Parliament as of writing that will legally end EU jurisdiction over the UK)[90] under UK national law,[91] which will ensure legal continuity on Brexit day. With respect to what will happen thereafter, the future status of law was further fleshed out in mid-March 2017, when the UK and the EU agreed to core provisions concerning EU27 citizens residing in the UK, and *vice versa*, in the "Draft Agreement on the Withdrawal of the United Kingdom of Great Britain and Northern Ireland from the European Union and the European Atomic Energy Community" (hereinafter "Draft Agreement").[92]

The Draft Agreement largely preserves the rights of EU27 citizens and their relatives (specified therein) who are lawfully present in the UK

---

https://www.llv.li/#/12119/residing-in-liechtenstein. However, this was likely only agreed to because of Lichtenstein's exceptionally small size. All Other EFTA States *generally* have Free Movement of People with the EU. *See* EUROPEAN COMMISSION, "Non-EU Nationals," Employment, Social Affairs & Inclusion," http://ec.europa.eu/social/main.jsp?catId=470&langId=en.

88 Dulewicz, *supra* note 87 at 35.

89 DEPARTMENT FOR EXITING THE EUROPEAN UNION, "Legislating for the United Kingdom's Withdrawal from the European Union," (Mar. 2017), 1.24(a) at 12, https://assets.publishing.service.gov.uk/government/uploads/system/uploads/attachment_data/file/604514/Great_repeal_bill_white_paper_print.pdf.

90 *Id.* at § 1.24(a) at 12.

91 The UK, like the US, is a dualist rather than monist state, requiring non self-executing treaties to be implemented independently through the national legislature.

92 Although the document is a draft, the drafters indicated which provisions have been agreed upon.

arrive in the UK prior to the withdrawal date, preserving rights for these people largely in line with the Citizens Rights Directive.[93] Such persons can reside in the UK and become permanent residents,[94] their working and non-discrimination rights pursuant to Article 45(3)-(4) TFEU are preserved, as is the mutual recognition of professional qualifications.[95] Additionally, the harmonised pension scheme pursuant to Directive EC 883/2004[96] will be grandfathered in.[97] In essence, any EU27 citizens who lawfully moves to the UK on a permanent basis will be treated as if the EU *acquis communautaire* on Free Movement (as it stands at the time of implementation) applies to him or her. Recently, many EU27 citizens, namely from Poland, have taken advantage of this development.[98] While a commendable stabilizing agreement, it does create a bizarre situation in which EU27 citizens arriving the moment just prior to and those arriving after Brexit Day, which currently stands at March 27, 2019, will essentially be subject to two different legal regimes and different sets of rights. If the cliff-edge scenario occurs, meaning no EU-UK deal concerning the rights of workers, an EU27 passenger who arrives in the UK the minute prior to the execution of Brexit will enjoy the rights afforded under the EU *acquis communautaire*, and those arriving a moment thereafter would be subject to the UK tiered immigration system, the five categories through which immigrant visas are issued in the UK (elaborated further below).

---

93 *See* "Draft Agreement on the withdrawal of the United Kingdom of Great Britain and Northern Ireland from the European Union and the European Atomic Energy Community," T50(2018)35 -Commission to EU27, Title II, Chapter 2 Arts. 9-10 at 16-21, (Mar. 19, 2018), https://ec.europa.eu/commission/sites/beta-political/files/draft_agreement_coloured.pdf.

94 *Id.* Art. 14 at 12.

95 *Id.* Art 26-27 at 20-21

96 *Id.* Art. 28(1)-(2) at 22.

97 *Id.* Chapter 2, I Art. 22(1) at 18. For specificity of these rights, *see generally id.* Art. 22 at 18.

98 *See* Jakub Ceglarz, *Polscy Emigranci Boją Się Brexitu. Ale Znaleźli na to Sposób*, MONEY.PL, (May 25, 2017), https://www.money.pl/gospodarka/unia-europejska/wiadomosci-/artykul/brexit-polacy-na-wyspach,179,0,2325683.html.

B. LOSS OF THE ACQUIS COMMUNAUTAIRE

In the absence of an association agreement preserving Free Movement of People or preferential treatment,[99] EU workers will be subject to the UK Immigration system. Even if the EU eventually successfully negotiations favourable treatment of prospective EU27 workers, it is unlikely that addressing migration will be considered the most pressing issue, and provided that it takes about ten years to create and implement an EU Commission Directive through the EU legislative process,[100] it is highly unlikely that a deal will be reached quickly in any case. Additionally, there no guarantee that the UK will agree to be bound by further developments in EU immigration law.[101] As the *acquis communautaire* develops over the course of time in the EU, differences between EU law and the law created by whatever provisions to which the UK and EU agree will apply to the UK, will become more pronounced over time unless the parties agree to periodic renegotiation of terms or harmonisation measures.

Even if Hard Brexit occurs, there are still some aspects of labour migration that are likely to be largely unaffected by the changing legal regime. Under UK immigration law, there are a plethora of family visas available for which Central European EU citizens may qualify given the significant number of EU27 citizens residing in the UK that already (or will soon) qualify as permanent residents in the UK; though many of these initially restrict ability to work in the UK.[102] EU anti-discrimination secondary law in *Köbler* situations, referenced *supra*, or similar situations involving mutual recognition of qualifications and work experience is likely to have a limited impact on the vast majority of potential central European workers as minimally-skilled workers in agriculture or construction would not necessarily rely on a long *curriculum vitae* of technical qualifications or past experience for their hiring. Also, given that many of the UK's low-wage A8 labourers do not arrive possessing

---

[99] Some scholars suggest that, as of 2016, the UK government favours some type of immigration agreement with the EU which would prioritize EU workers about those from Third countries. Fortes *supra* note 42 at 194.

[100] *See* ORGANIZATION FOR ECONOMIC CO-OPERATION AND DEVELOPMENT, "Recruiting Immigrant Workers: Europe 2016," at 69, https://read.oecd-ilibrary.org/social-issues-migration-health/recruiting-immigrant-workers-europe-2016_9789264257290-en#page1.

[101] Jarrod Tudor, *Working Across the Member States: The Free Movement of Workers in the European Union*, 8 CREIGHTON INT'L & COMP. L. J. 38, 51 (2017).

[102] The partners or spouses of permanent residents may apply for family visas *see* Immigration Rules Part 8: ¶ 227-89 "Family Visas: Apply, Extend, or Switch," THE HOME OFFICE OF THE UNITED KINGDOM, https://www.go v.uk/uk-family-visa/partner-spouse.

extensive English skills, as a related problem, migrant workers are unlikely to be significantly affected by loss of right to criminal proceedings in their choice of language[103] because UK domestic law protects this right.[104]

C. *THE UK IMMIGRATION SYSTEM*[105] *FOR THIRD COUNTRY NATIONALS*[106]

Since 2008,[107] the UK immigration system to which non-EU27 and non-EEA[108] are subject is based on a five-tiered classification. Currently, there are no specific avenues for low-skilled labour migration from non-EEA countries.[109] Like many immigration systems, the UK's immigration regime favours immigration from those at the highest point of the earning spectrum, recruiting skilled labourers who are unlikely to

---

103 "The answer to the question referred for a preliminary reference must therefore be that the principle of free movement of workers, as laid down in Article 48 of the Treaty and more particularly in Regulation No. 1612/68 of the Council, requires that a worker who is a national of one Member State and habitually resides in another Member State be entitled to require that criminal proceedings against him take place in a language other than the language normally used in proceedings before the court which tries him if workers who are nationals of the host Member State have that right in the same circumstances." C-137/84, *Ministère Public v. Robert Heinrich Maria Muntsch*, [1985] E.C.R. 2691 ¶ 18 at 2696.

104 Human Rights Act 1998, § 6(3)(e) (1998).

105 Immigration law is a dynamic field of law and the UK government regularly updates its regulations. The data referenced herein was accessed in March and April 2018 and may no longer be completely current as of publication. Those citing this data should visit the UK government website to ensure that figures are current.

106 In this context, "Third Countries" will exclude EEA states of Iceland, Norway, and Lichtenstein, as they are largely integrated into the "freedom of movement" scheme. As a caveat, many of the immigration requirements are subject to a complicated set of grandfather clauses and exceptions. While it is important to understand the limitations of generalizations, it is necessary to make generalizations insofar as it is possible to meaningfully speculate on the effect of subjecting A8 countries to the UK visa scheme. An editorial decision has been made to focus on "Tier 2 (general)" visas because that appears to be the visa category that would apply to the greatest number of A8 labour migrants in the UK.

107 Mimi Zou, *Employer Demand for 'Skilled' Migrant Workers*, *in* TEMPORARY LABOUR MIGRATION IN THE GLOBAL ERA (Joanna How & Rosemary Owns eds. 2016) at 117.

108 *See generally* AGREEMENT ON THE EUROPEAN ECONOMIC AREA, Arts. 28-30, at 13, (Jan. 1, 1994), http://www.efta.int/media/documents/legal-texts/eea/the-eea-agreement/-Main%20Text%20of%20the%20Agreement/EEAagreement.pdf. *See generally*, AGREEMENT BETWEEN THE EUROPEAN COMMUNITY AND ITS MEMBER STATES, OF THE ONE PART, AND THE SWISS CONFEDERATION, OF THE OTHER, ON THE FREE MOVEMENT OF PERSONS, Arts 1-16, *supra* note 32 at 6-19.

109 THE HOME OFFICE OF THE UNITED KINGDOM, The Tier 3 category visa has been removed from availability. *See* "Immigration Rules Part 6A: The Points-Based System," https://www.gov.uk/guidance/immigration-rules/immigration-rules-part-6a-the-points-based-system.

draw significantly from the public welfare system and likely to contribute significantly to the UK economy and welfare state through income and VAT tax, and disfavours lower-skilled migrant labour for its domestic workers. Tier one, three, and four are likely non-starters. Tier 5, the visa category for low-skilled workers has been suspended indefinitely. Tier 1 is reserved for those employing "exceptional talent" in the course of their work -not particularly relevant for the purposes of assessing post-Brexit impacts on the low-wage UK industry, and Tier 4 visas are reserved for students and therefore largely irrelevant for the purposes of this analysis. This leaves Tier 2 and Tier 5, which are reserved for a variety of specific types of work in various industries, and the categories relevant for the purposes of this section of the chapter.

1. Tier 5 Temporary Workers

Central European citizens do not qualify for the "Youth Mobility Scheme"[110] and therefore the relevant Tier 5 visa categories are limited to an existing exchange scheme.[111] Prospective migrants who attempt to work in the UK under this scheme must qualify for 30 points under ¶¶ 105-12 of Appendix A of the UK Immigration Rules (requiring, *inter alia*, pre-work sponsorship,[112] with extraordinary qualifications over permanent residents for sports and creativity-based work) [113] and also (¶¶ 8-9 of Appendix C)[114] (requiring that the employer "sponsor" be "A-rated" and willing to support the applicant up to £945 for the first month of employment.[115] Interestingly, however, minimum English proficiency is only required for Tier 1 and 2 visas.[116]

---

[110] THE HOME OFFICE OF THE UNITED KINGDOM, "Immigration Rules Appendix G: Youth Mobility Scheme," (Updated Jul. 6, 2016), https://www.gov.uk/guidance/immigration-rules/immigration-rules-appendix-g-youth-mobility-scheme.

[111] THE HOME OFFICE OF THE UNITED KINGDOM, "Tier 5 (Temporary Worker - Government Authorised Exchange) Visa," https://www.gov.uk/tier-5-government-authorised-exchange.

[112] *Id.* ¶¶ 109(a)-(b).

[113] *Id.* ¶ 111(a)(ii), (b)(iii).

[114] "Immigration Rules: Part 6A: The Points-Based System, 2016," *supra* note 109, ¶ 245ZO(b)-(c).

[115] *Id.*, "Immigration Rules Appendix C: Maintenance (Funds)," *supra* note 114 ¶¶ 8-9.

[116]," THE HOME OFFICE OF THE UNITED KINGDOM, "Immigration Rules Appendix B: English language ¶ 1, Tables 1-2, https://www.gov.uk/guidance/immigration-rules/immigration-rules-appendix-b-english-language.

2. Tier 2 Skilled Workers

"[F]or a temporary position, there's absolutely no way [to hire through Tier 2], we need someone tomorrow, not in 28 days' time . . .The social imperative, bringing down immigration, and the economic imperatives are completely at odds. We need these people. "[117]

Tier 2 appears to be the only existing UK visa category with any viable path for labour migrants in a post-transition Hard Brexit Regime. However, there are still significant challenges. In order to qualify for a Tier 2 visa, the applicant must, *inter alia*

- Not fall under general grounds for refusal[118]
- Obtain sponsorship from UK employer[119]
- Obtain "50 points" by satisfying the provision that the "job offer passes Resident Labour Market Test" with an "appropriate salary"[120] by meeting a narrow set of provisions.[121] The Resident Labour Test consists of *inter alia*
    - Satisfaction that "the Sponsor can show that no suitable settled worker is available to fill the job unless the job is in a PhD-level occupation shown in Table 1 of the codes of practice in Appendix J. Settled workers will not be considered unsuitable on the basis that they lack qualifications, experience or skills (including language skills) that were not specifically requested in the job advertisement."[122]
    - Job marketing restrictions including that the job is posted "at least 28 days within the 6 months immediately before

[117] Interview with David Orr, managing director of the UK packaging firm, Fencor. John Harris *Leavers Complain, but They've Shared the Benefits of Cheap EU Labour*, THE GUARDIAN, (Feb. 3, 2017), https://www.theguardian.com/commentisfree/2017/feb/03/leavers-cheap-eu-labour-workers-brexiters.

[118] *See* THE HOME OFFICE OF THE UNITED KINGDOM, "Immigration Rules Part 9: Grounds for Refusal," ¶¶ A320-234, https://www.gov.uk/guidance/immigration-rules/immigration-rules-part-9-grounds-for-refusal. This issue is likely not of great salience, as much general grounds for refusal revolves around criminal background and therefore would fall under public safely carve outs to limit Free Movement of People under the EU *acquis communautaire. See supra* note 13.

[119] *Id.* Art 245HB(a).

[120] *Id.*, "Immigration Rules Appendix A: Attributes," ¶¶ 76(a)-(b), 78, Table 11B, Table 11C.

[121] There are exceptions. However, these are relatively narrow carve outs mostly pertain to nurses in the NHS system. *See id.* ¶¶ 78(A)-(D).

[122] *Id.* Art. 78(d).

the Sponsor assigned the Certificate of Sponsorship to the applicant,"[123] and a requirement that the posting is in English (or Welsh if located in Wales)[124]

- Verify that the English skills of the applicant meet the CEFR B1 level[125]
- Meet the minimum salary -As of April 6, 2016, there is a minimum salary requirement, (excluding overtime bonuses etc.)[126] of £ 35,500[127]
- Exceptions are made for are a "shortage occupation" categories defined under Art. 78 of the Immigration Rules[128] or post-study work from UK university[129]
- The employer must pay an initial £1,000 (reduced to £ 364 for "small" businesses) "skills charge" and a periodic £ 500 (£ 182 for "small" businesses) every six months after the first year.[130]

---

123 *Id.* Art. 78 Table 11B. *See id.* for detailed specifications on marketing of jobs which are intended to qualify for "Tier 2 (general)" visa.

124 *Id.* at Art. 78(c).

125 THE HOME OFFICE OF THE UNITED KINGDOM, "Immigration Rules Appendix KoLL," Part 2.2 (b)-(c). This is the requirement that would apply to A8 members, as they are not English-speaking countries exempted from this provision under 202(a) of this section or Part 2.2(a)(iii)-(v).

126 *See id.* ¶ 245HF(d)(i)-(v).

127 *Id.* ¶ 245HF(d)(i)-(vi)(2). The published data in the UK's immigration regulations has announced as such: "(3) £35,800 if the date of application is on or after 6 April 2019, (4) £36,200 if the date of application is on or after 6 April 2020,(5) £36,900 if the date of application is on or after 6 April 2021,(6) £37,900 if the date of application is on or after 6 April 2022." *Id.* ¶ 245HF(d)(i)-(vi)(3)-(6). However, these figures are subject to a serious of complicated grandfather clauses and carve outs. *See generally id.* ¶ 245HF(e)-(g).

128 *Id.* Art. 78.

129 Art. 78B; *Id.* Art. 245HD(d).

130 THE HOME OFFICE OF THE UNITED KINGDOM, "UK Visa Sponsorship for Employers," https://www.gov.uk/uk-visa-sponsorship-employers/immigration-skills-charge. At 12.10£/hr, the average UK wage of a construction worker reported by one source, it would take slightly more than two weeks of 40-hour work weeks to reach £ 1,000. *Infra* note 174.

130 "Immigration Rules Appendix C: Maintenance (Funds)," *supra* note 114 ¶¶ 8-9.

IV. THE ECONOMIC CONSEQUENCES OF A HARD BREXIT'S EFFECT ON THE UK LOW-WAGE[131] LABOUR ECONOMY

A. *"BRITISH JOBS FOR BRITISH WORKERS"?[132] SECTORAL IMPACTS OF HARD BREXIT*

"*We are totally dependent on having access to non-U.K. [sic] members of the EU to come over and work.*"[133]

1. Strawberrexit? The UK Agriculture Industry & Brexit

Low-wage labour from Central Europe has allowed the UK to enjoy cheap agricultural goods,[134] but agricultural prices are increasing due to the labour shortages.[135] The UK agricultural sector is profoundly reliant upon A8 labour, and will experience serious challenges in the absence of a competent mitigating strategy to compensate for the loss or severe reduction of Free Movement of People from A8 Member States. In addition to potential shortages and higher prices of raw agricultural products and their derivatives that labour shortages will cause, agricultural sectors which are highly portable can locate to a more stable jurisdiction. Established orchards of stone fruits will probably stay put, notwithstanding the fact that there may not be sufficient pickers to harvest them, but annual crops such as strawberries, tomatoes, and rhubarb are highly mobile, and thus those industries are likely to relocate across the channel where they are certain to obtain the requisite labour they need.

It is reported that 65% of the agricultural workforce in the UK is comprised of non-UK European citizens[136] and 90% of the 80,000

---

[131] The focus of this paper is on lowest-wage sectors of the UK economy, however this is not to imply that there will not be substantial effects on highly-skilled and high wage sectors of the UK and wider European economy. For example, there could be a substantial effect on EU27 labour migrants working in finance in London. *See* Fortes, *supra* note 42 at 186.

[132] Brexit slogan.

[133] Paul Ames, *UK Farmers Wonder Who'll Get the Harvest In*, POLITICO, (Aug. 28, 2016), https://www.politico.eu/article/uk-farmers-wonder-wholl-get-the-harvest-in-agriculture-migration-brexit-labour/.

[134] These farms e.g. strawberry farms are going to close down if the current supply of cheap labour is not met. Lisa O'Carroll, *British Strawberries Could be Wiped Out by Brexit, Farming Leaders* Warn, THE GUARDIAN, (Jul. 20, 2016), https://www.theguardian.com/uk-news/2016/jul/20/brexit-farm-labour-shortages-fruit-vegetable-harvests-national-farmers-union.

[135] *Id.*

[136] This figure was published in 2017. McIndoe, Pledger, & Wright *supra* note 39 at 123.

seasonal workers are from Europe outside the UK.[137] Given that there is currently no path to such low-paid labour through the Tier System, it follows that 90% of seasonal workers are from EU27 or EFTA states. 30,000 EU27 migrants arrive in the UK annually as seasonal labourers.[138] Nearly all of the 26,000 seasonal labours employed in the tree-fruit-picking industry are from the EU27, (mostly A8 countries of Central and Eastern Europe), a figure which represents 28% of all of Britain's seasonal workers in general.[139] In 2016, it was estimated that the UK was experiencing an agricultural labour shortage of 20,000 jobs as of 2016,[140] and the National Farmers Union reported that seasonal worker migration fell by 17% in 2017.[141] The labour shortage is so drastic in this industry that part of the British agricultural sector could shift to the Low Countries,[142] which also compete for these workers.[143]

The UK berry-growing industry in particular may undergo particularly significant transformations due to Brexit and the attendant loss of Free Movement of People. As it stands, 100% of strawberry pickers in the UK hail from continental Europe.[144] Although the UK was able to meet 100% of its demand for blackberries, raspberries and strawberries through domestic production over a 10-15 year transition, as farmers plan ahead, to avoid the risk of a wasted crop caused by labour shortages, growers may also relocate *e.g.* to France,[145] prompting increased importation of fruits, particularly berries. In fact, the UK strawberry industry, a culturally significant icon of British culture, may transition to France in entirety.[146] In addition to higher labour costs for agricultural goods produced in the EU, the UK's withdrawal from the customs union[147] could result in more expensive agricultural products[148]

---

137 Data from source published in 2016. Kimiko De Freytas-Tamura, *supra* note 42.

138 O' Carroll, *supra*, note 135.

139 Kollewe, *supra* note 41.

140 Ames, *supra* note 133.

141 Claire Marshall, *European Fruit Pickers Shun Britain*, BBC, (Jun. 6, 2018), https://www.bbc.com/news/business-44230865.

142 *See* Kimiko De Freytas-Tamura, *supra* note 42. *See also* Ames, *supra* note 133.

143 Marshall, *supra* note 141.

144 *Id.*

145 O'Carroll, *supra*, note 134.

146 *See Id.*

147 The Customs Union is central to the Free Movement of Goods, one of the four underlying principles of the EU.

148 Currently, external duties on fresh raspberries and blackberries for Third Countries is at 8.8%, *ad valorem*. Taxation and Customs Commission, EUROPEAN COMMISSION, "TARIC Measure Information," (updated Jun. 5, 2018), http://ec.europa.eu-/taxation_customs/dds2/taric/measures.jsp?Lang=en&SimDate=20180605&Area=&MeasType=&StartPub=&EndPub=&MeasText=&GoodsText=&Taric=08102010&search_text=goods&textSearch=&LangDescr=en&OrderNum=&Regulation=&measStartDat=&measEndDat=. In this respect, Brexit presents an interesting opportunity, for

as UK-based growers move to the EU, noting that the EU has taken a firm position that it will not accept a customs union without preserving all four EU Freedoms.[149] This is a particularly salient point in the transformation of the agricultural economy of the UK seeing as the UK recently imported nearly three quarters of its agricultural products from the EU27.[150]

The UK must negotiate low tariff deals with Third Countries or the EU for agricultural imports because it is going to lose much of its domestic agricultural sector if it does not increase -much less *reduces*- migration in this agricultural sector. While the UK, outside the EU Customs Union, could set and impose its own tariffs to better protect or grow its agricultural sector, such a proposition could only be economically viable if suitable labour existed to work in the industry. On balance, it does appear that Britons should very well expect a substantial increase in price in their strawberries and cream.[151]

2. UK Construction Industry

A Hard Brexit will significantly affect the UK construction industry and housing market. The UK will be less able to quickly respond to "regional economic shocks in labour demand," exacerbating unmet demand for labour.[152] It is widely known and reported in UK media that the UK is experiencing a severe housing shortage. Not only is there a shortage of construction workers in the UK, there even are not enough UK nationals with the requisite masonry skills to address the crisis, a situation which will be worsened if Free Movement is curtailed.[153] One 2017 study by the Royal Institute of Chartered Surveyors indicated that

---

the growth in or development of new agricultural commodity-based derivatives contracts for those whose businesses are affected by the price of agricultural products in the UK, to hedge against the risk of dramatic increases in the prices of such commodities.

149 EURACTIV, *See Juncker Tells UK: No Single market without Free Movement of People*, (Jul. 26, 2016), https://www.euractiv.com/section/uk-europe/news/juncker-tells-uk-no-single-market-without-freedom-of-movement/.

150 Sarah Butler, *Price of Imported Fruit and Vegetables will Rise by up to 8% After Brexit*, THE GUARDIAN, (Mar. 28, 2017), https://www.theguardian.com/business/2017/mar-/29/brexit-fruit-vegetable-prices-uk-eu. Cross ref. *supra* note 148.

151 For further discussion on the potential impacts on the price of agricultural products in view of post-Brexit trade policy, *see generally* Peter Levell, Martin O'Connell & Kate Smith, "How Might Brexit Affect Food Prices," INSTITUTE FOR FISCAL STUDIES, (Jul. 27, 2017), https://www.ifs.org.uk/publications/9562.

152 Jarrod Tudor, *supra* note 102.

153 Dawn Foster, *A Hard Brexit Would Risk Deepening the Housing Crisis*, THE GUARDIAN, (Feb. 17, 2017), https://www.theguardian.com/housing-network/2017/feb/17/hard-brexit-worse-housing-crisis-eu-eib; Lucy Alderson & Geoff Wilkinson, *Hard Brexit Could Shrink Construction 9%, Warns Key Peer*, CONSTRUCTION NEWS, (Feb. 16, 2017), https://www.constructionnews.co.uk/markets/international/eu-referendum/hard-brexit-could-shrink-construction-by-9-warns-key-peer/10017326.article.

a Hard Brexit, *ergo* loss of access to the European Single Market may cost 175,000 jobs, which comprises 8% of the total UK construction labour force, and is cause for concern for the 30% of construction industry employers who employ non-UK labourers.[154] Furthermore, Arcadis, a construction consultant firm, foresees that "the introduction of a visa system could easily add hundreds of thousands of pounds to individual companies' costs,"[155] -all of which promise to exacerbate the housing shortage in the UK, driving up rent and hosing prices, decreasing Britons' disposable income and, in turn, the quality of life of the poorer segments of the British population.[156]

3. National Health System

Currently, 10% of NHS doctors, and 5% of the NHS general staff are non-UK EEA or EU27 nationals.[157] One third of doctors are retiring between 2017 and 2020, and the NHS experienced a 92% drop in registered nurses since the Brexit referendum.[158] The NHS is experiencing a shortage of 42,000 nurses, therapists and midwives, and at current rates of illness, will need to add 190,000 employees by 2027 to support the NHS.[159] Wages will have to increase garner more workers for the NHS, but it is reported that the public sector cannot afford an increase in wages.[160] Curtailing Free Movement will only complicate the strain on the system.

---

154 ROYAL INSTITUTE OF CHARTERED SURVEYORS, "UK Construction Industry Could Lose 8% of Workers Post-Brexit," (Mar. 15, 2017), http://www.rics.org/uk/news/news-insight/press-releases/uk-construction-industry-could-lose-8-of-workforce-post-brexit-new-rics-figures-reveal-/.

155 Kollewe, *supra* note 41.

156 *Id.*

157 McIndoe, Pledger, & Wright *supra* note 39 at 121.

158 *Id.*

159 Denis Campbell, *NHS Faces Acute and Growing Staffing Shortage, Warns Agency*, THE GUARDIAN, (Dec. 17, 2017), https://www.theguardian.com/society/2017/dec/13/nhs-faces-acute-and-growing-staffing-shortage-warns-agency.

160 *Id.*

B. *LEGAL OBSERVATIONS & RECOMMENDATIONS IN A POST-THE UK IMMIGRATION SYSTEM POST-BREXIT*

"There is an absolute requirement that the government has some sort of solution in place for seasonal work. It's not just horticulture, it's the care sector, hospitality sector and so many other places that are dependent on migrant workers"[161]

1. The UK Legal Regime is Unprepared to Meet Economic Demands Imposed by Hard Brexit

Even before any change in the legal regime occurs, the current massive outflow of migrants, Brexodous, is a significant problem for the UK economy because unless these migrants return to the UK before the end of the transition period, it will probably become substantially more difficult, if even at all possible, to immigrate to the UK to undertake the low-paid labour. Therefore, under a Hard Brexit regime, the outflow of low-wage workers acts as a one-way valve, further cementing the UK's labour shortages.

The forthcoming analysis is a hypothetical scenario in which the UK does not reach a deal granting favourable treatment to low-wage EU labourers who would not qualify for visas under the Tier system. As much as Brexit appears to be leaning "hard" on immigration, it promises even harder results on the UK economy. On balance, the UK faces a trifecta of woes: disinterest from its own labour market to meet its employers' demand, a mass "Brexodous" of EU workers triggered by an uncertain future and disillusionment with the UK -particularly among low-wage workers,[162] and a massive legal imposition on the low-wage economy in the post-transition period as a result of the inflexible tiered system. Recruiting labour in the UK has been more challenging due to lack of certainty over future rights of EU citizens without UK citizenship[163] and many are anticipating significant, if not crippling, labour shortages if Brexit takes effect with the current regime.[164] These

---

161 O 'Carroll, *supra,* note 135.

162 Kimiko De Freytas-Tamura, *supra* note 42; *See* Fortes, *supra* note 42 at 192. For example, a UK recruitment firm which largely draws upon Eastern European labour observed a sudden 50% decrease in applications; applications were reduced to a quarter on a year-on-year basis. John Harris, *supra* note 117.

163 Kollewe, *supra* note 41.

164 *See id.* For example, The Guardian reported that "Denis O'Donnell, who owns the Peruga's restaurant in Stockport in Cheshire, has already felt the pinch. He says: 'There has been a massive surge in demand for kitchen staff, and almost zero response to ads.' He recounts that at the last meeting of the British Hospitality Association, 'people were

effects are particularly pronounced "in agriculture, construction, hotels and restaurants, and in low-skill manufacturing sectors."[165] In fact, A8 low-wage labour is indispensable to the UK economy; a 2013 study indicated that A8 and A2 countries account for 28% of the shift-based low-skill labour in the UK.[166]

2. Overhauling the UK Immigration System to Accommodate the Post-Brexit UK Economy?

If Polish and other A8 low-wage workers apply through Tier 2, they may appear relatively more attractive because some employers demonstrate a preference for Third Country nationals whose legal right to remain in the UK is tied to their employment, rather than EU workers who can simply quit their job if a more attractive offer comes along in the UK[167] and who are generally free to remain in the UK, subject to the limitations set forth in the *acquis communautaire*. Obviously, employers prefer workers who are "locked into" a job once they arrive, and there have been indications of very extreme examples of labour poaching of A8 agricultural workers, which can present extreme consequences to agricultural businesses.[168] For this reason, UK employers in low-skilled sectors may continue to actively recruit for newly secure Polish labour and lobby the UK government for an expansion of the definition of Tier 2 "occupation shortage" jobs within the agricultural industry and an increase in the 20,700 cap on Tier 2 visas. Furthermore, many Polish workers who come to the UK obtain their job informally,[169] which means their job-seeking habits will need to change to accommodate the UK's tier system with respect to the advertising requirements of Tier 2 jobs under UK law. Additionally, for those who would qualify under Tier 2, there may be a bias towards pre-selected younger workers because they are "likely to be more 'flexible' and willing to work longer and unsociable

doing a lot of handwringing and saying: we can't get chefs.' He adds that people are going to 'ridiculous lengths' to get staff, like renting houses and bussing them in. . . . O'Donnell employs 24 people, including 10 full-time staff. Of those, four are EU nationals: an Italian husband and wife team, one of whom is *maître d'*; plus a Latvian and a Hungarian kitchen porter. He says these two are 'good, solid, reliable guys in their 60s. You won't get English guys in their 60s doing this job.'"

165 Brückner et al., *supra* note 39 168-69.

166 "Migrants in Low-Skilled Work the Growth of EU and non-EU Labour in Low-Skilled Jobs and its Impact on the UK," *supra* note 40 at 129.

167 *Id.* at 128.

168 Workers already set to arrive to work at one business can be poached by other employers promising higher wages. Reliance on secured labour in time-sensitive industries, such as quick-to-spoil agricultural products can cost hundreds of thousands of Dollars. Kimiko De Freytas-Tamura, *supra* note 42.

169 , "Migrants in Low-Skilled Work the Growth of EU and non-EU Labour in Low-Skilled Jobs and its Impact on the UK," *supra* note 40 at 116.

hours"[170] meaning that fewer older migrants would arrive in the UK in search of work. For those who qualify, even with the decline in the rate of net positive migration to the UK from A8, Hard Brexit will likely cause bottleneck for Tier 2, and to a lesser extent, Tier 5 visas, as they will be competing with the remainder of the world for a finite number of visas.

What is clear from an analysis of the needs of the low-wage sectors of the UK economy is that Brexit will do little to address the employment concerns of Britons. The widespread labour shortages indicate that unemployment in the UK is of a highly structural in nature, and using legal means to curb immigration will only exacerbate these labour shortages. While the aggregate effects of restricting Free Movement of People may result in a slight wage increase for the lowest-paid UK workers, scholars note the significant negative economic effect that it poses for the UK economy on balance, because "they are more likely to work and pay tax and less likely to use public services as they are younger and better educated than the UK-born."[171]

3. Economic Challenges Posed by the Tiered System's Minimum Salary Provisions

Even if Tier 3 were introduced, it would have to actually be constructed,[172] a process that will likely take significant time. Furthermore, Tier 3 would have to be radically different from the onerous visa system which is simply unworkable for these industries. The agricultural industry which is dependent on short-term, on-demand immediate labour[173] able to respond to a dynamic environment, cannot sustain business on the uncertainty that a requisite amount of foreign workers will be approved -and in requisite time! Moreover, it is manifestly impracticable to impose the types of charges and pre-conditions on employers that are anywhere near those required for employers to obtain legal sponsorship for their employees under Tier 2. Imagine an agricultural employer paying the minimum legal wage of 6.66 £/hr. for a Grade 1 or 7.42 £/hr. for a Grade 2 agricultural worker[174] or

---

[170] Zou, *supra* note 107 at 126. *See also* Bridget Anderson, *Migration, Immigration Controls and the Fashioning of Precarious Works*, 24 WORK, EMP. & SOC'Y 300 (2010).

[171] Fortes, *supra* note 42 at 196.

[172] "Tier 3 was never opened, and it has been fully deleted from the Immigration Rules, so there would need to be significant re-drafting to the rules for low skilled workers to have access to the [points-based system.] *Id.* at 123.

[173] *See e.g. Exodus of Foreign Workers Leaves British Employers in the Lurch*, N.Y. TIMES, (Dec. 16, 2017), https://www.nytimes.com/2017/12/16/world/europe/britain-european-union-farming-immigration-labour-shortage.html.

[174] Grade 1 agricultural workers characterize packers and harvesters. After 30 weeks, they have the right to training to qualify for grade 2. Additionally, Someone [independently] is also a grade 2 worker if he or she is generally unsupervised, drives a tractor, operates a powered, machine, or whose work involves contact with animals.

the average wage is 8.23 £/hr.,[175] or a construction contractor paying the average rate of 10.10£/hr.,[176] or a manufacturing employer paying an average hourly rate of 8.23£/hr., to an "assembly line" employee[177] all of whom likely face significant downward pressure on the price of their end products, justifying paying more than two-weeks' pay for an initial £ 1000 skills charge for the employee to obtain Tier 2 sponsorship, let alone the additional £ 500 required in 6-month increments thereafter.[178] Hiring such workers under these Third Country requirements is imposition which hardly appears economically rational to employers, and it will come as no comfort to those who need and recruit prospective employers subject to a skills charge that the Conservative/Unionists have pledged to double the initial skills charge to £ 2,000.[179] Similarly, any expansion of Tier 5 would likely have to drop or dramatically reduce the £ 945 guarantee provision[180] to be viable for low-paid work.

UK.GOV, "Agricultural Workers' Rights," https://www.gov.uk/agricultural-workers-rights/grades-and-categories. Rates are based on the 2018-2019 schedule. "AWB Agricultural rates of Pay Orders and Reports," Department of Agriculture, Environment and Rural Affairs, (Accessed May 10, 2018), https://www.daera-ni.gov.uk/articles/awb-agricultural-rates-pay-orders-and-reports.

[175]This was a reported figure appearing in July 2018. "Farm Worker Salary," PAYSCALE, (updated Jul. 21, 2018), https://www.payscale.com/research/UK/Job=Farm_Worker/Hourly_Rate. Another survey from 2013 data assessed the figure at higher 8.74 £/hr. "Pay Survey Who Gets What in the Farm Industry," FARMERS WEEKLY, (Jan. 1, 2014), http://www.fwi.co.uk/business/pay-survey-who-gets-what-in-the-farm-industry.htm. If it is correct that average wages are dropping, then the economic impracticability of fitting UK agricultural workers into the tiered scheme is made *a fortiori*.

[176] This was a reported figure appearing in July 2018. "Construction Worker Salary," PAYSCALE, (updated Jul. 21, 2018), https://www.payscale.com/research/UK/Job=Construction_Worker/Hourly_Rate. This figure may also have fallen. 484.10£/week averages to 12.10£/hr based on a 40-hour work week, according to data reported in 2003. https://www.constructionnews.co.uk/home/scaffolders-highest-paid-in-construction-industry/861457.article.

[177]"Assembly Line Worker, Factory Salary," PAYSCALE, (updated Jul. 21, 2018), https://www.payscale.com/research/UK/Job=Assembly_Line_Worker%2C_-Factory/Hourly_Rate.

[178] "UK Visa Sponsorship for Employers," *supra* note 131. At £ 10.10/hour, it would take more than two weeks of 40-hour work weeks to reach £ 1,000.

[179] Manifesto of the Conservative and Democratic Unionist Party, Forward Together Our Plan for a Stronger Britain and a Prosperous Future the Conservative and Unionist Party Manifesto 2017, (May 18, 2017), at 21, https://issuu.com/conservativeparty/docs-/ge2017_manifesto_a5_digital/12.

[180] "Immigration Rules Appendix C: Maintenance (Funds)," *supra* note 114 ¶¶ 8-9.

4. Economic Challenges Posed by the Tiered System's Narrow Job Categories and Stringent Quotas

Given the current nonexistence of Tier 3, and assuming, *ipso facto*, that EU27 nationals do not currently qualify for Tier 5 under UK law, Tier 2 is the scheme under which the majority of A8 and Central European workers that would qualify would fall. It is very difficult to assess how a typical Polish or similarly situated A8 worker would fall when his or her legal status is transposed into the UK immigration regime because EU citizens able to bypass the Tier system completely, however given the type of relatively low-wage, low-skill work that many Polish and other A8 workers undertake in the UK, it is probably most reasonable to assume that, in a situation in which there is no association agreement granting favourable rights to relatively low-skill, low-pay work, those workers who would qualify would fall into the "Tier 2 (general)" "worker visa category as[181] "Tier-2 general" and "Tier-2 shortage occupation," the visa sub-categories that would most readily lend themselves to low-skilled or low-paid agricultural, construction or similar work in the UK. Tier 2 consists of agriculture, construction, water infrastructure work, manufacturing,[182] household work, and "other service activities"[183] According to recent data available, 19% of approved applications were for jobs in "information and communication," 19% went to those in scientific and technical fields, 12% to finance-related jobs, 6% were allocated for public health and social positions, however only 4% were reserved within the manufacturing sector.[184]

It appears that were EU27 workers to be subject to the Tier system for Third Country nationals, most EU applicants would fall under "Tier

---

[181] For example, NHS demand is likely to be approved for EU nationals through skilled Tier 2. *See* THE HOME OFFICE OF THE UNITED KINGDOM, "Work," (Feb. 23, 2017), https://www.gov.uk/government/publications/immigration-statistics-october-to-december-2016/work. For a detailed guide on how the UK immigration authorities make these determinations, *see generally* MIGRATION ADVISORY COMMITTEE, "Assessing Labour Market Shortages A Methodology Update," (Jan. 2017), https://assets.publishing.service.gov.uk/government/uploads/system/uploads/attachment_data/file/586110/2017_01_26_MAC_report_Assessing_Labour_Market_Shortages.pdf.

[182] This is also salient in a macroeconomic context of the UK economy because, as of 2017, manufacturing comprised one tenth of the UK economy. Syrrakos, *supra* note 66 at 51.

[183] *See* THE HOME OFFICE OF THE UNITED KINGDOM, "Immigration Statistics," July to September 2017, Data Tables:, (Nov. 30, 2017), https://www.gov.uk/government/statistics/immigration-statistics-july-to-september-2017-data-tables.

[184] Zou, *supra* note 107 at 118.

2 (general)," of whom only 20,700 individual slots can be filled each year (not including dependents).[185] While it is possible that many A8 workers would qualify, simply raising the cap, even substantially, would not alleviate the economic pressures for cheap labour. First, many would outright fail to qualify[186] as agricultural workers and construction workers would clearly not meet minimum salary requirements.[187] Second, even with the most creative lawyering, it is not reasonably foreseeable that fruit-pickers and non-engineer construction workers could qualify under any definition of "highly skilled" in the Tier 2 visa application. In fact, Oxford University's Migration Observatory has determined that only 4% of non-UK European labourers would be able to obtain visas, were they suddenly subject to the Tier System for Third country nationals.[188]

If the UK government intends to retain Hard Brexit, it could expand the class of "shortage occupation" positions that already exist within its immigration system to meet economic demands, or do nothing and accept goods shortages, increased prices, and a reduced-growth economy. Even if the UK does relax its quota, it remains doubtful that the current tiered visa process, with all its regulations and requirements, is a workable solution given the high volume of short-term seasonable work. If the UK intends to calibrate Tier 2 to accommodate the economic needs that will be exacerbated through Hard Brexit, it could utilise the "shortage occupation" process, which can employ a focus group comprised of "employers, industry groups, trade unions and local authorities" and bypass the process of the "labour market test"[189] discussed in Section III. While this is certainly preferable to an alternative of no action, it requires an accurate estimation of future needs and actual projections of needs may be distorted by political interests. It would also necessarily need to drop any "skills-based" threshold.[190]

Industry has not been quiet about this reality. In addition to complaints from industry leaders voiced in the media, especially from the UK agricultural and construction industries, interested parties have made

---

[185] UK VISAS & IMMIGRATION, "UKVI quick guides: Skilled Workers (Tier 2)," (Sept. 2014), https://assets.publishing.service.gov.uk/government/uploads/system/uploads/attachment_data/file/398127/Quick_guide_Tier_2.pdf; Zou, *supra* note 107 at 116. There is no indication that these figures have been amended as of mid-May 2018.

[186] McIndoe, Pledger, & Wright *supra* note 39 at 122-23.

[187] *See infra*, Section III.

[188] McIndoe, Pledger, & Wright, *supra* note 39 at 123. This probably follows considering that in September 2013-2014, only 4% of Tier 2 reservations went to those working in the manufacturing industry. Zou, *supra* note 107 at 118.

[189] Zou, *supra* note 107 at 121-12.

[190] Either the UK should abandon the "skills" requirement under Tier 2, or keep Tier 2 as a means of immigration for truly "skilled" migrants and implement some other scheme to meet the demands of the UK economy.

their voices heard in the chambers of Whitehall. Russ Shaw, the founder of Tech London Advocates, a lobbying group for the technology industry, spoke to peers of the Parliamentary *EU Internal Market Sub-Committee*, specifically addressing his concerns about the anticipated detrimental effects of the 20,700 annual Tier 2 visa limits specifically on this industry.[191] Similar concerns were echoed in the "Food Supply Chain Manifesto," representing dozens of industry leaders.[192]

Perhaps the most sensible approach would be to allow a quota of "shortage occupations" which truly reflect the needs of the economy, irrespective of "“skill,” namely, agricultural, construction, and manufacturing workers. Currently, the UK government designates professions under "shortage occupation" as those relating to civil, mechanical, hydrological engineering, aeronautical maintenance, welding IT specialists, certain technical professions in healthcare, and all nursing positions; given the significant economic crisis that could result from lack of agricultural, construction and similar workers, it is almost comical to note that, even almost two years after the Brexit referendum result, the UK has not added designations for agricultural industries that may be forced to leave the UK due to severe insufficient labour, failing an agreement, yet it is evidently eminently important that it retains dancers, choreographers, chefs, graphic designers, and skilled orchestral musicians who are leaders, principals, sub-principals or numbered string positions" as those it deems in critically short supply in its Tier-2 "shortage occupation" designations.[193] Recently, The Conservative Manifesto has publicly acknowledged the need to face economic realities, at least in part. In the *Conservative and Unionist Party Manifesto 2017*, the Conservative Party pledged to work towards meeting the needs of the economy in the Brexit framework, however this was in within the context of "strategically important sectors" and the need for *skilled* work,[194] and explicitly referenced the intention to keep migration at net zero.[195]

---

[191] "Things on my wish list that could be addressed now -we need to immediately look at the Tier-2 cap. 20,700 Tier-2 visas is simply not enough . . . ." Derek du Preez, *Brexit – Tech Community Warns that Foreign Workers Now Thinking Twice About UK*, DIGINOMICA, (Feb. 8, 2018), https://government.diginomica.com/2018/02/08/brexit-tech-community-warns-foreign-workers-now-thinking-twice-uk.

[192] NATIONAL FARMERS' UNION OF ENGLAND AND WALES, "Food Supply Manifesto for a Successful Brexit," (May 2018), https://www.nfuonline.com/assets/107735.

[193] THE HOME OFFICE OF THE UNITED KINGDOM, "Immigration Rules Appendix K: Shortage Occupation List," (Updated Apr. 6, 2018), https://www.gov.uk/guidance/immigration-rules.

[194] "Forward Together Our Plan for a Stronger Britain and a Prosperous Future the Conservative and Unionist Party Manifesto 2017," *supra* note 179 at 21.

[195] *Id.*

5. A Bespoke UK- EU Association Agreement for Agricultural Work?

Alternately, the UK could ratify an association agreement with the EU, totally independent of the Tier system, which would allow the UK to meet its demand for EU labour. In fact, there have been recent calls to renew the seasonal worker program.[196] This would perhaps be a suitable possibility for Britons insofar as they have a strong preference for European, particularly Polish or A8 country labour[197] and will be much more economically efficient than managing visa approval process for every foreign seasonal worker.

If such a plan were implemented, however, the May government would lose a substantial, if not nearly all of its credibility if it were to agree to terms with the EU resembling Free Movement, especially considering that immigration was *the* salient issue in the electorate's decision to leave. Furthermore it would, more or less, demonstrate Brexit as a failure in practicality. Indeed, it is true that the May government can claim that Brexit allows the UK to re-exercise sovereignty over its territory and end CJEU jurisdiction over the UK. However, if it ratifies an association agreement with terms resembling Free Movement, the UK would essentially be giving up the Customs Union, Single Market, an untold number of mutual recognition agreements and access to the multitude of EU organisations, such as Euratom, without ending immigration in any significant measure, a severe political hazard for May's government. The Agriculture & Horticulture Development Board has suggested increasing productivity and incentivising UK workers to seek employment as suggestions in mitigating shortages in the agricultural industry.[198] However if it is true that Britons do not want these jobs, it seems unlikely that higher "productivity" expectations of workers would encourage Britons to work in agriculture. Automation however, is a suggestion of theirs[199] that may be viable.

---

196 De Freytas-Tamura, *supra* note 42.

197 There is significant evidence that there UK employers generally hold Polish workers in high regard due their assessment of them as having a strong work ethic. *See e.g.* studies of McCollum and Findlay, which find that "[e]vidence from research shows that employers of migrant workers, in particular of Central and Eastern European workers, perceived them to work harder and be more reliable than UK workers. These positive attributes may derive from the different frame of reference and consequent willingness to accommodate employers' demands and to accept pay and working conditions that would not be acceptable to local UK workers." "Migrants in Low-Skilled Work the Growth of EU and non-EU Labour in Low-Skilled Jobs and its Impact on the UK," *supra* note 40 at 118.

198 UK HOUSE OF COMMONS, "Brexit: Future UK Agricultural Policy," Briefing Paper No. 8218, (Jan. 31, 2018), at 32, https://www.parliament.uk/documents/commons-library/Brexit-UK-agriculture-policy-CBP-8218.pdf.

199 *Id.*

The UK government announced that it plans to release a White Paper specifically addressing an a-la-carte immigration bill.[200] To the dismay of segments of the UK business community, the Home Office has stated that it will not publicly publish its White Paper until a formal agreement been signed with the EU stipulating the terms of the transition period,[201] and whatever deal is reached is unlikely to satisfy industry if the current government remains in power and faithful to their pledge to reduce EU immigration.[202] Perhaps surprisingly however, the UK government may be warming to such an agreement, with hints that reconstituting the Seasonal Worker Program in some fashion is not off the table.[203] This possibility is elevated due to the UK Government's commitment to keep low-skilled agricultural labour sourced abroad from the EEA.[204] Given that it is practically inconceivable that the UK will simply provide *no* path for low-wage immigrant labour and that there are strong pressures to keep Brexit hard, the critical factor for the UK economy will ultimately be the scope of any such agreement on movement of labourers into the UK.

C. CONCLUSIONS, OBSERVATIONS

Those for whom the changing character of UK is of utmost concern and are willing to sacrifice economically to reduce the rate of change, Brexit, particularly Hard Brexit, may be characterised as a rational decision, however, the UK immigration scheme will need to implement serious interventions if it is to sustain its labour economy. Ultimately, the

---

200 *See* George Parker & Robert Wright, *Brexit Immigration White Paper to be Delayed until Autumn*, FINANCIAL TIMES, (Feb. 2, 2018), https://www.ft.com/content/c92d3418-0807-11e8-9650-9c0ad2d7c5b5.

201 Alan Travis, *Brexit Immigration Paper Delay Criticised by UK Businesses*, THE GUARDIAN, (Feb. 5, 2018), https://www.theguardian.com/politics/2018/feb/05/brexit-immigration-white-paper-uk-businesses-delay.

202 "Forward Together Our Plan for a Stronger Britain and a Prosperous Future the Conservative and Unionist Party Manifesto 2017," *supra* note 179 at 55.

203 "We will keep our position on seasonal workers under review. . . . [A] new SAWS could be introduced very quickly—in five or six months—once the need for such a scheme has been identified. I hope my hon. [sic] Friend is reassured that we will have the agility to meet those needs." PARLIAMENT OF THE UNITED KINGDOM, "Oral Answers to Questions, 'Support for Farmers,' Vol. 628," (Sept. 7, 2017), https://hansard.parliament.uk/Commons/2017-09-07/debates/07680A84-0304-4D21-931C-85696795F024/SupportForFarmers#contribution-9AE0826C-74F3-4F18-9617-1CA0FD48EC16.

204 "It remains the Government's policy not to operate migration schemes for non-EEA nationals coming to fill vacancies at lower skill levels while employers have unrestricted access to labour from elsewhere in the EU." "Brexit: Future UK Agricultural Policy," *supra* note 196 at 31.

ethos of Brexit and economic reality are fundamentally incompatible. However, the UK cannot have its tea (with strawberries) and drink it too. Either solution, overhauling the Tier system or a "soft" association agreement undermines one of Brexit's underlying main motivations, namely reducing immigration. In this sense, Brexit is truly a zero-sum game. It will have to either accept that that a significant section of its economy is heavily immigration-reliant and address the tensions between its native and foreign workers, to the degree that they exist, or alternatively, reduce the potential for immigration and accept a significantly altered legal environment prejudiced against the British consumer, and with scant evidence that central European migration even significantly undermines the position of the British worker. When viewed on the whole, a particularly Hard Brexit is likely to be a net negative for the UK and for the migrant workers who drive its economy.

1. Good News for Skilled Third country Nationals?

One of the consequences of a Hard Brexit is a narrowing in the gap of labour competition between the EU and Third Countries for those who qualify for the Tier System. If the UK does not have to apply the *acquis communautaire* to labour and employment, Third Country applications for work in the UK may be more competitive. Although EU nations will likely be given an advantage in the UK immigration application process (unless Brexit is maximally hard in this respect) and Central Europe will still be relatively protected from more stringent regulations levied upon non-EU nationals, a Hard Brexit would likely contribute towards narrowing the gap between EU27 Migration and Third Country labour migration. That is, whatever imposition Brexit imposes upon EU27/EEA workers, (from nearly none, where it stands by virtue of the EU *acquis communautaire*) the advantage over prospective Third Country narrows, assuming additional restrictions are no imposed upon prospective Third Country workers. Additionally, any application of the Tired system without changes which preference EU27/ETA workers will, of course, be good news for Tier-qualifying "skilled" third country nationals who wish to immigrate to the UK, they will be able to complete on the same footing for jobs in the UK. This is potentially salient observation for prospective African workers, as Europe is the migration destination for two thirds of African emigrants[205] and has

[205] "Immigrant Workers: Europe 2016," *supra* note 100 at 93. An interesting trend is that in countries which regulate immigration to generally only accept skilled and educated migrants, diaspora communities may be better educated and skilled than that of their home country, leading to brain-drain in the home country, and brain gain in the host country. With Free Movement of People, the opposite can occur, in which lower-educated people may seek opportunities abroad only as a "last resort," resulting in a less-educated diaspora population. This phenomenon was observed with respect to Estonian

been the most popular destination for migration, remaining at least above 60% between 2005 and 2010.[206] In fact, according to data collected by Gallup in a 2011 study, the UK was the most popular destination for permanent migration among potential migrants who have taken "concrete actions."[207] This is also a potentially salient development considering that there is a clear positive correlation between education attainment and desire to move to the EU/EFTA versus other destinations.[208] A similar study using data collected between 2011 and 2014 suggested that the UK was also the most popular target for temporary labour migration.[209] Of course none of this will be relevant if the Conservative/Unionist government achieves its goal of "bearing down" on Third Country Migration.[210]

immigration. *See Coping with Emigration in Baltic and Eastern European Countries*, *supra* note 66 at 32-33. Where this is the case, Hard Brexit will not improve the quality of the pool of workers for the Home country, however data indicate that this is unlikely to be the case, at least for Poland, the most important country with respect to Brexit in the context of this chapter. *See* , "Migrants in Low-Skilled Work the Growth of EU and non-EU Labour in Low-Skilled Jobs and its Impact on the UK," *supra* note 40, 169.

206 "Immigrant Workers: Europe 2016," *supra* note 100 at 92.

207 *Id.* at 104.

208 "The low-educated tend to express a preference for non-OECD destinations, chiefly in the Gulf Region, which reflects frequent migration patterns of less well educated workers from Asian and North African countries. As for the migrants educated to a medium level, 26% express a preference for EU/EEA . . . Among the highly educated, EU/EEA countries exert the greatest appeal with 27% of preferences, compared with the United States' 21%, and 24% for other OECD counties." "Immigrant Workers: Europe 2016," *supra* note 100 at 107-08. *See also id.* at 110.

209 *Id.* at 105.

210 "Forward Together Our Plan for a Stronger Britain and a Prosperous Future the Conservative and Unionist Party Manifesto 2017," *supra* note 179 at 54.

V. ECONOMIC AND POLITICAL EFFECTS OF A HARD BREXIT ON CENTRAL EUROPEAN MEMBER STATES EXPERIENCING DEMOGRAPHIC CRISES

"Brexit może być prezentem dla Polski"
(Brexit can be a present for Poland)[211]

[212]

Table 1.2. Overview of the economic effects of labour migration on Romania

Positive effects	Negative effects
Lower unemployment rates	Negative demographic trends (ageing, lack of territorial cohesion)
Decreased pressure on social protection budgets	Unbalanced distribution of the available workforce by sector and geographical area
Remittances support the improvement of living standards	Business losses due to wage pressure (especially prior to 2008) and reduced production
Workers abroad facilitate skill transfer and growth	Brain drain (loss of investment in education and training, lower competitiveness)
	A threat to the sustainability of social protection systems (pension, medical care)

Poland is haemorrhaging working age people at a catastrophic rate. The problem is particularly acute with respect to those more likely to be educated[213] and those who would otherwise contribute to Poland's social welfare system in the course of employment. The Central Statistical Office of Poland projects the Polish population to shrink by 2.4 million people by 2035,[214] and by 2050, Poland's population could decline by 4 million, the equivalent of three vovoidships. In the major Polish city of Łódź, for example, one fifth of the city's 1% annual decrease in population in recent decades is attributed to emigration.[215] This demographic trend is a concern that will become increasingly pressing as Poland's population ages and requires an increasing quantity of healthcare, home care, and related services attendant to an elderly

---

211 Agnieszka Bielewska, *Brexit Może Być Prezentem dla Polski*, SWPS UNIWERSYTET HUMANISYCZNOSPOLECZNY, (Jun. 23, 2016), https://www.swps.pl/nauka-i-badania/blog-naukowy/2446-brexit-moze-byc-prezentem-dla-polski.

212 Mereuta, supra note 64 at 18.

213 Brückner, *supra* note 39 at 164.

214 Magdalena Krukowska, *Polish Cities Begin to Fight for Fleeing Residents*, (Aug. 8, 2016), FINANCIAL OBSERVER, https://financialobserver.eu/poland/polish-cities-begin-to-fight-for-fleeing-residents/.

215 *Id.*

population, and of course, enough working people making regular contributions to the welfare state in order to pay for it all.

According to a 2009 study, massive emigration may have reduced Polish GDP by nearly 1%.[216] Furthermore, data indicate that there is a widespread issue filing vacancies in the Polish labour economy due to intra-EU migration, notably to Germany and the UK. [217] Despite Poland's remarkable economic growth in recent years, the Polish Union of Entrepreneurs and Employers believes that Poland will need to add five million workers to the Polish economy within two decades in order to sustain its growth.[218] Ukrainians and Belarusians have been filing in the labour shortages in Poland,[219] however this is insufficient to sustain Poland's economic growth, especially because the 500,000 Ukrainian labours have not been able to fill the high skills gap.[220] There is also a concern that sending countries experiencing a mass return via Brexodous will not benefit from "skills transfer," because the types of jobs undertaken in the UK did not contribute to skills enhancement.[221] The Baltic states are facing similar demographic-economic challenges. Lithuania is facing a demographic crisis[222] and has experienced a brain drain,[223] a situation that has also characterised Latvia by the conclusion of 2009.[224] One 2011 study even indicated that three

216 Brückner et al., *supra* note 39, at 84.

217 "The Talent Shortage Continues How the Ever Changing Role of HR Can Bridge the Gap," Report on Employment gaps for 2014, MANPOWER GROUP, at 3, https://www.manpowergroup.com/wps/wcm/connect/c2ddd2bc-fa8f-4d7f-8281-6bd96071a160/2014_Talent_Shortage_WP_US2.pdf?MOD=AJPERES&-CACHEID=c2ddd2bc-fa8f-4d7f-8281-6bd96071a160.

218 Dorota Bartyzel, *Poland Can't Get Enough of Polish Migrants*, BLOOMBERG, (Mar. 6, 2017), https://www.bloomberg.com/news/articles/2017-03-06/million-migrants-fleeing-putin-score-a-policy-jackpot-for-poland. *See also 'Come Back to Poland' Says Deputy Prime Minister*, (Mar. 17, 2016), http://www.bbc.com/news/world-europe-35837447.

219 REUTERS, *Will We Have Enough Ukrainians to Work for Us? Poland's Central Bank Head Wonders*, (Jan. 30, 2018), https://www.reuters.com/article/us-poland-economy-labour/will-we-have-enough-ukrainians-to-work-for-us-polands-central-bank-head-wonders-idUSKBN1FJ0V9.

220 *Id.* It will be interesting to observe whether loss of access to the UK labour market and Brexodous will create tension with these new Eastern European communities through labour competition.

221 OECD, "Coping with Emigration in Baltic and Eastern European Countries," (2013) at 18.

222 *Eastern Europe's Workers are Emigrating, but its Pensioners are Staying*, THE ECONOMIST, (Jan. 17, 2017), https://www.economist.com/news/europe/21714999-eus-newest-members-face-economic-decline-unless-they-woo-back-workers-or-recruit-immigrants.

223 *Id.*

224 Mihails Hazans, *Selectivity of Migrants from Baltic Countries Before and After Enlargement, in* EU LABOUR MIGRATION IN TROUBLED TIMES SKILLS MISMATCH, RETURN AND POLICY RESPONSES, 198.

out of every five Lithuanians under thirty years of age indicated a desire to emigrate.[225] Estonia, whose population had fallen by 7% in recent years through the combined effects of emigration and low birth rates,[226] has attempted to address the issue by essentially bribing its citizens to return home.[227] The issue of depopulation was deemed so severe that the Latvian government convened a meeting in 2012 to address the issue with respect to the Baltic States and kickstarted "initiatives to guarantee a healthy socio-economic future for Estonia, Latvia and Lithuania."[228] Although Brexit will not limit the free movement rights of EU citizens within the EU27, from the perspective of the interests of the state, A8 states, especially Poland, which are experiencing low birth rates and high rates of net emigration may stand to benefit from severely limited access to a popular labour market through amelioration of their *own* labour shortages. Significant loss of population contributes towards long-term instability of the state through reduced ability to fund social programs, and sending states may have neglected to focus on job-skill training for its workers as immigration was a simple means of dealing with unemployment.[229] The negative effects of over-emigration may also have been abated by the inflow of remittances,[230] meaning that a decline in remittances as a result of restricted access to the UK labour market and the resulting Brexodous could exacerbate demographic and unemployment issues in high net-remittance inflow A8 states, economic issues which were previously masked by remittances.[231]

---

225 *Coping with Emigration in Baltic and Eastern European Countries*, Organisation for Economic Co-operation and Development, (2013), *supra* note 66 at 56, http://dx.doi.org/10.1787/9789264204928-en. Data indicate that depopulation is a major concern among the Latvian population. *Id* at 63.

226 *Coping with Emigration in Baltic and Eastern European Countries*, *supra* note 66 at 30.

227 *Id.* at 22.

228 *Id.* at 14.

229 Concerning skills levels, EU Member States currently face little pressure for labour migration programmes to meet demand in unskilled jobs. While the low-educated population in Europe continues to decline in line with improving education and the shifting nature of the economy, migration channels such as family migration and humanitarian migration are substantial in a number of EU Member States. These channels are dominated by less educated migrants and will contribute to ensuring a sufficient supply of workers to meet demand in declining unskilled occupations." OECD, ""Recruiting Immigrant Workers: Europe 2016," *supra* note 100 at 36.

230 *See Coping with Emigration in Baltic and Eastern European Countries*, *supra* note 66 at 19- 20.

231 *See id.* at 37.

A. *A HARD BREXIT IN THE CONTEXT OF REMITTANCES*

Figure 3.10. Remittances in millions of litas and as a proportion of GDP

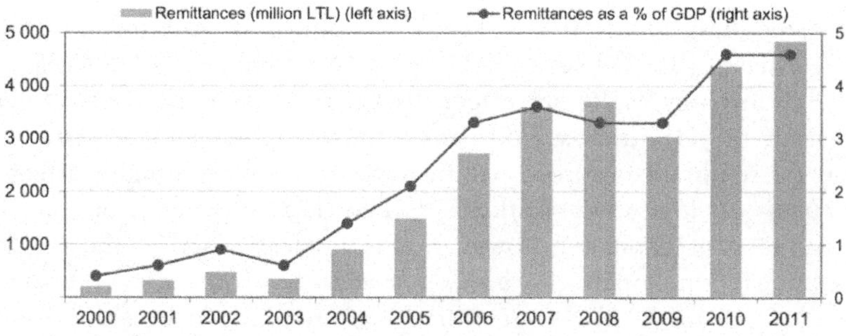

Source: Central Bank of the Republic of Lithuania; Statistics Lithuania.

Remittances, money which is earned in a foreign economy and spent in the economy of the home jurisdiction, contribute to increases in a country's capital account as net-foreign income from abroad, sometimes in enormous measure, raise gross national product, and can help counterbalance the potential risks for trade deficits. In a Hard Brexit or medium-hard Brexit scenario, Central European A8 Member States may see a reduced potential in growth of gross national product due to stagnant or diminished net foreign income from abroad (NFI) resulting from the tapering off of such remittances.

Net remittances from the UK to Poland in 2016 were about $1,102,000,000 and accounted for 21.33% of Poland's 2016 worldwide net remittances.[233] Net remittances from the UK to Lithuania in 2016 were $290,000,000 and accounted for 27.22% of Lithuania's 2016 worldwide net remittances.[234] Net remittances from the UK to Latvia in

---

232 *Id.* at 60.

233 Based on data supplied from Pew's 2016 remittances map, the 2016 net remittances from UK to Poland = [$1,134,000,000 (remittance inflow from UK to Poland) - $32,000,000 (remittance outflow from Poland to UK)] = $1,102,000,000. Poland's 2016 net remittances worldwide was ($6,712,000,000 (inflow) - $1,546,000,000 (outflow) = $5,166,000,000. The $1,102,000,000 net remittances from the UK/$5,166,000,000 worldwide net remittances to Poland = UK accounted for 21.33% of Poland's net remittances in 2016. Pew Research Center, "Remittance Flows Worldwide in 2016," (Jan. 23, 2018), http://www.pewglobal.org/interactives/remittance-map/.

234 Based on data supplied from Pew's 2016 remittances map, *id supra* note 231, the 2016 net remittances from UK to Lithuania = [$292,000,000 (inflow from UK) – $2,000,000 (outflow from UK)] = $290,000,000. Lithuania's 2016 net remittances worldwide was [$1,280,000,000 (inflow) - $213,000,000(outflow)] = $1,067,000,000. The $290,000,000 net remittances from UK/ 1,067,000,000 net remittances worldwide = UK accounts for 27.87% of Lithuania's net remittances.

2016 were at least $265,000,000 and accounted for at least 26.93% of Latvia's 2016 worldwide net remittances.[235] Net remittances from the UK to Romania accounted for 3.52 % of Romania's worldwide net remittances.[236]

This diminished NFI is likely to be significant due to the extreme difference in PPP between the UK and A8 economies,[237] and amplified by the currency multiplier effect discussed in Section II(A)[238] Finally, whether the UK imposes measures which render it more difficult to transfer remittances abroad will be a decision that can highly affect the calculus of low-wage workers.[239] The EU provides for the free movement of capital,[240] however it is unclear whether the UK will continue to maintain the *acquis communautaire* on capital. Assuming changes are made, low-wage workers are unlikely to be able to evade further restrictions on capital through the use of high-tech cryptocurrencies or complicated banking transactions as low-wage industries tend to be cash-based.

Even if prospective central European workers migrate to potentially higher-wage EU countries to work, notably Germany and The Netherlands[241] or other Eurozone Member States in which workers would not incur associated costs of converting currency earned to home currency, loss of access to the UK market is likely to increase competition in the EU27 because many would rather search for work rather than return to Poland, especially in view of the unpopularity of the ruling Polish party, PiS, among many Polish expatriates.[242] In fact, with the

---

235 Based on data supplied from Pew's 2016 remittances map, *id, supra* note 231, the 2016 net remittances from UK to Latvia = [$266,000,000 (inflow from UK) - >$1,000,000 (outflow from UK)] = ≥ $265,000,000. Latvia's 2016 net remittances worldwide was = [$1,269,000 (inflow) - $285,000,000 (outflow)] = $984,000,000]. ≥ $265,000,000 net from UK/ $984,000,000 of Latvia's worldwide net remittances) = UK accounts for at ≥ 26.93% of Latvia's net remittances.
Romania's 2016 net remittances from the UK were [106,000,000 (inflow from UK)- $3,000,000 (outflow to UK)] =$103,000,000

236 Romania's net remittance flow worldwide for 2016 =[$3,484,000,000 (inflow) - $560,000,000 (outflow)] = $2,924,000,000. $103,000,000 total net remittances from the UK/$2,924,000,000 total net remittance inflow worldwide = 3.52%. Interestingly, it is not the UK, but Italy which is the major EU remitter to Romania. Pew Remittance Map, *supra* note 231. As a general comment to these figures, *see* Section II(A), particularly *supra* note 65.

237 *See supra* section II(A).

238 *See id.*

239 "Remittance costs disproportionately affect lower-wage workers, since they remit smaller amounts and tend to use non-banking channels which carry higher costs." *Immigrant Workers: Europe 2016 supra* note 101 at 262.

240 TFEU, Art. 63(1), *supra* note 6 at 71.

241 *See* Kollewe, supra note 41.

242 *See id.*

commencement of Brexodous, it appears that workers have indeed begun to set their sights on Germany and the Low Countries.[243] Loss of access to the UK may result in a shortage of low-wage jobs in the EU27, prompting many to stay hope or return home, though if agricultural industries currently based in the EU relocate, the chance of this becoming a significant issue may be reduced.

If return patterns follow those observed from 1999-2009 of Poles living in other Member States,[244] those who are highly-skilled labour migrants and those with a university degree rather than vocational training are more likely to relocate to another country rather than simply return to Poland.[245] Conversely, however, between 2000-2010, Latvian immigrants were *less* likely to return if did not possess a university degree,[246] (but there has been a notable uptick in emigration among more skilled migrants.)[247] For those who stay, the "currency multiplier effect" of remittances may be reduced, *ceteris paribus*, by the Pound falling against the Euro.[248]

It appears that reducing emigration may have a net benefit for the long-term economic viability of A8 states, even with a potential decline in the growth, or even reduction, in net remittances. Hard Brexit could, at least in part, help stabilise the outflow of people, and prompt renewed effort of A8 governments with high levels of NFI by virtue of net remittances, to renew efforts to address structural problems which may have been abated by the palliative "release valve" of mass emigration to "solve" unemployment. This especially the case for countries like Lithuania, which appear to have not yet developed a cogent policy to deal with their demographic issues.[249] These are structural and demographic issues that countries must inevitably address, and relying on emigration to solve them is inevitably not viable in the long-term when the country becomes depopulated and cannot sustain its social services regime. The extent to which these developments will be positive or negative will turn on a number of factors which remain unknown, including the extent and

---

243 *See* Kollewe, *supra* note 41.

244 Marta Anacka & Agnieszka Fihel, *Return Migration to Poland in the Post-accession Period, in* EU LABOUR MIGRATION IN TROUBLED TIMES SKILLS MISMATCH, RETURN AND POLICY RESPONSES, 149 (Galgószi, Leschke & Watt, eds. 2012).

245 Additionally, for this 1999-2009 period, older migrants who are from more rural regions in Poland were more likely to return home (from other EU countries), particularly those from central voivodships of Dolnośląskie, Wielkopolskie, Łodzkie, Świętokrzyskie, and Lubelskie. *Id.* at 148, 158, 162-163.

246 *Id.* at 87.

247 Mihails Hazans, *supra* note 220, at 131-32.

248 *See* note 66.

249 *Coping with Emigration in Baltic and Eastern European Countries,* supra note 66 at 60-61. In the Polish context, *see infra* note 268.

immediacy of a change in population flows, remittances, effects of trade, and the timing thereof vis-à-vis each other. While there could be potential benefits for the A8, the UK's withdrawal from the EU is probably not the most harmonious and constructive way in which management of the demographic crisis could be achieved. Finally, any economic downturn is also likely to amplify "Brexodous" because the types of jobs A8 migrants undertake in the UK are particularly vulnerable to layoffs,[250] reducing remittances. Even if decline in remittances will be good for the long-term viability of the state, forcing growth at home and reducing dependence on the economies of other states, the transition will need to occur in incremental and manageable course, and provided that remittances from the UK account for such an enormous proportion of the total remittances and represent a significant quantity of GNP, the status of remittances will be an important factor to watch as Brexit unfolds in the Central European context.

---

250 This is because "[a]s a rule, migrants are the first to be fired, especially temporary, seasonal workers in sectors such as construction, manufacturing and tourism." "Coping with Emigration in Baltic and Eastern European Countries," *supra* note 66 at 51.

B. *A BREXITUNITY FOR SENDING STATES?*

"Talents Back Home!"[251]

Table 5.6. Programmes/initiatives targeting potential Polish return migrants

Name of the programme/ initiative	Institutions responsible	Main target groups	Time frame	Level of implementation
"Masz PLan na powrót?" [Have you got a PLan to return?]	Chancellory of the Prime Minister, Ministry of Labour and Social Policy, Centre of Human Resources Development	All migrants staying abroad, persons considering return to Poland and return migrants	Since September 2008 (still active)	National
Wracajdopolski.pl [ReturntoPoland.pl]	Hays Polska, Polish-British Chamber of Commerce	Polish migrants abroad, particularly highly skilled migrants	October 2007-11	National
"Zostań w Polsce – swoim szefem" [Become your own boss – stay in Poland]	Urząd Marszałkowski, Wyższa Szkoła Finansów i Prawa	Returnees in region of Mazovia (especially migrants aged 45 and over, women, and people who were forced to return due to loss of job abroad)	Since September 2010 (still active)	Regional
12 miast – wracać, ale dokąd? [The 12 cities – to go back, but where to?]	Poland Street Association (Polish NGO based in London), municipalities of 12 biggest Polish cities: Białystok, Bydgoszcz, Gdańsk, Katowice, Kraków, Lublin, Łódź, Poznań, Rzeszów, Szczecin, Warszawa i Wrocław	Polish migrants in the United Kingdom	January-August 2009 (stopped due to financial problems and economic downturn)	Regional
Powroty [Returns]	Fundacja Barka	Polish migrants in London (particularly if homeless)	Since January 2007 (still active)	Regional
Opolskie – tutaj zostaję ['Opolskie – here I stay']	Self-Government of Opole region, Regional Labour Office in Opole	Persons staying abroad, graduates, people looking for a job in the region	2009	Regional
Wrócić i co dalej? [To return and what next?]	Fundacja Fundusz Lokalny Ziemi Biłgorajskiej, Powiatowy Urząd Pracy, Biłgorajska Agencja Rozwoju Regionalnego	Young (below 35) Polish migrants and their families	January 2007-June 2009	Local

Source: Fiałkowska, K. and M. Szczepański (2012), "Labour Mobility Within the EU – Impacts of Return Migration. Poland Case Study", Eurofound – PPMI, unpublished manuscript.

1. The Welfare State

"I think Poland needs us to come back"[252]

The Polish welfare state may benefit from the hundreds of thousands or potentially millions of young working-age Poles who will may stay in Poland due to Brexit, and observation which may inform why the Polish government seems relatively unconcerned with the effects of Brexit on immigration rights.[253] Economics Professor Dr. Bielewska, an

---

251 *Id.*at 22.

252 In the words of Marta Tondera, a Polish expatriate who moved back to Poland. Joshua Chaffin, *Young Poles Leave UK to Return Home as Economy Booms*, FINANCIAL TIMES, (Oct. 27, 2017), https://www.ft.com/content/2329a046-ba6f-11e7-8c12-5661783e5589.

253 Polish leaders do not seem to consider continued unimpeded access to the UK labour market as a key priority. *See e.g. Poland's Interests Secured as Brexit Looms*, RADIO POLAND, (Dec. 15, 2017), http://www.thenews.pl/1/10/Artykul/340115.

immigration specialist at the University of Social Sciences and Humanities in Warsaw suggests that a Brexit-induced return could help address the demographic crisis facing Poland.[254]

In addressing demographic issues caused by a shrinking population, governments generally have three strategies available: raising birth rates, increasing immigration, or taking measures to reduce emigration. Currently, the Polish government is actively attempting to increase its birth rate.[255] The traditionalist and populist *Prawo i Sprawedliewość* or Law and Justice Party (PiS), which heavily identifies with conservative Catholic values, also touts increasing birth rates as one of its mandates. Its 2014 party platform even features an entire section dedicated to the Polish "demographic crisis."[256] The issue of emigration is particularly salient in the context of Poland's political environment because the current government is also focused on welfare-state initiates to encourage larger families.[257]

Indeed, the return of its working-age expatriates would be a welcome development to a government needing to fund expanded social programs, concerned with low-birth rates in the context of a demographic crisis, or perhaps even preserving the very viability of the nation. In a similar vein, from the Lithuanian government's perspective, restricted access to the UK may be positive because it probably needs to address its emigration in order to fund its new social programs.[258] Although increasing birth rates may be necessary for the long-term

---

[254] "Powrót migrantów, jeśli udałoby się ich później zatrzymać w Polsce, załagodziłby zbliżającą się do nas szybkimi krokami katastrofę demograficzną. Polska niedługo stanie się jednym z najstarszych demograficznie krajów w Europie i wynika to głównie z niskiej dzietności pokolenia wyżu demograficznego lat 80 ubiegłego wieku, a także z niskiej liczebności kolejnych kohort wiekowych *oraz emigracji ludzi młodych*." Bielewska, *supra* note 211. Emphasis added.

[255] Davis VanOpdorp, *Polish Government Urges its Citizens to Multiply like Rabbits*, DEUTSCHE WELLE, (Nov. 8, 2017), http://www.dw.com/en/polish-government-urges-citizens-to-multiply-like-rabbits/a-41300915.

[256] "Program Partii Prawo i Sprawiedliwość 2014," (2014) at 12. *See also id* at 13 (noting the crisis of demography, family, and parenthood. ("Możemy to wszystko osiągnąć, jeśli przełamiemy kryzys demografi czny, kryzys rodziny, kryzys rodzicielstwa i problem emigracji oraz tzw. pułapkę średniego rozwoju w gospodarce.") *See generally* "Rodzina to nie Wydatek, a Inwestycija," (May 9, 2018), http://pis.org.pl/aktualnosci/rodzina-to-nie-wydatek-a-inwestycja.

[257] *See generally* "Program Partii Parwo i Sprawiedliwość 2014," *supra* note 253; "Rodzina to nie Wydatek, a Inwestycija," *supra* note 252; James Traub, *The Party that Wants to Make Poland Great Again*, N.Y. TIMES, (Nov. 2, 2016), https://www.nytimes.com/2016/11/06/magazine/the-party-that-wants-to-make-poland-great-again.html.

[258] *See Lithuania Launces Poland-Inspired Family Benefits*, RADIO POLAND, (Feb. 2, 2018), http://www.thenews.pl/1/10/Artykul/342376,Lithuania-launches-Polishinspired-family-benefits.

viability of a country, increasing birth obviously does not address short term labour needs, and may not be able to counterbalance extreme rates of emigration, at least in the medium-term.[259] Ukrainian labours have been able to fill in some of the shortfall, however Ukrainian immigration has been insufficient to meet demand for labour in Poland,[260] with no intention of replacing its population with immigrants non-European, non-Christian immigrants,[261] so the return of Polish migrants would be welcomed in this context.

Loss of access to the UK labour market may also ease demographic tensions in countries, like Estonia, in which emigration is overwhelmingly male.[262] This may, in turn, abate any potential gender imbalance which may be contributing to low birth rates in sending-countries.[263] If gender imbalances are corrected through decreased gender-skewed migration, young citizens of A8 states may start families at home which may keep more potential migrants at home through community and family ties.[264]

In addition to Polish media reporting on the various potential benefits to Poland[265] of the return of its migrants, all the prospective immigrants who can no longer rely on the protection of EU law, may be incentivised to stay home rather than emigrate. However, this effect may be reduced by those who wish to emigrate simply deciding on other EU27 jurisdictions. While Section II(A) suggests that this will indeed be

---

259 Krukowska, *supra* note 212. 253; "Rodzina to nie Wydatek, a Inwestycija," *supra* note 252; James Traub, *The Party that Wants to Make Poland Great Again*, N.Y. TIMES, (Nov. 2, 2016), https://www.nytimes.com/2016/11/06/magazine/the-party-that-wants-to-make-poland-great-again.html.

259 *See Lithuania Launces Poland-Inspired Family Benefits*, RADIO POLAND, (Feb. 2, 2018), http://www.thenews.pl/1/10/Artykul/342376,Lithuania-launches-Polishinspired-family-benefits.

260 "Coping with Emigration in Baltic and Eastern European Countries," *supra* note 66 at 17.

261 RADIO POLAND, *Polish PM: We Cannot Accept Refugees* (May 16, 2017), http://www.thenews.pl/1/9/Artykul/307247,Polish-PM-We-cannot-accept-refugees. The ruling party in the Sejm and leader of the Polish government, *Prawo i Sprawedliewość* (PiS) position is largely in line with the opinion of its population. *See* VISEGRÁD GROUP, *Poland and Refugees: Some People More Welcome Than Others*, (July 25, 2017), http://www.visegradgroup.eu/poland-and-refugees-some.

262 *Coping with Emigration in Baltic and Eastern European Countries*, supra note 66 at 38.

263 Polish migrants who returned home also tended to skew male. *Id.* at 114.

264 However, the opposite may occur if there are not suitable employment opportunities at home.

265 *See e.g.* Bartłomej Niedziński, *Brexit. Czy Możemy na tym Skorzystać*, DZIENNIK, (Mar. 29, 2017), http://wiadomosci.dziennik.pl/opinie/artykuly/546114,brexit-polska-wielka-brytania-korzysc-zagrozenia-dla-polakow-opinia.html.

the result for many Poles residing in the UK, if there are similar phenomena in the EU27 or EEA, the UK's enormous economy and the strength of the British Pound are significant enough to conjecture that Hard Brexit would deter many from leaving, or at least significantly increase competition for work in the EU27, resulting in more A8 workers staying home, especially those who have a particular preference for the UK.

2. Hard Brexit and Domestic Political Issues

Hard Brexit, and its attendant effects on immigration could bear non-insignificant consequences for the domestic politics of sending states. The effect of Brexodous or reduced access to foreign labour markets may result in a rise in unemployment, even with the massive need for workers in the A8 States. This could result, for example, if Poles are, for whatever reason, unwilling to take jobs already available in Poland.[266] Indeed, managing emigration may be more desirable for the government rather than a mass return of UK-based workers because the current ruling party, Law and Justice (PiS), may fear that its Polish émigré voters in the UK may turn sour on the party if they return to a lower-wage environment, and therefore, it would be in the interests of the current government to secure the rights of those already in the UK to avoid the risk of a voting block becoming dissatisfied with the government.[267]

Bielewska suggests that immigration to the UK from Poland has lowered the Polish unemployment rate,[268] and even if Poland does not face the prospect of mass migration back, the government will still have a reduced ability to rely on migration as a solution to structural employment problems in the Polish economy in a Hard Brexit scenario. Returning migrants may also signal trouble for sending state governments as migrants who return home may be associated with higher rates of unemployment[269] and issues associated with reintegration into the Polish economy.[270]

Staying home may also result in a psychological reinvestment in the future of the home country. While European integration has created

---

266 Brexit is projected to increase unemployment in Poland. *See* Tudor, *supra* note 102 at 51.

267 *Eastern Europe's Workers are Emigrating, but its Pensioners are Staying*, *supra* note 218.

268 *See* Bielewska, *supra* note 211.

269 "Coping with Emigration in Baltic and Eastern European Countries," *supra* note 66 at 18.

270 This effect is partially attributable to the profile of Polish post-EU accession migrants, many of whom left Poland after completing their education without ever entering the Polish labour market. In such cases – especially if combined with depreciation of skills abroad – reintegration in Poland upon return can be extremely difficult. *Id.* at 117. This is particularly the case among lesser-educated returners. *Id.* at 118.

excellent opportunities to seamlessly match the different economic needs of Member States and forced government accountability through the construction of "vote with your feet" consequences to take effect vis-à-vis the marketplace of ideas, because it is easy for EU citizens dissatisfied with their governments to relocate within the EU, it must be admitted that reduced ability to migrate does have some potential positive advantages. Potential migrants who find it more costly or difficult to immigrate may be inclined to demand more of their governments and better hold them accountable if simply leaving is relatively onerous. If Hard Brexit takes hold, those who view their current governments with disfavour may pose a more serious threat to such governments because they may be more likely to engage in civil society through protest and political mobilisation rather than leaving.[271]

If anything is certain at this point, it is that the future is uncertain, and exactly what will happen, and with what severity is dependent upon an innumerate quantity of unknown variables interacting with each other. Despite the lack of clarity, the demographic situation facing Poland and the Baltic States is so severe that, whatever happens, any tightening of access to the UK labour market is likely to contribute towards the long-term viability of the welfare regime of Central European states, provided there are not major counteracting events.

VI. CONCLUDING OBSERVATIONS

A. *ILLEGAL IMMIGRATION*

In the absence of changes in national law serving as a "release valve" for the economic distortions Hard Brexit will manifest, there is a virtual certainty of increased illegal immigration. While this observation is not intended to encourage or excuse disregard for the UK's laws, Britons and the UK government must prepare for the practical reality that massive economic pressures of both promise of elevated earnings in the UK and the substantial demand for low-wage labour, especially A8 labour among the industry will not simply disappear when the UK severs itself from the Union. This could create problems, especially in the context of the

[271] This possible manifestation of Brexit is a particularly possible in Poland vis-à-vis the more progressive segments of its population. For example, it is noted that "coming to grips with Poland's right wing government has been more complicated. Its crackdown on the judiciary and women's rights has inflamed many liberal, well-educated poles," *Id.* For those returning from the UK, it may be an unwelcome transition to a more conservative political environment. *See id.*

passage of the harsh[272] Immigration Act of 2016.[273] The increase in illegal immigration is likely to increase the volume in the docket of immigration proceedings and demand for translators considering that many workers in industries most likely to be characterised by a relatively high incidence of illegal working will probably not have sufficient command of English to participate in legal proceedings in English.

B. *THE PENSION SCHEME*

There are a serious of other issues attendant to free movement of labourers that must be addressed prior to the date of withdrawal concerning those who arrive after the date withdrawal.[274] One of the most serious issues is the EU's harmonised pension scheme. Under EU rules provided for in Regulation EC 883/2004, contributions to national pensions systems have been harmonised allowing workers who move frequently to be able to draw on benefits in the state in which they retire because contributions made in any Member State are essentially aggregated.[275] Essentially, the entire EU is treated as a single country for the purpose of years counted towards paying into the Member State pension system.[276] It is unclear whether this harmonisation will continue. If it does not, it will discourage further immigration both ways as years worked in the foreign state will not count towards the required years if the worker intends to retire in different Member State. Similar issues arise with respect to harmonisation regarding working qualifications and health insurance schemes.

---

[272] The Act mandates that the Crown prosecutor ask the Court to consider the confiscation of wages earned in the course if illegal work. "Immigration Act of 2016," (34)(3)(5)-(7), available at http://www.legislation.gov.uk/ukpga/2016/19/pdfs/ukpga-_20160019_en.pdf. *See also* HOME OFFICE OF THE UNITED KINGDOM, "Immigration Act 2016 Factsheet – Illegal Working," (Section 34-38), (Jul. 2016), https://assets.-publishing.service.gov.uk/government/uploads/system/uploads/attachment_data-/file/537205/Immigration_Act_-_Part_1_-_Illegal_Working.pdf ("What are we going to do? Make it harder for people to live and work illegally in the UK. Impose tougher penalties and sanctions on rogue employers who exploit illegal migrants for their own gain. How are we going to do it? Make it a criminal offence to work illegally and seize wages from illegal working as the proceeds of crime."); Bogg, *supra* note 77 at 48.

[273] The Immigration Act of 2016 received Royal Assent on May 12, 2016. "Immigration Act of 2016," *supra* note 270.

[274] Those who arrive prior thereto will be subject to the harmonization scheme enumerated in EC 883/2004. See "Draft Agreement," Art. 28(1)-(2), at 22.

[275] *See* Stephanie Reynolds, *EU Citizens Living in the UK*, *in* THE UK AFTER BREXIT LEGAL AND POLICY CHALLENGES 196, (Michael Dougan ed. 2017).

[276] *Id.*

C. *INTRA-EU POLITICAL EFFECTS*

Another even more politically fraught issue will be the rights of frontier workers along the border between the Republic of Ireland and UK Northern Ireland and the implications on the Good Friday Agreement. Another political aspect of Brexit meriting further study is the political effect of the UK leaving the Union on sending states. It would be impossible to ignore the potential implications of the UK, as the most significant receiving state for Polish migrants, withdrawing from the EU during a time in which the relationship between Brussels and Warsaw is particularly nasty.[277] Brexit, moreover Hard Brexit, may increase Euroscepticism if it causes the populations of sending Member States to conclude that they lost a major advantage of belonging to the EU; with loss of access to the UK, they may see fewer advantages of cooperating with Brussels. If this is the case, current Eurosceptic government may further distance themselves from the EU. This is a challenge for which the EU and its supports should prepare.

D. *CONCLUSION*

The UK government deserves commendation for its willingness to negotiate level-headed, common-sense interim provisions for the immediate short term future, such as the "Draft Agreement," and Westminster's intent to transpose EU law into national law in the Repeal Bill. It is the UK's sovereign right to enter into and withdraw from treaties in accordance with domestic and international law. The risks and challenge posed by poorly-conceived mass migration are real and serious in any jurisdiction, and Britons are understandably concerned about the effect of immigration and frustrated by the unchecked rise of neoliberal "race to the bottom" economics which subordinate the welfare and quality of life of workers to multinational corporate profiteering. Civil society in all states *should* actively campaign for an economy which places a superior value of individual welfare and quality of life over corporate greed, a concerns Labour seems particularly keen on addressing. Malign employers who are found to be taking advantage of complaisant or desperate workers and unfairly undercutting legitimate employers[278] by

---

[277] In addition to a vicious row over the EU's migration policy between Visegrád and the EU, the European commission has initiated infringement proceedings against Poland for its highly questionable "reorganization" of its judiciary, since PiS has taken control of the Polish government.

[278] There is "considerable evidence" that some of these employers, especially in industries in which a large portion of migrant workers work, "are violating migrant workers' labour rights under UK law. . . .This raises questions about social justice towards often vulnerable migrant works. It also means that responsible employers find it difficult to

intentionally disregarding UK labour law should be dealt with harshly under the full force of British law.

However, a more desirable and stable means of addressing these concerns would have been to launch a campaign to better harmonise labour regulations at the EU level with these concerns in mind. Measures such as harmonising environmental protection, protection of public health and safety, and non-discrimination provisions through EU-wide directives and regulations in accordance with the Treaties have been successful at squaring the circle of balancing the potential for massive economic growth though the competition, innovation, and efficiency the free market offers with safeguarding the public and planet against the negative externalises of globalisation and deregulation. Additionally, the UK could have instead launched a purposeful effort to increase the competitiveness of British workers, for example, by undertaking measures designed to improve the "soft skills" of those who seek to enter industries in which such skills are highly valued.[279] Had the UK instead lobbied for better working conditions and protections for low-wage workers across the EU and succeeded, employers and industry would be forced to adapt to heightened standards or leave the EU completely, not simply hop across the English Channel or Irish Sea, as many will after Brexit.

Regrettably, it appears that the decision to leave the Union does nought to remedy the shortcomings of the modern economy, creates more legal and economic instability, and will create a liquidity crisis within the labour economy with only speculative positive externalities for the UK. Withdrawal from the EU in Hard Brexit fashion will do little, if anything at all to address the issues of structural employment within the UK economy. These businesses, subject to wider macroeconomic pressures, competition across the Channel, and dependent upon immediate short-term labour, will either go bankrupt or simply relocate to more favourable jurisdictions nearby because they will be unable to

---

compete with rouge employers. More generally, it has led to the perception that migrant workers are undercutting national workers and are thus, effectively, denying national workers jobs." Barnard, *supra* note 1 at 195.

[279] The Migration Advisory Committee concludes that the youth labour market is a concern. We do not find strong evidence that this is a consequence of the expansion of the EU in 2004. Schools presently have an incentive to boost the number of A* - C grades in GCSE exams. This may imply insufficient attention is given to those towards the bottom (and top) of the ability range. Many apprenticeships do not stretch the individual sufficiently and have too little employer input. Greater attention needs to be given to raising the awareness and adjusting aspirations towards available opportunities and improving the soft skills of those at the lower end of the ability range." MIGRATION ADVISORY COMMITTEE, "Migrants in Low-Skilled Work the Growth of EU and non-EU Labour in Low-Skilled Jobs and its Impact on the UK," *supra* note 40 at 10.

adapt their businesses models to the rigid and outdated strictures of the UK's tiered immigration system. As a result, UK agriculture production will relocate, transportation costs and associated tariffs on the goods which will now be produced outside of the UK will likely raise prices of goods in the UK, labour shortages will persist, the housing market will remain unable to keep up with demand, rents and housing prices will only worsen, and the wider economy will suffer. EU27 workers, unable to travel to the UK for short-term hassle-free labour that low-wage industries offer, will see a decrease in their employment prospects, and faced with a choice of committing to remain in the UK during the transition period or returning or staying home, many will likely opt to stay home, depriving the UK of a much-needed source of labour. While some may gain from Brexit in particular circumstances, more will lose because economic consensus is that Brexit will result in a substantial loss in GDP for both the UK and Europe, and globally. And although Hard Brexit may create positive externalities for A8 Member States, government policies that that succeed in keeping citizens at home when citizens have a genuine choice to stay or move abroad are preferable to a situation in which citizens stay home because simply their movement is restricted. All in all, there is indeed a strong case to be made that the UK's leaving the European Union was not the most constructive option available to address issues global economic challenges.

The misrepresentations and outright prevarications of some prominent figures within the Leave Campaign, which have relentlessly pursued an ill-conceived narrative about the "unelected autocrats in Brussels" controlling the destiny of Britons, persuaded UK voters to apply an obtuse remedy to complicated and nuanced problems. This will engender a sense of agency in the short term, but in the long-term, will bear out wide net-negative economic consequences, and generate ill-will between populations sharing common core values and geostrategic interests. Rather than reforming what many, perhaps correctly, view as a predatory economic system and focusing their ire on malign actors,[280] Brexit appears to have only made scapegoats out of foreigners,[281] especially the Poles, which is particularly regrettable given the historical emotional ties between the two nations.

The European Union as a multilateral instruction is perhaps the greatest political and legal achievement of modern history. Mere decades ago, it would have been inconceivable that the nationalism that left

---

[280] *See Barnard supra,* note 1 at 194.

[281] The widespread and anti-immigration response to labour issues leading up to and immediately after the Brexit referendum is clear evidence of this. *See Barnard supra,* note 1 at 194.

Europe in ashes and tens of millions dead in the wake of the Second World War would have given way to a level international cooperation which would culminate in the largest integrated economy in history and an international system conferring the greatest array of rights to its citizens of any jurisdiction ever created, rights which may dwindle as Eurosceptic movements gain success in Member State governments and the European Parliament. While nobody knows what developments will ultimately materialise, one hopes that the desires of the sovereigns can be reconciled with economic realities, and moreover, that the Union will demonstrate competence and leadership as it addresses the most significant challenge in its history.

CHAPTER 13: EU TRADE REMEDY POLICY IN THE WAKE OF BREXIT: A CASE STUDY OF THE STEEL INDUSTRY

SHENGXIANG NI

I. INTRODUCTION

Under the newly-released Draft Withdrawal Agreement,[1] no article addresses the difficult issue of trade remedies. Given that majority of the trade issues and the eventual permanent arrangements for the EU-UK relations are to be established[2] during the transition period, which commences after March 29, 2019 and lasts until December 31, 2020, the issues and the implications of trade remedies remain uncertain. In the midst of such uncertainty, and given the significant impact that Brexit will have on the trade remedies of both sides, this chapter seeks to explore the issue in depth and to offer a possible policy that the EU may adopt post-Brexit.

Trade remedies, or recognized by the European Commission as 'trade defenses,'[3] are actions such as anti-dumping duties or countervailing (anti-subsidy) duties imposed to protect the Union's producers from dumped or subsidized imported products. The decision to impose such trade defenses is taken after investigations regarding the products being allegedly dumped and the degree of injury being suffered by EU industries. In the past, investigations on products imported into all EU Members, including the UK, were conducted by the European Commission ("the Commission"). Upon investigations, the Commission was also responsible for calculating and imposing the appropriate dumping margin. Post-Brexit, this regime will require significant changes. For one, the Commission may not continue to maintain its current trade remedies since they reflect data from the UK, which will no longer be a part of the EU. The inclusion of UK data skews the past investigation

[1] Draft Agreement on the withdrawal of the United Kingdom of Great Britain and Northern Ireland from the European Union and the European Atomic Energy Community, EUROPEAN COMMISSION-EUROPEAN COMMISSION, https://ec.europa.eu/commission/publications/draft-agreement-withdrawal-united-kingdom-great-britain-and-northern-ireland-european-union-and-european-atomic-energy-community-0_en(last visited Apr 15, 2018).

[2] What is the Brexit "transition" phase?, BBC NEWS, February 1, 2018, http://www.bbc.com/news/uk-politics-42906950 (last visited Apr 28, 2018).

[3] Trade defence - Trade - European Commission, http://ec.europa.eu/trade/policy/accessing-markets/trade-defence/ (last visited Feb 26, 2018).

and if the Commission simply maintains the existing margins, it could be challenged by targeted companies and countries both within the EU and at the World Trade Organization (WTO). Secondly, on the UK side, Article 1 of Agreement on Implementation of Article VI of the General Agreement on Tariffs and Trade 1994 requires each imposing country to conduct its own investigations.[4] Post-Brexit, the UK will be subject to this provision, so may not maintain EU-imposed dumping margins, and will need to impose the remedies under its own system.[5]

There is also the question of whether the UK can maintain EU's dumping margins during the transition period, which is not provided for in the Draft Withdrawal Agreement. Legally speaking, it is unlikely that EU-imposed trade remedies will extend into the transition period, since the UK will not be a part of the EU after March 29, 2019. Further, even though the agreement to be reached during the transition period addresses trade remedies between the UK and EU, other countries and companies subject to anti-dumping or countervailing duties are not bound by this and can still be allowed to challenge the anti-dumping and countervailing duties imposed on the imports into the UK immediately after Brexit.

Given these questions and implications, this chapter contends that the EU needs to re-determine the findings behind each existing trade remedy. It examines those current remedies most affected and offers a method that the EU Commission could use to recalculate trade remedies on the basis of past statistics. In the meantime, it examines various criteria required under the EU and WTO laws to impose anti-dumping and countervailing duties, and examines their impact on the trade remedies in force.

This chapter will use the example of the steel industry as a model to illustrate how Brexit could affect the trade remedies on imports of steel into the EU and the UK. The EU steel industry is of strategic importance to the European Union's economy since it is closely linked to many downstream industries such as automotive, construction, and electronics.[6] "The EU is one of the main users of trade defense

---

[4] Agreement on Implementation of Article VI of the General Agreement on Tariffs and Trade 1994, https://www.wto.org/english/docs_e/legal_e/19-adp_01_e.htm - articleV (last visited Apr 28, 2018).

[5] Research into the design of the UK Trade Remedies Framework - GOV.UK,, https://www.gov.uk/government/publications/research-into-the-design-of-the-uk-trade-remedies-framework (last visited Jun 9, 2018).

[6] European Commission, THE EU STEEL INDUSTRY GROWTH, https://ec.europa.eu/growth/sectors/raw-materials/industries/metals/steel_en (last visited Mar 22, 2018).

instruments globally."[7] As the second largest producer of steel in the world, the EU has always been trying to protect and boost its steel industry through trade remedies against foreign imports.[8] As of January 31, 2018, there are 53 measures in place on steel and iron products, among which 27 measures are targeted at the products coming from China.[9] With so many foreign and domestic producers affected by trade defense measures, it is worth exploring the effect of Brexit on the EU's current trade remedies regarding the steel industry. Other industries may be also affected in a similar way.

II. BACKGROUND ON THE EU LAWS REGARDING TRADE REMEDIES

Before imposing trade remedies, the Commission needs to establish the existence of i) "dumping or subsidy," ii) "injury," and iii) "causal relationship between the dumped/subsidized imports and the injury."[10] To do so, the Commission sends questionnaires to the Union's producers (petitioners) and the foreign producers of the imported products (respondents) to collect statistics. Based on this data, the Commission determines whether the dumped or subsidized imports have caused the injury of the Union industry. Below is a background on the methodology used to investigate these elements.

A. *DUMPING DETERMINATION AND THE CALCULATION OF DUMPING MARGIN*

"A product can be considered 'dumped' where the export price of that product is less than its normal value…"[11] Article 2 (12) of Regulation 2016/1036 provides that "The dumping margin shall be the amount by which the normal value exceeds the export price. Where dumping margins vary, a weighted average dumping margin may be established."[12] "The Union Institutions calculate the dumping margin in specific amounts which are generally translated into percentage terms on

---

[7] Trade defence-Trade-European Commission, , http://ec.europa.eu/trade/policy/accessing-markets/trade-defence/ (last visited Feb 26, 2018).

[8] European Commission, THE EU STEEL INDUSTRY GROWTH, https://ec.europa.eu/growth/sectors/raw-materials/industries/metals/steel_en_(last visited Mar 22, 2018).

[9] European Commission, COMMISSION IMPOSES MEASURES ON CAST IRON PRODUCTS FROM CHINA, http://trade.ec.europa.eu/doclib/press/index.cfm?id=1790 (last visited Feb 26, 2018).

[10] *See*, PETER VAN DEN BOSSCHE & WERNER ZDOUC, THE LAW AND POLICY OF THE WORLD TRADE ORGANIZATION 1491 (4 ed.).

[11] *Id.* at 1490.

[12] REGULATION (EU) 2016/1036, 176 OJ L (2016), http://data.europa.eu/eli/reg/2016/1036/oj/eng (last visited Mar 17, 2018).

the basis of the CIF export price of the product under consideration."[13] After Brexit, the Commission should recalculate the dumping margin since usually the calculation is based on weighted-average export price (WAEP) and weighted-average dumping margin (WADM), which means the averaged "export price" or "dumping margin" of imports into the EU largely depends on the "weight" of imports in each transaction. Since the sales made in the UK were also accounted in the past investigation, the old WAEP and WADM need be recalculated post Brexit.

B. INJURY DETERMINATION

Article 3 (2) of Regulation 2016/1036[14] and Article 8 (1) of Regulation 2016/1037[15] provides the elements in the determination of injury, which reads "A determination of injury shall be based on positive evidence and shall involve an objective examination of: (a) the volume of the dumped/subsidized imports and the effect of the dumped/subsidized imports on prices in the Union market for like products; and (b) the consequent impact of those imports on the Union industry."[16] From this provision we know the three key elements of injury are the imports volume, prices, and the impact of those imports on the Union industry, which will all be subject to change in the recalculation.

Apart from these three key elements, the Commission also needs to determine whether the number of petitioners, usually the Union's producers of like products who compete with the imported products, are adequate enough to constitute the "Union industry."[17] Post-Brexit, the number of petitioners from the UK will be excluded, which could significantly affect industries of which many companies are based in the UK, such as steel.

Further, it is worth noting that after Brexit, the UK exports to the EU 27 when the past investigations were conducted become "non-subject imports." Although such imports will not affect the volume of dumped/subsidized imports into the EU 27 countries when the recalculation is conducted, adding the UK exports to the original non-subject imports into the EU could influence the re-determination of causal relationship. The larger volume of the non-subject imports serves

---

13 VAN BAEL & BELLIS (FIRM), EU ANTI-DUMPING AND OTHER TRADE DEFENCE INSTRUMENTS 128 (5 ed. 2011).

14 REGULATION (EU) 2016/1036, 176 OJ L (2016), http://data.europa.eu/eli/reg/2016/1036/oj/eng (last visited Mar 17, 2018).

15 REGULATION (EU) 2016/1037, 176 OJ L (2016), http://data.europa.eu/eli/reg/2016/1037/oj/eng (last visited Mar 17, 2018).

16 *Id.*

17 *See*, id.

as an alternative cause of the injury and it is harder for the Commission to decide whether the injury of the EU-27 was caused by the subject imports or the surging non-subject imports.

C. CAUSATION

The causal relationship should also be demonstrated between the dumped/subsidized imports and the injury under Article 3 (6) of Regulation 2016/1036[18] and Article 8 (5) of Regulation 2016/1037.[19] When deciding causation, Article 3 (7) of Regulation 2016/1036[20] and Article 8 (6) of Regulation 2016/1037[21] stipulate that contributory factors such as non-subject imports or decreasing demand of the domestic market should be considered so as to prevent the blurring of causation of the injury.

D. EXPIRY REVIEW AND INTERIM REVIEW

When the trade remedies are about to expire, expiry review could be initiated if "the expiry would be likely to lead to a continuation or recurrence of dumping/subsidization and injury."[22] The interim review also shall be initiated if the measure in force can't protect Union industry effectively or the injury no longer exists.[23]

Under Article 11 (2) of Regulation 2016/1036[24] and Article 18 of Regulation 2016/1037,[25] an expiry review could be initiated either by application, or by the initiative of the Commission. It is likely that after Brexit, many foreign producers suffering the higher duty of trade remedies may apply for the interim review and the Commission should investigate the latest situations of the EU-27 countries.

III. THE RE-DETERMINATION OF MATERIAL INJURY

As mentioned above, a determination of injury shall involve "the volume of the dumped/subsidized imports," "the effect of the dumped imports on prices in the Union market for like products" and "the consequent impact of those imports on the Union industry."[26] In addition, the injury is to the "Union industry," which under Article 4 and Article 9 of both Regulations, shall be interpreted as the "Union producers as a whole of the like products," or the producers "whose

---

18 *Supra note 14.*

19 *Supra note 15.*

20 *Supra note 14*

21 *Supra note 15.*

22 *Supra note 14; Supra note 15.*

23 *Id.*

24 *Supra note 14.*

25 *Supra note 15.*

26 *Supra note 14; Supra note 15.*

collective output of the products constitutes a major proportion of the total Union production."[27]

Many determining factors of the injury would be subject to the change. For example, the dumped volume into the EU would decrease when the amount imported into the UK is excluded; the Union industry will exclude the UK's producers; any imports from the UK, as mentioned above, will need to be evaluated as an alternative cause of injury. These changes will directly affect the determination of whether the EU 27 industry suffered from material injury in past investigations.

A. THE RE-DEFINITION OF THE UNION INDUSTRY

Under Article 5 (4) of Regulation 2016/1036[28] or Article 10 (6) of Regulation 2016/1037,[29] to be qualified as the Union industry, the collective output of the Union's producers who express support or opposition to the complaint shall constitute 50% of the total production of the like product in the Union, and for those producers who give support, their share of production of like product should be at least 25%.

1. The Exclusion of Production in the UK

The first issue the Commission needs to deal with is whether the remaining petitioners in the past investigations meet the requirement of the "Union industry" when the collective production of the UK's companies would be excluded from the total output of the EU, and the production of the UK supporters would also be subtracted from the EU supporters' production.

When we decide whether the petitioners' production is above the threshold of 25% of total production, the formula is the supporting companies' production divided by the Union's production.[30] Post-Brexit, the Commission needs to subtract the UK's production of like products from the total EU production of like products on the denominator as well as deduct the production of the UK's supporters' production of like products on the numerator to decide whether the ratio is over 25%. It is likely that in many cases, the petitioners may find it more difficult to meet the requirement of the Union industry after the recalculation when there are so many UK supporters are excluded from the numerator.

Most of the UK's producers of "domestic like products" are likely to be the supporters of the petition because the UK steel producers were anxious to impose trade remedies as much as possible against the foreign producers, owing to the fact they have always been suffering from the imports of steel from rest of the world. In 2016, Tata Steel, the top steel

---

[27] *Id.*

[28] *Supra note 14.*

[29] *Supra note 15.*

[30] *See,* supra note 14; supra note 15.

producer in the UK, announced "plans for 1050 job cuts, on top of the 1,200 it axed in October 2015 and the 720 it cut last summer"; Sahaviriyi Steel Industries, the second largest UK producer, also announced 2,200 job cuts.[31] In the meantime, the UK's steel producing companies complained that the anti-dumping and countervailing duties imposed at EU level are not high enough to protect the injured industry, and urged the UK government and other EU members to support the trade remedies.[32] Gareth Stace, director of UK Steel said: "The EU has been slower and the result is we're still haggling over tariffs and action to prevent unfairly traded Chinese steel. Britain and the EU need to stop treading on egg shells and take decisive action following America's impressive lead."[33]

When almost all the UK producers of like products support the petition, it is possible the numerator will decrease more sharply than the denominator in the recalculation, and as a result, the new ratio of the EU 27 is smaller than the previous ratio of the EU 28, which makes it more difficult to meet the requirement of 25%. Why does the numerator decrease more sharply than the denominator when both subtract a number related to the production of the UK's producers? This is because when almost all of the UK's producers are firm supporters of trade defense against other countries, the proportion of UK supporter's production to the total EU supporters' production(numerator) is greater than the proportion of total UK's like product production to the total EU's like product production (denominator). This means that the numerator subtracts a larger part of itself than the part that the denominator subtracts. The following hypothetical example fully illustrates this trend:

The UK's production of like products	0.1 million tons
The UK supporters' production of like products	0.09 million tons
The EU 28's production of like product	1 million tons

[31] Tim Bowler Lee Dave, *Britain's steel industry: What's going wrong?*, BBC NEWS, March 30, 2016, http://www.bbc.com/news/business-34581945 (last visited Mar 27, 2018).
[32] Vidya Ram, UK STEEL SECTOR FLAGS BILL 'LOWERING' TRADE DEFENCES, https://www.thehindubusinessline.com/companies/uk-steel-sector-flags-bill-lowering-trade-defences/article10020416.ece (last visited Apr 6, 2018).
[33] Julia Kollewe, UK AND EU URGED TO ACT ON CHINESE STEEL DUMPING AFTER US RAISES DUTY ON IMPORTS THE GUARDIAN (2016), http://www.theguardian.com/business/2016/may/18/uk-and-eu-urged-to-act-on-chinese-steel-dumping-after-us-hikes-duty-on-imports (last visited Mar 27, 2018).

The EU 28 supporters' production of like products	0.25 million tons
EU 28 supporters/EU 28 production	25%
EU 27 supporters/EU 27 production	(0.25-0.09)/(1-0.1) =17.7% $(\frac{0.09}{0.25} > \frac{0.1}{1})$

$$\frac{\textit{the EU supporter's production} - \textbf{UK supporter's prodiction}}{\textit{the total EU production} - \textbf{UK production}} = \frac{0.25 * (1 - 0.09/0.25)}{1 * (1 - 0.1/1)} = 17.7\%$$

In this hypothetical example, the EU 27's ratio is only 17.7% because 0.09/0.25 is larger than 0.1/1. Although in many practical cases the statistics can't be so perfect, and the comparison can't be so obvious, they at least reveal the trend that the requirement of 25% threshold may be harder for the EU 27 to meet, owing to the fact that the support for the petition might be greater in the UK than in the EU.

2. The Exclusion of Regional Market of the United Kingdom

Under certain exceptional circumstances, the Commission does not examine the injury of the whole union market, but several separate markets within the EU whose producers sell most of their production into such market and meet the demands within the market, pursuant to Article 4 (1) of Regulation 2016/1036 [34] and Article 9 (1) of Regulation 2016/1037. [35]

Although the Commission applies the provision only in exceptional circumstances,[36] so long as the UK was deemed as a separate regional market in any case, the anti-dumping and countervailing duties based on the regional market of the U.K. shall be removed post Brexit because the United Kingdom then will not be a part of the EU.

B. THE RE-CALCULATION OF IMPORTS VOLUME

Article 3 (3) of Regulation 2016/1036 [37] and Article 8 (2) of Regulation 2016/1037[38] provide that "With regard to the volume of the dumped/subsidized imports, consideration shall be given to whether there has been a significant increase in dumped/subsidized imports, either in absolute terms or relative to production or consumption in the Union."

Unlike the calculation of the Union industry mentioned above where we determine if the new petitioners can be over the threshold after

---

[34] *Supra note 14.*

[35] *Supra note 15.*

[36] *See*, VAN BAEL & BELLIS (FIRM), EU ANTI-DUMPING AND OTHER TRADE DEFENCE INSTRUMENTS 263 (5 ed. 2011).

[37] *Supra note 14.*

[38] *Supra note 15.*

subtracting the UK's petitioners, here the Commission needs to subtract the dumped volume into the UK and find out if there is a "significant increase" of the remaining dumped imports during the period of investigation (POI). In other words, the comparison is made between the dumped imports of like products into the new EU 27 countries in several consecutive years, and the Commission needs to examine if the "significant increases" still exist after the volume of UK's imported products is subtracted for each year during the POI.

With regards to the dumped/subsidized imports in absolute terms, the result depends on how many dumped/subsidized products into the UK are being subtracted. Theoretically, if the UK was a significant importer of these dumped products, and if the number of these products increased year by year during the POI, the exclusion of the UK's data may undermine the determination of "significant increase," and vice versa. In other words, if the UK imports more dumped or subsidized products than the previous years, the UK's suffering from a severe injury, and when it is excluded, the injury picture of the EU 27 countries is not so serious as the EU 28 countries before. Therefore, in cases where dumped imports into the UK kept increasing each year, the 'significant increase' as applied to EU 27 could be harder to be established. One instance of such a situation could be the definitive antidumping or countervailing duties imposed during the UK's steel crisis in 2016, when the UK's steel industry suffered a lot and received many dumped and subsidized imports. After subtracting the imports into the UK and comparing the imports volume into the new EU 27 in 2016 with that of 2015, the "significant increase" becomes harder to be maintained.

With regards to the imports volume relative to the production or consumption, the ratio of the imports to the production/consumption (market share of the imports) shall be taken into consideration.[39] Whether there are "significant increases" depend on both the numerator (imports volume) and the denominator (production or consumption). It is possible that when the UK imports more and produces or consumes less than the previous years within the POI, the ratio will not increase significantly or even decline compared to the last year after we subtract the UK's amount from both the numerator and the denominator, and there are no "significant increases." Similar to the analysis above, when the UK imports more and produces less than the previous year, the UK's suffering from a severe injury, and when it is excluded, the injury picture of the EU 27 countries is not so serious as the EU 28 countries before. As a result, the Commission may find it more difficult to find the

---

[39] *See*, VAN BAEL & BELLIS (FIRM), EU ANTI-DUMPING AND OTHER TRADE DEFENCE INSTRUMENTS 281 (5 ed. 2011).

"significant increase" in dumped imports. The following hypothetical chart could illustrate this trend:

	2015	2016	2017
The UK dumped imports	5,000 tons	15,000 tons	20,000 tons
The UK like products production	20,000 tons	15,000 tons	10,000 tons
The EU 28 dumped imports	50,000 tons	60,000 tons	65,000 tons
The EU 28 like products production	100,000 tons	100,000 tons	100,000 tons
EU 28 dumped imports/EU 28 like products production	50%	60%	70%

In the hypothetical chart above, we see that the dumped imports into the EU-28 countries experience a significant increase both in absolute terms and relative to like production within the EU.

	2015	2016	2017
The EU 27 dumped imports (exclude UK)	45,000 tons	45,000 tons	45,000 tons
The EU 27 like products production (exclude UK)	80,000 tons	85,000 tons	90,000 tons
EU 27 dumped imports/EU 27 like products production	56.25%	52.9%	50%

$$\left(\frac{EU\ imports - UK\ imports}{EU\ production(consumption) - UK\ production(consumption)} = EU\ 27\ relative\ imports\right)$$

However, there is no significant increase of the dumped import into the EU 27 in absolute terms or relative to the production when the UK's part is excluded. In the hypothetical statistics above, the UK receives more dumped imports than the year before (5,000 tons, 15,000 tons, 20,000 tons), but produces less production year by year (20,000 tons,

15,000 tons, 10,000 tons). Consequently, the EU 27 dumped imports do not increase year by year and the ratio of imports to the production even decreases (56.25%, 52.9%, 50%).

C. *THE RE-CALCULATION OF OTHER ECONOMIC FACTORS AND PRICES*

Aside from the dumped or subsidized volume and the steel price, Article 3 (5) of Regulation 2016/1036[40] and Article 8 (4) of Regulation 2016/1037[41] also list many other economic factors, such as the output, the costs of producing steel, the sales of the companies and so on, which the Commission examines in its determination of injury.

For those elements which can be adjusted by simply excluding the UK's part, the analysis will be similar to that of the "significant increase in imports volume" in Section B above. However, instead of evaluating "significant increases," the Commission only examines the general outlook of the injury suffered by the EU, usually reflected by the decline in the elements examined. For example, the injury picture can be better constructed when the number of workers decreases or the sale declines.

As in the analysis for "imports volume" in Section B above, the greater the injury suffered by the UK during the POI, the less clear it is to determine injury for EU 27. Usually the industry suffers severe injury in the form of retaining fewer workers, selling less steel, or generating less income compared to the previous years. Take the example of the workers:

	2015	2016	2017
The number of EU 28 workers for the like products	200,000	180,000	175,000
The number of UK workers for the like products	30,000	10,000	10,500
The number of EU 27 workers for the like products (exclude UK)	170,000	170,000	164,500

From the hypothetical statistics above, we can conclude that the EU 27's steel industry does not lose many jobs compared to previous years, but from the perspective of the EU 28's industry, it is evident that worker retention is on a steady decline. Majority of the injury from such laid-off workers is borne by the UK's steel industry, so after the UK is excluded,

---

40 *Supra note 14.*

41 *Supra note 15.*

the injury picture to the new EU 27 is not as significant as compared to EU 28.

However, for those elements which could not be adjusted by simply subtracting the UK's data, such as prices and costs of goods sold (COGS), the Commission may refer to questionnaires sent to relevant companies in EU 27. Based on these statistics collected, the Commission can reach a new averaged price of the new Union or a new COGS with the same calculation method used before, which excludes the UK's data.

D. THE RE-DETERMINATION OF CAUSATION

Under Article 3 (7) of Regulation 2016/1036[42] and Article 8 (6) of Regulation 2016/1037,[43] the Commission should not attribute the injury caused by other factors, such as non-subject imports, consumption, and other possible causation, to the investigated imports.

Usually foreign producers would argue that the injury of the Union industry is not caused by dumped or subsidized imports but other reasons, such as the non-subject imports, rising demand, or declining costs of steel in the Union's industry. Subject to the exclusion of the UK, many elements will also be affected. The Commission may reexamine the arguments put forward by the foreign producers and recalculate certain statistics on its initiative, if necessary, to determine if causation can still be established. For example, the Commission may take gain in non-subject imports into consideration when the UK exports to the EU are to be counted as non-subject imports in the recalculation, or to re-determine if the consumption of the EU 27 countries increased dramatically during the POI.

IV. THE RECALCULATION OF DUMPING MARGIN

As mentioned above, the dumping margin is usually the excess of normal value over export price divided by the export price. Article 2 (11) of Regulation 2016/1036 [44] provides that in most cases the dumping margin is based on the comparison of weighted average normal value and weighted average export price, or the comparison of normal value and export price on a transaction-by-transaction basis. Since "Dumping margins have traditionally been determined by a comparison of weighted average normal values to weighted average or individual export prices on a model-by-model basis," [45] this chapter only examines the former type

---

[42] *Supra note* 14.
[43] *Supra note 15.*
[44] *Supra note 14.*
[45] VAN BAEL & BELLIS (FIRM), EU ANTI-DUMPING AND OTHER TRADE DEFENCE INSTRUMENTS 131 (5 ed. 2011).

of comparison and illustrates how the exclusion of the sales into the UK will affect the determination of dumping margin.

A. *THE RE-CALCULATION OF WEIGHTED AVERAGE EXPORT PRICE (WAEP)*

To get the WAEP, first we need to multiply the export price by the sale volume of each transaction, divided by the total sale volume of all the transaction, and then add up the ratio of every transaction. In other words, "The weighted average export price is computed by multiplying each adjusted export price by its corresponding weights and summing up the results and dividing by 100." [46] The formula can be illustrated as the following:

$$\frac{EP\,1 * QTY\,1 + EP\,2 * QTY\,2 + \cdots EP\,n * QTY\,n}{QTY\,1 + QTY\,2 + \cdots QTY\,n} \quad or$$

$$EP\,1 * \frac{QTY\,1}{QTY\,1 + QTY\,2 + \cdots QTY\,n} + EP\,2 * \frac{QTY\,2}{QTY\,1 + QTY\,2 + \cdots QTY\,n} + \cdots EP\,n * \frac{QTY\,n}{QTY\,1 + QTY\,2 + \cdots QTY\,n}$$

As reflected above, the equation is a result of adding export prices in each transaction according to their weight. Among all the sales into the EU, the steel sold to the UK will be excluded from the formula and the WAEP of the rest EU 27 will be recalculated. Whether the comparison of the new WAEP and weighted average normal value will have a different result from the old comparison depends on the weight of the steel into the UK as well as the price of this steel. Theoretically, if the majority of steel was sold to the UK, then the export price of the sale into the UK has a "heavy weight" compared to the export price in other transactions. If at the same time, the difference between the "heavy weight" UK price and the price of the sale into the remaining EU 27 countries is great, then the WAEP of the new EU 27 will differ greatly from the previous EU 28 WAEP, and the result of its comparison with the normal value could be changed. For example, when the steel into the UK has a "heavy weight," and is priced much higher or lower than those dumped to the rest EU 27, then the new WAEP of the EU 27 would also fluctuate accordingly; if the volume into the UK was not so much compared to the total dumped volume into the rest EU27, then the previous WAEP would not be affected greatly. In the following hypothetical example, the products are only imported into three EU countries:

---

[46] CZAKO JUDITH, HUMAN JOHANN & MIRANDA JORGE, A HANDBOOK ON ANTI-DUMPING INVESTIGATIONS 121 (2003).

Sale	Import Quantity	Export price	Destination
1	600,000 tons	$10/ton	UK
2	200,000 tons	$2/ton	France
3	200,000 tons	$2/ton	Germany

Above, the weight of the imports into the UK is 60% and is priced much higher than imports into other countries. Therefore, the new WAEP is only 2 dollars per ton while the old one is 6.8 dollars/ton—a significant difference.

Sale	Import Quantity	Export price	Destination
1	600,000 tons	$2/tons	UK
2	200,000 tons	$10/tons	France
3	200,000 tons	$10/tons	Germany

In the hypothetical example above, it has the same result as the first chart because the weight of imports into the UK is much heavier than other imports and has a very different price, and thus the new WAEP is quite different from the old one (the WAEP of the EU 28 is 5.2$/ton, and the WAEP of the EU 27 amounts to 10$/ton).

Sale	Import Quantity	Export price	Destination
1	200,000 tons	$10/tons	UK
2	400,000 tons	$2/tons	France
3	400,000 tons	$2/tons	Germany

In the hypothetical example above, the price of the steel into the UK does not have a "heavy weight" so that the WAEP is not greatly affected due to the "light weight" of the price of the UK imports. The WAEP of the EU 28 is 3.6$/ton and the WAEP of the EU 27 is 2$/ton.

B. The Re-Calculation of Weighted Average Dumping Margin (WADM) and Anti-Dumping Duties

Before the Commission arrives at the WADM, it needs to know the dumping margin of every code of product dumped into the EU, and then multiply such margin with the corresponding share of the imported volume of such product in the total volume of the dumped products.[47] In the same vein as the WAEP, whether the past dumping margin would be dramatically changed mainly depends on the share of the dumped volume into the UK and the difference between the dumping margin of the sale into the UK and the sale into the EU27.

However, it is worth noting that when imposing the anti-dumping duty, the EU applies the "lesser duty rule." That is "the amount of the anti-dumping duty shall not exceed the dumping margin but that it should be less if such lesser duty rule would be adequate to remove the injury to the Union industry."[48] This means that the anti-dumping duty might remain the same even if the dumping margin declines after the re-calculation because the duty may be below the new dumping margin due to the lesser duty rule. Therefore, the adjustment of anti-dumping duties requires a case-by-case analysis.

V. WHAT THE COMMISSION WILL DO AFTER THE RECALCULATION

As illustrated above, for many cases the "significant increase in volume" will be undermined, the 25% threshold becomes more difficult to be met, or the dumping margin will decrease after the recalculation. Further, there is the question of what the Commission will do if i) it discovers that the share of supporters' production among the total EU 27 production is less than 25%, or ii) the new dumping margin is de minimis, or iii) that the majority of the injury was suffered by the UK and not the EU producers?

Theoretically, the Commission should eliminate the anti-dumping or countervailing duties when it finds out that the new analysis does not meet the requirement of imposing trade remedies since maintaining these remedies will violate both WTO rules and EU laws. However, in practice the Commission may not be willing to do so. Other countries may challenge these unrevised duties at the WTO, but such cases take a long time to settle. Further, even if the EU loses such WTO cases, it may only end up removing the additional duties in the specific case at issue, but not the other trade remedies in force. Alternatively, the EU may automatically remove all the unqualified trade remedies, just as in *EU - Cotton-type Bed Linen Case* where it changed its zeroing practice for all other cases and not just the one with India.[49] However, in light of the

---

[47] *Id.* at 126.

[48] VAN BAEL & BELLIS (FIRM), EU ANTI-DUMPING AND OTHER TRADE DEFENCE INSTRUMENTS 401 (5 ed. 2011).

[49] *See*, WTO | dispute settlement - the disputes - DS141, , https://www.wto.org/english/tratop_e/dispu_e/cases_e/ds141_e.htm (last visited Jun 4, 2018).

increasing trend of global protectionism, such severe modifications of existing trade remedies might be unlikely.

It is also relevant to consider what the Commission may do if the current anti-dumping and countervailing duties are not sufficient to compensate for the injury the EU 27 suffered after the recalculation. The exclusion of the UK provides a better picture of the injury, dumping or causation for the EU 27 countries. Under this circumstance, the Commission cannot impose higher anti-dumping or countervailing duties solely based on the recalculation, but must conduct a new investigation and collect new information if it wants to increase the duties. Therefore, the anti-dumping or countervailing duties cannot be increased without new investigations after Brexit.

VI. THE IMPLICATIONS OF BREXIT FOR THE NEW INVESTIGATION

For new investigations that the Commission will conduct post March 29, 2019, it will need to consider effects of Brexit in its investigation. Such new investigations will be necessary in situations where current antidumping duties expire, or where foreign steel exporters request an interim review on the trade remedies in force, or if the Commission initiates a new investigation against the imported steel. Below are relevant factors in such investigations.

A. THE EXCLUSION OF RELATED PARTIES IN THE EU WHEN IMPOSING TRADE REMEDIES AGAINST THE UK

Under Article 4 of Regulation 2016/1036 [50] and Article 9 of Regulation 2016/1037,[51] production of the EU's steel producers is to be excluded from total Union production if they are related to the foreign exporters or domestic importers, or if they are themselves the importers of dumped and subsidized products.

The UK can be exposed to the trade remedies imposed by the EU post Brexit. "We observe that around the world, members of FTAs (Free Trade Agreement) frequently use anti-dumping duties against one another—thus, the UK could easily become the target of antidumping duties into the EU."[52] The top five countries which received the UK's exported steel in 2016 were France, Germany, Turkey, Ireland, Netherlands, accounting for 52% of the UK's steel exporting volume at

---

50 *Supra note 14.*

51 *Supra note 15.*

52 Meredith Crowley, Giancarlo Corsetti, Oliver Exton & Lu Han, HOW DAMAGING WOULD A NCARLO CORSETTI, OLI LSE BREXIT (2018), http://blogs.lse.ac.uk/brexit/2018/01/24/how-damaging-would-a-no-deal-brexit-be/ (last visited Mar 29, 2018).

1.8 million tons.[53] Among these countries 4 are the current EU-28, and although Turkey is a candidate, it is still part of the European Union Customs Union.[54] There is no reason for the new EU not to consider taking some measures against the UK when so much steel is imported into the EU.

However, the determination of the Union industry becomes complicated when many steel companies in the EU and the UK are or may become related through mergers and acquisitions. In order to better deal with the challenges confronting the EU's steel industry, companies are seeking mergers and acquisitions to increase their competition. In 2017, Tata steel has announced a merger with the German steel manufacturer ThyssenKrupp, becoming the second largest producer in the EU.[55] The merger of companies between the UK and rest of the EU will qualify them as "related parties" because it indicates a certain degree of relationship and control between the companies who share the same interest. Therefore, in the new investigation against the UK, the Commission may exclude the production of many new EU 27 companies from the total Union production.

B. BLURRED CAUSATION

The Commission may find it harder to determine the causal relationship between the unfair trade practice and the injury. How to know whether the EU's steel industry is suffering from the unfair trade practice or Brexit, or their combined effects? The EU's steel producers may sell less due to the declining consumption, or other reasons caused by the Brexit. Combined with the increasing trend of global protectionism, Brexit may make the Commission more difficult to distinguish what causes the injury of the Union's industry.

VII. CONCLUSION

After the recalculation, many trade remedies may lose justification for the less convincing evidence of injury, dumping, or causation. As a general matter, when the UK suffered a lot and contributed a lot to the whole EU 28 injury picture in the past investigations, such as many UK companies supporting the petition, or many dumped/subsidized imports

---

[53] INTERNATIONAL TRADE ADMINISTRATION, STEEL EXPORTS REPORT: UNITED KINGDOM, https://www.trade.gov/steel/countries/pdfs/2016/q3/exports-uk.pdf.

[54] European Union Customs Union, WIKIPEDIA (2018), https://en.wikipedia.org/w/index.php?title=European_Union_Customs_Union&oldid=842332411 (last visited Jun 4, 2018).

[55] Tata Steel to merge European operations with ThyssenKrupp, THE GUARDIAN (2017), http://www.theguardian.com/business/2017/sep/20/tata-steel-merge-thyssenkrupp-job-losses-port-talbot (last visited Mar 29, 2018).

into the UK (heavy weight), the trade remedies relying on these investigations are more likely to lose justification. But when the UK's contribution to EU 28 injury was not significant, and the exclusion of the UK provides a more severe injury picture for the EU 27, the Commission cannot simply increase the current anti-dumping or countervailing duties. However, with so many cases which could potentially lose legal basis, the Commission may not be willing to eliminate all trade remedies in these cases and may just remove certain specific one only when other countries win the case in the forum of the WTO, unlike what they did after the dispute with India regarding the zeroing practice.

Besides the effect of Brexit on the existing trade remedies, it will also influence the future investigations of the Commission. Many EU 27 producers will be excluded in the investigation against the UK, and the Commission may find it more difficult to distinguish the causation post Brexit. Therefore, the Commission needs to realize the potential challenges and prepare for them as soon as possible.

CHAPTER 14: BREXIT AND BORDER SECURITY: IMPLICATIONS FOR EUROPOL AND MORE

SARAY LEON

This chapter will trace the development of border security cooperation within the European Union and the prospect for continuation after Brexit.

I. HISTORY AND EVOLUTION OF THE EUROPEAN UNION

The European Union (EU) was established with the purpose of eradicating the frequent wars between neighboring European countries, which culminated with World War II. In fact, by 1950, the European Coal and Steel Community (ECSC) laid its foundation by uniting the six founding European countries: Belgium, France, Germany, Italy, Luxembourg and the Netherlands.[1] During the 1960s, the EU member countries agreed to stop charging custom duties to one another when trading among themselves and to exercise joint control over food production, in order to ensure that every country had enough agricultural produce to feed its populace. The next surge of countries added to the EU occurred during the 1970s when Denmark, Ireland and the United Kingdom became members on January 1, 1973. During that time, the European Parliament had increased its influence in EU affairs and by 1979, all citizens were granted the right to elect their members directly.

The 1980s marked a significant period for the EU. During that decade, Greece became the 10th country to join the EU in 1981, with Spain and Portugal following five years later. Also of significant importance during this period was the enactment of the Single European Act (SEA) in February 1986. It was signed by the nine EU member states as well as Greece, Italy and Denmark.[2] The SEA's preamble emphasizes its member states' determination to transform their relations as a whole with the vision of creating a European Union. The preamble also focused on the two objectives of revising the Treaty of Rome, also

---

[1] European Union, *A peaceful Europe – the beginnings of cooperation* (last updated Sept. 5, 2017), https://europa.eu/european-union/about-eu/history/1945-1959_en (last visited July 17, 2018).

[2] EUR-Lex: Access to European Union Law, *The Single European Act* (last updated Oct. 26, 2010), https://eur- lex.europa.eu/legal-content/EN/TXT/?uri=LEGISSUM%3Axy0027 (last visited Apr. 15, 2018).

known as the 'Treaty Establishing the European Economic Community (EEC treaty)[3], which were: "to improve the economic and social situation by extending common policies and pursuing new objectives" and "to ensure a smoother functioning of the Communities".[4] The SEA was meant to add new momentum to European integration and to completing the internal market by amending the rules governing European institutions and expanding research and development, as well as common foreign and security policy.[5]

The SEA provided the basis for a six-year program aimed at identifying and addressing the problems with the free flow of trade across EU borders, which led to the creation of the 'Single Market,' an economic market that emphasized and protected the 'four freedoms' of: movement of goods, services, people and money.[6] The SEA's contribution to the transformation of the common market into the Single Market culminated in the 1992 Treaty of Maastricht on European Union, also known as the "Maastricht Treaty."[7]

The Maastricht Treaty was mainly the result of external and internal events. Externally, the collapse of communism in Eastern Europe and the outlook of German reunification led to a commitment to reinforce the European community's international position. Internally, the Member States wished to supplement the progress achieved by SEA with other reforms.

Additionally, the Maastricht Treaty introduced the concept of European citizenship, reinforced the powers of the European Parliament and launched the Economic and Monetary Union (EMU).[8] This framework proved to be of significant value to the economic and political expansion of the EU in the late 1990's and the 2000's as the EU's membership increased with three additional States—Austria, Finland and Sweden—and the free flow of European citizens and the newly-adopted currency, the Euro, across Member State borders.

Further, the Lisbon Treaty was proposed in 2007 as an international agreement that amended the Maastricht Treaty and the EEC with the goal of simplifying and streamlining the several institutions governing and

---

[3] EUR-Lex: Access to European Union Law, *Treaty of Rome (EEC)* (last updated Mar. 14, 2017), https://eur-lex.europa.eu/legal-content/EN/TXT/?uri=legissum:xy0023 (last visited July 20, 2018).

[4] *Id.*

[5] *Id.*

[6] European Union, *The History of the European Union: 1980-1989*, https://europa.eu/european-union/about- eu/history_en#1980_-_1989.

[7] EUR-Lex: Access to European Union Law, supra note 2.

[8] EUR-Lex: Access to European Union Law, *Treaty of Maastricht on European Union* (last updated Oct. 15, 2010), https://eur-lex.europa.eu/legal-content/EN/TXT/?uri=LEGISSUM:xy0026 (last visited Apr. 5, 2018).

overseeing the EU. The Lisbon Treaty was ratified by most member states in 20085 with the exception of Ireland, which rejected it altogether, and thus, jeopardized the entire treaty. Finally, toward the end of 2009, the Lisbon Treaty was ratified and entered into force by all 27 member states.[9]

II. EUROPOL AND THE EU

In its ten-year anniversary publication, Europol discussed the idea behind its inception as an organized police agency. What is known today as Europol dates back to the establishment of the Trevi group in the 1970s, which was set up by European Communities' interior and justice ministers to address concerns about international terrorism.[10] However, not long after its inception, Trevi extended its focus toward other areas of cross-border crime within the European community.[11] During the following decades, there were several talks about the need to formalize police cooperation between the several European communities. In 1991, the German chancellor called for the establishment of a European police agency that would mirror the American Federal Bureau of Investigation (FBI).[12] In 1992, this idea was given more substance in the Maastricht Treaty on the European Union.

The Maastricht Treaty culminated in the creation of a European Union that consisted of three significant pillars: the European Communities, Common Foreign and Security Policy (CFSP), and Police and Judicial Cooperation in Criminal Matters (PJCC)—formerly named Justice and Home Affairs (JHA). The first pillar of the EU consisted of the European Community, the ECSC and Euratom. It was concerned with the domains in which the Member States shared their sovereignty via the Community institutions. The second pillar established a common foreign and security policy, which replaced the provisions of the SEA and allowed Member States to take joint action in the field of foreign policy. The third and last pillar focused on Community cooperation in JHA. Europol was the byproduct of the EU's objective for its Third Pillar.

The Convention establishing Europol under Article K3 of the Maastricht Treaty was agreed in 1995 and into force on October 1, 1998.[13] Europol's main objective was to effectively carry out cross-border

---

[9] Michael Ray, ENCYCLOPEDIA BRITANNICA, *Lisbon Treaty: European Union*, https://www.britannica.com/event/Lisbon-Treaty (last visited July 19, 2018).

[10] Europol, Ten Years of Europol: 1999-2009 (2009), https://www.europol.europa.eu/sites/default/files/documents/anniversary-publication.pdf (last visited May 1, 2018).

[11] *Id.* at 15.

[12] *Id.*

[13] *Id.* at 18.

policing that would "prevent and combat unlawful drug trafficking in nuclear and radioactive substances, illegal money laundering, immigrant smuggling, trade in human beings and motor vehicle theft."[14] The Convention required each member state to designate a national unit to serve as a liaison between its own authorities and Europol. The national units would represent the interest of their authorities at Europol and help facilitate the flow of information between their authorities and Europol.[15]

A. EUROPOL KICKS OFF

After resolving some initial legal difficulties and adding some legal acts to the Convention, Europol commenced its full activities in July 1999.[16] Since July 1999, Europol has had the authority to deal with child abuse, terrorism, forgery of money and human trafficking, among other major crimes. The Convention gave Europol the authority to enter into cooperation agreements with third states and international organizations.[17]

During its initial years, Europol was faced with combating organized crime, drug- trafficking, illegal immigration, and the unstable situation in the Balkans.[18] However, Europol's agenda shifted greatly after the terrorist attacks on the World Trade Center and the Pentagon in the United States. The EU countries found a need to increase their vigilant efforts and work much more closely together in order to fight domestic and international crime.[19] In response, Europol set up a Counter Terrorism Task Force (CT Task Force), which focused on gather intelligence and conducting extensive analysis. However, the CT Task Force was dismantled once the immediate terrorist threat was believed to have subsided. Unfortunately, Europol found itself reactivating the CT Task Force in light of the terrorist attack on the Madrid train in March 2004.

The 2000's continued to pose a challenging era for the EU to provide its citizens with security and justice while combatting local and international crime, particularly terrorism. To make matters worse, the EU found itself at the epicenter of religious extremism and unrest in the Middle East resulting in an influx of refugees. The constantly shifting

---

[14] Peek J 'International Police Cooperation within Justified Political and Judicial Frameworks: Five Thesis on TREVI' in Monar J & Morgan R (eds.) '*The Third Pillar of the European Union*' (Brussels, European Interuniversity Press, 1994), at 252.
[15] Europol, *supra* note 8, at 18.
[16] University of Exeter, *History of Europol*, http://people.exeter.ac.uk/watupman/undergrad/pollard/html/history.htm#_ftn2.
[17] Europol, *supra* note 8, at 25.
[18] *Id.*
[19] European Union, *supra* note 5.

ideological and political scheme signified that Europol needed to enhance its international crime efforts. Fortunately, several new member states acceded to the European Union in May 2004, bringing with them national units with considerable experience in combatting these areas of crime in their territories.[20]

B. EUROPOL TAKES OFF

Along with its increased member statehood, Europol increased its anti-crime resources by expanding its Information Technology (IT) systems; thus, allowing it to provide a faster and more effective exchange of information between the national units and the law enforcement agencies of the member states.[21] In 2007, Europol's analysis system was enhanced with OASIS (Overall Analysis System for Investigation Support), which increased Europol's ability to match Intel and analytical information from different sources.[22] By 2008, Europol's communication network connected all member states to Europol, providing national units with access to all of Europol's information through messaging and telephone systems. Europol also created a crime scene website, in collaboration with the European Network of Forensic Science Institutes (ENFSI), which facilitated the sharing of information related to crime scene investigation and related techniques.[23]

Another very important anti-crime tool facilitated by Europol is the Organized Crime Threat Assessment (OCTA). OCTA's main objective is to identify and assess emerging threats, identify and categorize the structure of organized crime groups, the way they operate, their main criminal enterprises and the areas affected in the EU.[24] OCTA is an important component of the European Criminal Intelligence Model (EICM), which is considered by the EU as its business model for "intelligence-led policing."[25] The EICM is structured in six phases. First, Member States collect intelligence; second, Europol stores and analyzes the intelligence collected; third, the analysis produces two key sets of information: threat assessments in priority areas and a list of top criminals and target profiles; fourth, the Police Chief Task Force (PCTF) sets the enforcement strategy in priority areas; fifth, PCTF sub-groups task and coordinate investigations along with Member States' and EU resources

---

[20] Europol, *supra* note 8, at 48.
[21] *Id.* at 50.
[22] *Id.*
[23] Europol, *supra* note 8, at 51.
[24] *Id.* at 52.
[25] *Id.* at 53.

against top-listed criminals; and sixth, intelligence generated by investigations is recycled.[26]

Europol's anti-crime efforts also include a range of print and electronic publications to inform and support Member States and partner law enforcement agencies.[27] Of significance is the EU Terrorism Situation and Trend Report (TE-SAT). Since 2007, the TE-SAT has been informing Member States and partner law enforcement agencies about current trends in terrorism in the EU, as well as reporting on terrorist attacks and suspects arrested by category, such as terrorist group, political or religious ideology. The TE-SAT is an informative tool that reflects Europol's increased involvement in anti-terrorism activities over the past decade. In the foreword for its 2017 publication, TE-SAT's Director stated the following on the matter:

> "Over recent years the organisation's [sic] involvement in this area has seen a steep increase. The number of Europeans travelling as foreign terrorist fighters (FTFs) to the conflict areas in Syria and Iraq, the invasive use of the internet and social media in propaganda and recruitment activities, and the terrorist attacks in EU Member States directed or inspired by jihadist terrorist organisations [sic], have cause a major increase in the number of cases at Europol concerning "crimes committed or likely to be committed in the course of terrorist activities against life, limb, personal freedom or property" – a development that is not expected to come to a halt soon."[28]

This statement is only a glimpse into the severity of terrorism in the EU and the imminent threat that the various groups of terrorists pose to the law-abiding citizens of the European community.

III. TERRORISM IN THE EU

Europe has always been a fruitful ground for various forms of conflict and violent action, including non-international conflicts among neighboring countries as well as civil unrest and wars among citizens of the same country. However, the nature and activities surrounding some of these conflicts warrant further analysis and determination as to whether or not they would be more properly classified under terrorism. For example, the Irish War of Independence (1919-1921),[29] the First and Second Chechen Wars (1999-2009) and the War of Dagestan (1999).

---

[26] *Id.*

[27] *Id.* at 55.

[28] E.U. TE-SAT 2017, *Foreword of the Director* (2017), https://www.europol.europa.eu/activities-services/main- reports/eu-terrorism-situation-and-trend-report-te-sat-2017 (last visited May 10, 2018).

[29] The National Archives, *The Cabinet Papers: Nationalism and the War of Independence*,

There is an expansive history of terrorism across Western and Eastern Europe. Some terrorist attacks have been linked to nationalist and separatist movements, while others have been linked to political or religious extremism. According to the University of Maryland National Consortium for the Study of Terrorism and Responses to Terrorism, terrorism in Europe has killed over 11,000 persons in over 18,800 terrorist attacks since 1970.[30] From the 1970s to the early 1990s, western countries such as Northern Ireland and Spain were at the epicenter of terrorist attacks by its local separatist and extremist groups. Despite the fact that the number of deadly attacks in the western region fell drastically by the mid-1990s, the same could not be said for the eastern region. In the years after the fall of the Soviet Union, terrorist groups formed with some even receiving support from foreign extremist groups, including al-Qaeda.[31]

The 2001 terrorist attacks on the World Trade Center and the U.S. Pentagon reverberated around the world, leading to the realization that terrorism was becoming a global problem. Not long after the terrorist attacks on U.S. soil, Europe also fell victim to terrorism. On March 11, 2004, almost 200 people were killed when bombs detonated on four commuter trains in Madrid, Spain.[32] A little over a year later, on July 7, 2005, over 50 commuters were killed in London when four suicide bombers inspired by al-Qaeda blew themselves up on a bus and three subway trains.[33]

In March 2, 2011, an Islamic extremist, inspired by a fake video displaying American atrocities in Afghanistan, shot and injured several people at an airport in Frankfurt, Germany.[34] Eight months later, on November 2, 2011, the offices of Charlie Hebdo, a French satirical

---

http://www.nationalarchives.gov.uk/cabinetpapers/themes/nationalism-war-independence.htm (last visited Apr. 5, 2018). The Irish War of Independence was a brief but intense conflict following the 1916 Easter Rising—a rising tide of militant Irish nationalism that was countered with harsh treatment from British leaders, which further alienated the Irish and contributed to the radicalization of the nationalist party and the expansion of the Irish Republican Army (IRA). After several violent upsurges, including 'Bloody Sunday,' the British Cabinet reluctantly recognized that its authority in Ireland was collapsing and agreed to a truce in 1921, giving Ireland dominion status within the Empire.

[30] Chris Alcantara, THE WASHINGTON POST, *46 Years of Terrorist Attacks in Europe, Visualized*, (updated July 17, 2017), https://www.washingtonpost.com/graphics/world/a-history-of-terrorism-in-europe/. *See also* National Consortium for the Study of Terrorism and Responses to Terrorism: A Center of Excellence of the U.S. Department of Homeland Security, *Global Terrorism Database*, https://www.start.umd.edu/gtd/.

[31] *Id.*

[32] Bloomberg, *Recent Major Terror Attacks in Europe* (May 23, 2017), https://www.bloomberg.com/news/articles/2017-05-23/recent-major-attacks-in-europe (last visited May 1, 2018).

[33] *Id.*

[34] *Id.*

magazine, were firebombed in Paris, France in retaliation for running a caricature of the Islamic Prophet Muhammad on one of its covers.[35] Unfortunately, in January 2015, the offices of Charlie Hebdo once again suffered terrorist attacks by gun assault, in which Al-Qaeda claimed responsibility for the attack, also in retaliation for the magazine's depiction of Prophet Muhammad.[36] Later that year, Islamic State-linked extremists attacked several sites across Paris, France, including the Bataclan concert hall, killing 130 people.[37] The following year, on March 22, 2016, several suicide attacks on the airport and subway system of Brussels, Belgium killed over 30 people and left hundreds of innocent victims injured.[38] These attacks are just a few of the most serious and lethal terrorist attacks in recent European history and recent history.

IV. BREXIT: THE UK AND EU DIVORCE

On June 23, 2016, the United Kingdom voted through a referendum to leave the EU, a decision commonly known as Brexit. Following the referendum decision, several debates ensued surrounding pertinent topics such as trade, sovereignty, immigration, defense and security. Despite talks of uncertainty and speculation of withdrawing from Brexit, on March 28, 2017, British Prime Minister Theresa May formally began Britain's divorce from the EU, declaring: "The United Kingdom is leaving the European Union. This is an historic moment from which there can be no turning back."[39] In a hand-delivered, six-page letter to EU Council President Donald Tusk, PM May announced Britain's tortuous exit process and departure from the union it joined back in 1973 under Article 50 of the EU's Lisbon Treaty.[40] At that moment, the formal two-year exit process commenced.[41]

In her letter to President Tusk, PM May stressed a strong desire to negotiate Britain's divorce and the future trading relationship with the EU

---

[35] *Id.*
[36] *Id.*
[37] *Id.*
[38] *Id.*
[39] Guy Faulconbridge & Elizabeth Piper, REUTERS, *'No turning back': PM May triggers 'historic' Brexit* (Mar. 28, 2017), https://www.reuters.com/article/us-britain-eu/no-turning-back-pm-may-triggers-historic-brexit-idUSKBN16Z22G (last visited Apr. 10, 2018).
[40] THE LISBON TREATY, http://www.lisbon-treaty.org/wcm/the-lisbon-treaty.html (last visited Apr. 21, 2018). The Lisbon Treaty was signed on December 2007 by the heads of state and government of the then 27 EU Member States. The treaty was intended to reform the functioning of the EU following the two waves of enlargement since 2004 in which the EU membership expanded from 15 to 27 Member States. The Lisbon Treaty includes key changes aimed at increasing the consistency and coherence of the EU's external actions.
[41] *Id.*

during the two-year exit process; however, EU officials have opined that it will be difficult to do so.[42] "We believe it is necessary to agree to the terms of our future partnership alongside those of our withdrawal from the EU," said PM May in her letter to President Tusk, while emphasizing strong aspirations for establishing an ambitious free trade agreement with the EU, "If, however, we leave the European Union without an agreement the default position is that we would have to trade on World Trade Organisation [sic] terms," she added.[43]

In addition to discussing the need for establishing a positive and fruitful trade agreement with the EU through a special partnership, PM May also called for a clear and constructive relationship regarding security matters, "We want to agree a deep and special partnership between the UK and the EU, taking in both economic and security co-operation."[44] Recognizing that Britain's departure from the EU threatens to disrupt the security and counterterrorism efforts they hold in common. "We should work together to minimize disruption and give as much certainty as possible. Weakening our cooperation for the prosperity and protection of our citizens would be a costly mistake," PM May continued in her letter to President Tusk.[45]

In one of its latest reports on the future of the UK and the EU, the House of Commons' Exiting the European Union Committee concluded the following on security co-operation between UK and the EU:

> "Continuing security co-operation is a priority for both sides. Our predecessor Committee welcomed the Government's commitment to continuing co-operation with the EU27 on foreign policy and defence [sic] matters. That Committee called on the Government in March 2017 to set out some detail about how such co-operation could be made to work in practice, including the institutional and decision-making frameworks that would underpin it. It is regrettable that no response has yet been provided to that report and no detail has been set out. Our predecessor Committee also welcomed the Secretary of State's statement that the Government wants 'as far as is possible to replicate what we already have' in respect of Justice and Home Affairs Cooperation and concluded that the UK's relationship with the EU when outside should be one of partnership on the basis of shared values and co-operation. Maintaining this level of co-operation will require overcoming a number of technical

---

42 *Id.*

43 *Id.*

44 Exiting the European Union Committee, HOUSE OF COMMONS, *The future UK-EU relationship: Fourth Report of Session 2017-2019* (Apr. 4, 2018), at 28.

45 Faulconbridge, *supra* note 37.

> challenges in respect of agreeing data protection, judicial oversight and governance provisions. The Prime Minister's Munich speech acknowledges that the Government will be looking to find positive solutions to address these challenges."[46]

However, the UK's calls for a treaty or agreement on security and defense have been met with indifference across the European community. On February 17, 2018, PM May spoke at the Munich Security Conference, urging European partners to come to an agreement on a new security treaty—sooner, rather than later. PM May said that the UK had an "'unconditional' commitment to European security that would not change after the country's departure from the bloc."[47] PM May continued, "This cannot be a time when any of us allow competition between partners, rigid institutional restrictions or deep-seated ideology to inhibit our cooperation and jeopardize the security of our citizens."[48] In an effort to expedite agreement talks, PM May offered a grand and controversial concession—Britain would "respect" the jurisdiction of the European Court of Justice in exchange for a security agreement with the EU. This is an unpopular move among hardline advocates of Brexit, which stress that Britain should regain control of its laws and no longer be bound to the European court.[49] Nevertheless, Britain, a member of the Five Eyes, an intelligence alliance among Australia, Canada, New Zealand, the UK and the United States, has very good intelligence to offer its partners, especially those in the European region. Florence Gaub, deputy director of the European Union Institute for Security Studies (EUISS), agreed with PM May, stating "European fighters in ISIS don't make any distinction between the U.K. and the Continent. Brexit and the Channel don't matter to them."[50] Unfortunately, many in the audience were not receptive to PM May's pleadings. In fact, Mr. Wolfgang Ischinger, the chairman of the conference, said that Britain's decisions to leave the EU was regrettable. "Everything would be so much easier if you stayed," he said. Mr. Ischinger's comment was received with a louder and longer applause from the conference audience than that of PM May after her speech.[51] Other non-supporters of a security-based treaty stress that Britain is asking for a special deal, giving it more say in European

---

[46] Exiting the European Union Committee, *supra* note 41, at 58.

[47] Katrin Bennhold & Steven Erlanger, THE NEW YORK TIMES, *Theresa May, in Munich, Calls for Swift Security Pact and Offers Concession* (Feb. 17, 2018), https://www.nytimes.com/2018/02/17/world/europe/uk-theresa-may- munich.html (last visited May 10, 2018).

[48] *Id.*

[49] *Id.*

[50] *Id.*

[51] *Id.*

affairs than a third country would normally enjoy.[52] Despite the animosity, PM May continued to stress the importance of a security and defense treaty between the UK and EU. "The partnership that we need to create is one that offers UK and EU way to combine our efforts to greatest effect where this is in our shared interest," said PM May in Munich.[53]

Not surprisingly, the European Commission Draft Withdrawal Agreement on the withdrawal of the United Kingdom of Great Britain and Northern Ireland from the European Union and the European Atomic Energy Community ("Draft Withdrawal Agreement"), which was released ten days after the Munich conference on security, glossed over security and defense matters. Title V of the Draft Withdrawal Agreement only covers "Ongoing Police and Judicial Cooperation in Criminal Matters," wherein it outlines several Council Framework Decisions that continue to remain in effect until the end of the Brexit transition period. Some Articles of the Convention implementing the Schengen agreement remain in effect as well, such as "requests for assistance of "cross-border surveillance in accordance with Article 40(1) of the Schengen Implementing Convention *received before the end of the transition period*" (emphasis added) or "cross-border surveillance Article 40(2) of the Schengen Implementing Convention carried out without prior authorisation [sic] *that started before the end of the transition period*" (emphasis added).[54] The title also mentions mutual assistance and cooperation between customs.

Evidently, the Draft Withdrawal Agreement is left wanting on matters relating to security and defense, which is concerning, if not alarming.

V. BREXIT: TRAVEL AND BORDER PROTECTION

As previously mentioned, when it comes to Brexit and security and defense matters, there are several challenging areas that demand adequate attention, for example travel, border protection, data flow and sharing, crime-related prevention and enforcement efforts, and more. The United Kingdom of Great Britain and Northern Ireland, more commonly known as the United Kingdom (UK) and Britain, is comprised of several

---

[52] *Id.*

[53] *Id.*

[54] EUROPEAN COMMISSION, *European Commission Draft Withdrawal Agreement on the withdrawal of the United Kingdom of Great Britain and Norther Ireland from the European Union and the European Atomic Energy Community* (Feb. 28, 2018), https://ec.europa.eu/commission/publications/draft-withdrawal-agreement-withdrawal- united-kingdom-great-britain-and-northern-ireland-european-union-and-european-atomic-energy-community_en (last visited May 12, 2018).

countries: England, Scotland, Wales, and the province of Northern Ireland, which occupies the northeastern part of the island, and thus, borders the Republic of Ireland. In addition, the Channel Tunnel beneath the English Channel connects the UK with France. Moreover, its physical proximity to other countries makes Britain share maritime borders with Denmark, Germany, Belgium, Netherlands and Norway.[55]

Given its physical location, it is evident that matters relating to travel and border protection are important political spheres that require the attention and cooperation of the UK and the EU Member States. Post-Brexit, there will be changes that affect travel between EU Member States and the UK. Currently, UK citizens are entitled to travel anywhere in the EU simply by presenting their passport. Which means that a guard at the border of France, Spain or Italy would only verify that the travel documents being presented are valid. That would be the extent of the vetting process. However, once the UK leaves the EU, UK citizens will be regarded as "third-country nationals."[56]

As non-EU nationals, UK citizens, absent a future agreement with the EU, will not have an automatic right of admission into other EU countries, and vice-versa. Additionally, research indicates that third-country nationals tend to be disadvantaged in employment compared to their EU national counter-parts. Non-EU nationals in the EU had a labor market participation rate of 62% and an employment rate of 52% in 2001, while EU nationals came in at 69% and 64%, respectively.[57] Member States vary considerably in the way they conceive the integration of third-country nationals and in the extent to which they have developed and implemented integration policies. Some countries have a long experience in this area whereas others have only just started developing national policies.

Additionally, a European initiative to strengthen the EU's external borders, the European Travel Information and Authorisation System (ETIAS), is currently underway. The legal process to pass the ETIAS began in 2016, and the system is expected to be in place by 2020. ETIAS

---

55 NATIONS ONLINE, *Political Map of United Kingdom*, http://www.nationsonline.org/oneworld/map/united- kingdom-map.htm (last visited Apr. 20, 2018).

56 EUROFOUND, *EurWORK: Third-Country Nationals*, https:/ www.eurofound.europa.eu/observatories/eurwork/industrial-relations-dictionary/third-country-nationals (last visited Apr. 20, 2018). The term "third-country nationals" is used as a reference, usually in treaties, to a country that is not a member of the European Union. It is derivative of the phrase 'third country,' which is often used to refer to a country that is not party to an agreement between two countries.

57 *Id. See also* Commission of the European Communities, *Taking Stock of Five Years of the European Employment Strategy*, (2002), http://ec.europa.eu/transparency/regdoc/rep/1/2002/EN/1-2002-416-EN-F1-1.Pdf.

is a completely electronic system which will keep track of visitors from countries who do not need a visa to enter the Schengen Zone.[58] Through ETIAS, each applicant will undergo a detailed security check to determine whether they can be allowed entry into any Schengen Zone country.[59] Since citizens of countries who do not need a visa for travel purposes of up to 90 days in the EU do not need to go through a long process of applying for the visa, the ETIAS will ensure that these people are not a security threat. This travel authorization system will collect, track, and update necessary information regarding visitors to determine whether it is safe for them to enter Schengen Zone countries.[60] The ETIAS will be mainly used to facilitate commuting into and within Schengen Zone countries mainly for business, tourist, transit and medical purposes and it will be mandatory for all countries who are Schengen visa-free. Furthermore, it is important to keep in mind that the UK and the Republic of Ireland opted out from participating in the Schengen Agreement. Nevertheless, in light of Brexit, several member states and citizens wonder if the UK and the Republic of Ireland are going to reconsider their opt-out from the Schengen Agreement.

VI. CONCLUSION

Becoming a Schengen Member State would only address one aspect of the multifaceted concepts that entail national and international security and defense measures. As previously mentioned, data and intelligence collection and sharing are extremely important tools for effective national and international security and defense systems, especially in densely populated areas in Europe with transient citizens constantly flowing across borders, which is a perfect breeding ground for domestic and foreign terrorist groups seeking to wreak havoc in the name of their ideology or religious beliefs. As PM May has incessantly stressed, it is imperative that a UK-EU treaty focusing on security and defense measures is reached prior to the end of the transition period. Preferably, a treaty that would provide for the UK's continued participation and collaboration with Europol. Ultimately, European leaders need to set aside their political differences regarding Brexit and coalesce in the interest of safety and security. European leaders—whether UK or EU—

---

[58] Schengen Visa Info, https://www.schengenvisainfo.com/schengen-visa-countries-list/ (last visited Apr. 14, 2018). Over 400 million nationals in 26 Member States have the freedom of travelling across borders without passport checks and border control.

[59] *Id.* The 26 Member States include: Austria, Belgium, Czech Republic, Denmark, Estonia, Finland, France, Germany, Greece, Hungary, Iceland, Italy, Latvia, Lithuania, Luxembourg, Malta, Netherlands, Norway, Poland, Portugal, Slovakia, Slovenia, Spain, Sweden, Switzerland and Liechtenstein.

[60] *Id.*

need to make reaching an agreement on security and defense a matter of both domestic *and* international priority. Otherwise, there may be extreme and irreparable consequences.

PART III:

Future Relationships for the UK

Chapter 15: Private International Law After Brexit: Jurisdiction, Recognition, and Enforcement in Civil and Commercial Matters

Eike Bleckwenn

I. Introduction

A comprehensive system of private international law rules ensures seamless cooperation in cross-border disputes within the European Union (EU). This system is based on mutual trust and reciprocity which both rest on EU membership. Furthermore, European private international law is part of the common legal framework with the Court of Justice of the European Union (CJEU) as the final arbiter, ensuring the uniform application and interpretation of EU law throughout the union. With the prospective withdrawal of the United Kingdom (UK) from the EU, EU private international law will cease to apply vis-à-vis the UK, and the UK will become a third state relative to the remaining EU-27. Despite this divorce, many persons from both sides of the English Channel will continue to interact and do business with each other. Cross-border legal issues will continue to arise and require a legal framework to be resolved. The future framework operating between the UK and the EU will determine how frictionless such cross-border disputes remain, or how cumbersome and costly they may become.

Following a brief overview displaying the status quo and the changes that will occur regarding jurisdiction, recognition, and enforcement in civil and commercial matters due to Brexit (II), the possible solutions to avoid friction in the future cooperation will be analyzed. After looking at options based on the objectives set out by the parties, who both seem willing to reach a bespoke deal (III), the status and provisions of the currently negotiated draft withdrawal agreement on private international law will be analyzed to look for signs of a solution (IV). Given the number of obstacles that could hinder the parties in reaching an agreement, the potential for international treaties to replace the current framework in case of a "hard Brexit" will finally be analyzed (V). It will be shown that though there are numerous possible solutions to bridge the gaps that will arise after Brexit, all of them have serious drawbacks, and most of them conflict with one side's position regarding the future authority of the CJEU, a key issue for the parties to resolve. Without a deal, future cooperation will likely rest on international conventions, especially the Hague Choice of Court Convention. Additionally, the 1968 Brussels Convention might have a comeback that could prove difficult for the UK, since it would also mean that the CJEU jurisdiction would prevail post-Brexit. Given the number of problems and uncertainties that an uncoordinated withdrawal of the UK would cause for private international law matters, it becomes clear that a future cooperation on agreed terms would be beneficial for all involved.

II. EU PRIVATE INTERNATIONAL LAW AND BREXIT

Today's legal conflicts often involve foreign elements. Such a foreign link can add a number of problems to a dispute, most of which are resolved following private international law rules. According to the British understanding of the term,[1] three main issues of private international law can be distinguished: First, the questions of which country's courts are competent to hear a case and have jurisdiction over the parties. Second, the choice of law rules which determine the applicable laws that govern a dispute. And third, under which circumstances a judgment will be recognized and enforced in a foreign jurisdiction.[2]

A. THE STATUS QUO

While each nation applies its own private international law rules, the EU member states are bound by EU law that supersedes their national laws in European contexts. Over the last decades, the EU established a comprehensive regime harmonizing private international law across the union. Important rules with regard to civil and commercial matters are laid out in the Rome I[3] and Rome II Regulations[4] as well as in the Brussels I Recast Regulation[5] (Brussels Ia). While the Rome Regulations deal with choice of law for contractual and non-contractual obligations, Brussels Ia deals with jurisdiction, recognition, and enforcement of court decisions. Several additional, no less important EU private international law instruments complete the European set of rules.[6]

---

[1] *Rühl*, Private international law, foundations, p. 1380, in: Encyclopedia of Private International Law, Edward Elgar Publishing, https://www.e-elgar.com/shop/encyclopedia-of-private-international-law (1 June 2018).
[2] *Id.* pp. 1380-1381.
[3] Regulation EC 593/2008 http://data.europa.eu/eli/reg/2008/593/oj (1 June 2018).
[4] Regulation EC 864/2007 http://data.europa.eu/eli/reg/2007/864/oj (1 June 2018).
[5] Regulation EU 1215/2012 http://data.europa.eu/eli/reg/2012/1215/oj (1 June 2018).
[6] For a comprehensive list see UK Government, Providing a cross-border civil judicial cooperation framework, p. 1, https://assets.publishing.service.gov.uk/government/up-

This comprehensive EU private international law framework provides a high-level of certainty and essentially allows for free movement of judgments across the union.[7] It underpins the single market by allowing EU businesses to engage in cross-border transactions with confidence, preventing delays and reducing costs and uncertainty in cross-border disputes.[8] This framework is of particular importance to the UK, which, unlike any other country in the EU, is a main center for international dispute resolution.[9] Not only is English law[10] frequently the governing law of choice for commercial contracts,[11] but London courts are also often called upon to settle commercial disputes.[12] A strong legal service industry based on these choices is an integral part of the UK's economy, and with regard to European clients, it is largely founded on frictionless cross-border interaction thanks to EU private international law rules.[13] Therefore, much is at stake for the UK in light of the possible loss of access to the EU private international law instruments.

B. STATUS OF EU PRIVATE INTERNATIONAL LAW IN THE UK

To determine the future of EU law after Brexit, one first has to look at how EU law came into the UK.[14] Brussels Ia, as well as Rome I and

---

loads/system/uploads/attachment_data/file/639271/Providing_a_cross-border_civil_judicial_cooperation_framework.pdf (1 June 2018).

[7] *Hess/Requejo-Isidro,* Brexit – Immediate Consequences on the London Judicial Market, http://conflictoflaws.net/2016/brexit-immediate-consequences-on-the-london-judicial-market/ (1 June 2018).

[8] *Hess,* Should Arbitration and European Procedural Law be Separated or Coordinated? http://conflictoflaws.net/2010/guest-editorial-hess-should-arbitration-and-european-procedural-law-be-separated-or-coordinated/ (1 June 2018).

[9] *Rühl,* Oxford Business Law Blog, Brexit Negotiations Series: 'The Effect of Brexit on the Resolution of International Disputes, 13 April 2017, https://www.law.ox.ac.uk/business-law-blog/blog/2017/04/brexit-negotiations-series-'-effect-brexit-resolution-international (1 June 2018).

[10] It has to be kept in mind that when it comes to private international law rules post-Brexit, Scotland and Northern Ireland form separate jurisdictions within the UK, apart from England and Wales, see e.g., https://e-justice.europa.eu/content_which_law_will_apply-340-sc-maximizeMS_EJN-en.do?member=1 (1 June 2018).

[11] Following an International Arbitration Survey, English law governs 40% of global commercial arbitrations, http://www.arbitration.qmul.ac.uk/media/arbitration/docs/2010_InternationalArbitrationSurveyReport.pdf (1 June 2018).

[12] *Id.*

[13] The UK's position as a center of legal and judicial excellence, with experienced courts and lawyers as well as the English law and language are, of course, of major importance as well.

[14] *Hillman/Horlick,* Legal Aspects of Brexit, p. 3, https://scholarship.law.-georgetown.edu/facpub/2028/ (1 June 2018).

II, are EU regulations like most other EU private international law instruments.[15] This means that the UK did not need to transpose them into national law since EU regulations by definition enjoy general application throughout the union.[16] The flipside of this nexus with the EU treaties is that regulations cease to apply after the UK leaves the union.[17] With no national implementation act,[18] they will not form part of the UK's legal body after Brexit. And since the CJEU derives its authority from the EU treaties as well, leaving the union will also end the jurisdiction of the CJEU in the UK.[19] Without an agreement between the parties, there will furthermore not be any transition, since neither Article 50 of the Treaty on the European Union (TEU), which supersedes the otherwise applicable articles of the Vienna Convention on the Law of Treaties (VCLT),[20] nor the EU private international law instruments have transitory provisions.[21] It is therefore important to look at what will happen in the event of a disorderly Brexit with no future agreement.

C. EFFECTS OF BREXIT ON EU PRIVATE INTERNATIONAL LAW

How will losing EU private international law affect questions of jurisdiction, recognition, and enforcement in civil and commercial matters in practice? Currently, a judgment from UK courts essentially enjoys free

---

[15] See UK Government, *supra* note 6 at p. 3-4, listing only two EU directives and twelve EU regulations.

[16] EU regulations are binding in their entirety and directly applicable in all member states, see Art. 288(2) TFEU.

[17] See Art. 50(3) TEU.

[18] It has to be noted that the UK sometimes adopted implementing acts following its dualist approach, see e.g. http://www.legislation.gov.uk/uksi/2009/3064/contents/made for Rome I; however, according to the prevailing opinion those instruments still lose their binding force after Brexit, see *Hess,* Back to the Past: BREXIT und das europäische internationale Privat- und Verfahrensrecht', 36 Praxis des Internationalen Privat- und Verfahrensrechts (2016), p. 410; *Pilich,* Brexit and EU private international law: May the UK stay in? Maastricht Journal of European and Comparative Law 2017, p. 390 http://journals.sagepub.com/doi/pdf/10.1177/1023263X17722327 (1 June 2018).

[19] Leaving aside the jurisdiction regarding the 1968 Brussels Convention, more on that *infra* V.A.

[20] The TEU therefore supersedes Art. 54 et seq. VCLT since Art. 50 TEU is *lex specialis* vis-a-vis the VCLT, see *Ungerer,* Brexit von Brüssel und den anderen EU-Verordnungen zum Internationalen Zivilverfahrens- und Privatrecht, in: Kramme/Baldus/Schmidt-Kessel, Brexit und die juristischen Folgen, 2017, p. 305.

[21] *Id.* p. 306.

movement throughout the EU.[22] It can be enforced against a foreign entity throughout the union without significant additional time or costs.[23] Brussels Ia abolished the formal exequatur,[24] introducing an automatic recognition based on the presumption that a foreign judgment from another EU court is valid.[25] At the same time, the regulation limits the grounds to challenge the enforcement to an absolute minimum,[26] under no circumstance can another EU court review a decision as to its substance.[27]

With a "hard Brexit," meaning a Brexit without an agreement to provide for the future relationship between the EU and the UK,[28] Brussels Ia will automatically cease to apply. Court judgments from UK courts will neither be automatically recognized nor can they be easily enforced in EU member states. The presumption of validity will vanish, as will the limitation of grounds to prevent enforcement. In practice, it will again be necessary to employ foreign attorneys to seek recognition and enforcement of a UK judgment on a case by case basis.[29] Chances to obstruct enforcement of UK judgments will increase, and while the outcome of enforcement abroad will become less certain, loss of time and money seems guaranteed. The fact that the unharmonized system might yield different results when enforcing UK judgments in each of the 27 remaining EU member states due to different private international law rules in each of them and different international or bilateral conventions that may apply, will only exacerbate the problem.[30] Given the possible changes, it may even be questioned whether a previous choice for UK law and UK courts will remain valid. Though it depends on the circumstances of each contract, it seems rather unlikely that Brexit could lead to frustration of contract or trigger material adverse change clauses, at least when applying

---

[22] *Kramer*, Cross-Border Enforcement and the Brussels I-bis Regulation, Netherlands International Law Review 2013, Vol. 60 Issue 3, p. 344 https://ssrn.com/abstract=2372701 (1 June 2018).

[23] See for a detailed analysis of the status quo without Brussels Ia, *id.* at p. 363.

[24] See Art. 53 of Brussels Ia; more details on the exequatur procedure and its importance, *Id.* at p. 346.

[25] *Fitchen*, Brexit and EU private international law: cross-border judgments – unintended consequences http://www.scottishlegal.com/2016/07/08/blog-brexit-and-eu-private-international-law-cross-border-judgments-unintended-consequences/ (1 June 2018).

[26] See Art. 45 of Brussels Ia, http://data.europa.eu/eli/reg/2012/1215/oj (1 June 2018).

[27] See Art. 52 of Brussels Ia, *Id.*

[28] For the common understanding of the terms "soft Brexit" and "hard Brexit" see BBC http://www.bbc.com/news/uk-politics-37507129 (1 June 2018).

[29] See the hypothetical of *Fitchen, supra* note 25.

[30] *Id.*

UK law.[31] However, the result might look quite different in other jurisdictions, further adding to the uncertainties.[32]

To prevent this cliff edge scenarios in case of a disorderly exit of the UK,[33] both sides need to agree to a transition before the UK's withdrawal. And given the importance of the UK's legal sector to its economy, the UK does not want to sit at the sidelines; consequently, it has put forward a proposal illustrating what it is aiming for in the negotiation for a future partnership post-Brexit.[34]

D. What the UK Aims for in the Current Negotiations

According to a paper published by the UK government in August 2017, the UK seeks for a *"new, deep and special partnership with the EU."*[35] In its reply to the EU's position paper on judicial cooperation in civil and commercial matters published one month before, the UK laid out its own goal for cross-border civil judicial cooperation after Brexit. It wants to be outside the direct jurisdiction of the CJEU but seeks to agree on a new close and comprehensive arrangement on private international law with the EU.[36] While international conventions may provide a solution to some extent, the UK does not see them as yet capable of replacing the framework provided by EU law today.[37] The UK, therefore, seeks an agreement that reflects the current close cooperation in cross-border disputes,[38] as part of the "bespoke deal" that Prime Minister May's government is aiming for. However, there are numerous obstacles on the way to achieve this goal to continue the current close cooperation after Brexit.

---

31 See *Gray/Sanitt/Sheftel/Berwick*, Brexit – what might be the contractual consequences?, pp. 8-9 at http://www.nortonrosefulbright.com/files/lexisnexis-banking--financial-services-142370.PDF (1 June 2018).

32 Pointing to a different outcome in Germany compared with the UK: *Weller/ Gonzalo Casas*, Was macht der Brexit mit Dauerverträgen?, in: Frankfurter Allgemeine Zeitung, 7 June 2017, p. 18 (in German).

33 For Brexit cliff edge scenarios compare *Fitchen*, The PIL Consequences of Brexit, Nederlands Internationaal Privaatrecht, 35(3), p. 411 http://www.nipr-online.eu/Default.aspx?site_id=35&level1=15205 (1 June 2018).

34 UK Government, *supra* note 6.

35 *Id.* p. 1.

36 *Id.* p. 2.

37 *Id.* p. 6 para 18.

38 *Id*, p. 6 para 19.

III. A FUTURE AGREEMENT ON CROSS-BORDER CIVIL JUDICIAL COOPERATION

There are different ways in which the UK could theoretically achieve a close and comprehensive partnership with the EU in private international law.

A. AGREEMENT FOR CONTINUOUS APPLICATION OF CURRENT EU LAW

The most straightforward solution would be to agree to a continuous application of the current rules. This solution has not only support in the UK[39] but is also suggested by the EU for the transition period in their draft withdrawal agreement put forward in February 2018.[40] Continuing the current framework seems also possible in light of the fact that the EU did not want the UK to leave the union in the first place and that the UK freely chose to join the EU's civil judicial cooperation in the past. This was despite a special protocol negotiated as part of the 1997 Treaty of Amsterdam that kept the UK (and Ireland) from being bound by EU legislation in this area unless it gave notice of its wish to take part, often referred to as "Europe à la carte."[41] Despite this freedom, the UK did join almost every instrument introduced by the EU, except for matters related to Schengen,[42] and it was able to significantly influence the content of the EU legislation thanks to its unique position to opt in voluntarily.[43]

1. The EC-Denmark Agreement as a Blueprint

How could such future cooperation be achieved practically? The EC-Denmark Agreement is seen as a possible blueprint.[44] Denmark was unable to ratify the Maastricht Treaty and join the home affairs and justice pillar after a referendum in 1992.[45] To enable Denmark to join EU

---

[39] For example, the House of Commons Justice Committee argued for it, see Implications of Brexit for the justice system, p. 16 para 32 https://publications.parliament.uk/pa/cm201617/cmselect/cmjust/750/750.pdf (1 June 2018).

[40] See Title IV, Art. 62-65 of the EU's draft https://ec.europa.eu/commission/sites/beta-political/files/draft_withdrawal_agreement.pdf (1 June 2018).

[41] See *Hartley*, Balance of Competences in the EU: Private International Law, https://assets.publishing.service.gov.uk/government/uploads/system/uploads/attachment_data/file/279275/professor-trevor-hartley-evidence.pdf (1 June 2018).

[42] Schengen refers to an area made up of 26 European states that have officially abolished border control at their mutual borders, see https://ec.europa.eu/home-affairs/what-we-do/policies/borders-and-visas/schengen (1 June 2018).

[43] See for the (positive) impact *Pilich, supra* note 18, p. 7.

[44] House of Commons House of Commons Justice Committee, *supra* note 39.

[45] Denmark was able to ratify the Treaty after a second referendum in 1993, resulting in

private international law instruments nonetheless, the EC-Denmark Agreement of 2005 was concluded. Despite being praised as a ready-made precedent from which to draw inspiration,[46] this model comes with several obstacles for the UK. Not only does it leave Denmark essentially as a rule-taker, but it also requires accepting unconditional CJEU supremacy.[47] And while this may not be a problem for Denmark, still being part of the EU and subject to the CJEU jurisdiction anyway, this looks quite different from the UK's perspective.

2. The Role of the CJEU

It is the UK's position to end the direct jurisdiction of the CJEU in the UK.[48] Unlike private international law matters in particular, taking back control of the UK's laws generally was part of the Brexit campaign,[49] and has since evolved to a clear red-line after Theresa May was appointed prime minister.[50] The UK's rejection of the CJEU was fueled by an increasing influence of European law which, due to the various different legal cultures, often irritates the legal order in EU member states.[51] In part because of the different legal traditions on both sides of the English Channel,[52] CJEU judgments had a special impact on the UK, most notably, the European court struck down longstanding common law doctrines, for example, forum non conveniens and anti-suit injunctions.[53] Leaving the case law aside, there are several further reasons for the UK's criticism,[54] none of which will likely disappear after Brexit. In

---

the Edinburgh Agreement of 1992, since then, Denmark's relationship with the EU is governed by a specific protocol, see https://eur-lex.europa.eu/legal-content/EN/TXT/?uri=CELEX%3A12012E%2FPRO%2F22 (1 June 2018).

46 *Masters/McRae*, What Does Brexit Mean for the Brussels Regime? in: Journal of International Arbitration 33, Special Issue (2016), p. 485 https://www.kluwerlawonline.com/abstract.php?id=JOIA2016029 (1 June 2018).

47 The agreement will automatically terminate in case Denmark does not implement changes made by the EU, Art. 3(7)(c), 4(5)(b), 6(6) https://eur-lex.europa.eu/legal-content/EN/ALL/?uri=celex:22005A1116(01) (1 June 2018).

48 See UK Government *supra* note 6 p. 2 para 2.

49 Though the red-line regarding the CJEU only crystallized after the referendum, see https://www.ft.com/content/32cd1e87-c7d1-3026-86fc-bce5229711d1 (1 June 2018).

50 *Id.*

51 See *Teubner*, Legal Irritants: Good Faith in British Law or How Unifying Law Ends Up in New Differences (1998), Modern Law Review, Vol. 61, pp. 11-32, https://ssrn.com/abstract=876950 (1 June 2018).

52 While civil law systems dominate on the European continent, the UK is part of the common law tradition.

53 See ECJ C-281/02 – Owusu, para 37 and ECJ, C-159/02 - Turner, para 27.

54 Listing delays, lack of clarity and precision, and the mechanism to appoint judges, see *Hartley*, *supra* note 41 p. 4.

fact, continuous CJEU jurisdiction will be even less tolerable for the UK once it leaves the EU since it will no longer be a part of the court. The UK will not have a judge or advocate general[55] appointed from its ranks, making the jurisdiction of the CJEU, a then completely foreign court, even less acceptable.[56]

However, that the EU would agree to waive its requirement regarding the supremacy of the CJEU seems even more unlikely. The role of the CJEU as the only ultimate arbiter when it comes to the interpretation and application of EU law lies at the heart of EU legal framework. The EU has stressed the need to protect the autonomy of the union and its legal order from the outset of the Brexit negotiations,[57] and this position is again reflected in the currently negotiated draft withdrawal agreement.[58] While it never seemed likely that the EU would waive its request, the recent *Achmea* judgment of the European Court of Justice (ECJ) actually reinforced the EU's position, making clear that, based on Art. 344 TFEU, the European court itself will not accept any deviation from its role as the only final arbiter on questions of EU law.[59] The *Achmea* decision is neither an outlier nor can it be seen as a reaction to Brexit, though the judges certainly had Brexit in mind;[60] rather, *Achmea* builds on an earlier opinion handed down by the ECJ in 2013 which prohibited the transfer of competences on issues subject to EU law to any adjudicatory body operating outside of the union.[61] This obligation not to jeopardize the supremacy of the CJEU when it comes to interpreting the EU law will impact future international dispute resolution agreements by the EU, including a potential dispute resolution mechanism between the EU and

---

[55] On the role of the Advocate General compare *Burrows/Greaves,* The Advocate General and EC Law, 2007.

[56] Currently, the UK sends three judges to the CJEU, one judge to the ECJ and two justices to the General Court, which together make up the CJEU, see https://europa.eu/european-union/about-eu/institutions-bodies/court-justice_en (1 June 2018).

[57] European Council (Art. 50) guidelines for Brexit negotiations, http://www.consilium.europa.eu/en/press/press-releases/2017/04/29/euco-brexit-guidelines/ (1 June 2018).

[58] See Art. 62 marked in green in the current draft withdrawal agreement between the parties at https://ec.europa.eu/commission/sites/beta-political/files/draft_agreement_coloured.pdf (1 June 2018), for more see *infra* IV.

[59] See Case C-284/16 Slovak Republic v Achmea BV http://curia.europa.eu/juris/document/document.jsf?text=&docid=199968&pageIndex=0&doclang=en&mode=req&dir=&occ=first&part=1&cid=354883 (1 June 2018).

[60] *Hess,* The Fate of Investment Dispute Resolution after the Achmea Decision of the European Court of Justice (March 30, 2018) p. 20 https://ssrn.com/abstract=3152972 (1 June 2018).

[61] In that particular case, the adjudicatory body concerned was the European Court for Human Rights (ECtHR), see http://curia.europa.eu/juris/liste.jsf?num=C-2/13 (1 June 2018).

the UK after Brexit.[62] Any marginalization of the CJEU's role when EU law is concerned is not only undesirable from the EU's perspective, it is unlawful.[63] This is all the more important since the ECJ will have the last word regarding the compatibility of any agreement reached between the EU and the UK with EU law.[64] As a result, whenever the continuing application of EU private international law instruments is agreed between the EU and the UK, the UK would need to accept jurisdiction of the CJEU regarding any EU law concerned.

3. Political Willingness on Both Sides?

Even if the parties were to overcome this hurdle, it seems anything but certain that the EU would agree to continue the current application of private international law instruments vis-à-vis the UK. For one, it could be seen as cherry picking, especially given the significance of London as a hub for international dispute resolution, making this an issue with substantial economic relevance for the UK. Though the EU did not want the UK to leave the union in the first place and still would prefer the UK to remain an EU member state, as long as the UK stays on its path to depart from the union, the EU might have a stronger interest not to offer the UK a good deal on its way out. The general EU position is that a state that does not live up to the same obligations as an EU member state cannot have the same rights and enjoy the same benefits as a member state.[65] The EU fears that if it were to proceed differently, it would set a dangerous precedent, signaling other member states that it is indeed possible to leave the union and to keep aspects that are favorable while being able to get rid of others that are disliked. From Brussels' perspective, Brexit is therefore perceived as an existential threat to the European project,[66] which is why it is in the EU's interest not to indicate that leaving the union could be beneficial for the departing party. And thus far, there are no indications that the EU will not succeed in putting

---

[62] *Hess, supra* note 60.

[63] *Id.*

[64] Art. 218(11) TFEU empowers a member state, the European parliament, the council and the commission to obtain the opinion of the ECJ as to whether an agreement envisaged is compatible with the EU treaties. If the court finds that it is not, the agreement envisaged may not enter into force unless it or the EU treaties are revised.

[65] See the European Council Guidelines following the United Kingdom's notification under Art. 50 TEU, 29 April 2017, p. 3 para 1 https://www.consilium.europa.eu/media/21763/29-euco-art50-guidelinesen.pdf (1 June 2018).

[66] See https://www.theguardian.com/world/2016/sep/13/jean-claude-juncker-eu-is-facing-existential-crisis (1 June 2018).

its own interests first.[67] This effectively rules out any Brexit deal on private international law with terms more favorable than the EC-Denmark Agreement, since the EU would otherwise be treating a third state better than a member state.

Secondly, while the UK seems to acknowledge the importance of keeping or adequately replacing the EU's private international law instruments,[68] from the EU's perspective, there may even be an interest not to further strengthen but rather weaken London's dominant position on the cross-border judicial market. Several member states are already positioning themselves to attract parts of the UK's legal business in light of the uncertainty caused by Brexit, and those endeavors stand to benefit if the UK's position were further weakened. The very day after the UK sent its formal letter triggering Article 50 TEU to withdraw from the union in March 2017, the courts of Frankfurt, Germany, announced an initiative to strengthen its position as a European spot for commercial litigation.[69] A number of courts from other EU member states also started offering proceedings in commercial matters that are conducted in English.[70] French courts even went a step further, offering not only proceedings in English but also decisions on English law if it was chosen to govern the dispute.[71]

These undertakings are further supported by EU laws reflecting the genuine interest of the union not only to apply mandatory EU law in disputes related to the internal market but also to submit all such disputes to the jurisdiction of a court or arbitral tribunal located in an EU member state.[72] One example is the Markets in Financial Instruments Regulation (MiFIR) that requires third-country firms providing investment services

---

67 See the NY Times "*In Brexit Give-and-Take, Britain Gives and the E.U. Takes*" see https://www.nytimes.com/2018/03/21/world/europe/uk-brexit-summit-theresa-may.html (1 June 2018).

68 House of Commons Justice Committee, *supra* note 38, see also http://www.bbc.com/news/uk-politics-42979920 (1 June 2018).

69 See http://conflictoflaws.net/2017/the-justice-initiative-frankfurt-am-main-2017-law-made-in-frankfurt/ (1 June 2018).

70 Notably France, The Netherlands, Belgium, and Germany, see *Segger/Sandkühler*, Germany steps up the competition for international dispute resolution, https://www.lexology.com/library/detail.aspx?g=688df063-d19d-4259-8a15-73c4ffd1d43e (1 June 2018).

71 See http://www.bbc.com/news/uk-politics-42979920 (1 June 2018); other foreign courts will of course also decide cases if English - or any other foreign - law applies; however, the applicable procedural rules will be different compared to domestic law.

72 See *Hess/Requejo-Isidro*, *supra* note 7.

to offer to submit any disputes relating to such activities to the jurisdiction of a court or arbitral tribunal located in the EU.[73] After Brexit, London will be located in a third state and can no longer simply be chosen as forum for such disputes.[74] This example affecting not only litigation but also arbitration is particularly noteworthy since some suggest that arbitration in the UK could be a solution to the uncertainties with respect to UK litigation in light of Brexit. In addition, it already seems advisable to amend dispute resolution clauses in current financial instruments and securities where the selected forum is located in the UK, in favor of a forum located in one of the remaining 27 EU member states.[75] This is highlighting yet another problematic aspect of Brexit: the legal uncertainty concerning countless private legal instruments that reference UK law, which currently includes EU law but won't anymore after Brexit.[76]

B. A New, Deep and Special Partnership

Another solution is to negotiate a new agreement that covers private international law.[77] The UK seems to have such a goal in mind when promoting a new, deep and special partnership with the EU.[78] Negotiating such a partnership from scratch will, however, be challenging and time-consuming, and the current Brexit negotiations illustrate that progress can be scarce. EU negotiators indicate that even with the additional 21-month transition period currently contemplated in the draft withdrawal agreement which would last until the end of 2020, there may not be sufficient time to form such a new partnership.[79] Even less wide-ranging trade deals, such as CETA negotiated between the EU and Canada,

---

[73] See Art. 46(6) MiFIR, Regulation EU No 600/2014, http://eur-lex.europa.eu/eli/reg/2014/600/oj (1 June 2018).

[74] This includes the London Commercial Court with its large amount of cases involving international parties who's choice of English law is the only link to the UK courts, see https://www.thecityuk.com/assets/2016/Reports-PDF/UK-financial-and-related-professional-services-meeting-the-challenges-and-delivering-opportunities.pdf (1 June 2018).

[75] See *Hess*, Back to the past, https://www.mpg.de/10824865/back-to-the-past (1 June 2018).

[76] Another prominent example highlighting the issue of private instruments relying on EU law is the "Brexit clause" the Irish airline Ryanair plans to includes in ticket, see https://www.reuters.com/Art./uk-britain-eu-ryanair/ryanair-to-put-brexit-clause-into-ticket-sales-for-summer-2019-idUSKBN1FK1ZC (1 June 2018).

[77] *Rühl, supra* note 9.

[78] See UK Government, *supra* note 6.

[79] See https://www.reuters.com/Art./us-britain-eu-transition/britain-wants-to-discuss-length-of-brexit-transition-with-eu-idUSKCN1G51BT and https://www.theguardian.com/politics/2017/oct/23/brexit-transition-period-final-eu-trade-deal-theresa-may (1 June 2018).

or the free trade agreements reached with Korea and Japan, have all taken several years to negotiate and come into force. And the UK is aiming for a far more comprehensive deal especially with regard to trade in services.[80]

One might argue that reaching a deal should be easier, given that the EU and the UK are already in a close relationship. However, this might prove to be a disadvantage rather than an advantage; after all, divorces are rarely easier to negotiate compared to the initiation of a new partnership. And this comparison may well be appropriate since, from an economic standpoint, the new EU-UK relationship will in total not create benefits on either side; rather, economic losses are widely expected.[81] Moreover, negotiating the existing private international law instruments in the EU took years, even though they were based on earlier conventions such as the Rome and Brussels Convention. As a general rule, the more the UK tries to deviate from the existing instruments, making good on promises to take back control over its laws,[82] the more complicated the negotiations will get.

However, if the parties were to reach an agreement—which would also mean overcoming the hurdles mentioned for the continuous application of the current rules[83]—this could be a platform to openly address contentious issues, most notably anti-suit injunctions, disclosures and freezing orders, and schemes of arrangement in restructuring proceedings.[84] A main sticking point will be the CJEU jurisdiction and how, in absence of it, a divergence of court decisions can be prevented. Since this issue is addressed at length below,[85] it suffices to say that the solution provided for in the Lugano Convention, to require courts to "*pay due account*" to each other's precedents, might not provide a viable solution.

---

[80] CETA, the EU-Canada trade deal, has only a minimal section on financial services and requires Canadian firms to set up a EU presence and to comply with EU regulations, see https://www.reuters.com/Art./britain-eu/update-2-eu-offers-uk-limited-trade-deal-no-special-access-for-banks-idUSL5N1QP3BB (1 June 2018).

[81] *Posen,* Drawbridge Economics: The Brexit Reality Check Is Coming, https://piie.com/commentary/op-eds/drawbridge-economics-brexit-reality-check-coming; *Busch/Matthes*, Brexit - the economic impact: IW-Report, No. 10/2016 https://www.econstor.eu/bitstream/10419/157171/1/IW-Report-2016-10.pdf; OECD http://www.oecd.org/newsroom/oecd-study-finds-britons-will-be-paying-a-heavy-brexit-tax-for-many-years-if-uk-leaves-eu.htm (1 June 2018).

[82] See https://www.ft.com/content/32cd1e87-c7d1-3026-86fc-bce5229711d1 (1 June 2018).

[83] See *supra* III.A.2. and 3.

[84] *Hess,* The Unsuitability of the Lugano Convention (2007) to Serve as a Bridge between the UK and the EU after Brexit, MPILux Research Paper 2018 (2), https://ssrn.com/abstract=3118360 (1 June 2018).

[85] See the discussion *infra* at V.B.2.

A possible way forward could be to foresee renegotiation in case of considerable deviation in the case law, maybe even through a standing committee provided for under the agreement,[86] or setting up a separate dispute settlement body[87] or arbitration panels as currently discussed between Switzerland and the EU.[88] However, this will not be something that the parties will easily compromise on, and given the little attention that private international law issues have gotten in the past, it is doubtful that this will be high on the negotiator's agenda moving forward.

C. Rolling over EU Law as a Unilateral Solution

In case no agreement can be reached some suggest the UK could simply "roll-over" the EU law that will cease to apply in order to guard against consequences of a disorderly Brexit. Indeed, with the EU Withdrawal Bill,[89] the UK intends to address the loss of EU law by copying existing EU legislation across into domestic law. However, this unilateral step will not enable the UK to continue the current cooperation in private international law with the EU.

The UK will face the least difficulties with its already announced plan to incorporate the Rome I and II Regulations into domestic law.[90] This step would cover choice of law issues in contractual and non-contractual matters, and, due to the universal application of the Rome Regulations without any reciprocity requirement,[91] this would indeed keep the UK formally in sync with the EU. But as with many other issues of Brexit, simply rolling-over EU law entails several problems. [92] Most notably, it does not prevent divergence over time, be it due to different interpretation and application or later amendments on either side. Even if the UK were to implement future EU reforms, essentially becoming a rule taker,[93] the courts of the EU and UK may still interpret and apply the

---

[86] *Hess, supra* note 84, p. 9 in footnote 41.

[87] On this issue from the EU's perspective http://ec.europa.eu/trade/policy/accessing-markets/dispute-settlement/ (1 June 2018).

[88] See https://www.reuters.com/article/us-swiss-eu/most-swiss-back-plan-for-new-treaty-with-eu-poll-idUSKBN1I007D (1 June 2018).

[89] Initially called the Great Repeal Bill, see http://www.bbc.com/news/uk-politics-39266723 (1 June 2018).

[90] UK Government, *supra* note 6, p. 6 para 19.

[91] See Art. 2 of the Rome I Regulation *supra* note 3 and Art. 3 of the Rome II Regulation *supra* note 4.

[92] See, e.g., for problems with rolling over East African Community-European Union Economic Partnership Agreement, *Kent,* in: Hillman/Horlick, Legal Aspects of Brexit (*supra* note 14), Chapter 5 p. 64.

[93] This might not be a problem with regard to the Rome I and II Regulation due to little expectations for future changes.

laws differently. To ensure equal enforcement, the UK would have to follow future decisions of CJEU.

Finally, rolling-over EU law will not be a solution with regard to the scope of Brussels Ia, which relies on mutual trust and reciprocity that cannot be unilaterally generated by the UK.[94] To gain mutual recognition and enforcement of UK judgments throughout the EU, the deciding court has to be part of the EU, subject to EU law and CJEU supervision ensuring consistent application of EU rules across the member state's courts.[95] With regard to jurisdiction, Brussels Ia does not provide for universal application; rather, it distinguishes between EU member state courts and courts of third states. Therefore, an act of the English parliament cannot provide the reciprocity and mutual trust that underpins the mechanisms of Brussels Ia.[96] Even if the UK were to adopt similar rules, this would not automatically result in reciprocity from the EU's side without a mutual agreement on this issue.

IV. THE DRAFT WITHDRAWAL AGREEMENT

The current draft withdrawal agreement is an indicator of where the parties presently stand. The agreement seeks to treat the UK as if it were an EU member state until the end of 2020, providing access to the EU internal market and customs union largely on current terms to allow for a 21-month transition period from the withdrawal date.[97] The agreement is still a draft, and given the number of outstanding issues, it is important to highlight both parties' understanding that nothing is agreed until a complete deal has been reached.[98]

Title VI of the current draft deals with the future judicial cooperation in civil and commercial matters. Both sides agree on the continuous application of the Rome I and II Regulations in the UK throughout the transition period.[99] Given the previous announcement by the UK to keep those rules after Brexit,[100] this declaration comes as no surprise. However, on the continuing application of many other private international law instruments proposed by the EU, most notably of Brussels Ia,

---

[94] *Fitchen, supra* note 33, p. 417.

[95] *Hess,* supra note 8.

[96] House of Lords, European Union Committee, 17th Report of Session 2016–17, Brexit: justice for families, individuals and businesses?, p. 20 https://publications.parliament.uk/pa/ld201617/ldselect/ldeucom/134/134.pdf (1 June 2018).

[97] The withdrawal date will be on March 30, 2019 at 00:00 CET unless an extension will be agreed, see Art. 50 TEU.

[98] See the European Council (Art. 50) guidelines for Brexit *supra* note 57.

[99] Art. 62 marked in green, see https://ec.europa.eu/commission/sites/beta-political/files/draft_agreement_coloured.pdf (1 June 2018).

[100] See UK Government, *supra* note 6, p. 6 para 19.

no agreement has been reached yet. There is not even a consensus regarding the policy objectives; rather, the discussions between the parties are still ongoing.[101]

However, there are also signs of compromise on controversial issues. Most notably, article 126 provides for continuing power of the EU institutions as provided for in the EU treaties, which means in particular that the CJEU will have full jurisdiction over the UK during the transition period. This UK concession could pave the way for a further application of Brussels Ia during the transition period since it ensures that the requirements set out by the ECJ in the recent *Achmea* judgment will be met.[102]

However, when looking at the entire draft as it currently stands, it becomes clear that the consensus on continuous jurisdiction of the CJEU is limited. Multiple provisions in the current draft specify CJEU jurisdiction throughout or even beyond the transition period, and most of them have not been agreed to yet, signaling the UK's continuous commitment to end the CJEU supervision. There is disagreement especially over the question of supervision of the withdrawal agreement itself.[103]

The current state of negotiations shows that the European court continues to be a serious obstacle on the path to agreement. Since all solutions discussed so far give rise to serious problems, other options have to be analyzed to look for solutions in case no agreement can be reached.

V. INTERNATIONAL CONVENTIONS AS A WAY OUT IN CASE OF NO DEAL

International conventions could provide a way out, and the first to be considered is the Brussels Convention, since it could automatically apply after Brexit.[104]

---

[101] Art. 63 still in white, which, according to the guiding remarks, means that discussions are ongoing as no agreement has yet been found, see *supra* note 99.

[102] *Hess, supra* note 60, p. 20.

[103] See *supra* note 99, Art. 162 (p. 95) and Art. 163 (p. 95): the provisions drafted by the EU suggest that the CJEU issues the final judgment in case a committee representing both parties cannot reach a settlement within three months.

[104] For the sake of completeness, it should be noted that the UK entered into judgment recognition conventions that could become relevant post-Brexit, most notably with The Netherlands, Italy, Belgium, Austria, Norway and (West) Germany; those are predating the UK's accession to the Brussels Convention and will not be further addressed here.

A. THE 1968 BRUSSELS CONVENTION

The Brussels Convention on jurisdiction and the enforcement of judgments in civil and commercial matters (Brussels Convention)[105] was signed in 1968 by the six initial members of the European Economic Community (EEC), with the UK acceding in 1978.[106] Not the EEC as a whole but its member states adopted the convention in their own rights as individual states.[107] The Brussels Convention was the first to establish a comprehensive system for the allocation of jurisdiction and the reciprocal enforcement of judgments between its contracting states. Among EU member states, the convention was largely superseded by the Brussels I Regulation, which was adopted in 2001 and is currently in force in the form of its 2012 recast—Brussels Ia.[108] However, the Brussels I Regulations provide for a continuous application of the Brussels Convention where their territorial scope differs,[109] which is the case with regard to a few dependent overseas territories of EU member states.[110] This is also the reason why the Brussels Convention is still valid UK law today.[111]

1. Arguments for a Revival

The Brussels Convention was concluded for an unlimited period[112] and does not provide for its own termination provisions. Whether it will be applicable between the EU and the UK after Brexit, however, seems

---

[105] The convention consists of two additional protocols from 1968 and 1971, see the legal texts at https://curia.europa.eu/common/recdoc/convention/en/c-textes/_brux-textes.htm (1 June 2018)

[106] The Brussels Convention became part of UK law under the Civil Jurisdiction and Judgments Act 1982, see https://uk.practicallaw.thomsonreuters.com/0-205-5104?transitionType=Default&contextData=(sc.Default)&firstPage=true&bhcp=1 (1 June 2018).

[107] This was different regarding the most recent Lugano Convention and the Hague Convention on Choice of Court Agreements that were adopted by the European Community (EC) respective the EU for its member states, made possible in the Treaty of Amsterdam that added the required competences in the field of private international law.

[108] See Art. 68(1) of Regulation EU 1215/2012 http://data.europa.eu/eli/reg/2012/1215/oj (1 June 2018).

[109] *Masters/McRae*, *supra* note 46, p. 493; *Rothschild*, Jurisdiction and Brexit: Back to the Brussels Convention by default? https://brexit.law/2016/07/08/jurisdiction-and-brexit-back-to-the-brussels-convention-by-default/ (1 June 2018).

[110] Especially Aruba and French Overseas Collectives, see *Dickinson*, Back to the future: the UK's EU exit and the conflict of laws, Journal of Private International Law, 12:2, p. 204, https://doi.org/10.1080/17441048.2016.1209847 (1 June 2018).

[111] See Section 1(4) of the Civil Jurisdiction and Judgments Act 1982, providing for a hierarchy of the different Regulations and Conventions, and Section 2(1): "*The Brussels Conventions shall have the force of law in the United Kingdom, and judicial notice shall be taken of them.*" http://www.legislation.gov.uk/ukpga/1982/27/section/2 (1 June 2018).

[112] See Art. 66 of the Brussels Convention, *supra* note 105.

unclear.[113] One key question is if it was the intention of the EU and its member states to terminate the Brussels Convention in cases where the territory is now covered by Brussels Ia, or if the new EU regulation just added another layer, leaving the convention intact so that it continues to apply once the additional layer is removed.

As a multinational treaty, the Brussels Convention is part of public international law. And though neither the EU nor all contracting states signed on to the Vienna Convention on the Law of Treaties (VCLT),[114] the CJEU, being the final arbiter with regards to the Brussels Convention,[115] applies the VCLT when it reflects rules of customary international law.[116] This is the case for Article 59 VCLT which provides for an implied termination or suspension of a treaty by conclusion of a later treaty.[117] The question, therefore, is whether there was an implied termination in the meaning of this article.

The VCLT provides for an implied termination only if all parties concluded a later treaty, and (a) when this treaty covers the subject matter of the earlier treaty completely, or (b) when the provisions of the two treaties are completely incompatible, VCLT Art. 59(1). The latter alternative does not apply here since the Convention and Brussels Ia are compatible; in fact, they are intended to and do apply simultaneously. As for the first alternative, the better arguments do not support a termination after Brexit. First, neither Brussels I nor Brussels Ia, both being EU regulations, is a treaty within the meaning of VCLT Art. 59(1).[118] Secondly,

---

[113] Pro revival *Ungerer, supra* note 20; *Rothschild,* Jurisdiction and Brexit: Back to the Brussels Convention by default? https://brexit.law/2016/07/08/jurisdiction-and-brexit-back-to-the-brussels-convention-by-default/_(1 June 2018); listing arguments for both sides are *Fitchen, supra* note 33, p. 423; *Dickinson, supra* note 110, p. 204 et subsequent; *Masters/McRae, supra* note 46; against a revival *Hess, supra* note 18; *Pilich, supra* note 18, p. 714; *Rühl,* Judicial Cooperation In Civil And Commercial Matters After Brexit: Which Way Forward? International and Comparative Law Quarterly, 67(1), 99-128; *Rühl, supra* note 9.

[114] A notable exception among the EU member states is France, which has not signed the VCLT.

[115] See the 1971 Protocol *supra* note 105.

[116] See e.g., Case C-162/96 Racke v. Hauptzollamt (1998), para 24: "*[I]t should be noted that even though the Vienna Convention does not bind either the Community or all its Member States, a series of its provisions (...) reflect the rules of international law which lay down (...) the principle that a change of circumstances may entail the lapse or suspension of a treaty.*" https://eur-lex.europa.eu/legal-content/EN/TXT/?uri=CELEX%3A61996CJ0162 (1 June 2018).

[117] See *Dubuisson,* The Vienna Conventions on the Law of Treaties, Corten & Klein, 2011, Vol. II, Part V Art. 59.

[118] *Id.*; *Masters/McRae, supra* note 46, p. 493.

the EU that enacted those regulations is a body *sui generis*[119] and does not meet the definition of a state within the meaning of the VCLT. Thirdly, even if one were to apply the provision, Brussels Ia did not replace the Brussels Convention, since it does not cover the same territory, which is also why article 68 Brussels Ia states that the Brussels Convention will only be superseded as between EU member states, which the UK will no longer be after Brexit. Likewise, recital 23 Brussels Ia states that the Brussels Convention "*continues to apply*," indicating that outside the scope of EU law, the Brussels Convention remains the law of the land.[120] Fourthly, article 59 VCLT limits the scope of implied abrogation of a treaty to situations where all parties to the first treaty are parties to the subsequent treaty,[121] which is also not the case with respect to Brussels Ia and the Brussels Convention. Neither is the EU nor were the EC, or the EEC, party to the Brussels Convention; only some—not all[122]—of their member states are.[123] It can therefore well be argued that article 59(2) VCLT applies, which provides for a mere suspension of operation. Finally, it is unlikely that Brexit can be seen as another ground for termination, e.g., a fundamental change of circumstances that could, in combination with other circumstances, invoke a right to terminate following article 62 VCLT. Such a right requires that the circumstances be the essential basis for the consent of the parties to be bound by the treaty. However, it was not a condition that the UK join the Brussels Convention when it joined the EC, the EU predecessor at that time; rather, it was the motivation for doing so.[124]

2. Implications of the Uncertain Situation

It has to be noted that the question of whether the Brussels Convention will apply after Brexit is not as clear-cut as the arguments laid out above might suggest. The rather formal arguments listed leave room for an opposing view, especially based on the strong link between the EEC and EC treaties and the Brussels Convention.[125] For the purpose of this chapter, however, it suffices to say that there is a certain probability for

---

[119] *Hlavac,* Less than a State, More than an International Organization: The Sui Generis Nature of the European Union https://ssrn.com/abstract=1719308 ; *Phelan,* What Is Sui Generis About the European Union?, International Studies Review, Vol. 14, No. 3, pp. 367-385, http://www.jstor.org/stable/23280306 (1 June 2018).
[120] *Masters/McRae, supra* note 46, p. 493.
[121] See *Dubuisson, supra* note 117, p. 1339 para 33.
[122] The 13 EU member states that joined the union after 2004 are not party to the Brussels Convention.
[123] See *Fitchen, supra* note 33, p. 423.
[124] *Masters/McRae, supra* note 46, p. 493.
[125] See *Dickinson, supra* note 110, p. 205, listing four arguments the CJEU could make to rule against a revival.

its revival, which may well lead to disputes, not only in the UK but also in the member states that would be affected. In such cases, the CJEU will have the final say,[126] which is important for two reasons. First, it means that the CJEU would still have direct jurisdiction over UK courts. Secondly, and closely related to the first issue, UK courts would be prevented from applying common law doctrines. Specifically, *forum non conveniens* would not apply,[127] nor could anti-suit injunctions[128] be issued in cases where a court of another state party to the convention was first seized, since both decisions issued by the CJEU that currently prevent UK courts to do so were based on the Brussels Convention.

Would the Brussels Convention, if applicable, at least help the UK to bridge gaps resulting from Brexit? While it may provide some comfort since today's Brussels Ia is still founded on the rules of the Brussels Convention and given that the UK common law that could take its place instead has not been used much during the past decades, the benefit of applying the Brussels Convention appears limited at best. The 1968 document is largely outdated and does not contain the significant improvements that were made in the 2001 Brussels I and the 2012 Brussels Ia Regulation.[129] Finally, not all member states of the EU are contracting states: while the 14 EU member states that joined the EU before 2004 are, the 13 newer member states are not. Thus, the Brussels Convention would not apply vis-à-vis the latter.

Given the uncertainties linked to a possible revival of the Brussels Convention – the continuous CJEU oversight, its dated provisions, and the limited territorial scope – the UK is well advised to look for alternative solutions, which may be found in the Lugano Convention.

B. ACCESSION TO THE 2007 LUGANO CONVENTION

The 2007 Lugano Convention (Lugano II)[130] resembles the first 2001 Brussels I Regulation before its 2012 recast. It replaced its predecessor, the 1988 Lugano Convention,[131] which extends the rules on jurisdiction, recognition, and enforcement in civil and commercial matters

---

[126] *Id.*

[127] ECJ C-281/02 - Owusu, para 37, http://curia.europa.eu/juris/liste.jsf?language=en&num=C-281/02 (1 June 2018).

[128] ECJ, C-159/02 - Turner, para 27, http://curia.europa.eu/juris/liste.jsf?language=en&num=C-159/02 (1 June 2018).

[129] *Masters/McRae, supra* note 46, p. 492.

[130] See http://data.europa.eu/eli/convention/2007/712/oj (1 June 2018).

[131] The question can be raised if the 1988 Lugano Convention may spring to live after Brexit, however, the better arguments indicate a termination, see *Masters/McRae, supra* note 46, p. 494; *Dickinson, supra* note 110, p. 204.

from the 1968 Brussels Convention to members of the European Free Trade Association (EFTA). Lugano II was ratified by the EU with effect for all member states,[132] which means that the UK is not a member in its own right and will lose membership after Brexit.[133] However, the current draft withdrawal agreement provides for the right of the UK to negotiate international agreements even before its departure from the EU, which, inter alia, enables the UK to prepare to rejoin Lugano II. And the UK government announced that it indeed intends to do so.[134] Lugano II would then apply between the UK and all EU member states[135] as well as vis-à-vis all EFTA states except for Lichtenstein, providing an even wider territorial scope than an agreement with the EU alone does.[136]

Acceding to Lugano II is possible in two situations.[137] First, the convention can be joined by any member of the EFTA or the EU. Secondly, any third state may accede subject to the unanimous agreement of all contracting parties.[138] The latter will likely be the UK's only option, since becoming a full-fledged EFTA member would keep the UK in the single market requiring, among other things, continuous free movement of people,[139] which is a red-line for the UK. However, based on the political arguments made earlier,[140] it is anything but certain that there is the political will, especially from the EU's side, to have the UK rejoin Lugano II post-Brexit.[141]

1. Characteristics of the 2007 Lugano Convention

Assuming that the UK could rejoin Lugano II, this is often seen as a suitable solution to fill the gap that Brussels Ia will leave.[142] Though the UK government intends to continue to participate in Lugano II, it specifically sees this as the basis for judicial cooperation with Norway, Iceland, and Switzerland.[143] The main reason why the UK seems to prefer a

---

[132] See Art. 69(1) Lugano II.

[133] Except for Denmark which because if its specific status with regard to juridical cooperation had to become a party to the Lugano II Convention in its own right.

[134] See UK Government, *supra* note 6, p. 6 para 22.

[135] This would also include Denmark despite the fact that Denmark did not join the EU home affairs and justice pillar (see above III.1.a), since Denmark joined Lugano II in its own right, see Art. 69(1) Lugano II.

[136] *Masters/McRae*, *supra* note 46, p. 490.

[137] See Art. 71 Lugano II *supra* note 130.

[138] See Art. 72 Lugano II for the requirements including the formalities; *Masters/McRae*, *supra* note 46, p. 491.

[139] See http://www.efta.int/eea/policy-areas/persons (1 June 2018).

[140] See *supra* III.A.3.

[141] See *Hess*, *supra* note 18, pp. 414-415.

[142] See *Masters/McRae*, *supra* note 46, p. 487; *Rühl*, *supra* note 113, p. 120; *Dickinson*, Close the Door on Your Way Out, ZEuP 2017, p. 558.

[143] See UK Government, *supra* note 6, p. 6 para 22, while the use of Lugano II towards

different solution with the EU, though Lugano II could apply here as well, may well be the improvements achieved through Brussels Ia.[144] Those changes, which the UK had particularly lobbied for, would be lost since Lugano II is based on the earlier 2001 Brussels I Regulation. And there seems to be little prospect that the convention will be updated soon.[145] Important improvements missing are, among others, protection against the Italian torpedo,[146] as well as the abolishment of the exequatur.[147]

At the same time, a signature feature of Lugano II is that, unlike the Brussels Convention and Brussels Ia, it does not provide for CJEU supervision to ensure uniform interpretation. Following protocol 2 of the convention, the courts of all contracting states are only required to "*pay due account*" to the principles laid down by any relevant decision delivered by courts of the other contracting states concerning provisions of Lugano II.[148] This mechanism could help the UK keep its promise to end the CJEU jurisdiction over UK courts while also meet the EU's requirement to keep the European court as the only final arbiter of EU law.

2. An Illusion of Uniformity?

However, it is doubtful if this solution can effectively prevent divergence between the EU and UK courts. Most notably, the UK's common law system is uniquely different compared to all other Lugano II contracting states not subject to CJEU jurisdiction whose legal systems follow the civil law tradition. Given this general potential for greater discrepancies, it is important to consider what *paying due account* means in practice.

In essence, it is nothing more than a declaration of goodwill, coupled with an obligation to highlight and explain if a court intends to depart

---

the EU is not excluded, it is clear that the UK seeks a closer cooperation with the EU based on Brussels Ia.

144 See Art. 73(1) Brussels Ia: "*This Regulation shall not affect the application of the 2007 Lugano Convention.*"

145 The Standing Committee discussed options to bring Lugano II in line with Brussels Ia but made no recommendation, see https://www.bj.admin.ch/bj/en/home/wirtschaft/privatrecht/lugue-2007.html (1 June 2018).

146 Unlike Art 31(2) Brussels Ia Lugano II still gives priority to the court first seized despite an exclusive choice of court following *Gasser*. http://curia.europa.eu/juris/liste.jsf?language=en&num=C-116/02 (1 June 2018) on the Italian Torpedo *Panighetti*, Has London Outmaneuvered the Italian Torpedo? https://elibrary.law.psu.edu/arbitrationlawreview/vol5/iss1/15/ (1 June 2018).

147 Art. 39 Brussels Ia, *supra* note 5.

148 See Art. 1 of Protocol No 2 https://curia.europa.eu/common/recdoc/convention/en/c-textes/lug02-idx.htm_(1 June 2018).

from another court's previous decision.[149] This not only leaves the option to ignore the CJEU's precedents, but one also has to ask what would happen if a court were not even to make the effort—deliberately or negligently—to mention relevant decisions from other courts. Under Lugano II, not only is divergence possible, there is no explicit requirement to highlight it, not to mention that not doing so will have no direct consequences, leaving nothing but a weak declaration of willingness to follow other courts' precedents.[150]

A closer look at decisions from Swiss courts applying Lugano II seems to confirm this assumption, revealing that the mechanism provides for neither uniform nor cohered application of the convention.[151] While the Swiss courts do not deviate from core concepts thus far,[152] this might well prove to be different with respect to the UK given the greater differences in legal traditions that have to be bridged.[153] And preventing divergence is much more relevant when it comes to the UK, for two main reasons. First, while the population of Norway, Switzerland, and Iceland together is less than 14 million people, more than 65 million people live in the UK, resulting in considerably more lawsuits. Secondly, the UK is the major center for international dispute resolution in Europe, further increasing the number of relevant cases brought before UK courts, making divergence a much more important issue.

Since the accession of the UK to Lugano II will most likely require EU approval, this analysis provides further arguments why such EU approval may be withheld. Though the UK is currently party to Lugano II, the situation changes considerably after it leaves the EU, since it is also leaving CJEU oversight. At a bare minimum, the EU would be well advised to require a stronger mechanism to ensure coherent interpretation and application of Lugano II by EU and UK courts.[154] Otherwise, the parties may end up with nothing but an illusion of uniformity in the long run. At the same time, the UK itself should carefully weigh the benefits of joining Lugano II, since it would further prevent UK courts from using common law doctrines previously struck down by the CJEU, aligning

---

149 *Hess, supra* note 84, p. 5.

150 *Id.*

151 *Id.* p. 6, distinguishing between cases with an open as well as with not disclosed deviation from the CJEU.

152 *Id.* p. 6.

153 *Id.* p. 6 et subsequent, listing two examples: anti-suit injunctions and restructuring proceedings in the UK.

154 *Id.* p. 7-8; this might, on the other hand, provoke rejection on behalf of the UK, see *Beaumont*, Respecting Reverse Subsidiarity as an excellent strategy for the EU at The Hague Conference on Private International Law, p.4, https://www.abdn.ac.uk/law/documents/CPIL_Working_paper_2016_3_revised.pdf (1 June 2018).

the country with the European court in one way or another. While the revival of the 1968 Brussels Convention may yield a similar result vis-à-vis 13 EU member states, joining Lugano II would further cement this issue.

C. THE HAGUE CHOICE OF COURT CONVENTION

Given the number of difficulties that rejoining Lugano II would entail, it is sensible that the UK also announced its intention to remain a leading member in the Hague Conference and to participate in Hague Conventions which it already joined by virtue of its EU membership.[155] The 2005 Choice of Court Convention[156] will prove to be an especially useful tool post-Brexit when it comes to providing recognition and enforcement of exclusive choice of court agreements as well as judgments made by a court so chosen throughout the EU without CJEU oversight. Though the UK will lose its membership upon Brexit,[157] it will be able to ratify the convention without requiring consent by other parties.[158]

However, the Choice of Court Convention is much narrower in scope compared to Brussels Ia or Lugano II, since it only applies when the parties have implemented an exclusive choice of court provision in their contract.[159] Though the territorial scope of his convention is also limited, it would cover the EU without Denmark,[160] and additionally Mexico and Singapore.[161] Not covered would be the EFTA states. Others, most notably China and the United States, signed the convention, but did not ratify yet.

Three main features of the convention can be highlighted: First, the court of a signatory state exclusively chosen by the parties must hear the case and cannot declare *forum non conveniens* unless the court choice itself is null and void.[162] Second, parallel proceedings will be avoided since

155 See UK Government, *supra* note 6, p. 6 para 21 and 22.

156 See https://www.hcch.net/en/instruments/conventions/full-text/?cid=98; not to be confused with the *Hague Convention on the Recognition and Enforcement of Foreign Judgments in Civil and Commercial Matters* from 1971, which has not been widely ratified, see https://www.hcch.net/en/instruments/conventions/status-table/?cid=78 (1June 2018).

157 *Ahmed*, Brexit and English Jurisdiction Agreements, https://aberdeenunilaw.wordpress.com/2016/07/20/brexit-and-english-jurisdiction-agreements-a-look-into-the-post-referendum-legal-landscape/ (1 June 2018).

158 *Id.*

159 Future conventions might narrow the gap, see *Beaumont*, *supra* note 154 p. 4.

160 See recital 9 of the Council Decision https://eur-lex.europa.eu/legal-content/EN/TXT/?uri=celex%3A32014D0887 (1 June 2018).

161 For the Contracting States see https://www.hcch.net/en/instruments/conventions/status-table/?cid=98 (1 June 2018).

162 See Art. 5(1) and (2) of the Choice of Court Convention, *supra* note 156.

every court not chosen by the parties must suspend or dismiss proceedings if seized, subject only to limited exceptions.[163] Third, the convention provides for an international framework to recognize and enforce judgments issued by courts of other contracting states exclusively chosen by the parties.[164]

Despite its narrow scope, the UK would still significantly benefit from rejoining the convention. Almost every commercial contract provides for a choice of court clause, which will be deemed exclusive under the Choice of Court Convention as long as its permissiveness is not explicitly stated. Hence, if the parties continue to choose UK courts in their commercial contract, judgments would remain enforceable throughout most of the EU, protecting the UK's position as dominant litigation hub, especially in commercial contract matters. Additionally, UK courts may be able to issue anti-suit injunctions in case of exclusive court agreements in favor of them.[165] It must be noted, however, that if the Brussels Convention continues to apply, such practice could collide with the principle of mutual trust currently preventing UK courts from issuing anti-suit injunctions.[166]

All in all, the Hague Choice of Court Convention will be beneficial for the UK especially in case of a hard Brexit since the EU cannot stop the UK from rejoining it.[167] Once the UK is a party again, the convention will protect UK courts exclusively chosen by the parties and ensure enforcement of judgments handed down by UK courts throughout the EU, though not in Denmark or the EFTA states.[168]

VI. CONCLUSION

For over 70 years, the path of European national states has been to advance cooperation, to remove boundaries and to grow closer together. Brexit is the first major event in recent years that is heading in the opposite direction. Despite Brexit, both the EU and the UK publicly aim to

---

[163] See Art. 6 of the Choice of Court Convention, *supra* note 156, listing limited grounds for exceptions.

[164] See chapter III of the convention (Art. 8-15), *supra* note 156, with limited exceptions.

[165] Arguing for the possibility to issue anti-suit injunction are *Ahmed/Beaumont*, Exclusive choice of court agreements, Journal of Private International Law, 13:2, pp. 386-410, https://doi.org/10.1080/17441048.2017.1348782; see also *Ahmed/Beaumont,* I thought we were exclusive? Some issues with the Hague Convention on Choice of Court, Brussels Ia and Brexit, https://aberdeenunilaw.wordpress.com/tag/brussels-ia-regulation/ (1 June 2018).

[166] See ECJ, C-159/02 - Turner, para 27, http://curia.europa.eu/juris/liste.jsf?language=en&num=C-159/02 (1 June 2018).

[167] *Ahmed/Beaumont*, *supra* note 165, also on the differences when applying Brussels Ia.

[168] *Ahmed*, *supra* note 157.

remain a close partnership when it comes to future civil judicial cooperation. However, the devil is in the details, and a closer look at both sides' positions reveals several conflicting conditions, making it difficult to facilitate the UK's departure without both sides parting ways in their judicial cooperation as well.

This chapter has shown that though there are several ways to move forward, none meet both sides' requirements, and the jurisdiction of the CJEU is one major sticking point. The UK intends to end the influence of the European court. And after Brexit, when the UK has none of its judges remaining on the ECJ's bench, this will only become a more contentious issue. The EU, on the other hand, stands firmly behind its goal to protect the autonomy of the EU and its legal order, which includes the role of the CJEU as the final arbiter in cases where EU law is involved. The recent *Achmea* judgment cemented the EU's position even further, making it virtually impossible to apply EU law in the UK without CJEU oversight.

What possible ways out can be drawn from this analysis? During the transition period, the parties should agree to continue as much of the current legal framework as possible. Extending the presently applicable rules until a new final framework—in whatever form—will come into force saves all involved the need to adapt multiple times, causing nothing but additional friction, costs, and legal uncertainty. After all, uncertainty is one of the major threats businesses face when it comes to Brexit.

After Brexit, including a potential transition period, two possible scenarios can be anticipated. The first and most likely outcome would be a "soft Brexit" based on a mutual agreement between the parties including terms for private international law. While both sides would benefit from avoiding uncertainty, the UK stands to profit the most if it can secure the necessary framework to keep its position as the leading center for international dispute resolution. After all, when it comes to legal services relating to continental Europe, the UK's current position is largely based on EU private international law instruments. Another advantage of a mutual agreement is its possibility to provide for a smooth transition. Brexit does raise multiple questions, for example, what will happen with court proceedings instituted before Brexit that go beyond the divorce? What laws shall apply? Will the UK's courts still be required to refer to the ECJ in cases initiated before Brexit even if the referral only becomes necessary after the UK leaves the union? And will the UK's courts even be allowed to call upon the ECJ after the EU treaties providing for such right cease to apply? These and numerous other questions would ideally be resolved in a joint agreement between the parties.

As a general rule for the negotiations to reach a future deal, the deeper the continuous partnership—and the UK seeks a close partnership—the greater the likelihood that the CJEU will have to be part of the solution. With this being an Achilles' heel, it remains possible that no deal can be reached. This leads to the second scenario: a "hard Brexit." Without an agreement between the EU and the UK specifying their future cooperation regarding jurisdiction, recognition, and enforcement in civil and commercial matters, the only step the UK can currently take unilaterally is to join the Hague Conventions, most notably the Choice of Court Convention. While the 2007 Lugano II Convention requires the EU's approval and has several shortcomings, the 1968 Brussels Convention might only add to the complexity, posing difficult questions as to whether it will be revived and on top of it, maintaining CJEU supervision over UK courts.

In any event, no matter how "hard" the Brexit, CJEU case law will most likely remain relevant in the UK either way. Businesses that want to sell beyond the English Channel will have to respect EU standards as defined by the European court. Given this inherent limitation to take back control, some concessions might be worth making to reach a mutually beneficial deal.

CHAPTER 16: RULES OF ORIGIN: THE IMPACT ON POST-BREXIT TRADE

JACOB TRAVERS

I. INTRODUCTION

The trade relationship between the United Kingdom and the European Union has been a touchstone issue since the beginning of the Brexit referendum campaign. The supporters of Leave and Remain both used broad statements about trade as proof that their position would strengthen the UK in the long term. Although the exact date on which the UK will leave the EU depends on the outcome of negotiations, its swift approach makes clear the need to examine all aspects of UK trade. Minutiae that have long been the bailiwick of trade negotiators and lawyers now need to enter popular discourse to ensure that voters and their representatives can make informed decisions. This chapter will examine rules of origin and their implications for Brexit.

Every modern trade deal contains a lengthy section dedicated to rules of origin. These agreements describe rules of origin in great detail—the text defining the preferential system of rules of origin in NAFTA is around 200 pages.[1] Rules of origin are a critical part of determining the extent to which preferential trade agreements will create economic benefits.[2] The origin requirements differ from one agreement to the next.[3] Rules of origin have gained in popularity as a response to the lowering of other trade barriers.[4] Rules of origin were simpler to apply prior to the rise to prominence of extended, transnational supply chains.[5] Producers of goods with large numbers of components can now source those intermediate goods from all over the world—creating a global market for goods used at every step of production. And administrative burdens for companies rise when they have to comply with a variety of systems for determining the origin of a product.[6] The European Union has used its economic power to impose its preferred origin classification system on the countries it negotiates trade deals with. After exiting the

---

[1] Hatem Mabrouk, *Rules of Origin as International Trade Hindrances*, 5 ENTREPRENEURIAL BUS. L.J. 97, 165 (2010).

[2] PAUL BRENTON, RULES OF ORIGIN IN FREE TRADE AGREEMENTS 1 (2003).

[3] Mabrouk, *supra* note 1, at 165.

[4] *Id.* at 103.

[5] Joseph A. LaNasa III, *Rules of Origin and the Uruguay Round's Effectiveness in Harmonizing and Regulating them*, 90 AM. J. INT'L L. 625, 625 (1996).

[6] Mabrouk, *supra* note 1, at 165.

EU, the United Kingdom is unlikely to have enough economic power to dictate terms to its important trading partners.

II. WHAT ARE RULES OF ORIGIN?

Rules of origin come in two different forms—preferential and non-preferential. Non-preferential rules of origin are used for a variety of purposes, including gathering trade statistics, enforcing government procurement rules, and applying trade policy instruments such as anti-dumping and countervailing duties measures.[7] The European Union makes extensive use of these and they apply to trade between it and some major economies with which it does not have trade agreements, like the United States and China. Preferential rules of origin, however, will be the focus of this chapter. These are used to determine if a good originates from a country that has a special trading arrangement with the importing country.[8] These special trade arrangements include mutual agreements—such as regional trade agreements, free trade agreements, or customs unions—and unilaterally granted privileges—like the Generalized System of Preferences.[9] The rules of origin in the UK's current trade deals affect domestic production and economic output and that will not change. The only question is to what extent will the landscape on which companies in the UK operate transform because of the changes to future UK trade arrangements.

A. *THE LEGAL BASIS FOR RULES OF ORIGIN*

The modern world trading system is underpinned by the World Trade Organization (WTO). A fundamental goal of the General Agreement on Tariffs and Trade (GATT) and its successor, the WTO, was to encourage global trade. These agreements did this by introducing the most favored nation (MFN) principle requiring members to provide other members the same tariff rates.[10] However, article XXIV of the GATT creates an exception to the principle of nondiscrimination for free trade areas and customs unions—this allows for the use of restrictions like rules of origin.[11] The Uruguay Round of WTO negotiations concluded that "for the purposes…of this Agreement, rules

---

[7] Final Act Embodying the Results of the Uruguay Round of Multilateral Trade Negotiations, Apr. 15, 1994, 1868 U.N.T.S. 397 (1994), available at http://www.wto.org/english/docs_e/legal_e/22-roo.pdf [hereinafter Agreement on Rules of Origin].

[8] *Id.*

[9] *Id.*

[10] General Agreement on Tariffs and Trade, Oct. 30, 1947, 61 Stat. A-11, 55 U.N.T.S. 194, Art. I [hereinafter GATT].

[11] *Id.* at Art. XXIV.

of origin shall be defined as those laws, regulations and administrative determinations of general application applied by any Member to determine the country of origin of goods provided such rules of origin are not related to contractual or autonomous trade regimes leading to the granting of tariff preferences."[12] Rules of origin are necessary to ensure that the exporters in countries that are parties to trade agreements play by the rules, but they can also be employed to subvert the putative goal of lowering trade barriers for all.

The WTO has attempted to prevent members from using non-tariff barriers, like rules of origin, to counteract the effects of trade liberalization. The countries that were parties to the Uruguay Round agreed that rules of origin must be "objective, understandable and predictable."[13] The outcome of the negotiations stated that "...members shall ensure that...rules of origin are not used as instruments to pursue trade objectives directly or indirectly."[14] Given the history of countries creating trade deals that overly protected domestic industries, this was a worthy goal. Even after the Uruguay Round, however, rules of origin continue to be used as non-tariff barriers to protect domestic and regional interests at the cost of consumers and foreign producers.

B. HOW IS THE ORIGIN OF A PRODUCT DETERMINED?

Trade agreements use a variety of methods to determine if a good imported or exported from a country that is party to the agreement should be granted the status of originating from that country for the purpose of gaining preferential tariff rates. This is necessary because trade agreements require that all goods carry only one country of origin. The classification of a wholly obtained good, one that is grown or extracted (or made entirely from domestically grown or extracted materials), is straightforward. But most manufactured goods use at least some parts from abroad, so the sufficient processing or substantial transformation tests are frequently used to determine the origin of these goods.

C. CLASSIFICATION

The three main methods used for determining if sufficient processing or substantial transformation has occurred are (i) a change of tariff classification or heading, (ii) a set minimum amount of domestic value has been added, or (iii) a specific manufacturing process has

---

12 Agreement on Rules of Origin.

13 *Id.* at Article 9(c) (1986).

14 *Id.* at Art. II.

occurred.[15] The minimum amount of domestic value and specific manufacturing process tests are straightforward and as described by their names—although they can be complex as they relate to particular products. The change of tariff classification system utilizes the Harmonized System tariff classification produced by the World Customs Organization to measure the transformation of a product for origin purposes.[16] The change in tariff heading rule, which is favored in treaties of the European Union, requires a change in the four-digit heading of a good in the Harmonized System.[17] Most of the trade agreements of the EU utilize a combination of all three methods—change in tariff heading, minimum EU content, and a list of specific manufacturing processes—for determining if sufficient processing or a substantial transformation has occurred.[18] The *ad valorem*, or value-added, test provides finished goods manufacturers with more flexibility than the change of tariff category, or change of tariff heading, method for determining the origin of a product because it does not presumptively exclude intermediate goods manufacturers from third countries.[19]

D. CUMULATION

Because a goal of trade agreements is to encourage cross-border supply chains—agreements often include provisions that allow countries to count materials made by, or wholly obtained in, the other parties as domestic products for the purposes of origin certification. Bilateral cumulation is when country A and country B agree that their mutual imports will count as the domestic products of country A for the purposes of exporting the finished product to country B, and vice versa.[20]

Diagonal cumulation occurs in a regional trade agreement where all inputs from any regional trading partner count as the domestic product of the exporting country for the purpose of exports within the regional trade agreement.[21] If countries A, B, and C are parties to an agreement, diagonal cumulation would allow for the intermediate goods from country C to count as domestic goods of country B when used to create a finished good in country B that is then exported to country A. This could also hold true outside of regional trading scheme if C and B have

---

[15] BRENTON, *supra* note 2, at 2.

[16] Jong Bum Kim, *Exclusionary Rules of Origin of Mega-RTAs under WTO Law: Mega-RTA 'Fracturing' Its Overlapping* RTA, 17 WORLD TRADE REVIEW 121, 124 (2018).

[17] *Id.* at 124.

[18] BRENTON, *supra* note 2, at 2.

[19] Kim, *supra* note 16, at 138.

[20] BRENTON, *supra* note 2, at 2.

[21] *Id.* at 2.

a bilateral trade agreement and countries B and A also have a bilateral trade agreement that states that country A will allow for diagonal cumulation from country C into country B despite not being a party to the trade agreement between country C and country B.

Based on its current trade deals, the EU appears reluctant to include loose diagonal cumulation provisions.[22] The EU only permits diagonal cumulation when all countries concerned have aligned their rules of origin with those of the EU.[23] Unless the UK is treated differently from all other trading partners, the UK government will not be able to tailor the rules of origin provisions in new trade deals to specifically benefit domestic industry without risking falling out of the required lockstep with the EU.

Full cumulation allows for all processing activities carried out within any of the participating countries to count towards satisfying the origin requirement. If countries A, B, and C each perform a step of the production process that do not qualify as granting origin but all of the steps put together do, then full cumulation grants origin status.[24] This explanation is illustrative of the complications that modern rules of origin provisions create, not only during the negotiations between countries, but also for the companies that then must design their supply chains to maximize the benefit of new trade deals.

E. TOLERANCE AND ABSORPTION RULES

Tolerance and absorption are a set of sub-rules that simplify the process of determining origin slightly. Tolerance rules create an exception for inputs of non-originating materials that fall below a certain percentage of the finished product.[25] The absorption principle means that once a product has acquired originating status it will retain that status if used in further production steps—inputs lose their non-originating qualities once the product they are in qualifies as originating.[26]

F. PREVENTING TRADE DEFLECTION

An important role for rules of origin is to prevent the transshipment of goods. Countries justify the use of preferential rules of origin as

---

22 Peter Holmes & Michael Gasiorek, *Grandfathering Free Trade Agreements and Rules of Origin: What Might Appear Bilateral is in Fact Trilateral!*, UK TRADE POLICY OBSERVATORY (Sep. 27, 2017), https://blogs.sussex.ac.uk/uktpo/2017/09/27/grandfathering-ftas-and-roos/.

23 *Id.*.

24 BRENTON, *supra* note 2, at 2.

25 *Id.*

26 *Id.* at 3.

necessary to prevent trade deflection or transshipment of goods.[27] These are methods used by producers in countries that don't have trade agreements to take advantage of the trade preferences of others.[28] Members of a customs union all apply a common external tariff, so a good entering the customs union from a third country will pay the same duty no matter which country it uses for entry. But parties to free, or regional, trade agreements can set their own tariff schedules. So, country A may have a tariff on tomatoes that is 10% whereas country B has set its tariff at 5%. If country C, not a party to the trade agreement between A and B that has lowered the tariff to zero as between those countries, wants to export tomatoes to country A, it may try to transship the goods by exporting them to country B and paying the 5% tariff and then moving them from B to A with no tariff thereby paying a 5% tariff instead of a 10% tariff. Because the government of the United Kingdom has touted the fact that Brexit will allow it to negotiate new trade arrangements with the world, the European Union would be justified in worrying that the UK may be setting itself up to become a hub for transshipment of goods into the EU—this will increase the stringency of origin checks that the EU will want in place for all goods entering the EU from the UK.

III. THE IMPACT ON TRADE OF RULES OF ORIGIN

The proliferation of various types of rules of origin in different trade agreements increases the administrative and production costs for exporters of goods.[29] This raises the costs for exporting producers because their choice of suppliers is restricted.[30] When choosing inputs, firms must calculate the value of a lower tariff for an originating product and compare that to the increased cost of a qualifying input.[31] Producers with extensive supply chains face an increased burden under restrictive rules of origin regimes.[32]

A. *LEGAL IMPLICATIONS OF ENTERING THE WITHDRAWAL PERIOD*

The UK government has conducted itself in a way that assumes that the UK will be able to continue to take advantage of the trade deals

---

[27] *Id.* at 1.

[28] *Id.*

[29] Mabrouk, *supra* note 1, at 104.

[30] BRENTON, *supra* note 2, at 1.

[31] *Id.* at 3.

[32] *Id.* at 4.

between the EU and third countries—this is by no means a certainty.[33] Even if the government rolls over every trade agreement it is party to as a member of the EU, the UK will still bear additional costs from complying with new rules of origin requirements that may not mesh as they did before. Producers that serve both preferential and non-preferential trading partners face the possibility of having to tailor different input mixes to serve different end markets—reducing the value of economies of scale.[34]

It appears that the UK will continue to be part of the EU's Common Commercial Policy during the transition period, currently set to last from March 30, 2019 to December 31, 2020. Imports from countries that have free trade agreements with the EU will continue to arrive in the UK under those arrangements. But the UK needs to ensure that the goods of UK exporters will be treated the same as EU exports. According to WTO rules, if the UK does not have the necessary replacement trade deals ready on the first day of the transition period then it must trade with its previous trading partners on a most favored nation basis.[35] This means that UK products will face tariffs they currently do not have to pay and that the UK may have to collect tariffs on previously duty-free products.[36] In addition to the issues raised by trade with the EU, the UK does significant trade with non-EU countries. In 2015, non-EU countries with which the UK had trade agreements through the EU accounted for 15% of total UK trade.[37] This 15% of trade will suddenly face the additional costs of tariffs as well as new administrative burdens associated with verifying origin certificates. While it may seem like the UK could simply neglect to enforce its tariff regime, this would both violate its WTO commitments and lead to a crackdown at the border with the EU to prevent transshipment into the EU by third-party nationals.

The UK does not have the power to unilaterally extend its current trade agreements. The countries that have trade agreements with the EU would have to agree to new bilateral trade deals with the UK on day one of the transition.[38] The UK government may have proceeded as though this process of "grandfathering" will occur without any concessions.[39] While some countries may agree to this, others will surely look to

---

33 Holmes & Gasiorek, *supra* note 22.
34 BRENTON, *supra* note 2, at 4.
35 Holmes & Gasiorek, *supra* note 22.
36 *Id.*
37 *Id.*
38 *Id.*
39 *Id.*

improve their trading status with the UK.[40] If the UK exits the EU without a comprehensive trade agreement, many of its products will be required to pay the EU common external tariff. As of 2014, the EU had a trade-weighted average tariff for non-agricultural products of 2.3% and 8.5% for agricultural products.[41] Its lessened heft will make it an easy target for the leaders of countries—and the EU—that see more to gain from helping their domestic industries than aiding the UK in its effort to benefit from leaving the EU.

B. WHY ARE RULES OF ORIGIN IMPORTANT FOR BREXIT?

The careful and lengthy negotiations that surround origin requirements in major trade deals are indicative of their importance to domestic industries. Brexit will mark the first time that a developed nation drastically rewrites its own rules of origin vis-à-vis not just one country or bloc, but in relation to the whole world. The benefit of a preferential trade arrangement is typically the difference between the in-agreement tariff and the MFN tariff.[42] For most countries negotiating trade agreements any tariff rate below the MFN rate is a benefit to domestic producers. The many producers in the UK that focus on serving the European market, however, will face higher costs no matter what deal is reached because they currently face no tariffs when trading within the EU and thus any tariff will cut into profits.

C. THE UNITED KINGDOM'S TRADING RELATIONSHIP WITH THE EUROPEAN UNION

The European Union is the United Kingdom's most important trading partner. Trade in goods with the EU accounted for roughly 49% of all UK goods exports and about 55% of all UK goods imports during 2017.[43] This amounted to approximately 167 billion GBP of goods exported to the EU and approximately 262 billion GBP of goods imported from the EU.[44] These numbers are crucial when estimating the impact of rules of origin changes because UK trade within the European Customs Union currently operates with zero tariffs. If the rules of origin

---

[40] *Id.*

[41] House of Commons Library, Statistics on UK-EU Trade, Briefing Paper Number 7851, Dec. 19, 2017.

[42] Moshe Hirsch, *Rules of Origin as Trade or Foreign Policy Instruments? The European Union Policy on Products Manufactured in the Settlements in the West Bank and the Gaza Strip*, 26 FORDHAM INT'L L.J. 572, 575 (2003).

[43] Dominic Webb, *A UK-EU customs union?*, Briefing Paper Number 8290, House of Commons Library, pg. 6, Apr. 25 2018, https://researchbriefings.parliament.uk/-ResearchBriefing/Summary/CBP-8290.

[44] *Id.*

clauses in a future trade deal prevent some of these goods from receiving a zero tariff rate, then companies will either have to absorb the costs of the EU's MFN tariff rates or pass those on to consumers.

The industries that are most integrated into the European Single Market are at the greatest risk of being hurt by the inevitable changes that will accompany Brexit. Some industries in the UK rely heavily on exporting to the EU.[45] Measured by percentage of the sector's total revenue, a measure of impact on the particular industry rather than a measure of impact on UK GDP, mining and quarrying—oil, gas, and other extractive industries—have the highest level of exports to the EU, coming in at 43% of total revenues for 2013.[46] Manufacturing comes next with exports to the EU amounting to 21% of total revenues.[47]

The introduction of new trading arrangements and the changing costs of a variety of inputs will alter the trading landscape not only for producers in the UK but also for companies located in the EU. Trade diversion occurs when a regional importer utilizes goods from an inefficient regional source instead of from a more efficient source that is outside of the trade agreement.[48] So EU 27 importers may now alter their supply chains to source goods from EU 27 producers instead of the UK producers that they had been purchasing from—unless the UK producers can change their prices to accommodate the additional costs that would come from having to pay tariffs when their components cross the border.

D. SUPPLY CHAIN IMPLICATIONS

The expansion in supply chains has meant that governments increasingly need to worry about the economic health of domestic producers of intermediate goods. The importance of the proximity of a component producer to the factory that will create the finished product has decreased as movement of goods has become easier and cheaper. While rules of origin can be used for neutral or positive trade purposes,

---

45 *See generally* Frederico Mor, *Importance of trade with the EU for UK industries*, Briefing Paper Number 8065, House of Commons Library, August 1, 2017, http://researchbriefings.parliament.uk/ResearchBriefing/Summary/CBP-8065.

46 *Id.* The data in this paper come from the UK Office of National Statistics "UK input-output analytical tables for 2013" which was released on March 9, 2017. This is a comprehensive report of inputs and outputs for every product in the UK. The complexity of the underlying data explains the long lag time in reporting, but because there have not been revolutionary changes in the trading relationship between the EU and the UK I treat the

47 *Id.*

48 Mabrouk, *supra* note 1, at 133.

they can also be used to raise protectionist barriers.[49] They can be used to protect domestic makers of intermediate goods—the inputs for finished products.[50] These protectionist barriers accomplish this goal by increasing the cost of using an intermediate goods supplier located outside of a free trade area, regional trade arrangement, or a customs union as compared to the cost of purchasing the input of the same quality from a supplier inside the arrangement.

Global value chains are becoming increasingly important in the worldwide production of goods.[51] Global value chains allow finished goods producers to source materials and intermediate goods from the most competitive producers, factoring in both cost and quality.[52] UK producers that source inputs from the EU risk having their supply chains disrupted if tariffs are imposed on goods that are currently duty-free. The manufacturing industry faces the highest risk with 20% of non-staff production costs coming from EU imports in 2013.[53]

The use of rules of origin to induce manufacturers to use intermediate products from within the regional trade arrangement or customs union will necessarily harm the domestic producers in a country that leaves that arrangement.[54] After leaving the European customs union, UK producers will lose European business unless they can add sufficient value to overcome the application of the MFN tariff to products that will lose their European origin labelling.[55] Excluding gold and precious stones, the UK currently imports close to $80 billion of intermediate goods from non-EU countries.[56] Vehicles are one of the important sectors that utilizes these inputs.[57] And the EU applies an MFN tariff on automobiles of 10%.[58] This means the costs of failing to gain either EU origin or a newly negotiated UK origin would come at a hefty price. While some producers will be able to bear the costs, many industries—like automobile manufacturing—rely on high production volumes to create profits from products that are sold at tight margins.

---

[49] *Id.* at 103.

[50] BRENTON, *supra* note 2, at 1.

[51] Kim, *supra* note 16, at 121.

[52] *Id.* at 121-22.

[53] Mor, *supra* note 45.

[54] Mabrouk, *supra* note 1, at 118.

[55] *Id.* at 135-36.

[56] Holmes & Gasiorek, *supra* note 22.

[57] *Id.*

[58] *The World Trade Organisation: A Safety Net for a Post-Brexit UK Trade Policy?*, UK TRADE POLICY OBSERVATORY, Briefing Paper 1 (Jul. 201).

E. THE AUTOMOTIVE INDUSTRY AS AN EXAMPLE

Rules of origin in trade deals for the automotive industry tend to be complex and often include a minimum local content requirement. The EU's free trade agreement requires that 55% of the parts in a car must be local to qualify for the reduced tariff rate.[59] The UK may be able to negotiate a bilateral cumulation clause in a future, standalone free trade agreement with the EU—meaning that components sourced from the EU may count towards, not against, the local UK content requirement. This would solve the parts sourcing issue for cars sold in the UK and in the EU. It would not, however, allow the UK to unshackle its car manufacturing from Europe. Countries outside of the EU are unlikely to allow the UK to count EU parts towards the local content requirements in other free trade agreements. The scale of parts used in car manufacturing is difficult to comprehend. The UK's largest car plant, operated by Nissan, uses 5 million parts each day.[60] Sales of motor vehicles produced by the UK have doubled over the last seven years, according to the UK Office for National Statistics.[61] The EU receives over 50% of UK exports of automobiles. The second and third largest export markets for UK cars are the United States and China, respectively.[62] At present, the typical UK content for the purpose of rules of origin of a domestically-produced automobile is less than 20-25% of the vehicle.[63] The largest UK car manufacturers import up to 70% of their components from the EU.[64] In order to benefit most from future trade deals, the UK will have to negotiate trade deals with cumulation provisions that allow its manufacturers to count EU components as domestic.[65]

The automotive sector in the UK relies heavily on transnational supply chains. The crankshaft of the Mini—an iconic British car—is a model of this. The part is first created at a factory in France then shipped

---

59 Graham Ruddick & Philip Oltermann, *A Mini part's incredible journey shows how Brexit will hit the UK car industry*, THE GUARDIAN, March 3, 2017, https://www.theguardian.com/-business/2017/mar/03/brexit-uk-car-industry-mini-britain-eu.

60 *Id.*

61 https://www.ons.gov.uk/businessindustryandtrade/manufacturingandproduction industry/bulletins/ukmanufacturerssalesbyproductprodcom/2016intermediateand2015 finalresults.

62 https://www.statista.com/statistics/298970/destination-of-cars-exported-from-the-united-kingdom/

63 *The impact of Brexit on the automotive sector*, Fifth Report of Session 2017-19, House of Commons Business, Energy and Industrial Strategy Committee, para. 42 (Feb. 27, 2018), https://publications.parliament.uk/pa/cm201719/cmselect/cmbeis/379/379.pdf.

64 *Id.*

65 *Id.*

to the UK for further processing then on to Germany to be placed in the engine before the engine itself is shipped to the UK to be placed in a finished Mini. If the car is sold in the UK the part will have crossed international borders three times, but those models sold in continental Europe will cross four times.[66] Car production in the UK has expanded rapidly since the financial crisis of 2008. The UK produced 1.72 million cars in 2016—a 17 year-high. But this expansion has utilized close relationships with continental European suppliers.

F. THE EU-SOUTH KOREA TRADE AGREEMENT AS AN EXAMPLE

The cut and paste method of trade negotiations—simply replacing EU with UK in existing trade deals—may be appealing in sound bite form, but the devil is in the details. Peter Holmes and Michael Gasiorek, in their blog for the UK Trade Policy Observatory, break down one way in which rules of origin would prevent the UK from using the cut and paste method to replace the existing EU-South Korea free trade agreement with a new UK-South Korea free trade agreement.[67] The rules of origin regime in the EU-South Korea agreement allows for bilateral cumulation of goods for the production of automobiles.[68] This means that intermediate components from either an EU country or South Korea will be counted towards the percentage—40% is used as an example—of a car that is required to originate from within the FTA to gain preferential tariff treatment.[69] Pre-Brexit, a UK auto manufacturer can pay no tariff on a car exported to an EU country that uses 30% UK inputs and 20% South Korean inputs. After cutting and pasting the new trade agreement, that car exported from the UK to the EU will no longer qualify as originating from the UK. The 30% UK input will not satisfy the 40% threshold because the UK has separate trade deals with the EU and South Korea, which would not automatically grant origin status for the use of intermediate components of other countries.[70] The UK companies that produce for export have shaped their supply chains to maximize their economic opportunities within the existing set of trade agreements and privileges. Any new set of trading arrangements will force UK producers that source inputs from more than one trading partner to either change their existing supply chains or absorb the new tariff costs.

---

[66] Ruddick & Oltermann, *supra* note 59.
[67] Holmes & Gasiorek, *supra* note 22.
[68] *Id.*
[69] *Id.*
[70] *Id.*

G. *ADMINISTRATIVE BURDENS*

Membership in the EU Customs Union lowers administrative burdens. Because of the common external tariff, there are no checks for compliance with rules of origin on goods moving from one EU country to another.[71] Proving origin requires a number of administrative steps to provide the required documentation.[72] The limited information available on the administrative costs to gain origin preference suggests costs of around 3 percent of the value of the export.[73] This cost of proving origin is recognized to be higher in countries with poorly developed customs mechanisms.[74] Since 1993, no UK firms have had to prove the origin of their goods when selling into the EU.[75]

While the UK does have sophisticated trade with non-EU countries, exporters that have focused entirely on intra-EU trade will face the highest administrative burdens upon exit from the customs union.

The UK will have to build out its own customs infrastructure—e.g., personnel, IT systems—to handle EU trade that previously did not require origin checking. The lack of need for rules of origin checks within a customs union allows for trade that does not require physical checks.[76] Free trade agreements, however, do still require origin checks—introducing administrative burdens that add time and cost to the movement of goods.[77] Delays at the border between the European Union and Turkey illustrate the problems that come with the movement of goods between countries with anything short of the full integration that membership in the Customs Union and Single Market currently provides.[78]

Even goods imported to the EU from European Economic Area nations are required to prove their origin, regardless of whether they qualify for preferential treatment or not.[79] Proving the origin of a product typically requires that the exporter provide Certificates of Origin to the importer who then presents the Certificates to the relevant customs authorities.[80] Exporters bear the risk of private liability in the event that

---

71 Webb, *supra* note 43, at 7.

72 BRENTON, *supra* note 2, at 4.

73 *Id.*

74 *Id.*

75 Peter Holmes & Nick Jacob, *Certificates and Rules of Origin: The Experience of UK Firms*, Briefing Paper 15, UK TRADE POLICY OBSERVATORY, pg. 2 (Jan. 2018).

76 Webb, *supra* note 43, at 10.

77 *Id.*

78 *Id.* at 14.

79 Holmes & Jacob, *supra* note 76, at 2.

80 *Id.* at 3.

a false claim of origin is made under current UK foreign trade agreements.[81] This provides a strong incentive for exporters to study and comply with applicable regulations. The EU currently has an Approved Exporter status that EU firms can apply for that creates a streamlined system for certifying the origin of exported goods.[82] The EU has launched an online database of registered exporters into the EU—REX—that it plans for use for all future trade agreements.[83] Without the inclusion of a provision in a UK-EU trade deal, UK firms will no longer be able to participate in the Approved Exporter program. However, either that or the REX system could serve as the basis for expedited movement of goods in a future UK-EU FTA.

H. FOREIGN DIRECT INVESTMENT

Rules of origin can have an impact on foreign direct investment in countries. Stringent rules of origin in regional trade agreements can induce manufacturers that are located outside of the region to create facilities inside of the trade agreement to take advantage of lowered tariffs even if they would not make economic sense absent the stringent rules of origin requirements.[84] Multinational firms often rely on international networks to provide specific advantages.[85] These companies will make business decisions—such as factory placement—with rules of origin requirements in mind.[86]

If the UK leaves the European customs union without a bespoke deal keeping it inside of the union for the purpose of origin labelling—a virtual impossibility—UK producers of intermediate goods will be treated the same as producers from any other country. Producers of finished goods will have to reconsider the economics of sourcing intermediate goods from the UK because of the increased cost of tariffs and the potential to jeopardize the finished product's EU origin status depending on the percentage of the inputs that come from the UK.[87] Assuming that the UK leaves the customs union, changes to rules of origin provisions will require companies in the UK to perform costly examinations of supply chains and potentially lead to changes in input sourcing or necessitate selling products into different markets.[88] The fact

---

[81] *Id.* at 4.
[82] *Id.*
[83] *Id.*
[84] Mabrouk, *supra* note 1, at 151.
[85] BRENTON, *supra* note 2, at 4.
[86] *Id.* at 3.
[87] Mabrouk, *supra* note 1, at 151.
[88] *Id.* at 108.

that future trade arrangements are uncertain—heightened by the government's lack of clear signaling as to its ultimate goals and red lines—will inevitably affect the long-term decisions that companies make when deciding if they should invest in facilities within the UK.

I. FUTURE TRADE AGREEMENTS

The determination of origin for a product becomes more important with the increase in preferential trade agreements that give benefits to that origin.[89] The large number of preferential trade agreements negotiated by the EU—plus the intra-EU market—make EU origin very valuable for exporters. Many countries utilize trade agreements, and non-tariff barriers like rules of origin, to protect domestic interests.[90] Concessions were granted to the EU to gain access to that market; it is not clear why similar concessions would be granted to access the UK's much smaller market.

Stringent rules of origin in regional trade agreements can be used to protect the national products of some, but not all, of the constituent parties.[91] This means that when negotiating future trade deals, the UK will not be burdened by a need to protect the domestic industries of EU 27 countries and thus may be able to optimize its trading arrangements to protect only UK production. For example, the UK used to import cheap lamb from New Zealand, but after joining the EU the common external tariff was high enough that the UK shifted to importing lamb from France.[92] After Brexit, the UK will not have to participate in trade arrangements designed only to help the domestic producers of another country.

IV. CONCLUSION

Every trade agreement that the UK makes after Brexit will contain rules of origin provisions. The global trading system relies on these provisions to facilitate and monitor trade. And rules of origin are only one of a number of interlocking aspects of trade agreements. Simply replacing the words "the European Union" with "the United Kingdom of Great Britain and Northern Ireland" in current trade deals will not retain the status quo or improve economic conditions in the UK. As described above, this could cause UK exporters to lose out on tariff preferences and potentially encourage companies to move manufacturing outside of the country. The government of the UK and

---

[89] LaNasa, *supra* note 5, at 625.
[90] Mabrouk, *supra* note 1, at 151.
[91] *Id.* at 108.
[92] *Id.* at 147.

its trade negotiators must examine the origin provisions in its current agreements and seek to alter them to benefit the specific industries of the UK. Without tailoring these provisions to suit the needs of its economy, UK trade will not be helped—and will likely be harmed—by Brexit.

CHAPTER 17: THE UK'S DATA FUTURE: WILL BREXIT AFFECT THE UK'S TRAJECTORY IN A WORLD OF UNCERTAINTY?

PHILIPP RUPPERT

I. INTRODUCTION

The United Kingdom has long been a policy outlier in the European Union. Under the Labour governments of Blair and Brown, the UK voted against the majority in the European Council an average of 2.6% of the time, making it one of the most "dissenting" nations in the EU. This trend only picked up in 2009, when the Conservative government took over, raising the UK "dissent rate" to 12.3% between 2009 and 2015.[1] While there were a number of topics of disagreement, the question of how to treat data privacy has been consistently among them,[2] culminating in the United Kingdom partially halting enforcement of its Investigatory Powers Act (IPA) following the *Tele2 Sverige AB v Post-och telestyrelsen* decision,[3] in which the Court of Justice of the European Union (CJEU) invalidated the IPA's predecessor.

Since the IPA passed both legislative houses in the UK in 2016,[4] the EU's implementation of its General Data Protection Regulation (GDPR) in May 2018 has come closer,[5] and Data Privacy has become a global focus of political and social interest through a range of news,[6] such as the use of Facebook data by Cambridge Analytica in order to affect election results, or the increased publication of the Chinese Social Credit Score system. In light of this newfound awareness of data privacy issues

---

[1] Simon Hix, Sara Hagemann, *Is the UK a winner or loser in the EU Council?*, THE GUARDIAN (Nov. 2015), https://www.theguardian.com/world/datablog/2015/nov/02/is-uk-winner-or-loser-european-council.

[2] *Id.*

[3] Joined Cases C-203/15 and C-698/15, *Tele2Sverige AB and Watson and Others* (2016), ECLI:EU:C:2016:970.

[4] Ewen MacAskill, *'Extreme surveillance' becomes UK law with barely a whimper*, THE GUARDIAN (Nov. 1, 2016) https://www.theguardian.com/world/2016/nov-/19/extreme-surveillance-becomes-uk-law-with-barely-a-whimper.

[5] *Official Journal of the European Union*, Vol. L119 (4 May 2016), pp. 1-88.

[6] Reuters, *Amid global outcry, Facebook will introduce new features allowing users to download and delete their data*, SOUTH CHINA MORNING POST (April 2018), http://www.scmp.com/news/world/united-states-canada/article/2139334/amid-global-outcry-facebook-will-introduce-new.

and its increasing relevance as more data is collected, it is important to understand how Brexit will affect the future of data privacy in the UK, and how the movement toward data privacy might affect Brexit.

To this end, this chapter will first explain the legal and technological framework of data privacy and establish the various interests that companies, law enforcement, and citizens will likely have regarding the use of their data. The second part of the chapter will be dedicated to laying out the legal and political framework of the European Union and the United Kingdom regarding data security. In the third part, it will then be explored how these differences in policy will affect considerations during Brexit, and how Brexit may influence changes in policy. Ultimately, the chapter predicts that the United Kingdom is likely to shift its policy toward a stronger protection of its citizens data as a result of economic drivers in the Brexit process, as well as social and political drivers within its own borders.

II. DATA PRIVACY

Data privacy is an area that has become more relevant in recent years. With the emergence of data mining for commercial and public applications, many more organisations decided to record and collect data from their customers or constituencies. Consequently, 90% of all data in existence has been created in the past two years alone.[7] A large part of this data consists of records of human behaviour or interaction, such as conversations between people engaged in online, sales records of supermarkets, or health information of populations.

Based on such records, it is possible to track preferences, purchasing patterns, and health trends, making it possible to address wider societal concerns, but also creating implications regarding the individuals' right to privacy.[8] As such, the next parts will discuss what the right to privacy means and entails, and how data collection and mining may affect such rights.

---

[7] See, e.g. Julie Sobowale, *How artificial intelligence is transforming the legal profession*, ABA JOURNAL. (2016), http://www.abajournal.com/magazine/article/how_artificial_-intelligence_is_transforming_the_legal_profession.

[8] Christopher Wolf, The Commercial Use of Big Data Can Help Improve Equality, The New York Times (2014), https://www.nytimes.com/roomfordebate/2014/08/06/is-big-data-spreading-inequality/the-commercial-use-of-big-data-can-help-improve-equality.

A. *PRIVACY RIGHTS IN GENERAL*

While the legal right to privacy is relatively young, sociological and psychological papers indicate that the concept has existed before modern government,[9] and various definitions have been proposed. Considering the lack of such definitions in international law, this section will draw on the findings of other fields in order to determine a more general concept for the remaining chapter.

In a 1975 article, the philosopher James Rachels argues that some level of privacy was necessary in order to make the multifaceted nature of humans and their interactions possible.[10] Based on such an understanding of privacy as a necessity for the multifaceted human nature, sociological text have defined privacy as a person's ability to control the information they provide to each group of people, or selective self-presentation.[11] Considering that various groups across society represent "one-tracked and monopolistic" viewpoints, individuals often require the use of discretion and privacy to navigate the intricate web of social interaction, making it possible for them to exist on a spectrum in-between these viewpoints.[12]

However, this concept can likely also be expanded to society as a whole. It has been argued that "prohibition of political interference in legally recognized private spheres relieves the political system from decision making on a wide range of issues,"[13] making it clear that it is in the interest of society as a whole to create spheres of privacy, and implying that the current political system is not (yet) adapted to exercising expertise and influence in such areas.

Adding to this basis, Westin proposed four states of privacy in 1967: Solitude, anonymity, reserve, and intimacy.[14] In this context, solitude is seen as the removal from society and anonymity as that of having an impact on society without one's identity attached to it. Reserve represents a person's ability to control disclosure of information about themselves, while intimacy pertains to the sharing of information only within a chosen in-group environment. All four of these states can be seen as an individual's choice about how much of their identity they are willing to expose to other people.

---

[9] Philipp Ruppert, *Privacy, Tax Evasion, and the Development of Crypto Currencies*, 1 GEO. L. TECH. REV. 398, 405 (2017).

[10] James Rachels, *Why Privacy is Important*, 4 PHIL. & PUB. AFF. 323, 326 (1975).

[11] Katayoun Baghai, *Privacy as a Human Right: Sociological Theory*, 46 SOC'Y. 951, 956 (2012).

[12] *Id.* at 954.

[13] *Id.* at 957; G. Verschraegen, *Human Rights and Modern Society: A Sociological Analysis from the Perspective of Systems Theory*, 29 J. L. & SOC'Y. 258, 272 (2002).

[14] *See*, ALAN F. WESTIN, PRIVACY AND FREEDOM 31 (1967).

To conclude, this chapter will treat privacy as the ability of a person to control the level of disclosure of private information they choose in any given sphere, i.e., the reserve they exercise in different aspects of their social identity.

B. DATA INTERESTS

Having established the nature and international context of data privacy, it is important to realise how data can be used for socially and commercially beneficial purposes, why its collection is important, as well as how the use of data may infringe on the rights of individuals as defined above.

The use of data recording and collection in the digital sphere is generally aimed at recognising patterns. For example, consumer behaviour may be tracked by companies in order to determine similarities with other consumers, and therefore recommend "targeted advertising" for products that the consumer may not be aware of, but which similar consumers have enjoyed. Such an analysis may lead to better product targeting or better product innovation, better healthcare, more efficient stock trading, and various others.[15] It may also be used to detect and avoid fraud by consumers, a use very prevalent in the financial services industry, or to avoid behaviour the customer may later regret.

Going beyond the scope of a single company, the government may also have a legitimate interest in the use of such inferences in order to detect fraud, create early warning systems for outbreaks of disease, or find communications indicative of illegal behaviour.[16] Requiring for multiple collectors of data, such as companies, or government agencies to surrender access to their data, makes the inferences to be drawn by such a system even more powerful, allowing the government to get ahead of any misconduct.

The analysis of such patterns, however, can also lead to the inference of private information from seemingly harmless data, such as sexual orientation from purchasing patterns, or early Alzheimer's disease from key-click streams.[17] While it may be feasible for an individual to control what data he or she gives to a company, it will therefore be far more difficult if not impossible for the individual to assess what inferences will be drawn from this. This is especially true when looking at the

---

[15] President's Council of Advisors on Science and Technology, *Report to the President: Big Data and Privacy: A Technological Perspective*, EXECUTIVE OFFICE OF THE PRESIDENT 8 (2014).

[16] *Id.*

[17] *Id.*

government level, where an individual will likely not be aware of which set of input data the government will be able to access, or what this data will reveal in the aggregate.

While beyond the scope of this chapter, multiple recent developments, such as the Facebook/Cambridge Analytica misuse of social media data in order to affect political elections,[18] Palantir's secretive attempt to predict crime in New Orleans,[19] or the Social Credit Score introduced by China,[20] also suggest that data analysis at a societal scale may be a danger to democracy and a country's values itself.[21] In the case of the Facebook/Cambridge Analytica misuse of data, the latter company used psychological profiles it created from user data of the social network in order to target advertisements and (fake) news to individuals they had identified as being on the fence regarding the U.S. presidential election, as well as the Brexit referendum itself.[22] In the Palantir case, the company analysed patterns and individuals' profiles in order to predict which individuals will be likely to break the law in the near future and where crime may occur.[23] Finally, the Social Credit Score introduced in China analyses patterns, individual behaviour, and likelihood to abide by the law, such as jaywalking or defaulting on a loan, in order to determine an individual's trustworthiness, potentially barring them from participation in society, such as travel or their children's education.[24] While all three examples are vastly differently, they highlight the potential of mining personal data in fundamentally changing the shape of society itself.

Consequently, it is important in any discussion of data privacy to address the balance between legitimate interests of larger entities and the privacy right of individuals.

---

18 BBC NEWS, *Facebook-Cambridge Analytica Data Scandal* (2018), http://www.bbc.com/news/topics/c81zyn0888lt/facebook-cambridge-analytica-data-scandal.

19 Noah Feldman, *The Future of Policing Is Being Hashed Out in Secret*, BLOOMBERG (Feb 2018), https://www.bloomberg.com/view/articles/2018-02-28/artificial-intelligence-in-policing-advice-for-new-orleans-and-palantir.

20 Reuters Staff, *China to bar people with bad 'social credit' from planes, trains*, REUTERS (Mar 2018), https://www.reuters.com/article/us-china-credit/china-to-bar-people-with-bad-social-credit-from-planes-trains-idUSKCN1GS10S.

21 Tyler Grant, *The West could be closer to China's system of 'social credit scoring' than you think*, THE HILL (2018), http://thehill.com/opinion/technology/386524-the-west-could-be-closer-to-chinas-system-of-social-credit-scoring-than.

22 BBC NEWS, *Facebook-Cambridge Analytica Data Scandal, supra* note 15.

23 Feldman, *The Future of Policing, supra* note 16.

24 Reuters Staff, *social credit, supra* note 17.

C. DATA TRANSFERS

Having established the nature of privacy and what can be done with the data, it is also important to understand the logistical structure of concern. While data may be collected in one country, on its citizens, it can then be transferred to other countries in order to be processed.[25] A country could therefore have excellent laws regarding the privacy of its citizens inside of its own borders, but all of its efforts would be in vain once the data is transferred out. Consequently, a country has to ensure that the data of its citizens is either treated in accordance with its own policies, or not transferred out at all.

In this context, there are a number of possible avenues for data to be transferred:

A. Data may be transferred between states, in order to facilitate law enforcement or other government efforts.[26] While it is possible to merely transfer law enforcement conclusions or the data of suspicious actors, transferring a larger data set, such as the ID of all clients who have purchased "suspicious" goods, would allow joint mining, potentially leading to better inferences.

B. Data may be transferred from one company or entity within the country to another abroad. This could serve the purpose of joint mining between affiliates, of sending a data set to a company specialised in mining in order to receive the product, or of selling the data set to a third party which may use it for its own purposes.[27] Assuming that such data would include personal information (e.g. about the owner of a product), the transfers may not be allowed under certain regimes, or would have to be scraped of a number of attributes. This mode of transfer may, for example, be used for agreements between stock exchanges, banks, clearing houses and other financial actors regarding the detection of fraud across borders.

C. Data may be transferred from one country to another within the same company. This may be in order to get international statistics, or in order to allow for the creation of data specialised

---

[25] Jacques Bughin, Susan Lund, *The ascendancy of international data flows*, MCKINSEY (Jan 2017), https://www.mckinsey.com/mgi/overview/in-the-news/the-ascendancy-of-international-data-flows.

[26] Jennifer Daskal, *Law Enforcement Access to Data Across Borders: The Evolving Security and Rights Issues*, 8 Journal of National Security Law & Policy 473, 473 (2016).

[27] Business and Industry Advisory Committee to the OECD, *The Flow Of Data Across Borders: A BIAC Trade Committee Policy* Perspective, BIAC (2016), https://www.uscib.org/uscib-content/uploads/2016/03/2016_03_The-Flow-of-Data-Across-Borders_A-BIAC-Trade-Committee-Policy-Pe....pdf.

departments in a given country.[28] For example, Jaguar branch offices in Europe may collect information about repairs within their country and send them back to the company headquarters in the UK.

D. Data may also be transferred from one country to another in an interaction between the individual and a foreign country.[29] In such a scenario, a citizen of country 1 would directly provide his or her data to a company in country 2 in order to retain the company's services. This may be used when European companies use legal or financial services by firms in the UK, or when a European individual decides to open an account at a UK bank.

E. Finally, data may also be transferred between two individuals in different countries, with the company providing this service storing the communication on its own servers. While this would be analogous to scenario D, the exchange potentially includes a variety of interested states, complicating the question of applicable data protection laws.

While all of these scenarios implicate the transfer of personal data of one or multiple individuals across state lines, such crossing of borders will only be of concern if one or more of the involved countries have laws that would expose the data to less stringent privacy laws.

It is also important to set these scenarios into the context of data use: for scenario A, the transfer of data may be crucial to the effective operation of law enforcement and national security, as a number of acts that would be considered suspicious if taken together could be camouflaged by spreading them across countries. Likewise, scenarios B-E involve the transfer of data for commercial purposes which creates billions of dollars of revenue for companies in the countries in question.

III. LEGAL FRAMEWORK AND VALUES

A. PRIVACY RIGHTS IN INTERNATIONAL LAW

Since the intent of this chapter is to address privacy concerns in the context of Brexit, it is important to consider the cross-border implications of privacy. In this regard, the first starting point is

---

[28] DECHERT, LLC, *DATA TRANSFERS WITHIN A MULTINATIONAL GROUP* (2013), https://www.dechert.com/content/dam/dechert%20files/onpoint/2013/6/-data-transfers-within-a-multinational-group-safely-navigating/Data_Transfers_whitepaper.pdf.

[29] Yaki Faitelson, *Yes, The GDPR Will Affect Your U.S.-Based Business*, FORBES (Dec 2017), https://www.forbes.com/sites/forbestechcouncil/2017/12/04/yes-the-gdpr-will-affect-your-u-s-based-business/#5e900e0e6ff2.

international law. While there are a number of agreements and guidelines in this regard, none of them are legally binding.[30]

In particular, the United Nations has recently addressed the issue, adopting resolution 68/167 in December 2013. The resolution enshrines the right to privacy in the digital age under Article 12 of the Universal Declaration of Human rights, and in Article 17 of the International Covenant on Civil and Political Rights.[31] While these articles lay out the right to privacy as the right for a person not to be "subjected to arbitrary interference with his privacy, family, home or correspondence,"[32] this definition is broader than the conclusion reached above, and may be interpreted as requiring more than spying on, or collection of someone's data.

Beyond that, the Organization for Economic Co-operation and Development (OECD) has also compiled "Guidelines on the Protection of Privacy and Transborder Flows of Personal Data" to be used as tools to help "us think about and frame discussions about privacy."[33] While these guidelines do not define privacy, they create a framework for the OECD member states with regards to cross-border transfers of data, and generally emphasise security in their transmission.

While being generally vague and non-binding, these institutional guidelines lay out the general framework for countries to adopt their own privacy laws and suggest that the international community accepts that data privacy is a concern with consequences similar to offline privacy.

B. EU APPROACH/LAW

The first instance of the recognition of the need to protect personal data within the EU happened through the 1950 adoption of the Council of Europe Convention for the Protection of Human Rights and Fundamental Freedoms.[34] Furthering this recognition, the 1981 Convention for the Protection of Individuals with regard to Automatic Processing of Personal Data created a separate individual right to security in personal data.[35] At this point, the rights from the European

---

[30] Kriangsak Kittichaisaree & Christopher Kuner, "The Growing Importance of Data Protection in Public International Law," EJIL: TALK!: BLOG OF THE EUROPEAN JOURNAL OF INTERNATIONAL LAW (Oct. 14, 2015), http://www.ejiltalk.org-/the-growing-importance-of-data-protection-in-public-international-law/.

[31] G.A. Res. 68/167 (Dec. 18, 2013).

[32] G.A. Resolution 217 A (III); Resolution 2200 A (XXI), annex.

[33] OECD PRIVACY PRINCIPLES, http://oecdprivacy.org/

[34] EUROPEAN UNION DATA PROTECTION LEGISLATION, https://secure.edps.europa.eu/EDPSWEB/edps/EDPS/Dataprotection/QA/QA2.

[35] *Id.*

Convention on Human Rights (ECHR), the case law of the European Court of Justice (CJEU), and selected national legislation and constitutions are encompassed in the EU Charter of Fundamental Rights (the Charter).[36] The Charter acts as a quasi-constitution, with all decisions by the EU institutions and courts having to be consistent with the rights it affords to EU citizens.[37] The article concerned with data privacy in particular is article 8, which establishes the right to data protection, limits the use of data to specified purposes (as opposed to indiscriminate use), and requires the existence of an independent authority for oversight of the data use.[38]

Consistent with the EU Charter of Fundamental Rights, and more specifically, European data privacy is regulated by national privacy laws under the framework of the Data Protection Directive 95/46/EC of 1995 (DPD).[39] In addition to that, the E-Privacy Directive 2002/58/EC of 2002 governs electronic communications,[40] and the Framework Decision 2009/977/JHA of 2009 regulates protection of personal data with regard to criminal matters.[41]

In an effort to update these laws, the European council has adopted Directive 2016/680 and the General Data Protection Regulation (GDPR, Regulation 2016/679) in 2016.[42] The Directive regulates the security of individuals with regard to transfers of their personal data by government authorities for the purposes of the "prevention, investigation, detection or prosecution of criminal offenses or the execution of criminal penalties, including the safeguarding against and the prevention of threats to public security." As such, the Directive attempts to enable the cooperation of law enforcement across borders, while preventing security threats to information. States are obligated to have adopted national laws consistent with this Directive by May 2018.

---

[36] Shannon Togawa Mercer, *Chapter 16: Exploring the potential for coalescence and divergence in UK-EU data policy after Brexit*, in LEGAL ASPECTS OF BREXIT 181, 183 (Hillman & Horlick eds., 2017).

[37] National institutions and courts have to also have to keep their decisions consistent with the EU charter, if they are making decisions on EU directives or regulations, or national legislation implementing them.

[38] EUROPEAN COMMISSION, EU CHARTER OF FUNDAMENTAL RIGHTS.

[39] Council Directive 95/46/EC, 1995 O.J. (L 281) 31-50 (EC) .

[40] W. Scott Blackmer, *GDPR: Getting Ready for the New EU General Data Protection Regulation*, INFORMATION LAW GROUP (May 5, 2016), http://www.infolawgroup.com/-2016/05/articles/gdpr/gdpr-getting-ready-for-the-new-eu-general-data-protection-regulation/.

[41] United Kingdom Parliament, Brexit and Data Protection, 2016, Commons, 7838, at 3.

[42] *Official Journal of the European Union*, Vol. L119 (4 May 2016), pp. 1-88.

The GDPR, which will also come into effect in May 2018, is set to replace the DPD, and is globally considered the most progressive step in data privacy that has been taken so far.[43] The GDPR will extend extraterritorially in order to protect EU citizen's rights, applying to any company within or without the EU that is holding data (data controller) or using data (data processor) on EU individuals, if the company is offering goods or services or monitoring the behaviour of EU subjects.[44] Beyond that, the GDPR establishes a variety of legal obligations for data processors: the company must maintain a record of its processing operations for every controller, designate a data protection officer, conduct impact assessments for risky processing actions, implement data monitoring, and must notify the controllers if there are instances of data breaches.[45] The GDPR also requires explicit consent for the processing of sensitive data, and the burden is on the controller to prove that consent has been given. Finally, the GDPR also includes a "right to erasure", which has often been termed the "right to be forgotten" in previous court cases and can be considered an expansion of the right to have one's data rectified as granted by the Charter.[46] This means that data controllers have to remove the relevant data entries when consent is withdrawn, unless the data is considered to be in the public interest.[47]

In addition to EU Directives and Regulations, case law of the European Court of Justice (CJEU) interprets the Charter, and therefore establishes further rights for citizens. In *Maximillian Schrems v. Data Protection Commissioner* (2015) the CJEU held that "legislation permitting the public authorities to have access on a generalized basis to the content of electronic communications must be regarded as compromising the essence of the fundamental right to respect for private life."[48] This decision very strongly follows the Charter's wording of limiting data use to "specified purposes" but interprets the article broadly to include laws that allow for indiscriminate data collection.[49]

In two later cases, the CJEU has affirmed and expanded that holding, stating that indiscriminate data retention laws are impermissible

---

[43] Rowland Manthorpe, *Congress won't hurt Facebook and Zuck, but GDPR and Europe could*, WIRED (2018), http://www.wired.co.uk/article/facebook-mark-zuckerberg-congress-testimony-cambridge-analytica-gdpr-privacy.

[44] European Council REGULATION 2016/679.

[45] *Id.*

[46] Manthorpe, *Congress won't hurt Facebook, supra* note 39.

[47] European Council REGULATION 2016/679.

[48] Court of Justice of the European Union Press Release No 177/15, The Court of Justice declares that the Commission's US Safe Harbour Decision is invalid (Oct. 6, 2016).

[49] EUROPEAN COMMISSION, EU CHARTER OF FUNDAMENTAL RIGHTS.

under EU privacy legislation. In one of the cases, the Court stated that the Data Protection and Investigatory Powers Act (DRIPA) "exceeds the limit of what is strictly necessary and cannot be considered to be justified, within a democratic society."[50] In addition, the Court stated that any legislation adopted by an EU member state would have to "[limit the] retention of data . . . with respect to the categories of data to be retained, the means of communication affected, the persons concerned, and the retention period adopted, to what is strictly necessary."[51] This language is strongly overlapping with the language provided in the guidelines of the OECD as well as article 8 (2) of the Charter and can be considered to limit the disclosure and processing of any information to the single sphere of the individual that is concerned in the investigation.

Based on this legal framework, it can be said that the EU laws and decisions are strongly supporting the privacy rights of its citizens, while retaining law enforcement cut-outs. For example, the "right to be forgotten" allows citizens to manage their online and public identity and allows for them to change their opinions and expressed views over time, without having to fight an uphill battle against their own previous behaviours and statements. Likewise, the requirements for recordkeeping and reporting placed on data processors allows for individuals to at least retain a level of transparency regarding the use of their data.

C. UK APPROACH

1. Current equivalence with EU standards

Considering that the United Kingdom is still part of the European Union at the time of this chapter's submission, UK law currently conforms with EU standards mentioned above, and the UK has to fully comply with the requirements of the GDPR from May 2018 on until the end of March 2019 and will continue to do so based on the current state of the Withdrawal Agreement until the end of the transition period of 31st December 2021.[52]

In this regard, the DPD has been implemented by the Data Protection Act (DPA) of 1998,[53] and the Privacy and Electronic Communications Regulations (PECR) regulates private companies in a

---

[50] Joined Cases C-203/15 and C-698/15, *Tele2Sverige AB and Watson and Others*, 2016, ¶ 107, ECLI:EU:C:2016:970.

[51] *Id.*

[52] Draft Withdrawal Agreement, TF50 (2018) 35.

[53] *See* United Kingdom Parliament, Brexit and Data Protection, 2016, Commons, 7838, at 3.

number of ways to ensure privacy rights for individuals.[54] For example, the PECR regulates marketing, the use of online tracking technology (such as cookies), the security of electronic communications services, and the handling of location data, billing, identification, and directories of the customers of communications networks.

Additionally, the Investigatory Powers Act (IPA) passed both Houses of Parliament at the end of 2016.[55] The Act, which has been termed "Snooper's charter" by media outlets, consolidates the powers of government agencies to aggregate communications, requires for internet providers to retain web browsing records, enables the use of surveillance domestically, governs the questions of judicial approval for such measures, and creates the Investigatory Powers Commissioner in order to oversee their use.[56] Considering the wide range of data collection mandated under the Act, some of its provisions have been "mothballed" at this point in order to await the interpretation by national courts regarding how CJEU decisions about its predecessor DRIPA will affect the validity of the IPA.[57] While the similarities in the invalidated wording of DRIPA and the current wording of the IPA have prompted the mothballing and a government review of the Act, civil rights groups have contended that even with the updates suggested by the government, the Act would violate the Charter and CJEU decisions regarding data retention.[58]

Finally, the Data Protection Bill introduced into Parliament in late 2017 aims to implement GDPR and Directive 2016/680 in British domestic law.[59] While the bill has not yet received royal ascent at the time of submission of this chapter, it will have to be implemented by May 2018 in order to comply with the Directive. The Bill is also aimed at

---

[54] INFORMATION COMMISSIONER'S OFFICE: WHAT ARE PECR?, https://ico.org.uk/for-organisations/guide-to-pecr/introduction/what-are-pecr/

[55] Ewen MacAskill, *'Extreme surveillance' becomes UK law with barely a whimper*, THE GUARDIAN (Nov. 1, 2016) https://www.theguardian.com/world/2016/nov/19/-extreme-surveillance-becomes-uk-law-with-barely-a-whimper.

[56] *Id.*

[57] Kelly Fiveash, *UK forced to derail Snoopers' Charter blanket data slurp after EU ruling*, ArsTechnica (Feb 2017), https://arstechnica.com/tech-policy/2017/02/investigatory-powers-law-missing-draft-communications-data-code/.

[58] BBC News, *'Snoopers' Charter' changes put forward* (Dec 2017), http://www.bbc.com/news/technology-42195352.

[59] Annabelle Dickson, *What you need to know about the UK's Data Protection Bill*, POLITICO (Mar 2018), https://www.politico.eu/article/what-you-need-to-know-about-the-uks-data-protection-bill/.

providing an updated data protection regime post Brexit and the transition period.

2. The UK's post Brexit direction

Based on the UK's current compliance and the length of the transition period, 1st January 2021 will mark the first day of uncertainty regarding the UK's new direction in the protection of personal data. Looking at the currently available information, there are strong pulls in both directions, that of more government control and surveillance, as well as that of more privacy rights for citizens. This section aims to discuss the factors currently influencing the potential changes in British legislature in or after 2021.

The period immediately following the transition period will be governed by the withdrawal agreement. In the withdrawal agreement, Title VII addressed which law will govern the retention and processing of data transferred into the UK before the end of the transition period and based on the agreement following the transition period.[60] In this context, it is important to return to the previous discussion of modes of data transfers.

In particular, case A, the transfer and treatment of data between governments, is addressed in Title VII, and the colour-coding of the passage suggests that the application of EU law to such data has been agreed to by the UK on the policy level.[61] Case D, the provision of personal data to a foreign (i.e. British) company by the individual him or herself, is covered by the extraterritorial application of the GDPR in general and will apply to UK companies independent from the direction the UK will be taking regarding data protection.[62]

The remaining 3 possibilities for data transfer, however, are less clearly agreed to. While article 67 of the Withdrawal Agreement lays out the considerations regarding the protection of personal data, the article states that "Union law on the protection of personal data shall apply in the United Kingdom in respect of . . . data subjects outside the United Kingdom, provided that the personal data: (a) were processed in accordance with Union law in the United Kingdom before the end of the transition period; or (b) are processed in the United Kingdom after the end of the transition period on the basis of this Agreement."[63]

---

[60] Draft Withdrawal Agreement, TF50 (2018) 35; In the Withdrawal Agreement, the European Union as the drafter used colour coding in order to differentiate between passages that the UK had agreed to at a negotiator level (green), at a policy level (yellow), or that had been proposed by the EU without agreement from the UK (white).

[61] *Id.*

[62] *Id.*

[63] *Id.*

Considering the extraterritorial application of the GDPR in general, part (a) of this article seems somewhat redundant. Since the GDPR will apply to companies in third party states that retain or process the personal information of EU citizens, the information of EU citizens already stored in the UK should be no exception. Part (b), however, may apply EU law to transfers of data under cases B and C if they were done "on the basis of this Agreement". Since the article is colour-coded to indicate that it has been added by the European drafters and has not yet been agreed to by the UK, UK opposition is most likely to part (b), suggesting that the UK could have plans for laws that would be incompatible with the application of EU standards.

Possible designs for such legislation may be seen in the IPA and its proposed changes. As mentioned in the discussion above, the IPA contains language which very closely resembles the language of DRIPA, invalidated by the CJEU in its previous decision. In particular, the bulk warrants authorised under part 6, the retention notices authorised under part 4, and the wide-sweeping authority of the Secretary of State to authorise under section 19 either of the aforementioned, will likely go against the set of EU laws governing their citizen's data privacy.[64] While the government's proposed changes after the CJEU decision regarding DRIPA fix some of the issues (such as limiting the ability to authorise such measures to investigate more minor offences like tax avoidance), it is unlikely that the IPA after the implementation of such changes would be in compliance with the EU standards.[65] An additional indication is also given by the Data Protection Bill, which includes major carve-outs that would allow the UK government to avoid GDPR transparency requirements in case of immigration issues, or when the data is held by organisations addressing national security concerns.[66] Taken together, the UK rules seem to grant the government wide authorities to collect and retain personal data or force companies to retain data the government may wish to inspect later. Consequently, specific orders by the UK government could violate EU citizen's rights, and the EU is unlikely to consider the laws to create a stable enough regime to protect its citizen's data.

While it may be possible that the IPA and Data Protection Bill will be amended to narrow their scope in order to be more aligned with EU rules, the manifesto of the Conservative Party would suggest that

---

[64] Investigatory Powers Act (2016).

[65] Andrew D. Murray, *Data transfers between the EU and UK post Brexit?*, 7 International Data Privacy Law 149, 149 (2017).

[66] Dickson, *What you need to know about the UK's Data Protection Bill*, *supra* note 55.

political intent is a shift toward more surveillance in general.[67] A frequently quoted excerpt from the manifesto sets the tone in this regard: "Some people say that it is not for the government to regulate when it comes to the technology and the internet. We disagree."[68] Giving details on that intent, the government has already mentioned plans to force encrypted content and communications providers to build backdoors for law enforcement purposes into their security, and the idea of banning non-compliant services has been circulated.[69] Additionally, government officials have proposed the monitoring and ban of negative content on social networks, as well as the blocking of certain sites, for example with pornographic content.[70]

One indication of this political will in particular is seen in the "European Union (Withdrawal) Bill" (formerly Great Repeal Bill), which specifically attempted to repeal the Charter of Fundamental Rights instead of passing it into UK law like the majority of other laws.[71] While the government contended that the Charter was not necessary as all rights were already covered by domestic law, a member of the House of the Lords commented after the reading of the bill "If, as the Government suggests, the Charter of Fundamental Rights adds nothing to the content of EU law which is being retained, we do not understand why an exception [to repeal it, unlike other EU laws] needs to be made for it."[72]

Indeed, one possible explanation is given by an opponent of the Charter, the Chairman of the European Scrutiny Committee, Sir Bill Cash MP: "the Charter of Fundamental Rights is dealt a fatal blow by the arguments for Parliamentary Sovereignty."[73] Parliamentary Sovereignty is the British concept of the parliament's absolute power; if an act is passed by parliament, it is the supreme law of the land, and cannot be invalidated by the judiciary on grounds of previous or superseding law.[74]

---

67 Jay McGregor, *Why Are UK Prime Minister Theresa May's Web Regulation Plans Still A Thing?*, Forbes (Jun 2017), https://www.forbes.com/sites/jaymcgregor/2017/-06/30/why-are-theresa-mays-web-regulation-plans-still-a-thing/#7452c56030fe

68 Conservative Party Manifesto, 82, https://www.conservatives.com/manifesto

69 Andrew Griffin, Theresa May to create new internet that would be controlled and regulated by government, The Independent (2017), https://www.independent.co.uk/-life-style/gadgets-and-tech/news/theresa-may-internet-conservatives-government-a7744176.html.

70 *Id.*

71 European Union (Withdrawal) Bill, Bill 5, 57/1.

72 UK Parliament, *Chapter 6: Charter of Fundamental Rights*, https://publications.parliament.uk/pa/ld201719/ldselect/ldconst/69/6909.htm.

73 Sir Bill Cash MP, *Lord Goldsmith previously fought the Charter of Fundamental Rights, what's changed?* (April 2018), https://brexitcentral.com/lord-goldsmith-fought-charter-fundamental-rights-whats-changed/.

74 *Id.*

Considering the Charter's history and status in the European Union, he argues that the Charter, if transferred into domestic law, may create a precedent for the judiciary to overturn laws on the basis of the Charter being more "fundamental" in nature.[75] While the Charter generally only affects EU laws and national laws based on EU directives, most EU laws will be transferred to being domestic law by the UK, and those laws would still make reference to, and be backed by, the Charter.[76] The attempt to repeal the Charter by the government may therefore be seen as an attempt to regain Parliamentary Sovereignty in principle – but this sovereignty would only be necessary in practice if they intended to act contrary to EU standards.

Despite the strong push by the government to repeal the Charter, the House of Lords has currently defeated that part of the European Union (Withdrawal) Bill and has sent it back to the House of Commons for review.[77] While the House of Lords has previous given in to political pressure on Bills it has sent back, the cross-party majority of 71 votes and strong opinions on both side may suggest that it will hold its ground regarding the Charter.[78]

Based on its passing of the IPA, the Data Protection Bill, attempted repeal of the Charter, as well as its political intent, the UK under the conservatives seems to be strongly pro-surveillance/law enforcement. However, the implementation of the GDPR during the transition period, current state of the Withdrawal Agreement, and opposition to the repeal of the Charter in the House of Lords may create political inertia to lowering existing citizen's rights.

IV. THE IMPACT OF BREXIT

Considering the new EU GDPR will secure the rights of EU citizen's anywhere, data sharing by the EU will be limited to countries with similarly high standards. While the Withdrawal Agreement indicates that there is agreement between the EU and the UK on sharing data related to law enforcement (case A), the future of access to personal data for UK companies is less certain. In order for UK companies to retain access

---

[75] *Id.*

[76] Joelle Grogan, *The good, the bad and the ugly arguments for ditching the EU Charter of Fundamental Rights*, LSE Brexit Blog (February 2018), http://blogs.lse.ac.uk/brexit/2018/02/01/the-good-the-bad-and-the-ugly-arguments-for-ditching-the-eu-charter-of-fundamental-rights/.

[77] UK Parliament, *Chapter 6: Charter of Fundamental Rights*, *supra* note 68.

[78] BBC News, EU Withdrawal Bill suffers third Lords defeat on human rights charter (April 2018), http://www.bbc.com/news/uk-politics-43872520.

to transfers of data on EU citizens, the country will have to have a similar legal regime, or it will risk jeopardising much of its cross-border commerce in services and data processing.

A. LEGAL MECHANISMS:

The EU already has a number of mechanisms in place in order to allow access to its citizens' data from third party countries. Three of them in particular might be used in order to allow UK companies to gain access to the data:[79]

1. Adequacy decision. The European Commission (EC) may determine whether a third country's laws are considered "adequate" by EU standards. This process requires a qualified majority decision by the Commission, based on a wholistic approach, and is valid for 4 years following such a decision. Considering the previous CJEU decisions regarding indiscriminate data collection, it is unlikely that the UK would receive an adequacy judgement if it pursued the political direction that has shown through in its adoption of the IPA, European Union (Withdrawal) Bill, and manifesto.[80]

   Should an adequacy decision be made by the EC, data transfers of all 5 cases discussed above would be able to happen without further steps being necessary on behalf of the companies or governments. While this would create the most practical and efficient framework for data transfers between the UK and EU, the UK's direction regarding data privacy may make the framework less stable than it would be with other third parties:

   The CJEU established in *Schrems* that national supervisory authorities are permitted to review the level of protection provided by a data recipient country, even if an adequacy decision has been found by the EC.[81] As a result, such an adequacy decision would be continuously subject to review by the national supervisory authorities of the member states in case any of their citizen's makes a claim that his or her data is being misused. Assuming that the UK's existing law would suffice for an adequacy decision, any specific order given under the laws would therefore create a possible cause for withdrawal of the adequacy decision, creating uncertain grounds.

---

[79] Dr. Detlev Gabel, Tim Hickman, *Cross-Border Data Transfers – Unlocking the EU General Data Protection Regulation*, WHITE & CASE (2017), https://www.whitecase.com-/publications/article/chapter-13-cross-border-data-transfers-unlocking-eu-general-data-protection.

[80] Andrew D. Murray, *Data transfers between the EU and UK, supra* note 61.

[81] Case C-362/14, Maximilian Schrems v Data Protection Commissioner 2015, ECLI:EU:C:2015:650.

While this system would likely be favoured by British companies, EU companies and EU governments, as it allows for the easiest free transfer of data, the British government would have to change its direction regarding the increase of surveillance powers in order for the adequacy decision to become a feasible option.

2. Binding Corporate Rules. An additional possibility would be for companies to establish an EU subsidiary and apply for recognition of its "Binding Corporate Rule". This system allows for a company to establish a set of rules regarding the transfer, processing, and security across borders, as long as the data stays inside of the company.[82] While companies may attempt to gain the ability to transfer data under this regime, it is important to note that this scenario would only affect case C of the previous examples, and would therefore be a very limited solution to begin with. Additionally, the wide-ranging authority of the UK government to access the data held by companies would likely mean that a company would be unable to abide by both the Binding Corporate Rules approved by the EU and by requests for data by the government. Considering the likely conflicts with the data access provision of the IPA and the governments intent on forcing companies to have backdoors to their encrypted data are therefore likely indications that Binding Corporate Rules will be an unlikely medium for data transfers.

3. Bespoke agreement. The final option would be for the UK to negotiate a bespoke agreement for access to data, possibly as part of a larger trade deal. However, it would be unlikely for the EU to accept such an agreement without further concessions on the part of the UK, as the EU's own Charter of Fundamental Rights would require it to protect its citizens' data.[83] Consequently, neither its institutions nor its member states would have the authority to lower the threshold of data protection expected from the UK without repealing or changing the Charter first.

In summary, the mechanism currently employed by the EU to grant data access to the UK will likely not allow for the EU to share its data with the UK under the legislature intended to be implemented by the Conservative Party. While some limited transfers could occur under

---

[82] European Commission, *Binding Corporate Rules*, https://ec.europa.eu/info/law/law-topic/data-protection/data-transfers-outside-eu/binding-corporate-rules_en.

[83] European Commission, *When does the Charter apply?*, https://ec.europa.eu/info/aid-development-cooperation-fundamental-rights/your-rights-eu/eu-charter-fundamental-rights/when-does-charter-apply_en.

divergent data protection regimes, it is unlikely that existing levels of data exchange could be facilitated if the UK law diverged to the extent that it could not receive an adequacy decision.

B. *ECONOMIC CONSIDERATIONS*

While the legal mechanism will likely prevent the data sharing under the Conservative Party's plans, it is in the economic interest of both sides to enable the free flow of data.

The market in direct services between EU and UK, which is approximately £100 billion in size, will likely be affected by the lack of data flow.[84] Since financial services, legal services, and data processing companies, many of which are located in the UK, all depend on transfer of data between their location of operation and supplier-, client-, and partner firms in the EU, it is likely that a blocking of the data transfers would result in many of them leaving to the EU or having to downsize their operations. These transfers all fall under case B in the previous discussion and present a major part of the UK economy in business to business services.

Further, a number of UK companies are currently transferring EU citizens' data to third countries through the Binding Corporate Rules scheme, having applied to this through, and with their status being administered by, the UK Data Protection Agency (DPA).[85] Since the UK will become a third country, its DPA will cease to have the authority to provide this status absent a bespoke agreement based on strong equivalence of laws, and the companies will have to create a subsidiary in the EU or move their status to one of their subsidiaries in a member state. These scenarios fall under case C, and represent a more certain, but less impactful section of economic problems created by Brexit's new data law divergence.

Finally, there is the unlikely but possible scenario of the UK diverging too strongly from EU standards to even support case D transfers. While most countries in the world, including the U.S., are in no danger of having legal regimes that will create a dilemma for companies as to whether to comply with GDPR or their domestic laws,[86] the UK's plans for the weakening of encryption may qualify, if implemented in an extreme fashion: Assuming that a company is keeping data on their EU clients on UK servers, a UK decision to force them to

[84] United Kingdom Parliament: Economic Policy and Statistics Section, In brief: UK-EU Economic Relations, 2016, Commons 06091, at 6.

[85] European Commission, *Binding Corporate Rules*, supra note 82.

[86] Yaki Faitelson, *Yes, The GDPR Will Affect Your U.S.-Based Business, supra* note 26.

weaken their encryption, or to retain their data in order for the government to get access may create a situation in which a company will have to choose between compliance with GDPR requirements, such as the right to erasure, or compliance with UK domestic law, such as the notice to retain the data. While the occurrence of such a scenario is exceedingly unlikely, it would force rational companies to outsource their data storage to non-UK servers in order to avoid liability.

Overall, it is in the UK's economic interest to keep its domestic data protection laws equivalent to those of the EU, and even mild divergence would interfere with vast parts of the economy. Considering that the UK will be in compliance with GDPR requirements until the end of the transition period, however, will likely create economic inertia, as any change will be perceived as the direct result of actions taken by the UK government.

C. POLITICAL DIFFICULTIES

Even if the UK should decide to abandon its plans of stronger data regulation in order to gain access to EU data, any of the mechanisms described above would subject UK laws and procedures to the "whims" of EC or CJEU insofar as both branches of the EU could revoke the adequacy decision, bringing about the consequences described above. Considering that the political interpretation of Brexit was to avoid such an outcome, there will likely be backlash to such a decision.[87]

Likewise, the intent of the conservative party, as discussed in the UK approach section above, goes towards more surveillance, and many of the political forces will likely try to continue along this path. While the possible retention of the Charter of Fundamental Rights may create more inertia against the conservative party's direction, the perception of still adhering to the EU Charter, and potential persuasive nature of CJEU decisions regarding matters based on the Charter will likely create even more political backlash.

Nevertheless, the current outcry over data protection problems might mean that not having EU equivalence and instead creating the regime intended by the Conservative Party will create issues with the public as well,[88] especially in the face of the Cambridge Analytica

---

[87] Brian Flanagan, *The strange case of Brexit and British sovereignty*, RTE (Mar 2018), https://www.rte.ie/eile/brainstorm/2018/0301/944407-the-strange-case-of-brexit-and-british-sovereignty/.

[88] Reuters, *Amid global outcry, Facebook will introduce new features allowing users to download and delete their data*, SOUTH CHINA MORNING POST (April 2018),

meddling in the referendum having potentially affected the Brexit results in the first place. Creating even stronger controls will likely alienate especially the younger voters who are used to a free internet and who have been affected by the Facebook/Cambridge Analytica scandal, which would create incentives for the weakened Conservative Party to avoid such a route.

In this context, it might even be possible for the government to use the public outcry over data protection in order to justify a system of UK equivalence to the EU rules, as well as the perceived submission to EC and CJEU. Such a political move could capitalise on the current scandals over data privacy and suggest that the referendum has to be reinterpreted in light of their occurrence.

V. CONCLUSION

Looking at the data protection and privacy trends within EU and UK, it is unlikely the UK will to be able to gain access to EU data transfers without a major change in political direction. With the current global data protection trend, it is likely that the UK will not be politically able to follow the direction chosen by the Conservative Party. In the face of that inability, it is likely that the UK will attempt to benefit their economy instead and pursue EU equivalence in its data protection laws. Nevertheless, it would appear that recent developments regarding data privacy have put the Conservative Party in a lose-lose situation, and as such, they will either frustrate many of the voters who were hoping to avoid being controlled "by Brussels", or instead frustrate many of the voters who are concerned by the implication of the scandals.

Ultimately, the UK's agreement to align itself with the EU data protection standards before its exit from the Union may give the biggest indication of where the UK will go: After institutions and companies will have gone through major efforts to create a GDPR compliant system, their inertia and the general economic incentive to be aligned with the EU will likely lead to the UK retaining an equivalent structure. Beyond the positive economic effect, the wide-reaching positive reactions to the GDPR in light of the Facebook scandal, and potential adoption by the US of similar standards, may also give an indication that the regime would be the best option for British citizens independently of Brexit.

---

http://www.scmp.com/news/world/united-states-canada/article/2139334/amid-global-outcry-facebook-will-introduce-new.

CHAPTER 18: THE SPECIAL RELATIONSHIP IN THE DIGITAL AGE: EXAMINING U.S.-UK DIGITAL TRADE POST-BREXIT

KANZANIRA THORINGTON

On 27 February 2018, British Secretary of State for International Trade, Liam Fox delivered a speech outlining the UK government's position on the country's commercial policy and the future of the United Kingdom ("UK") in the global economy.[1] In his speech, Secretary Fox emphasized the need for the UK to remain competitive in the fast-growing digital economy. For Secretary Fox, the UK's exit from the European Union ("EU") presents an opportunity for the country to break away from the "rigidity" of Brussels' trade practices and forge its own path as a "global leader in digital trade."[2] Specifically, the UK can now embrace a more flexible trade agenda when it comes to negotiating agreements with third-party countries, namely the United States ("U.S.").[3] It is true that as an EU Member State the UK's ability to engage in the global digital economy has been constrained by the bloc's policy positions. The UK's ability to participate in digital trade with countries outside the EU is completely subject to the European Commission's third party country adequacy decisions.[4] Brexit may appear to provide the UK with the opportunity to finally strike out on its own, but as the UK withdraws from the EU it has become increasingly apparent that negotiating its own international digital trade arrangements may be more complex than the picture presented by Secretary Fox.

After the EU, the UK's most important digital trading partner is the U.S.[5] Digital trade between the U.S. and the UK is currently governed by the EU-U.S. Privacy Shield, a transatlantic data transfer regime that allows U.S. companies to access and process data from EU Member

---

[1] Liam Fox, "Britain's Trading Future" (speech, Bloomberg London, London, UK) February 27, 2018. https://www.gov.uk/government/speeches/britains-trading-future.

[2] *Id.*

[3] *Id.*

[4] Nigel Cory, "Cross-Border Data Flows: Where Are the Barriers, and What Do They Cost?," *Information Technology & Innovation Foundation*, May 1, 2017. http://www2.itif.org/2017-cross-border-data-flows.pdf?_ga=2.96308312.574869217.1524777720-1691918850.1523900938.

[5] Kati Suominen. "Where the Money Is: The Transatlantic Digital Market," *Center for Strategic & International Studies,* October 12, 2017. https://www.csis.org/blogs/future-digital-trade-policy-and-role-us-and-uk/where-money-transatlantic-digital-market.

States. However, once the UK officially leaves the EU it will no longer be subject to the Privacy Shield and will have no arranged mechanism to continue its digital trade relationship with the U.S.[6] Despite the fact that the future of U.S.-UK commercial activity depends on the continuance of unhindered and uninterrupted cross-border data flows, the UK has not put forward any coherent plans to ensure this outcome.

To maintain the status-quo the UK will have to negotiate its own data transfer deal with the U.S. Furthermore, the UK will also have to balance any U.S. digital trade agreements with its current and future obligations to the EU. This chapter seeks to address the dilemma the British government faces in negotiating a digital trade regime with a key trading partner as well as provide possible solutions for the UK. Part I of this chapter provides a brief introduction to digital trade and an overview of the U.S.-UK. digital trade regime. Part II describes the limitations the UK will face in its data transfer negotiations with the U.S. Part III outlines the different options the UK has to prevent a disruption to U.S.-UK data flows. Finally, Part IV examines how a free trade agreement between the U.S. and UK will impact the nature of digital trade between the two countries, and the challenges it could present to the UK's future relationship with the EU.

I. BACKGROUND INFORMATION

A. *WHAT IS DIGITAL TRADE?*

Technological advancements and the rise of digital platforms have transformed global trade in the 21st century. In 2016, the economic impact of the Internet was estimated to be $4.2 trillion, equivalent to the world's fifth largest economy, and today a growing share of global trade flows are digital.[7] While there is no single description of digital trade, there is a general consensus that it includes digital transactions in goods and services delivered digitally or physically between consumers, businesses and governments.[8] The scope of digital trade ranges from digitally-enabled purchases of digital services and goods, such as financial services or a purchase of on an e-book, to digitally-enabled physically delivered goods and services, such as an online purchase of a piece of

---

[6] Hayley Evans and Shannon Togawa Mercer, "No Privacy Shield, No Parachute?: The Brexit Cliff Edge and Data Regulation, *Lawfare* (blog), November 30, 2017. https://www.lawfareblog.com/no-privacy-shield-no-parachute-brexit-cliff-edge-and-data-regulation.

[7] Rachel F. Fefer, Shayerah Ilias Akhtar, and Wayne M. Morrison, "Digital Trade and U.S. Trade Policy," *Congressional Research Service*, June 6, 2017. https://www.hsdl.org/-?view&did=801365.

[8] Javier López González and Marie-Agnes Jouanjean, "Digital Trade: Developing a Framework for Analysis," *OECD Trade Policy Papers*, No. 205, (Paris: OECD Publishing), 2017. http://dx.doi.org/10.1787/524c8c83-en.

clothing or booking a hotel through an online matching service.[9] Even more, digital platforms and lower transportation costs allow for a larger number of smaller and low-valued packages to be traded, which is particularly beneficial for small and medium sized enterprises (SMEs). Specifically, the rise of digital marketplaces such as Amazon and eBay provide SMEs unprecedented access to foreign markets and consumers.[10]

The flow of data, or information, across borders is imperative to the success of the global digital economy. Data is at the core of every digital trade transaction. Data-transfers not only connect businesses and individuals, but also organize the flow of goods and services. Companies use data to monitor supply chains and manage global workforces as well as process personal data to adapt their services and products to customers.[11] Between 2005 and 2014, the volume of global data flows increased 45-fold,[12] and continues to grow faster than the overall rate of global trade.[13] While cross-border data flows are essential to sustain the development of the global digital economy, they also create challenges for governments and policymakers. Digital trade issues extend across various policy areas, including trade, data protection and national security, and as such many countries have increased regulation around cross-border data transfers. While many countries see these limitations on digital trade and data flows as necessary protection for consumers, others view these actions as unnecessary barriers to trade.

B. HOW IS IT REGULATED?

Despite the rapid expansion of the digital economy, there is no global regulatory framework for digital trade or data flows. Current multilateral trade rules were negotiated during the early stages of the digital economy and while the WTO framework briefly acknowledged digital trade in a 1998 work program on e-commerce,[14] there has been little advancement on the multilateral level to address digital trade rules.[15] As a result, countries have increasingly utilized bilateral and plurilateral trade agreements to develop digital trade rules and tackle emerging trade barriers. Simultaneously, there has been a surge in unilateral data flow regulation, such as restricting the flow of cross-border data for privacy

---

[9] *Id.*
[10] *Id.*
[11] Cory, *supra* note 4.
[12] Fefer, Akhtar, and Morrison, *supra* note 7.
[13] Cory, *supra* note 4.
[14] Electronic Commerce, *World Trade Organization.* https://www.wto.org/english/-thewto_e/whatis_e/tif_e/bey4_e.htm.
[15] Fefer, Akhtar, and Morrison, *supra* note 7.

and security reasons.[16] Two major actors in this area are the U.S. and the EU. While the U.S. uses its trade agreements to advocate for the free flow of data, the EU—which considers the right to privacy a fundamental human right—seeks the global harmonization of privacy regimes that matches its own system.

Since the 1990s, the EU has significantly shaped the global privacy debate. Its 1995 Data Protection Directive ("DPD") and the new General Data Protection Regulation ("GDPR"), seek to create "de facto international benchmarks" for corporate processing of personal data.[17] EU data protection law establishes an internal market that allows the free flow of personal data between countries located in the European Economic Area ("EEA") and restricts the transfer of such data to third countries. Under DPD and the GDPR, personal data may only be freely transferred (without any further safeguards) to third countries that the European Commission finds can provide an adequate level of protection of EU data. Therefore, if a third country wants unrestrained access to EU data to better facilitate digital trade, the country will have to demonstrate to the Commission that it provides a level of protection "essentially equivalent to that guaranteed within the [EU]."[18] To date, the EU has only granted an adequacy decision to twelve countries.[19] Although the U.S. is included in this short list of approved countries, the EU has not completely recognized the U.S. approach to privacy protection as "adequate."

After the DPD was passed in 1995, it became evident that the U.S. did not provide the necessary level of protection for personal data. As a federal system with a sectoral approach to data protection, the Commission found U.S. law did not meet the requirements set out by the EU's sweeping data protection regulation.[20] Nevertheless, in order to safeguard the development of transatlantic digital trade, the U.S. and the EU developed the Safe Harbor Agreement, a mechanism that allowed American companies to voluntarily sign up to EU data protection

---

16 *Id.*

17 Paul M. Schwartz, "The EU-U.S. Privacy Collision: A Turn to Institutions and Procedures," *Harvard Law Review* 126, no. 7 (2013): 1966-2009. https://harvardlawreview.org/wp-content/uploads/pdfs/vol126_schwartz.pdf.

18 Judgment of 6 October 2015, *Maximillian Schrems v Irish Data Protection Commissioner,* C-362/14, EU:C:2015:650, paragraph 73. https://eur-lex.europa.eu/legal-content/EN/ALL/?uri=CELEX:62014CJ0362.

19 Cory, *supra* note 4.

20 Jacque Borgeois, Cameron F. Kerry, William R.M. Long, Maarten Meulenbelt, and Alan Charles Raul, "Essentially Equivalent: A comparison of the legal orders for privacy and data protection in the European Union and the United States," *Sidley Austin LLP,* January 25, 2016. https://www.sidley.com/-/media/publications/essentially-equivalent--final.pdf?la=en.

principles and access EU data.[21] After almost fifteen years of operation, the Safe Harbor Agreement was invalidated by the 2015 Court of Justice of the European Union ("CJEU") decision in *Maximillian Schrems v Irish Data Protection Commissioner*, in light of the 2013 Snowden revelations which exposed U.S. government access to and surveillance of EU data. In order to preserve data flows between the two regions, the U.S. and the EU quickly negotiated the Privacy Shield agreement, adopted in 2016. The Privacy Shield operates similarly to the Safe Harbor framework in that certified corporations agree to abide by and uphold EU data protection principles; however, the new regime also imposes stricter data protection obligations than its predecessor,[22] such as more rigorous onward transfer requirements for third-party processing of EU data.[23]

Most recently, with the GDPR, which took effect on May 25, 2018, the EU has expanded the global application of its data protection regime. Unlike the DPD, which only applies to organizations within the EU, the GDPR applies to any organization—either within or outside the EU—that processes personal data of individuals in the EU where the processing is related "to the offering of goods or services" (even if it is free).[24] Thus for many U.S. companies, the GDPR will put further constraints on their EU digital trade activities as any U.S. organization that seeks to operate in the EU or engage in a digital transaction with an EU customer will be subject to the GDPR.

Though the EU's measures may aim to tackle genuine policy concerns, the resulting disruption to data flows has serious economic consequences and hinders the expansion of global digital economy. Many U.S. information and communication technology ("ICT") firms in particular have criticized emerging trade barriers, such as limitations to cross-border data flows, as inhibiting the growth of their commercial practices in foreign markets.[25] In part due to the increasingly influential

---

21 Lauren B. Movius and Nathalie Krup, "U.S. and EU Privacy Policy: Comparison of Regulatory Approaches," *International Journal of Communication* 3 (2009): 169-187. http://ijoc.org/index.php/ijoc/article/view/405/305.

22 Victoria A. Espinel, "Privacy Shield: A strong framework for transatlantic digital trade," *Euractiv*, September 19, 2017. https://www.euractiv.com/section/data-protection/opinion/privacy-shield-a-strong-framework-for-transatlantic-digital-trade/.

23 Julia Fioretti and Dustin Volz, "Privacy group launches legal challenge against EU-U.S. data pact," *Reuters*, October 26, 2016. https://www.reuters.com/article/us-eu-dataprotection-usa-idUSKCN12Q2JK.

24 Patrick Van Eecke, "Data Protection Laws of the World: EU Regulation" *DLA Piper*, https://www.dlapiperdataprotection.com/index.html?t=eu-section&c=AU.

25 Shamel Azmeh and Christopher Foster, "The TPP and the digital trade agenda: Digital industrial policy and Silicon Valley's influence on new trade agreements," *LSE Working Paper Series*, no. 16 (2016). http://www.lse.ac.uk/international-development/Assets/-Documents/PDFs/Working-Papers/WP175.pdf.

lobbying efforts of American ICT companies, such as Google and Facebook, the U.S. has incorporated digital trade as a part of its overall trade policy agenda.[26] Pursuant to its "digital trade agenda" the U.S. uses trade agreements to push for the free flow of data. For example, the U.S. was the driving force behind the e-commerce chapter of the Trans-Pacific Partnership Agreement, which includes provisions prohibiting barriers to cross-border data flows.[27] Specifically, Article 14.11 of the TPP agreement states that participating countries "shall allow the cross-border transfer of information by electronic means, including personal information when this activity is for the conduct of the business."[28] Although the U.S. is no longer party to the agreement, TPP (signed by 11 Asian-Pacific countries on March 8, 2018 in Santiago, Chile) is a testament to the U.S.'s ability to set norms for the global digital economy. In contrast to the EU's strategy of restricting access to its digital market on the basis of privacy, the U.S.'s digital trade agenda promotes open markets and free-flow of data between countries.[29] While the Privacy Shield combines the U.S. and EU's divergent approaches to data flow regulation, the development of the U.S. digital trade agenda and growing integration of the global digital economy could leave countries which wish to engage in preferential digital trade with both regions in a difficult position.

C. WHY FOCUS ON U.S.-UK DIGITAL TRADE?

U.S.-UK relations, also known as the "special relationship," is defined by shared historical, political and linguistic ties that have fostered a deepened economic relationship between the two countries. As a member of the EU, the UK has always had a strong relationship with the U.S. in terms of trade, and the UK is often viewed by the U.S. as a liberalizing force within the bloc.[30] As the UK withdraws from the EU, the U.S. anticipates a continued close economic relationship with the UK. Both U.S. President Donald Trump and British Prime Minister Theresa May have advocated for a U.S.-UK free trade agreement ("FTA") once the UK has left the EU.[31]

Any talks between the U.S. and the UK on the future of their economic relationship will have to consider U.S.-UK digital trade.

---

[26] *Id.*
[27] *Id.*
[28] Chapter 14 of Trans-Pacific Partnership Agreement (TPP). https://ustr.gov/sites/default/files/TPP-Final-Text-Electronic-Commerce.pdf
[29] Cory, *supra* note 4.
[30] Shayerah Ilias Akhtar, "U.S.-UK Free Trade Agreement: Prospects and Issues for Congress," *Congressional Research Service*, April 14, 2017. https://fas.org/sgp/-crs/row/R44817.pdf.
[31] *Id.*

Through its EU membership, the UK has been able to use Safe Harbor and the Privacy Shield to participate in the flourishing transatlantic economy. Within this framework, the U.S. and the UK have a particularly lucrative relationship. The majority of transatlantic flows originate from the UK,[32] and the U.S. and the UK are each other's top trading partners of online goods and services.[33] In terms of e-commerce, 70% of UK e-commerce shoppers use U.S. e-commerce sites and 49% of American consumers use UK sites.[34] Even more, the UK is the U.S.'s biggest trading partner of digitally-enabled services—it is responsible for 23 percent of U.S. exports and 29 percent of U.S. imports of digitally deliverable services from the EU.[35]

II. THE UK'S DILEMMA

According to UK tech industry experts, the Privacy Shield is "disproportionately important for the UK within the EU."[36] Cross-border data flows are essential for the UK-U.S. economic relationship, and the EU-U.S. data transfer agreement has enabled the development and growth of U.S.-UK digital trade. Nevertheless, once the UK leaves the EU it will no longer be subject to the Privacy Shield and will be considered a third party in terms of data transfers between the EU and the U.S.[37] There are growing concerns that "Brexit day" will mean the end of UK-U.S. data flows, jeopardizing digital trade between the two countries.[38] Although British Minister for Digital Economy, Matt Hancock remains hopeful that the UK and the U.S. will create their own system to maintain "the same unhindered flow of data," the UK government has yet to propose any comprehensive solutions.[39] This is particularly concerning as any U.S.-UK arrangement will be further complicated by the Withdrawal Agreement and any data transfer arrangement the UK makes with the EU.

Although UK-U.S. data flows are important to the British economy, 75 percent of the UK's cross border data flows are with the other EU member states, and as such the UK government will prioritize an EU

---

32 House of Lords European Union Committee, "Brexit: the EU data protection package," *House of Lords*, 3rd Report of Session 2017-2019, July 18, 2017. https://publications.parliament.uk/pa/ld201719/ldselect/ldeucom/7/7.pdf.

33 Suominen, *supra* note 5.

34 *Id.*

35 *Id.*

36 House of Lords European Union Committee, *supra* note 32.

37 Evans and Mercer, *supra* note 6.

38 *Id.*

39 *Id.*

data-transfer agreement over any future U.S. negotiations.[40] Prime Minister May has stated maintaining EU-UK data flows is one of the "five foundations" of the UK's future relationship with the EU; however, the exact nature of the UK-EU data flows post-Brexit remains uncertain.[41] In its guidelines for future withdrawal negotiations with the UK, the EU states that any future UK-EU data flows would be governed by an adequacy decision.[42][43] The UK has proposed developing a "novel, bespoke data sharing agreement with the EU."[44] In a May 2018 position paper on the future of UK-EU data protection, the British government stressed the need to preserve the legal certainty and efficiency of data flows post-Brexit.[45] As such, the UK proposes a future data sharing arrangement that goes beyond the current adequacy decision framework provided to other third countries, and one that cannot be unilaterally rescinded by the EU.[46] Specifically, this enhanced adequacy model will ensure the high standards of protection for data flows and continued regulatory cooperation with the European Data Protection Board and the UK's Information Commissioner's Office—the largest data protection authority in the EU.[47]

Despite the UK's confidence, an adequacy decision—allowing the free flow of data between the UK and other EEA member states—is by no means guaranteed. It is still unclear if the UK's future data protection framework will meet the EU's standards. With its recent Data Protection

---

[40] Department for Exiting the European Union, "The exchange and protection of personal data: A Future Partnership Paper," *HM Government,* August 24, 2017. https://assets.publishing.service.gov.uk/government/uploads/system/uploads/attachment_data/file/639853/The_exchange_and_protection_of_personal_data.pdf.

[41] Mark Scott and Annabelle Dickson, "Brexit threat to data flows," *Politico Europe*, March 9, 2018. https://www.politico.eu/article/uk-eu-theresa-may-brexit-brussels-michel-barnier-data-protection-privacy-flows/.

[42] European Council, "European Council (Art. 50) (23 March 2018)-Guidelines," *European Union,* March 23 2018. http://www.consilium.europa.eu//media/33458/23-euco-art50-guidelines.pdf

[43] Shannon Togawa Mercer, "Brexit: One Year Anniversary," *Lawfare* (blog), April 2, 2018. https://www.lawfareblog.com/brexit-one-year-anniversary.

[44] Hayley Evans, "Summary: United Kingdom Data Protection Bill," *Lawfare* (blog), November 30, 2017. https://www.lawfareblog.com/summary-united-kingdom-data-protection-bill.

[45] Edouard de Nyary Comandini and Christopher M. Loeffler, "No Post-Brexit Arrangement on Data Protection Will Affect UK-EU Trade," *The Trade and Manufacturing Monitor* (blog), July 27, 2018. https://www.ustrademonitor.com.

[46] Id.

[47] Department for Exiting the European Union, "Framework for the UK-EU Partnership Data Protection," *HM Government,* May 23, 2018. https://www.gov.uk/government/publications/framework-for-the-uk-eu-partnership-data-protection.

Act 2018 (received Royal Assent on 23 May 2018),[48] the UK has incorporated the GDPR into its national legislation.[49] Additionally, Article 67 of the EU Withdrawal Agreement states the EU data protection law will continue to apply in the UK during the transition period from March 29, 2019 to December 31, 2020.[50] Although this provision is subject to further negotiation,[51] it is likely in the UK's best interest to remain regulatory aligned with the EU to secure an adequacy decision. However, there are still some contingencies that could impact a UK adequacy decision, including the UK's data protection laws after the transition period as well as any data flow agreements it makes with outside countries.[52]

So what does this mean for U.S.-UK digital trade? While the UK will no longer be a member of the EU, as pointed out by the House of Lords EU Committee and evidenced by the Withdrawal Agreement, there is "no prospect of a clean break" with the EU on data protection law post-Brexit.[53] An adequacy decision means that EU institutions, such as the European Data Protection Board and the CJEU, will continue to influence UK data protection law. The UK will have to follow any alterations made in EU law in order to maintain the necessary level of protection to facilitate EU-UK data flows. Even more, an adequacy decision also means that the UK will have to consider how any changes in national practice could impact its adequacy status.[54] Thus, in any future digital trade arrangement with the U.S., it will be imperative for the UK to prove the U.S. can establish the same level of protection ensured under the Privacy Shield. In other words, if the UK takes a "lax approach" to onward data transfers to the U.S.,[55] or negotiates a U.S.-UK digital trade deal that does not meet the EU's protection standards, it could endanger the country's future relationship with the EU.[56]

---

[48] Katie Lamb, "Introducing the Data Protection Act 2018!," *Lexology,* June 6, 2018. https://www.lexology.com/library/detail.aspx?g=b66f89d5-6834-4ef6-9320-9b72f4972195.

[49] *Id.*

[50] Draft Agreement on the withdrawal of the United Kingdom of Great Britain and Northern Ireland from the European Union and the European Atomic Energy Community (Draft Withdrawal Agreement), *European Union,* March 19, 2018. https://ec.europa.eu/commission/sites/beta-political/files/draft_agreement_coloured.pdf

[51] David Allen Green, "A Brexit withdrawal agreement in name only," *The Financial Times,* March 20, 2018. https://www.ft.com/content/38570c12-2b92-11e8-9b4b-bc4b9f08f381.

[52] Department for Exiting the European Union, *supra* note 40.

[53] *Id.*

[54] *Id.*

[55] *Id.*

[56] *Id.*

In negotiating a U.S.-UK digital trade deal, the UK will have to juggle its EU commitments with a U.S. digital trade agenda. Fortunately for the UK, the Withdrawal Agreement may provide the UK more time to develop a future arrangement with the U.S. As all provisions of EU law governing the protection of personal data shall apply during the transition period,[57] subject to possible further negotiation, the UK should be considered a party of the Privacy Shield throughout the transition period, and there will not be a disruption in U.S.-UK data flows (and digital trade) until after December 31, 2020. Additionally, under the Withdrawal Agreement the UK and the EU have fully agreed that the UK will be able to negotiate its own international agreements during the transition period,[58] meaning the UK will be able to benefit from the Privacy Shield while developing its own agreement with the U.S. for the purposes of data transfers and digital trade.

III. LEGAL OPTIONS FOR U.S.-UK DIGITAL TRADE POST-BREXIT

A. *STANDARD CONTRACTUAL CLAUSES*

One way the U.S. and the UK could prevent a disruption to digital trade flows is to rely on market solutions, such as standard contractual clauses ("SCCs"). SCCs are popular safeguard measures used by companies to transfer data out of the EEA to third countries that have not obtained an adequacy decision from the European Commission.[59] SCCs are essentially provisions within a contract between a data exporter and importer, obligating the parties to guarantee an adequate level of protection for the personal data involved in the transaction.[60] If the U.S. and the UK are unable to develop a data-transfer deal before the UK is forced to leave the Privacy Shield, companies can use SCCs as an EU-approved mechanism to continue digital trade flows between the two countries.

Despite their popularity, SCCs may not be a sustainable solution for U.S.-UK digital trade. Although SCCs are an attractive option for large multinational corporations, they are particularly burdensome for SMEs in terms of the legal costs associated with their implementation.[61] If the U.S. and the UK solely relied on SCCs for data transfers, it would

---

[57] Article 67, Draft Withdrawal Agreement.

[58] Article 124(4), Draft Withdrawal Agreement.

[59] Department for Exiting the European Union, *supra* note 40.

[60] Caroline Krass, Jason N. Kleinwaks, Ahmed Baladi and Emmanuelle Bartoli, "The General Data Protection Regulation: A Primer for U.S.-Based Organizations That Handle EU Personal Data," *Compliance & Enforcement of NYU School of Law* (blog), December 11, 2017, https://wp.nyu.edu/compliance_enforcement/2017/12/11/the-general-data-protection-regulation-a-primer-for-u-s-based-organizations-that-handle-eu-personal-data/.

[61] Department for Exiting the European Union, *supra* note 40.

seriously hinder SMEs' ability to engage on cross-border digital trade.[62] Even more, while SCCs are currently accepted under EU law, there are growing concerns of their ability to adequately protect personal data transferred outside the EEA. Most recently, the Irish High Court in *Data Protection Commissioner v Facebook Ireland Limited and Maximillian Schrems,* has referred the issues of SCCs to the CJEU which will examine the continued validity of SCCs under EU law.[63] In its invalidation of the Safe Harbor Principles, the CJEU has already demonstrated its ability to disregard the security of transatlantic data flows to protect EU personal data, thus an invalidation of the SCCs scheme is possible. Therefore, while the UK could use SCCs to maintain U.S.-UK digital trade and remain compliant with EU data protection standards, the unknown future of this mechanism under EU law makes SCCs an unfavorable solution.

B. U.S.-UK FREE TRADE AGREEMENT

After Prime Minister May and President Trump agreed to begin informal talks for a future U.S.-UK trade agreement, the UK and U.S. established a Trade and Investment Working Group to support U.S.-UK commercial activity (including digital trade) throughout the Brexit process as well as "lay the groundwork" for a potential U.S.-UK FTA.[64] As the U.S. and the UK are already preparing for an FTA, simply incorporating a digital trade provision into the trade agreement appears to be an effective solution to ensure continued digital flows. However, it is not that simple. Relying on an FTA as a mechanism for U.S.-UK digital trade flows presents both short term and long-term problems (discussed in Part IV) for the UK.

In the short term, an FTA is not a practical solution to guarantee digital trade flows between the U.S. and the UK come Brexit day. As mentioned above, once the UK is no longer subject to the Privacy Shield (either on May 29, 2019 or the end of the transition period), it will need an immediate solution to prevent the disruption of digital trade with the U.S. While in theory the Withdrawal Agreement gives the UK the ability to negotiate a U.S. digital trade deal before the country leaves the Privacy Shield framework,[65] in practice this strategy is not attainable. The UK's ability to enter into international agreements during the transition period

---

[62] *Id.*

[63] Glyn Moody, "Bad News for 'Privacy Shield': As Expected, the EU's Top Court Will Examine Legality of Sending Personal Data to US," *Techdirt,* April 16, 2018. https://www.techdirt.com/articles/20180413/07033939620/bad-news-privacy-shield-as-expected-eus-top-court-will-examine-legality-sending-personal-data-to-us.shtml.

[64] *Id.*

[65] Article 124, Draft Withdrawal Agreement.

has been criticized as an "illusory power" as third party trading partners will not strike a deal with the UK until its future trading relationship with the EU is defined.[66] Additionally, even if the U.S. is willing to enter formal trade negotiations with the UK, it is highly unlikely that a U.S.-UK FTA will conclude and go into effect before December 31, 2020. For example, the U.S.-South Korea FTA took five years to finalize.[67] Therefore, even if the UK and the U.S. develop an FTA it cannot serve as an immediate solution for post-Brexit digital trade flows.

C. U.S.-UK PRIVACY SHIELD

Finally, the U.S. and the UK could develop their own data sharing arrangement, similar to the present Swiss-U.S. Privacy Shield, to facilitate data flows and encourage digital trade. Although the country is not a member of the EU or the EEA, Switzerland has an adequacy decision from the EU allowing a free flow of data between the two territories without any further safeguards.[68] As Switzerland is not subject to the EU-U.S. Privacy Shield, it was compelled to create its own data sharing arrangement with the U.S. to maintain Swiss-U.S. digital trade flows as well as preserve its EU adequacy decision.[69]

A U.S.-UK Privacy Shield is likely the best option for the UK. In terms of administrative ease, it is preferable to SCCs. While smaller companies can be weighed down by the cost and complexity of SCCs, it would be relatively easy for UK companies to comply with a U.S.-UK Privacy Shield. Currently, a U.S. company that is already self-certified under the EU-U.S. Privacy Shield can simply sign up to the Swiss-U.S. framework by logging into its Privacy Shield Account and clicking on the Swiss Privacy Shield option.[70] Additionally, a U.S.-UK framework could provide the UK some flexibility in its data sharing relationship with the U.S. The Swiss Privacy Shield is largely aligned with the EU-U.S. Privacy Shield, however, there are small discrepancies between the two regimes.[71] For example, the Swiss-U.S. Privacy Shield defines "sensitive data" differently from the EU-U.S. Privacy Shield.[72] This means that the UK

---

[66] Green, *supra* note 49.
[67] Evans and Mercer, *supra* note 6.
[68] Undine von Diemar, Todd S. McClelland, and Jennifer C. Everett, "A New Swiss-U.S. Privacy Shield Replaces the U.S.-Swiss Safe Harbor," *Jones Day*, January 2017. http://www.jonesday.com/files/Publication/2f2b104a-14a0-4923-9dbd-8b45fc0154b8/Presentation/PublicationAttachment/4e6be4d8-a4c1-4448-8a0b-9a8b18a470a2/New_Swiss-US_Privacy_Shield.pdf.
[69] *Id.*
[70] Swiss-U.S. Privacy Shield FAQs, *International Trade Administration*, https://www.privacyshield.gov/Swiss-US-Privacy-Shield-FAQs.
[71] Evans and Mercer, *supra* note 6.
[72] *Id.*

would be able to negotiate a data sharing agreement with the U.S. that would be largely but not strictly consistent with the EU-U.S. Privacy Shield, providing the UK with some discretionary power while also settling concerns about its EU adequacy status.

Although the U.S.-UK Privacy Shield is arguably the best course of action for the UK, there are dangers in aligning its U.S. data sharing framework so closely to that of the EU. For example, although Switzerland is not subject to the CJEU, the invalidation of the Safe Harbor Principles in *Schrems* indirectly impacted Swiss-U.S. data flows. In order to preserve its adequacy decision, Switzerland's data protection laws on cross-border data flows closely mirror the EU's.[73] Thus, when EU-U.S. Safe Harbor was deemed inadequate, the Swiss-EU Safe Harbor regime (the predecessor the Swiss-U.S. Privacy Shield) was subsequently invalidated by Swiss data protection authorities.[74] Therefore, in modeling its future U.S.-UK Privacy Shield on the Swiss option, the UK would essentially risk putting its ability to transfer data to the U.S. in the hands of EU institutions.

IV. LONG TERM PROBLEM OF U.S.-UK FREE TRADE AGREEMENT

Even if the U.S. and the UK are able to come to some arrangement to maintain digital trade flows once the UK leaves the EU, it does not mean that the digital trade issue between the two countries is completely resolved as a digital trade provision in a future U.S.-UK FTA will likely have long-term implications for the UK. As mentioned above, since TPP the U.S. has used bilateral and plurilateral trade agreements to promote its digital agenda. Additionally, the recent 2018 United States Trade Representative ("USTR") Agenda highlights the need to incorporate digital trade provisions into the renegotiated North-America Free Trade Agreement ("NAFTA"),[75] a move that is supported by several members of Congress.[76]

---

[73] K Royal, "Are the Swiss and EU Data Transfer Requirements Different?" *Lexology*, August 21, 2017. https://www.lexology.com/library/detail.aspx?g=dbaca74f-c6f9-42bc-8e40-dfd8c84a717a.

[74] Steven R. Chabinsky, Detlev Gabel, Jeremy Apple, "Swiss-U.S. Privacy Shield: Key Similarities, Key Distinctions with the EU-US Approach," *White & Case*, April 10, 2017. https://www.whitecase.com/publications/article/swiss-us-privacy-shield-key-similarities-key-distinctions-eu-us-approach.

[75] Robert E. Lighthizer, "The President's 2018 Trade Policy Agenda," *United States Trade Representative*, March 2018. https://ustr.gov/sites/default/files/files/Press/Reports/2018/AR/2018%20Annual%20Report%20I.pdf.

[76] Susan Delbene, "A new NAFTA for the digital age," *The Hill*, January 25, 2018. http://thehill.com/blogs/congress-blog/economy-budget/370572-a-new-nafta-for-the-digital-age.

It is important to note that the U.S.'s digital trade agenda not only pushes for a free flow of cross-border data transfers, but also encourages a greater recognition of its privacy framework. For example, while TPP's e-commerce chapter requires all participating countries to have privacy regulations for the protection of personal data, the trade agreement does not advocate for the adoption of a particular regulatory regime.[77] Therefore, even a country such as the U.S. with a "sectoral-specific" privacy regime would have sufficient privacy protection under the TPP agreement.[78] Even more, Article 14.8(5) of TPP specifically recognizes the right of each participating country to "take different legal approaches to protecting personal information" and encouraging each Party to develop mechanisms "to promote compatibility between [the] different regimes."[79] This is a stark distinction from the EU's policy of limiting data flows to countries that demonstrate an adequate level of protection. Unlike the EU which deems the U.S.'s sectoral approach to privacy protection inadequate, the liberal language of Chapter 14 (pushed by American negotiators) requires TPP countries to allow the free flow of data to other participating countries providing *any* degree of privacy protection.

Under the new "America-first" platform of the current administration, the U.S. will undoubtedly push for greater digital market access and free flow of data in any trade agreement with the UK. If U.S. negotiators insist on including a digital trade provision (akin to the TPP e-commerce chapter) in a U.S.-UK FTA, the UK will be forced into a difficult negotiating position as it will be forced to recognize the U.S. privacy regime for the purposes of commercial data transfers. Such action by the UK would almost certainly put any EU adequacy decision or any other data transfer agreement with the EU at risk.

So where does this leave the UK? If the U.S. and the UK are not able to come to an agreement on digital trade it could possibly halt the entire FTA negotiation process. Both the U.S. and the UK have consistently stressed the importance of digital trade to their future trade policy so it is unlikely that a future trade agreement between the two countries would move forward without it. While FTA talks on data flows will be difficult for the UK, it is not necessarily impossible for the country to create a digital trade arrangement with the U.S. and meet EU privacy protection standards. Currently, Japan is in the process of a creating a

---

[77] Sam Klein, "The Data is in the Details: Cross-Border Data Flows and the Trans-Pacific Partnership," *The Diplomat,* November 23, 2015. https://thediplomat.com/2015/11/-the-data-is-in-the-details-cross-border-data-flows-and-the-trans-pacific-partnership/.

[78] *Id.*

[79] Article 14.8(5), TPP.

data protection system that can balance its TPP commitments on data flows and achieve an EU adequacy decision.[80]

In December 2017, the EU and Japan finalized their FTA, the Economic Partnership Agreement.[81] In a joint statement on their FTA the two countries committed themselves to "ensuring a high level of privacy and security of personal data…as a central factor of consumer trust in the digital economy, which also further facilitate mutual data flows."[82] After months of working together to update Japan's data protection laws, on July 17, 2018, the EU and Japan concluded their negotiations on data protection and established reciprocal recognition of an adequate level of protection, enabling a free flow of data between the regions.[83][84] Notably, while the EU has previously granted unilateral adequacy decisions, this agreement marks the first time the EU and a third country have agreed to a mutual recognition of an adequate level of data protection. To meet EU standards, Japan has agreed to implement additional measures to protect EU citizens' personal data, including stricter conditions for onward transfers of EU personal data to third countries, enhancing the protection of "sensitive data", and developing a complaint-management system for EU citizens.[85]

Despite its new commitments to the EU, as a participating member of TPP, Japan is bound to enable the free flow of cross-border data to other TPP countries that offer some level of privacy protection, even if these safeguards do not meet EU standards. Thus, in carrying out its obligations under TPP, Japan could be jeopardizing its adequacy decision with the EU. As Japan's TPP data flow commitments were largely shaped by the U.S. digital agenda, Japan is currently facing the challenge the UK will encounter in its FTA negotiations with the U.S. on digital trade.

It remains unclear how Japan plans to juggle its data flow relationship with the EU and its fellow TPP members. The EU-Japan deal still faces several obstacles, such EU privacy advocates' criticism of

---

80 Yumi Watanabe, "Japan EU Data Transfers—Mutual adequacy findings under APPI and GDPR," *Lexology*, April 9, 2018. https://www.lexology.com/library/-detail.aspx?g=c6694994-d3d0-4f00-b0c2-0f389d40c3f3.

81 *Id.*

82 Marija Bartl and Kristina Irion, "The Japan EU Economic Partnership Agreement: Flows of Personal Data to the Land of the Rising Sun," *The University of Amsterdam,* October 25, 2017.

83 Watanabe, *supra* note 78.

84 Stéphanie de Smedt, Yves Van Couter and Lola Lenfant, "EU and Japan agree on free flows of personal data-Will South Korea be next in line?" *Lexology,* July 26, 2018. https://www.lexology.com/library/detail.aspx?g=b26f3e13-84f1-4b34-9450-8453663493f0.

85 Id.

the agreement and Japan's treatment of sensitive personal information.[86] Furthermore, Japan's adequacy decision must be reviewed by the European Data Protection Board as well as receive approval from European Parliament's Committee on Civil Liberties, Justice and Home Affairs, which has recently passed a resolution to suspend the EU-U.S. Privacy Shield.[87] Nevertheless, any solutions Japan may develop to address these forthcoming challenges could be a guide for the UK in shaping its digital trade relationships with the EU and U.S.

V. CONCLUSION

Although the British government claims Brexit will allow the UK to emerge as a global digital innovator, it is clear that the UK's digital trade policy will be heavily constrained by the EU's data protection standards and the U.S. digital trade agenda. Frankly, the UK has missed its window to become a rule-maker in the global digital economy, and after Brexit the country will be caught in between two contradicting data protection regimes. Unfortunately for the UK, the EU has proved itself unyielding in its position on cross-border data flows, and the U.S. may use a UK-U.S. FTA as an opportunity to push its own agenda against the EU's growing regulatory dominance in the global digital economy. While the UK appears to be at a crossroads, its digital trade future is not necessarily hopeless. The UK can swiftly develop a U.S.-UK Privacy Shield that can ensure U.S.-UK digital trade flows do not end abruptly on Brexit day while also maintaining the necessary EU safeguards. Even more, the UK is not alone in its dilemma as other countries such as Japan are navigating between U.S. and EU norms on data flows and digital trade. Nevertheless, moving forward into and beyond the transition period the UK-U.S. digital trade relationship will continue to be shaped (either directly or indirectly) by EU institutions as the UK prioritizes its data flow and digital trade relationship with the EU.

---

[86] Mehreen Khan, "EU strikes data deal with Japan with UK looking on," *The Financial Times*, July 17, 2018. https://www.ft.com/content/d5b40334-8961-11e8-b18d-0181731a0340.

[87] Glyn Moody, "EU And Japan Agree To Free Data Flows, Just As Tottering Privacy Shield Framework Threatens Transatlantic Transfers," *TechDirt*, July 26, 2018. https://www.techdirt.com/articles/20180720/06192740272/eu-japan-agree-to-free-data-flows-just-as-tottering-privacy-shield-framework-threatens-transatlantic-transfers.shtml.

CHAPTER 19: THE FUTURE FREE TRADE AGREEMENT BETWEEN THE UNITED KINGDOM AND CHINA AFTER BREXIT

MINXI WANG

I. INTRODUCTION

As the UK prepares for its official exit from the EU, slated for March 29, 2019, it is in the process of negotiating with the EU as well as other countries in a bid to boost trade opportunities post-Brexit. One of the key countries that the UK is working to build a stronger partnership with is China,[1] which in 2016, was the seventh largest export market for the United Kingdom (4.4 percent of United Kingdom exports) and the second largest import market for United Kingdom (9.4 percent of United Kingdom imports).[2] So, at the beginning of 2018, Prime Minister Theresa May took her first foreign visit to China after the Brexit Referendum seeking to discuss the possibility of an "ambitious" post-Brexit deal with President Xi Jingping. May expressed the possibility of securing a comprehensive free trade agreement (FTA) between the two countries,[3] one that would further open China's markets to the UK.[4] Given the economic success and leaders' announcement of a "golden era" between the UK and China, this chapter will focus on a future free trade agreement between the two countries and discuss the elements that must be included in this agreement.

A free trade agreement often covers a wide array of issues, including goods, services, investments, intellectual property, e-commerce digital trade, dispute resolution, etc., among others, but for purposes of brevity, this chapter focuses on three important parts under a FTA: tariff elimination, rules of origins, and dispute settlement clauses. Part II explores the background of the economic relation between China and the UK and some issues that need to be considered before signing such a trade deal, especially as they are affected by the latest EU-UK

---

[1] China here refers to mainland China.

[2] Department for International Trade / Department for Business Strategy (UK) Energy and Industrial, INTERNATIONAL TRADE IN GOODS AND SERVICES BASED ON UN COMTRADE DATA, http://comtrade.un.org/labs/BIS-trade-in-goods (last visited Mar 29, 2018).

[3] Katya Adler, *May hails "first step" to China trade deal*, BBC NEWS, February 1, 2018, http://www.bbc.com/news/uk-politics-42897705 (last visited Mar 29, 2018).

[4] *Id. at para. 3.*57

negotiation. Part III concentrates on goods clauses within the future FTA, with a focus on tariff elimination and rules of origin. Part IV examines a potential dispute settlement clause, explaining the status quo in the EU, UK, and China. These chapters also provide some suggestions to be included in the future China-UK FTA, by using China-EU FTAs as references, and modifying them to the unique Brexit circumstances.

II. A COMPREHENSIVE FTA OR A SHALLOW FTA IN THE FUTURE?

A. WHEN CAN THE UK SIGN A FORMALIZED DEAL WITH CHINA?

One of the key reasons behind the Brexit vote was the UK's push to exit the EU customs union and the single market and to seek its own trade deals with third countries, which could be more flexible and efficient[5] than the broader EU agreements. However, the UK cannot implement any agreements with third parties immediately upon leaving the EU on March 29, 2019, which is when the two-year negotiating window ends with the EU.[6] First, according to Article 124, Section 4 of the Draft Withdrawal Agreement,

> Notwithstanding paragraph 3, during the transition period, the United Kingdom may negotiate, sign and ratify international agreements entered into in its own capacity in the areas of exclusive competence of the Union, provided those agreements do not enter into force or apply during the transition period, unless so authorized by the Union.[7]

Therefore, the UK has to wait until after December 31, 2020, which is when the 21-month transition period ends.[8] What's more, under WTO rules, "in practice, the UK would have to detach itself from the EU and regularize its position within the WTO before it could sign its own trade agreements, including with the EU."[9] That is to say, although the UK

---

[5] *May hails "first step" to China trade deal*, *supra* note 3, at para. 2.

[6] Brexit timeline: UK's departure from the EU - BBC News, http://www.bbc.com/news/uk-politics-43546199 (last visited Apr 29, 2018).

[7] Draft Agreement on the withdrawal of the United Kingdom of Great Britain and Northern Ireland from the European Union and the European Atomic Energy Community, EUROPEAN COMMISSION - EUROPEAN COMMISSION, https://ec.europa.eu/commission/publications/draft-agreement-withdrawal-united-kingdom-great-britain-and-northern-ireland-european-union-and-european-atomic-energy-community-0_en (last visited Apr 10, 2018).

[8] *Id. at article 121 transition period.*

[9] Alan Beattie, *Brexit and the WTO option: Key questions about a looming challenge*, FTCOM LOND. (2016),

can negotiate the contents of a future FTA with China, there is no administrative capacity and legal authority to sign a formalized deal until January 2021.[10]

B. ECONOMIC RELATIONS BETWEEN THE UK AND CHINA

Regardless of the approach used to leave the EU, soft Brexit or hard Brexit,[11] winning the right to independently deal with the third countries is the UK government's ambition. Around the globe, China, the world's second biggest economy, has great market demand. In 2016, China was the second largest export market for the EU[12] and the seventh largest export market for the United Kingdom in trade in goods.[13] What's more, ratifying a FTA with China is conducive to reducing the UK-China trade deficit. Since market reforms and liberalization in China, the trade deficit in goods between the two countries has increased year by year.[14] Statistics from 2016 show that the deficit of the UK's trade in goods with China was up to -€36.95bn, which was one of the largest trade deficits among European countries.[15] Therefore, trade under a FTA, through eliminating tariff rates, simplifying rules of origin, and improving dispute settlement mechanism, among others, can to some extent solve this deficit problem.

As for China, it currently views FTAs as an effective approach to integrate into the global economy and strengthen economic cooperation with other countries, as well as an important supplement to the multilateral trading system. Currently, China has 14 existing FTAs, 11

---

https://search.proquest.com/docview/1810682086/citation/393F4999AB124038PQ/1 (last visited Apr 10, 2018).

[10] Trade deals with third countries – UK in a changing Europe, , http://ukandeu.ac.uk/explainers/trade-deals-with-third-countries/ (last visited Apr 1, 2018).

[11] Soft Brexit means the UK still keeps a close relationship with the EU, through some form of membership of the EU single market; while hard Brexit refers that the UK would trade with the EU under the WTO rules, as if it were any other country outside the EU. What are the Brexit options? BBC NEWS, June 12, 2017, http://www.bbc.com/news/uk-politics-37507129 (last visited Apr 30, 2018).

[12] WTO | Publications, https://www.wto.org/english/res_e/publications_e/-world_tariff_profiles17_e.htm (last visited Apr 10, 2018).

[13] China was the 2nd largest export market for United Kingdom (9.8 percent of United Kingdom exports; $5bn), Strategy (UK), *supra* note 2.

[14] Despite a large proportion of China exports to the UK, China accounts for just a small proportion of British exports, 3.1 percent in 2016, compared with 43 percent for the European Union. The U.K. Seeks a Free Trade Deal with China, FORTUNE, http://fortune.com/2018/01/30/britain-free-trade-deal-china/ (last visited Apr 18, 2018).

[15] China-EU international trade in goods statistics—Statistics Explained, http://ec.europa.eu/eurostat/statistics-explained/index.php/China-EU_-_international_trade_in_goods_statistics (last visited Apr 14, 2018).

FTAs under negotiation, and 9 FTAs under consideration.[16] Accordingly, depending on economic factors and both countries' attitudes, signing a FTA could accelerate the UK-China "golden era" into a higher level.

C. RELEVANT ISSUES AFFECTING A POTENTIAL FTA

Despite the great benefits from a FTA, both China and the UK governments should also consider several issues. First, it is uncertain when this FTA could be formally implemented, which could take a long time not only because the UK is restrained by its transition period, but also because it needs to participate in several rounds of negotiations before achieving an agreement.[17] Given the time-consuming nature of negotiating a new FTA, the UK government's push for a comprehensive FTA with China could be stalled.

Second, some domestic industries may be hurt by a FTA. Through reducing tariff rates, making concessions in market access, and liberalizing sectors such as services under a FTA, foreign products may become more competitive and appealing in local markets. This could hurt domestic industries, therefore protecting such local is a heated issue of concern.

Third, UK exporters may not be able to rely much on China's market. Take South Korea as an example. In 2016, China was the largest export and import market for South Korea[18] under the China-Korea FTA. However, after the deployment of Terminal High Attitude Area Defense (THAAD[19]) in 2017, Beijing decided to expand the scope of sanctions to Seoul. According to the central bank in Seoul, in dollar terms, South Korea looked worse off, taking a $4.7 billion hit from the drop in tourism alone. When combined with the falling sales of South Korean cars, cosmetics and other goods in China, the dispute could cut 0.3

---

[16] China FTA Network, http://fta.mofcom.gov.cn/topic/ennorway.shtml (last visited Feb 24, 2018).

[17] For example, China and South Korea spent over three years and went through 14 rounds of negotiations to ratify their FTA, while the China-Switzerland FTA was enacted similarly —more than three years' negotiation and up to eight rounds. *Id.*

[18] Strategy (UK), *supra* note 2.

[19] "The US Army's Terminal High-Altitude Area Defense (THAAD) system that has been deployed in South Korea is designed to shoot down ballistic missiles in the terminal phase of their approach to a target. As a result, China has protested fiercely, insisting that THAAD's radar can be used to monitor the movements of its military within China and that the deployment will further destabilize the region."
Julian Ryall, WHAT IS THAAD? SOUTH KOREA'S BEST DEFENSE AGAINST A MISSILE ATTACK THE TELEGRAPH, https://www.telegraph.co.uk/news/0/thaad-south-koreas-best-defence-against-missile-attack/ (last visited Jun 4, 2018).

percentage point from GDP growth in 2017.[20] Therefore, the UK must be cautious of China's unpredictable policies and avoid making the Chinese market its primary target.

Finally, the UK should also keep an eye on their competitors—their neighbors, like France and Germany. [21] The IMF's Direction of Trade statistics show that "for most of the period between 2000 and 2015, China's imports from Germany, France, and Italy grew faster than those from the UK. The absence of an EU-China FTA did not appear to be hampering exporters from those countries."[22] That is to say, this potential China-UK FTA shall contain more competitive and attractive aspects to guarantee the UK's development in economy and trade.

In summary, negotiating a comprehensive FTA is a better choice. Around the globe, adding WTO-Plus provisions, that is provisions terms that go above and beyond the scope of the WTO agreements, to FTAs is a common trend. It includes not only traditional items like goods and services, but also broader elements like a dispute settlement mechanism and as demonstrated in the China-Korea FTA co-production on film. [23] The more aspects in a FTA, the easier to integrate both countries' economies. What's more, signing a deep FTA can help the UK to improve a balance in trade, dealing with the trade deficit and becoming more competitive among the countries in Europe.

III. GOODS CLAUSE IN THE FUTURE FTA

A. *TARIFF ELIMINATION ISSUES*

1. Current Situations in Trade in Goods

On the basis of World Tariff Profiles 2017 published by the WTO, the EU's simple average most favored nation (MFN) tariff rate was 5.2 percent and China's was 9.9 percent.[24] As for agricultural production, EU's was 11.1 percent while China's was 15.5 percent.[25] According to statistics, assuming that the UK chooses to inherit the EU's schedule

---

[20] China's Missile Sanctions Are Taking a Heavy Toll on Both Koreas, BLOOMBERG.COM, August 29, 2017, https://www.bloomberg.com/news/articles/2017-08-29/china-s-missile-sanctions-are-taking-a-heavy-toll-on-both-koreas (last visited Apr 10, 2018).

[21] Among EU Member States, Germany is the largest importer (EUR 70 billion) from and largest exporter (EUR 77 billion) to China and has the largest trade surplus with China (EUR 7 billion).

China-EU - international trade in goods statistics - Statistics Explained, *supra* note 17.

[22] Cpianalysis, BREXIT, CHINA AND THE PROSPECTS FOR AN FTA CHINA POLICY INSTITUTE: ANALYSIS (2017), https://cpianalysis.org/2017/02/28/brexit-china-and-the-prospects-for-an-fta/ (last visited Apr 8, 2018).

[23] China FTA Network, *supra* note 16.

[24] World Tariff Profiles 2017, 250 (2017).

[25] *Id.*

under hard Brexit, customs duties will be imposed.[26] As for agricultural products, since the EU-27 is the biggest vegetable and fruit supplier of the UK,[27] the relatively high tariff, compared with zero tariff in the customs union, may cause domestic price inflation in necessaries. Therefore, negotiating an agreement with China can fill this gap because China is an agricultural country with high yield, especially in fruit and vegetable.[28] As for China, it also can be the UK's ideal export market not only because it is a leading importer of animal products, including beef and lamb, but also because signing a FTA may encourage the Chinese government to reduce its import control and customs duties.

As for the annual trade amount, the EU has been China's biggest trading partner, 514.6 billion Euros of trade volume of both import and export in 2016 and China now is the EU's second-biggest trading partner behind the United States.[29] The UK had a relatively large share of the EU imports from China, accounting for 15.4 percent (€53.2bn in 2016), while the UK's exports had comparatively lower absolute values among the EU-28, only 9.6 percent (€16.3bn).[30] In 2016, the UK's top three imports of goods from China were electrical and electronic equipment, nuclear reactors, and furniture and prefabricated buildings.[31] In the same year, the UK's top three exports of goods to China were vehicles, mineral fuels, and nuclear reactors.[32] Among these commodities, China was the United Kingdom's second largest exporting partner for vehicles other than railway (9.8 percent of the UK's exports) behind the United States, and was the largest import market for electrical, electronic equipment (23.6 percent of the UK's imports) for the UK.[33] This data demonstrates that manufactured goods and non-agricultural products dominate trade

---

[26] What are the Brexit options? BBC NEWS, June 12, 2017, http://www.bbc.com/news/uk-politics-37507129 (last visited Apr 30, 2018).

[27] Matthew Taylor, MOST OF UK'S FRUIT AND VEG IS FROM OTHER EU NATIONS "SO BREXIT IMPACT MAY BE DRAMATIC" THE GUARDIAN (2017), http://www.theguardian.com/environment/2017/nov/01/most-of-uks-fruit-and-veg-is-from-other-eu-nations-so-brexit-impact-may-be-dramatic (last visited Apr 30, 2018).

[28] Since 1993, the output of fruits and vegetables in China has ranked first in the world for several consecutive years. China's fruits and vegetables production and market analysis, http://www.frtchina.com/Helps/zhongguoguoshuchanxi.html (last visited Apr 30, 2018).

[29] China-EU - international trade in goods statistics - Statistics Explained, *supra* note 15.

[30] *Id.*

[31] *Id.*

[32] Department for International Trade / Department for Business Strategy (UK) Energy and Industrial, INTERNATIONAL TRADE IN GOODS AND SERVICES BASED ON UN COMTRADE DATA, http://comtrade.un.org/labs/BIS-trade-in-goods (last visited Mar 29, 2018).

[33] More information and data can be searched through International trade in goods and services based on UN Comtrade data, *Id.*

between the two countries. Therefore, in the future FTA, the clauses of the tariff elimination or reduction can concentrate more on these items, depending on great demand in the markets.

The China-Switzerland FTA, which came into effect in 2014, is a useful model for a future China-UK FTA. Although Switzerland is neither a member of the EU nor a member of the European Economic Area (EEA), this trade pact is a helpful reference because it was the first FTA signed between China and a country in continental Europe.[34] Further, it has been significant to the economic development of both countries. Statistics show that in the first three quarters of 2016, despite the recession of global economy, the total volume of trade between two countries was 25.42 billion US dollars, a rise of 9.4 percent on the previous year.[35] Therefore, if the UK wants to obtain more benefits and reduce the trade deficit with China, negotiating a trade agreement is the best policy forward.

2. Suggestions and Implications

First, while eliminating tariffs is a good policy forward, China and the UK could negotiate an initial general benchmark of tariff elimination. In other words, this means that the majority of customs duties on goods will be removed only after a period of time starting from the entry into force of the FTA. This transition period is necessary because a sudden and drastic tariff elimination would lead to an influx of imports that could have a detrimental impact on domestic industries. This is especially true for the UK, since Brexit may have a negative impact on domestic industries and uncertainty in international trade and politics, so negotiating an interim is a wise choice.

To be specific, a suitable interim agreement would be to reduce 90 percent tariff lines to zero within 10 years. Confirming a benchmark should depend on several factors, like experience from existing FTAs, domestic industries conditions, market demand, and current bilateral trade situations. According to China's existing FTAs, the general principle is "90 percent tariff lines within ten years' benchmark", which means tariff rates will be reduced to a similar level after the decade of implementation.[36] On the EU side, the process tends to be faster, like

---

[34] Switzerland Becomes First Mainland European Nation to Start Free Trade Agreement with China, INTERNATIONAL BUSINESS TIMES UK (2014), https://www.ibtimes.co.uk/switzerland-becomes-first-mainland-european-nation-start-free-trade-agreement-china-1455068 (last visited Apr 30, 2018).

[35] China FTA Network, *supra* note 16.

[36] It is China's general principle that 90 percent tariff lines realize full liberalization within 10 years on China side. For example: China-Singapore FTA—92.2 percent; China-Peru FTA—93.07 percent; China-New Zealand FTA—97.1 percent; China-Australia FTA—96.8 percent.

the EU-South Korea FTA which would eliminate 98.7 percent of duties in trade within 5 years from the date of entry.[37] But based on China's experience, eliminating the remaining 10 percent tariff lines may need more time, especially for some highly sensitive goods. In the China-South Korea FTA, which has the largest trade volume among all China's FTAs, tariff lines are to be reduced to zero within 20 years. Such long transition periods work to protect domestic industries while markets open on a big scale. By contrast, the China-UK FTA may not require such a long period since the trade volume between the two countries is not large. Consequently, and due to a variety of factors, the China-UK FTA can apply the general principle in tariff rates elimination clauses.

Second, as mentioned above, manufactured products dominate trade between two countries right now. Given this trend, China and the UK could curtail the transitional period of manufactured products, making it shorter than for some highly sensitively products, such as agricultural products. If the customs duties could be eliminated as soon as possible, consumers in FTA partner countries would benefit more on commodities with lower price and at the same time manufacturers could profit on increasing demands. For example, China was the UK's second largest exporting market for vehicles other than railway, but China's average MFN in vehicles is 16 percent and MFN of Chinese consumers' most purchased motor is even up to 25 percent[38] in 2016. Therefore, if the tariff line reduces to zero in several years, more automobiles will export to China at a more attractive price, which can achieve a win-win situation. What's more, according to other China's existing FTAs, it is common to eliminate the tariff line of vehicles in a comparably short transitional period, such as 2 years under the China-Chile FTA and the China-Singapore FTA, and 5 years under the China-Australia FTA.[39] Hence, considering actual demands and practical operation in existing FTAs, generally, the transitional periods of manufactured products in tariff elimination can be shortened.

Gu Minkang; Yan Rong, The Free Trade Agreement between China and Korea - What Should Be Included in the FTA, 11 J. World Investment & Trade 1059 (2010)

[37] "What's more, a limited number of highly sensitive agricultural and fisheries products have transitional periods longer than 7 years."
EU-SOUTH KOREA FREE TRADE AGREEMENT: A QUICK READING GUIDE http://trade.ec.europa.eu/doclib/docs/2009/october/tradoc_145203.pdf (last visited Apr 15, 2018).

[38] World Tariff Profiles 2017, *supra* note 24.

[39] The data are collected from China's tariff elimination schedule with other FTA partners. What's more, for electrical, electronic equipment, China was the largest importing market for the UK which has been mentioned above. And this chapter thinks that short transitional periods can also apply here because of large market demands and the similar operation in the EU FTAs.

Third, as for agricultural products, in most cases, the transitional periods are longer than non-agricultural products.[40] States seek to control the import of these sensitive goods to protect interests of domestic agricultural and industrial labor. Such a provision could be adopted in the China-UK FTA. However, depending on the current situation, some products could realize full liberalization within relatively short years due to market demands. Fruits, vegetables, and beef will be analyzed below.

Fruits and vegetables imported to the UK meet the standard of tariff elimination in advance for two reasons. On one hand, importing fruits and vegetables from China can satisfy great and immediate market demands in the UK after Brexit. In the past two decades, Britain's dependence on fruit and vegetable imports has become more and more serious. The self-sufficiency rate of vegetables is only 58 percent, while that of fruits is only 11 percent.[41] And the EU-27, especially Spain, is its biggest supplier.[42] However, after Brexit, if the customs duties are imposed, it will have a negative impact on domestic price. Therefore, importing fruits and vegetables with lower tariff rates from China can, to some extent, solve this serious problem. On the other hand, China has a high agricultural yield, especially in fruit and vegetable,[43] which can help its FTA partners. South Korea is a good instance. In 2017, the imports of fruits and vegetables from China reached US$634 million, an increase of 12.6 percent over the FTA's entry into force.[44] So, reducing tariff of vegetables and fruits within a short period of time can fill the vacancy of the UK market and maintain its stability.

Beef exported to China also should not take a long time to realize the full liberalization. Although China is self-sufficient in most agricultural products, it is the leading global beef importer in the world, which is expected to increase its beef imports significantly.[45] And for

---

[40] The Free Trade Agreement between China and Korea - What Should Be Included in the FTA, *supra* note 36, at 1069.

[41] Britain will turn to import fruits and vegetables in Africa after Brexit, China Daily News, http://world.chinadaily.com.cn/2016-09/22/content_26865990.htm (last visited Apr 18, 2018).

[42] MOST OF UK'S FRUIT AND VEG IS FROM OTHER EU NATIONS "SO BREXIT IMPACT MAY BE DRAMATIC" THE GUARDIAN (2017), *supra note* 27.

[43] China's fruits and vegetables production and market analysis, *supra* note 28, *at Para.1.*

[44] Statistics: From January to October 2017, Korea's imports of fruits and vegetables from China has increased significantly, Yonhap News Agency, http://chinese.yonhapnews.co.kr/allheadlines/2018/01/29/0200000000ACK20180129000200881.HTML (last visited Apr 18, 2018).

[45] What might Brexit mean for UK trade in agricultural products? Agricultural & Horticulture Development Board, https://ahdb.org.uk/documents/Horizon_Brexit_-Analysis_Report-Oct2016.pdf (last visited Apr 18, 2018)

Britain, the EU-27 now is its major beef exported market.[46] However, if the result is hard Brexit after negotiation, beef exported from the UK may not as attractive as right now due to the imposed tariff. Then the EU may cooperate with other FTA partners to deal with beef trade, which could contribute to big loss in the UK's beef industry. Hence, transferring beef markets to China with preferential customs duties can be advantageous to it. However, how to compete with other beef exporters is another question. Australia is currently China's largest source of beef imports and the average tariff of 15 percent of beef will fall to zero within 10 years.[47] Facing such a strong competitor, Britain should try to negotiate a shorter period to succeed in the Chinese market.

In summary, market demands are the top priority. In other words, whether to reduce customs duties to zero within a certain period mainly depends on market demands. What's more, all the statements analyzed above are based on hard Brexit, which means the UK has its own schedule under WTO rules. By contrast, if Britain finally signs a FTA with the EU-27 (soft Brexit), China and the UK will still have many cooperating opportunities, depending on relatively low labor costs and China's Belt and Road program.

B. RULES OF ORIGIN

1. Rules of Origin and Implementation Procedures

Rules of origin are an integral part of international trade because they determine where items come from and ascertain the corresponding preferential tariff rates.[48] Only after confirming a product's origin, which meets the requirement under a trade agreement, tariff elimination can be applied if it is on the preferential list. In other words, rules of origins are the premise of customs duty reduction. If products are all made in a FTA partner country, they will qualify. In most cases, products would be listed clearly in the wholly obtained goods clause, such as plants, animals, fish and natural recourses, which also include in China's FTAs and the EU's FTAs with the third country.[49]

However, the assessment is complicated in today's globalized world where a finished commodity, especially non-agricultural ones, has been

---

[46] Scheherazade Daneshkhu, LUCRATIVE BRITISH MEAT EXPORTS TO US SET TO RESUME FINANCIAL TIMES (2016), https://www.ft.com/content/85a95b60-53ed-11e6-9664-e0bdc13c3bef (last visited Apr 30, 2018).

[47] South Korean beauty instrument Australian beef cuts to zero in 10 years - ICEach.com, http://www.chinanews.com/life/2015/12-21/7680188.shtml (last visited Apr 18, 2018).

[48] Rules of origin in an EU-UK FTA, A 'hidden hard Brexit' for food and drink exporters, food &drink federation, https://www.fdf.org.uk/corporate_pubs/FDF-Rules-of-origin-report.pdf

[49] The statement is summarized through comparing different existing FTAs.

processed in several countries before it is prepared for exporting.[50] How does one evaluate whether a product has been substantively processed? Different FTAs contain different rules. According to most of China's FTAs, there are two approaches. One is adopting the regional value content rule (RVC%) as the main criteria.[51] It is a quantitative test to assess a certain percent of originating content. According to the China-Singapore FTA, it shall be calculated on the basis of a general formula: $RVC\% = \frac{V-VNM}{V} * 100$. "V means the value of the good adjusted on a Free on Board (FOB) basis; and VNM shall be the Cost, Insurance and Freight (CIF) value at the time of importation of the materials or the earliest ascertained price paid for the materials of undetermined origin in the territory of the Party where the working or processing takes place. And the percentage of regional value content shall not be less than 40 percent."[52] Besides Singapore, China-South Korea FTA and China-Chile FTA apply similar rules with different value-added criteria.[53] The other FTAs are required to meet one of the three rules, i) a regional value content rule (RVC), or ii) a change in tariff classification rule, or iii) a process requirement rule which are involved in the annex of products specific rules of origin list. The last two rules mainly refer to the tariff headings or subheadings' change of goods, as evaluated by importers.[54] The alternatives make the criteria more flexible, so some FTAs prefer to choose this approach to solve the problem of long distance in trade, such as in the China-Australia FTA and China-New Zealand FTA.[55] And under the EU's existing FTAs, in most cases, a good is substantively changed if it satisfies one of the three standards: the tariff heading change, the value-added criterion, and the certain technical criteria.[56] Therefore, based on the similar grounds in identifying the rules of origin in China and the EU FTAs, it turns to be comparatively easy to negotiate this chapter in the China-UK FTA.

2. Suggestions and Implications

The basic principle of rules of origin clauses in the future UK-China

---

[50] Mark Neville, HOW THE TARIFF SHIFT RULE WORKS IN A FREE TRADE AGREEMENT (FTA), https://www.shippingsolutions.com/how-the-tariff-shift-rule-works-in-a-free-trade-agreement-fta (last visited Apr 16, 2018).

[51] Gu Minkang; Yan Rong, The Free Trade Agreement between China and Korea - What Should Be Included in the FTA, 11 J. World Investment & Trade 1059 (2010), at 1071.

[52] China FTA Network, *supra* note 16.

[53] *Id.*

[54] Process requirement rule is applied to some specific goods, such as chemical products.

[55] This is because depending on remote locations, there is no practical way to move back and forth. China FTA Network, *supra* note 16.

[56] How to use EU free trade agreements and save duty costs, National Board of Trade Sweden, http://unctad.org/en/PublicationsLibrary/EU_2017d1_en.pdf (last visited Apr 16, 2018)

FTA can refer to the rules under WTO, ensuring transparency in international trade and avoiding complicated standards to restrict trade and increase the cost.[57] This is because negotiating relatively simple criteria in rules of origin will benefit exporters and importers in FTA partners countries. In order to make rules easier and more flexible, there are several suggestions as follows.

First, in the wholly obtained goods clauses, the China-UK FTA can use the majority of existing FTAs as reference because they often involve some similar provisions, including the origin of agricultural products, such as harvested plants and animals raised in the partner country, and the origin of the specific natural recourses. But the high-sea fishing part is an exception. There are three different approaches in China's existing FTAs. First, under the China-Singapore FTA, "products of sea fishing and other marine products taken from the high seas by vessels registered with a Party or entitled to fly the flag of that Party."[58] With an "or", the first rule is relatively flexible. Second, according to the China-Australia FTA, the standard becomes strict: "goods (fish, shellfish, plant and other marine life) taken from the high seas by a vessel registered with a Party and flying its flag."[59] Compared with the first one, it is a stricter rule, narrowing down the scope of wholly obtained high-sea fishing products. The last approach only requires a vessel flying its flag, which can be found in the China-Chile FTA.[60] As for the China-UK FTA, because of the uncertainty in fishing policy after the transition period,[61] it is better to have a relatively flexible rule, referring to the first approach. Through restrictions, the UK can benefit more in exporting sea fishing products and other marine goods to China.

What's more, if products combine originating and non-originating contents, it will be more beneficial to apply the standard for alternatives, involving a regional value content rule (RVC), a change in tariff classification rule, and a process requirement rule. Through this method, China and the UK can promote the strengths and avoid the shortages in the rules of origin chapter. Each rule has its disadvantages. The process of calculating the regional value content is more complicated and time-consuming than the other two because of two variables in the formula, the FOB value of the finished goods, and the CIF value at the time of

[57] WTO | legal texts—A Summary of the Final Act of the Uruguay Round, , https://www.wto.org/english/docs_e/legal_e/ursum_e.htm#iAgreement (last visited Apr 17, 2018).

[58] China FTA Network, *supra* note 16.

[59] *Id.*

[60] *Id.*

[61] According to the recent EU-UK negotiation, the EU-27 can still obtain fishing opportunities in the UK fishing water under Article 125 section 1 of the Withdrawal Agreement. But after the transition period, it is still uncertain.

importation of the materials, which have to be evaluated by customs. But the other two rules are less objective than the RVC rule because whether a product satisfies the rules of origin depends on importers who may make an unfair decision for some reasons like domestic industries protection or current policies. Therefore, based on negotiating a simple, efficient, flexible and predictable rule, the criteria for alternatives is much more proper.

IV. DISPUTE SETTLEMENT CLAUSE IN THE FTA

A. *STATUS QUO OF DISPUTE RESOLUTION UNDER CHINA'S AND THE EU'S EXISTING FTAS*

Dispute settlement is a necessary element under the China-UK FTA so as to ensure rapid resolution of conflicts. It appears that WTO Members may have recourse to non-WTO dispute settlement forums, and so China and the UK may regulate the terms of a dispute settlement mechanism in the FTA. Neither authority nor prohibition can be found in the WTO rules regarding the negotiation of dispute settlement mechanisms under FTAs. Article XXIV of the General Agreement on Tariff and Trade (GATT)[62] contains an exception of the MFN clause when Members are dealing with FTAs, and Article V of the General Agreement on Trade in Service (GATS)[63] also provides the similar rule, recognizing the rights of Members to liberalize trade in services under preferential trade agreements. Therefore, based on these two provisions and subsequent WTO jurisprudence.[64] WTO Members are allowed to sign their own bilateral or multilateral deals, which suggests that their preferential trade agreements can contain different dispute settlement mechanisms.[65]

In all of the EU's FTAs since 2000, the dispute settlement clauses are based on the model of the WTO dispute settlement understanding, including consultations, conciliation, mediation, requests for a panel, and others. China's FTAs share the same model. Despite such trends, the lack of a legal process is a problem that cannot be overlooked. The Chinese approach has been to solve disputes with trading partners

---

[62] WTO | GATT documents, , https://www.wto.org/english/docs_e/gattdocs_e.htm (last visited Apr 15, 2018).

[63] WTO | Services: General Agreement on Trade in Services, https://www.wto.org/-english/tratop_e/serv_e/gatsintr_e.htm (last visited Apr 15, 2018).

[64] WTO | dispute settlement - the disputes - DS457, , https://www.wto.org/-english/tratop_e/dispu_e/cases_e/ds457_e.htm (last visited Jun 10, 2018).

[65] The Dispute Settlement Mechanism of Free Trade Agreements and Its Relationship with WTO Law, http://www.zoomlaw.net/files/16-1138-37481.php (last visited Apr 15, 2018)

through political approaches, like cooperation and consultation in the very early step of dispute resolution, instead of undergoing legal proceedings and enforcing a final report. For example, the dispute settlement clauses in the China-Chile FTA, which entered into force in 2006 and in the China-Pakistan, which entered into force in 2009, have never been used.[66] Therefore, the future FTA should improve the dispute settlement mechanism, making it more practical and effective.

B. SUGGESTIONS AND IMPLICATIONS

Although there is great variation among dispute resolution clauses, they still serve as useful models for the China-UK FTA negotiation. The first task is to decide the type of the dispute settlement mechanism. A common way stipulated in most of EU's existing FTAs with third countries (e.g. the EU-South Korea FTA) is referral to an ad hoc arbitral panel that takes the WTO dispute settlement rules as a reference.[67] All of China's existing FTAs also administer disputes to ad hoc arbitral panels. Given this trend, as well as the flexibility associated with ad hoc tribunals, such a mechanism would be appropriate in the China-UK FTA. China and the UK could specify the scope, the standing, and detailed procedures of the dispute settlement in a way that would facilitate efficient and transparent dispute resolution. Currently, standing to initiate cases pursuant to FTA clauses is limited to states. Although this may seem restrictive, since organizations and individuals are prevented from bringing claims to an arbitral tribunal under an FTA, it may still be best and most efficient to limit the FTA dispute settlement forum to state-to-state disputes.

Finally, dispute settlement clauses also specify whether the final report awarded by the arbitral panel is formal or not. Legal provisions are usually examined on the basis of three criteria—obligation, precision, and delegation.[68] These factors can also be applied in framing dispute settlement provisions.[69] Precision means whether the clauses are concise and clear enough, which is essential to avoid disagreements caused by vague language. Adopting language from the WTO dispute settlement

---

[66] China FTA Network, *supra* note 16.

[67] Dispute Settlement Mechanisms in Free Trade Agreements, TRADELAB, https://tradelab.legal.io/guide/57e3e094e4a9945f6a00000c/Dispute+Settlement+Mechanisms+in+Free+Trade+Agreements (last visited Apr 5, 2018).

[68] Goldstein, J., Kahler, M., Keohane, R., & Slaughter, A. (2000). Introduction: Legalization and World Politics. *International Organization, 54*(3), 385-399. doi:10.1162/002081800551262

[69] The form choice of dispute settlement mechanism in the China Free Trade Zone, Zhao Jun & Wei Jinshen, http://crs.shisu.edu.cn/_upload/article/c8/a6-/102cc1534cb8bb4eb9254ee50289/92b80f84-c71c-45c3-bd36-7163103b188d.pdf (last visited Apr 5, 2018).

understanding, which is a mature and tested system into the future China-UK FTA is a guaranteed way to meet the precision test. Delegation means whether the parties would authorize the third party to handle disputes. The China-UK FTA will meet this standard if it chooses an ad hoc arbitral panel as the type of dispute settlement mechanism. Finally, obligation refers to whether the final reports from the arbitral panel is binding or not, which is equivalent to whether the report is formal or not. Formal clauses and informal clauses coexist in China's FTAs, therefore deciding which one would be most appropriate in the China-UK FTA is a core issue. This chapter argues that the future FTA should adopt the formal one since it assures predictability and reliability. Although informal dispute settlement mechanisms, like the one in the China-Chile FTA and the China-New Zealand FTA, can offer flexibility, formal mechanisms work better to avoid potential disagreements over language and any violations. Since China and the UK hope to enhance cooperation, especially in trade, a formal dispute settlement mechanism can protect the interests and rights of exporters and importers.[70]

V. CONCLUSION

Brexit necessarily requires the UK to shift its attention outside the EU for future trade, and China promises an excellent option. Obtaining a comprehensive FTA with China could open markets with the world's second largest economy, boosting joint trade, deepening bilateral economic cooperation, and potentially reducing the costs and losses from exiting the single market with the EU.

Admittedly, market liberalization and elimination of trade barriers as early as possible are the top priorities, but it is advisable that the UK and China consider their national conditions, actual capabilities, and apply mechanisms that also protect some special domestic industries. For example, in China-South Korea FTA, Korea government gave up huge vehicle market in China to protect its highly sensitive product—rice in tariff elimination clause.[71] In conclusion, Brexit can be seen as a new start of Sino-Britain cooperation and implementing a comprehensive free trade agreement can accelerate the realization of "Golden Era."

---

[70] *Id.*

[71] China, South Korea sign "substantial conclusion" of free trade deal, REUTERS, November 10, 2014, https://www.reuters.com/article/us-southkorea-china-trade/south-korea-effectively-reaches-free-trade-deal-with-china-idUSKCN0IU02Z20141110 (last visited Apr 30, 2018).

Institute of International Economic Law—
Georgetown Law

600 New Jersey Avenue, NW
Washington, DC 20001
www.iiel.org
Email: lawiiel@georgetown.edu

The Institute of International Economic Law is the focal point for the study of international economic law at Georgetown University.

It is also one of the leading centers for international economic law and policy in the world.

Originally focused on trade, the Institute now boasts leading capabilities and international renown in a range of areas including investment and financial regulation, tax, business and monetary law. The Institute actively approaches these fields as interrelated and at times overlapping policy spheres that impact how law is devised, practiced and enforced.

The IIEL's reputation in trade, financial regulation, arbitration, tax and transnational business stems directly from the scholarly work and real world contributions of our faculty. More than any other institute in the field, the IIEL's instructors are leading scholars and thinkers who routinely participate in the highest level policy discussions on each of the core fields of international economic law. Their writings are in law reviews, think tank policy pieces, op-eds and Congressional testimony consistently, and help shape national and international economic affairs. In the classroom, students gain an insider and cutting edge look into international economic rulemaking.

Alongside IIEL's instructors and administrators are nearly a dozen additional visiting researchers, adjunct and visiting professors who teach international economic law courses for our students.

IIEL Faculty & Professional Staff

Chris Brummer—IIEL Faculty Director; International Financial Regulation and Monetary Affairs, and International Trade
Grant Aldonas—IIEL Executive Director; International Trade, WTO, International Business Transactions
Lilian Faulhaber—International Law, Taxation
Michael Gadbaw—International Trade and International Business
Anna Gelpern—International Financial Regulation; Sovereign Debt and International Monetary Affairs
Itai Grinberg—International Tax, International Tax Policy, Tax Reform
Daniel Heath—International Monetary Affairs and International Trade
Jennifer Hillman—International Trade, WTO, and International Business Transactions
Joost Pauwelyn—International Trade, International Investment, and Public International Law
Alvaro Santos—International Trade, Economic Development, Transnational Labor Law and the Future of NAFTA
David Stewart—International Business, Public International Law and National Security
Robert Thompson—Business Organizations and Securities Regulation
Anne Marie Whitesell—International Arbitration, Dispute Resolution, and International Negotiations
Christine Washington—Director, Programs & External Affairs
Jacquelyn Williams—Program Associate

Made in the USA
Monee, IL
08 November 2026

67378670R00246